THE HUMAN POTENTIAL FOR PEACE

THE HUMAN POTENTIAL FOR PEACE

An Anthropological Challenge to Assumptions about War and Violence

Douglas P. Fry

Åbo Akademi University & University of Arizona

New York Oxford
OXFORD UNIVERSITY PRESS
2006

Oxford University Press, Inc., publishes works that further Oxford University's objective of excellence in research, scholarship, and education.

Oxford New York
Auckland Cape Town Dar es Salaam Hong Kong Karachi
Kuala Lumpur Madrid Melbourne Mexico City Nairobi
New Delhi Shanghai Taipei Toronto

With offices in
Argentina Austria Brazil Chile Czech Republic France Greece
Guatemala Hungary Italy Japan Poland Portugal Singapore
South Korea Switzerland Thailand Turkey Ukraine Vietnam

Published by Oxford University Press, Inc.
198 Madison Avenue, New York, New York 10016
http://www.oup.com

Library of Congress Cataloging-in-Publication Data

Fry, Douglas P., 1953-
The human potential for peace : an anthropological challenge to assumptions about war and violence / by Douglas P. Fry.
p. cm.
Includes bibliographical references and index.
ISBN 13: 978-0-19-518177-7 (alk. paper) – ISBN 13: 978-0-19-518178-4 (pbk. : alk. paper)
1. Violence. 2. War. 3. Peace. 4. Social control. 5. Intergroup relations. I. Title.

GN495.2.F79 2005
303.6–dc22 2004063133

Printing number: 9 8 7 6 5 4 3 2

Printed in the United States of America
on acid-free paper

With love and gratitude
to my dearest Sirpa

And also with love to those who
have nurtured the peace in me:
my father, Brooks,
my mother, Carol, and
my second mother, Miriam

Contents

Foreword

The assumption that all societies are necessarily aggressive not only is incorrect but also poses a danger to world peace. The empirical evidence that this assumption is not correct is lucidly set out in the pages that follow. Its dangerous nature also requires emphasis.

During the Cold War, both sides built up enormous arsenals of nuclear weapons. Seen from the outside, the escalation lacked rationality. Each side came to have a nuclear firepower many, many times greater than that necessary to deter the other side from making a preemptive strike. Indeed, an all-out nuclear exchange would almost certainly have involved the end of civilization over the world as a whole. There were many reasons for this escalation, but it was presented at times by politicians on both sides as necessary on the view that humans are inherently and inevitably aggressive and that sooner or later a first strike by the other side was inevitable unless the opponents were deterred from striking by fear of retribution.

Toward the end of the Cold War a group of scientists produced a statement, subsequently adopted and disseminated by UNESCO as the Seville Declaration, summarizing the scientific evidence against the view that we have an inherent tendency to make war. The view that aggression is inevitable is not the only view that is incorrect. It is worthwhile considering some other points of relevance to Professor Fry's book. First, the view that human aggressiveness makes war inevitable involves a conceptual confusion. It is necessary to distinguish between aggressive behavior, which refer to actions intended to harm others, and aggressiveness, the propensity or motivation to show aggressive behavior. War involves aggressive behavior in that the combatants try to harm each other, but how it is motivated is another issue. In general, aggressive behavior is a tool that is used for a number of purposes. It may be motivated by a desire to obtain something possessed by another individual, by fear, by a desire to show off, or, of special importance in modern war, by duty. The bomb aimer who presses a bomb release does so primarily because it is his duty, not (usually) because he wants to kill civilians on the ground. The tank commander goes into battle not with a desire to kill, kill, kill, but to do his duty. The motivations of the politician who declares war, the commander who orders the destruction of an enemy post, and the infantryman who fires his AK 47 are all different. And only rarely is there a simple desire to kill—when there is, as at My Lai in the Vietnam War, it is usually not condoned.

So the immediate causes of war lie with the politicians, generals, despots, revolutionaries, or tribal leaders, not with those who do the actual fighting. And such leaders may in turn be motivated by rational considerations of policy, by popular opinion, by greed, by not knowing what else to do, and in many other ways. It is much more correct to say that war causes aggression than that aggressiveness causes war.

But, more importantly, humans are not solely aggressive. We do indeed have propensities to behave assertively and aggressively, but we also have propensities to behave prosocially and cooperatively, with kindness and consideration for others. Social life would not be possible if these prosocial tendencies did not predominate over selfish assertiveness and aggressiveness. Indeed, even war involves cooperation with one's fellows, and war fighting usually involves at least as much cooperation with members of one's own group as aggression toward others.

The emphasis on the inevitably of aggression comes mainly from two sources. First, the media are full of reports of murders, muggings, and rapes, but these are reported primarily because they are relatively rare. If murders were an everyday occurrence, they would lose much of their interest. Meanwhile the thousands of acts of human kindness and generosity that occur every day go unreported. We forget the essential goodness of humankind.

The second source of the emphasis on inevitability comes from the Christian doctrine of original sin. Few people may believe in it, but the view that evil is endemic has become embedded in our society. And such a view can be enhanced by the difficulty of bringing up children. Of course children express their needs and desires, and these may be contrary to those of their parents. But as developmental psychologists have increasingly emphasized, children also want to please their parents and to be seen to be good. Wordsworth was nearer the truth when he described the newborn as "trailing clouds of glory."

So humans are not inevitably aggressive, and aggressiveness does not cause wars. But that does not mean that there are not connections of several kinds. Even in modern war aggressiveness, the desire to harm the enemy, sometimes surfaces. Indeed, in the days of hand-to-hand fighting soldiers were taught to arouse their own aggressiveness. But it was the state of war that decreed that they should do so, not their aggressiveness that caused the war. And war propaganda is sometimes designed to arouse aggressiveness—as when the enemy is portrayed as evil and subhuman.

In conclusion, the very existence of human societies depends on the preponderance of prosocial tendencies over assertive and aggressive ones. Humans do not inevitably show aggressive behavior, and aggressiveness does not cause wars. But we must remember that the balance is a fine one. The incidence of wars and the millions who have died in wars during the last century show that aggressive behavior directed toward those seen as belonging to another group is an ever-present possibility. That is why this scholarly book, summarizing evidence from such diverse sources to show that peaceful societies have existed and can exist, is so important. It represents a unique and important contribution to what must be the goal of us all—the abolition of war.

Robert A. Hinde
University of Cambridge

Preface

When I first began studying anthropology, one aspect of the discipline that appealed to me was its breadth. Anthropology addresses big questions. Where did we come from? What is our nature? What does it mean to be human? Why do we behave the way we do? What are the prospects for our future? Anthropology, literally the "study of humankind," lends itself to a *macroscopic perspective*. It focuses not just on the present but also on the past. It seeks to understand specific cultures as well as recurring patterns that span societies. Anthropology simultaneously embraces the biosocial diversity and uniformity of humanity.

There is a natural tendency to think in terms of the "here and now." But as we enter the 21st century, many of the challenges facing humanity demand a broader context. The macroscopic perspective of anthropology, with its expansive time frame and culturally comparative orientation, can provide unique insights into the nature of war and the potential for peace. A cross-cultural perspective shows, for instance, that humans everywhere seek justice—although the paths to justice vary. Some entail violence, but others do not. Much violence, in fact, stems from people defending their rights or attempting to correct injustices. Anthropological and historical cases show that it is possible to replace violent means of justice seeking with nonviolent approaches. Herein lies a broader lesson for creating and maintaining peace.

A macroscopic anthropological view suggests that it would be possible to replace the institution of war with more effective, less brutal ways of seeking security, defending rights, and providing justice for the people of this planet. In an era of nuclear missiles and other weapons of mass destruction, trying to achieve security through the threat or use of military force is like trying to perform heart surgery with a chainsaw. For the good of us all, we must replace the war system with viable institutions for creating peace, delivering justice, and guaranteeing security.

In adopting a view that spans millennia and crosses cultural space, I draw on data from many anthropological fields: archaeology, hunter-gatherer research, ethnographic descriptions of particular societies, comparative cross-cultural studies, research on socialization and cultural belief systems, and applied anthropology (a field that focuses on "real-world" problem solving). The book also includes theory and data from fields beyond anthropology—for example, behavioral ecology, game theory, animal research, and evolutionary biology. The goal is to attain a view of the human capacities for violence and peace that is as complete and integrated as possible. Traditionally, war has received the lion's share of anthropological attention. This book, while not neglecting war, begins to correct this imbalance by placing the primary emphasis on peace.

Two themes span the covers of this book. The first theme is that violence and warfare are neither natural nor inevitable. To the contrary, humans have a great capacity for dealing with conflicts nonviolently. The second theme is that cultural beliefs about the naturalness of violence and war continue to bias interpretations, affect our views of human nature, and may even close our minds to the possibilities of developing alternatives to war and violence.

Following the introduction of these themes in chapter 1, the first example of the human potential for peace, Brazil's Upper Xingu peace system, is considered in chapter 2. This peace system and others like it demonstrate that war is not an inevitable result of intersocietal contact. In chapter 3, the human potential for peace is further illustrated with ethnographic examples of how people handle conflicts without violence through group discussion, mediation, avoidance, negotiation, toleration, judicial contests, payment of compensation, appeal to arbitrators, use of courts, and so forth.

In chapter 4, a focus on two Mexican Zapotec communities introduces the concept of cultural belief system and highlights the poignant influences of social learning on how people deal with conflict. Building on these ideas, chapter 5 presents a continuum model as a useful way to conceptualize the variability in peacefulness–aggressiveness across human societies. The documentation of over 80 societies that have very low levels of aggression—those near the peaceful end of the cross-cultural continuum—again demonstrates that humans have a substantial potential for peace. Chapter 6 describes in greater detail three internally peaceful societies—the Semai of Malaysia, the Ifaluk of Micronesia, and Norwegians. One lesson is that dealing with conflict without violence is not merely a utopian dream: Numerous peaceful societies exist.

Chapter 7 begins an anthropoligical consideration of warfare, including the biasing effects that cultural beliefs have on our study and perceptions of war. The cross-cultural and archaeological data contradict assumptions that war is natural, universal, and ancient. Furthermore, as explored in chapter 8, war increases with the degree of social complexity. This finding has been replicated across various anthropological studies, yet its importance is not widely appreciated beyond anthropology. Methods of seeking justice also relate to social complexity. The book's second theme about cultural beliefs biasing interpretations reemerges in chapter 9 with a strange tale of scholarly misrepresentation.

Was the past really as warlike as some Westerners assume? A careful weighing of the available archaeological data on the antiquity of warfare in chapter 10 reveals that warfare actually is very recent in a prehistoric sense, a finding that jibes with the association between war and social complexity previously noted in chapter 8. Chapter 11 illustrates how some Western observers project martial images and war vocabulary onto indigenous phenomena, such as revenge homicide, which actually are quite different from warfare. Chapter 12 surveys conflict management among the hunter-gatherers of Aboriginal Australia. The human potential for peace is reflected in the diverse and creative ways that Australian Aborigines prevent and contain violence. Prior to the arrival of Europeans, this entire continent consisted of hunter-gatherer societies, and, significantly, warfare was a rare anomaly. This observation casts doubt on presumptions that warfare was a predominant pattern among foraging bands of the evolutionary past.

Chapters 13 and 14 directly critique a widely held view about the prevalence of violence and warfare in the human past. When assumptions about the past are compared with actual data on nomadic hunter-gatherer bands—the best model of social life in past millennia before the rise of agriculture—it becomes apparent that the assumptions are extremely unrealistic. Chapter 15 continues the critical examination of implausible assumptions by focusing on a particular often-cited study of violence among the South American Yanomamö. In chapter 16, several conflict management case studies of nomadic hunter-gatherer societies are presented. Two conclusions are that, as in Aboriginal Australia, war is rare at this band level of social organization and that conflicts tend to be between particular individuals, not entire groups. Chapters 17 and 18 suggest an alternative evolutionary perspective on human aggression. This new perspective proposes that individual aggression in humans, as in various species, is a product of natural and sexual selection, but that *warfare* is not. Chapter 19 reviews and summarizes the various lines of evidence that support the book's tandem themes. Chapter 20 then explores anthropological implications for enhancing peace in the 21st century.

In my experience, some people, accustomed to the international war system, assume that it simply is not possible to find better ways to resolve differences and to assure security. However, the wealth of anthropological data considered in this book suggests otherwise. Humans have a tremendous capacity for resolving conflicts without violence. In today's world, we need to apply these skills in new ways and on a grander scale. We need to think in new, bolder ways about creating realistic alternatives to war. Too often, short-term, shallow security analyses prevail over more comprehensive planning for a secure future. Rather than focusing exclusively on narrow issues, such as how many fighter jets to order this year, we need to address a set of broader, critically important questions that are relevant to providing genuine, long-term safety and security for the people of the planet that are crying out for serious consideration: How can we improve the quality of life for all humanity; reduce the social and economic inequalities that foment hostility, hatred, and terrorism; and create new procedures and institutions for providing justice and resolving differences without war? In short, at the global level, how can we replace the law of force with the force of law?

A central goal of this book is to thoroughly explore how anthropology contributes to understanding war and peace. I hope to challenge existing ways of thinking about war, peace, security, and justice. These are topics that concern each and every one of us on this interdependent planet, where we all breathe the same air and would perish together in the same nuclear winter.

With the hope of communicating to a readership well beyond anthropology, including students from various fields, I have avoided using technical jargon whenever possible and, when needed, have attempted to explain key concepts clearly. I hope that students and other readers will find the book thought provoking. I am fully aware that some ideas are controversial. By questioning traditional thinking, I hope that the book will provoke reflection, discussion, and debate.

ACKNOWLEDGMENTS

Many friends and colleagues graciously have engaged in discussions on relevant topics or provided bibliographic and other useful information. For their assistance, I thank John Archer, Ofer Bar-Yosef, Megan Biesele, Bruce Bonta, Chris Boehm, Mark Davis,

Bob Dentan, Brooks Fry, Kathy Fry, Sirpa Fry, Peter Gardner, Jonathan Haas, Marvin Harris, Bob Hitchcock, Allen Johnson, Ray Kelly, Sue Kent, Hanna Korpela, Joyce Marcus, Carolyn Nordstrom, Carl O'Nell, John Paddock, Fred Rawski, Carole Robarchek, Clay Robarchek, Heikki Sarmaja, Cliff Sather, Kenneth Smail, Les Sponsel, Jukka-Pekka Takala, and Bob Tonkinson. This book also has benefited from the wisdom of many fine teachers. Richard K. Farnham, Paul L. Jamison, Robert J. Meier, Craig Nelson, and Donald Symons deserve special thanks for their influences on my intellectual development.

I owe warm thanks to my wife, Sirpa Fry, and my father, Brooks Fry, for their unfaltering support during the entire writing project. Sirpa has heard, repeatedly I'm afraid, about the trials and tribulations of working on a project of this nature. As a psychologist, Sirpa knows how to listen. Additionally she always has offered sound, supportive advice and honest, helpful reactions to my prose, for which I am most grateful. My father has been a fountain of wisdom. He has provided keen insights on many topics. I have always been impressed with his ability to draw connections between seemingly unrelated topics and to consider an array of information from diverse fields. I'll leave it to the reader to judge whether I have "inherited" some of this inclusive analytical style.

As any writer knows, a work benefits substantially from feedback. The following persons generously read and commented on one or more draft chapters: John Archer, Roger Archer, Jan Beatty, Bruce Bonta, James Côté, Bob Dentan, Carol Ember, Mel Ember, Brian Ferguson, Brooks Fry, Sirpa Fry, Agustin Fuentes, Robert Hinde, Paul Jamison, Ray Kelly, Hanna Korpela, Joyce Marcus, Heikki Sarmaja, Peter K. Smith, Jukka-Pekka Takala, Bob Tonkinson, Jim Welch, and several reviewers—Nancy Ries, Colgate University; Brian Ferguson, Rutgers University; Frans B. M. de Waal, Living Links, Yerkes Primate Center, Emory University; Catherine Lutz, Watson Institute, Brown University; and Leslie E. Sponsel, University of Hawaii. I thank these colleagues for their helpful suggestions, most of which have been incorporated into the book. Bruce Bonta, Heikki Sarmaja, Peter K. Smith, and Jukka-Pekka Takala deserve additional thanks for critically reading all or much of the book in draft form and for offering valuable feedback. I alone take responsibility, of course, for any deficiencies that remain in this work.

The proposal of new interpretations at times requires the critiquing of existing views. My goal is to raise issues about the validity of assumptions, the soundness of methodological procedures, and the logic of interpretations and, in some cases, to call attention to the existence of overlooked evidence, but certainly *not* to find fault with other writers *as persons*. I emphasize this point because one reader of this manuscript misinterpreted my critique of a particular study as an ad hominem attack against the author of the work. This is not my intention. Aside from keeping the focus of the critiques on the works themselves, not particular persons, I develop the theme that prevailing cultural beliefs, which are largely taken for granted, creep into scientific interpretations in various ways. This theme, as reflecting a general phenomenon, certainly is not ad hominem.

I am extremely grateful for the financial and institutional support received from granting agencies and my universities. At Åbo Akademi University in Finland, Kaj Björkqvist, Karin Österman, and Camilla Westermark have consistently encouraged my research on peace. At the Bureau of Applied Research in Anthropology at the University of Arizona, I thank Tim Finan for his supportive collegiality and Maria Rodriguez for her efficiency and numerous favors. The researching and writing of the book was greatly facilitated by a grant expressly for this purpose from the United States Institute of Peace (grant number 023-99F). In particular, I thank David Smock, former director of the grants program, for his initial interest in this anthropological project and April Hall, grants administrator, for her efficient and friendly assistance with implementing the project.

Additionally, some material presented in the book was collected over the course of several research projects supported by the National Science Foundation (grant numbers 81-17478, 97-10071, and 03-13670), the Wenner-Gren Foundation for Anthropological Research (grant number 4117), and an Indiana University Skomp Fellowship (number 26-235-77). I am very grateful to these institutions for supporting my research on human aggression and conflict resolution over the years. It should also be clear that the opinions expressed in this book do not necessarily reflect the views of these granting agencies. The librarians at the University of Helsinki and the Ethnology Collection of the Finnish Literary Society (SKS) have provided extremely efficient service, for which I am most appreciative. I especially thank Terttu Kaivola for digging out countless journal articles from the shelves of the SKS collection and for her helpfulness overall.

Turning to visual images, a number of colleagues have generously provided photographs. Individual credits appear in photo captions, but additionally I would like to express my special gratitude to Chris Boehm, Kirk Endicott, Peter Gardner, Tom Gregor, Mari Laaksonen, Catherine Lutz, Peter Meylan, Clay Robarchek, Heikki Sarmaja, Jukka-Pekka Takala, and Bob Tonkinson for providing photographs. Julie Brown of the Peabody Museum at Harvard University also deserves a thank-you for her help in providing illustrations.

I cannot imagine a more supportive editor than Jan Beatty at Oxford University Press. It has been a delight to work with her. I thank Jan not only for her initial and continuing enthusiasm over the book but also for her astute observations and guidance. Others in the editorial and production departments at Oxford also have made important contributions to the book. I thank Talia Krohn for consistently providing excellent advice and efficiently addressing a mountain of questions. I thank Christine D'Antonio for so ably steering the book through the production process, and Michele F. Kornegay for excellent copyediting on the entire manuscript.

Karstula, Finland
Summer 2004

CHAPTER 1

QUESTIONING THE WAR ASSUMPTION

> Many ideas in science seemed crazy at one time but are now regarded as being settled, either having been laid to rest (as in the case of cold fusion) or firmly established (as in the case of plate tectonics, which grew out of an earlier "crazy" theory of continental drift). . . . But, even the weirdest theories of science must pass one rigorous test or be discarded: their predictions must be in agreement with phenomena observed in the physical world.
>
> ROBERT EHRLICH[1]

Several years ago, as I was reading an intriguing book by primatologist Frans de Waal called *Peacemaking among Primates,* I realized that de Waal had hit upon a valuable new perspective.[2] *Getting along, reconciling,* and *peacemaking* are very common and extremely important aspects of social behavior in many primate species, and this conclusion also applies to humans. Violence tends to grab the headlines, but violence constitutes only a minute part of social life. To focus too much attention on the aggression is to totally miss the "big picture."

A batch of recent books purports to tell us how violent humans really are—at least how violent *men* really are—sometimes in melodramatic terms: "We live in a world in which cheaters, robbers, rapists, murderers, and warmongers lurk in every human landscape," writes primatologist Michael Ghiglieri in *The Dark Side of Man.* Lawrence Keeley, in *War before Civilization,* forges a thesis that warfare is old and widespread. Psychologist David Buss writes in an evolutionary psychology textbook that "Human recorded history, including hundreds of ethnographies of tribal cultures around the globe, reveals male coalitional warfare to be pervasive across cultures worldwide." In *Demonic Males,* primatologist Richard Wrangham and writer Dale Peterson argue that human warfare has ancient evolutionary roots: "chimpanzee-like violence preceded and paved the way for human war, making modern humans the dazed survivors of a continuous, 5-million-year habit of lethal aggression."[3]

With some variation from author to author, this overall perspective makes certain claims. Violence and warfare are ubiquitous or nearly so. Humanity is warlike. Consequently, peaceful societies are dismissed as virtually or totally nonexistent. Some authors propose that even the simplest cultures, nomadic hunting-and-gathering (foraging) bands, are warlike. Keeley, for example, writes, "there is nothing inherently peaceful about hunting-gathering or band society." Wrangham and Peterson assert that "no truly peaceful foraging people has ever been found or described in detail." As a theme spanning such arguments, not only is warfare viewed as pervasive across cultures, but it also is seen as an extremely ancient practice. Finally, some authors propose that warring, assaulting, raping, and murdering have an instinctual basis or that evolutionary processes have favored human violence and warfare.[4]

In this book, I will propose an idea that at first may seem improbable, namely, that the view that humans are fundamentally warlike stems much more from the *cultural beliefs* of the writers than from "phenomena observed in the physical world"—from data, in other words.[5] Indisputably, humans are capable of engaging in interpersonal and group violence from rape and murder to war and genocide. Nonetheless, the dark-sided, demonic view of humanity, especially male humanity, so stridently advocated in some recent writing, goes far beyond the anthropological facts. It is time for a careful reassessment of the anthropological evidence related to war, violence, and peace. I will argue that the human potential for peace is underappreciated, whereas violence and warfare are emphasized, exaggerated, and thus *naturalized*. Naturalizing war and violence can help to create a self-fulfilling prophecy: *If war is seen as natural, then there is little point in trying to prevent, reduce, or abolish it. Consequently, the acceptance of war as a social institution facilitates its continuance*. Viewing warfare as fundamentally human may help to justify going to war as "just doing what comes naturally."

A thorough reconsideration of the anthropological data suggests that this view of humanity as essentially violent and warmongering is simply wrong. Warfare is no more natural than, say, slavery. Just over 150 years ago Frederick Douglass, himself born into slavery, published his moving autobiography chronicling the almost unimaginable inhumanities inflicted on slaves in the United States. It is important to remember that in Douglass' time, many people viewed this cruel institution as normal and socially justifiable. A common view was that some races were clearly superior to others and that slavery reflected this *natural* order. Obviously, cultural beliefs accepting slavery as an institution have changed dramatically over the course of the 19th and 20th centuries. Upon closer scientific examination, war might turn out to be no more "natural" than slavery. Anthropology provides a wealth of evidence relevant to evaluating this issue, but interestingly, these data typically have been ignored. Could this reflect, in part at least, a common belief that we already *know* the answer about humanity's warlike nature?[6]

In this book, we will see the pervasiveness and sometimes subtlety of cultural beliefs that violence and war are embedded in human nature. The recent crop of writings advocating a dark-sided, demonic view actually has a long line of historical predecessors in Western tradition. Thomas Hobbes philosophized in *Leviathan* on the natural state of war, William James saw humans as naturally bellicose, and Sigmund Freud devised a death instinct to account for some forms of human destructiveness.[7] It is an obvious yet often ignored fact that, as human beings, scientists and scholars are members of a culture, too. Like everyone else, they are exposed to cultural traditions and worldviews that influence their thinking and perceptions. When the learned and shared beliefs of a culture hold that humans are innately pugnacious, inevitably violent, instinctively warlike, and so on, the persons socialized in such settings, whether scientists or nonscientists, tend to accept such views without much question.

One example of how cultural beliefs about the naturalness of war and violence are reflected in scholarship involves the landmark treatise, *A Study of War,* by judicial scholar Quincy Wright.[8] As we will consider in greater detail later, Wright observed that some societies in his large cross-cultural sample were nonwarring but, nonetheless, classified the whole sample within four categories called political war, economic war, social war, and defensive war. Consequently, the nonwarring societies were labeled as engaging in at least defensive war, because there simply were no alternatives like *peaceful* or *nonwarring* in the classificatory scheme. This is analogous to labeling *everybody* as being sick, for instance, as *critically ill, chronically ill, periodically ill,* or *undiagnosed,* with no category for *healthy*. Such labels subtly imply that illness is the *natural state of affairs*. Wright's war classification scheme is merely one example of research that seems to reflect a *belief bias* in Western culture that war is natural.

Another example involves the inordinate amount of attention given to one anthropological article on the South American Yanomamö.[9] The article purports to show that men who have killed someone have more children than men who have not killed anyone. This particular finding has achieved "celebrity status," being reiterated in writings on war and violence again and again. In such discussions, a recurring implication is that this particular finding tells us something important about evolution and human nature. At the same time, published critiques of the article tend to go unmentioned. This book will offer a new analysis of these controversial findings.

Similarly, a primatological finding that has been played up as having the utmost relevance for understanding the origin of human warfare is that chimpanzees at Gombe Reserve in Tanzania killed off members of a neighboring group, one-by-one. But why should this particular observation on *chimpanzees* be repeatedly touted as so important for understanding *humans?* And why do writers taking this approach simultaneously just brush over unaggressive bonobos—a species that is just as closely related to humans as are chimpanzees—and instead link humans to so-called killer chimps? De Waal points out that "had bonobos been known earlier, reconstructions of human evolution might have emphasized sexual relations, equality between males and females, and the origin of the family, instead of war, hunting, tool technology, and other masculine fortes."[10]

In researching this book, I have encountered example after example of how primatological, archaeological, and cultural findings have been interpreted so as to bring them into correspondence with prevailing cultural beliefs about the warlike nature of humanity. At the beginning of the project, I did not anticipate encountering such a pervasive bias in this direction.

At one level, this book presents a critical reexamination of previous interpretations of human aggression and warfare. In some cases, I question the validity of underlying assumptions, critique methodology, or point out how interpretations overstep the facts. Criticism and skepticism are normal in science and scholarship. If the practice of science moves us gradually closer to a true understanding of the world—and I believe that it does—then ideally the omission of information that contradicts one's a priori views or the misrepresentation of facts should have no place in science. Scientific discovery does not advance through such practices. One case of misrepresentation and distortion that I discovered while working on this book is so egregious, in my opinion, that I have devoted most of a chapter to sorting out the facts from the fantasy. Fortunately, blatant omissions and deliberate distortions of information are relatively rare in scientific research and reporting. Consequently, the more common challenge when reading reports involves assessing the methodology and weighing the findings, interpretations, and conclusions from a particular work against existing theory and the results of other studies. Probably the most difficult challenge in the scientific endeavor is to minimize the effects of one's own biases and unwarranted assumptions.

This book also presents copious anthropological findings. A wealth of cross-cultural information exists on conflict management, reconciliation, peacemaking, and related topics from around the world, but it is scattered across a vast number of library shelves. I have drawn on this bounty of anthropological sources, for instance, to illustrate that peacemaking and conflict-resolving patterns exist across cultures, to document that numerous nonwarring societies exist, to illustrate key features of internally peaceful societies, and to explore the nature of peace and aggression among nomadic hunter-gatherers. Some chapters have numerous short anthropological examples and other chapters have longer cultural case studies. I have drawn on my own field studies among the Zapotec of Mexico as well. Additionally, findings from comparative, cross-cultural research projects of other researchers are presented. In short, this book rests soundly on anthropological data, documented in the notes and bibliography.

By now the reader may have surmised that some of the ideas in this book go against traditional thinking. Challenging an established view will undoubtedly generate controversy, which can be beneficial. At the same time, I have come to realize that controversies tend to become polarized. Shades of gray are forcefully relabeled as either black or white. The middle ground evaporates and recondenses at the poles representing the most extreme views. One conflict resolution specialist at a conference a few years ago referred to the polarization process as "hardening of the categories." Semantic confusion often enters the picture also as people "talk past each other." Therefore, I have attempted to express my ideas as precisely as possible with the hope of communicating exactly what I mean to say. For example, when I express the conclusion, based on an evaluation of several lines of evidence, that warfare was a rare anomaly through most of prehistory, I am *not* implying the nonexistence of all forms of violence—fights, murders, executions—over evolutionary time. Similarly, when I conclude that *warfare* is not an evolutionary adaptation, I am in fact talking about warfare (*not* all forms of human aggression). Additionally, in arguing that *warfare* is not an evolutionary *adaptation,* I am not dismissing evolution theory in general, the concept of adaptation, Charles Darwin, or all academic disciplines that take evolutionary approaches. When I suggest that humanity *could* abolish the institution of warfare, my conclusion is based on a study of the anthropological material, not a blind faith that humans are angels. There will always be a need for police and jails, laws and courts, and arbitrators and mediators. Abolishing war will not mean an end to conflict. What I will propose by the end of the book is that anthropology shows humans to have the *capacity* to replace the institution of war with international conflict resolution procedures that could assure effective dispute resolution, human rights protection, and security for the people of the world—social features that are sorely underdeveloped in the current international *war system.* This conclusion, as we will see, stems from a comprehensive review of the anthropological data on conflict management, social organization, and human evolution. Such a macroscopic anthropological perspective, spanning evolutionary time and cross-cultural space, leads to a consideration of future *potentials* for peace that is considerably broader than most current-day political perspectives and, I think, very valuable.

A sleuthing analogy may help to clarify what I am attempting to accomplish in this book. Imagine that Holmes and Watson don't know the sex of a person who has just moved into their neighborhood, but they have heard that the new neighbor lives alone. Walking by the house on Saturday afternoon, they observe the following clues. The name on the mailbox says "Tyler Geoffrey." The pickup truck parked in front of the house has a somewhat sexist bumper sticker that, in advertising "Carol's Pizzeria," attempts to humorously equate women with pizza. Glancing in the side window of the truck, Holmes astutely observes that the driver's seat is adjusted far back from the steering wheel. Based on these facts, the obvious conclusion is that the new neighbor is a man. It seems crazy to argue that a tall, pickup-driving, sexist person named Tyler might be a woman.

In this book, we are confronted in the broadest terms with two rival interpretations of human nature and the potential for peace. According to the first view, humans (especially human males) are a bloodthirsty mob, prone to be violent and warlike by nature. Advocates of this dark-sided, demonic view attempt to link chimpanzee and human violence, discuss sex differences, and recount a litany of barbarity, atrocity, and brutality as incontrovertible evidence that this portrait of humanity is accurate. The validity of this view may seem rather obvious. However, a different—but *not* polar opposite—perspective is taken in this book. According to this second perspective, clearly humans are capable of a great deal of violence, but they also have a huge capacity for peace. And specifically, a reexamination of the evidence leads to the conclusion that humans are *not* warlike *by nature*. I realize this may sound like an improbable idea at first. If so, I must beg for indulgence and propose that we reexamine *which perspective is best supported by the available ethnographic, cross-cultural, and archaeological evidence.*

To express a question in terms of our sleuthing analogy, how solid is the *seemingly obvious* conclusion that Holmes and Watson's new neighbor is a man? Bear in mind that they haven't actually seen the person. They are basing their conclusion on circumstantial evidence alone. Thus we can begin to question assumptions. What if Tyler Geoffrey was the previous resident's name? What if Tyler in this case actually is the name of a woman? What if the pickup truck belongs to someone else? Or, assuming that the truck in fact does belong to the new neighbor, aren't some women tall? And don't some women drive pickup trucks? It is even possible, although perhaps not probable, that a woman could own a truck displaying a bumper sticker that most women would shun. What if she borrowed the truck from a male friend for moving? The main point is this: The initial "obvious" conclusion rests on a set of assumptions and may be absolutely wrong.

In this book, I advocate a healthy skepticism about traditional views. I propose that, paralleling the circumstantial evidence in our analogy, the evidentiary base supporting the dark-sided, demonic view of humanity is in fact very limited. And, as unlikely as it might sound at first, I suggest that some of the assumptions of the neo-Hobbesian view are flawed. In this book, we will consider specific instances where underlying assumptions turn out to be very unrealistic. We will question the logic of some explanations, asking, for instance: Are conclusions actually in accordance with the data? Are all the relevant data considered? How do proponents of a particular interpretation deal with data that contradict their perspective?

In our analogy, Holmes and Watson realize that if they really want to be sure that their new neighbor is a man, they should look for more tangible clues. Watson proposes that they knock on the door and say, "Welcome to the neighborhood." Unfortunately, no one comes to the door, but while they are waiting, Holmes surveys the interior of the house through an adjacent front window. Watson knocks a second time and looks displeased, noticing that Holmes is not-so-subtly peering through the window. In this book also, we are going to look for more clues, more evidence, to better understand the human potential for peace and the nature of human violence.

Holmes has noticed a small table, near the front door and partly under the front window. Holmes also can see across the living room to a bar-height kitchen counter. On the table near the front door Holmes notes a hairbrush with long dark hairs, a makeup kit, and a key ring containing five keys and a small plastic figure of Snoopy. Scattered on the living room sofa, which faces toward the window, Holmes spies a violet sweater, the unread daily newspaper, a cookbook, and two magazines—*Better Homes and Gardens* and a *Glamour* with model Heather Graham on the cover. The room has various cardboard moving boxes, some open, some sealed. A signed photograph of actor Jeremy Irons protrudes from one of them. Looking across the living room, Holmes scans a miscellaneous assortment of small items on the kitchen counter. One item in particular catches Holmes' attention, a plastic bottle brightly labeled "Multivitamins plus Iron."

In light of this more extensive investigation, Holmes and Watson are ready to modify their initial conclusion. They still have not been able to gather all of the information they hoped for—meeting the new neighbor face-to-face—but they have been able to collect many new clues by looking in the window. Moreover, they have *weighed* the importance of different types of information in their minds to arrive at a comprehensive judgement. Watson remarks to Holmes as they continue their walk, "I've seen more women driving pickup trucks than single men's homes with stuff like that." Holmes replies, "Precisely, Watson. And also consider the types of things that were *not* there."

Anthropology provides a great deal of data that has either not been considered at all or else has been simply dismissed by advocates of the dark-sided demonic view. After a fresh, comprehensive consideration of the facts, I hope to convince the reader that a new perspective in fact makes a lot of sense. As physicist Robert Ehrlich points out, "the nice thing about ideas in the sciences is that they can be supported or refuted by data."[11]

Anthropology offers much more than interesting—at times even exotic—tales from other cultures, some of which we will explore. Anthropological data are directly relevant to questions of war and peace. Toward the end of the book, we will consider practical applications of a macroscopic anthropological perspective for understanding, preventing, and diminishing violence and war.

A PREVIEW OF COMING ATTRACTIONS

This book has both a major and a secondary theme. The major theme is that humans have a great capacity for dealing with conflict without using violence. This *human potential for peace,* I suggest, is greatly underappreciated in comparison to a contrasting, more traditional set of beliefs in Western thinking that fixate on the human capacity for violence. Secondarily, the book explores some of the ways that the prevailing belief system with its emphasis on violence and war continues to bias interpretations of prehistory, the ethnographic record, and human nature in many subtle and not-so-subtle ways.

In chapter 2, the human potential for peace is introduced by examining a *peace system.* The societies of the Upper Xingu River basin in Brazil devalue aggression and do not make war on each other. Peace systems such as this one show that war is not an inevitable outcome of intergroup contact. Also in chapter 2, we review the prevalent kinds of human social organization, because social organization is crucial to understanding cross-cultural patterns of conflict management as well as warfare.

Chapter 3 illustrates the human capacity for resolving conflicts without violence. Short ethnographic examples from diverse cultural settings illustrate the widespread use of conflict *avoidance* and *toleration*. Additionally, ethnographic data suggest that *third-party assisted conflict management* among humans is the rule, not the exception. *Belief systems* and *conflict prevention* also are considered.

In chapter 4, I use my fieldwork in two adjacent Zapotec communities as a backdrop for making several broader points. First, a comparison of these two communities, San Andrés and La Paz, highlights the importance of socialization processes on children's learning of aggressive and nonaggressive behavior. San Andrés has a higher level of aggression than does La Paz—more physical fights, wife beatings, corporal punishment, and homicides. Already by the three- to eight-year age range, children in San Andrés and La Paz show statistically significant differences in rates of aggressive behavior that parallel the overall community patterns. Social learning environments clearly have enormous effects on individual conduct and can favor peacefulness or, at least in some social situations, aggressiveness. Second, the Zapotec research serves as a way to further explore the key concept of *cultural belief system*. A focus on differences between San Andrés and La Paz related to aggression, jealousy, gender equality, and sex roles, among other topics, illustrates the concept. Later in the book, I bring the concept close to home by suggesting that the widespread views in Western culture about the great antiquity and the naturalness of warfare also can be seen as elements of a cultural belief system. The idea *making the invisible visible* alludes to the manner in which cultural belief systems are largely taken for granted by the cultural insiders—the holders of the shared beliefs—whether we are referring to beliefs about jealousy in San Andrés or beliefs about human nature shared by many Westerners. Third, the Zapotec research serves to introduce the idea of *cultural variation in levels and expression of aggression*. Even at an intracultural level represented by San Andrés and La Paz, human communities can differ markedly in degrees of peacefulness.

Chapter 5 proposes that a *cross-cultural peacefulness–aggressiveness continuum* is a useful way to conceptualize variability across human societies. Near one end of the cross-cultural continuum, societies have very low levels of physical aggression. This chapter relates to both of the book's themes. First, the documentation of over 80 societies that have very low levels of aggression—those near the peaceful end of the cross-cultural continuum—again demonstrates the human potential for peace. Second, the existence of numerous highly peaceful societies calls into question the veracity of Western beliefs about natural human belligerency.

Chapter 6 describes three peaceful societies in greater detail: the Semai of Malaysia, the Ifaluk of Micronesia, and Norwegians. These cultures have belief systems that promote nonviolent behavior, as do most internally peaceful societies. The Semai and the Ifaluk cases in particular debunk the idea of universal male violence. The Norwegian example additionally shows that modern nations can achieve extremely low levels of aggression in social life.

With chapter 7, the book shifts toward a consideration of war. A huge amount of anthropological data speaks to questions of war, peace, and human nature. The data contradict assertions that war is natural, universal, and ancient. Several cross-cultural studies of warfare are reviewed and in some cases methodological issues are raised for the reader's consideration. Cross-cultural studies as a group show war to be common among societies, but not universal. A listing of over 70 nonwarring societies from around the globe demonstrates clearly that war is not an inevitable feature of human existence.

Chapter 8 shows that war relates to *social organization,* as do other features of conflict management. War increases with the degree of social complexity. This finding has been replicated repeatedly across anthropological studies, yet its importance for understanding the origin of war is not widely appreciated beyond anthropology. To give this point emphasis, I've titled the chapter "Social Organization Matters!" I also highlight the critically important distinction between *simple nomadic hunter-gatherer bands* and *complex sedentary hunter-gatherers.* Nomadic bands tend to be *nonwarring,* whereas complex hunter-gatherers are often *warlike.* A great deal of confusion and needless debate continues about the peacefulness versus warlikeness of *hunter-gatherers,* because very different types of societies, *nomadic bands* versus *hierarchical chiefdoms,* are mixed together under the same label. Again, at this more specific level, *social organization matters!* All hunter-gatherers are *not* the same when it comes to war and peace.

Chapter 9 features Richard Wrangham, Dale Peterson, Margaret Mead, and Derek Freeman in an academic tango of a most unusual nature. I won't give away the story, but simply foreshadow that this cautionary tale has relevance to both themes of the book.

Chapter 10 raises the question: Was the past really as warlike as some Westerners assume? An archaeological review reveals an interesting pattern: Time and again gruesome interpretations of the human past have turned out to be wrong. We consider a handful of such cases. This chapter also examines archaeological data on the antiquity of warfare. The oldest archaeological evidence of war is extremely recent, within the last 10,000 years or so, corresponding with the development of agriculture and associated dramatic changes in human lifestyle.

Chapter 11 makes a straightforward yet important point. Western observers routinely misapply martial language, appropriate to their own warring cultural tradition, when describing social phenomena in other cultures that in reality have nothing to do with *warfare.*

Chapter 12 explores the *peace system* of the Australian Aborigines. For many millennia prior to the arrival of Europeans in Australia, the island-continent was the realm of largely nomadic hunter-gatherers, unencroached upon by agricultural or herding peoples. The ethnographic material on Australian Aborigine societies shows a highly consistent pattern: *Warfare was a rare anomaly.* Are there more general lessons here about the human past? For more than 99 percent of prehistory, all of humanity lived as nomadic hunter-gatherers. The fact that the Australian Aborigines were basically nonwarring suggests an intriguing question: Could the same have been true for most of human prehistory—prior to the rise of agriculture—elsewhere on the planet as well? The Australian Aborigine peace system, like the worldwide archaeological record, suggests that such a possibility is not as far-fetched as it might at first seem.

Chapters 13 and 14 return us to questioning assumptions about human belligerence by scrutinizing the Pervasive Intergroup Hostility Model of human prehistory. As the name implies, the Pervasive Intergroup Hostility Model asserts that the human past was conflict-laden and often violent. However, an examination of recurring social patterns seen among simple nomadic foragers suggests a very different picture of the human past. When the assumptions of the Pervasive Intergroup Hostility Model are evaluated by comparing them with actual data on simple nomadic hunter-gatherers, it becomes apparent that the model is extremely unrealistic. At the same time, many of the model's presumptions *do* correspond with today's world. Whereas the Pervasive Intergroup Hostility Model mirrors current political, demographic, and social conditions, it is a *very implausible* portrayal of humanity's nomadic hunter-gatherer past.

Chapter 15 continues the critical examination of implausible assumptions. In a series of publications, Napoleon Chagnon reports that among the South American Yanomamö, killers have *three times* as many children as men who have not killed.[12] These findings have proliferated in the literature and are often emphasized in evolutionary discussions of warfare or violence.[13] In this chapter, I explore a series of conceptual, methodological, and analytical problems with these Yanomamö findings. To mention one major problem, the reproductive advantage originally emphasized by Chagnon for participating in a killing turns out to have been greatly inflated, in part because an average age difference of *at least 10 years* between killers and nonkillers was not adequately taken into consideration. Not surprisingly, older Yanomamö men average more children than younger men, whether or not they have participated in a killing.[14]

Having critiqued the Pervasive Intergroup Hostility Model overall and more particularly the Yanomamö findings on the alleged reproductive advantage of killers, I turn, in chapter 16, to laying the groundwork for an alternative approach. Nomadic foragers, while not living representatives of prehistoric societies, are, nonetheless, the most defendable choice among the various types of human societies to use in making inferences about past lifeways. Five nomadic hunter-gatherer conflict management case studies are presented. Key observations paralleling those on nomadic forager bands of Australia are that war is rare or lacking and conflicts tend to be between particular individuals, not entire groups.

Chapters 17 and 18 provide an alternative perspective on human aggression. The theoretical argument draws on evolutionary theory, game theory, the behavioral ecology of animal conflict, and patterns in data on simple hunter-gatherer societies. This multifaceted perspective suggests that *individual aggression* in humans, as in various species, is a product of natural and sexual selection. However, the same conclusion cannot logically be made related to *human warfare*. Aggression is certainly not a fixed response, but rather, variable in its expression—or lack of expression. Furthermore, there are both empirical and theoretical reasons for suggesting that *restraint* against engaging in aggression has been favored by selection over evolutionary time. In science, interpretations should correspond as closely as possible to the available data. I suggest that this alternative perspective on human warfare and violence fits the facts much better than dark-sided demonic views, the Pervasive Intergroup Hostility Model, or generalizations based on problematic Yanomamö findings. This alternative perspective is *not* antievolutionary. It does involve viewing the evidence in a new way and including evidence that has traditionally been ignored. Finally, this perspective attempts to balance the acknowledged human capacity for aggression with the underappreciated human potential for peace.

Chapter 19 summarizes the arguments presented throughout the book. We return to the Holmes and Watson sleuthing analogy as a device for making concluding points about assumptions, models, facts, and beliefs.

Chapter 20 explores the crucial practical question: What insights does anthropology offer for creating a more peaceful world? Margaret Mead once expressed, "One of the principal contributions of anthropology should be to distill from our available treasure house of small and unusual social models . . . new combinations and new forms that will release us from our historically limited imaginations."[15] The anthropological literature on war, peace, conflict, and conflict management suggests a variety of insights for building and preserving peace. In this book, by drawing comprehensively on anthropological material, I suggest that *potentially* war could be eliminated and replaced by effective conflict management procedures and institutions.

In addition to offering a macroscopic perspective on the human potential for peace, anthropology provides certain insights that could prove helpful in moving humanity beyond war. Some of the anthropological ideas include enhancing crosscutting ties among social groups, recognizing the new reality of global interdependence and the consequential necessity of acting cooperatively, adopting new attitudes and cultural beliefs appropriate to an interdependent world that promote nonviolent conflict resolution practices and no longer accept warfare as a legitimate activity, and creating overarching authority structures for effective governance and conflict management. The demonstrated cross-cultural relationship between the complexity of social organization and the use of authoritative judicial procedures provides us with a valuable insight about the *potential* of international institutions to provide security, assure justice, and resolve disputes in the 21st century and beyond. Rather than jumping immediately into the exploration of real-world applications such as these, we must begin by building a necessary foundation by considering the anthropological findings on conflict and peace from diverse cultural settings and across millennia.

CHAPTER 2

THE PEACE SYSTEM OF THE UPPER XINGU

> In the Waurá view, self-control over violent aggressive impulses, compassion for children, and acceptance of the responsibility to share material wealth are all basic attributes of human beings.
>
> EMILIENNE IRELAND[1]

Terms like *aggression* and *conflict* have multiple meanings and applications in daily speech. The word *aggression,* for instance, can suitably apply to a schoolyard fight, the unrelenting persistence of a telephone solicitor, spouse abuse, or Hitler's invasion of Poland. The term *conflict,* likewise, can refer to phenomena as disparate as psychic turmoil and warfare.

Conflict is defined in this book as "a perceived divergence of interests—where interests are broadly conceptualized to include values, needs, goals, and wishes—between two or more parties, often accompanied by feelings of anger or hostility."[2] *Aggression* means the infliction of harm, pain, or injury on other individuals. Sometimes aggression is subdivided into verbal and physical aggression. *A central point is that conflict need not involve any aggression whatsoever.* Thus, aggression and conflict are *not* synonymous.

In this book, the term *violence* is reserved for severe forms of *physical aggression.* Thus, simply shouting angrily at someone without any physical contact is neither physical aggression nor violence. Shouting is verbal aggression. If the verbal tirade escalates to include some relatively mild contact, such as slapping or pushing, this physical aggression generally would not be considered serious enough to warrant calling it violence. Violence entails forceful attacks, usually with weapons that can result in serious injuries or death.

Although violence may be one of the most noticeable and destructive ways through which people handle conflict, a close examination of cross-cultural data reveals that *people usually deal with conflicts without violence.* Humans have a remarkable capacity for getting along with each other peacefully, preventing physical aggression, limiting the scope and spread of violence, and restoring peace following aggression.[3] Shortly we will consider an illustration of this human potential for peace—an intertribal peace system in Brazil's Upper Xingu River basin.

The suggestion that peacefulness and the nonviolent handling of conflict predominate in human affairs might seem to be contradicted by daily observations, especially to people who have become accustomed to Hollywood films and daily newscasts stuffed with images of murders, rapes, riots, and wars. A study of over 2000 television programs aired between 1973 and 1993 on major networks in the United States found that more than 60 percent featured violence and over 50 percent of the leading characters in these shows were involved in violence.[4] However, as professors of criminal justice Bahram Haghighi and Jon Sorensen write, "the media tend to distort the types of criminal victimization occurring and exaggerate true accounts of criminal victimization in the community."[5] In other words, violence-saturated programming can contribute to a false, unrealistically violent, picture of the world.

In actuality, the vast majority of people on the planet awake on a typical morning and live through a *violence-free day*—and this experience generally continues day after day. The overwhelming majority of humanity spends an average day without inflicting any physical aggression on anyone, without being the victim of physical aggression, and, in all likelihood, without even witnessing any physical aggression *with their own eyes* among the hundreds or thousands of persons they encounter. Perhaps surprisingly, this generalization holds in even the most violent cultures on earth. Clayton and Carole Robarchek conducted fieldwork among a culture, the Waorani of Ecuador, where over 60 percent of the deaths in the last several generations were violent ones. Yet the Robarcheks report that "even during this period when the raiding was comparatively intense, years passed between raids." And while the rate of spearings had markedly decreased by the time the Robarcheks did fieldwork—and the reasons for this huge reduction in killing is an intriguing story that I'll save for later—*the Robarcheks never actually saw the Waorani kill anyone*. Furthermore, they note that Waorani "child socialization is indulgent and non-punitive, both husbands and wives care for children, and children's relations with both parents are warm and affectionate." They also report that "we saw no violence between spouses. . . . The only overt violence that we saw during both of our field trips was one instance of a child attacking his brother." Daily life is tranquil.[6]

Bruce Knauft provides another paradoxical case of a peaceful violent culture, the Gebusi of New Guinea.[7] The Gebusi are tranquil in daily life; at the same time, their homicide rate is one of the highest in the world. A third illustration comes from my research in a Mexican Zapotec community referred to as San Andrés (see chapter 4). Interspersed between periodic acts of physical aggression such as fistfights, wife beatings, and the physical punishment of children, most typical daily scenes are peaceful. These examples illustrate that whereas violence undeniably does occur at times, *it is not as prevalent as people sometimes assume, even in so-called violent cultures*. At times, discussion of crime and crime statistics exaggerate violence. In order to "see" the daily violence, more often than not, one relies on images relayed by the news crews scouring the planet for video footage of mayhem from war zones, riots, terrorist attacks, or sensational crime scenes.

In actuality, one can travel from continent to continent and personally observe hundreds of thousands of humans interacting nonviolently. Even if searching for conflict, an observer may find people talking over their differences, ridiculing a rival, persuading and coaxing someone, and perhaps arguing. A traveling observer also may find people negotiating solutions to their disputes, agreeing to provide compensation for damages, reaching compromises, while perhaps also reconciling and forgiving one another, all without violence, within families and among friends, neighbors, associates, acquaintances, and strangers. In contrast to violence, such pervasive human activities rarely make the news. Additionally, time and again, individuals from various cultures simply walk away from conflict—and such widespread avoidance and toleration tend to be both invisible and considered unnewsworthy. Dealing with interpersonal and intergroup conflict is an important part of daily human existence but is largely just taken for granted.

A PEACE SYSTEM

Buell Quain began studying the Trumaí people of Brazil's Upper Xingu River basin in August 1938. His fieldwork was interrupted, and in 1939 before he was able to return to his study, he died. Quain's mother carefully organized and typed her son's handwritten diary and field notes before giving them to Professor Charles Wagley with the hope that her son's material would prove of some anthropological significance. Wagley asked then graduate student Robert Murphy—who later became known for his work among another Brazilian people, the Mundurucú—to attempt to organize Quain's notes for publication. Aside from being an interesting ethnography, the resulting book, *The Trumaí Indians of Central Brazil,* published in 1955 under joint authorship, is somewhat unusual because Murphy had never met coauthor Quain! Murphy comments that "the information is Quain's product, its ordering into a coherent description of Trumaí culture mine."[8]

In 1938, Quain had observed that the Trumaí and the other tribes of the Upper Xingu River basin, although sometimes raided by outside tribes, did not make war on each other. "Intertribal bonds within the upper Xingú Basin were based on peaceful relations between the tribes. These tribes formed part of a bounded social system in which groups outside the area did not take part."[9]

In fact, even earlier, the first European to visit the Upper Xingu, German explorer Karl von den Steiner, first in 1884 and again in 1887, had found a cluster of peoples representing four different language groups participating in a broader, peaceful social system.[10] Thomas Gregor, who has conducted fieldwork among the peoples of the present-day Xingu tribes, especially among the Mehinaku, observes, "What is striking about the Xinguanos is that they are peaceful. During the one hundred years over which we have records there is no evidence of warfare among the Xingu groups. To be sure there have been instances of witchcraft killings across tribal lines, and rare defensive reactions to assaults from the war-like tribes outside the Xingu basin. But there is no tradition of violence among Xingu communities."[11]

The single-village tribes within the Upper Xingu River basin have a combined population of 1200.[12] The Carib language family is represented by the Kuikuru, Kalapalo, Nafukuá, and Matipú tribes; Arawak-speakers include the Mehinaku, Wauja/Waurá, and the Yawalapití/Yaulapití; Tupian language speakers are the Kamayura/Kamaiyura and the Aultí; and the Trumaí studied by Quain speak a language of the same name.[13]

Although there are variations among the groups, certain commonalties of culture exist.[14] The Xinguanos are slash-and-burn horticulturalists, planting manioc and maize as their primary crops.[15] The men clear patches of forest for gardens that are then worked by the women. Hunting tends not to be of much importance, but fishing contributes a substantial amount of protein to the diet. About 20 percent of the men are "chiefs," but in fact chiefs wield virtually no power.[16] They suggest activities and attempt to persuade others to follow particular courses of action, but if others don't go along, the chiefs have no way of forcing the villagers to comply with their wishes. Head chiefs give regular public speeches, lecturing to their villagers. Above all else, chiefs should be generous to the people, not show anger, and set an example of peaceful, lawful conduct. Gregor writes that among the Mehinaku, a chief "approximates the idealized father in that he represents prosocial values and the repression of antisocial impulses."[17]

Despite their different languages and dialects, the single-village tribes of the Upper Xingu River basin are interconnected through trade, intermarriage, and ceremonial commonalties. Shortly we will consider how interdependencies contribute to the maintenance of the peace system. We also will consider how two mutually reinforcing value orientations—one that directly encourages peaceful conduct and a second that strongly devalues violence—operate toward the same end of preventing war among the tribes of the Upper Xingu. First, however, the sexuality of the Xingu peoples deserves a brief consideration, for although there is a great deal of adultery, the expression of jealousy through male–male violence rarely occurs.

Xinguanos are both active and relatively open regarding sex. In the words of one man, "Good fish get dull, but sex is always fun."[18] Mehinaku men are described as "perpetually sexual," and both Trumaí men and women, according to Murphy and Quain, have "a frank and honest interest" in sex.[19] In Kalapalo language, the word for coitus literally means "to eat something sweet."[20] Sexual relations between unmarried persons is expected and "subject to little or no public censure."[21] "So casual is the attitude toward premarital courtship that girls are said to unabashedly return from an assignation smeared with their boyfriend's body paint," writes Gregor of the Mehinaku.[22] Kalapalo girls, who according to custom are supposed to remain in seclusion behind a dividing wall in their family huts, surreptitiously receive visits by lovers.[23] Quain was apparently surprised by the openness with which one young Trumaí man in particular kept him updated on this sexual adventures, and recounts how this man just "borrowed" Quain's hut one evening to have noisy intercourse with one of his girlfriends amongst Quain's kitchen paraphernalia.[24]

Adultery is common, especially, but not exclusively, on the part of husbands. Quain observed that a Trumaí chief, Maibu, was one of the most avid adulterers, regularly carrying on affairs with unmarried women and also with another man's wife when her husband was away from the village. Ellen Basso concludes that virtually all Kalapalo have at least one extramarital lover, and some people have many extramarital partners, usually from several tribes. Of the Mehinaku, Gregor reports that among 37 adults, approximately 88 extramarital affairs were being conducted at a given point in time. Among 20 men, the number of ongoing affairs ranged from a low of one to a high of ten. Three of 17 women were not engaged in extramarital relationships, whereas the remaining women had between 3 and 14 lovers each. Infidelity is clearly the rule, not the exception. Men typically were motivated to have an affair out of sexual desire, whereas the women's reasons for engaging in liaisons tended to be multifaceted: for social contact with the men, to receive gifts from their lovers, and for sexual enjoyment. By the way, a typical and much appreciated gift given by a man to his lover is a freshly caught fish. Even in light of the number of sexual partners available to most Mehinaku, the men report that they would like to have sex more often. In fact, the males complain that women are stingy with their genitals. This is balanced by the female complaint, as expressed among the Trumaí, that they have to "dispense their favors to too many men too often."[25]

The regular social interaction among Xinguanos from different tribes facilitates finding sexual partners beyond one's own village. Interaction has the potential for reducing intertribal prejudices, a point illustrated as a Mehinaku man recounts his attitude change about the Carib language: "I ate their food, had sex with their women, and learned their words. Now I think their language is beautiful."[26]

Gregor comments that the Mehinaku children, while imitating adult activities during their play, adopt the roles of wives and husbands, shamans and chiefs, as well as extramarital lovers. "A Mehinaku child grows up in an erotically charged social environment. Living on close terms with his sexually active older kin and occasionally following them out to the garden to watch their assignations, a ten-year-old child is already a sophisticate by American standards."[27]

What about jealousy among the Xinguanos? Jealous husbands usually do not physically attack rivals, but they may beat their wives. Certainly there are differences among individuals and possibly among the different Xingu tribes in this regard. Murphy and Quain tell that a jealous Trumaí wife might not speak to her husband's lover and possibly attack the woman by pulling her hair.[28] No Trumaí wife was ever seen attacking her adulterous husband, although they usually seem bothered by the affair. One woman, however, merely chuckled at her husband's sexual pursuits. This type of reaction may even be typical among Yawalapití wives.[29] The fact that a jealous husband might beat his wife is reported for the Trumaí, Yawalapití, and Mehinaku, but it also is clear that husbands often just "look the other way."[30] Jealousy tends to diminish with age. Gertrude Dole writes of the Kuikuru that "A jealous bride may fight with her unfaithful husband early in their marriage, but older couples merely tolerate mutual infidelity. Hence an extraordinary amount of extramarital sexual relations occurs without causing open hostility."[31] Among the Mehinaku, "extramarital affairs seldom provoke serious confrontations. . . . Jealousy is tempered by social pressure that enjoins discretion in managing affairs and avoiding confrontations."[32] Similarly, the expression of physical aggression over a woman, or for any reason, is considered socially unacceptable among the Trumaí. Instead, an angry husband may deliver a public harangue at the man he knows or suspects to be having an affair with his wife.[33]

Gregor considers additional complexities of Mehinaku sexuality in his book, *Anxious Pleasures,* and in various publications he addresses other aspects of Xinguano culture, including the ways in which these tribes maintain the peace. Over several periods of fieldwork, Gregor lived among the Mehinaku and the Yawalapití, visited most of the other Xingu tribes, and interviewed persons from all of them. On the basis of his research, Gregor concludes that the institutional basis of the Xingu peace system rests on three pillars: intervillage trade, intermarriage, and ceremonial interconnections. The value system also plays an important role in preserving the peace.[34]

Persons in each tribe produce specialized items to trade with people from other groups. The Wauja make pottery. The Tupian-speaking Kamayurá specialize in making hardwood bows from *pau d'arco* trees that grow in their area. The Carib-speaking tribes such as the Kalapalo and Kuikuru make highly valued shell necklaces and waistbands. The Arawak-speaking Yawalapití also make shell decorations. The Trumaí formerly made stone axes but by the time of Quain's fieldwork had shifted to salt production as a trade specialty. Likewise, the Mehinaku make salt from water hyacinth plants, a trade specialty that requires a substantial input in labor.[35]

The production specialties of the tribes and the elaborate system of exchange among them combine to build bridges and interdependencies that contribute to peace. Murphy and Quain state: "No aspect of trade was recognized as divorced from personal relations."[36] The point that Xinguanos use the exchange of specialized goods to cement social relationships across village lines is highlighted by the fact that for the most part the production monopolies result from social arrangements rather than from exclusive access to specialized knowledge or the control of particular critical resources. Gregor sums up the important features of reciprocal exchange among persons of the different tribes, emphasizing that the system represents much more than mere economic transactions:

> Trade means trust, since items offered may not be reciprocated for several months or more. Trade means mutual appreciation, since craft objects, unlike our manufactures, are an extension of the self which the maker hopes will be admired. Trade is a social relationship that is valued in and of itself, and is a conscious reason for maintaining monopolies. As one of my informants explained to me: "They have things that are really beautiful, and we have things that they like. And so we trade and that is good."[37]

Widespread intermarriage also contributes to the maintenance of peaceful relations among the cultures of the Upper Xingu.[38] The dominant pattern is for the wife to shift residence to join her husband's village, although on occasion the man will move to his wife's tribe. The Yawalapití, for example, do not marry other persons from their own village, seeking spouses instead among the Kamayurá, Kuikuru, Kalapalo, and Mehinaku.[39] Among the Kuikuru, 30 percent of marriages are with persons from other tribes, and among the Mehinaku, the figure is about 35 percent.[40] A man with parents from two different tribes expressed his intertribal identity as he gestured, dividing his body down the middle, "This side . . . Mehinaku. That side is Waurá."[41] The result of this long-standing pattern of intertribal marriages is that persons with multiple identifications and numerous ties of kinship interlink the Xingu societies. The presence of relatives, trading partners, and friends in the other tribes is a huge disincentive for making war among these interconnected social groups.

The third pillar of peace involves the ceremonial and ritual interdependencies that the Xingu tribes have created and vigorously nourish. Gregor describes one ritual, called *Yawari,* that includes mock aggression between pairs of relatives from different tribes. The ritual can be seen as a controlled expression of antagonism that ends with a reaffirmation of friendly, nonhostile intentions (see Figure 2.1).[42]

A different ceremony involving the simultaneous inauguration of chiefs and the mourning of passed chiefs requires the participation of all the tribes.[43] The ceremony reinforces for the participants that they are all part of a larger, peaceful social system. As one Xinguano expresses, "We don't make war; we have festivals for the chiefs to which all of the villages come. We sing, dance, trade and wrestle."[44]

Intertribal trading relationships, marriages and the resulting kinship ties, and ceremonial bonds are only part of the Xingu peace system.[45] Additionally, a set of shared values promotes peaceful conduct and simultaneously discourages acts of violence, including war. In the Xingu value orientation, peace is moral, whereas war and violence

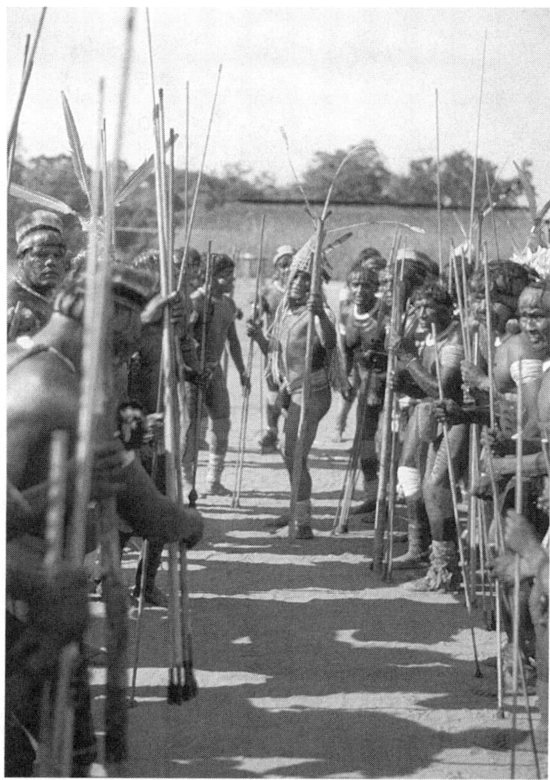

Figure 2.1 Men of the Yawalapití and Mehinaku tribes engage in the Yawari ritual in 1989. In turn, paired opponents hurl and parry wax-tipped arrows as they stand at opposite ends of a narrow corridor formed by observing men. The wax-tipped arrows, which both opponents are holding in the photo, do not cause serious damage. After this exchange of ritualized and limited aggression, the opponents reaffirm their bonds of kinship and friendship. (Photo courtesy of Thomas Gregor.)

are immoral. A person gains prestige and respect through being tranquil and self-controlled. Social approval flows to persons who refrain from violence. An ideal person is generous, avoids confrontation with others, remains calm even if angry, and forsakes interpersonal aggression.[46] Gregor writes that "the good citizen is therefore peaceful in response to both the moral imperative of peace and the aesthetics of behavior."[47] Carneiro reports that "the Kuikuru are strongly socialized from childhood to be amiable and to refrain from expressing anger. Indeed, fights among men in the village are unknown."[48] An acceptable, if not encouraged, practice among the Mehinaku as well as other groups is to move to another village to leave conflict behind.[49] Furthermore, the warrior role is neither valued nor rewarded.[50]

Although generally peaceful places, Xingu villages are not totally free of hostility and competition. Thefts occur, spouses sometimes express jealousy, and people are fearful of witchcraft.[51] Among the Trumaí, a typical outlet for hostility or anger is to deliver

Figure 2.2 During Mehinaku wrestling matches, opponents vigorously struggle for advantage. Everyone in the village knows who the champion wrestlers are. Of the highly skilled wrestler, Tom Gregor writes, "Likened to the anaconda in the quickness of his holds and the way he 'ties up' his opponents, he commands fear and respect. To the women, he is 'beautiful' (*awitsiri*), in demand as a paramour and husband." (Photo courtesy of Thomas Gregor; quote from Gregor 1985:96.)

a public harangue. Rivalries also are expressed competitively, yet nonviolently, through the regular wrestling matches that occur between persons of the same or neighboring villages.[52] To the Xingu, expressing their anger through wrestling allows it to subside. "When our bellies are 'hot with anger' we wrestle and the anger is gone."[53] Wrestling matches can be seen as the Olympics of the Xingu world (see Figure 2.2).

In addition to the positive value that Xinguanos place on calm and peaceful conduct, they also hold antiwar and antiviolent values. It should be remembered that even though Xinguanos are against war, they have defended themselves periodically from raiding by tribes such as the Suyá, Shavante, and Txicão who live outside the Xingu basin. Murphy and Quain point out that the Trumaí gain no prestige from warfare: "Trumaí men showed scars of old wounds to Quain, but only to impress him with the hostility of other tribes. To the Trumaí, warfare was an occasion for fear, and not an opportunity to enhance one's status." Gregor reaches a similar conclusion, and Emilienne Ireland explains that for the Wauja, violence and war are morally degrading: "Far from viewing physical aggression with awe and admiration, they see it as pathetic and a mark of failed leadership. The Wauja term for warrior or soldier, *peyeteki yekeho,* can be translated as 'man whose greatest talent is losing his self control.' "[54]

In the belief systems of the Xingu tribes, three categories of humans exist: (1) peaceful peoples of the Xingu basin, (2) wild and warlike Indians from beyond the Xingu area, and (3) all non-Indians, or, basically, the "whites." Interestingly, the concept of "wild Indian" reinforces the antiwar and antiviolent value orientation of the Xingu people, and they use this stereotypical image as a point of contrast to what they see as their morally superior peaceful, civilized way of life. For example, people from the Xingu Arawak-speaking villages explained the violent nature of the wild Indian to Gregor as follows: "He beats his children. He rapes his wife. He shoots arrows at the white man's planes. He splits peoples' heads with clubs. He kidnaps children and burns villages. He kills his own kin. War for him is a festival." Clearly the Xinguanos view the wild Indians with disdain. But this is not the main point. As the antithesis of their own peaceful way of life, Xinguanos evoke their stereotype of repulsive, violent wild Indians, not as an excuse to fight them, but instead to remind themselves and to teach their children that warfare and violence are morally repugnant activities, inappropriate within Xinguano society.[55]

Another manifestation of the antiwar, antiviolent ethos is the way that most of the Upper Xingu tribes regard blood. Blood, whether human or animal, is a vile contaminant that can cause illness. Among the Mehinaku blood evokes revulsion and disgust. Mehinaku men who decades ago had defended the Xingu peoples against the "wild" Txicão Indians had to take special medicine to rid themselves of the defiling blood before they could resume normal village life.[56] The Mehinaku also have taboos against eating most animals, and those they do eat are cooked thoroughly to remove the last traces of blood.[57] Somewhat relatedly, the Kalapalo believe that hunting is violence and should be avoided.[58] Thus the constellation of beliefs about blood and the associated feelings of aversion and disgust reinforce the broader moral sentiment that killing and war are wrongful, dangerous acts to be avoided except under the most dire circumstances, such as in defense of one's life and family.

The Wauja antiviolent beliefs as well as their view of blood are reflected in the following myth about how the three different kinds of humanity received their basic characters from the Sun.

> The Sun offers a rifle to the ancestor of the Wauja, but the Wauja merely turns it over in his hands, not knowing how to use it. The Sun takes the rifle from the Wauja and offers it to the ancestor of the warlike Indians who live to the north of the Wauja. This Indian is also baffled by the rifle, and so the Sun takes it away again and this time hands it to the ancestor of the whiteman.
>
> . . . Next the Sun passed around a gourd dipper from which each man was asked to drink. The ancestor of the Wauja approached, but found to his horror that the dipper was filled to the brim with blood. He refused to touch it, but when the warlike Indian was offered the dipper, he readily drank from it. When the Sun finally offered the dipper of blood to the whiteman, he drank it down greedily in great gulps.
>
> That is why the whiteman and the warlike Indian tribes are so violent today; even in ancient times, they were thirsty for the taste of blood. To the Wauja, however, the Sun gave a dipper of manioc porridge. And that is why the Wauja drink manioc porridge today, and why they are not a brutal and violent people.[59]

Institutionally, friendly peaceful interaction among the tribes in the Upper Xingu basin is created and re-created on a daily basis through exchange, kinship, and ritual. Unlike a prevalent Western view that the roots of war lie in some uniformly violent human nature, Xinguanos differentiate between their own civilized, peaceful nature and the violent natures of wild Indians and whites. War and violence constitute uncivilized, immoral conduct.

The Xingu peace system was already firmly in place when first observed over 100 years ago, and since that time there have been no acts of war among these tribes.[60] The system, however, does not protect the Xinguanos from violence originating outside its boundaries, either by wild Indians or whites. Thus Xinguanos periodically have had to defend themselves from attacks by outsiders. A lesson to deduce is that to be truly effective, a peace system must be inclusive, incorporating any groups on the periphery.

SOCIAL ORGANIZATION

The Upper Xingu peace system presents just one illustration of the human potential for peace. In the next chapter, we will consider the wealth of ways that humans handle conflict without violence across different types of *social organization*. Therefore, as a useful precursor to this discussion, we will now briefly consider the major kinds of human social organization.

Service proposes four basic categories of human social organization: bands, tribes, chiefdoms, and states. Christopher Boehm makes finer distinctions, describing *nomadic hunter-gatherers* (corresponding to Service's *bands*), *acephalous tribes* and *big-man societies* (together roughly corresponding to Service's *tribes*), *sedentary foragers* and *chiefdoms* (called *chiefdoms* by Service), and *primitive kingdoms, ancient civilizations,* and *modern states* (all variants of *states,* in Service's system).[61]

For the most part, the four-part scheme of Service serves our purposes as we consider conflict management in the next chapter and violence and warfare later in the book.[62] Bands are small in size (generally with about 25–50 members), are politically egalitarian, lack clear leadership, are nomadic or semi-nomadic, and engage in hunting-and-gathering as a subsistence strategy. Individuals shift readily among different bands. Consequently, anthropologists refer to band composition as being flexible and in flux. Additionally, band society lacks ranked social statuses or classes and tends not to be subdivided into corporate subgroups—or, social segments—on the basis of kinship or other distinctions. As we shall see later in the book, this last point, although often ignored, is of critical importance in understanding patterns of human aggressive behavior. Nomadic, egalitarian, hunter-gatherer band society is the oldest and simplest form of human social organization, extending back over humanity's evolutionary past. Anthropologists often note that members of the human line have spent over 99 percent of their existence on the planet living in nomadic bands.

Tribes tend to be sedentary and typically engage in hoe-farming horticulture. Tribal settlements may contain 100 or more persons. Although *headmen, big men,* and other leadership roles tend to emerge in tribal societies, the leadership is weak. Tribal leaders attempt to exert their will through the art of persuasion and by leading through example, since they lack, for the most part, other forms of coercive power. Boehm uses of the term *acephalous,* or headless, to reflect the lack of authority among tribal leaders. Headmen among the South American Yanomamö, a tribal society that we will consider later, typify this pattern of weak leadership. The absence of positions of strong authority really means that tribal social organization remains largely egalitarian. Unlike bands, however, tribes tend to be segmented politically into lineages—societal subgroups with membership based on descent from a common ancestor—clans, or other kinship distinctions.

Evolutionarily, sedentary, horticultural tribes represent a recent form of social organization compared to nomadic hunter-gatherer bands.

Chiefdoms exhibit considerable variability, although the existence of a social hierarchy is a distinguishing feature. Some chiefdoms vest minor authority in the chiefs, whereas in other cases, chiefs wield considerable authority. Chiefs are entitled to special privileges. Commoners pay tribute to chiefs, some of which the chiefs then redistribute back to their subjects. The economies of chiefdoms tend to be based on farming or fishing.

Boehm's scheme makes special mention of *sedentary foragers,* or, to use an alternative name, *complex hunter-gatherers.*[63] In considering conflict management and warfare from an anthropological viewpoint, it is absolutely critical *not* to confuse nomadic hunter-gatherer bands with complex, sedentary, hunter-gatherers. These types of societies are as different as night and day. Complex sedentary hunter-gatherers are socially ranked societies with rulers and commoners, and sometimes slaves as well. Population densities tend to be higher than in nomadic hunter-gatherer societies. Complex hunter-gatherers exploit rich natural resources such as the salmon runs in the rivers of the North American Northwest Coast. Ethnographically, this type of society is very rare, limited to groups like the Ainu of Japan and a cluster of North American Northwest Coast societies.[64] Archaeological evidence shows the development of complex sedentary hunter-gatherer social organization to be recent, arising in particular places only within the last 25,000 years, yet most typically within the last 13,000 years or so.[65]

As recently as 5,000 to 6,000 years ago some early chiefdoms underwent further organizational transformations. The world's first states were born. In the evolutionary history of the human species, this development of civilizations occurred only "yesterday," some 3,000 to 4,000 years B.C. The economy of states rests on agriculture. Rulers of states wield considerably more coercive power than do the rulers of chiefdoms. Economic specialization, social class distinctions, centralized political and military organization, the use of writing and mathematics, urbanization, large-scale irrigation of crops, and the development of bureaucracy characterize states, ancient and modern.[66] In reference to the present, Boehm notes that "modern democracies may temper individual power with checks and balances, but centralized power still exists and is backed by coercive force supplied by professional policemen and soldiers."[67]

CHAPTER 3

TAKEN FOR GRANTED

The Human Potential for Peace

> To irrigate both pieces of land that the two [Nubian] men farmed, the water had to be channeled first into one ditch and then into another. One of the men was always accusing the other of taking more than his share of water. An uncle overheard the shouting one day. He found a large, flat stone and put it on its side in the middle of the canal. This effectively divided the water into two streams, thus putting an end to the cause of the contention. . . . Most frequently, arguments between kinfolk are resolved quickly by a third, usually older relative.
>
> ROBERT FERNEA[1]

Conflict is an inevitable feature of social life, but clearly *physical aggression is not the only option for dealing with conflict.* Ethnographic accounts from around the globe reveal a wealth of conflict management possibilities such as "putting a stone in the middle" that do not involve violence. A cross-cultural perspective substantiates not only the human potential for violence but also the human potential for handling conflict nonviolently.

Of course, cultures prescribe particular favored ways for dealing with conflict.[2] Nonetheless, cross-cultural comparisons reveal general approaches to conflict management. In separate writings, Klaus-Friedrich Koch, Donald Black, and Laura Nader and Harry Todd categorize conflict management into the following five approaches: self-redress (self-help), avoidance, toleration, negotiation, and third-party assisted settlement (Box 3.1).[3]

Some approaches to conflict management span different kinds of social organization, from bands and tribes to chiefdoms and states. Descriptions of third parties intervening to separate disputants, for example, occur within all types of societies. However, certain approaches to conflict management are deeply affected by social organization. In turn, we will explore avoidance, toleration, negotiation, several kinds of third-party assisted settlement, and then cultural beliefs related to handling conflict. Self-redress can involve the use of physical aggression and will be considered in more detail in future chapters.

AVOIDANCE

Avoidance entails ceasing or limiting interaction with a disputant, either temporarily or permanently. The use of avoidance in response to conflict is extremely widespread and probably occurs in all social groups. As an approach to conflict, avoidance can be seen

BOX 3.1 MAJOR APPROACHES TO CONFLICT MANAGEMENT

Unilateral and Bilateral Approaches

1. *Avoidance.* Disputants cease to interact or limit their interaction, either temporarily or permanently.
2. *Toleration.* The issue in dispute is ignored as the relationship is simply continued.
3. *Negotiation.* Disputants interact to form mutually acceptable compromises or solutions. Negotiation often involves the giving and accepting of compensation.
4. *Self-Redress* (also called *self-help* and *coercion*). One disputant takes unilateral action in an attempt to prevail in a dispute or to punish another.

The Trilateral Approach

5. *Settlement.* A third party deals with a dispute. Settlement can take several forms, of which the following are common:
    - *Friendly Peacemaking.* The third party merely separates or distracts disputants.
    - *Mediation.* The third party facilitates the negotiation process.
    - *Arbitration.* The third party renders a decision, but lacks the power to enforce it.
    - *Adjudication.* The third party renders a decision and has the power to enforce it.
    - *Repressive Peacemaking.* The third party uses force or the threat of force to stifle a dispute.

as a means to *prevent* aggression. Persons who avoid each other preclude the possibility of physical altercations. As Brian Ferguson points out, avoidance at a group level is much less costly than war. He provides a list of ethnographic cases to illustrate that "when people feel in danger of being attacked, they move to a safer location. Flight is preferred to fight." Along similar lines, Robert Dentan suggests that the Semai avoidance strategy of fleeing deep into the forest when confronted with slave raiders has been extremely adaptive.[4]

Avoidance takes various forms. First, it can be short-term or long lasting. Second, it can involve only two persons or, more broadly, encompass groups of people. Third, it can entail the moving away of an individual (with or without supporters), or it can involve social manifestations (such as not speaking) in order to create psychosocial distance. An incident among the Mbuti of Africa illustrates short-term, social manifestations of avoidance. After receiving a whipping with thorny branches as a punishment for stealing food, a man fled into the forest. Colin Turnbull reports how "He stayed in the forest for nearly twenty-four hours, and when he came back the next night he went straight to his hut, unseen, and lay down to sleep. . . . I heard him crying softly because even his brother wouldn't speak to him."[5]

As a generalization, the duration of avoidance tends to be inversely related to the importance of the relationship. That is, the period of avoidance tends to be shorter among interdependent persons than among independent ones. Mbuti foragers are interdependent upon one another, and in the incident just recounted, the food thief and the other band members reconciled the next day. In other settings, among distant, independent individuals, avoidance may become an ongoing, permanent response, as when a restaurant patron, displeased with a meal, adheres to her decision never to return to the establishment. Ethnographic illustrations of avoidance are presented in Box 3.2.

BOX 3.2 ETHNOGRAPHIC ILLUSTRATIONS OF FOUR TYPES OF AVOIDANCE

I. Interpersonal Avoidance

1. Informal (i.e., simply avoiding contact)

Andamanese of the Andaman Islands, South Asia: "Direct confrontation is avoided, and 'going away'—that is, leaving the source and scene of conflict for a short time—is encouraged."[1]

Grand Valley Dani of New Guinea: "The most common Dani way of coping with conflict is simple withdrawal. At a very early stage in conflict one party simply moves away from the situation. Individuals do it and groups do it."[2]

Norwegians: "An old Norwegian proverb, 'Love thy neighbor but keep the gate,' reflects this need for maintaining a certain distance in possibly conflictual social relations."[3]

Samoans of Oceania: "Often conflicts of personality between young people of the same age in a household are not so tempered [as between members of different generations], but the removal of one party to the conflict, the individual with the weakest claim upon the household, is here also the most frequent solution. . . . Resentment is expressed by subdued grumblings and any strong resentment results in the angry one's leaving the household or sometimes the village."[4]

Thai Villagers of Southeast Asia: One of several devices that control the expression of aggression is "leaving the field at the slightest hint of provocation (whether the provocation is intended or not). . . . Over and over again, villagers indicate that they prefer not to have any relationship at all than to have one that is even tinged with hostility."[5]

Toraja of Indonesia: "Toraja villagers generally prefer to avoid the people with whom they are in conflict rather than to confront them directly."[6]

2. Formal (i.e., a specific cultural term or concept exists)

Javanese of Indonesia: "Interpersonal conflict, anger, and aggression are repressed or avoided in Javanese society. . . . The major method of handling interpersonal conflict is by not speaking to one another (*satru*)."[7]

Jalé of New Guinea: The avoidance relationship (called *héléroxo*) "demonstrates anger and communicates grievances, but reduces the danger of a violent confrontation. . . . Typically, the parties no longer speak to each other, cease to share food, and avoid sitting or sleeping close to each other. . . . An avoidance relationship may last from a few days to several years."[8]

Fijians of Oceania: "One of the most effective sanctions is the offended's avoidance of the offender and the village talk or gossip (and subtle avoidance on the part of other villagers) that accompanies the initiation of an avoidance relationship. . . . It is consonant with the Fijian emphasis on non-confrontation and restraint in one's dealings with others."[9]

Finnish Gypsies: "Controlled avoidance by the feuding families has much the same function as does feuding itself. By voluntarily moving away, and thereafter avoiding contact in every way with the offended family, the killer's family 'pleads guilty' . . . It is the responsibility of other people in a group of gypsies to see that members of two feuding families do not come near one another."[10]

Sama Dilaut: "Such a relationship is called *magbanta,* and those who stand in it refer to each other as *banta.* The relationship is dyadic and banta no longer exchange words."[11]

II. Intergroup Avoidance

1. Group Fission

Birhors of India: "In case there is a conflict within the *tanda* [band], which is again a rare event, the *tanda* splits, and one group moves to another camp."[12]

Ju/'hoansi of the African Kalahari: "When arguments develop and there is no clear right or wrong side, the usual solution is for one of the parties to leave the group, moving off to another band where he and his sympathizers have friends and relatives."[13] "When an argument is too serious to be dissipated by rough good humor it is far simpler to split the camp then to stay together and fight it out. Old N!eisi explained it this way: 'In the case of arguments in the camp, we sit down and talk it out, and bring in others who know more to listen. But with people like myself who don't want trouble, we will just pack up and go away.' "[14]

Netsilik Inuit of Northern Canada: "Whenever a situation came up in which an individual disliked somebody or a group of people in the band, he often pitched his tent or built his igloo at the opposite extremity of the camp or moved to another settlement altogether."[15]

Paliyan of India: ". . . different rates of pay lead to bitter words and the formation of factions. Half the community left that evening. When they returned two weeks later the wounds were not entirely healed so the other half left for a week."[16]

Tewa Pueblo of the American Southwest: "Internal conflict that resulted in fissioning could be resolved by a group leaving their natal Pueblo and establishing a new one elsewhere."[17]

Yanomamö of Brazil and Venezuela: "The kinsmen of the dead man were then ordered to leave the village before there was further bloodshed."[18]

2. Flight or Maintaining Distance

Semai of Malaysia: "The avoidance may be overt, as when people, especially women and children, flee at the approach of strangers."[19]

Buid of the Philippines: "The socially approved response to aggression is avoidance or even flight."[20]

Hare of Northern Canada: "In their relations with others, especially the Inuit, the Hare traditionally have possessed a reputation for timidity. They have withdrawn rather than fought."[21]

Jahai of Malaysia: "The Jahai are known for their shyness toward outsiders. . . . In times of conflict, the Jahai withdraw rather than fight."[22]

Kubu of Sumatra: "Avoidance constitutes a basic strategic ingredient in the way these Kubu have adapted to the reality and perceptions of external dangers."[23] "They are so afraid of seeing any one not of their own race, that if suddenly met or come up with in the forest, they will drop everything and flee away."[24]

Sources: 1. Pandya 1992:10. 2. Heider 1979:86. 3. Dobinson 2004:161. 4. Mead 1973:121, 123. 5. Phillips 1974:184. 6. Hollan 1997:64. 7. Martin 1993:113. 8. Koch 1974:74–75; also cf. Koch et al. 1977. 9. Hickson 1986:284. 10. Grönfors 1977:119, 122. 11. Sather 2004:142. 12. Sinha 1972:395. 13. Draper 1978:43. 14. Lee 1972:360. 15. Balikci 1970:192. 16. Gardner 1972:432. 17. Jacobs 1991:349. 18. Chagnon 1992a:189. 19. Dentan 2004:180. 20. Gibson 1989:66. 21. Krech 1991:141. 22. Sluys 1999:307, 310. 23. Sandbukt 1988:111. 24. Forbes 1885:122.

Certain forms of social organization appear conducive to a group fissioning type of avoidance. Nomadic hunter-gatherers relatively easily can separate into subgroups. As Bernard Arcand notes, "like other communities of hunter-gatherers that are said to 'vote with their feet,' the Cuiva [of South America] tend to vote with their paddles: conflicting parties will simply part and travel to distant areas of the territory, where they will remain until a time when much is forgotten and the quarrel has turned trivial."[6]

TOLERATION

In toleration, the issue causing the conflict "is simply ignored, and the relationship with the offending party is continued." Sociologist Donald Black views toleration as the most prevalent response by aggrieved persons everywhere. He points out that persons tend to favor toleration in personal relationships that fall on opposite ends of the intimacy scale; that is, toleration is frequent in the closest relationships and also among those most distant.[7]

Some cultures place special emphasis on toleration, encouraging it as a favored response to conflict. For instance, the Piro of Peru advocate both toleration and avoidance: "It is the custom to 'forget' offenses or to move away from the village."[8]

Among Finns, toleration and avoidance are regularly employed approaches to conflict. There is a reluctance in the culture to criticize others openly or to complain. Thus a common response to frustration caused by another person is just to put up with the situation. A second option is to make indirect, soft suggestions, in hopes that the other person will catch on that there is a problem and do something to correct it. The person distressed at the behavior of another often finds it too difficult to say something directly. During an ethnographic interview, I proposed that "Many of these things are just 'let go.' In other words, people do nothing." The informant responded: "That is the basic way. Like a pendant: 'That's the Finnish way.' . . . You try to avoid the conflict as long as possible, whatever it is, both of you. That is the basic rule number one." Although the interviewee uses the word "avoid" in his answer, his meaning implies toleration as defined here, because the idea is that both parties are dodging the conflict, not necessarily avoiding each other, although this certainly happens too.

Helena Norberg-Hodge provides an excellent ethnographic illustration of toleration and the underlying cultural attitude expressed in the phrase, "we have to live together," among Ladakhi villagers living near the India-Pakistan border.

> Sonam and his neighbor had asked the carpenter to make some window frames; they were both building extensions to their houses. When the carpenter was finished, he brought all the frames to the neighbor. A few days later, I went with Sonam to collect them. Some were missing; his neighbor had used more than he had ordered. This was a considerable inconvenience to Sonam since he could do no further construction work until the frames were in place, and it was going to take several weeks to have new ones made. Yet he showed no signs of resentment or anger. When I suggested to him that his neighbor had behaved badly, he simply said, "Maybe he needed them more urgently than I did." "Aren't you going to ask for an explanation?" I asked. Sonam just smiled and shrugged his shoulders: "Chi choen? ('What's the point?') Anyway, we have to live together."[9]

As one reads the ethnographic literature, it is easy to spot examples of avoidance and toleration. By definition, these approaches to conflict do not entail any physical aggression. Avoidance and toleration also *prevent* the spread of a conflict to other persons.

NEGOTIATION

Negotiation entails handling a dispute by the disputants themselves and generally results in compromises or mutually agreeable nonviolent solutions. Often one party agrees to compensate the other for damages. The expression of remorse or the offering of an apology during the negotiation process can facilitate a resolution, as can occur among G/wi foragers of Africa when one disputant "apologizes or makes other reparation, thus ending the affair." For the Japanese, offering an apology has been shown experimentally to reduce the chance of subsequent aggression toward the apologizer. Among Fijians, a special apology ritual called the *i soro* formally puts an end to a conflict.[10]

The Kpelle of Liberia convened moots to deal with conflicts, and apologies are part of the "restoration of harmony within the group." James Gibbs explains:

> This apology takes the form of the giving of token gifts to the wronged person by the guilty party. These may be an item of clothing, a few coins, clean hulled rice, or a

> combination of all three. It is also customary for the winning party in accepting the gifts of apology to give, in return, a smaller token such as a twenty-five cent piece to show his "white heart" or good will.

The apology and gift exchange clearly prevent further conflict, for, as Gibbs explains, "the public offering and acceptance of the tokens of apology indicate that each party has no further grievances and that the settlement is satisfactory and mutually acceptable."[11]

In northern Mexico, a Tarahumara man named Seleronius once killed a neighbor's cow that had entered his cornfield. Seleronius realized that he had overreacted and went to see his neighbor. He offered his neighbor a burro in compensation, and Seleronius' neighbor, taking into consideration the initial crop damage, accepted the burro. Through this personal negotiation, the problem was resolved and further trouble between them was averted.[12]

With or without an expression of apology or remorse, paying of compensation can prevent violence. The Yurok of California regularly negotiated payments necessary to balance wrongdoings. During the negotiation process, each side pressed its case and resisted pressure from the other, eventually resulting in some compromises, with payments then given in general accordance with an unwritten code of compensation. The killing of a socially respected man resulted in the payment of more indemnity than when the victim had less social status. In the former case, compensation was 15 strings of shells, perhaps also an obsidian blade and a headband decorated with woodpecker scalps, and the giving of one daughter in marriage. A lower status man was worth only 10 strings of shells. "A seduction followed by pregnancy cost five strings of dentalium [shell] or twenty woodpecker scalps. . . . If a man beat his wife, she might go to her parents, who might keep her until the husband had paid them certain damages; then he might retake her."[13]

As among the Yurok, the Comanche of North America also negotiated compensation to end disputes. In neither Yurok nor Comanche society did judges make rulings because there were no judges. The only way to reach an agreement was to negotiate. Warfare and raiding were central to the Comanche way of life, bravery was highly valued, and a man who had been wronged by another was obligated by custom and social pressure to seek compensation from the offender. Adamson Hoebel explains the general process was for the wronged individual to demand specific damages. Sometimes the aggrieved person went to negotiate with a plaintiff himself, and in other circumstances he sent representatives to bargain in his place or brought allies along with him to do the actual bargaining as he waited on the sidelines. Outbreaks of violence were possible, but many grievances were settled via negotiation instead of through physical means. In the following case, a husband sends his unfaithful wife to collect damages on his behalf from her lover:

> [The husband] went by the tipi of a young man and heard his wife's voice inside. Looking in stealthily, he saw the pair lying together.
>
> . . . When the woman came home . . . he pulled out his knife and cut her hair off close to the scalp, then cut her skirt short. In this bedraggled state he drove her through the camp with his whip. When they came by her lover's tipi the husband bade his wife call to him to come and see her. She called, but her lover did not appear.
>
> Her husband then sent her to collect damages from him. He demanded six horses, a saddle, bridle, and war costume. When she appeared before the young man in her sad state he was sorry for her and said, "You look so pitiful; you may have anything you want that I have!"

> His mother loaded his horse with all his portable belongings, and the wife led it publicly through the camp to her husband. This satisfied him, so he kept her as a wife.[14]

In contrast to many dramatizations of the in flagrante delicto scenario, it is interesting that in this real-world example, from a warrior culture, of a husband catching his wife in the act, he does not immediately explode in violence against either the lover or his wife but simply returns home. In place of violence, the irate husband focuses on severely humiliating his wife and attaining material compensation from her lover. The lover also is apparently not eager to engage in a physical confrontation. He avoids a face-to-face encounter with the husband by remaining inside his tipi. He also finds a face-saving way to pay compensation, by managing to cast his actions as resulting from sympathy for his lover rather than a need to pay off her husband to protect his own hide.

SETTLEMENT

Humans are group-living, social beings, connected to each other in webs of social relationships. Two themes that recur in ethnographic discussions of conflict include the importance of restoring the relationship between disputants to normal and of preserving harmony within the group as a whole.[15] Anthropologists often remark that reconciling disputants is more important than determining who is right and who is wrong.

By definition, the settlement approach to conflict resolution involves third parties (Box 3.1). Black proposes a scheme with five third-party settlement roles: (1) friendly peacemaker, (2) mediator, (3) arbitrator, (4) adjudicator, and (5) repressive peacemaker.[16] The first two roles are well represented across all levels of social organization, from forager bands to modern industrial states. The last two roles become more common as the complexity of social organization increases.

Friendly Peacemaking

Friendly peacemakers simply separate or distract adversaries and do not delve into the issues of the conflict. More often than not, friendly peacemakers have a close relationship with one or both antagonists and they are concerned about the well-being of one or both adversaries. Robin Fox tells how friendly peacemakers separate disputants among the Irish of Tory Island: "[The antagonists] were pulled back, dusted down, showered with nonstop advice, and implored to cool down and go home."[17]

While working in the Zapotec community of San Andrés, I had the occasion to witness various fistfights, generally between inebriated men during celebrations (Figure 3.1). Soon after blows were exchanged, friendly peacemakers descended on the combatants and pulled them apart before either received serious injuries. During the first couple of witnessed fights, I confronted the dilemma as to whether or not I should attempt to separate the antagonists. Then I caught on to the pattern. It was the role of the closest relatives on the scene to restrain the contestants, and the physical separation takes place after a few rather ineffective punches have been exchanged. Not once in perhaps a dozen witnessed fights did the relatives of the combatants join the fray as partisans—rather, their intention clearly was to pull their intimate out of the fight.

Having realized the way this system worked, I nonetheless was caught by surprise on a particular occasion. During a Saint's Day celebration, a friend of mine, Samuel,

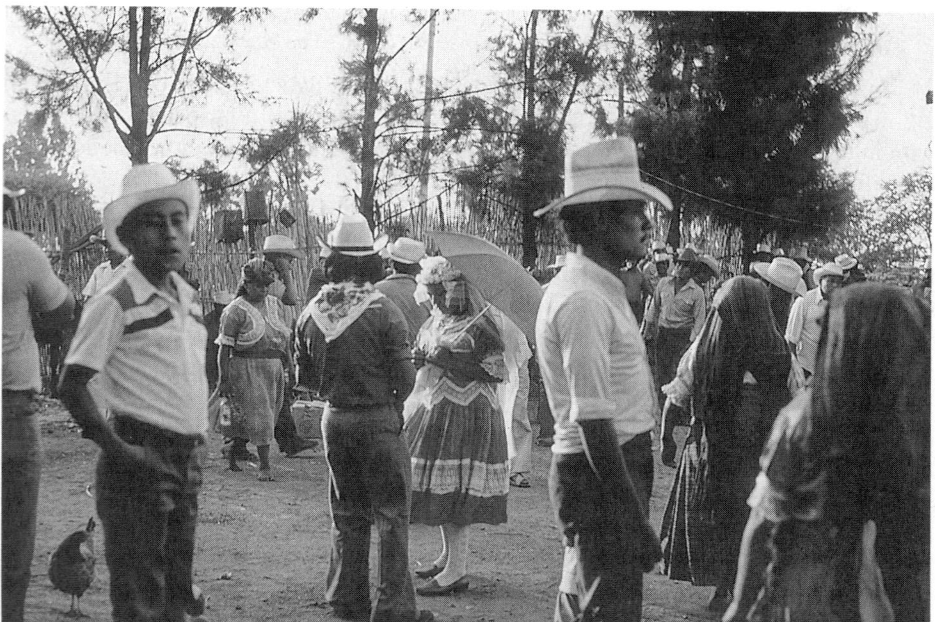

Figure 3.1 Guests dance during a wedding celebration in San Andrés. The bride, with a parasol, and groom are dancing together in the center. It is considered improper for dance partners to converse with each other. At weddings, funerals, and Saint's Day celebrations, guests are provided abundant quantities of alcohol. At such events, physical altercations are more common in San Andrés than in neighboring La Paz. (D. P. Fry photo collection.)

drew my attention to a man who had returned to the community for the fiesta, telling me that this guy was an aggressive bastard. Samuel pointed out the long scar on the man's face and relayed the details of a particularly nasty fight in which the man's opponent had slashed him with scissors.

Later that evening, the inebriated scar-faced man was dancing with my former wife. Mid-dance, he made a drunken lunge at her, wrapping his arms around her waist as he dropped to a kneeling position, his face pressed into her pubic region. Clearly my wife was not happy with this intimate contact. I rushed over, embraced the guy from behind, and tried to drag him off of my wife, but he held tight. I had no intention of getting into a fight with him. I simply wanted to untangle him from my distressed wife. And here is when I received a surprise that made perfect sense only after reflection: Two or three of my Zapotec friends grabbed onto me and hauled me away, leaving the drunken guy still wrapped around my wife. In amazement, I thought: "Why in hell are you pulling *me* away!" Others then helped my wife out of her predicament.

In San Andrés, men are very jealous. In fact, many fights and some murders stem from jealousy. After the shock wore off, I realized that I had been the recipient of friendly peacemaking. Concerned for my well-being, my Zapotec friends were preventing me from doing what they thought was likely to be my next move—in other words, what a typical San Andrés husband seeing his wife in the lustful embrace of another man would likely do—go for blood. And since this particular guy already had a reputation as an aggressive troublemaker, their perceived need to protect me from myself was all the more urgent.

To shift cultures, I also have seen instances of friendly peacemaking on the late-night Helsinki streets. The pattern is similar to that observed among the Tory Island Irish, the San Andrés Zapotec, and elsewhere: Finnish buddies attempt to keep their friends from getting hurt or arrested for fighting. Friendly peacemakers separate disputants and attempt to keep irate antagonists from actually exchanging blows or at least from delivering effective punches. It is also noteworthy that the antagonists generally are careful, even when drunk, not to hit their friendly peacemakers. This suggests that they are not totally without self-restraint.

Friendly peacemakers need not always separate antagonists by physical means—distraction also can be an effective technique. Among the Mae Enga of New Guinea, if tempers begin to flare during the peacemaking process, a third party will launch into an irrelevant, even mildly humorous speech, consequently allowing overly excited members of the group once again to get their emotions under control.[18]

Ronald Berndt reports the use of humor among several Australian Aborigine groups to forestall aggression. In northern Arnhem Land, for example, someone interrupts a quarrel by adopting the role of a clown. "The general loud laughter from everyone keeps the angry one from committing any overt act; and since the clown and his audience express no hostility, the offended man cannot cause trouble."[19]

Friendly peacemaking occurs around the world (see Box 3.3). The ethnographic observations of how *real people* respond to a fight often contradict the popular Hollywood scenario in which heroes and heroines plunge wholeheartedly into the fray.

BOX 3.3 FRIENDLY PEACEMAKING: ETHNOGRAPHIC EXAMPLES

Andamanese, Asia (separation, persuasion)[1]

Australian Aborigines of Arnhem Land, Australia (separation)[2]

Cheyenne, North America (separation, persuasion)[3]

Finns, Europe (separation, persuasion)[4]

Gugadja, Australia (separation)[5]

Irish of Tory Island, Europe (separation, persuasion)[6]

Jalé, Oceania (separation, persuasion)[7]

Japanese, Asia (separation)[8]

Jaraldi, Australia (distraction)[9]

Jívaro, South America (unspecified)[10]

Ju/'hoansi (also spelled Ju/wasi; formerly called the !Kung or Kung), Africa (unspecified,[11] distraction,[12] persuasion)[13]

Mae Enga, Oceania (distraction)[14]

Mardudjara, Australia (separation)[15]

Mbuti, Africa (separation, distraction)[16]

Montenegrins, Europe (separation, persuasion)[17]

Murngin/Yolngu, Australia (separation, persuasion)[18]

Netsilik, North America (separation)[19]

Nootka, North America (separation)[20]

Nubians, Africa (separation, persuasion)[21]

Paliyan, Asia (distraction)[22]

Shavante, South America (separation)[23]

Siriono, South America (persuasion)[24]

Slavey, North America (separation, distraction)[25]

Tahitians, Oceania (separation)[26]

Tarahumara, Middle America (separation)[27]

Tlingit, North America (separation—via evoking supernatural symbol)[28]

Tristan da Cunha Islanders, South Atlantic (distraction)[29]

Walmadjeri, Australia (separation)[30]

Yahgan, South America (separation, persuasion)[31]

Yanomamö, South America (separation)[32]

Zapotec of San Andrés, Middle America (separation, persuasion)[33]

Sources: 1. Man 1932:42. 2. Burbank 1992, 1994:79; Berndt 1965:182. 3. Hoebel 1967b:162. 4. Fry 2001a. 5. Berndt 1972:203. 6. Fox 1989:159–163. 7. Koch 1974:73. 8. Black 1993:110. 9. Berndt 1965:181; Coon 1971:254. 10. Harner 1972:193. 11. Draper 1978:43. 12. Lee 1972:360. 13. E. Thomas 1994:76. 14. Meggitt 1977:119. 15. Tonkinson 1978:119, 125. 16. Turnbull 1961:123, 124, 1965a:189, 201, 203, 208; see also Black 1993:109. 17. Boehm 1987:95–98, text and photos; see also Figure 8.3. 18. Warner 1969:156, 174; Williams 1991:226. 19. Balikci 1970:174. 20. Coon 1971:262. 21. Fernea 1973:22. 22. Gardner 1972:426; 1995:7. 23. Maybury-Lewis 1974:180. 24. Holmberg 1969:156. 25. Helm 1961:106–107. 26. Levy 1975:283. 27. Pastron 1974:393. 28. Redfield 1967:23. 29. Bonta 1996:407. 30. Berndt 1972:203. 31. Cooper 1946a:95; Coon 1971:248–249; Gusinde 1937:894, 895. 32. Asch & Chagnon 1975. 33. Fry 1990:336.

Mediation

In mediation, neutral third parties help disputants to reach agreements. P. H. Gulliver views mediation as the intervention of a third party into the negotiation process. Mediators do not make judgments and they lack the authority to impose agreements on disputants, but they may use coercion to push for agreements.[20]

Mediation occurs in a large number of cultures. People in many herding and horticultural tribal societies rely on mediation, often as an alternative to aggressive self-redress, while peasant agriculturalists, nowadays residing within the jurisdiction of nation-states, sometimes use mediation in preference to pursuing a grievance through governmental courts.[21] Multiple mediators often assist in settlements. For example, several elders typically mediate disputes among the East Indians of Fiji, Paliyans of India,

Dou Donggo of Indonesia, Limbus of Nepal, Abkhazians of the Caucasus, and Nubians of Egypt.[22]

Traditionally, native Hawaiian families practiced mediation in a dispute-resolution meeting called *ho'oponopono,* and variations of the procedure remain in use today. In the traditional belief system, "holding a grudge or failing to forgive was considered a grievous offense that threatened the spiritual, physical, and emotional health of the family." An elder family member serves as the *ho'oponopono* leader (*haku*). During the meeting, the family members do not talk directly to each other, except when they are asking for forgiveness or making an apology. Instead, each person speaks to the *haku.* A low level of emotionality is expected of the family members, and the process of channeling all conversation through the *haku* helps to minimize emotional outbursts.[23]

The *ho'oponopono* has four stages.[24] The first phase consists of an opening prayer and a review of the conflict. In the second stage, the problem is discussed. The third phase entails resolving the conflict through apology and mutual forgiving. The final stage includes a summary of what has occurred during the *ho'oponopono* and a reaffirmation of the spiritual and emotional unity of the family. In the following example, the opening prayer contains a statement of the objectives of the *ho'oponopono,* the rules to be followed, and an expression of the anticipated positive outcome.

> Dear Lord, we thank thee for this opportunity to get together as an *'ohana,* a family. It was obvious during this morning that many things were happening to our family. People were getting at one another and things weren't right. As You know, we need to restore harmony within our family in order for us to continue on. Dear Lord, as we get together in this *ho'oponopono,* give us the strength and wisdom and understanding to be able to lay the problems out and identify what the problems all are. Give us also the understanding and the know-how to be able to discuss things freely without hurting one another, and to say things in a way that makes for understanding. And, dear Lord, give us the opportunity, so that as one is talking about the problem, that the others will sit quietly and listen with an open ear, so that they can understand as to how the other one perceives what is happening. And, dear Lord, after we've identified it all, may we be able to open our hearts to one another, to forgive each other, so that we can then carry on. Always, we ask in Thy holy name. Amen.[25]

Among the Semai of Malaysia, the overriding tendency is for people to cooperate, avoid conflicts, and interact nonviolently. Through enculturation, children internalize the Semai values and perceptions of the world. They learn to avoid conflicts whenever possible and to suppress feelings of anger (Figure 3.2).[26]

On occasions when conflict cannot be avoided, the headman convenes a dispute resolution assembly called the *becharaa'*.[27] The disputants, their relatives, and any other members of the community who choose to attend meet at the house of the headman. After some initial socializing, several elder members of the band each present lengthy monologues referring to the interdependence of all members of the community. All persons are reminded that the maintenance of harmony is of primary importance.

Following these reiterations of community values, one disputant begins to discuss the conflict. Next the other party offers a portrayal of the dispute. Others join in, expressing opinions or perhaps asking questions. The disputants do not confront each other or argue; rather, they calmly address the gathered assembly. The *becharaa'* continues without ceasing for hours or even several days and nights. The headman's household

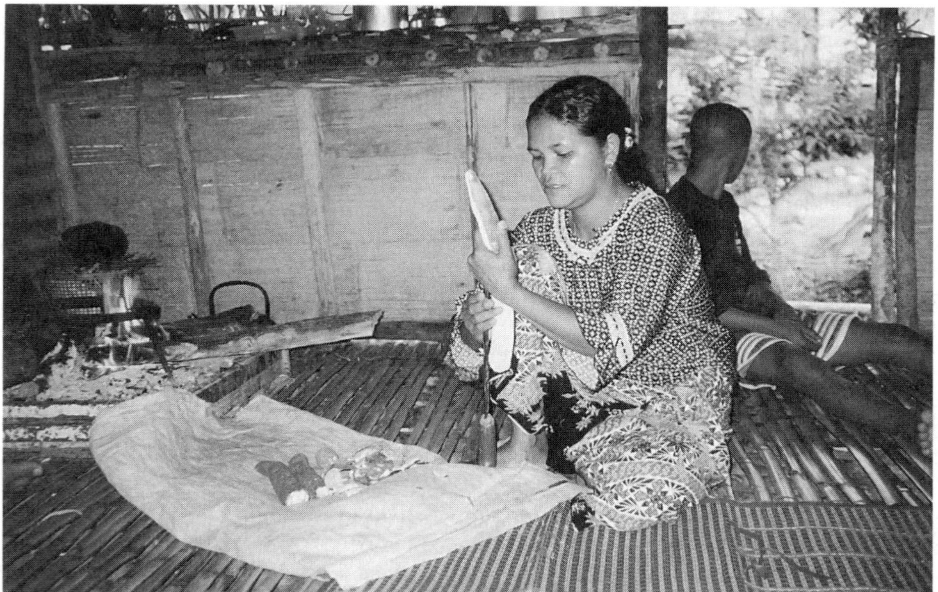

Figure 3.2 A Semai woman prepares food. The Semai strongly value social harmony and use a type of mediation-arbitration assembly called the *becharaa'* to resolve disputes nonviolently. (Photo courtesy of Mari Laaksonen.)

provides food, and people may nap from time to time on the floor as the discussion continues.

Robarchek explains that during the *becharaa'*, all events related to the dispute are explored from "every conceivable perspective in a kind of marathon encounter group. Every possible explanation is offered, every imaginable motive introduced, every conceivable mitigating circumstance examined . . . until finally a point is reached where there is simply nothing left to say." The headman then lectures one or both of the parties, noting their guilt in the matter, instructing them in how they should have acted differently, and directing them not to repeat such mistakes. The headman and other elders again offer monologues reaffirming the paramount necessity of maintaining the unity and harmony of the band. Robarchek emphasizes that, through the *becharaa'*, the Semai are able to deal nonviolently with serious conflicts—involving property ownership, infidelity, divorce, land claims, and so on—so as to dissipate anger, deal effectively with the basis of the conflict, promote the reconciliation of the disputants, reconfirm and reinforce the interdependence of all members of the band, and reiterate the need for social harmony.[28]

Arbitration

In arbitration, a third party renders a decision but lacks the power to enforce it. Each Bedouin tribe has several respected men who act as arbitrators. By mutual consent, disputants appear before an arbitrator. Why should disputants adhere to the arbitrator's decision if the arbitrator lacks power to enforce it? The answer involves social pressure *from one's own relatives.*

Central to Bedouin social structure are what Frank Stewart calls *blood money groups* that usually are related to each other through descent from a common male ancestor. Members of a blood money group support each other's interests and share each other's liabilities; as a Bedouin saying expresses, "they pursue and they are pursued together." A disputant's blood money group, his closest allies in life, have the power to pressure him to comply with an arbitrator's ruling.[29]

The pacification of blood feuds in Montenegro during the 1800s provides an illustration of how arbitration can restore the peace.[30] The arbitrators, called *Kmets,* assembled as the Court of Good Men. *Kmets* were of high status and had nonpartisan reputations. Boehm emphasizes that the central goal of the *Kmets* was to bring about a compromise and contribute to the social harmony of the overall community. The words of one *Kmet* conveys the goal of the Court of Good Men:

> Never is judging going to be, for one side or the other, exactly what they want: but rather it must be according to what people know and are able to do and to discover. It would be an evil thing if one party to a legal case were to go home singing and the other lamenting. . . . For us, the task is to see clearly with our minds and to make the decision that we see as being most appropriate, to ensure that two embroiled brastvos [clans] come to peace with one another and that other honorable men will not look askance at what we have done.[31]

As arbitrators, the Court of Good Men exerted as much moral authority as they could. Boehm suggests that the amount of pressure brought to bear on the feuding parties from their own groups to end the conflict increased in proportion to the necessity of cooperation between the two groups overall.[32]

From various ethnographic sources, it is apparent that disputants abide by an arbitrator's decision for any number of reasons: due to the pressure of public opinion or influence from relatives, because they believe the arbitrator's ruling is fair, to maintain a good reputation, or to avoid facing harmful consequences such as the violence of blood feuding or the expense of pursuing the matter in court. Even though arbitrators lack direct power to enforce their decisions, the arbitration process can provide a viable alternative to violence.

Adjudication

Adjudication may be even better for delivering justice because judges not only make rulings but also possess the power to enforce them. Commonly employed in the Western world, adjudication is probably familiar to most readers. Black points out that adjudication can occur in settings beyond the courtroom, for instance, "in families, particularly those with a patriarchal structure, and organizations such as business firms and voluntary associations in which judgements against members may ultimately be enforced with expulsion."[33]

Max Gluckman describes the judicial system of the Lozi kingdom in what is now Zambia. For at least 200 years, this African kingdom has had a hierarchy of courts. The primary goal of the judges is to reconcile disputants and correct errant behavior.

> Large parts of the judgements read like sermons. . . . The standards publicly stated for the parties are the norms involved in their social positions and relationships. . . . The essence of the judicial process is to state these norms to the world and to assess against

> them the behaviour of the parties in a specific series of situations. The aim of the judicial process is that when the parties have had their rightdoings and wrongdoings indicated to them, they will be reconciled and live together harmoniously in the future.[34]

In Mexico, local community courts among the indigenous groups such as the Tarahumara, Huichol, and Zapotec stem from colonial times and further illustrate the process of adjudication.[35] Every Tarahumara group, for instance, has a head official, called the *gobernador.* During trials, the *gobernador* is the true judge, while other officials sit in advisory capacities. The *gobernador* hears the evidence, rules on the guilt or innocence of the accused, and when necessary dictates a punishment. The typical punishment is a public whipping. Sometimes the court also rules that a defendant should pay compensation to a plaintiff. Additionally, the *gobernador* delivers a sermonlike lecture, a *nawésoli.* To a Tarahumara, appearing in court is to be avoided, not simply due to the pain of physical punishment or damage to one's pocketbook if fined, but also due to the risk of public humiliation and harm to one's reputation. The social disgrace of receiving a public scolding from the *gobernador* "stings almost as sharply as the whip."[36]

Repressive Peacemaking

Repressive peacemaking is the most authoritative third-party settlement role and treats fighting itself as an offense to be punished, *regardless of the reasons for the dispute.* Repressive peacemaking occurs when colonial powers or national governments unilaterally impose peace on feuding or warring indigenous peoples.[37] For instance, Koch reports how "the Jalé of the Jaxólé Valley realized that a new kind of stranger [the New Guinea government police] who neither spoke nor understood their language would punish any form of violent behavior."[38]

Among the Yukaghir reindeer hunters of northeastern Siberia, traditionally the brother of a murder victim or another relative could seek blood vengeance. "He does not kill directly, but requires from the murderer an explanation of his act, not infrequently letting him off with a ransom," explains Waldemar Jochelson. The repressive peacemaking concept is illustrated by the fact that after the Russians subjugated the peoples in this area, the Yukaghir discontinued the practice of seeking blood vengeance, fearing punishment by Russian authorities through the newly imposed court and penal system. As Jochelson explains, "the manners of the Yukaghir have become much milder."[39]

CULTURAL BELIEFS AND AGGRESSION PREVENTION

Belief Systems

Belief systems can facilitate the prevention or limitation of aggression, but they also can facilitate the expression of aggression. For instance, belief systems in some cultures allow for seeking vengeance, whereas other belief systems do not. Some belief systems hold that it is a husband's right to beat his wife, but in other cultures spousal violence runs counter to what is viewed as acceptable. Some cultures have beliefs that anger can lead to illness, and such views may have an inhibiting effect on expressing anger or acting aggressively.[40]

When individuals grow up in a particular society, they internalize the shared beliefs of the culture. Internalized beliefs form a guide for how to behave in given situations. Belief systems can contribute to the prevention and limitation of aggression in several ways. First, belief systems can directly encourage nonviolent behavior. Second, cultural beliefs can favor avoidance or toleration as preferred responses to conflict. Third, belief systems can encourage self-control, inhibition of anger, or the denial of hostile feelings.

Beliefs Favoring Nonviolence

Some belief systems strongly devalue the expression of violence, and therefore might be termed *antiviolent,* whereas other belief systems positively advocate *nonviolent* behavior. As individuals internalize antiviolent or nonviolent beliefs, they become reluctant to engage in violence. After surveying much anthropological information on societies with low levels of aggression, Bruce Bonta concludes that the existence of a *nonviolent belief system* is a feature shared by nearly all cultures that exhibit extremely low levels of physical aggression. For instance, the *becharaa'*-using Semai are nonviolent in belief and behavior. Another peaceful Malaysian culture, the Chewong, also has a belief system that emphasizes nonviolence: "To remain and confront the aggressors is not a viable alternative."[41]

North American religious groups such as the Amish and Hutterites have pacifistic beliefs and very low levels of violence in their communities. The Hutterites, now numbering about 30,000, have never had a homicide in their history. To take an example from South America, the Panare "are brought up to believe that any form of violence is the height of immoral behavior." Paul Henley, who refers to the "pacific nature" of the Panare, came across only one incident involving physical aggression, a beating, after more than 18 months of fieldwork among these people. Among the Wáiwai, also of South America, antiviolent beliefs play an important role in the prevention of aggression. Catherine Howard tells that "overt conflict, aggression, or discord are highly censured. The Wáiwai ethos rests on the contrast between being *tawake,* 'peaceful, sociable,' and *tîrwoñe,* 'angry, hostile.' Society is considered viable only if its members control their desires, meet obligations to others, and shun confrontations."[42]

Beliefs Favoring Toleration or Avoidance as Preferred Ways to Handle Conflict

Belief systems that favor the handling of conflict through toleration—simply putting up with an undesirable situation—would seem to prevent physical aggression. The Semai belief system favors toleration. As Robarchek notes, Semai "go to great lengths to avoid conflict and will usually tolerate annoyances and sacrifice personal interest rather than precipitate an open confrontation." Cultures that emphasize toleration include the Andamanese of South Asia, La Paz Zapotec of Middle America, Batek Semang of the Southeast Asia, Bukidon of Southeast Asia, Doukhobors of North America, Ladakh of South Asia, Montagnais-Naskapi of North America, Seri of Middle America, Sherpa of South Asia, and Tanna Islanders of Oceania, among others.[43]

We have seen that avoidance entails the cessation or the limitation of interaction with another person, either temporarily or permanently. Obviously, people who strive to avoid each other make physical aggression less likely. In some cases, such as among

Finnish gypsies locked in a blood feud relationship, maintaining avoidance is the acceptable alternative to seeking blood revenge. The Hill Pandaram of southern India have "a value system that puts a premium on the avoidance of aggression and conflict; like other foragers, the Hill Pandaram tend to avoid conflict by separation and by flight." Similarly, the belief system of the Central Thai helps keep the peace through "a Buddhist value system, which places a premium on avoiding conflict and fleeing rather than fighting." The essential point is that some cultural belief systems encourage toleration and avoidance in response to conflict, and this helps to prevent and limit aggression.[44]

Beliefs That Emphasize Self-Control and the Denial of Anger

Beliefs favoring the self-control of anger also may help prevent aggression.[45] In reference to the West Greenland Inuit, Inge Kleivan writes, "Children must learn to control themselves and not show open aggressiveness." Pertaining to the Canadian Inuit, one "way of avoiding confrontations was to deny that one was unhappy, angry, dissatisfied, resentful—to 'forget' the situation." For the Ju/wasi (or Ju/'hoansi) foragers of the African Kalahari, "Self-discipline pervaded everyday life, so people virtually never showed hunger or pain, let alone anger." Among the Toraja of Indonesia, "Anger (*senko*) is one of the 'hot' emotional states most feared and avoided." Regarding the Thai, Herbert Phillips reports that "more than half the informants describe people who hide their feelings as 'good,' 'persons who do not want to cause trouble,' 'just men,' and perhaps most cogently from a Thai point of view, 'persons who realize that hiding one's feelings is a virtue that helps men to live together happily.' " Related to the Tarahumara of Mexico, "it is common for the Tarahumara systematically to deny their feelings of hostility." And for the La Paz Zapotec, Carl O'Nell explains that "people are particularly loath to admit to anger even at times when an observer might think anger is justified."[46]

My own fieldwork in La Paz reinforces not only O'Nell's observation about the denial of anger, but also that La Pazians sometimes deny that a conflict even exists at all. Anthropologists, like children, must learn a totally new system of beliefs. One way we do this is by making mistakes—and then, hopefully, learning from them.

When I first visited Zapotec villages, well off the beaten path of tourists and other foreigners, children usually appeared from all quarters to have a look at the "strange creature." It was both amusing and a little uncomfortable to be the center of such attention, surrounded by curious faces, some staring, some chanting *gring, gring, gring*—the Zapotec shortening of the Mexican slang word for North American, *gringo.* Such was my initial reception in San Andrés and to a lesser degree in neighboring La Paz. Children in La Paz are more respectful to visitors. But with time, most of my novelty wore off in both communities. This was fortunate because I planned to make naturalistic observations of children's behavior, especially their playfighting and aggression, in these community settings.

After many months of establishing rapport, I began to select representative samples of 24 children in each community, ages three to eight, which I hoped to observe systematically. With the help of field assistants, I made visits to the parents of the children, explained my interest in children's behavior, and requested permission to come to their households from time to time to see what the children were doing. I explained that I would usually come with an assistant from the community and we would simply observe the children, noting by tape recorder or on paper what was going on. In nearly all cases, parents gave permission.

We got off to a good start with the observations, with most children not paying much attention to us, but then I noticed that one otherwise-helpful field assistant in La Paz was speaking so as to draw too much attention to our child-watching activities. I mentioned this to him a couple of times to no avail. The other assistants easily had caught on that we should not "advertise" to the children that we had come to observe them, so as not to unduly affect their behavior, but Tomas continued to make loud declarations such as, "We are here to watch the children." If children heard this, depending on their reactions, we had to scrap the observation or else hang around waiting until they seemed to forget about us. This situation was less than ideal.

Ironically, these events ended up demonstrating one very important way that the La Paz Zapotec deal with conflict: by denying that it even exists. After several frustrating observation visits, I sat down with Tomas to have a chat and find some solution to this problem. To my utter amazement he adamantly insisted that, "There is no problem." So I said, "Well, I'm afraid that there is." "No, there isn't any problem," he continued to insist, "everything is going fine." After the frustrating discussion, I realized that in trying to talk openly about the issue—my American approach for dealing with this sort of problem—I got nowhere because my problem-solving style violated an important La Pazian rule: *Deny that a conflict even exists.*

Methodologically, it was important to have as negligible an influence as possible on the children we were observing. So I reassigned Tomas to a census project and worked with a different assistant who was more discrete when conducting child observations. This plan worked well.

The conflict with Tomas provided an unanticipated insight about how people in La Paz keep the peace. If both parties cooperate in denying that a conflict even exists, then this can help to prevent aggression and conflict escalation. *Cooperative denial* seems to be a psychosocial mechanism used by La Pazians to prevent aggression and the persistence of disputes.

Cooperative denial and similar processes have interacting psychological and social dimensions. For denial as an *individual process* to work effectively, it must also become part of the belief system and a *social process* wherein persons cooperate with each other in order to deny jointly that there is a problem. Children growing up in the La Paz social environment, as well as an outsider like me, must learn the social rule: *Deny that a conflict even exists* (Figure 3.3). I learned the rule only by breaking it in my conversation with Tomas.

POINTS TO HIGHLIGHT

A major reason for illustrating with cultural examples the diverse ways that humans deal with conflict is to highlight that violence, as a form of self-redress, is only one option among various possibilities. Undeniably, humans engage in acts of physical aggression, but they also regularly deal with conflicts in other ways. At least some other approaches are not as noticeable as violence, but this does not mean that they are unusual or ineffective ways to deal with conflict. Indeed, toleration, avoidance, negotiation, and third-party assisted settlement would seem to be less costly and more effective than aggression in many situations.

Figure 3.3 In La Paz and San Andrés, children have ample opportunities to observe and imitate adult behavior and to internalize community values and beliefs. In La Paz, for example, children learn that denial and avoidance are favored responses to conflict. (D. P. Fry photo collection.)

Recent research shows that some species of nonhuman primates engage in peacemaking and reconciliation.[47] Maintaining good relationships with other group members is important. Research also shows that individuals are more likely to reconcile after aggression when their relationship is valuable.[48] De Waal suggests that "the *relational model* views aggressive behavior as resulting from conflicts of interest between individuals who share a history (and a future). It assumes an equilibrium between tendencies that pull individuals apart and those that bring them together."[49]

Maintaining valuable social relationships clearly is important among humans. Dealing with conflict through aggression may harm relationships in ways that avoidance, toleration, negotiation, and settlement options do not. Portrayals of human nature that magnify violence, decontextualized from a consideration of the importance of relationships within which it occurs, are one-sided. An overemphasis on violence obscures how humans manage to live peacefully together most of the time. A more realistic perspective also takes into account human restraints on violence, the myriad regularly practiced conflict management approaches, aggression prevention activities, and reconciliation strategies, all occurring every day around the world. Certainly, violence is part of the human species' profile, but it is only part of the picture. A balanced view of human nature also recognizes the substantial capability that people have for limiting and dealing with conflicts without force.

CHAPTER 4

MAKING THE INVISIBLE VISIBLE

Belief Systems in San Andrés and La Paz

Respect for the rights of others is peace.

BENITO JUÁREZ[1]

Benito Juárez was a Zapotec-speaker from the Mexican State of Oaxaca who served as the president of Mexico in the mid-1800s and implemented important social reforms.[2] In the 1980s, I went to Oaxaca to conduct anthropological fieldwork in two adjacent Zapotec communities for which I use the pseudonyms San Andrés and La Paz. Reminiscent of the words of Benito Juárez, the Zapotec of these communities place a high value on respect. They believe that people should not infringe upon the rights of others. As Juárez expressed, this type of respect is concordant with peaceful social relations. The Zapotec emphasis on respect can be viewed as an ideal, a statement on the way people *should* behave toward one another. In the course of daily interaction, however, the ideal may not always be attained. The Zapotec realize that if respect breaks down violence becomes a possibility.

But now a puzzle presents itself. The people of San Andrés and La Paz regularly express the virtues of acting respectfully, but the citizens of La Paz take Benito Juárez's credo more seriously that do the people of San Andrés. Individuals from San Andrés are more likely to abandon this ideal in daily life by exchanging insults, lying, arguing, getting into fights, and destroying another person's property than are the La Paz Zapotec, who largely succeed in living in accordance with an ethic of respect. San Andrés has a substantially higher level of physical aggression than La Paz, as shown by comparing the number of fistfights, child punishment episodes, wife beatings, assaults, and murders in the two communities. Moreover, the citizens of La Paz maintain a self-image of themselves as nonjealous and nonviolent. By contrast, the people of San Andrés hold a community image that incorporates a certain amount of physical aggression. In San Andrés, people express that avenging a relative's murder is one path to justice, that killing a rival out of jealousy is understandable, and that fighting—especially among intoxicated persons—is simply to be expected. It would seem that the people of San Andrés have ambivalent beliefs about expressing aggression, and they do *not* hold a nonviolent image of their community analogous to the one held in La Paz.

In this chapter, I will try to unravel the puzzle as to why the San Andrés Zapotec are more aggressive than their neighbors in La Paz. But there are at least two questions here. What types of processes perpetuate greater or lesser amounts of aggression? And how did differences in peacefulness–aggressiveness come about in the first place? For the first question, we have some answers, but for the second, we are left with hypotheses. The answers we do have involve a process usually taken for granted: the potent impact of cultural belief systems on our daily perceptions, thinking, and actions. The members of any given culture share a wide number of beliefs that they simply tend not to question. One way to realize the presence and power of certain beliefs is to spend some time in a different culture. A consideration of the La Paz and San Andrés Zapotec illustrates the power of belief systems and shows how internalized beliefs guide human behavior.

SO NEAR AND YET SO FAR

Status and Rights of Women

Marked differences exist between La Paz and San Andrés in terms of how women and men interact. In San Andrés, the cultural pattern is for men not to trust their wives. The San Andrés men exhibit patterns of control over women involving fear, containment, and sometimes force. For example, a 65-year-old husband explained that "when I get very mad—well, the men, when they get very mad, they grab a stick and they hit them [their wives], but only two or three blows."[3] By contrast, women in La Paz are much closer in status to the men. Mutual respect is expected within husband–wife relationships and between the sexes generally.

In San Andrés most young wives have to ask their husband's permission to go on an errand. Middle-aged wives do not necessarily have to ask permission, but they are expected to keep their husbands informed as to their whereabouts. Generally, premenopausal women do not leave home very often. They lack the freedom to do so. In La Paz, by contrast, women regularly visit each other and go on errands upon their own discretion. A young wife should keep her mother-in-law informed as to her visiting plans, but women in La Paz enjoy much greater freedom of movement than do their counterparts from San Andrés.

Divergent patterns of interaction between women and men at weddings and other celebrations also show the higher degree of respect shown to women in La Paz than in San Andrés. When guests arrive at a wedding in San Andrés, the men and women separate. Men sit on benches, chairs, or logs; women sit on woven reed mats on the dirt floor (Figure 4.1). Under comparable circumstances in La Paz, women and men sit together in chairs. Furthermore, in La Paz, women and men talk with each other.

As a cultural outsider to both Zapotec communities, I learned that when passing women on the street in La Paz it was courteous and expected to say hello and perhaps exchange a few words of conversation. This conversational pattern was not very different from what I was accustomed to in United States culture. In San Andrés, by contrast, I realized rather quickly that my friendly greetings to women were unreciprocated. Women avoided eye contact and hurried on their way without saying a word. As these experiences continued, I caught on that in San Andrés a man should ignore women in most public contexts. I was not the only person to realize that the rules of interaction between men and women differed between San Andrés and La Paz. One day, three La Paz women packed up a burro with the pottery they had made and walked over to

Figure 4.1 At a celebration in San Andrés, rather than socializing in mixed company, women and men separate. The men are pictured eating together outside as the women socialize in the kitchen. (D. P. Fry photo collection.)

San Andrés to sell their wares. The La Paz women were struck by the fact that the San Andrés men they encountered would not stop and talk with them: "All they said was 'Good afternoon,' and then looked down and away."

Jealousy

> O, beware, my lord, of jealousy! It is the green-eyed monster which doth mock the meat it feeds on.
>
> —*Othello*, Act 3, Scene 3

As I lived in both communities, gradually it became obvious that a cloud of jealousy hangs in the air over San Andrés and shadows the interactions between the sexes. Men are suspicious of their wives and women are wary of their husbands. In San Andrés, if a man suspects his wife of infidelity or even just flirting he may beat her. Flirting, San Andrés style, may involve nothing more than exchanging a quick glance with a man, a nonverbal signal that may be charged with sexual meaning within this system of restricted contact. Women usually act prudently.

Clearly, jealousy is not compatible with mutual respect. One young husband from San Andrés remarked that "All women are bad!" I asked him why. "Because they will have sex with other men." On a different occasion, the same husband bragged to me that he had girlfriends. To his thinking, there was nothing bad about that.

Upon first arriving in San Andrés, one aspect of my culture shock involved learning how to relate to women. In fact, it would be more accurate to say learning how *not* to relate to women. At first it was difficult to fathom that I should ignore all women I passed on the street, not attempt to talk to a friend's wife if I arrived at their house when he was not at home, and never smile at a woman while dancing with her at a party. Dancing in San Andrés, by the way, entails no physical contact of any sort and, if done properly, should involve only a barest minimum of eye contact. Basically, men and women shuffle about, with little or no attempt to coordinate one's own movements with those of one's partner. It is also typical for a woman while dancing to display facial expressions that alternate among boredom, pain, and disgust. There should be no indication that she might be enjoying the dance. Coming from a culture where men and women regularly converse and smile at each other, I found that my spontaneous inclinations to say hello to women or smile at them while dancing were totally inappropriate within the San Andrés social setting. I had to learn quickly to change a lifelong pattern of interaction that I had simply taken for granted as *natural*. My belief system was clearly very different from that of the San Andrés Zapotec in this regard.

One of my field assistants in San Andrés, a good-natured fellow who was not particularly jealous by community standards, one day volunteered some friendly advice to me:

> I order my wife, if I am not home and someone comes to the gate, say, "What do you want?" If the person seems legitimate, say a time when I'll be home. If the person has no reason to be there, just walk away. If the person keeps talking and talking, leave him. Walk away and shut the door of the house. Be especially careful if the person is a "stranger" [that is, a nonrelative]. If he is a *compadre* or relative, be careful also—just to be safe.

My friend then suggested that I order my wife—his wording—to take similar precautions.

My wife was never seriously accosted, but on two occasions males of widely different ages came to our house in my absence with the clear intention of having sex with her. One seemed to be contemplating using force to get what he wanted. Fortunately, through quick thinking, she successfully managed to get rid of her unwanted guests on both occasions. Other women warned her never to go to the river by herself because she might be "pricked by the animals," ostensibly referring to biting insects. However, the real meaning of their play on words was clear.

We both had trouble adjusting to a social setting where interactions among women and men were so restricted and where distrust, jealousy, and intrigue formed a cultural backdrop for interactions between the sexes. The fact that I managed to adopt patterns of interaction appropriate to San Andrés beliefs was driven home to me during one of my first visits to La Paz. I had by this time become accustomed to San Andrés women, whose husbands were not home, tersely and at times even frantically yelling to me "He's not here! He's not here!" before they darted from view. Therefore, as I walked down a street in La Paz, I was very surprised to see a woman beckoning me to come into her compound. I hesitated, unwilling to respond immediately to what I suspected to be a socially inappropriate, sexually provocative invitation. But then a man appeared and also beckoned me to enter, so I did, still thinking the woman's behavior had been odd.

Another afternoon I returned to this friendly household for a follow-up visit with Carlos and Dominga. Again Dominga eagerly invited me into the compound and then directly into her house. She began to chat with me. My emotional reaction is the revealing part of this story, because it shows that I had become *resocialized* to a San Andrés way of thinking—that is, into the San Andrés belief system regarding what constitutes proper male–female interaction. I became more and more anxious with each passing minute and fidgeted in my chair. This whole situation *felt* very wrong. What was I doing here! After all, I was sitting and talking with a lone woman in her house! How inappropriate! Of course, images of a jealous Carlos came to mind. What would I say if he suddenly appeared? How would I handle that situation? Would he become violent? On another front, I was worried that this situation could ruin my chances for establishing trust with members of the community in order to conduct field research in La Paz. I speculated that almost certainly gossiping neighbors had seen me enter the house *alone with Dominga* minutes before! In that case, gossip about our love affair no doubt was already spreading with the speed of voice from compound to compound. I had to get out of there fast!

Subsequently, I realized that Dominga was neither unusually bold *by La Paz standards* nor signaling any sexual interest by inviting me into her house for a chat. She was simply being friendly and hospitable. I was misinterpreting the situation by thinking like a person from San Andrés! As similar events recurred in La Paz, I realized that without a doubt, La Paz lacked the belief system regarding jealousy that I had already become accustomed to in San Andrés. I recorded in my field notes, for example:

> I went by a La Paz house where the young wife said her husband was out of town. I was amazed when she invited me in to take a picture. I was also amazed the other day when two women, a mother and a daughter, alone in their compound, invited me in to have some *tejate* [a cold maize-cacao beverage]. . . . This sure is not San Andrés. Aren't the wives here afraid of their husband's beatings—or at least of malicious gossip?

Becoming Visible

The broader point of these experiences is that they illustrate how when we remain within our native culture, we take our *shared* beliefs more or less for granted. However, when we visit another culture, suddenly many of our beliefs become visible because they no longer fit the new social circumstances. A further look at the beliefs and behaviors in San Andrés and La Paz not only provides insights about peace and violence within these Zapotec communities but also more generally shows how many of the shared beliefs and behavior patterns that we largely *just accept as natural* are more arbitrary than we probably imagined. In future chapters we will consider a major implication of this phenomenon. Scientists and scholars, like humans everywhere, are affected by the largely invisible influences of cultural belief systems on their thinking. Regarding war and peace, many writings seem to be affected more by underlying cultural beliefs as to the warlike and violent nature of humanity than by an objective examination of the available data.

A consideration of San Andrés and La Paz may help to make the invisible visible. Clearly there are differences between San Andrés and La Paz, but these communities also are similar in many ways. The adjacent communities are in the semiarid Valley of Oaxaca about 1,700 meters above sea level. A small central plaza in each community is roughly ringed by an elementary school, a local government hall, a couple of tiny stores, and a

Catholic church. Each evening, local officials who serve without pay for one- to three-year elected terms congregate in the government hall to attend to community business.

Both communities consist of Zapotec peasant farmers. There are no non-Zapotecs, large-landowners, or political bosses in either community. Nearly all marriages are between women and men of the same community. Men and teenage boys in both places periodically search for wage labor in Oaxaca City and elsewhere. The people in both communities are near the low end of the socioeconomic scale for Mexico overall. Electrical service and piped water are fairly recent improvements in both places, village streets are unpaved, and the typical diet consists primarily of tortillas and beans, with squash, wild greens, chilies, fruit, and eggs being eaten less often. A small amount of meat may be available once a week, or so.

San Andrés with about 3,000 inhabitants is larger than La Paz, which has a population closer to 2,000 persons. In both places, everybody knows everyone else. La Paz women have a long tradition of making pottery, a craft specialization that has made women economically important for several hundred years. Historically, the women of San Andrés have had no comparable manner of bringing cash, or trade goods, into their households. San Andrés men, on the other hand, have a long history of working as wage laborers in nearby metal ore mines, an activity that ceased in the 1970s. In recent times, some women from San Andrés have managed to earn small amounts of money by selling their homemade tortillas in the marketplaces of Oaxaca City. I should make clear that changes continue to come rapidly to rural Mexican communities like San Andrés and La Paz and throughout these pages the descriptions—although presented in the present tense—apply to the time of my fieldwork in the 1980s. With ease of readability in mind, I've adopted a more personal, less technical style of presentation here than in previous academic publications.[4]

DIFFERENT LEARNING ENVIRONMENTS

In both San Andrés and La Paz, children have ample opportunity to observe the social world of adults and to learn the system of beliefs existing in their respective communities. For instance, usually in the company of adults, children go on errands, pay visits to other households, go to the fields, attend community celebrations and private parties, and travel to marketplaces in other towns. Typically, children and their elders eat together in the kitchen and sleep in the same one-room house. In other words, individuals have little privacy in these communities, and children are observing and imitating adult behavior on a daily basis.

Although sharing a broader Zapotec culture, the residents of La Paz clearly are less aggressive than the people of San Andrés. During celebrations, large quantities of beer and mescal are consumed. In San Andrés, fighting often breaks out, but in La Paz, fighting is much less likely.[5] Furthermore, when fights do occur, the participants tend to follow different scripts in the two communities. In San Andrés, intoxicated men punch and grapple with each other and then are pulled apart by *other people*. In La Paz, almost as rapidly as a fight begins, it is over. The tendency is for at least one participant to leave of *his own accord*. Again, in both communities, such events are likely to take place under the watchful eyes of children.

O'Nell worked in La Paz in the 1960s. My experiences are in agreement with O'Nell's observation that, regarding animosities and quarrels in La Paz, "relatively few of these problems have led to physical violence." In La Paz, I never saw sober individuals engage in physical aggression; in San Andrés such fighting did occur, although less frequently than when individuals were intoxicated. Judicial records in the district archives tell a corresponding story: San Andrés has a much higher assault rate than does La Paz.[6]

Murder

> For murder, though it have no tongue, will speak with most miraculous organ.
>
> *Hamlet*, act 2, scene 2

Regarding lethal violence, the district judicial archives show San Andrés to have had an average homicide rate more than five times that of La Paz between the 1920s and 1960s. The San Andrés rate was 18.1 compared to the La Paz rate of 3.4 per 100,000 persons per year.[7] For sake of comparison, the homicide rate in the United States in recent decades generally has varied around 8–10 per 100,000 persons per annum.[8]

During fieldwork in 1981–1983, I gathered ethnographic data on homicides that had taken place in recent years, and the ethnographic information corresponds with the community differences in the judicial archives. Persons in La Paz reported that no murders had occurred within memory. By contrast, the accounts of killings by several San Andrés informants suggest that homicides have occurred about every three to five years in preceding decades. During a field trip in 1986, a reliable La Paz informant noted that there still had not been any murders in La Paz for a very long time. By contrast, in San Andrés, a man had just been killed a few days before my arrival. A second possible homicide in San Andrés was less clear-cut, because two versions of the same event were circulating through the community. In one account, the victim had been clubbed; in the other, he had fallen and hit his head.

Most of the San Andrés killings stem from disputes between men over a woman. The following account summarizes an informant's description of two associated homicides. The first originates in jealousy and the second in revenge. Both are typical San Andrés killings in that men are the victims and killers. The use of an ambush is also common, and killers are usually sober at the time of the killing, although their victims may be drunk. It would seem that killings in San Andrés result more often from premeditation than fits of passion.

> A young married man and an older fellow were talking—joking—about each other's spouses. The older man said that the younger man's wife was attractive and then he started to say things that were a little too pointed. The young man began to get jealous; he did not think the joking was funny anymore. Later, a problem developed over the young woman's shawl. The wife had wrapped a tortilla in her shawl, as is sometimes done to transport food. A dog stole the shawl and ran out into the street to get at the food wrapped inside.
>
> Coincidentally, the older man who had joked with the young man before about how much he liked the young man's wife, how she was so beautiful, and everything, came and picked up the shawl.
>
> When the young husband discovered somehow that the other man had his wife's shawl, he waited his opportunity. The older fellow used to go to the hills to hunt, sometimes at night. When the jealous husband saw his rival leaving to go hunting, he went to a companion, "Come with me to do this work that I must do." The two young men went

up to the hills together and waited in a spot where nobody usually passed. They killed the hunter when he came by and left the body in the hills. It wasn't until a day or two later that other people found the corpse. Nobody knew who had killed the man, and the young husband continued working as if nothing had happened.

Then the son of the victim, who had been away working in Mexico City, returned and wanted justice done. He went to see a specialist to determine who had killed his father. The murderer decided to leave town, but about a year later he returned to San Andrés. One time as he went to haul a load of water for the animals, the son of his victim waited with his rifle by the street where he would pass on his return. He shot him from about 15 meters distance, in the back, killing him. Justice done, the young man returned to Mexico City and has remained there ever since. And with that, the feud ended between the two families. The peace was restored.

When a murder occurs in a small Zapotec community such as San Andrés, people talk about it for weeks. The omnipresent children of the community are privy to the talk regarding the details of the wounds and the nature of the crime scene, debates about motives, evaluations of guilt or innocence of particular suspects, or, when the perpetrator is known, as is usually the case, whether or not the killing could be considered justified, or at least understandable. Therefore, with killings occurring about every three to five years, a typical childhood within the San Andrés learning environment includes personal knowledge of several murders, whereas by comparison, most La Paz children pass their entire childhood without any homicides having occurred in their community. In other words, the children get very different ideas about the *meaning and conceivability of homicide* in their respective communities. Community expectations about homicide might be expressed roughly as "regrettable but predictable" in San Andrés and "horrible and unexpected" in La Paz.

San Andrés, while not being an extremely violent place, has a markedly higher level of physical aggression than tranquil La Paz. Additionally, a fair amount of the aggression in San Andrés—especially wife beatings, fistfights, and murders—involves jealousy. People in La Paz maintain an image of themselves as respectful, cooperative, nonjealous, and nonviolent. The children of La Paz hear adults expressing this kind of peaceful community self-image in the course of everyday conversations as they are growing up. Several kilometers away, the children growing up in San Andrés hear their elders voicing beliefs that reflect how jealousy and violence are *natural* aspects of life in their community. Hence, the people of San Andrés do not hold consistent beliefs as to the peaceful nature of their community. A comparison of the two places leads to the conclusion that children growing up in these communities are exposed not only to different levels of aggression within the community learning environments, but also to rather different cultural belief systems regarding jealousy, the expression of aggression, and the importance of living in accordance with an ideal of respect.

Childrearing: Beliefs and Practices

Several types of data gathered in San Andrés and La Paz illustrate how socialization and enculturation patterns perpetuate peaceful social life in La Paz to a greater extent than in San Andrés. Observing that physical punishment of children is absent or very rare in some cultures with low levels of aggression, I predicted that parents in La Paz would employ less physical punishment than parents from San Andrés, and furthermore that

La Paz parents would favor verbal means of disciplining their children. During fieldwork, I gathered attitudinal data through structured interviews and behavioral data via both casual and very systematic behavior observations of children.[9]

The analysis of responses to interview questions reveals that parents from San Andrés advocate the use of physical punishment very significantly more often than do respondents from La Paz.[10] Typical San Andrés responses were: "Hit him then so that he grows up with some discipline," and "Hit her so she will have a little respect." By contrast, the most favored reaction to children's misbehavior among the La Paz parents is to talk, tell, show, correct, and educate the children—in other words, to use positive verbal responses. One La Paz father told how he would talk to a disobedient son, and in his speech, the core value of *respect* and adherence to proper father and son roles are emphasized: "Listen son, if you do not obey . . . I am not able to assist you. . . . You, as my son, ought to [have] respect. . . . You ought to respect my words, because you know that your father and your mother are the ones that raise you." Other La Paz respondents also regularly mentioned respect, for example: "Teach them . . . so that they have respect. Educate them." And La Pazian nonviolent thinking regarding child training was expressed by a father who explained that, "One must explain to the child with love, with patience . . . so that he is educated more." Some La Paz respondents also mentioned the importance of setting a good example for their children.

Figure 4.2 graphically portrays the major differences in approaches to child discipline between San Andrés and La Paz. In neither community do respondents advocate

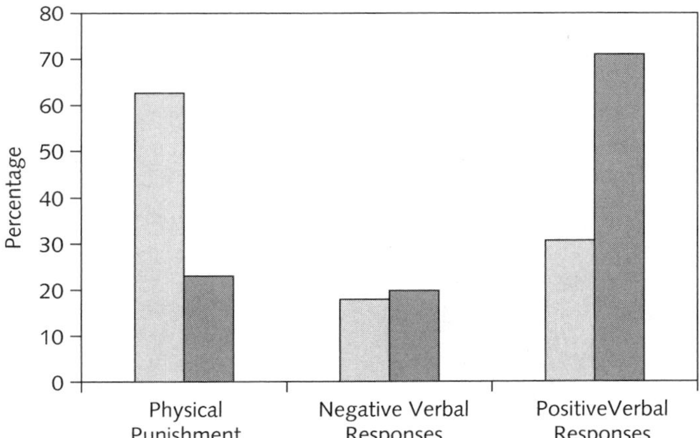

Figure 4.2 Disciplinary approaches advocated in San Andrés and La Paz. The kinds of disciplinary approaches advocated by parents in San Andrés (light bars) and in La Paz (dark bars) differ from each other regarding types of child misconduct such as lying, fighting, stealing, being disobedient, and not doing assigned chores based on an analysis of the verbs used by respondents. Physical Punishment verbs include to hit, to punish physically, and to strike with a stick. Negative Verbal Responses include to scold, to compel, and to threaten. Positive Verbal Responses include to say or tell, to correct with words, to educate, to teach, to show, to talk to, and to explain. Clearly, San Andrés parents favor Physical Punishment, whereas La Paz parents favor Positive Verbal Responses. Since the three categories of response are not mutually exclusive, the column percentages for each community sum to over 100 percent. See Fry 1993a for additional discussion.

much use of negative verbal approaches, such as scolding or threatening children, but San Andrés respondents clearly favor physical punishment, while La Paz respondents lean strongly toward positive verbal responses.[11]

Ethnographic observations correspond with the attitudes and beliefs voiced by the fathers. During fieldwork, under comparable observation situations, I personally witnessed 11 child beatings in San Andrés, in addition to other types of aggression directed at children such as throwing rocks at them, but in La Paz I never observed a child receiving a beating or any other type of physical aggression from an adult. On two occasions, La Paz parents were seen threatening children with a beating, but they did not actually punish the children. O'Nell's observations in La Paz in the 1960s are parallel to mine. He has written, "the physical disciplining of a child might be undertaken with a *vara* (cane), reported to be so by fathers *but never observed*."[12] Thus O'Nell's and my own findings lead to the same conclusion: Corporal punishment of children in La Paz is very rare.

During a visit to La Paz in 1991, I was talking with the mother of one of the boys I had systematically observed in my study of children's behavior. I remembered with some sentimentality going high into the hills to observe Marcos herding goats with other boys. Now the boy was 14 years old, and Natalia was saying how she had had to give him a beating. My ears picked up. "How often do you beat him?" She answered that this was the only time. I double-checked to be sure I had understood correctly. Natalia affirmed that this beating was Marcos' *first and only beating of his childhood!* It occurred to me that he must have really done something wrong, so I asked, "What did he do?" The mother's reply reflects once again the importance of avoiding aggression in La Paz: "He got into a fight with another boy." I must wonder if receiving one and only one beating in the course of an entire childhood would have a very strong psychological impact in conveying the seriousness of one's misdeed—fighting in this case.

The parents in San Andrés and La Paz also hold markedly different opinions as to the nature of children, and this relates to their expectations about children's behavior. In San Andrés, a fair amount of disobedience is tolerated as *natural* among children. The people of San Andrés view children as mischievous and somewhat uncontrollable, and the children live up to these expectations. In comparison, the Zapotec of La Paz perceive children as basically well-behaved. La Paz adults believe that children *naturally* will learn how to act correctly and show respect. La Paz children typically do fulfill their elders' expectations.

It would seem that the positive verbal approaches as well as positive parental expectations help La Paz children develop their own *internal* controls against acting aggressively.[13] La Paz parents explain the consequences of misdeeds to children and convey in both words and actions the ideals of respect and nonviolence. One father, for example, said, "If my boy sees that I . . . do not have respect for other persons, well . . . he thus acquires the same sentiment. But if I have respect for others, well, he imitates me. . . . Above all, the father must make himself an example, by showing how to respect." By contrast, the heavy reliance on physical punishment in San Andrés may not be conducive to the internalization of a comparable degree of self-restraint against aggression. Physical punishment reflects an *external* locus of control, and thus San Andrés children may come to expect a controlling response from others, rather than developing as strongly their own self-restraints. Additionally, as San Andrés adults model physical aggression during punishment episodes and at other times, the children are presented with a message that sometimes aggression is acceptable.[14]

One line of evidence in support of this interpretation involves the behavior of young children in San Andrés and La Paz.[15] As mentioned in the previous chapter, I conducted systematic behavior observations on samples of three- to eight-year-old children from both communities in order to record data on fighting and play fighting behavior (such as beats, slaps, kicks, and so on). The samples of children were similar in sex composition, average age, the age of their parents, number of siblings, and economic standing of the families within the community. Whenever the child who was being observed engaged in aggression or play aggression, the details of the interaction were recorded, including the identities of the interactants and any facial expressions or gestures.[16]

Children's Aggression

> Beware of entrance to a quarrel.
>
> *Hamlet*, act 1, scene 3

Children from San Andrés participated in significantly more play aggression than the La Paz children, about twice as much in a typical hour. Likewise, the rate of aggression was significantly higher in San Andrés than in La Paz (see Table 4.1). In both communities, children engaged in more play aggression than aggression.

Some aggression consisted of *physical* contacts (e.g., punches and kicks), while other instances blended *noncontact* threatening (e.g., a raised arm with the intention to beat) with contact aggression. Of course, noncontact threatening is less severe than actually striking blows. In San Andrés, only about 10 percent of aggression simultaneously included threatening. In La Paz, however, 63 percent of aggression simultaneously included threatening. The mixing of noncontact threatening with physical aggression over half the time in La Paz is another indication—along with the significantly lower rate of aggression among the La Paz sample to begin with—of the La Paz children's *internal* restraint against actually engaging in physical aggression.

TABLE 4.1 Rates of play aggression and aggression in San Andrés and La Paz

Episodes per Hour	San Andrés (n = 24)	La Paz (n = 24)	Statistical Significance (two-tailed)
Rate of Play Aggression			
Mean	6.90	3.71	$p < .0001$
Standard deviation	6.80	4.00	
Rate of Aggression			
Mean	0.78	0.39	$p = .005$
Standard deviation	1.00	0.70	

These findings suggest an overall reluctance on the part of La Paz children to participate in play fighting and real fighting, relative to the San Andrés children, an intercommunity difference that also appears to strengthen with age. These differences in children's behavior correspond with the interpretation that different beliefs and values regarding the expression of aggression are internalized in these two communities. Prevalent attitudes regarding what constitutes acceptable behavior, shared expectations about the nature of the citizenry, and overall images of the community's aggressiveness and peacefulness are all elements of a child's learning environment. Through socialization, even by the three- to eight-year-old age range, La Paz children have begun to develop internal controls against engaging in both play fighting and real fighting (Figure 4.3).[17]

Figure 4.3 The systematic sampling and recording of behavior allows statistical comparisons to be made between different groups. Behavior observations reveal that San Andrés children engage in significantly more aggression than do La Paz children, a difference that parallels the overall contrasts in adult behavior between these communities. (D. P. Fry photo collection.)

MULTICAUSALITY AND MULTIDIMENSIONALITY

If we ask what accounts for the differences in levels of aggression between San Andrés and La Paz, we can address the question in different ways. Answers dealing with the *maintenance* or *perpetuation* of differences are fairly clear. The data are consistent with socialization or social learning theories.

Sociologist Suzanne Steinmetz found that conflict resolution styles tend to be passed from generation to generation within families in the United States. Steinmetz discovered that when parents used *discussion* to deal with conflicts with their children, then the children tend to adopt discussion as an approach to conflicts also. Similarly, *verbal aggression* and *physical aggression* tend to be taken up by children if these approaches to conflict were used by their parents.[18]

Similar social learning processes could account for the overall community differences in conflict resolution styles between San Andrés and La Paz. Children maturing within these communities are socialized to act in ways that are accepted, expected, and rewarded by other community members. Children from San Andrés see adults fighting at parties and at other times, witness teenagers fighting and roughhousing, see their peers receiving beatings, and on occasion feel the lashes from a rod themselves.

Psychological research shows that if parents or other adults use physical punishment, there is a tendency for the recipient child to imitate the adult and act aggressively.[19] In La Paz, the adults that children imitate hardly ever use physical punishment and rarely strike other persons. As we have seen, in the uncommon instance that people become involved in a physical confrontation, almost certainly while intoxicated, one or both are likely to separate of their own accord.[20] As a pattern, adults in La Paz model nonaggressive behavior for their children.

Shared attitudes and beliefs regarding what constitutes acceptable behavior within the community, common expectations about the nature of one's fellow citizens, and overall beliefs as to the aggressiveness or peacefulness of the community constitute elements of a child's learning environment. The findings that the children of La Paz actually engage in less play aggression and serious aggression than do children in San Andrés clearly support a social learning, socialization interpretation. Individuals growing up in the La Paz social environment, beginning in early childhood and continuing even into adulthood, internalize and act in accordance with a belief system that discourages physical aggression and encourages respectful conduct in social interactions. Unlike their neighbors in San Andrés, citizens of La Paz do not talk with resigned acceptance of disrespectful, aggressive, jealous persons existing in their community. As psychologist Rowell Huesmann notes, children are more likely to internalize *scripts* for behavior that are in accordance with social norms.[21] Acting aggressively runs counter to La Pazian social norms.

Turning to the question of how differences between San Andrés and La Paz have originated, some ideas can be proposed as *hypotheses* rather than definitive answers. It may be important, for example, that citizens of La Paz have more land on the average than do the people of San Andrés. About one-third of San Andrés families own one hectare of land, or less, whereas in La Paz, about one-sixth of the families are in the same land-poor situation. Perhaps more prevalent land shortages among San Andrés families, especially over recent generations, have resulted in a higher level of hostility in San Andrés than in La Paz, tensions that can shatter the peace. However, when disputes do occur over land in San Andrés, they are between individuals, not community factions as sometimes occur in other Mexican communities, and this limits bloodshed.[22]

As we have seen, sex roles and patterns of interaction between women and men differ markedly between these two Zapotec communities.[23] La Paz men treat women with greater respect and less violence than do the men of San Andrés. Might the origin of these differences stem, in part, from differing economic factors? For hundreds of years, La Paz women have produced pottery for trade or sale with the result that they have a long-standing history of bringing goods and money into their households.[24] Historically, the situation has been very different in San Andrés. The women have lacked a way to make regular contributions through trade goods or cash to the household income. The men, by contrast, have brought in wages from their work in the mines. Could these long-standing economic differences underlie or contribute to the divergent systems of belief and behavior related to jealousy, respect, and aggression that are manifested between the sexes? La Paz men value and are in awe of the women's pottery-producing skills, which are passed from mother to daughter. More than once, men explained to me that women can make pottery, but that they can't. In other words, community histories, patterns of household economics, and beliefs involving equality, respect, and jealousy may all interrelate with each other in explaining why La Paz women are largely immune to the types of forceful and fearful controls that San Andrés men employ against women (Figure 4.4).

Figure 4.4 The women of La Paz have a long-standing tradition of making and selling pottery. The La Paz men appreciate this special skill of the women. In La Paz, in contrast to San Andrés, men are not overly jealous. As a rule, La Paz men and women get along well. (D. P. Fry photo collection.)

This brings us back to a consideration of jealousy. Not only does the jealousy-ridden belief system in San Andrés result in more wife abuse than in La Paz, but many of the San Andrés fistfights and killings stem from jealousy.[25] In La Paz, shared beliefs hold jealousy to be an emotion of youth that rarely leads to aggression. Whereas the origin of differences in such beliefs between the two communities, along with the very different patterns of interaction between women and men, remain unclear, it is nonetheless apparent that new generations of children growing up in each place learn these beliefs and behaviors, thus perpetuating the divergent social patterns. An interaction of several factors over time almost certainly has led to the marked intercommunity differences between San Andrés and La Paz.[26]

SOME BROADER IMPLICATIONS

What are the broader implications of this Zapotec research? First, the findings illustrate the general principle that humans are learners par excellence. Socialization and social learning processes have huge effects on human beliefs and behavior. The statistically significant differences in rates of children's aggression and playfighting between San Andrés and La Paz provide hard data that illustrate this point. Clearly, human aggression is not an immutable behavioral response, but, to the contrary, varies greatly across different social learning environments.

This leads to a second point. San Andrés and La Paz show that cultural beliefs and behavior vary, even among neighboring communities *within* the same overall culture. We will consider in the next chapter how the cross-cultural variability in aggression and peacefulness is even greater *among different cultures*. At one end of the cross-cultural spectrum, some societies have exceedingly low levels of physical aggression, whereas at the other end of the continuum, other societies have much higher levels of aggression. As we saw in chapter 2, however, even within violent societies, much daily behavior is peaceful.

A third generally applicable point is that peacefulness stems from multiple factors. The comparison of San Andrés and La Paz suggests that various interacting variables most likely contribute to intercommunity contrasts in peacefulness. The differences in aggression between three- to eight-year-old children of San Andrés and La Paz show that by an early age individuals are internalizing different beliefs as to the appropriateness or inappropriateness of engaging in aggression within their social group. In all likelihood, however, La Paz is less violent than San Andrés not only because of divergent social learning and socialization processes between the two communities, but also because of various interacting economic, social, and historical variables. The Zapotec study thus suggests a general point: A multicausal perspective on peace and aggression will be useful as we consider these topics in other human societies.

A final implication of the Zapotec research involves the concept of cultural belief system. Each culture has a constellation of beliefs that are learned and shared. The members of a given culture rarely question the veracity of the shared beliefs. In large part, the elements of the belief system are simply taken for granted by persons who have grown up within the culture. Most cultural beliefs are *invisible* to the persons who hold them. Going to live within a society that is very different from one's own can *make the invisible visible.* We have seen how a constellation of beliefs in San Andrés related to jealousy, sex roles, and culturally appropriate patterns of female–male social interaction differs dramatically from the beliefs on such topics held both in La Paz and in the United States. I have related how, as a newcomer to the San Andrés cultural landscape, I did not immediately realize that acts like smiling at a woman or attempting to engage her in friendly conversation would be tantamount to making a sexual advance *within the context of her belief system.* I learned quickly that local beliefs differed greatly from my own beliefs about the appropriateness of engaging in casual conversation with members of the opposite sex. In future chapters, we will return to the largely taken-for-granted nature of cultural beliefs and the challenge of *making the invisible visible,* but within a new context. We will consider whether many statements about war made by members of Western society reflect presumptions based on their belief system rather than on an objective evaluation of data on warfare. We will attempt to untangle how much "knowledge" about warfare has a basis in *fact* and how much reflects instead cultural beliefs that upon closer examination are greatly at odds with the actual anthropological data on war.

CHAPTER 5

THE CROSS-CULTURAL PEACEFULNESS–AGGRESSIVENESS CONTINUUM

> In November of 1913, a 47-year-old Icelandic woman poisoned her brother for financial gain. . . . It was dark November again, 16 years later, when a 19-year-old burglar was surprised at his work, and beat to death the man who interrupted him. The reason that these two cases are noteworthy is that they are the only two homicides known to have taken place in the little island nation of Iceland in the first 40 years of this century. . . . The two Icelandic cases between 1900 and 1939 represent a rate of 0.5 homicides per *million* persons per annum.
>
> MARTIN DALY AND MARGO WILSON[1]

Internally peaceful societies—cultures with extremely low levels of physical aggression and belief systems that favor nonviolence—can be found in various parts of the world. Many internally peaceful societies also do not engage in warfare, but some do, often for defensive reasons.[2] Internally peaceful societies tend to have values, attitudes, socialization practices, and conflict resolution procedures that emphasize nonviolent approaches to social tensions.[3] They are likely to be small communities with egalitarian social structures that promote cooperation, generalized sharing, and decision-making through group consensus. However, some such societies are not so small. Icelanders, Norwegians, and the Japanese, for instance, shun physical aggression and in fact have low levels of internal violence in their societies.

Descriptive and culturally comparative studies provide complementary perspectives on the high degree of variability in physical aggression from one society to the next. *The overall conclusion is that humans clearly are capable of creating societies with very little violence and of dealing with conflicts without violence.* This statement is by no means utopian, because numerous internally peaceful societies already exist. One reason that it is necessary and important to document this basic ethnographic fact is that assertions to the contrary continue to be made.[4] As we shall see, peaceful societies are not such a rarity after all.

A PEACEFULNESS–AGGRESSIVENESS CONTINUUM

A prism offers a new perspective on the nature of visible light, revealing to the human eye a spectrum of colors that grade one into the next. Analogously, a cross-cultural perspective enlightens by revealing that the amount of physical aggression manifested within societies is highly variable. Each society can be viewed as occupying a position on a spectrum that ranges between notable violence at one end and the *virtual* absence of physical aggression at the other, with most societies falling between the extremes. This variation is illustrated by the findings of political scientist Marc Ross, who developed composite scales for internal and external conflict. Ross scored 90 preindustrial societies for seven measures of conflict and then combined these variables statistically to derive an overall *internal conflict score* for each society.[5] Of Ross' seven internal conflict variables, one assessed, for example, how often individual disputants resorted to physical force, and another variable involved the society's frequency of internal war. The internal conflict score included measures of physical aggression and nonphysical conflict. Ross also developed an *external conflict score* for each society, this time based on three variables, to assess the degree of conflict between each society and its neighbors. He discovered that levels of internal and external conflict are statistically correlated. That is, levels of internal and external conflict *tend* to correspond with each other, although there are various exceptions to the pattern.[6]

Returning to our focus on internal conflict, I have used the data from Ross' study to illustrate visually the cross-cultural spectrum for internal conflict.[7] As is shown in Figure 5.1, the internal conflict scores range between –5 (low internal conflict) and +6 (high internal conflict). Of the Lepcha of the Himalayas, one of the seven societies scored as –5, Ross writes:

> Overt conflicts are relatively few and not very severe on the rare occasions when they occur. Theft is virtually unknown and the last authenticated murder took place *two centuries* before Gorer's fieldwork in the 1930's. . . . Quarreling is so strongly disapproved that it is the responsibility of all to make every effort to prevent disputes or to stop them once they have broken out.[8]

Jumping to the opposite end of the spectrum, Ross writes about the Jívaro of Ecuador, scored as a +6: "concerns about conflict and violence affect most aspects of daily life. There is little institutionalized cooperation and little interpersonal trust. As a result, individuals, with some assistance from close kin and occasional friends, seek security in personal achievements and the establishment of reputations for aggressiveness. Feuding is pervasive and constant attention to possible threats is necessary for survival."[9]

It is interesting that there are more cultures at the peaceful end of the continuum in Figure 5.1 than at the high internal conflict end. Fourteen societies (16 percent of the sample) received the lowest or second lowest score, whereas only six (seven percent of the sample) received the highest or second highest score. Otherwise, with some rises and dips, the cultures are rather evenly distributed across the spectrum of internal conflict. However, as pointed out in chapter 2, even so-called aggressive societies are not violent most of the time.

Visualizing such a continuum is useful for several reasons. It suggests that dichotomizing between peaceful and aggressive cultures is an oversimplified distortion. Where should one make such a split between peaceful and aggressive anyhow? Any

								Amhara			
								Aweikoma	Otoro		
		Aztec	Cuna			Andamanese		Gheg Albanians	Shilluk		
		Basseri	Korean			Aymara		Goajiro	Maasai		
		Buganda	Bambara			Copper Eskimo		Iban	Somali		
Burusho	*Balinese*	Carib	Miskito			Negri		Kurds	Egyptian		
Cayapa	Chiricahua	Huron	Rural Irish	Lozi	Azande	Maori		Lakher	Rwala		
Havasupi	Gond	Fon	Yokuts	Hausa	Comanche	Marshalese	Ainu	Nyakusa	Orokaiva		
Lepcha	Gros Ventre	*!Kung*	Yahgan	Warrau	Gilyak	Mende	Belacoola	Samoans	Kapauku	Abipon	
Papago	*Mbuti*	Lamet	*Lapp*	Ingalik	Kazak	Slave	Manus	Tiv	Fijian	Ifugao	
Semang	Mundurucú	Pawnee	*Saulteaux*	Toradja	Kikuyu	Trobriand	Suku	Tiwi	Klamath	Riffian	Jivaro
Timbira	Santal	*Tikopia*	Vietnamese	Eyak	Nambicuara	Yurok	Tallensi	Yapese	Mapuche	Shavante	Teda
−5	−4	−3	−2	−1	0	+1	+2	+3	+4	+5	+6

Low Internal Conflict — High Internal Conflict

Internal Conflict Score

Figure 5.1 A cross-cultural peacefulness–aggressiveness continuum. Cultures appearing in italic type are listed in Box 5.1, the Internally Peaceful Societies List. The societal names used by Ross 1993a are retained in this figure (for example, !Kung instead of Ju/'hoansi) to avoid any confusion that might result from changing names or their spellings. (Source: Internal Conflict Scores from Ross 1993a: Appendix A, rounded to the nearest whole number.)

decision is arbitrary. At the same time it is clear that relative to the vast majority of the cultures in the middle range of the continuum, at one end of the spectrum societies are very peaceful, and at the other end of the spectrum societies have much higher levels of aggression. The peacefulness–aggressiveness continuum shows the wide range of societal possibilities.

Another point is that the peacefulness–aggressiveness of a given society is not immutably fixed through time. Shifts toward violence and shifts toward peacefulness occur over years, generations, and centuries.[10] The fact that a culture has a high level of physical aggression today does not preclude a change toward peacefulness in the future. For example, Carole and Clay Robarchek describe how the Waorani of Ecuador managed to decrease their initially high rate of homicide *by over 90 percent* in just a few years (see Figure 5.2).[11]

> The catalyst that began the transformation of the Waorani culture of war was the entry into Waorani territory of two North American Protestant missionary women accompanied by two Waorani women. . . . As bands became convinced that the feuding could stop, peace became a goal in its own right, even superseding the desire for revenge. . . . The killing stopped because the Waorani themselves made a conscious decision to end it.[12]

Figure 5.2 A Waorani woman strips fibers, the first step in making string for weaving hammocks and carrying bags, as other family members rest in the background. Revenge homicides ran rampant in Waorani society, until, as Clayton and Carole Robarchek explain, "the killing stopped because the Waorani themselves made a conscious decision to end it." (Photo courtesy of Clayton A. Robarchek and Carole J. Robarchek; quote from Robarchek & Robarchek 1996b:72–73.)

A similar case of a community plagued by murders and brutal maimings that managed to supplant violent practices with more peaceful ones comes from a Chatino village in southern Mexico studied by James Greenberg. The community brought about land reforms and enacted new laws. In a movement initiated by village women who were "sick of seeing their men killed in blood feuds," the majority of the village came to support the passing and subsequent strict enforcement of an ordinance banning alcohol consumption and the carrying of weapons. Greenberg writes, "These measures were effective and put an end to the blood feuding and factionalism in the village."[13]

Roy Willis tells of another transformation away from violence toward peace. He explains that the Fipa of Tanzania are a people "who in the middle of the nineteenth century emerged from a period of conflict and civil war to construct a peaceful, orderly, and prosperous society."[14] History and anthropology provide various examples of societies replacing violent practices and institutions with more peaceful social patterns, sometimes with remarkable rapidity.[15]

GROWING INTEREST IN PEACEFUL SOCIETIES

Being interested in peaceful societies, I have observed a puzzling phenomenon: Some people seem uncomfortable with the idea that peaceful societies exist, and a few authors have even attempted to argue that peaceful societies are only an illusion.[16] A major problem with this argument is that a great deal of anthropological evidence contradicts it.

Interest in peaceful societies seems to be increasing, as indicated by a flowering of recent publications.[17] Over the decades of the 20th century, many societies with low levels of internal physical aggression have been studied and described, despite the fact that direct research on peace and nonviolence is in large part a recent development.[18] In 1994, Leslie Sponsel commented, "Nonviolent and peaceful societies appear to be rare—not because they are, in fact, rare, but because nonviolence and peace are so rarely considered in research, the media, and other arenas."[19]

In a classic article, H. Thoden van Velzen and W. van Wetering classified 20 societies as internally peaceful. In 1978, David Fabbro summarized information on seven peaceful societies, the Mbuti, Ju/'hoansi (!Kung), Semai, Siriono, Copper Inuit, Hutterites, and Tristan da Cunha Islanders—all of which shunned war and collective internal violence, had low levels of interpersonal violence, and tended to lack social structures that institutionalized violence.[20]

The same year, Ashley Montagu edited a book called *Learning Non-Aggression,* in which contributors paid special attention to how children are socialized in certain societies with low levels of aggression.[21] Montagu and my father were friends before I even knew what the word "anthropology" meant. Aside from his prolific and widely appreciated scholarship, Montagu was respected for his humanitarianism and known for his wit. Long after retiring from his university position, he quipped that he had been "institutionally uncommitted for many years."[22] On being famous he joked: "Fame is when a lot of people you don't know know your name." At age 91, in the midst of working on two books, he remarked, "I'm always doing so many things—like the gallant young man who jumped on his horse and galloped off in *all* directions." His diverse legacy of publications, many concerned with improving the human condition, such as those on race and racism, certainly support his self-assessment.[23] When asked about overpopulation in 1996, he commented that he didn't see much hope for the world, but nonetheless felt that he had to work for a better future—then added: "Besides, maybe I'm wrong. I've been wrong before." Such openmindedness is especially appropriate for a scientist.

In 1989, 11 years after Montagu's *Learning Non-Aggression* was published, information on some additional peaceful cultures such as the Buid, Chewong, Piaroa, and the La Paz Zapotec appeared in a book called *Societies at Peace,* edited by Signe Howell and Roy Willis. The chapter on La Paz is by friend and colleague Carl O'Nell, who worked in La Paz before I did. Carl and his wife Nancy first took me to La Paz and introduced me to their Zapotec friends. I remember bumping along in a rented yellow VW beetle that turned gradually brown as we neared La Paz on the hot and dusty dirt road. I remain grateful to Carl for generously facilitating my studies in La Paz in numerous ways.[24]

Also in 1989, David Levinson published the results of a systematic cross-cultural study on family violence—specifically, wife and husband beating, physical punishment of children, and sibling fighting. Levinson found that in 16 of 90 societies, or 18 percent of the sample, "family violence of any kind is virtually nonexistent." In these 16 societies, physical fighting among men also tended to occur only rarely if at all; Levinson comments that the tendency is that "men resolve disputes with other men peacefully." These findings are in accordance with the continuum of peacefulness–aggressiveness model discussed earlier—here focusing on the most peaceful 18 percent of a sample, which, by the way, is different from the sample of 90 societies used by Ross.[25]

In 1993, Bruce Bonta's *Peaceful Peoples: An Annotated Bibliography* came out, providing thorough annotations of the literature on over 40 highly peaceful societies. Contributors to Leslie Sponsel and Thomas Gregor's 1994 edited volume, *The Anthropology of Peace and Nonviolence,* discussed theoretical issues and provided additional data on cultures with low levels of internal aggression, such as the Semai, La Paz Zapotec, and certain Inuit bands. The next year, Johan van der Dennen published a two-volume work, *The Origin of War,* in which a comprehensive chapter focuses on peace and peaceful societies.[26]

In 1996, Tom Gregor, one of the anthropologists who studied the Upper Xingu peace system, edited *A Natural History of Peace,* which includes a comparison of Mehinaku and Semai societies. The book also contains a thought-provoking anthropological overview of humanity's peace potential by Les Sponsel. The late 1990s and early 2000s also saw the publication of many works on peaceful societies, including those by Bruce Bonta, Bob Dentan, Peter Gardner, Clay Robarchek, Les Sponsel, and myself. A book called *Keeping the Peace: Conflict Resolution and Peaceful Societies around the World,* which Graham Kemp and I coedit, focuses on how peaceful people *manage conflict without violence* and includes chapters on the Nubians of Africa, Hopi of North America, Mardu of Australia, Paliyan of South Asia, Sama Dilaut sea nomads of South East Asia, Rotuman Islanders of Oceania, and Norwegians of Europe, among others. Gregor is currently writing a book on the Xingu peace system.[27] In January 2005, Bruce Bonta inaugurated the internet site www.peacefulsocieties.org, an excellent resource on peaceful societies.

PEACEFUL SOCIETIES: NOT SUCH A RARE BREED AFTER ALL

It is important to state explicitly that no internally peaceful society is expected to be absolutely devoid of *all forms* of aggression at *all times.*[28] Levinson suggests that it is "useful to think of nonviolent cultures as cultures where violence does not occur often, where it is not valued and is openly discouraged, where violence-inducing events in other cultures are reacted to nonviolently, and where violence is considered deviant."[29] Furthermore, internally peaceful societies are anticipated to show some variation in the types of rare aggression that do occur. For example, some peaceful cultures might have relatively more or less spousal aggression, physical punishment of children, or homicide than do other peaceful societies.[30] As a group, however, internally peaceful societies, although not identical regarding all types of behavior, share the observable feature of having very low levels of physical aggression in comparison to most other societies. In internally peaceful societies, nearly all conflicts are dealt with in nonviolent ways, for instance, by moving away, tolerating a problem, discussing an issue in order to find a solution, letting others mediate a dispute, and so on. *Thus the essential point is that physical aggression is strongly discouraged and in fact occurs only very rarely.*

In researching this book, I began compiling a list of internally peaceful societies. Currently there are over 80 societies on the list, as shown in Box 5.1. The decision to

BOX 5.1 INTERNALLY PEACEFUL SOCIETIES: DESCRIPTIVE SOURCES AND COMPARATIVE RATINGS

Peaceful societies are characterized by an extremely low level of physical aggression among their members as well as beliefs that favor nonviolent behavior and do not accept aggression. From a comparative, cross-cultural perspective, internally peaceful societies cluster near the peaceful end of a peacefulness–aggressiveness continuum. As in all societies, conflicts occur in peaceful societies. However, in peaceful societies conflicts are almost always handled nonviolently. No peaceful society is absolutely "violence free." Rather, acts of violence in peaceful societies are extremely rare and strongly devalued. Undoubtedly, additional internally peaceful societies exist beyond those on this list. Generally, primary sources and sources with the most information are listed first; useful secondary sources follow in some cases. When ratings from cross-cultural studies exist, they appear in italics.

Africa: Fipa/Ufipa,[1] G/wi,[2] Ju/'hoansi/Ju/wasi (formerly called !Kung or Kung),[3] Kongo/BaKongo,[4] Mbuti,[5] Nubians,[6] Tristan da Cunha[7]

Asia: Akha,[8] Alangan Agta,[9] Bajau Laut/Sama Dilaut,[10] Balinese,[11] Batak Agta,[12] Batek,[13] Birhor,[14] Buid,[15] Central Thai,[16] Chewong,[17] Hanunóo,[18] Iraya Agta,[19] Irula,[20] Japan,[21] Jahai,[22] Kadar,[23] Kua Sai Chinese,[24] Ladakhi/Ladaki,[25] Lepchas,[26] Malapandaram/Hill Pandaram,[27] Mamanua Agta,[28] Mentawei Islanders,[29] Nayaka/Naikens,[30] Palawan Agta,[31] Paliyan,[32] Punan/Penan (especially Eastern groups),[33] Semai Senoi,[34] Semang,[35] Sherpa,[36] Subanun,[37] Sulod,[38] Tagbanua/Tagbanuwa Agta,[39] Taubuid Agta,[40] Temiar Senoi,[41] Tiruray Agta,[42] Toda,[43] Toraja,[44] Veddahs/Vedda,[45] Wana,[46] Yames/Yami,[47] Yanadi[48]

Europe: Danes,[49] Icelanders,[50] Norwegians,[51] Saami/Lapps[52]

North America: Amish,[53] Canadian Inuit (specifically, Utkuhikhalingmiut and Qipisamiut),[54] Dogrib,[55] Greenland Inuit (East & West),[56] Hopi,[57] Hutterites,[58] Koksoagmyut/Hudson Bay Inuit,[59] Mandan,[60] Montagnais-Naskapi,[61] Papago,[62]

Polar Eskimo/Inughuit,[63] Saulteaux,[64] Taos Pueblo,[65] Tewa Pueblo,[66] Zapotec of "La Paz,"[67] Zuni[68]

Oceania: Arapesh,[69] Ifaluk,[70] Mardu/Mardudjara,[71] Rotuma Islanders (Fiji),[72] Tahitians,[73] Tanna Islanders,[74] Tikana (New Ireland),[75] Tikopia,[76] Wape[77]

South America: Cayapa,[78] Kuikuru,[79] Panare,[80] Pemon,[81] Piaroa,[82] Siriono,[83] Trio,[84] Wáiwai,[85] Wauja/Waura[86]

Sources: 1. Willis 1989, 1995:99; see also Bonta 1993. 2. Silberbauer 1972, 1981; see also Bonta 1993. 3. Draper 1978; Lee 1979: esp. Chapter 13, 1993: esp. Chapter 7; Howell 1979; E. Thomas 1959:21–24, 1994; see also Fabbro 1978; Kent 1989; Murdock 1934; for further discussion: Knauft 1987; Konner 1982:204. 4. MacGaffey 1995; see also Dennen 1995:626. 5. Turnbull 1961, 1965a, 1965b, 1968b:341, 1978; see also Bonta 1993; Fabbro 1978. 6. R. Fernea 1973, 2004; E. & R. Fernea 1991; see also Bonta 1993, 1996. 7. Loudon 1970; Munch 1974; Munch & Marske 1981:163, 165, 168; see also Bonta 1993. 8. Kammerer 1993:13. 9. Dennen 1995:652–653. 10. Sather 1975:11, 1993:34, 2004; Clifford Sather, personal communication. 11. Howe 1989; McCauley 1993:37; see also Bonta 1993, 1997:317; Hollan 1988:52–53; *Masumura 1977 internal violence score = low; Ross 1993a internal conflict score = –4; Ember & Ember 1992a assault score = low, homicide score = "don't know."* 12. Warren 1975a; Dennen 1995:652–653. 13. Karen Endicott 1984:6; Kirk Endicott 1979, 1983, 1988, 1993:235; see also Bonta 1993. 14. Sinha 1972; see also Bonta 1993; 15. Gibson 1989, 1990; see also Bonta 1993. 16. Phillips 1974; Martin & Levinson 1993:71; *Levinson 1989 family violence score = 1 (no or rare), male fighting score = 1 (nonviolent, ritualized, or self-directed).* 17. Howell 1988:150, 1989; see also Bonta 1993. 18. Conklin 1954; LeBar 1975a:76; Hockings 1993:91. 19. Dennen 1995:652–653. 20. Nobel & Jebados 1992:107; Murdock 1934:110; Zvelebil 1988; see also Hockings 1992:15, 17; Wolf 1992:137. 21. Kidder & Hostetler 1990; Lock 1993; Krauss, Rohlen, & Steinhoff 1984; Lebra 1984; Archer & Gartner 1984; see also Knauft 1987: Table 2; *Masumura 1977 internal violence score = low; Ember & Ember 1992a assault score = low, homicide score = low.* 22. Sluys 1999:307, 310, 2000; see also Endicott 1983, 1993. 23. Ehrenfels 1952, cited in Bonta 1997:318; see also Bonta 1993; Gardner 1966:402. 24. Ward 1970; see also Bonta 1993. 25. Mann 1986; Norberg-Hodge 1991; see also Dennen 1995:646; Holsti 1913. 26. Gorer 1967; DiMaggio 1992:149; see also Bonta 1993; Ember & Ember 1994a; Montagu 1978b:5; Ross 1993a:89–92; *Thoden van Velzen & van Wetering 1960 rating = peaceful; Masumura 1977 internal violence score = low; Ross 1993a internal conflict score = –5; Palmer 1965 murder score = 2 out of 21; Ember & Ember 1992a assault score = low, homicide score = low.* 27. Morris 1977: esp. 230, 237–238, 1982, 1992:100; see also Bonta 1993, 1996; Dennen 1995:648; Gardner 1966:402. 28. Dennen 1995:652–653; see also Maceda 1975. 29. Nooy-Palm 1972:43; see also Dennen 1995:650; Holsti 1913. 30. Bird-David 1992; see also Bonta 1993, 1997. 31. Dennen 1995:652–653; see also Warren 1975b. 32. Gardner 1966:402, 1972: for example, see 425, 1985:413–416, 1995, 1999:263; 2000a, 2000b: esp. Chapters 5 and 6, 2004. 33. Hose 1894:157–158; Needham 1972:180; see also Holsti 1913:71; Montagu 1978b:5. 34. Dentan 1968, 1978, 1988, 1991, 1992, 1993, 1995, 1999:419, 420, 2000, 2001a, 2004; Dentan & Williams-Hunt 1999; Gregor & Robarchek 1996; Robarchek 1979, 1980, 1986, 1989, 1990, 1994, 1997; Robarchek & Robarchek 1992, 1996a, 1998b; Robarchek & Dentan 1987. 35. LeBar et al. 1964:185; Kirk Endicott 1993; Murdock 1934:94–95, 100; Schebesta 1929:280; see also Dennen 1995:660–661; Endicott 1983; Holsti 1913; *Ross 1993a internal conflict score = –5; Ember & Ember 1992a assault score = low, homicide score = low.* 36. Paul 1977:176, 1992:259; Ortner 1978, 1989; Fürer-Haimendorf 1984. 37. Frake 1960:52, 1980a:133, 135, 1980b:105, 1993:245; LeBar 1975b:34; see also Dennen 1995:652–653. 38. Dentan 1992. 39. Warren 1975c:67; Dennen 1995:652–653. 40. Dennen 1995:652–653. 41. Benjamin 1993; Roseman 1990:232–233. 42. Dennen 1995:652–653; 43. Rivers 1986; Walker 1986: esp. 91–96, 1992:297; see also Montagu 1976, 1978b:5; Murdock 1934; Holsti 1913; *Ember & Ember 1992a assault score = low, homicide score = low.* 44. Hollan 1988, 1997; 45. Seligmann & Seligmann 1969:34; Stegeborn 1999:271; see also Davie 1929; Hobhouse 1956:105; Holsti 1913:71; Levinson 1994:122; Lesser 1967:94; Montagu 1978b:5; *Ember & Ember 1992a assault score = low, homicide score = low.* 46. Dentan 1992; Frederick Rawski, personal communication. 47. Le Bar 1975c; Montagu 1978b:5. 48. Raghaviah 1962; see also Bonta 1993, 1996; Gardner 1966:403. 49. Anderson & Anderson 1992; Archer & Gartner 1984; Gudjónsson & Pétursson 1990. 50. Durrenburger and Beierle 1992; Gudjónsson & Pétursson 1990; Daly & Wilson 1988; Archer & Gartner 1984. 51. Archer & Gartner 1984; Aubert 1969; Barth 1952;

Dobinson 2004; Gudjónsson & Pétursson 1990; Gullestad 1991; Hollos 1970, 1974; Larson 1992; Ross 1993a, 1993b; *Yearbook of Nordic Statistics* 1994:338. 52. Pelto 1962:101, 135–140; Itkonen 1984:288–295; Anderson & Beach 1992:222; Ingold 1976; see also Davie 1929:49; Holsti 1913; Montagu 1976:187; *Ross 1993a internal conflict score = –2; Levinson 1989 family violence score = 1 (no or rare), male fighting score = 1 (nonviolent, ritualized, or self-directed); Palmer 1965 murder score = 0 out of 21; Ember & Ember 1992a assault score = low, homicide score = low.* 53. Hostetler 1983a:3, 25, 29, 38, 43, 1991; Kidder & Hostetler 1990; see also Bonta 1993, 1996, 1997; Dentan 1994. 54. Briggs 1970, 1978, 1994. 55. Helm 1972:79–81, 1991:89. 56. Nansen 1893; Kleivan 1991; see also Dennen 1995. 57. Cox 1973: Chapter 5; Schlegel 2004; Simmons 1942:10–11; see also Montagu 1976:21, 1978b:5; Murdock 1934:337; Thoden van Velzen & van Wetering 1960:190–191; *Levinson 1989 family violence score = not reported, Male fighting score = not reported;* Palmer 1965 murder score = 3 out of 21. 58. Hostetler & Huntington 1968; Hostetler 1974, 1983b:3, 17, 1991:154; see also Bonta 1993; Fabbro 1978; Montagu 1976:21. 59. Dennen 1995:640–641. 60. Schneider 1991:215; Thoden van Velzen & van Wetering 1960:188; *Thoden van Velzen & van Wetering 1960 rating = peaceful.* 61. Driver 1969:313; Leacock 1981; Lips 1947:399, 402, 469–472; Reid 1991; Speck 1935: for example, see 27, 31, 44; see also Bonta 1993, 1997; Hallowell 1974:277; *Levinson 1989 family violence score = not reported, male fighting score = not reported; Ember & Ember 1992a assault score = low, homicide score = low.* 62. Underhill 1939:11, 13, 22, 24, 89, 113–121, 1946; see also Levinson 1994:122, 124; Montagu 1978b:5; *Thoden van Velzen & van Wetering 1960 rating = peaceful; Ross 1993a internal conflict score = –5; Levinson 1989 family violence score = 1.25 (no or rare), male fighting score = 1 (nonviolent, ritualized, or self-directed); Palmer 1965 murder score = 6 out of 21; Ember & Ember 1992a assault score = low, homicide score = low.* 63. Gilberg 1984, 1991; Murdock 1934:210–211. 64. Hallowell 1974: esp. 278; see also Holsti 1913; *Ross 1993a internal conflict score = –2; Ember & Ember 1992a assault score = low-moderate, homicide score = low.* 65. Jorgensen 1980:244–245, Map CU181; Montagu 1978b:5; see also Dozier 1983:78–82 for further discussion; *Palmer 1965 murder score = 3 out of 21.* 66. Jacobs 1991:349; see also Montagu 1978b:5. 67. Fry 1988, 1992b, 1993a, 1994, 1999a, 2004b; O'Nell 1979, 1981, 1986, 1989. 68. Goldman 1961; Montagu 1976:21, 1978b:5; see also Bonta 1993; Dennen 1995:673; Redfield 1967:7–8; Thoden van Velzen & van Wetering 1960:169; *Masumura 1977 internal violence score = low; Palmer 1965 murder score = 3 out of 21; Ember & Ember 1992a assault score = low, homicide score = low.* 69. Mead 1961a; see also Montagu 1976:187, 1978b:5; *Minturn et al. 1969 rape score = 2 (rape does not occur but the concept is present).* 70. Burrows 1952; Lutz 1982, 1983, 1988:esp. 136–138 & 174–182; Spiro 1952; see also Bonta 1993, 1996, 1997; Betzig & Wichimai 1991; *Thoden van Velzen & van Wetering 1960 rating = peaceful; Minturn et al. 1969 rape score = 2 (rape does not occur but the concept is present); Palmer 1965 murder score = 2 out of 21.* 71. Tonkinson 1978, 1991, 2004. 72. Howard 1990, 1991:282, 2004. 73. Levy 1975, 1978. 74. Lindstrom 1991:314–315. 75. Billings 1991: for example, see 252, 253. 76. Firth 1957, 1967; *Masumura 1977 internal violence score = low; Ross 1993a internal conflict score = –3; Levinson 1989 family violence score = not reported, male fighting score = not reported; Palmer 1965 murder score = 0 out of 21; Ember & Ember 1992a assault score = not reported, homicide score = moderate.* 77. Mitchell 1991:372, 1999; see also Mitchell 1978. 78. Barrett 1925; Murra 1948:282; see also Altschuler 1964, 1967, 1970; *Masumura 1977 internal violence score = low; Ross 1993a internal conflict score = –5; Ember & Ember 1992a assault score = low, homicide score = low.* 79. Carneiro 1994a:208; see also Dole 1966. 80. Henley 1982:153, 1994:266. 81. D. Thomas 1982, 1994:272–273. 82. Overing 1986, 1989; Zent 1994; see also Bonta 1993. 83. Holmberg 1969; see also Dentan 1992; Fabbro 1978. 84. Rivière 1994:336. 85. Howard 1994:347–348; see also Campbell 1995: Chapter 4. 86. Gregor 1994b; Ireland 1988, 1991.

include a given society on the list rests on anthropological information about the nonviolent beliefs and low levels of physical aggression expressed within the culture. The Piaroa of South America, for example, meet the criteria for inclusion based on Joanna Overing's descriptions, such as: "Piaroaland is almost free of all forms of physical violence, a place where children, teenagers, and adults alike never express anger through physical means. . . . Since the Piaroa totally disallow physical violence, and children are never physically punished, the children have no model of such action."[31] A sampling of other such anthropological descriptions appears in Box 5.2.

BOX 5.2 A SAMPLING OF QUOTATIONS ABOUT INTERNALLY PEACEFUL SOCIETIES

Tahitians of Oceania, fishing and farming economy: "Available statistics on crime and suicide, impressions of administrators, and my own observations during a period of more than two years in a rural village and a small enclave in urban Papeete indicate . . . an extreme lack of angry, hostile, destructive behavior."[1]

Chewong of Malaysia, hunting-and-gathering and shifting cultivation: "Anger is ignored as much as possible, as with angry children, but when it becomes too manifest, people physically remove themselves, just as they flee from outsiders. . . . Their mythology has no instances of human physical violence. I asked about murder. They insisted it never happened."[2]

Pemon of South America, slash-and-burn cultivation, fishing, and hunting-and-gathering: "The Pemon do not approve of anger or displays of hostility. . . . The dispersion of settlements acts in concert with the tendency to avoid interaction between disputants to ensure that the main means of social control is not allowing the conflict to break out in the open in the first place. . . . Homicide is very rare."[3]

Hutterites of North America, collectivist agriculture: "In their history there has never been a homicide."[4]

Trio of South America, slash-and-burn cultivation and hunting-and-gathering: "The Trio lack tolerance for conflict, and the tendency is always to move in order to avoid confrontation. . . . Cases of physical violence are rare."[5]

BaKongo of Africa, wage labor in urban areas and cultivation in rural areas: "The BaKongo have a reputation as a nonviolent people. Physical violence is, in fact, rare among them, although they think of themselves as under constant attack by hostile relatives and neighbors, 'witches' exercising occult powers. Appropriate committees of elders mediate disputes, and diviners may be consulted in serious cases; often the diviner is a 'prophet' (*ngunza*) of a Christian denomination."[6]

Paliyan of South Asia, foraging: "Regarding their avoidance of competition, it is of first importance that Paliyans assert an explicit code of nonviolence."[7]

Central Thai of Asia, wet-rice agriculture: "To a large extent, social control is maintained by a Buddhist value system, which places a premium on avoiding and fleeing rather than fighting."[8] "The most obvious fact about aggression in Bang Chan is that villagers cannot tolerate its spontaneous, direct expression in face-to-face relationships."[9]

Panaré of South America, slash-and-burn cultivation, fishing, and hunting-and-gathering: "Far from producing a state of anarchy in which life is nasty, brutish and short, this atomistic social organization underlies a way of life in which there is very little interpersonal aggression and very few disputes, for the simple reason that the grounds for conflict are few."[10]

Toraja of Indonesia, rice farming: "[The Toraja devalue] anger and hostility and successfully control overtly aggressive behavior through a number of cultural practices."[11]

Iceland of the North Atlantic, industrial fishing economy: "In 1985 the annual homicide rate per 100,000 inhabitants was just over 0.6 for Iceland. . . . About one third of the offenders had been either psychotic or mentally subnormal at the time of the homicide or committed suicide shortly after the act."[12]

Wape of New Guinea, slash-and-burn horticulture: "During my fieldwork, I never saw a physical fight between men, between women, or even between children. The preferred Wape response to potential violence is conciliatory, not confrontational."[13]

Wauja of South America, slash-and-burn horticulture and fishing: "Important to their identity as Wauja is their rejection of war and violence as behavior befitting honorable people. . . . Far from viewing physical aggression with awe and admiration, they see it as pathetic and a mark of failed leadership."[14]

Rotuma Islanders of Oceania, gardening and fishing: "Some of the central factors that keep disputes from escalating into violent confrontations . . . include a pattern of socialization that minimizes aggressive dispositions, a set of culturally sanctioned beliefs that promises immanent justice for wrongdoing, social provision for mediation when impasses occur, and perhaps most importantly, the custom of *faksoro*—a ritual of apology that, under most circumstances, must be accepted by the aggrieved party. . . . The results of this socialization pattern are a people who are socially sensitive, ready to react defensively when their sense of autonomy is threatened, but definitively nonviolent in disposition."[15]

Kuikuru of South America, slash-and-burn cultivation: "Fights among men in the village are unknown. A dislike of being thought stingy, quarrelsome, or aggressive keeps village life running smoothly."[16]

Lepchas of South Asia, agriculture and hunting: "For the Lepchas quarrelling is not natural or inevitable, but a deplorable accident which it is everybody's business to stop."[17]

Hopi of North America, horticulture: "Interpersonal violence was rare among Hopis until recently."[18]

Hanunóo of the Philippines, shifting cultivation: "Peaceful settlement is invariably reached after much heated but physically harmless discussion, presided over by the eldest relatives of the principals. . . . Murder is rare. . . . The last known attempted murder (by barbed arrow) was in the late 1930s."[19]

Tristan da Cunha Islanders of the South Atlantic, farming and marine resources: "The Tristan islanders have justly won the reputation of being a very peace-loving people. . . . As one villager expressed it: 'The worst thing you can do on Tristan is to be unkind to someone.'"[20]

Sources: 1. Levy 1978:224. 2. Howell 1989:55. 3. D. Thomas 1994:272–273. 4. Hostetler 1983b:3. 5. Rivière 1994:336. 6. MacGaffey 1995:168. 7. Gardner 1972:425. 8. Martin & Levinson 1993:71. 9. Phillips 1974:184. 10. Henley 1982:153. 11. Hollan 1988:54. 12. Gudjónsson & Pétursson 1990:50, 52. 13. Mitchell 1999:101. 14. Ireland 1991:57, 58. 15. Howard 1990:268, 269; see also Howard 2004. 16. Carneiro 1994a:208. 17. Gorer 1967:142. 18. Cox 1968:chapter 5; see also Schlegel 2004. 19. Conklin 1954:48. 20 Munch & Marske 1981:165.

Within anthropology, cross-cultural research usually entails the examination of data archives on a sample of societies. In preparing this chapter, I reviewed published cross-cultural studies on homicide, assaults, family violence, and other types of aggression. These cross-cultural studies are (1) Thoden van Velzen and van Wetering's classification of peaceful and nonpeaceful societies; (2) Wilfred Masumura's dichotomous ratings for low versus high internal violence; (3) Marc Ross' numerical scores for internal conflict; (4) Leigh Minturn, Martin Grosse, and Santoah Haider's ratings of rape frequency; (5) David Levinson's scores for family violence and male fighting; (6) Stuart Palmer's homicide scores; and (7) Carol and Melvin Ember's assessment of individual homicides and assaults. As we consider the findings of these studies in relation to the internally peaceful societies listed in Box 5.1, certain points should be kept in mind. The methods used to sample the cross-cultural material vary from one study to the next. Sample sizes also vary. And relevant data for certain cultures sometimes are missing or not reported. Watch for the pattern that emerges from the following summaries.[32]

Of 20 societies that Thoden van Velzen and van Wetering classify as *peaceful,* 5 are included in the list of internally peaceful societies. On the other hand, none of the 31 societies that they list as *nonpeaceful* appear in Box 5.1.[33]

Of 21 societies that Masumura rates as having *low internal violence,* 7 are included in Box 5.1. On the other hand, none of the 26 societies that he rates as having *high internal violence* appear on the list.[34]

Of 90 societies that Ross ranks in terms of internal conflict, 10 are included in Box 5.1. Four of these 10 receive the lowest possible score for *internal conflict* (–5); two each receive scores of –4, –3, and –2 on the scale that ranges between a low of –5 and a high of +6 (these 10 societies appear in italic type in Figure 5.1).[35]

Of 43 societies that Minturn and her colleagues rated for frequency of rape, three societies also are listed in Box 5.1. Two of these received the rating *rape does not occur but the concept is present* and the third society was scored *rape is very rare.*[36]

Of 90 societies scored for family violence and for male fighting by Levinson, 10 are included in Box 5.1. Unfortunately for the current purposes, Levinson does not publish ratings for all 10 cases. However, he reports that 6 of the 10 societies have *no or rare family violence* and 5 of these have the lowest possible male fighting score, defined as *nonviolent, ritualized competition, or violence directed only at self or own property* (for the sixth case, relevant data are reported to be missing).[37]

Of 40 societies that Palmer rates for *murder* using a 0- to 21-point scoring system, 8 appear in Box 5.1.[38] All 8 are below the median value of 8.4 on Palmer's murder scoring system. Furthermore, 7 of these 8 have murder scores so low as to also be below the value 3.7, the median of the subsample of the 21 lowest scoring societies. The Lapps (Saami) and the Tikopia Islanders receive murder ratings of 0, indicating that murders are rated as virtually absent (see Figure 5.3).[39]

Of 186 societies rated for individual homicide and assault by Ember and Ember, 16 societies appear in Box 5.1. Available information allowed the Embers to rate 14 of the 16 societies on a three-point *low-moderate-high* homicide scale. All 14 received a *low* homicide rating. On the same *low-moderate-high* scale for assault, 11 of the same 16 societies received a *low* rating, 2 received an intermediate rating of *low-moderate,* and the remaining 3 were rated *moderate.*[40]

Figure 5.3 Saami reindeer herders in northern Finland in the early 1980s take a break from identifying the herds with cuts marks to the animals' ears. In a cross-cultural study of lethal violence, Stuart Palmer reports that homicide among the Saami is virtually nonexistent. The Saami are also nonwarring and nonfeuding. Pertti Pelto concludes that nonaggressiveness is an important aspect of the male gender role in Saami culture. (Photo courtesy of Heikki Sarmaja; see Anderson & Beach 1992:222; Palmer 1965; Pelto 1962.)

What conclusions can be drawn from the cross-cultural studies? The initial decision to include any given culture on the list of internally peaceful societies was dependent on the written *descriptions* of the culture (such as those illustrated in Box 5.2). When information from one or more of the seven cross-cultural studies was available, the cross-cultural ratings almost always supported the idea that cultures on the list are internally peaceful *in a culturally comparative sense also.* That is, these cultures very consistently received low aggression ratings within *a culturally comparative framework.* This is analogous to the *descriptive* exclamation by a person coming into the house on a hard winter's day—"It's bitter cold out there!"—being given a broader *comparative* frame of reference as the TV news reports that it is the coldest day on record since 1953. Both types of information help us to reach a conclusion. In the weather example, we decide to stay indoors. When evaluating the Ifaluk of Micronesia, for example, the ethnographic descriptions by three anthropologists and ratings in three cross-cultural studies suggest *descriptively and comparatively* that the Ifaluk are an internally peaceful society.[41]

The length of the provisional list of internally peaceful societies suggests that there is no shortage of internally peaceful societies in the world. I have no doubt that further checking of anthropological sources will result in other peaceful cultures being added to the list.

Visualizing societies along a peacefulness–aggressiveness continuum is useful. It helps to shatter the dichotomous illusion that societies are *either* aggressive *or* peaceful. It also shows that humans have the capacity to create societies with very low levels of violence. The existence of over 80 such internally peaceful societies proves that creating nonviolent social life is entirely within the human potential and not merely a utopian fantasy.[42]

CHAPTER 6

PEACE STORIES

> Often experiences abroad had widened women's horizons. They had learned about cultural differences and about the relativity of danger. They described cultural differences . . . strengthened by a belief that Finnish women are independent and courageous and that their society supports their independent mobility and gender equality.
>
> HILLE KOSKELA[1]

I moved to Helsinki several years ago, having been attracted to Finland by the wonderful woman who is now my wife. Helsinki is the capital and largest city in Finland with a population of over one-half million. When I first arrived, I was repeatedly surprised to see lone women walking on the streets late at night virtually anywhere in the city. Gradually I realized that my surprise was due to perceiving Helsinki through "American eyes." Over the years, I have had numerous occasions to realize that most women in the United States are concerned, if not fearful, about being out alone in urban areas at night. I have observed that some American women carry whistles, pepper sprays, and hand guns. At university campuses in the States, I have seen that self-defense courses are offered regularly and that escort services are provided for lone women needing to move around the campus at night. I have overheard women complaining that street lighting should be better. In short, as a *cultural insider* I simply absorbed and stored this type of information.

The situation in Finland, however, is somewhat different. Finnish geographer Hille Koskela observes that "it is quite common for women to go out without male company, and to stay out until the latest restaurants close at 4 a.m. and, as a consequence, the landscape of Finnish cities at night is not obviously gendered."[2] Sociologist Jukka-Pekka Takala and I decided to gather some quantified data on this topic. From counts at randomly drawn locations, we found that women constituted 42 percent of the persons on the streets at night, and focusing on lone individuals only, we found that one-third of the unaccompanied persons were women.[3] As both Koskela's comments and my initial impressions had suggested, this amounts to a substantial number of women out on their own. By the way, the rate of reported rapes in Finland in recent years is about one-fifth the number reported in the United States, although in both countries the number of rapes resulting from an attack by a stranger represents a minority of assaults.[4]

On a visit to a University of California campus library a couple of years ago, I pointed to a sign offering escort protection for women students leaving the library at night and asked my Helsinki born-and-raised wife, "What does this mean?" My anthropological hunch turned out to be correct. The purpose of the sign made no sense to a

Finn. My wife had never heard of this strange escort idea and had a hard time believing that such a service was really being offered.

I tell these stories for two reasons. First, they raise the hypothesis, subject to further investigation, that Finland and the United States may be located at somewhat different points on the cross-cultural peacefulness–aggressiveness continuum. However, I think a second point is more important: The stories illustrate the tendency for people, including theorists on violence like myself, to *assume* that cultural circumstances are basically similar across societies until faced with experiential evidence to the contrary. Thus I just *assumed* that Finnish women would avoid going out by themselves on the streets of Helsinki late at night because I had learned that this is the case in much of urban America. My Finnish wife *just assumed* that American women would leave the university library in California at night by themselves with confidence and in relative safety—why not? Such assumptions are in accordance with her lifelong experiences in comparatively safer Finland.

To further consider the implication of this idea, I suspect that much theorizing about aggression rests on similar hidden assumptions that patterns of violence are more or less the same everywhere, even though we might know intellectually that this is not exactly true. The same type of assumption that makes it hard for Americans to understand the confidence with which numerous Finnish women travel at night on their own also makes it hard, I suspect, for Americans to readily comprehend that certain other cultures really have much less violence than their own society. For that matter, certain cultures have less violence than Finland.

A case in point is the Semai of Malaysia. Semai culture demonstrates the human capacity to construct an almost totally nonviolent social existence. The Ifaluk of Micronesia provide further evidence that it is possible to create a peaceful society. And a consideration of Norway suggests that modern nations also can achieve low levels of violence. As a theme crosscutting these case studies, the presence of a nonviolent belief system is perhaps the most critical feature.[5] These three societies, like numerous other peaceful societies listed in the previous chapter, show that implicit and explicit assumptions about the cross-cultural ubiquity of violence are simply wrong. Theories about universal human violence are exaggerated and culture bound.

THE SEMAI OF MALAYSIA

Clayton Robarchek describes the Semai as "one of the least violent societies known to anthropology," and Robert Dentan writes of the Semai that "they seem to have worked out ways of handling human violence which technologically more 'advanced' people might envy." The Semai live in egalitarian bands, seldom consisting of more than 100 persons, and sustain themselves through a combination of swidden gardening, hunting, fishing, and gathering. A Semai headman (a position occasionally filled by a woman) lacks formal institutionalized power but exercises limited moral authority over the members of the band.[6]

Based on independent anthropological studies, Carole and Clay Robarchek and Bob Dentan arrive at similar conclusions regarding the peacefulness of Semai society. Dentan explains that violence terrifies the Semai, adults do not strike each other, and physical force is not used to punish children, aside from the mildest pinching or patting on the hand.[7] One Semai told Dentan: "We're very careful about hurting people. We avoid it. . . . The Jungle People [Communist terrorists] killed a *mnaleeh* [nubile girl], but we gave them tapioca and other food when they passed through. We really hate getting mixed up in other people's fights [uses the Malay word *gadoh*]. We want to live *slamad,* in peace and security."[8]

The Robarcheks concur with Dentan's assessments of Semai nonviolence. They explain, "husbands and wives do not assault one another, parents do not physically punish their children, neighbors do not fight with one another, and homicide is so rare as to be virtually nonexistent."[9]

Unfortunately, a grossly exaggerated Semai homicide rate has found its way into the literature, causing confusion. The Robarcheks explain that this error resulted from someone mistakenly using a population figure for the Semai of 300, instead of 15,000, thus producing a homicide rate, based on two murders between 1955 and 1977, that is *about 50 times too high.*[10] When Dentan recalculated the Semai homicide rate based on two murders over the same time period, but now using correct population figures, he got 0.56 per 100,000 per annum—a very low rate if compared with various other societies.[11] Furthermore, one of the two so-called homicides actually involved the abandonment of a terminally ill person.[12] To play devil's advocate, even when two unsubstantiated, or rumored, cases are added to the first two, the resulting homicide rate based on four killings remains very low—now about 1 homicide per 100,000 per year.[13]

Regrettably, the 50-times-too-high calculation continues to mislead. Raymond Kelly relies on the bogus homicide rate in his intriguing book *Warless Societies and the Origin of War,* as does Keeley when he writes that the Semai "homicide rate was numerically significant."[14] In actuality, of course, Dentan's corrections show the Semai homicide rate to be extremely low—not even remotely close to the erroneous figure. Additionally, the Semai have no history of warring or feuding.

As one elderly man expressed: "We don't fight people, we fight the trees and the animals of the forest."[16] Clay Robarchek elaborates, explaining that Semai cultural beliefs and values preclude violent behaviors:

> Most Semai men would probably like to have sex with more women than they do. Yet no Semai man ever gets up one morning, turns to his brother-in-law and says, "Let's get a bunch of the guys together and go raid the next valley and see if we can kill some people and steal some women." For Semai, murder and rape are simply not legitimate means to any ends, no matter how "objectively" desirable.[17]

Dentan and Robarchek independently have discussed socialization processes through which Semai children learn and adopt nonviolent attitudes and behavior (see Figure 6.1). For example, Semai children, who themselves are not the recipients of corporal punishment, acquire the Semai belief that being hit may cause a child to become ill and die. Robarchek concludes that, "for developing children, the learning of aggressive behavior by observation and imitation is almost entirely precluded. . . . The image of the world, of human goals, and of the means of attaining them that is presented to Semai children simply does not include violence as a behavioral alternative."[18]

The Semai fear aggression and violence. They also feel intensely threatened by any type of interpersonal conflict. When Robarchek orally administered a sentence-completion test to a sample of Semai, the findings clearly indicated the critical importance for the Semai of maintaining harmony in interpersonal relations. In completing

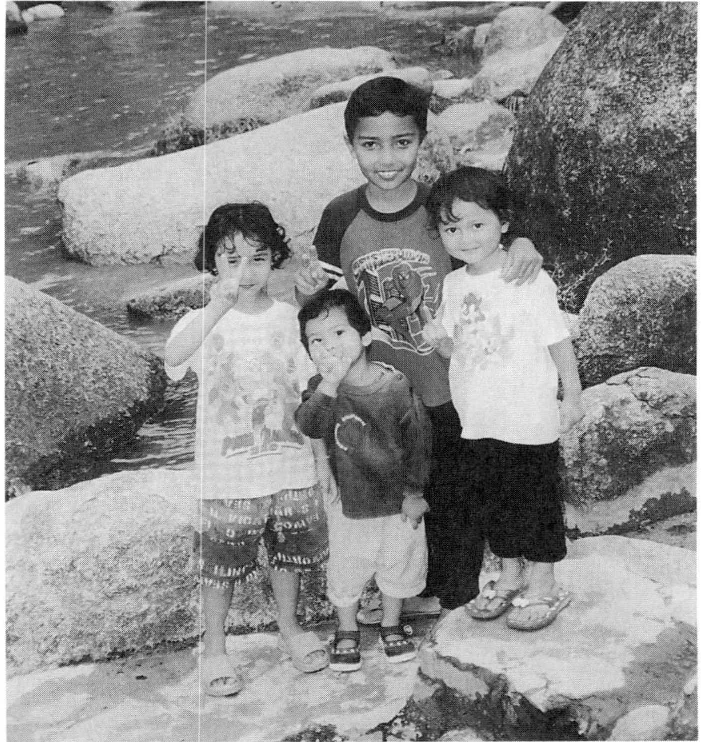

Figure 6.1 Wearing *Power Ranger* and *Spiderman* T-shirts, children from nonviolent Semai culture flash peace signs to a Western visitor in 2004. Will the Semai retain their nonviolent lifestyle in the face of an increasing onslaught of outside influences and social disruptions? (Photo courtesy of Mari Laaksonen; see Dentan 2004 and Cultural Survival in the Appendix.)

the sentence "more than anything else, he/she is afraid of . . ." the most commonly expressed fear was "a conflict," outnumbering the responses for "malevolent spirits," "tigers," and "death" *combined.*[19]

The fact that Semai are nonviolent does not mean that disputes never arise within the band—they do. Rather, it shows that the Semai rarely use aggression to deal with conflict. In Semai society, as in any human society, perceived and actual divergences of interests occur. Spouses are unfaithful, someone's goats invade another person's garden causing crop damage, somebody is offended by the words of another, and so on. The Semai "usually tolerate annoyances and sacrifice personal interests rather than precipitate an open confrontation."[20] Much of the time people deny or suppress angry feelings. Dentan observes, for instance, that "the Semai do not say, 'Anger is bad.' They say, 'We do not get angry,' and an obviously angry man will flatly deny his anger."[21]

Clay Robarchek reports that when an owner of some fruit trees discovered that someone was coming in the night and taking his fruit, he went to build a temporary shelter in the forest so he could spend the night and protect his fruit from theft. As he was in the process of building the shelter, he talked a great deal about his intention to guard the trees so that everybody in the band became aware of his plan to camp-out near his fruit trees. He did not want to run any danger of actually surprising the thief. Robarchek explains the strategy as one that sidestepped open confrontation while simultaneously protecting the resource: "He wished only to stop the theft, not to discover or catch the thief; for if he were to confront the thief, their relations would be disrupted."[22]

Conflict makes Semai very uneasy. They relocate to avoid external threats to the band and respond to conflict within the band by denying and suppressing anger, tolerating uncomfortable situations, and, when necessary, employing the *becharaa'* dispute resolution assembly, described in chapter 3, to reconcile disputants and restore an atmosphere of harmony within the band.

IFALUK OF MICRONESIA

The people of Ifaluk live on a one-half-square-mile coral atoll located midway between the Islands of Truk and Yap in Micronesia. Ifaluk is another society that contradicts the assumption of ubiquitous human violence. In 1947–1948 Edwin Burrows and Melford Spiro studied the people of Ifaluk, then numbering about 250 persons. Thirty years later, Catherine Lutz conducted fieldwork on Ifaluk, at a time when the population was over 400. All three anthropologists were impressed with the lack of physical aggression among these people, who make their living by growing taro, fishing, and gathering coconuts and breadfruit (see Figure 6.2). In the Ifaluk belief system, ghosts often act violently, but people do not. Burrows has this to say:

> What is striking about Ifaluk . . . is the fact that there is no discrepancy between its cultural values (the ideal culture) and its actual behavioral patterns (the real culture). Not one individual could remember a single case of murder, rape, robbery, or fighting; nor did the ethnographer witness such behavior in his seven-month study. It was almost impossible to convey to the people the concept of murder, the thought of wantonly killing another person is so completely alien to their thinking.[23]

Spiro is in total agreement with Burrows. He writes, "This culture is particularly notable for its ethic of nonaggression, and its emphasis on helpfulness, sharing, and cooperation." Spiro elaborates, "No display of aggression is permitted in interpersonal relationships; and in fact, no aggression is displayed at all." In a cross-cultural study of rape, Minturn and her colleagues rated Ifaluk as one of the societies where rape simply does not occur.[24]

Thirty years later, the observations of Lutz on Ifaluk agree with her anthropological predecessors. "Murder is unknown; the most serious incident of aggression in a year involved the touching of one man's shoulder by another, a violation that resulted in the immediate payment of a severe fine."[25] Lutz explains that serious violence was almost inconceivable to the people of Ifaluk: "The horror that the idea of violence evokes for the Ifaluk was evident in their discussions of the rumored aggressive tendencies of Americans and some other groups. Several people checked with me to see if the stories they had heard about the existence of murder in the United States were in fact true."[26] This represents an interesting turnaround from the beliefs of some Westerners who assume the opposite, namely, that violence must be prevalent in every human society.[27] It is also reminiscent of the stories related at the opening of this chapter as to how I had

Figure 6.2 A cooperative fishing circle on Ifaluk Atoll in the Pacific. The people of Ifaluk do not allow aggression to damage their social net. Melford Spiro observes that "the culture is particularly notable for its ethic of nonaggression and its emphasis on helpfulness, sharing, and cooperation." (Photo courtesy of Catherine Lutz; quote from Spiro 1952:497.)

perceived Finland with "American eyes," and my wife in turn perceived the United States through "Finnish eyes." We both simply made implicit assumptions that what we knew about our native societies also would apply in another society. Returning to Ifaluk, the field research of Burrows, Spiro, and Lutz suggest that, counter to assumptions of universal violence, Ifaluk represents one of many societies wherein physical aggression is extremely rare.[28]

If one belongs to a culture where certain types of physical aggression—for example, corporal punishment of children, spouse abuse, fistfights, assaults—are known to occur with some periodicity, it may be difficult to understand the strength of the Ifaluk fear and revulsion toward physical aggression. With the repeated exposure to media depictions of violence, most members of Western culture have been desensitized to at least media portrayals of brutality in a way that the people of Ifaluk have not. For the Ifaluk, according to Lutz, the culturally acceptable reaction to violence, for both men and women, is not to counterattack, but rather to experience horror and to want to escape from the aggression. For example, Lutz relates the stress felt by the people of Ifaluk upon viewing the movies that the U.S. Navy vessels brought to the atoll, ironically on "good will" visits, in the years following World War II. Decades later, Lutz recounts how persons "frequently talk about their panic on seeing people shot and beaten in those movies and relate how some individuals were terrified for days afterwards. In a few such cases, the persons become ill, and in many others, refused to see movies that arrived in later years." It seems that by talking about the aggression of other people, such as portrayed in U.S. movies, the Ifaluk reinforce for themselves their nonaggressive beliefs and also mentally rehearse flight responses. "In these rehearsals, they remind themselves and each other of the horrible consequences of violence which is casually accepted."[29]

Ifaluk society is organized hierarchically, wherein each person is ranked relative to others within eight matrilineal clans, and the clans also are ranked in relation to one another.[30] The chiefs who head the highest-ranking clans govern the island. Chiefs organize and supervise communal endeavors, but in fact have few privileges.[31] Persons of high rank are expected to behave politely and beneficently toward persons of lower rank. Prevalent values on Ifaluk include cooperation and sharing, and the ideal personality is one that radiates calmness, or is *maluwelu*.[32] "It is said that *maluwelu* individuals are extremely pleasant to be around, as they are not 'hot-tempered' (*sigsig*), and use highly valued respect behaviors and polite talk when interacting with others."[33]

As Lutz makes clear, nonaggressiveness does not necessarily imply that anger is absent.[34] The people of Ifaluk express anger (*song*) in a particular way, as moral outrage or "justifiable anger," when another person violates a social norm or breaks a taboo.[35] *Song* is considered by the Ifaluk to be appropriately experienced by higher-ranking individuals, who generally have greater moral legitimacy, toward lower ranking persons. Parents are expected to express *song* when their children misbehave. And since aggression constitutes misbehavior, parents use their justifiable anger, *song,* to strongly socialize the children not to act aggressively.

The people of Ifaluk—like the Semai, La Paz Zapotec, and many other peaceful peoples—have a belief system that inhibits physical aggression. On Ifaluk, as in any society, disputes and disagreements arise, but, with the rarest of exceptions, do not lead to aggression. Persons growing up on Ifaluk are socialized into a hierarchical social order that does not allow for the expression of physical aggression. Children learn that physical aggression results in adults expressing justifiable anger (*song*) toward them, and they come to experience anxiety if they misbehave. They see practically no examples of physical aggression, internalize nonviolent values, and learn to deal with conflicts in the ways that are considered acceptable in Ifaluk society.

NORWEGIANS: A NATION AT PEACE

Norway fits the criteria of an internally peaceful society: Physical aggression is strongly looked-down upon and in fact seldom occurs. The population of about 4.5 million Norwegians is relatively homogeneous in terms of many cultural and ethnic features, and Norway lacks a prominent class structure.[36] The country has a high standard of living.[37] In 1995, 39 percent of the parliamentarians were women—compared to 11 percent in the United States Congress and Senate the same year.[38]

Cross-national comparisons show Norway to have low scores on various measures of internal violence, number of labor strikes, suicide, and homicide.[39] Statistics on violent crime show low rates of assault, rape, and homicide in comparison to many other European countries.[40] As in many European countries, Norwegian homicide rates have increased over the last 30 or 40 years. However, despite gradual increases, current homicide rates per 100,000 per year for Norway remain very low: 0.6 in 1960, 0.2 in 1965,

TABLE 6.1 Homicide Rates in Norway and Several Comparison Countries

Norway	Denmark	Finland	United States	El Salvador	Colombia
1.4	1.1	4.1	10.0	40.0	49.0

Note: All rates are per 100,000 persons per year for the year 1990, except for Colombia where the rate is for 1988.

Sources: Yearbook of Nordic Statistics 1994 for Norway, Denmark, and Finland; *Statistical Abstract of the United States* 1996 for the United States; Ghiglieri 1999:117 for El Salvador and Colombia.

0.2 in 1970, 0.8 in 1975, 1.1 in 1980, 1.3 in 1985, and 1.4 in 1990. For comparison, homicide rates for several other countries are presented in Table 6.1 for the year 1990.

Political scientist Kristin Dobinson discusses various lines of evidence suggesting that peacefulness is highly valued in Norwegian culture. After noting that the prime minister emphasized peace in a recent speech, Dobinson elaborates:

> The point is not only that peace is highly valued in Norwegian society and a central element in Norwegians' self-understandings, but also that dominant discourses reinforce this self-image of Norwegians as essentially peace-loving. It can be argued that a dominant discourse of this kind also perpetuates societal peacefulness. Other representations of the society could have been chosen (for instance emphasizing its economic prosperity) but have not been. For a dominant discourse on national identity to catch on, it must not only be persuasive, but it must also represent a society in a way that accords with the group's deeply embedded notions of what constitutes its identity and culture. The fact that these discursive representations of Norway as peaceful are so widespread suggests that this image *does* resonate with a majority of the population.[41]

On the basis of almost two years of fieldwork in rural Norway, Marida Hollos reports that "public fights or arguments are unheard of, [and] murder is non-existent." In reference to the whole country, Ross emphasizes that levels of conflict are very low and that "even when Viking warriors were feared throughout Europe the domestic society was relatively peaceful." Ross also refers to work from the 1980s by Ralph Bolton, who found few aggressive models in Norwegian popular culture. Bolton's study, for instance, reports how Norwegians rated the Hollywood movie *E.T.* as too violent for children under the age of 12.[42]

Part and parcel of the Norwegian belief system are values that emphasize conformity, nonconfrontation, the control of emotions, and the shunning of physical aggression (see Figure 6.3).[43] Hollos findings also illustrate the value Norwegians place on emotional control, conformity, and the avoidance of conflictual confrontation.[44] The family farm is the basic economic unit in the community that Hollos refers to as Flathill. At the time of her study, there were approximately 300 persons living on some 70 farms in the area. As in the mountain region called Sollia that was studied by Fredrik Barth, farmers in Flathill practice dairy farming and timbering to make a living.[45] The values of self-reliance, equality, and community unity are clearly apparent. Class distinctions are absent and people view each other as equals. Simultaneously, there is strong pressure to conform to local customs, practices, and norms. Innovation is discouraged. The emphasis is on fitting in and presenting a unified view of the community to the outside world.

Figure 6.3 Each Norwegian city, such as Bergen, pictured here, has a conflict council whose legal mandate is to mediate interpersonal disputes involving youths. Kristin Dobinson reports, for Norway overall, that 89 percent of such youth mediations in 2001 led to agreements, of which nearly 80 percent were honored by the disputants. (Photo courtesy of Jukka-Pekka Takala; see Dobinson 2004:163.)

The work of Hollos and others suggests several interacting ingredients in the Norwegian formula for peace. First, not only physical aggression but also the direct expression of conflict generally is highly discouraged. Simultaneously, nonviolence, nonconfrontation, and the nonexpression of emotion are strongly valued, reinforced, and modeled by elders to the young. For example, Hollos explains that an implicit rule for interaction within Flathill families, which is similar to the La Paz Zapotec pattern of *cooperative denial,* is that as long as no one actually mentions a problem, then everyone acts as if there is no problem. "There are no open fights or conflicts, only smoldering resentments which never get resolved but never get out of hand and thereby make coexistence impossible." Writing about Norwegian culture overall, Gullestad correspondingly notes the importance placed on "avoiding open personal conflicts."[46]

Second, children are socialized to develop self-control over their emotions generally, including anger. "Even the most important news items, such as the arrival of a guest, death in the family or the impending birth of a new child are announced with as little emotionality as possible. People are reluctant to show joy, sorrow or worry in front of the other family members." Such restraint is also apparent in public interaction. Topics of conversation are neutral; statements are indirect and generally stripped of emotional expressiveness. Social interactions tend to be very formal and follow conventional rules of interaction. The rather rare visits to private homes are noteworthy for "their interminable length, by constant smiling. . . . There is a constant effort to show agreement with the people present and one feels that they are invited specifically for the purpose of being shown how much they are agreed with." This seems to illustrate a Norwegian version of *toleration,* relevant both to dealing with and preventing conflict.[47]

Third, the strategy of *avoidance* is widely practiced under conditions of conflict or potential conflict.[48] In Flathill, even on the family farm, people rarely work together, thus minimizing the chances for any disagreement. Barth mentions what might seem to be an extreme case of avoidance: "One farmer, quite well thought of, has literally no interaction with people, other than for economic reasons."[49] Gullestad's research led her to similar conclusions about the Norwegian use of avoidance, reporting the attitude that people who are slow to take "little hints" should be avoided, an observation that suggests the conflict preventive aspect of avoidance as discussed in chapter 3.[50]

Fourth, the notable *pressures on individuals to conform* relate to the low level of physical aggression among Norwegians. Within family, community, and society, individuals are pressured by others to follow group standards that favor nonconfrontation and nonaggressiveness. Hollos explains: "The pressure to conform to community norms is not only from the outside but from the inside of the family as well. Since community values place so much emphasis on conformity, non-conformity by itself becomes a serious offense. Deviants expect no sympathy from the rest of the community, nor from their family."[51] Fear of being the subject of gossip seems to play a large role in evoking conformity, especially in the rural setting.

A final point that seems conducive to the Norwegian variety of nonaggressiveness involves *socializing individuals to feel psychologically dependent* upon others in the family and community. The running of the family farm, for instance, makes each person dependent on the rest of the family. Gender-based work specialization exists with men doing the heavier labor. Additionally, young daughters-in-law focus on raising the children and household tasks, whereas the mothers-in-law engage in milking twice daily and related dairying chores. One indication of the high degree of interdependence between spouses in rural settings is that divorces in the communities studied by Barth and Hollos were virtually nonexistent.[52] Economic and emotional interdependence within families and to a lesser degree psychosocial dependence on other community members exert pressures on individuals to follow the cultural prohibitions against physical aggression and to otherwise conform to social expectations.

RETURNING TO HIDDEN ASSUMPTIONS

The members of some internally peaceful societies know that certain other cultures are more aggressive than their own. They may reinforce their own nonviolent beliefs and behaviors by contrasting themselves to the aggressive Other. La Paz Zapotec point to adjacent San Andrés as a reminder to themselves not to be like their disrespectful, swearing, jealous, violent, and occasionally homicidal neighbors. Semai shun the violence of Malays. The Ifaluk contrast themselves to the fearsomely aggressive Americans. Gregor explains the beliefs of the peaceful Upper Xingu tribes:

> In ancient times, according to one of the Xingu origin myths, the Sun created three races of humankind, including Xinguanos, "wild Indians," and whites. Recognizing the

> warlike nature of whites and wild Indians, he assigned them to separate worlds and even separate afterlives, well away from the headwaters of the Xingu River and the "Village in the Sky" above it.[53]

Ghiglieri assumes that it is valid to impose a bellicose view of human nature—a view that happens to be somewhat comparable to how the Xinguanos perceive the nature of "wild Indians" and whites—onto all humanity, without checking the ethnographic spectrum to see if it really fits. Thus he asserts that "*murder is encoded into the human psyche,*" "robbery, like murder, is universal," "both jealousy itself and jealousy murder are *common,*" "because rape is so widespread and rampant around the planet, by males both human and nonhuman, it is clearly a male biological adaptation," and, "are men born to be lethally violent? The answer is yes. Aggression is programmed by our DNA." These statements and others like them are absolutely contradicted by a wealth of available data from other cultures. As quipped by David Pilbeam in another context, but with relevance here, theories that are relatively unconstrained by data "often said far more about the theorists than they have about what actually happened."[54]

If it were true that humans are violent by nature or possess instincts that push them to violence, then logically societies with extremely low levels of physical aggression simply should not exist. The fact that such societies *do* exist contradicts such bloodthirsty images of humanity. Internally peaceful societies can be found in all quarters of the globe. In the previous chapter, over 80 examples were presented. Many are nomadic foraging bands, whereas others are horticultural societies, communities of peasant farmers, or even modern nations. Nearly all internally peaceful societies, as part of their belief systems, devalue physical aggression, value nonviolence, or both. Individuals in such societies internalize nonviolent beliefs, reiterate their views as they go about their daily lives, generally act in accordance with their shared and internalized beliefs, and, in the case of any deviance, apply social pressure to the errant individual to conform to the nonviolent ways of the group.

The result is that physical aggression is extremely rare. Several anthropologists, for example, clocked in thousands of hours of observation time over many months on Ifaluk and the only physical aggression seen was one event involving touching on the shoulders and two instances of child discipline. And as discussed in chapter 4, neither O'Nell nor I ever saw a child being beaten in La Paz and rarely witnessed other kinds of physical aggression. Nonviolent social life is possible, and, as the lengthy list of internally peaceful societies indicates, peaceful societies are not really as rare as is sometimes *assumed.* Erroneous overgeneralizations about the cross-cultural pervasiveness of violence, such as those by Ghiglieri, reflect *culturally based assumptions* similar in nature to those that my wife and I fell victim to in the stories recounted at the beginning of the chapter.[55]

Persons living in internally peaceful societies are not free of frustrations, hurt feelings, or hostility. But frustrated, angry, or hostile persons in these societies do not express themselves through physical aggression. As influenced by their particular belief system, people may deny the feelings altogether, put up with the situation, leave the group to "cool off," express their feelings via gossip, use supernatural means to punish someone, let others mediate their dispute, talk out the situation, destroy property, and so on. Similarly, internally peaceful societies are not free of conflict. As we have seen, conflict can be dealt with in various paths other than through physical aggression. The existence of conflict in a society is expected and does not mean that violence inevitably will result. The Semai may engage in a *becharaa'* to resolve their differences. Individuals disputing the ownership of a piece of land on Ifaluk accept the ruling of a chief. Norwegians avoid and tolerate, then perhaps mediate, and less often adjudicate.[56] Conflict is *not* identical to physical aggression. In internally peaceful societies, physical aggression is not considered an allowable option and in fact hardly ever occurs. Might we someday be able to say the same about how conflict is handled within the international community?

CHAPTER 7

A HOBBESIAN BELIEF SYSTEM?

On the Supposed Naturalness of War

> During the time men live without a common power to keep them all in awe, they are in that condition which is called war; and such a war, as is of every man, against every man. . . . No arts; no letters; no society; and which is worst of all, continual fear, and danger of violent death; and life of man, solitary, poor, nasty, brutish and short.
>
> THOMAS HOBBES, *LEVIATHAN*, 1651[1]

Several years ago, in a city park by the shore of Tampa Bay in Florida, I was chatting with a senior citizen. The discussion turned to war and human nature, and the elderly man, who had lived through World War II as well as the Korean, Vietnam, and Gulf wars, among others, expressed with certainty, "There always has been war and there always will be war."

At about the same time, I noticed how the screenwriters of the television comedy series *Murphy Brown* wrote into an episode statements as to the inevitability and naturalness of war. And on this same theme, a college student I know remarked that she was tired of debating with her roommate, who firmly believed humans to be naturally warlike.

As an anthropologist accustomed to thinking about culture, I recognized that such statements by members of my own culture reflect a commonly shared, although in this case not unanimous, cultural belief about human nature. Cultural belief systems contain "notions of the nature and attributes of humanity. They decide whether we are good, evil, or neutral," notes Marilyn Grunkemeyer.[2] As learned and shared phenomena, "belief systems tend for the most part to reside at the level of assumptions and presuppositions."[3] Certain beliefs may diverge sharply from empirical observations, but nonetheless the members of a culture tend not to question the validity of such beliefs, having simply adopted them as part of their cultural heritage. The senior citizen's statement that "there always has been war and there always will be war" is a reflection of a shared belief whose veracity is assumed and widely accepted without systematic testing. For this man and many other people, the supposed truth of the statement is patently obvious.

In separate studies, college students from Connecticut and Florida filled out attitude surveys designed to assess beliefs about war and human nature.[4] Respondents were asked if they agreed that "Human beings have an instinct for war" and that "War is an intrinsic part of human nature." In both places, approximately half the students linked war to instinct and human nature. Approximately 10 percent of the Florida students, depending on the question, answered "don't know," leaving roughly 40 percent of the students *disagreeing* with the statements. I suspect that beliefs as to the naturalness of war and aggression may be even more common among the general population than among university students, because courses that question Hobbesian views of human nature can be found on most university campuses.

Beliefs about human nature and war also are implicitly reflected in many Western writings about war, including those by scientists and scholars as notable as Thomas Hobbes, Jonathan Swift, William James, Sigmund Freud, and Francis Crick, who like other people tend to accept their culture's belief system without much question.[5] Semai tend not to question the existence of supernatural spirits called *mara'*.[6] Zapotec tend not to question that a sudden fright can cause a disease called *susto*.[7] So it is with cultural beliefs; they are simply accepted by cultural insiders most of the time. First, here is a set of quotations, some historical and some recent, that are in accordance with the cultural belief that war is an intrinsic aspect of human nature.

> Life was a continual free fight, and beyond the limited and temporary relations of the family, the Hobbesian war of each against all was the normal state of existence.[8]

> What does seem clear to trained observation is the universal belligerency of primitive mankind. Not only is war to be seen everywhere, but it is war more atrocious than we, with our ideas, can easily conceive.[9]

> Our ancestors have bred pugnacity into our bone and marrow and thousands of years of peace won't breed it out of us.[10]

> The blood-bespattered, slaughter-gutted archives of human history from the earliest Egyptian and Sumerian records to the most recent atrocities of the Second World War accord with early universal cannibalism, with animal and human sacrificial practices or their substitutes in formalized religions and with the world-wide scalping, head-hunting, body-mutilating and necrophilic practices of mankind in proclaiming this common bloodlust differentiator, this predaceous habit, this mark of Cain that separates man dietetically from his anthropoidal relatives [for example, chimpanzees, bonobos, and gorillas] and allies him rather with the deadliest Carnivora.[11]

> Are human beings innately aggressive? This is a favorite question of college seminars and cocktail party conversations, and one that raises emotion in political ideologues of all stripes. The answer to it is yes. Throughout history, warfare, representing only the most organized technique of aggression, has been endemic to every form of society, from hunter-gatherer bands to industrial states.[12]

> Optimism is a wonderful emotion. But the vision of paradise that comes from balmy islands of the South Seas is flatly challenged by the ubiquity of warfare and violence across time and space.[13]

> While some authors . . . suggest that the origins of war are simply prehistoric, an evolutionary or behavioral ecologist would argue that by any functional definition, war—lethal conflict—is older than humanity itself.[14]

> We can only conclude that *war is both a significant and a natural state of affairs erupting periodically between social groups of Homo sapiens*. . . . War is a male reproductive strategy.[15]

The views of biologists (Bobbi Low and Edward O. Wilson), primatologists (Michael Ghiglieri and Richard Wrangham), scholars from 100 years ago (Sir Henry Maine, Thomas Huxley, and William James), a writer (Dale Peterson), and an anatomist-turned-paleontologist (Raymond Dart) are represented in these quotations. Philosopher Thomas Hobbes is quoted in the chapter epigraph.[16] With literary embellishments and academic jargon added in some cases, these quotations parallel the statement of our senior citizen in that they reflect a culturally based belief whose truth appears self-evident. Interestingly, none of these quotations are written by cultural anthropologists, members of the academic discipline most familiar with warfare from a cross-cultural perspective. As reflected in the next set of quotations, persons most knowledgeable about the wide range of ethnographic data, typically but not exclusively cultural anthropologists, tend to reach a very different conclusion about the ubiquity and naturalness of war.

> Warfare is reported absent for example among the Andaman Islanders, the Arunta, the Eskimos, the Mission Indians, the Semang, the Todas, the Western Shoshoni and the Yahgan. . . . Evidently, conquest warfare and its modern development of war to advance national interests is not an inherent, inevitable feature of human social life—too many societies have existed in human history without it.[17]

> There is nothing either in the nature of war or in the nature of humanity that makes war inevitable. . . . Wars have an ancient history. They go back to the first city-states, and in the form of raiding earlier than that. Few states have ever existed that have not engaged in warfare. Such facts, however, do not mean that belligerency is either principally or in part due to instinctual drives.[18]

> Such war, let us not forget, made a very late appearance in human evolution. It could not occur before such high differentiation in types of culture as that of nomadic pastoralism and sedentary agricultural pursuits. . . . We have shown that war cannot be regarded as a fiat of human destiny, in that it could be related to biological needs or immutable psychological drives.[19]

> Warfare is by no means universal. . . . Many of the simplest peoples known either lack it entirely, or at least rarely engage in it. Even if some kind of *fighting* occurs in virtually all human groups, this fighting is not necessarily war.[20]

> Even *if* aggression is a universal human trait, war is not. "Warlike" societies fight only occasionally, and many societies have no war at all.[21]

> *War is not a cultural universal.* In particular, war seems to be most frequent and intense in the state level of sociopolitical organization, a relatively recent and short phase of cultural evolution that may eventually be transcended through further evolution. Nevertheless, there are civilizations that have experienced centuries or even millennia of relative peace.[22]

> The key point for our purposes is that—excepting a single late Upper Paleolithic site—archaeological evidence points to a commencement of warfare that post-dates the development of agriculture. This strongly implies that earlier hunter-gatherer societies were warless and that the Paleolithic (extending from 2,900,000 to 10,000 BP [before the present]) was a time of universal peace. Warfare then originates rather abruptly.[23]

> Pacifistic societies also occur (if uncommonly) at every level of social and economic complexity. . . . The idea that violent conflicts between groups is an inevitable consequence of being human or of social life itself is simply wrong.[24]

The first set of quotations reflects a view that war is part-and-parcel of being human, spans many millennia, and is a cross-cultural universal. Such beliefs imply the inevitability of war. Furthermore, the beliefs reflected in the first set of quotations recur *over centuries* of Western thinking.[25]

By contrast, the second set of quotations portrays war as having a recent origin, in large part following the development of agriculture, and points out that war does not occur in all cultures. It follows that war is not inevitable.

Shouldn't we be able to resolve this issue by examining the available evidence? Physicist Robert Ehrlich's comment, quoted in chapter 1, bears repeating: "The nice thing about ideas in the sciences is that they can be supported or refuted by data."[26] Do all societies engage in war, or do they not? Is there evidence of war predating agriculture, or is there not? In the remainder of this chapter, we will examine cross-cultural data to assess the important question as to whether warfare occurs in all cultures or not. In future chapters, we will consider data on the antiquity of war.

WARFARE AND FEUDING FROM A CROSS-CULTURAL PERSPECTIVE

According to Robert Textor's *A Cross-Cultural Summary,* in a sample of 45 societies, "warfare is prevalent" in 34 and "not prevalent" in the remaining 9.[27] The nine societies without prevalent warfare are the Ainu, Andamanese, Aranda, Lapps, Semang, Toda, Vedda, Yahgan, and Yukaghir. Drawing on data reported in a separate study of 32 societies, Textor lists eight societies where "warfare is common or chronic" and 24 where "warfare is rare or infrequent."[28] The societies coded as having rare or infrequent warfare are the Ainu, Andamanese, Apinaye, Balinese, Carib, Cayapa, Choroti, Chuckchee, Cuna, Gond, Hano, Huichol, Kazak, Khalka, Lamba, Lepcha, Naskapi, Samoyed, Tanala, Tarahumara, Tehuelche, Toda, Yakut, and Zuni. Whereas these findings suggest that some societies are much less warlike than others, they do not clearly address the question as to whether war is always present or not.

Keith Otterbein has been studying war, feuding, and other forms of violence, usually from a culturally comparative point of view, since the 1960s.[29] Beginning in his early studies, Otterbein makes distinctions among feuding, internal war, and external war.[30] Otterbein defines *feuding* as blood revenge that follows a homicide.[31] Thus feuding entails a patterned form of reciprocal homicides. Otterbein defines warfare as "armed combat between political communities."[32] More specifically, *internal war* refers to war between political communities within the same culture, and *external war* refers to warfare between political communities that are *not* within the same cultural unit. Otterbein's findings speak to the question: Do all cultures have war?

In a sample of 50 cultures, Otterbein found that 36 percent infrequently or never engaged in internal war.[33] Regarding external war, Otterbein rated each culture in two ways, for the frequency with which they *attacked* communities from other cultures and for the frequency with which they *were attacked* by communities of other cultures. The assumption seems to be that, if attacked, societies will fight to defend themselves, which is undoubtedly often the case, but there are also various accounts of people simply moving away from aggressive neighbors rather than holding firm and fighting back—for example, various Amazonian societies, including the Yanomamö,[34] the Buid of the Philippines,[35] the Kubu of Sumatra,[36] and various aboriginal Malaysia peoples.[37] In any case, 48 percent of the sample were attacked infrequently or never and 40 percent attacked other cultures infrequently or never.[38]

If we examine the three warfare subcategories in relation to each other, we find that 10 percent (5 of 50) of the societies infrequently or never engage in *any* internal or external war (either attacking or being attacked). Next, if we ask how many of these societies fit the "never" part of the rating, the answer is that war is absent from 4 societies of these 50—in other words, from eight percent of the sample.[39]

Clearly, the vast majority of Otterbein's sample engaged in either internal or external warfare, but a few of the societies did not engage in any type of war. However, before reaching a conclusion that about eight percent of societies lack war, a methodological complication should be mentioned. The manner in which this sample was assembled—*with the goal of studying war*—would seem to favor the inclusion of warring cultures. This is the case because Otterbein rejected many potential societies before arriving at the final sample of 50. One of the criteria among several that he used for dropping societies from the sample was if data on war were lacking. "In all, 61 societies were dropped from the sample . . . and 24 because data on military organization, tactics, and the causes of war were not in the sources."[40]

One plausible reason that information on war would be lacking from ethnographic sources is that war actually is absent or rare in the culture and therefore there are no details to portray. Ethnographers are more apt to describe the aspects of the culture that they observe rather than enumerate traits that are absent. In other words, lack of data on war in an ethnographic source may reflect an actual rarity or absence of war in that society. Thus due to the manner in which societies were excluded from the sample, the percentage of societies actually lacking war may be higher than the eight percent suggested by Otterbein's final sample. In a recent review on the study of war within anthropology, Otterbein reaches the overall assessment that "some conditions lead to war, some do not. I see great variation in the nature and frequency of war."[41]

Harold Driver also distinguished between war that occurs between true political organizations and feuds that occur between families or other kin groups. In his extensive overview, *Indians of North America,* Driver concludes that whereas feuding sometimes existed, "most of the peoples of the Arctic, Great Basin, Northeast Mexico, and probably Baja California lacked true warfare before European contact." Moreover, Driver summarizes that for the North American Sub-Arctic region, Northwest Coast, Plateau Region of the Northwest, California, and the Southwest, whereas some societies in these immense regions did make war, "at the same time, all these areas included some peoples with little in the way of violence, raids, or feuds, and no hostilities pretentious enough to be labeled war."[42]

Joseph Jorgensen and his collaborators surveyed 172 societies of western North America and conclude:

> One of the most obvious and interesting aspects of the cultures of western North America's Indians at the time of contact with Europeans was that so few societies actually engaged in persistent offensive warfare, or even raiding, yet the prospects of armed altercations deeply influenced the internal organizations and external relations of these aboriginal societies.[43]

In another cross-cultural study, Carol and Melvin Ember, like Keith Otterbein, made use of a distinction between internal war and external war. Unlike Otterbein, however, the Embers did not drop cultural cases that lacked information on war. The Embers coded 186 societies in the Standard Cross-Cultural Sample (SCCS), a set of primarily preindustrial societies widely used by cross-cultural researchers.[44]

The Embers present their findings on the frequency of war in two ways: first, for all the societies in the sample, and second, for only the societies not pacified by an external power such as a colonial or national government. For the whole sample, warfare was reported as "absent or rare" in 28 percent of the societies ("absent" means absent, and "rare" means less than once in ten years). This is a much higher percentage than in the Otterbein sample. For nonpacified societies only, the Embers found warfare to be "absent or rare" in nine percent of the 186 societies.[45]

Again in this case, drawing conclusions about warfare frequency turns out to have an added wrinkle or two. In contrast to Otterbein and many other anthropologists, the Embers defined "war" so broadly as to encompass feuding and revenge killings if undertaken by more than one person.[46] That the Embers are including feuding and revenge killings in their tally of "war" events is not readily apparent, but this is an absolutely crucial point to consider when assessing the meaning of their findings on the frequency of so-called war.

In their writings, Ember and Ember very consistently define war "as socially organized armed combat between members of different territorial units (communities or aggregates of communities)."[47] From this phrasing, it is not apparent that their definition includes feuding and revenge homicides. However, in one of their articles, the Embers explain their definition of war more completely than in their other reports:

> War is defined as socially organized armed combat between members of different territorial units (communities or aggregates of communities). In the ethnographic record, such combat usually involves groups on both sides, but a warfare event could involve the ambush of a single person of an "enemy" group. Thus the phrase "socially organized" means that there is a group of *combatants* on at least one of the "sides." This definition of warfare focuses on the behavior of groups, not on their presumed or reported motives for attacking and killing. Thus, *we do not distinguish between warfare and feuding ("blood revenge"),* as Otterbein does.[48]

In my opinion, with all due respect to the Embers, counting feuds as "war" represents a mixing of the proverbial apples and oranges. As Boehm points out, "Feuding is quite different from all-out warfare for several reasons: feuding is limited to one or two killings at a time; only one side takes the offensive at a time; and there is no necessary political objective beyond the maintenance of honor."[49]

Counting feuding and revenge killings directed at particular individuals as "warfare events" increases the number of societies that are reported to practice "war," by this expansive definition, and similarly this tallying procedure inflates estimates as to how often this so-called war is reported to occur within particular societies. For example, the "war" that the Embers report as occurring "every year" for the Andamanese and slightly more often than "once in every 3 to 10 years" for the Yahgan is mostly based on instances of blood revenge and feuding between disgruntled *individuals,* perhaps aided by their kin.[50] In other words, what the Embers call *warfare frequency* for the Andaman Islanders and Yahgan more precisely represents a frequency estimate for brawls, homicides, and revenge killings *combined.*

This conclusion rests on multiple sources. Alfred Radcliffe-Brown writes, based on his own fieldwork, that "Quarrels between individuals, as we have seen, were often taken up by friends on each side. . . . In some instances there appears to have been feuds of long standing; in others there was a quarrel, a fight or two, and the enemies made peace with one another, until a fresh cause of disagreement should arise."[51] After describing activities consistent with feuding and revenge killings, Radcliffe-Brown writes that "fighting on a large scale seems to have been unknown amongst the Andamanese." A quotation by Lesser given earlier in this chapter specifically mentions both the Andaman Islanders and the Yahgan as cultures where *warfare is absent*. L. T. Hobhouse reaches the conclusion that the Andaman Islanders had *feuds* but that "war between whole tribes does not seem to have occurred." Similarly, Service concludes that among the Andaman Islanders, "true warfare did not exist, and there was not even much fighting or feuding."[52]

Related to the Yahgan, John Cooper reports the occurrence of feuding and blood revenge only, and states directly that "organized warfare did not exist." Martin Gusinde explains that due to the absence of chiefly authority, military weapons, forts, and so forth, "gatherings of many people to warfare would therefore have been impossible. There are no reports anywhere concerning them." Based on a comprehensive review of the ethnographic information on the Yahgan, Service offers the assessment: "There is no organized warfare of any kind." The forgoing assessments suggest that the Embers' "war" frequency ratings for both these societies, and perhaps some others in their sample, are based on some combination of revenge homicide, feuding, and nonlethal brawls, but not actually on warfare as usually conceived.[53]

This discussion illustrates the importance of clearly specifying the manner in which war is being defined. If acts of feuding and blood revenge are counted as "war," the final frequency tally for this so-called warfare will be higher, as the Andaman Islander and Yahgan cases suggest, than if feuding is conceptually distinguished from "war." Either way, *the basis of the count should be clearly specified, because such definitional issues relate to the interpretations we derive from the findings*. Try this thought experiment on yourself: When you read that a given culture makes *war* every year, what mental image do you form? On the basis of what the word *war* connotes to most people, you probably picture substantially more bloodshed than when you next read the clarification that *feuding events or even a single revenge killing* constitutes the type of so-called war that is being counted as occurring every year in the culture.

The overall conclusion about the absence and rarity of "war" based on the Ember and Ember study can be stated as follows. *Even when "war" is defined so broadly as to include individual instances of blood revenge and feuding, it is still "absent or rare" in 9 percent to 28 percent of the societies in a large cross-cultural representative sample of societies, depending on whether one includes only "unpacified" societies or all the societies in the sample.*

The Embers' point about taking pacification into account when assessing the frequency of war may be a good one, at least in certain cases. However, as Ferguson points out, in some situations so-called pacification had the opposite effect: "The old imperialist rationale that state expansion stops local fighting is contradicted by a great number of detailed ethnohistorical studies (e.g., Ferguson and Whitehead 1992a; Ferguson and Farragher 1988:242–254) which document the opposite effect. Initially, state encroachment is far more likely to intensify conflict than suppress it."[54]

Returning to the importance of distinguishing between war and feud, van der Dennen points out: "In war—as contrasted with a feud–violence is relatively 'promiscuous': Anyone of the opposing community may be defined as an 'enemy' and thus be a potential victim. In a feud, the concept of enemy—and potential victim—is more restricted and selective: A particular member or members of a particular kinship group, family or clan." In fact, anthropologists, like other people, generally differentiate between war and feud as distinct phenomena.[55]

Cross-cultural studies of feuding show that rates of occurrence vary from one society to the next, and that *feuding, like warfare, is not present in all societies*. For a sample of 50 cultures, Keith and Charlotte Otterbein found blood feuding to be frequent in only eight societies (16 percent), infrequent in 14 (28 percent), and absent in the remaining 28 societies (56 percent). Psychologists Karen Ericksen and Heather Horton investigated blood feuding in the 186 societies of the SCCS, the same sample used by the Embers in their study of warfare. They found that the classic blood feud—that is, when both the malefactor and his relatives are considered to be appropriate targets of vengeance—exists in 34.5 percent of the societies. Overall, some form of kin group vengeance was *considered legitimate* in 54 percent of the cross-cultural sample and not legitimate in the remaining 46 percent of the societies.[56]

Even in societies where kin group vengeance was socially permitted, by no means was it always carried out. In the societies where kin group vengeance was legitimately allowed, it was considered to be a moral imperative in 42 percent of the cultures and presumably often occurred in such cases; was viewed as the most appropriate course of action in 16 percent; was seen as merely one possibility among other options, depending upon circumstances, in 20 percent; and was used only as the option of last resort in 22 percent of the cases. As Boehm notes, "systems of feuding are really not so wild and uncontrolled as they may have appeared."[57] Of the 46 percent of the overall sample of societies wherein kin group vengeance was *not* socially legitimate, the vast majority (81 percent) employed third-party assisted dispute settlement processes of various types, whereas individual self-redress tended to occur in the absence of third-party mechanisms, as in some hunting-and-gathering societies.[58] Viewing these two cross-cultural studies of feuding together, it is clear that approximately half of the societies allow blood feuding and half do not, and even when socially permitted, other approaches for dealing with grievances are often adopted in place of seeking vengeance. As we will explore further in chapter 8, feuding can be seen as a judicial mechanism—a way that aggrieved parties seek their own justice.

In one of the quotations cited earlier in this chapter, Low equated "war" with "lethal conflict."[59] By such a general standard, the killing of even one individual by another, even within the same society, could be counted as an act of "war." Is it really in accordance with a popularly shared concept of "war" to include all cases of lethal aggression? Is it "war" when an English woman poisons her husband? Is it war when South American bandits rob and kill their victims on a deserted highway? Is it war when an Australian Aborigine hunter, accompanied by his brother, gives chase to the man who ran off with his wife, catches up with the lovers, and spears his rival? With poetic license, we might employ martial vocabulary and imagery to such acts of lethal conflict: In the first event, "the *battle* of the sexes" has gone too far; the second could be called "an *ambush*"; and the third could be labeled a dastardly "*sneak attack*." However, these lethal conflicts are clearly homicides, not "war" as generally conceived. Defining war so broadly as to encompass a plethora of individual and group conflict behaviors (e.g., murder, robbery-homicide, revenge killings, and feud), which stem from diverse motivations and are often in-group events, can facilitate making the claim for the universality of "war." But clearly such word games are machinations that distort the concept of war. When examined more closely, much of the aggressive behavior subsumed under sweeping definitions of war, such as "lethal conflict," do not correspond with a general impression of what actually constitutes "war."

> The problem of the definition of "war," including "primitive war," is not merely a topic of sterile academic debate or trivial casuistry. On the contrary, it is of paramount importance within a general theoretical framework concerning the problem whether war existed at the dawn of [hu]mankind's evolution.[60]

A definition of warfare offered by Roy Prosterman is in correspondence with the common usage of the word and is specific enough to capture important features of *war* that differentiate it from the homicide and revenge killings that are aimed at a specific individual or kin group. According to Prosterman, war is

> a group activity, carried on by members of one community against members of another community, in which it is the primary purpose to inflict serious injury or death on multiple nonspecified members of that other community, or in which the primary purpose makes it highly likely that serious injury or death will be inflicted on multiple nonspecified members of that community in the accomplishment of that primary purpose.[61]

Thus Prosterman's definition highlights that war is a group activity, occurs between communities, is *not* focused against a particular individual or that person's kin group—as occurs in feuding—but rather is focused against nonspecified members of another community and is geared toward either the killing of people or achieving some goal that makes the killing of people likely. Prosterman's definition is useful because it clearly excludes individual homicides on the one hand and feuding on the other and consequently clarifies that war entails *relatively impersonal lethal aggression between communities*. Prosterman's definition of war is more detailed than Otterbein's "armed combat between political communities," but nonetheless these definitions are in rough correspondence. Moreover, Prosterman's definition of war, which excludes individual homicides, even if committed by more than one person, contrasts with that of the Embers.[62]

NONWARRING CULTURES

While researching this book, I decided to start compiling a list of cultures that were nonwarring according to a Prosterman/Otterbein type of definition of war, that is, by definitions that correspond with a general conception of war as distinct from both homicide and feud (see Box 7.1). Consequently, some of the cultures have feuding or blood revenge. However, the majority do not feud. When there was ambiguity in the ethnographic information as to whether violence was feud or war, I did *not* include the culture on the list even when feuding, not war, seemed to be the most appropriate classification. Thus, I opted for a conservative approach if there was any degree of uncertainty. This conservatism is illustrated, for example, by the fact I did not include the Alor of Melanesia on

BOX 7.1 NONWARRING SOCIETIES

The listed societies are *nonwarring* in accordance with Prosterman's and Otterbein's definitions of war that differentiate *warfare* from *feuding*.[1] Many of the societies do not engage in feuding either, but a few do, such as the Andaman Islanders mentioned in this chapter. Some of the nonwarring societies also are internally peaceful and therefore appear in Box 5.1. When applicable, *external conflict scores* from Ross' study are listed.[2] Citations include primary or secondary sources, or both, depending on the case in question. A sampling of descriptive ethnographic statements about nonwarring societies appears in Box 7.2.

Africa and the Middle East: Dorobo,[3] Fipa,[4] Guanches of the Canary Islands,[5] G/wi,[6] Hadza,[7] Ju/'hoansi (!Kung),[8] Mandaeans/Subba,[9] Mbuti,[10] Nubians,[11] Tristan da Cunha[12]

Asia: Andaman Islanders,[13] Badaga,[14] Baiga,[15] Batak Agta,[16] Batek,[17] Birhor,[18] Buid,[19] Central Thai,[20] Chewong,[21] Hanunóo,[22] Irula,[23] Jahai,[24] Kadar,[25] Kota,[26] Kubu,[27] Kurumbas,[28] Ladaki/Ladakhi,[29] Lepcha,[30] Malapantaram/Hill Pandaram,[31] Naikens/Nayaka,[32] Palawan,[33] Paliyan,[34] Penan/Punan,[35] Sama Dilaut/Bajau Laut,[36] Semai,[37] Semang,[38] Sherpa,[39] Subanun,[40] Toda,[41] Veddah/Vedda,[42] Yanadi[43]

Europe: Saami/Lapps[44]

North America: Central Inuit,[45] Columbia,[46] Copper Inuit,[47] Greenland Inuit,[48] Kawaiisu,[49] Kaibab and most other Southern Paiute groups,[50] Karok,[51] Mission Indians,[52] Point Barrow Inuit,[53] Polar Eskimo,[54] Sanpoil,[55] Saulteaux,[56] Shoshone,[57] Slave/Slavey,[58] Southern Paiute (see Kaibab Paiute), Wenatchi[59]

Oceania: Arunta/Aranda,[60] Australian Aborigines generally,[61] Ifaluk,[62] Mardudjara/Mardu,[63] Tikopia,[64] Tiwi[65]

South America: Cayapa,[66] Curetu,[67] Matsigenka/Machiguenga,[68] Panare,[69] Paumari,[70] Pemon,[71] Piaroa,[72] Siriono,[73] Waíwai,[74] Warao/Warrau,[75] Yahgan[76]

Sources: 1. Prosterman 1972; Otterbein 1970. 2. Ross 1993a. 3. Huntingford 1954:132–136; Otterbein 1970:20; see also Blackburn 1982; Woodburn 1988:47. 4. Willis 1989. 5. Dennen 1995:638; see also Davie 1929; Estevez 1992. 6. Silberbauer 1972, 1981: esp. Chapter 4. 7. Woodburn 1968a:157–158; Dennen 1995:638–639; see also Marlowe 2002:274. 8. Lee 1979: Chapter 13, 1993: Chapter 7; Draper 1975:86; Marshall 1976:53; Robert Hitchcock personal communication 2002; Thomas 1959:21–24; see also Johnson & Earle 1987:38, 47; Keeley 1996:29; Fabbro 1978; Sponsel 1996b:110; Ury 1999:50; one of the four societies rated as having the lowest external conflict score of the sample by Ross 1993a: Appendix A. 9. Drower 1962:1, 14, 15, 48. 10. Turnbull 1965a:218–223, 1968b:341; Fabbro 1978; Keeley 1996:30; one of the four societies rated as having the lowest external conflict score of the sample by Ross 1993a: Appendix A. 11. Fernea 1973, 2004:120; see also Fernea & Fernea 1991. 12. Loudon 1970; Munch 1974; Munch & Marske 1981. 13. Radcliffe-Brown 1922:49–50, 84–87; Pandya 1992:11; see also Man 1932:135–136; Hobhouse 1956:105; Service 1966:110, 1971b:49; Simmons 1937: Code Table; Textor 1967: Table 417; external conflict score is intermediate, Ross 1993a: Appendix A. 14. Hockings 1980, 1992:15, 17; Murdock 1934:110. 15. Montagu 1976:268–269, 1994:xii. 16. Warren 1975a. 17. Karen Endicott 1984:6; Kirk Endicott 1983:224, 238, 1993:235. 18. Sinha 1972:390, 392–393. 19. Gibson 1989, 1990:130–133. 20. Phillips 1974; Martin & Levinson 1993:71. 21. Howell 1988:150, 1989. 22. Conklin 1954:48–49; LeBar 1975:76; Hockings 1993:91. 23. Zvelebil 1988; Murdock 1934:110; also see Hockings 1992:15, 17; Wolf 1992:137. 24. Sluys 1999:307, 310; see also Endicott 1993. 25. Gardner 1966:402; also see Bonta 1997:318. 26. Wolf

1992:137; Murdock 1934:110. 27. Forbes 1885; Hobhouse 1956:108; Hobhouse et al. 1910:229; Sandbukt 1988. 28. Dick 1992:143; Hockings 1992:15, 17. 29. Mann 1986; Holsti 1913:72; Dennen 1995:646; see also Norberg-Hodge 1991. 30. Gorer 1967: esp. Chapter 1; DiMaggio 1992:149; see also Ember & Ember 1994a:642; Montagu 1976:185, 1978b:5; Textor 1967: Table 418; one of four societies rated as having the lowest external conflict score of the sample by Ross 1993a: Appendix A. 31. Morris 1977:230, 237–238, 1992:100; Bonta 1996; Gardner 1966:402; Dennen 1995:648. 32. Dennen 1995:651; also cf. Bird-David 1992:196. 33. Warren 1975b. 34. Gardner 1966:402, 1972: e.g., 425, 1985:413–416, 421, 1999:263, 2000a:232, 2000b: Chapters 5 and 6, 2004:58. 35. Hose 1894:157–158; Needham 1972:180; Hobhouse et al. 1910:229; Holsti 1913:71. 36. Sather 1975:11; 1993:34, 2004; personal communication 2000. 37. Dentan 1968:58, 1978:97, 1999: e.g., 419, 420, 2004; Gregor & Robarchek 1996:161; Robarchek 1990; Robarchek & Dentan 1987; see also Endicott 1983:231–233, 237–238. 38. LeBar et al. 1964:185; Karen Endicott 1984:6; Kirk Endicott 1983:224, 238, 1993:235; Schebesta 1929:280; see also Hobhouse et al. 1910:229; Holsti 1913; Murdock 1934:94–95; Simmons 1937: Code Table; Textor 1967: Table 417; external conflict score is in the lowest seven percent of the sample, Ross 1993a: Appendix A. 39. Paul 1992:259; Fürer-Haimendorf 1984. 40. Frake 1960:53, 1980a:133, 1980b:105. 41. Rivers 1986; Walker 1992:297; Murdock 1934:110; Holsti 1913:72; Textor 1967: Table 417; Otterbein 1970:20. 42. Seligmann & Seligmann 1969:34; Davie 1929:50–51; Lesser 1968:94; Hobhouse 1956:105; Stegeborn 1999:271; Davie 1929:50–51; Levinson 1994:122; Holsti 1913:71; Textor 1967: Tables 417 and 418. 43. Raghaviah 1962; Gardner 1966:403; see also Bonta 1996:411–412; Dennen 1995:672. 44. Anderson & Beach 1992:222; Holsti 1913:71; Montagu 1976:270; see also Ingold 1976; Textor 1967: Table 417; Davie 1929:49; external conflict score is in the lowest 14 percent of the sample, Ross 1993a: Appendix A. 45. Boas 1964:57; see also Davie 1929:47; Hoebel 1967b:82–83. 46. Jorgensen 1980:503–507, 509–515, 613–614, cf. 316. 47. Damas 1972, 1991; see also Fabbro 1978; Keeley 1996:28, 29; Otterbein 1970:20; external conflict score is in the lowest 14 percent of the sample, Ross 1993a: Appendix A. 48. Nansen 1893:162; Kleivan 1991:378; Irwin 1990:194; Dennen 1995:640; see also Davie 1929:46–47. 49. Zigmond 1986:399. 50. Keeley 1996:28, 30, 205; Kelly & Fowler 1986:368–370, 381–382; Fowler 1991:332. 51. Bright 1991:177. 52. Lesser 1968:94. 53. Hobhouse et al. 1910:229. 54. Murdock 1934:210–211; Simmons 1937: Code Table; see also Keeley 1996:30; Irwin 1990:194–196; Gilberg 1984, 1991. 55. Ray 1980:114–115; Ruby & Brown 1989:127, 138, 163–164, 172; Jorgensen 1980: 503, 505–507, 509–515, 613–614, see 316; Dennen 1995:659. 56. Hallowell 1974:278; see also Holsti 1913. 57. Specifically the Panamint, Battle Mountain, Hukundika, and Gosiute Shoshone groups: Jorgensen 1980:503–507, 509–515, 613–614, see 316; see also Johnson & Earle 1987:33; Keeley 1996:28, 30, 205; Service 1966:95; Thomas et al. 1986:275, 277; Steward in Wolf 2001:195. 58. Mason 1946 quoted in Kelly 2000:53; Kelly 2000:53; Asch 1981:343; Asch & Smith 1999:48; Rushforth 1991:320; see also Helm 1991:87; Krech 1991:139, 141; Savishinsky 1974:65–66 in the Human Relations Area Files (HRAF) on the Hare, a subgroup and/or closely related group to the Slave. 59. Jorgensen 1980:505–507, 509–515, 613–614, see 316; Keeley 1996:205. 60. Spencer & Gillen 1927:27–28; see also Service 1971b:18; Murdock 1934:45; Textor 1967: Table 417. 61. See chapter 12; also C. Berndt 1978; R. Berndt 1965; Davie 1929:52; Wheeler 1910; Dennen 1995:620–621. 62. Burrows 1952:23; Dennen 1995:640; also see Spiro 1952 and Lutz 1988:136, 184–185. 63. Tonkinson 1978:118, 2004:93; Keeley 1996:30. 64. Firth 1957, 1967; Kirch 1997; Otterbein 1970:20; see also Keeley 1996:28; one of the four societies rated as having the lowest external conflict score of the sample, Ross 1993a: Appendix A. 65. Hart & Pilling 1979:85, 79–87; Hart, Pilling, & Goodale 1988:93–95; Goodale 1991:329; see the further discussions of this interesting ethnographic case in chapters 11 and 12. 66. Barrett 1925; Murra 1948:282; see also Altschuler 1964, 1967, 1970; Keeley 1996:28, 205; Textor 1967: Table 418; external conflict score in the lowest seven percent of the sample, Ross 1993a: Appendix A. 67. Hobhouse et al. 1910:229. 68. Johnson 1983:62–63; Johnson & Earle 1987:65, 74, 82; Allen Johnson, personal communication, 2003. 69. Henley 1982, 1994:266. 70. Hobhouse et al. 1910:229 and references therein; Dennen 1995:656. 71. Thomas 1994:272–273. 72. Overing 1989. 73. Holmberg 1969; Morey & Marwitt 1975:447; see also Fabbro 1978. 74. Howard 1991:347–348; Fock 1963:6–9, 231–239; see also Campbell 1995: Chapter 4. 75. Heinen 1994:359; Turrado Moreno 1945:298; see also Morey & Marwitt 1975:447; Wilbert 1993. 76. Gusinde 1937:885, 893; Cooper 1946a:95; Hobhouse 1956:111; Service 1966:97, 1971b:35; Textor 1967: Table 417; external conflict score is in the lowest 14 percent of the sample, Ross 1993a: Appendix A.

the list because ethnographer Cora Du Bois uses the word "war" when describing violence that in actuality seems more like blood feuding than war.[63] Likewise, if an ethnographer reported that a particular society is "not warlike" but failed to elaborate, I did *not* add that culture to the list. Rather, I looked for direct statements to the effect that the culture lacks war, these people do not engage in warfare, the people respond to threats from other groups by moving elsewhere rather than fighting, and so on.

Clear statements as to the nonwarring characteristics of a culture are illustrated by the following examples, first by Julian Steward on the Shoshone of North America, and second by Gregor and Robarchek on the Semai of Malaysia.

> In aboriginal times most of the Shoshonean people had no national or tribal warfare. There were no territorial rights to be defended, no military honors to be gained, and no means of organizing groups of individuals for concerted action. When war parties of neighboring peoples invaded their country, the Shoshoneans ran away more often than they fought. Hostilities generally consisted of feuds, not organized military action, and they resulted largely from the suspicion of witchcraft and from women stealing.[64]

> Violence within and between Semai communities is nearly nonexistent. . . . Semai settlements were subject to slave raids by Malays and others. Neither Malay nor colonial histories nor the oral history of the Semai themselves report active resistance to these incursions. The Semai response was always a disorganized and headlong flight into the forest.[65]

Additional descriptions related to nonwarring cultures appear in Box 7.2. When possible, I checked multiple primary and secondary sources to validate the nonwarring nature of given cultures on the list. In situations where a source reported that a society

BOX 7.2 A SAMPLING OF ETHNOGRAPHIC STATEMENTS ABOUT NONWARRING CULTURES

"There is no ethnographic evidence to suggest the existence of long-standing intergroup animosity akin to feud [among the Mardu]. There is no word for either feud or warfare in the language of the desert people. Their accounts of conflicts are phrased in kinship terms and on an interpersonal or interfamily rather than intergroup level."[1]

"Warfare in the sense of organized intertribal struggle is unknown [among the Arunta]. What fighting there is, is better understood as an aspect of juridical procedure than as war."[2]

"All informants denied that any major conflict had occurred 'as long as could be remembered.' Admirable relations existed between the Sanpoil and all of their immediate neighbors."[3]

"These people [the Saulteaux] have never engaged in war with the whites or with other Indian tribes."[4]

"There is no warfare in their [Machiguenga] region, no villages or superordinate political structures, no lineages or other named social groupings beyond the household, and a very loose 'kindred.'"[5]

"Warfare, either actual or traditional, is absent [among the Hanunóo]."[6]

"There are no [Hanunóo] classes, no servants, no officials, and no warfare."[7]

"Relations with Subanun of the same or other groups are invariably devoid of warfare and class distinctions. . . . Social relationships, unmarred by warfare, extend outward along ties of proximity and bilateral kinship."[8]

"The classical example of the absence of war is that of the Eskimos. Among the Greenlanders warfare is unknown. . . . A similar situation prevails among the Central Eskimos, of whom Boas writes, 'Real wars or fights between settlements, I believe, have never happened, but contests have always been confined to single families.'"[9]

"[The Veddahs] live so peacefully together that one seldom hears of quarrels among them and never of war."[10]

"I can report a complete absence of feuding within Paliyan society and a corresponding total lack of warfare."[11]

"There is no evidence of Semang warring with one another or with non-Semang."[12]

"The Semang is not aggressive or cruel, but, on the contrary, very shy and timid toward strangers."[13]

"The Jahai are known for their shyness toward outsiders, their non-violent, non-competitive attitude, and their strong focus on sharing. . . . In times of conflict, the Jahai withdraw rather than fight."[14]

"Among the Andamanese quarrels between groups sometimes lead to bloodshed, and thus to feuds, which might continue for months or even years. . . . War between whole tribes does not seem to have occurred."[15]

Sources: 1. Tonkinson 1978:118 on the Mardudjara/Mardu of Australia. 2. Service 1971b:18 on the Arunta of Australia. 3. Ray 1980:114 on the Sanpoil of North America. 4. Hallowell 1974:278 on the Saulteaux of North America. 5. Johnson 1983:61, 63 on the Machiguenga of South America. 6. LeBar 1975:76 on the Hanunóo of Southeast Asia. 7. Conklin 1954:49 on the Hanunóo of Southeast Asia. 8. Frake 1960:52, 1980a:133 on the Subanun of Southeast Asia. 9. Davie 1929:46, 47; see also Boas 1964:57 on the Greenland and Central Canadian Inuit of North America. 10. Van Goens, writing in the 17th century, on the Veddahs of Asia, quoted in Davie 1929:50. 11. Gardner 2004:58 on the Paliyan of South Asia. 12. LeBar et al. 1964:185 on the Semang of Southeast Asia. 13. Schebesta 1929:280 on the Semang of Southeast Asia. 14. Sluys 1999:307, 310 on the Jahai of Southeast Asia. 15. Hobhouse 1956:105 on the Andaman Islanders.

is now peaceful but practiced war in the relatively recent past, I did *not* include the culture on the list. Thus I attempted to rule out cultures that are nonwarring due to relatively recent historical developments.

By using these conservative selection criteria, in several months' time I was able to locate over 70 nonwarring cultures. The sources of information for each nonwarring culture are included in Box 7.1. The list is far from exhaustive because it includes only the cultures that I was able to locate in a limited amount of time. Although not included on the list, certain religious "enclave societies"—groups existing within larger societies—such as the Amish, Hutterites, and Quakers, also have pacifist belief systems and consistently have forsaken warfare.[66]

Certain nations also have not been involved in warfare for very long periods of time. Sweden has not been to war in over 170 years; Switzerland, known for its neutrality and aided by natural mountain barriers, has not engaged in war for almost 200 years; and Iceland has been at peace for over 700 years.[67] In recent history, 20 countries have experienced periods without war that have lasted at least 100 years.[68] Costa Rica abolished its military after World War II—a very concrete statement of the country's intention not to engage in war. Former Costa Rican President Oscar Arias writes, "The stability of Costa Rican democracy stems primarily from the fact that it possesses no military institutions. . . . Costa Rica serves as an example of peace and democracy in a region of war and dictatorship."[69]

We began this chapter by noting that some Westerners—from scholars and scientists to senior citizens and students—espouse beliefs as to the naturalness and universality of war. I raised the possibility that such views, rather than being based on an objective evaluation of the data, instead might be part of a cultural belief system that includes a warlike image of humanity and a corresponding assumption that war occurs in all cultures. However, as we have seen, it is easy to find dissenting opinions from cultural anthropologists and others who have actually evaluated the cross-cultural evidence on this issue. Those most familiar with the relevant data tend to reach the conclusion that war is not a human universal.[70]

The cross-cultural studies by Otterbein and the Embers correspond with the list containing over 70 nonwarring cultures by pointing to the same conclusion: *Many nonwarring cultures do in fact exist*.[71] Nonwarring societies are not merely figments of the imagination. Most known cultures do engage in warfare, but some do not. Thus the belief that war is a universal feature of societies everywhere, as expressed by numerous persons including some eminent thinkers such as Thomas Huxley and Edward O. Wilson, is, nonetheless, false. It would seem that the presupposed "truth" of this belief about war and human nature, as an aspect of a broader cultural belief system, is simply accepted as self-evident by many people. Actively checking the validity of this belief against the available anthropological evidence, if such an endeavor ever comes to mind in the first place, might seem superfluous. Burrows, who worked on Ifaluk, offers a conclusion that is apropos: "We generally assume that we know, from . . . observation, what is universally human. But a little scrutiny will show that such conclusions are based only on experience with one culture, our own. We assume that what is familiar, unless obviously shaped by special conditions, is universal."[72]

CHAPTER 8

SOCIAL ORGANIZATION MATTERS!

> The Batek abhor interpersonal violence and have generally fled from their enemies rather than fighting back. I once asked a Batek man why their ancestors had not shot the Malay slave-raiders, who plagued them until the 1920s . . . with poisoned blowpipe darts. His shocked answer was: "Because it would kill them!"
>
> KIRK ENDICOTT[1]

In the midst of World War II, Quincy Wright published a magnum opus called *The Study of War*. The two-volume work, totaling well over a thousand pages, draws on information from fields as diverse as psychology, sociology, anthropology, history, and political science, as well as from Wright's own discipline, international law. In considering anthropological data, Wright and his team of assistants adopted the large cross-cultural sample assembled by Leonard T. Hobhouse, Gerald Wheeler, and Morris Ginsberg some 27 years before.[2]

From the Hobhouse, Wheeler, and Ginsberg sample, Wright was able to rate the vast majority of the societies, 590 in all, regarding warfare.[3] Thirty societies (5 percent of the total) were found to have *no war*—that is, the literature revealed no evidence of warfare, no military organization, and no special weapons. Another 346 societies (59 percent of the sample) were rated "to be unwarlike or to engage only in mild warfare," provided that "no indication was found of fighting for definite economic or political purposes in the more specialized literature."[4] Combining the *no war* and *unwarlike* categories shows that nearly two-thirds of the total sample (64 percent) were nonwarring or mild-warring. The rest of the sample were determined by Wright to engage in war for economic or political purposes (29 percent and 7 percent of the total, respectively).

It is also important that a substantial number of the so-called *unwarlike* groups engaged in feuding, *and nothing more*. If we conceptually untangle feuding from warring—as I've argued we should—then the societies that Wright coded as *unwarlike* based solely on descriptions of feuding should more appropriately be thought of as nonwarring. But putting this issue aside for the time being, Wright's findings highlight a very important point: *War is either lacking or mild in the majority of cultures!* The cross-cultural picture is not nearly as Hobbesian as is often assumed.

However, there is much more to this story. First, the classification scheme that Wright devised incorporates the term *war* into *all possible categories*. Thus the societies determined by Wright to have *no war* are referred to by the label *defensive war*. The societies defined as *unwarlike* or having *only mild warfare* (which amounts, again, to nothing more than feuding in some cases) are classified under the label *social war*. The *social war* category is a mixed bag of small-scale night raids, blood-revenge expeditions, headhunting parties, individual duels or contests, and pitched battles. In other words, *social war* clearly catches *feuds as well as war* and perhaps also encompasses *revenge homicides and juridical contests,* the latter being, in reality, a mechanism for resolving conflict. The meanings of Wright's remaining two categories of war are more straightforward; *economic war* entails economic objectives, military training, and mass tactics, and *political war* has political aims, usually sought through the use of standing armies. The main point is that Wright's labeling scheme manages to include *all* 590 societies under the war umbrella. Readers must study the "fine print" in a footnote to get a detailed description of what the categories of warfare actually entail.[5]

The label *defensive war* is perhaps the most problematic. How does Wright justify putting a war label on societies that are described as lacking warfare *and* feuding? Wright writes, "these people have no military organization or military weapons and do not fight unless actually attacked, in which case they make spontaneous use of available tools and hunting weapons to defend themselves but regard this necessity as a misfortune."[6] At first, this justification may sound plausible, but Wright presents no actual *evidence* of defensive fighting having occurred in any of the *no war* societies on his list. Wright seems to have overlooked the possibility that a group might flee or move away if attacked, rather than fight back.

This raises a question. Could Wright's *defensive war* category stem more from an *assumption* about what nonwarring peoples might do if attacked than on what the actual data show nonwarring peoples typically do? If we turn to ethnographic reports on the societies to which Wright applies the *defensive war* classification, such as the Semang, Jakun, Kubu, Batua (Batwa), and "Sakai" societies (such as the Semai), the typical pattern is one of avoidance and retreat, *not* defensive fighting.[7] The Greenland Inuit bands, another group classified by Wright as engaging in *defensive war,* lived within a nonwarring social system and had no need to defend themselves or to flee.[8] Additionally, avoidance and retreat have been reported for many other societies, most of them bands or tribes, including the Aweikoma, Buid, Chewong, Dorobo, Guayaki, Jahai, Northeastern Dene societies—such as the Hare, Dogrib, Yellowknife, Chipewyan, and Slavey—Panare, Shoshone, Siriono, and Wáiwai, among others.[9]

In Western thinking, it may be *cowardly* to flee or move away from danger, but not all peoples think like Westerners! Fleeing is often seen as simply sensible.[10] Belief systems differ regarding the value placed on fighting or fleeing. As we have seen, they also differ regarding the acceptability of violence. Recall the words of the Batek hunter who was quoted in the chapter epigraph. He was shocked at the question as to why poisoned blowpipe darts had not been used against slave raiders. Additionally, whereas Westerners come from an agricultural tradition associated with defending particular *pieces of land,* many other societies do not. Moving away may involve a consciously chosen and sensible alternative to fighting. My point is not that nonwarring groups *never* defend themselves if attacked, but rather that Wright greatly overemphasizes this aggressive response, probably based on his own Western assumptions, when he creates the category called *defensive war* and then puts *all* nonwarring societies into the category.[11] An examination of the ethnographic record does not support the viability of this assumption.

A second point to explore is whether there are grounds for updating some of the ratings assigned by Wright. Ethnographic information shows that some societies originally coded as warring in actuality do *not* war or feud. The Kadar (Kardar), Kurumba (Korumba), and Yanadi, for example, were coded by Wright as practicing *economic war,* but further ethnographic study shows that these groups are in actuality nonwarring.[12]

A strong case can be made for upgrading certain societies to *defensive war* status—that is, engaging in *no war and no feuding*. Without a doubt, the Paliyan (Paniyan) and Birhor are nonwarring and nonfeuding.[13] Geoffrey Gorer has shown that the Lepchas do not feud or make war.[14] The neighboring Toda, Badaga (Badoga), Irulas, and Kurumbas (the last one of these four having been mentioned earlier) lack war and feuding; only the killings of suspected sorcerers, homicides in other words, have been reported.[15] The Baiga (Bygas) also appear deserving of the *no war* rating instead of the *social war (unwarlike)* coding given to them by Wright.[16] A reevaluation also seems to be called for regarding Wright's classification of *all* Australian Aborigines in the sample as having *social war*. *Social war* probably *is* appropriate for some Australian Aborigine societies wherein feuding is documented. However, not *all* Australian Aborigines engage in feuding, a point illustrated by the nonwarring and nonfeuding Mardudjara.[17] The Mardudjara and other such Australian cases more appropriately fit the *no war and no feud* criteria of Wright's *defensive war*. In sum, based on a number of specific examples just mentioned, sixty-some years after Wright reported the results of this mammoth warfare categorization project, it now seems clear that a number of societies that fully meet the criteria of the *defensive war* category—having *no war and no feuding*—have been listed under inappropriate labels.

As a related point, we may also return to the question: How many *unwarlike* ratings—that is, Wright's *social war* codings—are due *only* to the presence of feuding in the society? A quick overview of Wright's classifications again suggests that a number of Australian Aborigine societies and perhaps some other cultures such as the Badjus, Veddahs, and Algonquins, among others, have been coded as having *social war* based on the presence of feuding alone. A careful updating of Wright's classifications based on more extensive ethnographic data would be needed to address this issue.

What can we conclude from all this? Despite Wright's labels that imply that some kind of warfare exists in all 590 societies, a closer look at the categories reveals that by Wright's own definitions, 64 percent of the cross-cultural sample are *not warring or unwarlike*. Some of the *social war* societies practice mild forms of warfare, such as headhunting, but some others are classified under *social war* solely on the basis of feuding. We have explored the conceptual differences between warfare and feuding and argued that feuding should not be subsumed under the label of war. In any case, *Wright's findings show the cross-cultural spectrum of human societies to be less warlike than typically assumed*. This important observation has not received much attention, perhaps in part because Wright labeled *all* societies as practicing some form of "war." Furthermore, Wright's category *defensive war* assumes that *all* societies would use a counterattack option while ignoring other possible responses to attack such as fleeing. Finally, a more extensive consideration of ethnographic data suggests that Wright's *no war and no feuding* classification has been short-changed as societies appropriate to this category were mistakenly placed in other categories. Do we see in Wright's scheme a set of Hobbesian assumptions that lead, in this case rather subtly, to overemphasizing warfare and underappreciating peace?[18]

TYPES OF SOCIAL ORGANIZATION

In chapter 2, bands, tribes, chiefdoms, and states were introduced as the major types of human social organization. Social organization must be taken into consideration by anyone who is interested in the origin of war or human justice seeking and conflict management.

In bands and tribes, leadership and political power are weak and dispersed, or *uncentralized*. By contrast, in chiefdoms and especially in states, political power is *centralized* at the top of a social hierarchy.[19] In other words, social relations in bands and tribes are relatively egalitarian compared to those within chiefdoms and states that are structured according to ranks or social classes.[20] Relatedly, hunting-and-gathering societies are of two general types: *Simple nomadic hunter-gatherers* have the *band* type of social organization and are egalitarian, whereas *complex sedentary hunter-gatherers* are small-scale *chiefdoms* due to the presence of social classes or status hierarchies.

THE LINK BETWEEN WARFARE AND SOCIAL ORGANIZATION

From examining the list of nonwarring cultures presented in chapter 7, an interesting observation emerges. Approximately half the nonwarring cultures on the list are band-living simple hunter-gatherers. This observation suggests a question: Is the presence or absence of warfare related to type of social organization?

A number of studies suggests that the answer is *yes*. Sociopolitical complexity and warfare do go hand-in-hand.[21] After reviewing cross-cultural studies on this topic, van der Dennen expresses that "one of the most consistent and robust findings is the correlation between 'primitivity' and absence of war or low-level warfare, or in other words, the correlation between war and civilization."[22] Reading the trends in the worldwide archaeological record, Jonathan Haas correspondingly concludes that "the level, intensity, and impact of warfare tend to increase as cultural systems become more complex."[23]

Bands

Steve Reyna presents a clear overview of the types of aggression and reasons for fighting found at different levels of social organization.[24] Reyna suggests that the *modes of social domination* differ greatly between uncentralized bands and tribes and centralized chiefdoms and states. Seeing the forest as well as the trees, Reyna proposes that even when aggression occurs in band society, it is relatively harmless. People sometimes fight, but grudges are personal affairs. In bands, *most* fighting is between individuals and is nonlethal, although killings can occur. Violence, notes Reyna, is relatively ineffective for controlling people within the egalitarian band type of social organization. In a culturally comparative sense, the title of Elizabeth Thomas' classic book on the Ju/'hoansi (!Kung) hunter-gatherers of the African Kalahari, *The Harmless People,* is apt even in the face of the occasional fights and homicides that occur within this band society.[25] Ju/'hoansi violence is rare and comparatively speaking doesn't amount to much, as we shall consider further in chapter 16.

Bronislaw Malinowski made an observation that is apropos to simple nomadic hunter-gatherers: "Under conditions where portable wealth does not exist; where food is too perishable and too clumsy to be accumulated and transported; where slavery is of no value because every individual consumes exactly as much as he produces—force is a useless implement for the transfer of wealth."[26]

Tribes

Turning to tribal social organization, Reyna points out that aggression still stems from personal grudges, but now can involve *kin militia*.[27] Groups of fighters tend to be related in tribal society because tribal communities are organized on the basis of kin groups. The term *kin militia* is appropriate because fighting groups can be temporarily assembled on the basis of kinship ties. In tribal societies, there are no professional standing armies and no hierarchical military structures. Fighting most often involves brawls and raids, and less often small-scale battles.

Reyna writes of tribes that "the organized means of violence in such polities, though more effective than those found in bands, were still harmless when compared to those found in centralized polities."[28] For example, when the tribal Yanomamö go on a raid, no one has the power to command obedience. Typically, raiders drop out and return home with excuses such as having sore feet or stomach aches.[29] Command structure and authority are very weakly developed within tribal society.

Chiefdoms

Within the centralized polities of chiefdoms, *chiefly militias* come into play. The leaders and military specialists have authority to command obedience from the ranks, as illustrated in large chiefdoms such as Tahiti, Tonga, Fiji, and Hawaii.[30] With chiefdoms, battles become more common than within tribal social organization.

Mead describes warfare between relatively simple village chiefdoms in the eastern part of Samoa. In Fitiuta, a council of 17 members made war-related decisions. Surprise attacks were preferred but arranged battles also took place. When opposing sides met in combat, each group used distinctive headbands or face-paint so as to differentiate more easily friend from foe. Clubs, spears, and shields of bamboo were employed during fighting.[31]

In some large-scale chiefdoms, such as Fiji with its six social classes, warfare involved large, bloody battles. Fijian chiefs tried to put as many men into combat as possible. Although standing armies did not exist and there was no formal draft, every man was expected to fight when ordered onto the field by his chief. Robert Carneiro explains, "Warfare among the Fijians was all-out and bloody, with no respect shown for sex or age. Women and children were killed ruthlessly and indiscriminately." The status and power of a chief could rise with success in war; victory could result in greater prestige, an expanded domain, and more tribute-paying subjects. On Fiji, cannibalism accompanied warfare. Commoners were allowed to feast on slain enemies, and human flesh became a favorite delicacy of some Fijian chiefs. Perhaps the all-time Fijian record was held by a chief named Ra Undreundre, whose self-tallied count of persons consumed came to 900.[32]

Warfare among the chiefdoms of *complex hunter-gatherer* societies deserves special note. Complex hunter-gatherers are rare, exemplified most notably by a cluster of societies from the Northwest Coast of North America such as the Bella Coola, Haida, Klallam, Kwakiutl, Nootka, Tlingit, and Tsimshian.[33] As we shall consider in chapter 10, complex hunter-gatherer societies appear only very recently in archaeological time.[34]

Service points out that along the coastal strip between Northern California and Southern Alaska, nature provided "hunting-fishing societies with an abundance of food and materials perhaps unsurpassed anywhere in the world, and, consequently, with a standard of living which can be matched only by societies possessing agriculture and domestic animals." Ferguson provides a thorough examination of warfare among some of the chiefdoms of the North American Northwest Coast. The complex hunter-gatherers of this cultural area shared certain features: They subsisted largely on marine resources (such as abundant and highly valued salmon runs), lived in hierarchical class societies (consisting of chiefs or nobles, commoners, and often slaves), had highly developed arts, rituals, and economies based on the redistribution of goods, and, last but not least, engaged in warfare (see Figure 8.1).[35]

In this region, archaeological evidence suggests warfare over at least 3,000 years, extending into historical times. Attacks often were carried out by sea, as raiders paddled scores or even hundreds of miles carrying their provisions with them. "War parties varied in size from a few canoes to huge flotillas with many hundred men. . . . Generally, the attitude toward war was pragmatic. Tactics were tailored to maximize enemy casualties and captives," writes Ferguson.[36] Wars apparently stemmed from multiple motivations such as gaining access to bountiful resources like salmon runs, acquiring slaves, exacting revenge for past wrongs, and gaining additional territory to support expanding populations.

Figure 8.1 This drawing of a Nootka house from 1778 by John Webber shows living units for multiple families. As complex hunter-gatherers from the Northwest Coast of North America, the Nootka stored food (note the supply of dried fish hanging from the rafters), lived in villages, had chiefs, and made war. Compare this large, solid Nootka residence to the Batek hut pictured in Figure 14.1, whose small size and comparatively basic construction are features typical of shelters constructed by simple nomadic hunter-gatherers. (Photo courtesy of Harvard University's Peabody Museum of Archaeology and Ethnology; see Kelly 1995.)

TABLE 8.1 Contrasts between complex and simple hunter-gatherers

Variable	Simple Hunter-Gatherers	Complex Hunter-Gatherers
Primary food	Terrestrial game	Marine resources or plants
Food storage	Very rare	Typical
Mobility	Nomadic or semi-nomadic	Settled or mostly settled
Population	Low population densities	Higher population densities
Political system	Egalitarian	Hierarchical with classes based on wealth or heredity
Social structure	Absence of social segments	Lineages in some cases
Slavery	Absent	Frequent
Competition	Not accepted	Encouraged
Warfare	Rare	Common

Source: Table adapted from Kelly 1995:294: Table 8.1.

A Comparison of Simple and Complex Hunter-Gatherers

Before considering states, it is important to review several differences between simple hunter-gatherers (as archetypal nomadic *bands*) and complex hunter-gatherers (as low-level *chiefdoms*). Robert Kelly notes that the image of simple hunter-gatherers entails "small, *peaceful,* nomadic bands, men and women with few possession[s] and who are equal in wealth, opportunity, and status."[37] Kelly next generalizes that "complex hunter-gatherers are nonegalitarian societies, whose elites possess slaves, *fight wars,* and overtly seek prestige."[38] Some distinguishing points are summarized in Table 8.1. One important observation is that lumping simple and complex forager societies together and then trying to make catchall generalizations about *hunter-gatherer peace and war* is an undertaking that is doomed to create confusion from the start.[39] We will return to this topic in more detail in chapter 14.

Kelly's assessment about warfare occurring in complex hunter-gatherer societies more regularly than in simple hunter-gatherer bands can be systematically tested.[40] Recall that a cross-cultural sample, the SCCS, representing 186 cultural provinces of the world exists.[41] Separately, George Murdock has published coded information on hundreds of societies, for instance, on how people make a living; in what type of settlements people live; whether or not a society has a class system and, if so, what type; whether horses are used in the society; and so forth.[42]

If we define hunter-gatherer societies as having *at most* five percent subsistence dependence on agriculture and animal husbandry, the SCCS contains 35 hunter-gatherer societies. By examining other Murdock codes, these hunter-gatherer societies can be divided into three subgroups.[43] Simple hunter-gatherers are those societies rated as nomadic or semi-nomadic, lacking domestic animals including horses, and lacking class distinctions. Complex hunter-gatherers are those rated as *not* being nomadic or as having social class distinctions. Equestrian hunter-gatherers, those societies relying on horses for hunting, are a third type of society of very recent origin. These ratings yield 21 simple hunter-gatherer societies, nine complex hunter-gatherer societies, and five equestrian hunter-gatherer societies. It is possible also to use ethnographic information for each society to classify it as *warring* or *nonwarring* according to Prosterman's definition of war.[44] Table 8.2 provides codes, warring/nonwarring ratings, and corresponding references for each of the 35 societies.

The essential finding is that all the complex hunter-gatherers and all the equestrian hunter-gatherers make war, whereas a majority of the simple hunter-gatherers do not. It appears that both social complexity and adoption of the horse greatly increase the

TABLE 8.2 Warfare among simple nomadic hunter-gatherers compared with other kinds of hunter-gatherers

The sample constitutes all 35 hunter-gatherer societies in the Standard Cross-Cultural Sample. The Prosterman definition of warfare, discussed in chapter 7, is used in the construction of this table.

Society (SCCS number)	Settlement Code[a]	Social Class Code[b]	Equestrian	Warfare
Simple Nomadic Hunter-Gatherers				
!Kung[1] (2) (Ju/'hoansi)	B	O	No	No
Hadza[2] (9)	B	O	No	No
Mbuti[3] (13)	B	O	No	No
Semang[4] (77)	B	O	No	No
Andamanese[5] (79)	S	O	No	No
Vedda[6] (80)	S	O	No	No
Tiwi[7] (90)	B	O	No	No
Aranda/Arunta[8] (91)	B	O	No	No
Copper Eskimo[9] (124)	S	O	No	No
Saulteaux[10] (127)	S	O	No	No
Slave[11] (128) (Slavey)	S	O	No	No
Paiute[12] (137)	S	O	No	No
Yahgan[13] (186)	B	O	No	No
Gilyak[14] (119)	S	O	No	Yes
Yukaghir[15] (120)	S	O	No	Yes
Ingalik[16] (122)	S	O	No	Yes
Montagnais[17] (125)	B	O	No	Yes
Micmac[18] (126)	S	O	No	Yes
Kaska[19] (129)	S	O	No	Yes
Botocudo[20] (178)	B	O	No	Yes
Aweikoma[21] (180)	B	O	No	Yes
Complex Hunter-Gatherers				
Aleut[22](123)	V	O	No	Yes
Eyak[23] (130)	V	W	No	Yes
Haida[24] (131)	V	D	No	Yes
Bella Coola[25] (132)	V	D	No	Yes
Twana[26] (133)	T	W	No	Yes
Yurok[27] (134)	V	W	No	Yes
Eastern Pomo[28] (135)	T	W	No	Yes
Yokuts[29] (136)	S	W	No	Yes
Klamath[30] (138)	S	W	No	Yes

TABLE 8.2 *(Continued)*

Society (SCCS number)	Settlement Code[a]	Social Class Code[b]	Equestrian	Warfare
Equestrian Hunter-Gatherers				
Kutenai[31] (139)	B	O	Yes	Yes
Gros Ventre[32] (140)	B	O	Yes	Yes
Comanche[33] (147)	B	O	Yes	Yes
Chiricahua Apache[34] (148)	B	O	Yes	Yes
Tehuelche[35] (185)	B	O	Yes	Yes

[a] The settlement codes, Murdock's column 30 (see 1981:99), are as follows: B = "Fully migratory or nomadic bands"; S = "Seminomadic communities whose members wander in bands for at least half the year but occupy a fixed settlement at some season or seasons, e.g., recurrently occupied winter quarters"; T = "Semisedentary communities whose members shift from one to another fixed settlement at different seasons, or who occupy more or less permanently a single settlement from which a substantial proportion of the population departs seasonally to occupy shifting camps, e.g., during transhumance"; V = "Compact and relatively permanent settlements, i.e., nucleated villages and towns."

[b] Class stratification codes, Murdock's column 67 (see 1981:101–102), are as follows: O = "Absence of significant class distinctions among freemen . . . ignoring variations in individual repute achieved through skill, valor, piety, or wisdom"; D = "Dual stratification into a hereditary aristocracy and a lower class of ordinary commoners or freemen, where traditionally ascribed noble status is at least as decisive as control over scarce resources"; W = "Wealth distinctions, based on the possession or distribution of property, present and socially important but not crystallized into distinct and hereditary social classes."

Sources: 1. Lee 1979, 1993; Thomas 1959:21–24; Draper 1975:86. 2. Woodburn 1968a:157–158. 3. Turnbull 1965a:218–223; 1968b:341. 4. LeBar et al. 1964:185; Endicott 1983:224, 238; 1993:235; Schebesta 1929:280. 5. Radcliffe-Brown 1922:49–50, 84-87; Pandya 1992:11. 6. Seligmann & Seligmann 1969:34; Davie 1929:50–51; Hobhouse 1956:105; Stegeborn 1999:271. 7. Hart & Pilling 1979:85, 79–87; Hart, Pilling, & Goodale 1988:93–95; Goodale 1991:329. 8. Spencer & Gillen 1927:27–28. 9. Damas 1972, 1991. 10. Hallowell 1974:278. 11. Kelly 2000:53; Asch & Smith 1999:48; Asch 1981:343; Rushforth 1991. 12. Kelly & Fowler 1986:368–370; Fowler 1991:332. 13. Cooper 1946a:95; Gusinde 1937:885, 893. 14. Shternberg 1999 & 1933 in the HRAF. 15. Jochelson 1926:118. 16. Osgood 1958:61–65. 17. Lips 1947:399; Leacock 1978:249. 18. Le Clercq 1910 in HRAF:237, 265–270; Wallis & Wallis 1955. 19. Honigmann 1954:88–98. 20. Métraux 1946a:467, 1946c:536. 21. Métraux 1946a:467; Henry 1941 in the HRAF:55, 89–90. 22. Veltre 1991:16. 23. Birket-Smith & de Laguna 1938:145–152, 464–468. 24. Swanton 1975:54–56; Ferguson 1984b; Murdock 1934:241; Donald 2000. 25. Ferguson 1984b. 26. Elmendorf 1974: Chapter 11, 1993. 27. Hester 1991:395; McCorkle 1978; see also Kroeber 1953:49–52; Elmendorf 1974:466 note 4; Spier 1930 in the electronic version of the Human Relations Area Files (eHRAF):24. 28. Gifford 1926 in eHRAF:342; Oswalt 1991:295; McCorkle 1978. 29. Gayton 1948 in eHRAF:9; McCorkle 1978. 30. Spier 1930 in eHRAF:24–25; Martin 1991:192. 31. Turney-High 1941:161–169; Secoy 1992:33. 32. Kehoe 1999. 33. Hoebel 1967a, 1967b; Kehoe 1999; Wallace & Hoebel 1952. 34. Basso 1971. 35. Musters 1873 in HRAF:60, 97, 148–149, 231, 322–324.

chance of warfare. Combining the relatively small number of complex and equestrian groups together allows a statistical comparison to be made between simple nomadic hunter-gatherers versus the other types of hunter-gatherer societies. As shown in Table 8.3, the results are very significant.[45]

Finally, a couple of words about differences in war *intensity and severity* between simple and complex hunter-gatherers are in order. The ethnographic descriptions suggest an overall pattern: Warfare among complex hunter-gatherers tends to be more serious than among simple hunter-gatherers. For example, Eleanor Leacock writes of nomadic Montagnais-Naskapi bands that "warfare was minimal or nonexistent."[46] Similarly, Jules Henry's portrayal of the nomadic Aweikoma suggests more instances of murder

TABLE 8.3 Warring versus nonwarring and type of society

Simple nomadic hunter-gatherers are in the top row. Other types of hunter-gatherers are in the bottom row. Following Prosterman and Otterbein, war is defined as involving armed combat between political communities and *not* merely as feuding and revenge homicide (see chapter 7 for discussion). Societies are classified based on Murdock's codes as presented in Table 8.2. The results are highly significant.

Nonwarring (n = 13)		Warring (n = 22)	
Simple Hunter-Gatherers			
!Kung	Aranda	Montagnais	Gilyak
Hadza	Copper Eskimo	Ingalik	Micmac
Mbuti	Andamanese	Botocudo	Kaska
Semang	Saulteaux	Aweikoma	Yukaghir
Vedda	Paiute		
Tiwi	Yahgan		
Slave			
Other Hunter-Gatherers			
		Bella Coola	Haida
		Gros Ventre	Yurok
		Comanche	Yokuts
		Chiricahua	Kutenai
		Tehuelche	Twana
		Klamath	Eyak
		Eastern Pomo	Aleut

Fisher's exact test (one-tailed) probability, $p = .0001$.

and feuding than warfare, although Henry makes reference to ancient enemies: "[The Aweikoma] have no idea of coming together and forming a solid unit against an outside aggressor. For them there was safety only in wakefulness and flight. Whoever pursues them constantly has them at his mercy, for they become panic-stricken and never turn to face their pursuers until they are brought to bay like hunted animals."[47]

Regarding the Gilyak, Lev Shternberg singles out two motivations for "war" among these simple hunter-gatherers: competition over a woman and avenging the death of a clan member. Shternberg writes, "Indeed, what the Gilyak called wars in ancient times were in fact nothing more than sporadic clan skirmishes motivated by vengeance or, even more frequently, were over women. The Gilyak have never known war as a profession."[48]

Turning to complex hunter-gatherer societies, we see, as a *pattern,* an increase in the severity of fighting. Murdock calls the complex hunting-and-gathering Haida "the Vikings of the coast" and reports that "they fight amongst themselves over real or fancied injuries, and they wage relentless war, partly for revenge but mainly for plunder, against the Tlingits, Tsimshian, and Bellabella." Marlene Martin reports that the Klamath, a hunter-gatherer society from Oregon and northern California that had given up nomadism, had chiefs, valued wealth, and evidenced a number of other cultural features typical of the complex hunter-gatherer societies of the Northwest Coastal region, warred for revenge, plunder, and slaves. Their enemies included the Shasta, Takelma, Kalapuya, and other groups. The raiding and warring of equestrian groups such as the Comanche and Chiricahua Apache also are well known. These examples suggest an overall pattern. Not only is war more likely to exist in complex and equestrian hunter-gatherer societies than in simple foraging bands, but also if warfare is practiced by simple nomadic foragers, it tends to be less severe than in other kinds of hunter-gatherer societies.[49]

States

Readers are probably intimately familiar with the state form of social organization because today's world is divided into nation-states. State sociopolitical organization, which most people simply take for granted today, is actually a *very recent* social development. The first archaic states arose a mere 5,000–6,000 years ago, and the birth of the nation-state is usually attributed to the year A.D. 1648 with the signing of the Treaty of Westphalia—a mere 350-some years ago.

States, ancient and modern, tend to have large permanent armies led by military specialists operating within hierarchical command structures.[50] Under such conditions, elaborate military campaigns and protracted wars are possible. The recent military outlay of one current nation-state, the United States, is unprecedented in the history of the world, exceeding 300 billion dollars a year.[51] The differences in fighting tactics between bands and tribal societies and those used by even small states are immense. The tribal Yanomamö's typical tactic is for raiders to hide outside an enemy village in the predawn hours, attempt to kill some unlucky person leaving the village at daybreak, and then run for their lives.[52] But returning to the military apparatus of the state, Reyna uses a specific case to illustrate a broader idea: "Caesar's legions did not ambush a few Gauls and then run for home. Rather, they stayed for the duration—the remaining five hundred years of the empire."[53]

SOCIAL ORGANIZATION AND SEEKING JUSTICE

Social organization also relates to seeking justice.[54] In uncentralized bands and tribes, rarely does anyone command enough influence to enforce a judgment. Courts of law, judicial authorities, police, mental hospitals, and prisons are all lacking. Within chiefdoms and states, adjudication becomes feasible with the advent of the social hierarchy. Those at the top have the authority to judge and the power to enforce their rulings. It is not uncommon to read in ethnographic accounts of chiefs imposing judgments. After all, the power to make rulings and to sentence commoners are marks of chiefly authority. On the Pacific Island called Tikopia, chiefs sometimes settle land disputes; among the Nootka of the Northwest Coast of North America, the head chief could sentence a malefactor to death (see Figure 8.2).[55]

We have seen that humans use a wide array of nonviolent methods to deal with conflicts on a daily basis. Across all levels of social organization, people practice avoidance, toleration, and negotiation. Avoidance is particularly easy to employ within band society as antagonists simply separate into different groups.

The third-party roles of *friendly peacemaker* and *mediator* are also widespread across the ethnographic spectrum. A recurrent theme, as we considered in chapter 3, is that friendly peacemakers intervene to separate or distract antagonists, either before or during physical altercations. Across different forms of social organization, third parties also act as mediators and assist disputants in finding mutually acceptable solutions to their problems.[56] In short, informal friendly peacemakers and mediators are present and

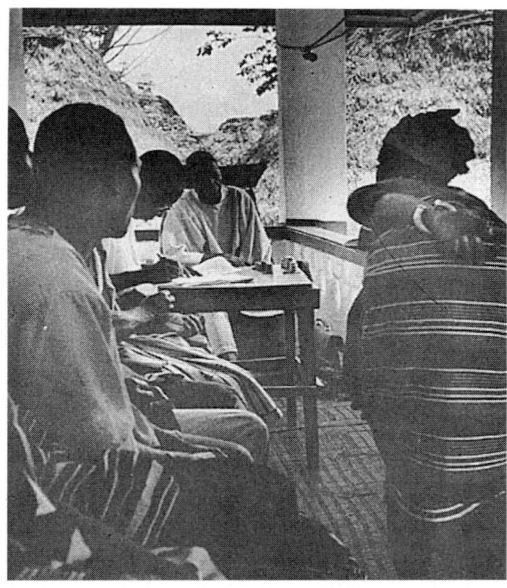

Figure 8.2 Adjudication is most typical within chiefdoms and states. Among the Kpelle of Liberia, paramount chiefs preside as judges over civil cases involving, for instance, physical assault, breach of contract, or disputes between men over a woman. Sanctions handed down by the chiefly judge may include orders to pay damages to plaintiffs, assessments of fines, and the imposition of short jail sentences. A paramount chief, in the role of judge, is seated at a table as he listens to a witness during a trial. (Photo from *Peoples of Africa* by James L. Gibbs, copyright © 1965 by Holt, Rinehart and Winston, Inc., renewed 1993 by James Lowell Gibbs, Jr., reprinted by permission of the publisher.)

active everywhere. Furthermore, in some societies mediation processes have become institutionalized—as in the *becharaa'* assembly of the Semai; the *ho'oponopono* of Hawaiian families; the *pancayat* of Indians living on Fiji and elsewhere; the *tultulan,* or collective discussion, of the Buid of the Philippines; and *school* and *community mediation programs* in countries such as Finland, Norway, and the United States.[57]

Although violence may be the most noticeable way through which people handle conflict, an examination of cross-cultural data reveals that people usually deal with conflicts without using any physical aggression at all. Humans have a great capacity for getting along with each other peacefully, preventing physical aggression, limiting the scope and spread of violence when it does break out, and restoring peace following aggression.[58]

Taking Justice into One's Own Hands

What about violent approaches to seeking justice? Anthropologists use the term *self-redress* for when a person with a grievance takes unilateral action against another individual. *Self-redress* is a coercive approach and sometimes involves violence. If violence is not directly used, then the threat of violence may linger in the background. The phrase "taking justice into one's own hands" catches the essence of *self-redress,* whether lethal or not.

One problem with using *self-redress* is that the actor's "justice" may be perceived by the recipient as "un-just," as an unwarranted or overzealous attack. This is one reason why self-redress can lead to the escalation of conflict. Consider the following example from Jan Brögger's fieldwork in southern Italy. To make charcoal, Domenico cut down some trees along the property line he shared with Guiseppe. Guiseppe requested some of the charcoal, thinking he had partial claim to this common resource, but Domenico refused to give him any. As a result of an ensuing argument, Guiseppe became furious and stole some of Domenico's rabbits. Domenico retaliated by cutting down Guiseppe's vineyard late one night. Ultimately, an enraged Guiseppe killed Domenico.[59]

Diverse ethnographic accounts suggest that people know the dangers set in motion by the use of self-redress and more often than not seek to avoid unbridled cycles of violence. Boehm comments on the paradox. Among tribal Montenegrins—a culture that placed great value on defending one's honor—disputes very rarely led to lethal blood feuds (see Figure 8.3).

> As a self-assertive Montenegrin warrior, then, a man's mission was to maximize his own reputation and honor at the same time that he minimized the risk of getting himself killed from ambush or of getting his kinsmen or tribe into deep trouble. . . . With a warrior people who played this game very hard, it would not be surprising if there were quite a large number of feuds; indeed, what is remarkable is that there were relatively few.[60]

Figure 8.3 Montenegrins of the Balkans are a tribal society divided into social segments called *brastvos,* or clans. During blood feuds in former times, the principle of social substitutability applied. In an incident witnessed by Christopher Boehm, a dozen or so men limit the movement of an angry man: "Almost all of the men who are restraining the quarreler are members of his clan and therefore are expected to watch out for his welfare. In traditional times, if he had injured or killed someone, his own clan brothers might have been liable for retaliatory homicide." Thus the members of the disputant's clan, as *interested* third parties, are engaging in *friendly peacemaking* as they keep an antagonist away from his rival. (Photo courtesy of Christopher Boehm; quote from Boehm 1987:98.)

Is there a relationship between the use of self-redress and type of social organization? Based on a careful examination of systems of justice in 650 societies representing different kinds of social organization, Hobhouse, Wheeler, and Ginsberg reached a conclusion in 1915 that has stood the test of time. Self-redress is most common among hunter-gatherer subsistence systems and steadily *decreases* in use as patterns of subsistence shift toward agriculture or herding. In their large cross-cultural sample, Hobhouse and his colleagues found self-redress to be present in about 90 percent of the simplest hunter-gatherer societies but in less than 15 percent of the most agriculturally reliant societies. These researchers concluded that "as we mount the [economic/social organizational] scale there is more government and more of the public administration of justice within society."[61]

A half century later, Hoebel expressed a similar conclusion about how law and justice are painted across the wide canvas of social organization: "the tendency is to shift the privilege rights of prosecution and imposition of legal sanctions from the *individual* [as in self-redress] and his *kin-group* [as in feuding] over to clearly defined *public officials* representing the society as such [as in courts of law]."[62] The main point is that the key administrators of justice sequentially change as social complexity increases from the individual, then to kin groups, and eventually to public officials.

Based on data from the 186 societies in the SCCS, Ericksen and Horton reach conclusions about vengeance-seeking that correspond with the earlier findings of Hobhouse and his colleagues and substantiate the generalizations offered by Hoebel. Ericksen and Horton report that *individual* self-redress is about seven times more likely among hunter-gatherer *band* societies than in all other types of societies. Additionally, Ericksen and Horton compared the likelihood of self-redress in unstratified or egalitarian societies—that is, the pattern typically found in uncentralized bands and tribes—and in stratified or hierarchical societies—basically, chiefdoms and states—and found over five times the self-redress among the unstratified group. Finally, Ericksen and Horton found adjudication to dominate in the most complex type of political economies. In other words, well-developed chiefdoms and states usurp from individuals and kin groups the right to administer justice. In modern states, homicides rarely result in individual acts of self-redress or in feuding between kin groups. Instead, most citizens accept that the administration of justice lies in the hands of the state. Should a person take the law into his or her own hands, the state judicial system treats such acts of self-redress as new crimes, not as the legitimate administration of justice. States claim the right and duty to administer justice.[63]

Chagnon recounts an anecdote that highlights the difference between seeking justice via revenge, as in self-redress and feuding, approaches that are common in uncentralized societies, and the adjudicatory mechanisms found in hierarchical societies such as states, as represented by Venezuela in this account:

> A particularly acute insight into the power of law to thwart killing for revenge was provided to me by a young Yanomamö man in 1987. He had been taught Spanish by missionaries and sent to the territorial capital for training in practical nursing. There he discovered police and laws. He excitedly told me that he had visited the town's largest *pata* (the territorial governor) and urged him to make law and police available to his people so that they would not have to engage any longer in their wars of revenge and have to

> live in constant fear. Many of his close kinsmen had died violently and had, in turn, exacted lethal revenge; he worried about being a potential target of retaliations and made it known to all that he would have nothing to do with raiding.[64]

On Feuding

As the foregoing discussion demonstrates, *individual* self-redress is relatively more likely in band societies than in hierarchical societies. However, feuding that pits kin group against kin group is *not* typical of foraging bands for the simple reason that most band societies lack cohesive kin organizations.[65] As will be documented in chapter 13, band societies tend not to exclusively emphasize either matrilineal or patrilineal kinship segments, but instead pay attention to both mother's and father's descent lines. What this means is that in a majority of simple forager societies, each person thinks in terms of his or her own unique set of relatives. Of course, the kin networks of two individuals may overlap, but even two brothers in most cases will have different kin networks after marriage due to each having a different set of in-laws. In short, the individually oriented patterns of kinship in band society cut across various nomadic groups, creating webs of *interlinking ties among different bands.*

Another way of putting this is that simple nomadic foraging bands are more likely to be *unsegmented,* or only weakly segmented, compared to other types of societies that have clear subunits such as lineages or clans.[66] Raymond Kelly points out that in unsegmented societies, "a homicide is consequently likely to be perceived and experienced as an individual loss shared with some kin rather than as an injury to a group."[67] This is a main reason why *individual* self-redress occurs more frequently than protracted feuding in simple band societies that tend to lack the types of well-developed social segments typically present in more complex societies.[68]

Once social segmentation enters the picture, a killing is perceived as a loss not only to the victim's immediate family, but more generally to members of the same patrilineage, subclan, clan, and so on. In seeking revenge, the victim's larger kin organization may target *anyone* belonging to the killer's social segment. Following the lead of Meyer Fortes, Kelly refers to this phenomenon as *social substitutability*. In segmented societies that allow payback killings, it is likely that the particular malefactor is no longer the only legitimate target of revenge.[69]

To highlight another recurring pattern among simple nomadic foragers, *the targets of lethal revenge tend to be the killers themselves.*[70] This tendency is clearly apparent, for example, in Ju/'hoansi homicide data.[71] Of 22 homicides, 11 were initial homicides.[72] Revenge was sought against four of the killers, attempts that ultimately led to 11 more violent deaths, including the four killers themselves, one relative of a killer, and several revenge-seekers and bystanders. Much of the bloodshed revolved around repeated attempts to execute two of the original four killers, who were notoriously violent men.[73]

In simple nomadic band societies that either lack social segments or in which they are only weakly developed, at times justice is achieved when a killer is killed.[74] A balance is restored between two families and this typically ends the matter. In segmented societies, whether tribes or chiefdoms, retaliatory justice seeking may alternate back and forth between feuding clans or lineages. Each killing prompts a retaliation, which in turn prompts

TABLE 8.4 A model of lethal aggression in relation to social organization

	Nomadic Hunter-Gatherer Bands	Tribes	Chiefdoms	States
Self-redress revenge homicide	*Typical*	Variable	Rare	Rare
Feud	Rare	*Typical*	Variable	Rare
Warfare	Rare	Variable	*Typical*	*Typical*

Individual self-redress homicide is typical of simple nomadic hunter-gatherer society. Such societies tend to lack the corporate kin groups (e.g., clans and patrilineages) that typify tribal society. In tribal society, revenge seeking shifts from individuals to kin groups and thus feuding becomes possible. Feuding is repressed once central authority develops, as within chiefdoms and, especially, states. A series of cross-cultural studies show that warfare is most common and most fully developed in chiefdoms and states. This model is intended to reflect the broad cross-cultural patterns or central tendencies, not invariable, universal features. See the chapter text for further discussion.

a counter-retaliation and then a counter-counter-retaliation. In other words, social substitutability can facilitate feuding. Among nation-states, social substitutability can facilitate war, as one act of violence (for instance, a terrorist attack) provokes retaliation *not* solely against the actual perpetrators, but against anyone labeled as belonging to the same national or religious group as the attackers. Clearly the idea of social substitutability has great relevance for understanding some types of warfare and intergroup violence in today's world.

Table 8.4 summarizes this cross-cultural model of how social organization relates to individual lethal self-redress, feud, and war. Lethal individual self-redress, although not universally present, is typical of bands, feuds are typical in tribes, and warfare is typical in chiefdoms and states. Table 8.4 reflects relative *tendencies* that are apparent across numerous anthropological studies, not absolutes.[75] Adding social organization to the equation and untangling individual self-redress, feud, and war from one another expands our knowledge about overall patterns of lethal conflict.

The case involving the Italian peasants, Domenico and Guiseppe, illustrates the danger of unilaterally seeking justice through revenge whether by self-redress, feud, or war.[76] One party's justice seeking may precipitate retaliation from the other side, leading to a spiral of escalating abuses.[77] Conflict resolution, a social art highly developed in humans, offers alternative paths to justice that make unnecessary the violence of self-redress, feud, and war. The cross-cultural data demonstrate the wealth of nonviolent approaches that humans regularly employ to make the balance—to attain just solutions to conflicts—without breaking the peace.[78]

A central challenge of the 21st century is to extend to the international level—*among* nation-states—the types of conflict resolution and judicial procedures that effectively provide justice and keep the peace *within* democratic nation-states today. The same inherent problems of attaining justice in band society occur within an international system that lacks overarching authority and that allows self-redress in the form of war-making among nations. As Hoebel points out, the seeking of justice through self-redress among the equestrian Comanche is "exactly comparable to that observed among nations which recognize certain practices of international law, but which reserve to themselves the sovereign right to resort to force if things don't suit them. Then, in the words of [a Comanche man named] Post Oak Jim, 'Lots of trouble, lots of people hurt.'"[79]

IMPLICATIONS

Patterns of fighting, conflict management, and justice seeking all relate to social organization. As we will consider in future chapters, some theorists of warfare have ignored social organization and in so doing have made a host of untenable assumptions. Overlooking social organization has led to speculations, for instance, as to the importance of military leadership among hunter-gatherer *bands* in the human past. Such ideas are dubious from the onset due to the virtual absence of authoritative leadership in band society. In theorizing about the nature of warfare and the nature of human nature, we ignore social organization only at our peril.

In egalitarian band society each person exercises a high degree of personal autonomy. In nomadic band society, authority is minimal and leadership is weak. Whereas no one has the authority to adjudicate disputes or hand down enforceable judgments, neither does anyone have the authority to order others into military action. A further ramification of high personal autonomy in band society is that each individual is largely left up to his or her own devices in pursuing personal grievances. Additionally, patrilineal and matrilineal kin segments either are lacking or only weakly developed, and this is one of several factors that works against the development of social substitutability and kin-based collective military action. The other side of the coin is that *individual* self-redress is more common in forager bands than in other types of societies, and, not surprisingly given the personal nature of disputes and lack of lineage development, the desired target of self-redress tends to be the actual perpetrator of a misdeed.

In tribal society, leadership is only slightly more developed than in bands. Individuals still have a high level of personal autonomy. Both bands and tribes lack social hierarchies and class stratification. However, tribal societies, in contrast to most bands, tend to be segmented into subunits on the basis of kinship. Individual grievances can become the basis for feuds between kin groups, spreading well beyond the original disputants themselves. It is this type of kin-based feuding that the Yanomamö man in Chagnon's story would like the Venezuelan nation-state to step in and stop.[80]

Stratified, centralized societies—chiefdoms and states—present a very mixed blessing. Social stratification and resulting positions of leadership open the door for a plethora of injustices and cruelties that come with warfare, slavery, and other types of exploitation by unchecked power-wielders. As Reyna emphasizes, in centralized polities, the power of some people to dominate and control others increases many times over what is possible at the level of bands and tribes.[81]

Modern democracies attempt to prevent the most flagrant abuses of power and to protect the rights of citizens. With increasing authority and leadership, adjudication of disputes also becomes feasible, largely eliminating justice seeking through individual self-redress and kin-group feuding. Herein lies an important message: *The types of judicial principles currently used within nation-states theoretically could be applied among nation-states to create institutions for resolving disputes and assuring international justice that do not rely on each nation's self-claimed right to use force.* This judicial solution repeatedly has been implemented within democratic nation-states as an alternative to self-redress. The idea also offers a viable alternative to the current global self-redress war system, under which, to again quote Post Oak Jim, "lots of trouble, lots of people hurt."

CHAPTER 9

PARADISE DENIED

A Bizarre Case of Skullduggery

> Peaceable preindustrial people constitute a nuisance to most theories of warfare and they are thus either "explained away," denied, or negated.
>
> JOHAN VAN DER DENNEN[1]

In *Demonic Males,* Wrangham and Peterson attempt to convince their readers that human and chimpanzee violence stem directly from an ancestral ape common to both species. They propose that human males are violent by temperament, and that modern humans are "the dazed survivors of a continuous, 5-million-year habit of lethal aggression."[2] Later they suggest that "This notion of the violent male seems reasonable to anyone familiar with crime statistics, and explains why we can't find paradise on earth."[3] Wrangham and Peterson are linking two propositions. The first proposition, that human males engage in severe physical aggression on the average more than do human females, is supported by much evidence including crime statistics from diverse countries.[4] However, the second proposition regarding the absence of "paradise," or, more precisely, that "neither in history nor around the globe today is there evidence of a truly peaceful society," obviously *is false*.[5]

First and most importantly, as we have seen, this second proposition is contradicted by the existence of numerous societies with extremely low levels of internal violence and a substantial assemblage of societies that rarely or never engage in war. Additionally, there are problems of logic here—as becomes apparent if we consider an analogy involving female and male height. The evidence showing that within given societies males are taller on the average than females cannot be used as an argument that societies with relatively short people do not exist. That is, evidence of sex differences *within* societies (for example, height or crime rates) does not in and of itself speak to the amount of variability (in height or crime rates) that exists *among* societies. Sex differences in male and female height no more demonstrate that Efe pygmies do not exist than sex differences in male and female crime rates demonstrate that peaceful societies do not exist. This point is illustrated visually in Figure 9.1.

Wrangham and Peterson are aware that the existence of nonwarring cultures and internally peaceful societies contradict their assertion about the "ubiquity of warfare and violence across time and space."[6] Their solution to this mismatch between their views and the anthropological data is to omit relevant information from the discussion

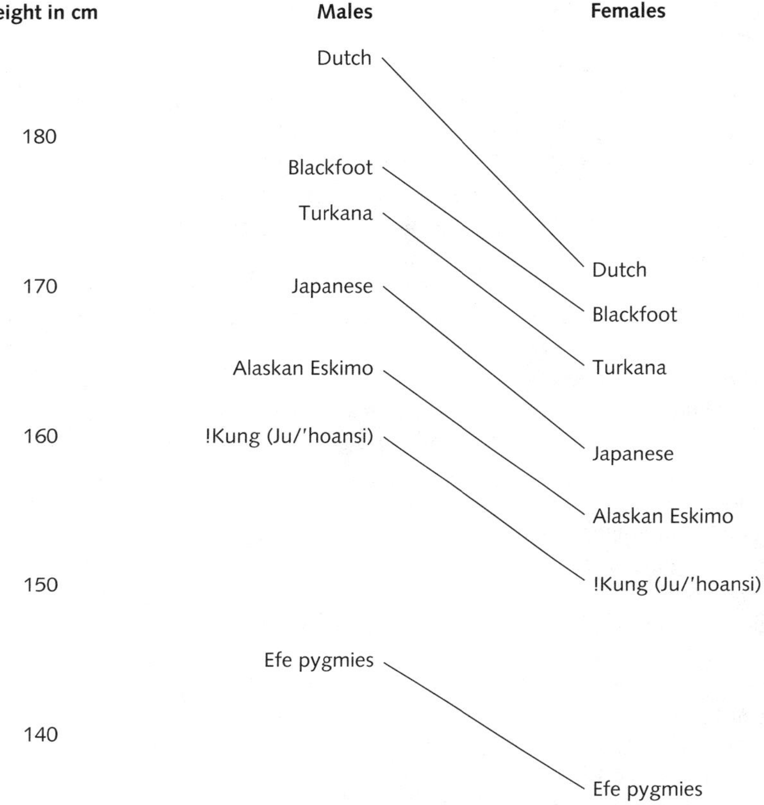

Figure 9.1 Sex differences in average adult height in representative populations. Adult height is affected by a number of interacting variables, including genetics, hormones, disease, and diet (see Stinson 2000). Across many societies, a recurring pattern is evident: The male *average* height is greater than the female *average* height. This does not mean, of course, that every woman in a given population is shorter than every man. The figure shows that average height differences also occur *from one population to the next* for both males and females. The figure illustrates visually that it is illogical to conclude that relatively short-statured populations, such as the Efe pygmies, do not exist based on sex differences in average stature that recur across populations. Likewise, it is illogical to conclude that populations with extremely low homicide rates, such as the Semai or Norwegians, do not exist based on sex differences in committing homicide. (Sources: Jamison 1978: Table 4.1; Stinson 2000: Figure 12.1.)

and to make assertions that simply are not supported by the facts.[7] In attempting to use Samoa as a showcase example to argue a thesis that peaceful cultures are only, in their words, "paradise imagined," Wrangham and Peterson rely heavily on Derek Freeman's lambasting of Margaret Mead's work.[8] The Samoan critique turns out to be built on sand. Before we delve into a strange tale involving myth-weaver Freeman, a couple of preliminary observations about the treatment of peaceful societies in *Demonic Males* are warranted.

In attempting to make peaceful societies disappear, Wrangham and Peterson simply ignore the bulk of the data. To take a specific instance, they mention and dismiss the nonviolent, nonwarring Semai in one paragraph, citing only one reference on this culture. More generally, Wrangham and Peterson ignore nearly all of the sources on peaceful societies published prior to their book, including dozens of articles and relevant books such as Montagu's *Learning Non-Aggression,* Howell and Willis' *Societies at Peace,* Bonta's *Peaceful Peoples,* and Sponsel and Gregor's *Anthropology of Peace and Nonviolence*. When Wrangham and Peterson assume that "no truly peaceful foraging people has ever been found or described in detail," they are wrong on both counts.[9]

Wrangham and Peterson do relate amusing stories about how artist Paul Gauguin and novelist Herman Melville searched in vain for paradise in the South Seas. Supposedly, these stories are offered to add weight to their thesis that a peaceful paradise does not really exist. While the Gauguin and Melville vignettes are interesting, obviously they are poetry, not hard evidence that human males have a violent temperament. An argument that peaceful cultures do not exist cannot rest upon the disillusionment of artists and novelists.

Besides the omissions of relevant information, another problem in *Demonic Males* is the recurring manner in which assertions overstep the facts. As primatologist Robert Sussman clearly documents, Wrangham and Peterson misrepresent the data on chimpanzee aggression.[10]

Another interpretation that oversteps the relevant evidence is when Wrangham and Peterson explain away the peacefulness of four cultures as being due to extreme geographical isolation from other groups. Specifically, Wrangham and Peterson assert that the Toda of India, the Tikopia of Oceania, the Dorobo of Africa, and the Copper Eskimo of North America "had no regular military organizations or warrior class, apparently as a consequence of finding themselves situated, like Switzerland, in extreme geographical isolation from their neighbors."[11] In a general context, Ferguson notes how patterns of trade and intergroup contact link not only local bands but also continents, and he quips: "An 'isolated tribe' is an oxymoron."[12] Are Wrangham and Peterson on solid ground when they emphasize that the four societies in question are extremely isolated?

The Toda clearly are *not* extremely isolated from their neighbors. They live in peaceful association with several neighboring societies—the Kotas, Badagas, Kurumbas, and Irulas—in an area of southern India called the Nilgiri Hills.[13] None of these societies, by the way, engage in warfare.[14] In his classic ethnographic monograph on the Todas originally published in 1906, W. H. R. Rivers devotes an entire chapter to "Relations with Other Tribes." Rivers explains, "The tribes with which the Todas come into contact habitually are the Badagas and Kotas, while their points of contact with Kurumbas and Irulas are much less important."[15] Clearly Wrangham and Peterson's argument that the Toda live in "extreme geographical isolation from their neighbors" does not hold water.[16]

Regarding the Tikopia, their closest neighbors are the Anuta on an island 70 miles away, which at first sounds distant until one finds out that the Anuta are the neighbors of the Tikopia, "*with whom they intermarry*."[17] How can the Tikopia be close enough to intermarry with the Anuta yet too isolated to make war with them? Whereas any island is isolated to some degree, the *extreme isolation* idea begins to founder in this case also. An additional point to keep in mind is that Pacific islanders are known for their ability to traverse long distances of ocean for purposes of visitation, trade, and war.[18]

In the third case, checking the original sources on the Dorobo reveals that these people live in proximity to the Nandi, Maasi, Tuken, Kipsikis, and other cultural groups. G. W. B. Huntingford conducted fieldwork among the Dorobo in 1938–1939, and his findings clearly show that the Dorobo are not extremely isolated from their neighbors. Huntingford reports that the Dorobo speak dialects of the neighboring Nandi language, suggesting long-standing culture contact, and, furthermore, that the Dorobo intermarry with Nandi and related Keyo and Terik groups. Hence, Wrangham and Peterson's assertion that extreme geographical isolation from neighbors is the reason that the Dorobo do not go to war simply *misses the mark*.[19]

Perhaps geographical isolation does figure into the Copper Eskimos' lack of war, but on the other hand, the Copper Eskimos did have periodic contact with the Netsilik Inuit and the Caribou Inuit.[20] Furthermore, as thoroughly discussed by C. Irwin, for example, there are various other factors to consider regarding the lack of war among the Inuit of the Central Arctic.[21] Clearly, isolation sometimes *can* play a role in preventing war, such as among Polar Eskimos (a group not mentioned by Wrangham and Peterson). However, this extreme isolation explanation fits *only partially or not at all* the four cultures to which Wrangham and Peterson apply it. The main point is that Wrangham and Peterson give the impression that these cultures lack warfare *only because* they are extremely isolated with no neighboring groups to fight—an argument that is clearly contradicted by the facts.

Logically, one cannot prove that no cultures are peaceful by demonstrating that one particular culture turns out not to be peaceful. In emphasizing Samoa to bolster their assertion that peaceful societies in general do not exist, Wrangham and Peterson claim that Mead had erroneously portrayed Samoa as peaceful. They write that Mead thought Samoans had "no war gods, no wars, little serious contention or hatred or violence, and so on."[22]

As I first read Wrangham and Peterson's portrayal of Mead's work, it seemed to me that something strange was going on here. Years ago as an undergraduate student, I had read Mead's classic *Coming of Age in Samoa* and I had no recollection that she in any way emphasized Samoan culture as unaggressive or as lacking war. Furthermore, I could think of no relevant anthropological source that listed Samoa as low in violence and lacking war. I reasoned that if Mead had *really* argued that the Samoans were so peaceful, other anthropologists writing about aggression and peace at least would have mentioned the Samoans. I checked some likely anthropological sources—such as those by Lesser, Montagu, and Sponsel—and found no references to the Samoans as particularly peaceful peoples.[23]

Puzzled by Wrangham and Peterson's assertion that Mead saw the Samoans as lacking war and generally peaceful, I first pulled Freeman's book off the shelf and compared Wrangham and Peterson's discussion in their chapter "Paradise Imagined" with Freeman's chapter called "Aggressive Behavior and Warfare." It became clear that Wrangham and Peterson basically summarize Freeman's chapter, drawing almost exclusively upon it for their critical comments on Mead's work. Both sources argue that Mead saw Samoans as unaggressive, and both sources emphatically, in biting style, rule that she was absolutely wrong.[24]

Next, I dug out my old paperback copy of *Coming of Age in Samoa*. It was a sunny Saturday afternoon and as I sat on the living room couch, I hoped to get some clarification on this puzzle. In a quick perusal, I found no statements about Samoan culture generally being peaceful or unaggressive in *Coming of Age in Samoa*. This is very interesting, I thought, in light of Wrangham and Peterson's numerous references to the book. I looked up *war* in the index of Mead's famous book and found a statement "cannibalism, war, blood revenge . . . all these have vanished."[25] Ah ha, clearly Mead acknowledged that the Samoans made war in the past. Is it as simple as Mead saying Samoans don't make war *nowadays* and Wrangham and Peterson leaving out the *nowadays?* But why does Freeman devote many pages of his chapter quoting historical sources to document that Samoans engaged in war while Mead obviously acknowledges that war had existed in the past?

My level of curiosity rose several marks and I went back to Freeman's direct quotations of Mead, many also identically reproduced by Wrangham and Peterson, to attempt to find the quotes in Mead's actual writings. First, I noticed that Freeman put quotation marks around one word, namely, "unaggressiveness." *Why put quotation marks around just one word?* It also caught my attention that some of Freeman's other quotes from Mead were only phrases and fragments, sometimes repeated several times. For example, Freeman quoted the *three* words "slight and spasmodic" *three* times to ostensibly encapsulate Mead's view of Samoan war.[26]

To clearly show Freeman's somewhat unusual technique of linking together multiple short quotations, usually from different sources, as well as to present Freeman's chapter thesis in his own words, I quote the first paragraph from "Aggressive Behavior and Warfare":

> In her depiction of the ease and casualness of their society, Mead, as we have seen, gave special emphasis to the "unaggressiveness" of the Samoans, describing them as "one of the most amiable, least contentious, and most peaceful peoples in the world." They were, she reiterated in 1950, a "peaceful and constructive people" among whom warfare had been "stylized as part of the interrelationship between villages that were ceremonial rivals and occasioned few casualties." These assertions, on which Mead so relied in her general theorizing about Samoa, are markedly at variance with the facts of Samoan history.[27]

From the sources that Freeman provides in a footnote, I noticed that *none* of these quotations came from *Coming of Age in Samoa,* the work emphasized by Wrangham and Peterson.[28] I happened to have one source, *Sex and Temperament in Three Primitive Societies,* in my bookshelf.[29] I knew that Samoa is *not* one of the three cultures treated in this Mead classic—again a little strange, I thought—and I proceeded to the page cited by Freeman. The word "unaggressiveness" occurs only one time on the page within the *only* sentence that mentions Samoa. It is located in the last section of Mead's book in a discussion of her findings. Mead writes that different age groups, sex groups, castes, occupations, and so on in societies generally may display different personality traits, and then she uses the Samoan example: "So the Samoans decree that all young people must show the personality trait of *unaggressiveness* and punish with opprobrium the aggressive child who displays traits regarded as appropriate only in titled middle-aged men."[30] *The contexts of both the word "unaggressiveness" within the sentence, and the context of the sentence within the paragraph, clearly show that Mead is not—contrary to what Freeman writes—giving "special emphasis to the 'unaggressiveness' of the Samoans."*[31] Mead states that aggressiveness by titled middle-aged men *may be culturally appropriate,* but that the same type of behavior in *young people* should be punished.

Freeman, in quoting one and only one word from the sentence, ignores the original context and meaning of Mead's sentence completely, totally altering its meaning! Furthermore, how does a *one-sentence example* pertaining to Samoa in a book on three other cultures count as a *special emphasis?* I was stunned by this discovery. *How could Freeman do something like this?*

In amazement, I realized that I must go to the other original sources and look for the origin of a possible myth, for in light of this discovery, an answer to the puzzle occurred to me: Could Wrangham and Peterson simply be retelling a myth, *totally created by Freeman*, that Mead emphasized Samoan unaggressiveness? If Freeman really had created this myth, then the subtitle of his book suddenly took on a new irony: *The Making and Unmaking of an Anthropological Myth.* Indeed! Since Freeman's misuse of the word "unaggressiveness" was so *outrageous,* then perhaps he had twisted Mead's words to suit his own ends in other places also.

After spending some time on this mystery, I realized that if one does not return to Mead's original writings, then Freeman's writing can seem very convincing. For one thing, Freeman's book is replete with actual, although usually short, quotations from Mead. The key, however, is to investigate the contexts of the short quotes: What is in the part of Mead's sentence that Freeman omits? What is the meaning of the surrounding text in general? What caveats and explicit limitations related to the quote does Freeman simply not mention? What additional information in the work is simply ignored by Freeman?

Contrary to Freeman's assertions, Mead makes repeated reference to Samoan aggression in her writings, including the existence of feuds; intervillage brawls; club fights between village champions; youth gang hostility, rivalry, and fighting; fist fights and quarrels among children; and women's aggression—all of which Freeman fails to mention. Here are some specifics:

1. "The two sexes go about in play gangs and throw sticks and stones at each other. This play becomes more vigorous after dark, when opposing gangs can actually give battle without disturbing their elders."[32]
2. "Married women will quarrel over the actual possession of a man, and even come to blows or bite each others' noses or ears."[33]
3. "Within one district there theoretically should not have been war, or the theft of a taupou [virgin daughter of a chief]—a method by which the aumaga [male youth group] of one village displayed its superiority over the aumaga of another village—nor should there have been clashes between the aumagas of two villages within a district. All these did sometimes occur, however, but they were regarded as rather lamentable."[34]

These descriptions and others like them, which are simply ignored by Freeman, open his thesis that Mead emphasized Samoan unaggressiveness to serious doubt. *Coming of Age in Samoa* adds to the doubt, for it also is replete with examples of aggression, as illustrated by the following quotations:

1. "A girl whose father has beaten her over severely in the morning will be found living in haughty sanctuary, two hundred feet away, in a different household."[35]
2. "She has been married at sixteen and against her will to a man much older than herself who had beaten her for her childish ways."[36]

3. "A man who commits adultery with a chief's wife was beaten and banished, sometimes even drowned by the outraged community, but the woman was only cast out by her husband."[37]

Clearly such examples strongly contradict Freeman's contention that Mead placed special emphasis on the "unaggressiveness" of Samoans. And what is the quality of Freeman's evidence that Mead supposedly did this? *Basically Freeman just tells us so.*

In the same sentence where Freeman abuses Mead's meaning of "unaggressiveness," he also quotes her as describing Samoans as "one of the most amiable, least contentious, and most peaceful peoples in the world." If, as Freeman contends, this unaggressive view of Samoans was so important to Mead's theorizing about Samoa, then why does Freeman have to cite a quotation from a two-page book review published in 1931 in the magazine *The Nation* to bolster his contention? If Freeman's assertion were correct, then shouldn't Mead's books and articles be brimming over with quotable-quotes on Samoan peacefulness that Freeman could cite? A book review in a popular magazine hardly seems a likely place for Mead or anyone else to engage in important general theorizing, as Freeman puts it.[38]

So, what is the actual context of Mead's quote? In the book review, Mead is summarizing the thesis of N. A. Rowe's *Samoa under the Sailing Gods,* an interpretation with which she largely concurs, that the actions of an inept, repressive colonial governor provoked Samoans to civil strife. Mead describes how

> the numbers of malcontents, under his [the governor's] efficient goading, swelled from a handful of Samoans to all but the entire population; plantations suffered, trade suffered, the League of Nations was annoyed at such unrest in a mandatory; and finally the New Zealand government had to import white police to end the violent disagreements which a few tactful words could have kept from ever beginning.[39]

Mead continues directly with the sentence that Freeman, and then Wrangham and Peterson, quote *only one part of:* "It is a local enough tale, this story of how a white governor, mad for recognition of his reforms and improvements, shattered the peace and prosperity of one of the most amiable, least contentious, and most peaceful peoples in the world."[40]

That's it! Mead's point is to chastise poor colonial administration, not to engage in general theorizing about Samoans as an unaggressive people. In no way does Mead develop the thesis that Freeman attributes to her. It is simply not there! To the contrary, as Mead relates episodes of violence discussed in the book she is reviewing, she clearly does not view the Samoans as unaggressive or incapable of violence. She refers to native unrest, the possibility of native attack, and violent disagreements. Mead's point is not to emphasize Samoan peacefulness as a cultural trait, but rather to relay the account told in the book she is reviewing "of the few years which transformed a happy, self-supporting colony into a comic-opera set . . . [torn] between hysterical officials and proud and determined natives."[41]

These examples of skullduggery show that Freeman does not always respect the textual context of quoted words and phrases within sentences or the meaning of the words and phrases within the broader context of the surrounding discussion. James Côté and Paul Shankman independently have made similar observations about other aspects of Freeman's writings.[42]

One reason for my shock when I realized that Freeman was so drastically twisting Mead's meanings was due to an underlying, implicit assumption that academics and readers in general share: an expectation that scholars attempt to accurately represent the work they cite. But in the two examples just considered, Freeman blatantly distorts Mead's original meanings. Such *outrageous* distortions in academia are rare enough that it seems to me that readers are not inclined to suspect misrepresentations *of this magnitude*. Thus while Freeman's book has received abundant commentary, it would appear that few have thought it necessary to check Freeman's representations of Mead's writings against her actual prose.[43]

A brief consideration of the Samoan *war versus no war* issue can cap this discussion. Mead *does not* write that warfare never occurred on Manu'a or elsewhere in Samoa. Mead *does* explain her reasons for concluding that past warfare was intermittent and not particularly elaborated on Manu'a, the part of Samoa where she worked. Freeman, however, grossly oversimplifies Mead's writings, collecting short quotations and stringing them together into an incomplete portrayal of Mead's perspective on war.[44]

If Freeman were more balanced in presenting Mead's writings, instead of just repeating the same mini-quotes such as "slight and spasmodic," "no war priests" (a point Freeman does *not* dispute, by the way), "no war gods," and the like, he also might have quoted Mead, for example, that, on Manu'a,

> position in war was a function of a man's place in the social organization. In each *fono* [chiefly governing council] there was one division whose men acted as *muao* or *lagitau,* (advanced guards and spies). The function of heralds was called *taliga i le taua*. There was no captain or general. In Fitiuta [village] a special council of seventeen (*fono fale-ula tau aitu*) met at night and presided over the warfare.[45]

A more balanced consideration of Mead's writings on Manu'an warfare also might have mentioned, for example, her description of the war clubs, spears, and shields used in combat; her comments about tactics such as the Manu'an preference for surprise attacks; and the additional information she includes, such as: "Women were sometimes taken captive, tribute demanded, changes in the social organization made, or indignities inflicted like singeing off the hair of the vanquished."[46] Additionally, Freeman's emphasis on the "slight and spasmodic" might have been tempered by acknowledging Mead's contrast of Manu'a with other parts of Samoa:

> Our records for the Western Islands are complicated by the presence of white men of different nationalities who themselves continuously incited the natives to trouble and supplied firearms to them, so that it is difficult to obtain any picture of the normal course of life before white interference. The reverberations of international rivalry did not reach Manu'a importantly, so the material there can be used with more credibility.[47]

In short, moving beyond Freeman's favorite selection of quotes to consider *what else* Mead actually wrote on war is very revealing.[48] Clearly Mead saw war on Manu'a as less developed than elsewhere in Samoa, but Freeman's portrayal of her perspective is simplistic and biased. When Mead's actual prose dealing with war is consulted, Freeman's assertion that Mead placed *special emphasis* on Samoan unaggressive and peacefulness weighs in somewhere between questionable and ridiculous.

An examination of Mead's writings also shows that she provides clear time and place specifications for her statements, which Freeman routinely disregards.[49] Mead is explicit that *Coming of Age in Samoa* is set in the 1920s, the period of her fieldwork: "The reader must not mistake the conditions which have been described for the aboriginal ones, nor for typical primitive ones."[50]

Wrangham and Peterson, drawing heavily on Freeman, apparently do not realize that the citing of historical examples of Samoan war from the 18th and 19th centuries actually poses no contradiction to what Mead actually writes in *Coming of Age in Samoa* and elsewhere, because Mead neither states nor implies that war didn't exist *in the past*. Wrangham and Peterson also disregard Mead's clear time-frame specifications when they write, for instance, that "Mead's generalizations about the peacefulness of Samoan society—no war gods, *no wars,* little serious contention or hatred or violence, and so on—are all, according to a wealth of historical, anthropological, and contemporary information, wrong."[51] The historical accounts of Samoan warfare enumerated by Freeman and reiterated by Wrangham and Peterson do not contradict Mead's straightforward observation that long before the 1920s warfare had been abolished![52]

Another element of the time context fallacy is reflected in the quotation from the preceding paragraph in which Wrangham and Peterson refer to "contemporary information." Freeman discusses Samoan crime statistics from the 1960s and 1970s, and Wrangham and Peterson repeat some of this contemporary information. Besides the fact that most of these crime statistics are *from a different part of Samoa* than where Mead worked, crime statistics are known to vary over time.[53] It is unreasonable to conclude that crime statistics reported for a period 40 or 50 years different from the period in question—and for a different part of Samoa—can prove generalizations wrong about the period in question. However, while these time and place points are valid, this is *not* the main issue. The critical point to keep in mind is that, contrary to Freeman's contention, *Mead did not emphasize the unaggressiveness of Samoans in the first place.* Therefore, forgetting for a moment the time and place context problems, *the occurrence of violent crime in Samoa cannot show Mead to be wrong about emphasizing something she never in fact emphasized!*

THE UNMAKING OF THE MYTH-WEAVER

Wrangham and Peterson were looking for an example to support their assertion that peaceful societies do not exist. It is understandable that they would assume that Freeman adheres to the normal practices for quotation and fair representation of the work of another scholar—an assumption most people reasonably make all the time. However, the assumption that Freeman fairly represents Mead's writings on aggression and war is false. Specifically, Freeman's quoting of the one word "unaggressiveness" as if it represents Mead's general theorizing about Samoans is astounding nonsense—as is his distorting use of the one phrase from a book review in a popular magazine as if it represents Mead's general theorizing or view of Samoans. Moreover, Freeman's representation of what Mead wrote on Samoan war is biased. As a final abuse to Mead's work, Wrangham and Peterson even exaggerate the myth that Freeman weaves when they mistakenly claim that Mead denied Samoans had war at all. What a tangled web! Mead must be turning over in her grave.[54]

Another point is perhaps already obvious. In that Freeman so misrepresented Mead's writings regarding Samoan warfare and aggression, it would be wise to double-check his representations of Mead's work on other topics as well. Shankman raises a companion point: "Relatively few reviewers of Freeman's argument have raised the possibility that substantial portions of his factual portrayal of Samoa may be inaccurate."[55]

Of course, this bizarre case of skullduggery in no way argues against the existence of peaceful societies. As we have seen, numerous peaceful societies really do exist, but Samoa—contrary to what Freeman and then Wrangham and Peterson assert—was never proposed by Mead (or anyone else, as far as I know) to be a good example of one of them. It is simply illogical to suggest that by debunking Samoan peacefulness, or the peacefulness of any particular society for that matter, one can convincingly demonstrate that *all* peaceful societies are only paradise imagined.

CHAPTER 10

RE-CREATING THE PAST IN OUR OWN IMAGE

> At the heart of science is an essential balance between two seemingly contradictory attitudes—an openness to new ideas, no matter how bizarre or counterintuitive, and the most ruthlessly skeptical scrutiny of *all* ideas, old and new.
>
> CARL SAGAN[1]

Born on a family farm in Ohio in 1869, my grandfather, Francis Pottenger, developed an interest in medicine, and eventually became a specialist in the treatment of tuberculosis.[2] "Grampy" actively practiced medicine until the age of 91. In my youth, I heard my father tell a story that my grandfather had related to him about the leading 19th-century pathologist, Virchow. I later discovered that my grandfather had written the story down:

> Koch wanted to demonstrate the tubercle bacillus to Virchow and invited him to his laboratory. When Virchow refused to go, Cohnheim urged him to do so, telling him it was his duty to see the demonstration. Finally, he succeeded in gaining Virchow's consent. Consent it was, too, for Virchow felt it was real condescension on his part to honor one of whose work he did not approve, one whom in derision he called "the boy from the country."
>
> He took to Koch's laboratory the microscope he had used so successfully in examining pathological tissues, and asked Koch to show the bacillus on it. Koch explained that the bacillus was so small that it required special staining and a high-powered microscope to show it. Whereupon Virchow, pointing to his low-power microscope, said: *"What that microscope does not show does not exist."*
>
> We are apt to think that a scientist always welcomes truth, but at times, he, too, may close his mind and obstruct progress.[3]

Persons who presume a cross-cultural universality of war often assume that war, as a "natural" attribute of humankind, also is an extremely ancient practice. War was stated to be "older than humanity itself."[4] However, such presumptions are *not* in accordance with the worldwide archaeological record. With the story about Doctor Virchow in mind, let us begin this exploration of the antiquity of war with a tale about how preexisting beliefs can affect one's interpretation of the past.

In 1925, a young anatomy professor, Raymond Dart, reported the discovery of an extraordinary fossil skull from a South African limestone quarry at Taung (see Box 10.1). The specimen was clearly a primate juvenile. The face and most of the lower jaw were intact, and the dimensions of the skull had been preserved by an extraordinary stroke of good fortune as minerals had entered the brain case during fossilization and hardened to form a cast of the brain. Dart realized that the "Taung child" fossil showed both apelike and humanlike features; gave it the scientific name *Australopithecus africanus,* literally, "southern ape of Africa"; and argued that this creature may have been an ancient ancestor to humanity.

BOX 10.1 THE CAST OF CHARACTERS

Three broad trends are apparent in the fossil record over the last several million years of human evolution: a shift from walking on all fours to bipedalism, overall reduction in tooth size, and enlargement of the brain. From about five million years ago and continuing to about two million years ago, a variety of ancestral forms, collectively called australopithecines, lived on the African continent. As shown by fossilized footprints and anatomical studies, well before 3.7 million years ago these human-precursors walked erect (Figure 10.1). Australopithecine brain size was close to that of the modern chimpanzee, and the australopithecine brain-to-body ratio was substantially smaller than that of modern humans.

Slightly before two million years ago, larger-brained forms, the first representatives of the genus *Homo,* made their appearance. From this point onward, the brain-to-body ratio steadily increased over time, as did the sophistication of stone tools in the fossil record. Teeth also continued to become smaller over the long haul within the genus *Homo.*

Figure 10.1 At a site called Laetoli in Tanzania, footprints preserved in volcanic ash provide clear evidence that by 3.7 million years ago, australopithecines walked upright. (Photo courtesy of Peter A. Meylan.)

Specimens of hominids—a general term for likely human ancestors—that date roughly between 1.5 million to about 350,000 years ago are classified within the species *Homo erectus*. Later *Homo erectus* specimens had substantially larger brains than the earliest *Homo erectus* fossils. *Homo erectus* occupied parts of Asia and Africa, and some sites suggest the possibility that these hominids used fire. The facial features of *Homo erectus,* especially of the oldest specimens, were robust compared to modern humans.

Early forms of our own species, *Homo sapiens,* sometimes referred to as *archaic Homo sapiens,* followed and may have overlapped with the very last of the *Homo erectus* fossils. The fact that the species name *Homo sapiens* is used for this class of ancestors beginning with specimens that date somewhat more than 200,000 years ago reflects the fact that they were anatomically very similar to current-day people. From at least 40,000 years ago, *modern Homo sapiens,* or anatomically modern humans, are clearly represented in the archaeological record. The Neanderthals were a variation of *Homo sapiens* found in parts of Europe and the Middle East, dating roughly between 75,000 and 40,000 years ago. The Neanderthals have sparked much debate.[1] Were these burly hominids ancestral to modern humans, or were they offshoots that became extinct? Did Neanderthals mate and merge with other groups of *Homo sapiens,* were they outcompeted in the search for game and eventually displaced, were they violently wiped out, or did they simply evolve more gracile-modern appearances? At least one point is clear: No archaeological evidence has been found to support the suggestion that the Neanderthals were victims of genocide.

One other point about the prehistoric world merits emphasis, an observation that may be difficult for people today, crowded on an earth populated by six *billion,* to visualize: Over several million years, hominids and then humans had a lot of space. It was not until about 11,000 to 12,000 years ago, just before the development of agriculture, that the entire population of the planet reached seven million.[2]

Sources: 1. Clark 2002. 2. Binford 2001: Chapter 5.

However, at the time, most experts dismissed Dart's conclusions largely because the "Taung child" did not fit their preconceived ideas about humanity's past.[5] The Taung specimen lacked the large brain that many experts were certain must have developed very early in human evolution. Additionally, expert opinion at that time held that Asia, not Africa, was the continent where humanity had its roots, due in part to the earlier discovery of *Homo erectus* fossils in Java. Influenced by such erroneous assumptions, many leaders in the field dismissed Dart's important find as merely a fossil ape with minimal relevance to the understanding of human origins.

Eventually, the physical evidence of the Taung skull itself, in conjunction with the discovery of additional australopithecine specimens and a more general shift in paleontological thinking, won out over erroneous preconceptions. The moral to the story is that preconceived beliefs can cloud an objective evaluation of the evidence. This lesson foreshadows our main story about Raymond Dart.

Following the Taung discovery, first Robert Bloom and later Dart himself searched for and found additional australopithecine fossils. Some specimens were classified as belonging to the same species as the Taung child, *Australopithecus africanus,* and other fossils eventually were given the species name *Australopithecus robustus*—or "robust southern ape." These australopithecine fossils from South Africa are roughly two to three million years old. Subsequently, australopithecine remains have been found in other parts of Africa that are even older.

Whereas Dart had been absolutely correct in his assessment of the importance of the Taung child to an understanding of human evolution, his reconstructions of australopithecine behavior revealed both that he had an active imagination and that he lacked an understanding of fossilization processes. Joseph Birdsell recounts how he once asked Dart what percentage of the australopithecines he thought had been murdered. "Why, all of them, of course," Dart replied. Perhaps Dart's answer should not be taken absolutely literally; nonetheless, in his writings, Dart argued that specimen after specimen showed evidence of having met violent ends.[6]

Dart interpreted fractured fossil skulls and shattered bones as indisputable evidence that humanity's earliest ancestors were killers of both animal prey and of each other, proving humanity's "carnivorous, and cannibalistic origin."[7] Dart noted that 80 percent of the ancient baboon skulls found with the australopithecine specimens from three sites appeared to have had their heads bashed in.[8] Many of the baboons and some of the australopithecines showed a particular type of fractured skull consisting of paired depressions or holes.[9] Dart interpreted the puncture holes in one australopithecine skull as a deliberate mutilation of a victim for ritualistic purposes.[10]

Dart argued that the paired depression damage on baboon and australopithecine skulls resulted from the australopithecine hunter-murderers' preference for using particular large animal leg bones as bludgeons, because this type of bone happens to have two bony projections that might make paired indentations if wielded just right.[11] The following examples illustrate how Dart wrote murder into his description of broken bones. He concluded that one hominid skull fragment shows "a severing transverse blow with bludgeon on the vertex and tearing apart of the front and back halves of the broken skull."[12] Another australopithecine, according to Dart, supposedly died from a "vertical blow in the left parietal region [the left side of the head] with a rock."[13] Dart also thought that the Taung child had succumbed to a blow to the head. Thus in Dart's view, at least some species of australopithecines were chronic head-bashers of baboons and of each other, or, in Dart's imaginative prose, "confirmed killers: carnivorous creatures, that seized living quarries by violence, battered them to death, tore apart their broken bodies, dismembered them limb for limb, slaking their ravenous thirst with the hot blood of victims and greedily devouring livid writhing flesh."[14]

Writer Robert Ardrey enthusiastically publicized the killer-ape interpretation of humanity's predecessors.[15] Did film director Stanley Kubrick read Dart or Ardrey? The opening scenes of Kubrick's 1968 blockbuster film *2001, A Space Odyssey,* portray an ancestral ape wreaking havoc with a bone-turned-weapon. Later in the movie, a group of these human ancestors brandish bone bludgeons in an attack on their unarmed rivals, beat the opposing group's leader to death, and drive the rest away from a waterhole. How many persons have had *their own images* of humanity's past shaped by viewing such vivid, dramatic, fictional portrayals of prehistoric violence?

Dart's reconstruction of human ancestors as violent "killer-apes" may have seemed plausible to Ardrey, Kubrick, and many other people, but his interpretations of damaged skulls as indicating widespread murder and cannibalism were questioned by physical anthropologists such as Sherry Washburn and Carlton Coon.[16] Eventually, further research revealed that Dart's gruesome reconstructions were a fantasy. Some of the shattering of the bones and skulls resulted from natural geological processes that occurred during fossilization as piles of rock and dirt compressed the specimens over many millennia. As for the various baboon skulls and occasional australopithecine specimens with paired depression fractures or holes, C. K. Brain examined the collections of animal bones more extensively than Dart had done and arrived at a more plausible explanation for much of this damage: large predators. Brain demonstrated that an extinct leopard species, whose remains were found at the same geological layer as the australopithecines, had projecting canine teeth that correspond with the paired puncture holes on skulls.[17] Thus the evidence suggests that predators were eating the ancient baboons and the australopithecines alike. The forces of geology then continued the destructive processes begun by the predators so that two to three million years later most of the australopithecine skeletal remains showed major damage. The murderous, cannibalistic killer-apes that Dart so vividly portrayed in fact turned out to have been merely lunch for leopards.

What we read into the past depends in part on our culturally based beliefs about human nature. A quotation by Dart was included among the set of quoted beliefs as to the universality and antiquity of war at the beginning of chapter 7. Dart's dramatic passage was the one that played up universal early cannibalism, the slaughter-gutted archives of history, worldwide scalping and head-hunting, and other gruesome images. Dart, as a member of Western culture, apparently shared with many other people a set of Hobbesian beliefs about the natural aggressiveness of humans. Such beliefs, I suggest, played a significant role in Dart's creation of australopithecine cannibalistic murderers. John Durant poses a key question: "Could it be that, like 'primitive' myths, theories of human evolution reinforce the value-systems of their creators by reflecting historically their image of themselves and of the society in which they live?" Durant continues: "Time and again, ideas about human origins turn out on closer examination to tell us as much about the present as about the past, as much about our own experiences as about those of our remote ancestors."[18]

Unlike Virchow, Dart *was* willing to look through the high-powered microscope (see Figure 10.2). After weighing the evidence presented in Brain's careful study, Dart changed his mind! To his credit, Dart conceded that Brain's conclusions were sounder than his own.[19] Could it be—especially after Dart himself had experienced firsthand the closed-mindedness of leading scientists who had dismissed for decades his Taung skull as unimportant because it did not match their opinions about human evolution—that Dart had become keenly aware of the power of preconceptions to bias one's own interpretations? Perhaps such insights helped him, years later, to change his own mind about australopithecine bloodlust.

Whereas Dart's cannibalistic, killer-ape portrayal of the australopithecines of two to three million years ago cannot be substantiated by the evidence, there is much indisputable archaeological evidence of violence, including warfare, in the very recent past.[20] For instance, Maria Ostendorf Smith reports on violence apparent in seven

Figure 10.2 This reconstruction of the past illustrates how the paired puncture holes on the skull of an australopithecine specimen were likely made by the protruding lower canine teeth of an extinct leopard. Fossil remains of both species co-occur at the site. (Redrawn with permission from C. K. Brain, 1970, "New finds at the Swartkrans australopithecine site," *Nature* 225: 1112–1119.)

archaeological sites in western Tennessee mostly dating between about 2,750 and 4,500 years ago.[21] Ten out of 439 skeletons show uncontestable evidence of lethal violence, including projectile points within the skeletons, cutmarks indicative of scalping or dismemberment, and stab wounds. All ten victims were male. The question remains whether these men were the victims of revenge homicide, feud, or war. Relating to part of the Northwest Coast of North America, Herbert Maschner notes *changes* in the archaeological record over recent millennia.[22] About 5,000 years ago, primarily non-lethal injuries, such as those from club blows, appear on skeletal remains. Then, by 1,500–1,800 years ago, evidence of warfare becomes clearly apparent. By this time, there are defensive sites, larger villages built in defensible locations, and a decline in population.

Keeley argues that evidence of warfare has sometimes been overlooked. As an example, Keeley suggests that despite clear archaeological indications of warfare among the Classic Maya—fortifications and countless depictions of war captives and armed soldiers—he and others largely dismissed such evidence as "unrepresentative, ambiguous, or insignificant."[23]

Another example illustrating Keeley's point comes to mind from my experience in the Mexican highlands of Oaxaca (Figure 10.3). At the awe-inspiring mountaintop archaeological site called Monte Albán—the center of the ancient Zapotec civilization—huge stones with carved depictions of human figures can be found amidst the temples of the central plaza. These stylized human portraits at first were referred to by the festive

Figure 10.3 By the time of Christ, ancient Zapotec civilization was already flourishing in the Oaxacan highlands of Mexico. The capital of the ancient state, Monte Albán, was built in an easily defensible location on a string of three mountaintops that command spectacular views in all directions. Monte Albán's main plaza includes many temples, a large ball court, subterranean passageways, and a distinct arrow-shaped building, shown here, which may have had important astronomical purposes. (D. P. Fry photo collection.)

name "dancers" (*danzantes*). However, in line with Keeley's point, the obvious facts that many so-called dancers have closed eyes, as in death, are naked, and have had their genitals mutilated combine to suggest that these are the images of the militarily vanquished (Figure 10.4).[24]

Whereas Keeley is undoubtedly correct in his assertion that archaeologists in some instances literally and figuratively have turned war captives into dancers, there also are many cases, and probably more numerous instances, where the reverse has occurred. In addition to the Dart case just considered, excavators have regularly "seen" violence where none in fact existed. The first interpretations of the *Homo erectus* fossils from a site called Zhoukoudian in China held that these human predecessors hunted and consumed each other. This interpretation was widely accepted for several decades. However, in a scenario reminiscent of how Brain showed Dart's fanciful interpretations to be based on misunderstandings of geological and fossilization processes, subsequent careful analysis by Lewis Binford and Chuan Ho revealed absolutely no support for cannibalism at Zhoukoudian. Archaeology and related sciences have greatly increased in sophistication since the Zhoukoudian fossils were unearthed just before World War II. Benefiting from the development of new analytical methods and the accumulation of knowledge about fossilization processes, Binford and Ho demonstrated that the type

Figure 10.4 As is typical of states, the ancient Zapotec civilization engaged in warfare. A collection of human figures carved on large stones and originally mounted in rows on the side of a temple at Monte Albán appear to depict the corpses of vanquished enemies. Note the closed eyes and denigrating elements (such as nudity and genital removal or mutilation), which are typical features of these misnamed *danzantes*. (D. P. Fry photo collection.)

of bone breakage and other observations that previously were assumed to have resulted from cannibalism were actually attributable to natural processes.[25]

The next tale began somewhat over 50,000 years ago in Europe. When a skull of a male Neanderthal was discovered in 1939 in a cave south of Rome at Monte Circeo, lying in a circle of stones in the presence of no other bones, its right side smashed and its *foramen magnum* (Latin for the "big hole" at the base of the skull through which the spinal cord connects to the brain) artificially enlarged, excavator Alberto Carlo Blanc interpreted the findings as a clear case of human sacrifice, the man having been killed by a skull-shattering blow. Paul Bahn comments, "Many popular works on prehistory have accepted this view unquestioningly."[26]

However, two recent reanalyses of the facts, by Mary Stiner and by Tim White and Nicholas Toth, show this interpretation to be based more on speculation than on precise observations of the site and skull itself.[27] An investigation of the cave geology shows that the circle of rocks is consistent with patterns formed by landslides. In fact, the so-called circle of stones forms an irregular cluster, not a circle, giving no indication of human arrangement. Whereas Blanc had given little attention to evidence of carnivores in the cave, the new investigators noted the presence of hundreds of bones, many gnawed, and fossilized hyaena feces, called coprolites. Stiner concludes, based on a detailed study of the great number of animal bones in the cave, that the so-called Neanderthal ritual chamber appears in fact to be "a spotted hyaena maturity den."[28] The edges of the enlarged *foramen magnum* lack any stone tool cutmarks or tool scraping marks that would be apparent had hominids actually removed the brain for cannibalistic purposes. On the other hand, White and Toth note that "the damage to the cranium is consistent with damage caused by carnivore chewing."[29] In short, there is absolutely no evidence for murder or cannibalism related to the Monte Circeo skull.[30]

William Ury summarizes the outcome of comprehensive work by White and Toth: "In specimen after specimen for which the claim of violence had been made, they reviewed the evidence and found alternative explanations equally or more persuasive."[31] In one case, for example, previous researchers had interpreted marks on a Neanderthal skull, referred to as Engis 2, as showing that the person had been scalped. White and Toth present a set of super-enlarged photographs to argue convincingly that the marks resulted from repairing, making casts of the skull, and otherwise working with the cranium in the laboratory. Their conclusion: "None of the marks have anything to do with prehistoric behavior."

ASSUMPTIONS COME TUMBLING DOWN

> Now Jericho was shut up inside and out because of the Israelites; no one came out and no one went in. . . . As soon as the people heard the sound of the trumpets, they raised a great shout, and the wall fell down flat; so the people charged straight ahead into the city and captured it. Then they devoted to destruction by the edge of the sword all in the city, both men and women, young and old, oxen, sheep, and donkeys.
>
> Old Testament, Joshua 6:1, 20–21

The famous walls of Jericho have been generally accepted as the first clear evidence of warfare, dating from 9,000 to 9,500 years ago.[33] However, accepting this apparently obvious interpretation may be jumping the gun. Marilyn Roper provides a thorough consideration of the famous walls, and by the end of her discussion, she has, like a good defense attorney, cast a "shadow of doubt" on their supposed military function.[34] Her central observation is that absolutely no other indications of war are present besides three so-called fortifications: the walls themselves, a so-called moat, and a tower. There are no indications of war injuries among the skeletal remains. There is no evidence of major fires having destroyed the village. There is no evidence of a rapid change of artifacts reflecting an invasion of the village. Furthermore, five other sites in the region dating from the same time period have no walls around them. This observation raises the question: If there had been a threat of warfare in the region, why would only Jericho have fortifications? Moreover, there is no archaeological evidence of the existence of a plausible "enemy" having been in the region at the time when the walls were constructed. Roper also points out that the so-called moat didn't actually surround the site.[35] Why only construct a partial moat? The walls themselves also may not have gone the full circumference of the site, but the subsequent construction of a road on one side of the village complicates obtaining a clear answer to this question.

C. Richards challenges Roper for questioning the accepted military explanation of Jericho's walls: "It seems to me that the burden of proof should be on those who think there was NO early warfare, rather than the reverse. . . . All this contradicts the principle of parsimony. Why strain and resort to complex explanations when there is a simpler one—warfare?"[36]

Two comments come to mind. First, we have just considered how several simple, or "obvious," explanations have tumbled in the face of more sophisticated analyses of the evidence. Thus the *simple* explanation for the walls of Jericho, warfare, may not be the *correct* explanation. Second, in light of our consideration of how implicit assumptions about the nature of humanity may affect interpretations of the past—remember Dart—another comment by Richards hints at a similar connection: "Man has fought for so many varied reasons that it is highly risky to overlook or reject outright the possibility of some built-in tendency toward war in man's genes or in some universal characteristic of human life such as long dependency, the frustrations of social living, and so on."[37] Such beliefs may predispose Richards toward "seeing" evidence of war in the walls of Jericho.

If we open our minds to the possibility that the large, solid walls at Jericho might not be fortifications, then we are left with the critical question: Why were they built? Ofer Bar-Yosef asked exactly this question and came up with what at first sounds like a truly crazy idea.[38] Remembering, however, that the now accepted idea of continental drift also seemed totally bizarre when it was first suggested, let's consider Bar-Yosef's idea. Bar-Yosef turned his eye to the physical geography and climatology of the famous site. He observed that other archeological sites in the region, when located near streambeds, called *wadis* in this part of the world, were partially or entirely covered with accumulated debris from flooding, mudflows, or sheetwash. So was Jericho.

Wadis are similar to the arroyos of the southwestern United States. They are dry most of the time but can flash flood during downpours in the rainy season, moving tons of sand, rock, and silt to downstream locations. Bar-Yosef observed that Jericho is located on a sloping plain, and that Wadi el-Mafjar descends from the hills into a drainage basin close to the Jericho site. Climatological indicators suggest the seventh millennium B.C. was wetter than today, and additionally, Bar-Yosef writes, "that the wadis of the region once carried more water than they do today seems obvious from the erosion reported by Kenyon [an excavator of Jericho in the 1950s] on the northern edge of the [Jericho] mound."[39]

Bar-Yosef writes that if one supposes the walls to have been built as fortifications, then a series of nagging, unanswered questions present themselves. Why would there be no evidence of enemies? As debris gradually accumulated both inside and outside the Jericho walls while the site was inhabited—thus making them easily scalable by supposed enemies—why didn't the inhabitants immediately build the walls higher or remove the debris from outside the wall? Why were no other sites in the region fortified until a couple of millennia after the Jericho walls were built? In other words, why would Jericho be the only settlement in the region fearful of enemy attack? Why would a fortification tower be constructed *inside* the wall in such a way as to preclude using it to protect the wall from attackers? On the other hand, once the assumption that the walls served a military purpose is lifted, answers to the forgoing questions become clear.

"Given all the available data," concludes Bar-Yosef, "it seems that a plausible alternative interpretation for the Neolithic walls of Jericho is that they were built in stages as a defense system against floods and mudflows. . . . [The response of the inhabitants] was to build a wall and then, when necessary, dig a ditch."[40] While the jury is still out, the flood control explanation seems to account for the data more thoroughly than the fortification explanation. In light of Roper's questioning and Bar-Yosef's reevaluation of the facts, the fortification explanation may be yet another example of how the past has been "violencified," rather than "pacified," by interpretations that rest more on assumption and speculation than a careful analysis of the data.

THE EARLIEST EVIDENCE OF WAR

Worldwide, the archaeological site with the earliest indications of *possible* war or feuding is a cemetery dated between 12,000 and 14,000 years ago. Excavations of this ancient burial site, Jebel Sahaba in Sudanese Nubia near the Nile, revealed that 24 out of 59 skeletons showed evidence of violence. This is a very high percentage of violent deaths in a skeletal population, and some scholars attribute it to warfare or feuding, while others caution that homicides and executions cannot be ruled out. *Thus the evidence of war from this site is ambiguous.* Clearly, all the deaths did not occur on a single occasion. The next earliest indications of warfare, including the ambiguous walls of Jericho, are more recent than 10,000 years ago.

After reviewing the archaeological evidence on prehistoric homicides and warfare, Keeley reaches the conclusion "that homicide has been practiced since the appearance of modern humankind and that warfare is documented in the archaeological record of the *past 10,000 years* in every well-studied region." I would not be surprised if occasional homicides occurred long before the emergence of modern humans. In fact, Roper's review of published sources suggests that homicides did occur even before modern humans arrived on the scene some 40,000 to 50,000 years ago.[41]

Our current focus, however, is on the antiquity of *warfare,* not the antiquity of murder. Otterbein points out that Keeley, in a section of his book titled "Prehistoric War," includes archaeological instances of homicide and "violent death" (a rather ambiguous term) along with the evidence for warfare.[42] In other words, many of the examples Keeley mentions under the label "Prehistoric War" actually are not war at all.[43] Otterbein criticizes Keeley for surreptitiously shifting concepts: "I object to sliding from 'violent death' in the Paleolithic to 'warfare' in the Late Paleolithic without comment upon his changing use of terminology."[44] Furthermore, pertaining to the same section of Keeley's book, Raymond Kelly questions Keeley's assertion that certain European mass burials are probably the result of war:

> Communicable disease and starvation provide highly plausible alternative explanations for multiple burials and even mass graves. In winter there is no inducement to prompt burial, especially during a time of general illness and famine. . . . Multiple burials should not be interpreted as evidence of war *unless skeletal indications of trauma or proximate projectile points support this.*[45]

In essence, Keeley intermingles archaeological examples of individual homicides, sometimes ambiguous cases of "violent death," and perhaps even nonviolent deaths due to starvation and disease with the archaeological examples of warfare, all under the title "Prehistoric War." Obviously, this can give an impression that there is more evidence for warfare, and older evidence for warfare, than actually exists. However, despite this unfortunate exaggeration of warfare, and this is really the crucial point, Keeley reports no solid evidence of *warfare,* anywhere in the world, older than about 10,000 years *before present,* or B.P., in archaeological lingo.

The archaeological record also yields additional important data related to the first evidence of warfare, namely, insights about the development of social systems. In chapter 8, we considered two types of hunter-gatherer social organization, simple and complex. Simple hunter-gatherer band societies are nomadic and egalitarian; they lack ranked social hierarchies and well-defined position of leadership or authority. By contrast, complex hunter-gatherers have partially or totally given up the nomadic lifestyle and tend to be found in areas of bountiful, consistent resources such as rich marine environments. Ethnographically, complex hunter-gatherer societies are rare.[46] Knauft explains that complex hunter-gatherer societies "may exhibit elaborate economic and political status-differentiation systems, including rank distinctions and chiefs."[47] Thus, they are not egalitarian. Service classifies such societies as chiefdoms.[48]

As considered in chapter 8, findings on the hunter-gatherers in the SCCS correspond with Robert Kelly's observation that warfare is *rare* among simple egalitarian hunter-gatherers and *common* among complex hunter-gatherer societies.[49] Evidence suggests that the simple tends to precede the complex, and, archaeologically speaking, complexity is *very recent.* From diverse parts of the planet, archaeological sequences tell similar stories. Knauft explains: "Complex hunter-gatherers were most common after 12,500 BP, usually transitional between simple hunter-gathering and agricultural systems." This observation is of *central importance* as we consider the origin of war, for as we saw in chapter 8, it makes little sense to talk about war divorced from social organization.[50]

So, broadly speaking, the archaeological record shows a recurrent pattern. The nomadic hunter-gatherer band was *the* form of human social organization until just before the *agricultural revolution.*[51] However, agriculture didn't just appear overnight and then spread instantly to all corners of the globe.

Whereas the development of agriculture is correctly heralded as a landmark in world prehistory, bringing innumerable changes to the human species, the *preagricultural revolution,* the emergence of complex hunter-gathering societies in some places, also can be viewed as a monumental transformation in human existence.[52] Donald Henry comments on the magnitude of the change from a simple nomadic existence to a settled pattern of complex hunting-and-gathering:

> The replacement of simple hunting-gathering societies composed of small, highly mobile, materially impoverished, egalitarian groups by a society that was characterized by large, sedentary, materially rich and socially stratified communities represented a dramatic shift from an adaptive system that had enjoyed several million years of success.[53]

The shift thus involved many interrelated changes in the way people lived, made a living, and interacted with other persons in society. The typical archaeological signs of social complexity include higher population density than among simple hunter-gatherers, larger settlement size, the presence of permanent shelters and ceremonial areas, development of artistic styles, and differences among individual burials within the society regarding the amount of grave goods, grave location, and elaboration of grave preparation.[54] Variability in burial features indicates the presence of a social hierarchy as high-status persons are entombed in more elaborate ways than commoners.

In one archaeological time sequence from an area of the eastern Mediterranean referred to as the Levant, the shift from simple foraging to complex hunting-and-gathering and then subsequently to agriculture occurred over the period 14,000 to 10,000 years ago and is clearly shown in the archeological record.[55] In this particular sequence, there is no archaeological indication of warfare whatsoever for either the earlier simple hunter-gatherers or the subsequent more complex hunter-gatherers.[56] Along with social complexity in this case, long-distance trade becomes apparent.

Recall Maschner's report, considered earlier, on an archaeological time sequence for the Northwest Coast of North America extending from 11,000 years ago to European contact about 200 years ago.[57] Starting at about 5,500 to 5,000 years B.P. and continuing for at least a couple millennia the skeletal evidence of aggression consists almost exclusively of *nonlethal* injuries—and there are not many of these. Such facts do not suggest warfare. Maschner sees these nonlethal injuries as reflecting club blows, and he suggests (based on the rarity of injuries that caused death) that conflict may have been largely symbolic.[58] On the basis of ethnographic accounts (as we will consider in subsequent chapters), the lack of any archaeological evidence indicative of warfare, and the rarity of the injuries themselves, I suggest that this evidence is consistent with acts of individual aggression, perhaps in the form of contests. By contrast, warfare appears later in this particular prehistoric sequence corresponding with a variety of societal changes, and large-scale war is evident only in the last 1,800–1,500 years B.P. For this area, Maschner links warfare and complexity: "The first large villages appear, status differences become apparent, a heavy emphasis on marine subsistence develops, and warfare becomes visible in the archaeological record."[59]

Roper notes that the archaeological record of the Near East shows no evidence of warfare at 12,000 years B.P., then gives way to sparse evidence for war by about 9,500 years B.P., followed by clear evidence of spreading and intensifying warfare in more recent times. In the Near East, between 12,000 and 10,000 years B.P., hunting-and-gathering subsistence patterns gave way to a new economy based on plant and animal domestication. The nature of living sites, human skeletal remains, and cultural sequence data, such as pottery and architectural styles, show the development of warfare over several millennia.[60]

At the early stages, 12,000 to 9,500 years B.P., occupation sites were out in the open and defensive structures were lacking. This suggests the absence of war. At the intermediate stages, 9,500 to 7,000 years B.P., an increasing number of sites show walls and ditches, some of which certainly relate to defense. At later stages, 7,000 to 6,300 years ago, the presence of defensive structures at certain sites along a major trade route is indisputable.[61]

The skeletal remains show a corresponding sequence over these millennia, beginning with a few isolated instances of skeletal damage and ending with clear evidence of village massacres. Early evidence of village fires shows a pattern of cultural continuity after a conflagration, suggesting that most or all fires resulted from accidents, not village sacking. Later in the archaeological sequence, however, warfare is suggested by the fact that village-destroying fires sometimes were followed in the archaeological sequence by changes in artifacts, such as pottery styles, once the site was reoccupied, supposedly by the invaders.

Beginning about 7,000 years B.P., a prehistoric group of people known as the Halafians appeared in parts of Mesopotamia, Syria, and Turkey.[62] The arrival of Halafian culture was accompanied by evidence of violence, suggestive of an invasion by this new group. For instance, two Samarran sites, Chagar Bazar and Sakce Gözü, were destroyed and immediately Halafian cultural elements appeared in the archaeological stratigraphy of these locations.

Not only do we have evidence of warfare, but the archaeological record also provides information about the likely reasons for war. Roper writes, "It is significant that all the sites that exhibit destruction or have fortifications are located on the east-west overland trade route. . . . One may hypothesize that the Halafians wanted and took control of a portion of this great trade route."[63]

During the same time period, 7,000 to 6,300 years ago, an unfortified village site called Mersin suddenly shows indisputable evidence of war. The anomaly of burned skeletal remains, something different from previous times, caught the attention of the excavator John Garstang, who explains, "we see evidence of disrespect and a mass burying of human bodies, a practice altogether unknown upon our site, which betrays violence and suggests the presence of an enemy. . . . We are forced to conclude that a fight had occurred with strangers who celebrated their victory with this holocaust."[64]

The site was immediately rebuilt as a fortress that eventually included a military garrison. The archaeological evidence clearly shows warfare after 7,000 years B.P., and additionally, the military garrison indicates the presence of professional warriors, a feature associated with a well-developed sociopolitical hierarchy. In subsequent millennia, warfare in the Near East became all the more prevalent, "not only involving the Ubadians (whose culture gave rise to the first civilization, Sumerian, in southern Mesopotamia) but other culture groups as well. . . . Fortifications became the rule rather than the exception."[65]

The Anasazi were the prehistoric ancestors of the current Pueblo people of the American Southwest. After a century of research, the archaeological record for this region is particularly rich. Jonathan Haas explains that "the chronological, palaeoenvironmental and archaeological records from the south-west provide a level of detail that allows us to see both the presence and absence of prehistoric warfare, and to examine closely the causes, nature and evolution of warfare on local and regional levels."[66]

The transition from nomadic foraging to settled farming took place over a thousand years, concurrent with population growth and climatic change. Between A.D. 500 and A.D. 700, several distinct branches of Anasazi culture developed. Goods were actively exchanged among the settled villages. The archaeological evidence between A.D. 700 and about A.D. 1200 shows no signs of warfare.[67]

Beginning about A.D. 1150, the climate in this area began to change. The pattern of precipitation switched from winter-dominant to summer-dominant, resulting in a drop in the water table, an increase in soil erosion, and a reduction in the amount of land suitable for growing crops. Haas explains that "high population coupled with a deteriorating environment led to severe economic stress among the Anasazi. . . . The conditions were finally sufficiently harsh for a major outbreak of warfare in the Anasazi region."[68]

Evidence of warfare is unmistakable by A.D. 1260. Arrowheads pierce skeletons, skeletons lack skulls, and skulls lack skeletons. Some villages have been destroyed, others have constructed protective palisades, and still others have moved to highly defensible locations. The famous Southwestern cliff dwellings epitomize secure living sites. Then, after about 50 years of warfare, the Anasazi heartland was simply abandoned. There is no evidence of genocide or a widespread massacre; rather, by A.D. 1300, the Anasazi simply moved to other parts of the Southwest, and then their involvement in warfare decreased. Haas summarizes:

> Anasazi co-existed peacefully with culturally different groups around their borders for more than a thousand years, and within the Anasazi culture area, ethnically distinct groups lived side by side for centuries, generation after generation, with absolutely no signs of organized conflict or war. The violence markers of raiding, killing, and burning appear only very late in Anasazi culture, as a complex response to changing demographic patterns and a prolonged period of severe environmental stress.[69]

Kent Flannery and Joyce Marcus report no evidence for group conflict among the small nomadic bands that foraged in the Valley of Oaxaca in southern Mexico between 10,000 and 4,000 years B.P.[70] Toward the end of this period, the transition from hunting-and-gathering to sedentary villages was underway. By 2,800 to 2,450 years B.P., three rival chiefly centers existed in the Valley of Oaxaca, buffered from each other by unoccupied zones. Near the end of this period, one center called San José Mogote was attacked and its main temple burned. The survivors relocated to the mountaintop called Monte Albán and began constructing defensive walls, some three kilometers in length. Eventually, Monte Albán became the capital of the prehistoric Zapotec state. By the period 2,000 to 1,700 years B.P., the state expanded geographically some 150 kilometers beyond the Valley of Oaxaca. Flannery and Marcus mention evidence of the professionalization of the Zapotec army, and they think it was likely that "by 2,000 BP, only 1,200 years since the first palisaded village, the Zapotec were already waging war on the scale witnessed by the 16th-century Spaniards."[71]

The foregoing archaeological time sequences illustrate how warfare may originate in particular areas and increase along with the development of sociopolitical complexity. These examples show a recurring sequence. First, among simple nomadic foragers there is no archaeological evidence for warfare. Evidence of violence exists in some cases, but when the telltale evidence of war is lacking, warfare cannot simply be assumed to have existed on the basis of sporadic cases of violence. Then, as some hunter-gatherer societies make changes toward increasing complexity, sometimes, but not always, warfare makes an appearance in the archaeological record.[72] With the development of states, the archaeological record often shows increases in the frequency and intensification of war, phenomena that also may be exacerbated by population pressures or environmental change, as in the Anasazi case.

Specialists who have evaluated the archaeological evidence regarding warfare have reached similar conclusions. Recall that Keeley, who is *emphasizing warfare,* pins down the time frame for warfare as *within the last 10,000 years*.[73] Correspondingly, Haas summarizes the big picture as follows:

> Archaeologically, there is negligible evidence for any kind of warfare anywhere in the world before about 10,000 years ago. . . . It was only about 10,000 years ago that the niches of the world were filled in through gradual population growth, and people had to develop new settlement and subsistence strategies to extract adequate resources from decreased territory. . . . The archaeological record indicates that endemic warfare was much more the exception than the rule until the first appearance of state level societies between 4,000 and 2,000 BC [or 4,000 to 6,000 years B.P.] in the centers of the world "civilization."[74]

Roper concludes her seminal article on prehistoric violence as follows:

> The known cranial remains of australopithecines, *H. erectus,* Neanderthals (progressive and classic), and Pleistocene *H. sapiens* are surveyed here. . . . The author's determination is that, although there seems to be sound evidence for sporadic intrahuman killing, the known data is not sufficient to document warfare.[75]

An excerpt from Kelly's *Warless Societies and the Origin of War* corresponds with the conclusions reached by Keeley, Haas, and Roper, among others—Boehm, Ferguson, Otterbein, Sponsel, and Ury, for example—that the earliest evidence for warfare is, archeologically speaking, very recent.

> The archaeological record provides very little clear-cut evidence of warfare within hunting and gathering populations prior to the development of agriculture. . . . By 5,000 to 4,300 BC [7,000 to 6,300 years B.P.], fortifications, garrisons, and site destruction at a number of locations in the Near East provide archaeological evidence for a more general prevalence of warfare. . . . In the relatively brief span of 4,500 years, a global condition of warlessness that had persisted for several million years thus gives way to chronic warfare that arises initially in the Near East and subsequently in other regions where a similar sequence of transformative events is reduplicated.[77]

In Figure 10.5, the oldest evidence for warfare is put in time perspective. Clearly, war is a very recent development. The archaeological record documents that war becomes more frequent and intensifies with the development of the state level of sociopolitical organization a mere 4,000 to 6,000 years ago.

Regarding the lack of any indications of warfare in the archaeological record much beyond the 10,000-year mark, it has sometimes been said that the absence of evidence is not evidence of absence. However, as archaeological data have accumulated from all corners of the world, it is now clear that warfare does leave archaeological marks.[78] Unambiguous fortifications around settlements, specialized weapons such as clubs and daggers not used for hunting, depictions of martial scenes in artwork, a substantial number of burials with projectile points either embedded in the bones or else lying within the frames of skeletons, evidence of massive fires followed by a change in cultural artifacts, a reduced number of male remains buried in cemeteries that suggests significant male death elsewhere, and *repetition of such findings across the archaeological sites of an area*—these and other indicators suggest that warfare was present. And when multiple lines of such evidence point in the same direction, we can be fairly certain that warfare was occurring.

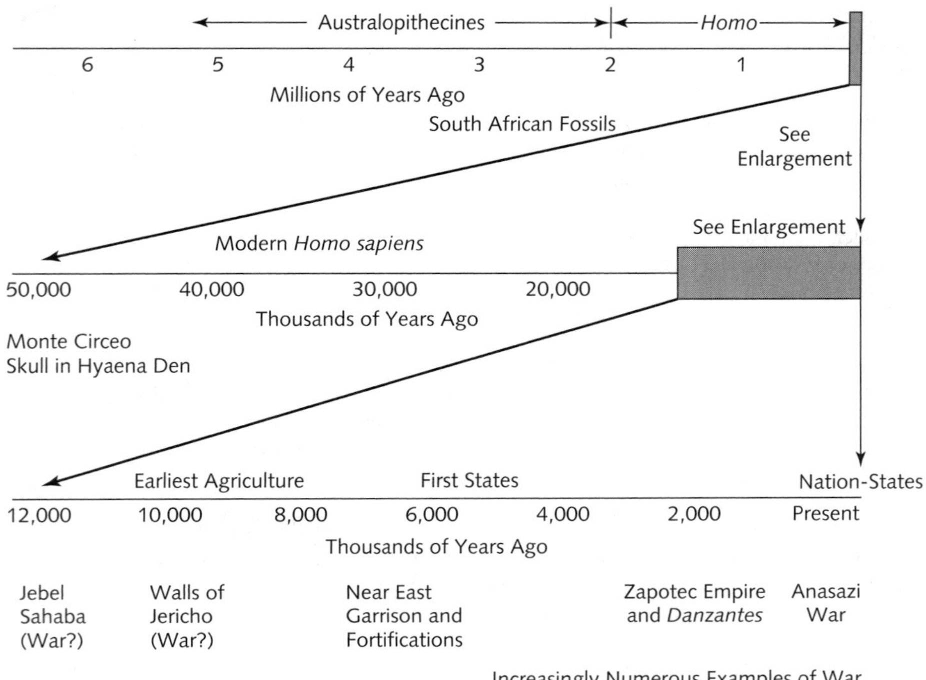

Figure 10.5 War and the evolutionary time line. Lawrence Keeley is correct when he points out that some war existed before civilization, that is, before the development of states. However, when viewed in the time frame of human evolution, civilization is an extremely recent development (dating from only 6,000 years ago at the earliest). Human precursors within the genus *Australopithecus* are five to six million years old. With relatively small brains, the australopithecines walked erect on two legs. The genus *Homo* is about two million years old and shows an increased brain size–to–body size ratio over time, the first evidence of developed stone tool manufacture, and the first controlled use of fire. The species *Homo erectus* preceded *Homo sapiens* in time. "Archaic" *Homo sapiens* dates from at least 200,000 years ago, while anatomically modern *Homo sapiens,* or, modern humans, appear in the archaeological record only in the last 40,000 to 50,000 years. Agriculture was developed during the last 10,000 years, the time period corresponding with the first archaeological indications of warfare. The first states, early civilizations in other words, appeared about 5,000 to 6,000 years B.P. (or 3,000 to 4,000 B.C.). From this period onward, there are ample examples of warfare in the archaeological record. The rest of the story, literally, is history—and thus, archaeologically speaking, very recent.

On the other hand, when we have an archaeological record with no such indicators of warfare, this tells us something real as well. Ferguson points out, "If we were talking about anything less ideologically weighted than war, such as the origin of agriculture or settled village living, no one would take seriously a claim that such *might* have existed in distant millennia. The time of origin would be simply, uncontroversially fixed at the point of the earliest evidence."[79]

Aside from what the archaeological record tells us, there also are a series of compelling, logical reasons that explain why warfare was only a rare anomaly during all but the last tiny fraction of human prehistory. For one thing, the social organization of simple nomadic hunter-gatherers, the only form of social organization for the vast majority of human prehistory, is simply not conducive to making war. We have already considered in chapter 8 how an association between warfare and the complexity of social organization has been replicated in many studies.[80] In the next several chapters, we will explore in greater detail why the paucity of warfare prior to the agricultural revolution makes a great deal of sense based on what we know about nomadic hunter-gatherer social organization and lifestyle. Ferguson concludes:

> Perhaps the most significant general finding of this volume [on prehistoric violence and war] is that violence and war leave recoverable traces. Not surprising, perhaps, but influential theories rise on the premise that "absence of evidence is not evidence of absence." While still true for particular cases, that axiom must be reconsidered as a generalization. . . . The maxim that absence of evidence is not evidence of absence remains valid for any particular dig, and for those areas with limited data. But where a cultural tradition is known from many sites and skeletons, absence of any sort of evidence suggesting war can indeed be taken as reasonable evidence of war's absence.[81]

In this chapter, as in chapter 7, we have considered *beliefs* and *facts*. I have suggested that beliefs about violence and war are not necessarily linked very closely to the observable facts. Cultural belief systems include presuppositions about human nature. Consequently, beliefs that war is an intrinsic part of human nature, that humans are naturally aggressive or have instincts for war, and the like tend to be accepted along with other aspects of a cultural belief system. However, turning to facts, a careful examination of cross-cultural data in chapter 7 showed that warfare, while common, is not a cultural universal. We have seen that, in actuality, many nonwarring cultures exist. Similarly, the belief that "there always has been war" does not correspond with the archaeological facts of the matter. The earliest clear evidence for warfare dates from about 10,000 years ago, and war becomes more common with the rise of the state several millennia later. After reviewing the archaeological record, Sponsel reaches the conclusion that "During the hunter-gatherer stage of cultural evolution, which dominated 99 percent of human existence on the planet . . . lack of archaeological evidence for warfare suggests that it was *rare or absent for most of human prehistory*."[82] Keeley might see Sponsel as attempting to pacify the past, but on the other hand, recall that Otterbein caught Keeley exaggerating the evidence for warfare by including under the label *prehistoric war* archaeologically older cases of *homicide* and *violent death*. When it comes down to the actual archaeological evidence, however, Keeley acknowledges the very recent time frame for warfare.[83] Sponsel's conclusion about the rarity or absence of warfare for most of prehistory, while perhaps contradicting popular *beliefs* as to the great antiquity of war, nonetheless is in accordance with the archaeological *facts*. Scientific understanding moves forward not by clinging tenaciously to fondly held beliefs but by constantly questioning old ideas and evaluating interpretations in light of the available data. And this returns us to our chapter-opening story. Dart's acknowledgment that Brain's reinterpretation of the australopithecine fossil evidence made more sense than his own is a case of scientific open-mindedness at its best.

CHAPTER 11

CULTURAL PROJECTIONS

> Our ordinary life still swarms with them [projections]. You can find them spread out in the newspapers, in books, rumours, and ordinary social gossip. All gaps in our actual knowledge are still filled out with projections. We are still so sure we know what other people think or what their true character is. . . . We are still swamped with projected illusions.
>
> CARL G. JUNG[1]

What do the following descriptions of hunter-gatherer aggression have in common? In the *Handbook of South American Indians* under a topical heading called "Warfare," Junius Bird writes of the Alacaluf:

> Crude spears, arrows, and clubs painted red were stuck into the ground around a roughly carved figure of wood as a *declaration of war* or as a warning of attack. . . . A man once stole another man's wife. The husband tried to get her back by force, but was beaten off by his competitor. He returned in the night with his brother and placed one red wooden replica of the *tant-tarrh* [spear] . . . at either end of the hut and behind it. Thus, having given a warning that he would try to kill the man, the latter's relatives could not hold him accountable. The two brothers subsequently ambushed the rival and killed him with a spear. The woman was blamed and beaten.[2]

Jane Goodale provides the following description of events among the Tiwi of northern Australia:

> According to my informant (a middle-aged woman), the husband whose wife had eloped would call a meeting and ask for help from his local sib and phratry members. If necessary, he would send a messenger to invite distant members of his sib and phratry to join the battle. The "enemy" (the lover's "people": his sib and phratry) would also be sent a message. The messenger was painted red, white, black, and yellow, and carried a single unbarbed "mangrove" spear. He announced the time and place for the battle. . . . When everyone had arrived, my informant continued, they lined up on opposing sides and the battle began.
>
> First a *young boy* from each side advanced and threw a spear. Then two more youngsters exchanged spears, and then a third pair. After this exchange of spears everyone threw his spear. When one side decided that they had had enough, an old man carried a white flag between the two lines and said, "You have won, we lose." Then they all camped. Next morning they had a little fight and went home. My informant finished her description at this point, and I had to ask her who got the wife, the husband or the lover, in the case either side won. She informed me that in either case the lover kept the wife,

> for the fight was not over who got to keep the woman but only for the husband's "honor," and after the fight the trouble must be forgotten. I suspect that my informant's account of the legal outcome of such a battle may have been personally prejudiced, as she had eloped three times successfully![3]

Finally, an account by William Bright pertains to the Karok of California[4]:

> A *person* could commit trespass or murder without being stigmatized as a criminal, but he could expect to be "called to account" in quite a literal sense—being required to "pay for his misdeeds," not by undergoing punishment, but by paying indemnity in the form of shell money or other valuables. If anyone refused to pay, he was likely to be killed by the people he had offended; and this killing could in turn result either in indemnification, or in further violence between the *families* concerned.
>
> What is sometimes referred to as "war" in northwest California was simply this type of retaliatory activity, expanded to involve fellow villagers of the aggrieved parties. Such *feuds* could be settled with the aid of a go-between, who was paid for his services. When a settlement was arranged, the opposing parties would face each other, the men doing an armed "war dance" in front of the settlement money while singing songs to insult the other side. If the women were successful in restraining the men from further violence, the settlement would conclude with an exchange and breaking of weapons.[5]

In these three cases, the disputes are basically between *individuals*. In the Alacaluf case, a dispute between two men over a woman is labeled as something that it clearly is not—warfare. Despite the use of the phrase "declaration of war," this is a case of homicide, clear and simple. Furthermore, the homicidal self-redress is apparently conducted in accordance with Alacaluf legal procedure so as to prevent retaliatory violence. The bloodshed could have been averted, supposedly, if the woman had returned to her husband.

Similarly, in the Tiwi example, the use of words like "battle" and "enemy" again suggests a warlike nature to a dispute that is in reality a fight between two men over a woman. The informant sees the so-called battle as being for the honor of the deserted husband. On the other hand, it may be a contest, as hinted at by Goodale, wherein the husband has a chance to regain his wife. Either way, it is important to explain that throwing spears in the manner described is *not* as serious as it might seem to a reader from another culture. Most male Australian Aborigines are skilled both at "throwing to miss" and, on the receiving end, dodging spears.[6] Victoria Burbank reports that in a settled Aboriginal community, "when men take up spears, more often than not, no one is injured."[7] That even *young boys* throw spears in the described event, that there is *no loss of life or even bloodshed,* and that the two groups *camp together* overnight, along with the initial observation that the cause of the dispute is between two individuals—all these points combine to show that something very different than warfare is actually going on here.

The Karok example is slightly different because the author himself clearly spells out how events that other people have "referred to as 'war'" in fact involve individual and family feuds and their settlement.[8] The Karok, like some Australian Aborigine societies, have developed a system of paying compensation to a victim's family in the case of homicide or paying the victim of lesser crimes for damages inflicted by *one person on another* so as to forestall additional violence. The so-called Karok war-dance, much like the so-called battle among the Tiwi, has ritualistic elements designed to *end the troubles once and for all between disputing parties.* They appropriately can be called dispute settlement procedures or juridical encounters, but not warfare.

The broader point is far from trivial. Whether due to misperceptions, projections, or poetic descriptions, conflicts in band societies are regularly presented as "warfare." It is not difficult to find examples of this "warification" phenomenon when reading ethnographic material, especially if written by nonanthropologists such as colonial administrators, missionaries, or early travelers.[9] Many descriptions penned by Westerners contain vocabularies of war—for instance, *warfare, battle, enemy, declaration of war, war parties, war paint,* and the like—that are imprecisely or inappropriately applied to disputes. This use of language implies *warring* when in actuality two *individuals,* perhaps aided by kin, are fighting or, ironically, engaging in procedures to settle disputes without bloodshed. Descriptions of this kind help to re-create the "savage" in our own preconceived warlike image, as the Western concept of war is projected onto indigenous activities.

As an undergraduate student at the University of California in Santa Barbara, I took an anthropology course from Service called "Law and War." Recently my class notes surfaced and I looked them over with fond amusement. I had enjoyed Service's lectures. My notes now reminded me that Service had emphasized, "People have lived in hunter-gatherer bands for 99.87% of human existence." (I gather the .87 part was Service's way of having a little fun as he highlighted the magnitude of humanity's nomadic hunter-gatherer heritage to his students.) He had explained that in simple hunter-gatherer bands, leadership is weak and based on charisma, not authority. Relationships are familistic and egalitarian; moreover, everybody knows everybody else in band society. Generosity is highly valued. And when it comes to "warfare," hunter-gatherer bands engage in little more than, in Service's words, "feuds and Saturday night brawls." Later, I discovered that Service also had emphasized the individual nature of simple hunter-gatherer disputes in *The Hunters*:

> Usually the occasion for any kind of battle or threat of battle is some kind of personal conflict, often caused by an elopement, or an illegal love affair of some kind, or simply an insult. There seems to be no evidence whatsoever in any of the band societies under review that warfare is actually undertaken for economic reasons, such as for booty or territorial acquisition.[10]

Service's observation that in hunter-gatherer band society disputes are *personal* has major implications, because it suggests that those who attempt to explain the biological evolution of human *warfare* are asking the wrong question. They are starting with the presumption that ancestral hunter-gatherer bands actually *had wars*, and then are going on to explain *warring* as an evolved adaptation. Instead of simply *presuming* that warfare has existed as a typical pattern in band society over countless millennia to gain territory, capture women, obtain scarce resources, wipe out the enemy, or whatever, wouldn't it make more sense to put the horse back in front of the cart by asking: What types of disputes do nomadic hunter-gatherers actually have? How do they deal with them?

I propose that by carefully examining the nomadic forager data for patterns—for recurring themes—we can reconstruct in broad outline the typical social features of ancestral humans. Bringing together the important features of this reconstructed social environment, on the one hand, and evolutionary theory, on the other, leads to the suggestion that certain types of aggression and associated behaviors, but *not warfare,* were favored by natural selection over millennia. It is also likely, as we shall see in future chapters, that in ancestral hunter-gatherer bands, overly aggressive individuals were selected *against,* that is, disfavored in comparison to less aggressive individuals.

CHAPTER 12

ABORIGINAL AUSTRALIA

A Continent of Unwarlike Hunter-Gatherers

> First encounters with the desert people are vividly remembered: the rapid realization, as you are touched, squeezed, and discussed, that as one of the first whites they have seen, you are at least as interesting an oddity to them as they to you; their complete unselfconsciousness about nudity (and on a winter's morning you wonder how can they be so warm in their bare skins while you're freezing in every piece of clothing you have with you); the pungent smell of grease and ochre [used as body lotion for medicinal-spiritual reasons], the matted hair, the wads of tobacco that are taken from the mouth or from behind the ear and generously offered (Will refusal offend? Is *this* what our teachers meant when they said rapport must be established regardless?); the way they constantly use their lips in indicating direction, which will soon become so habitual that you continue to do it back in "civilization," providing further proof that anthropologists are crazy (or become so, after fieldwork).
>
> ROBERT TONKINSON[1]

The island continent of Australia is immense—about as large as the contiguous 48 United States—and before the arrival of the Europeans, Australia supported an Aboriginal population of at least 300,000 persons, but more likely up to 750,000 persons, speaking well over 200 mutually unintelligible languages.[2] In an area this large, it is not surprising that numerous ecological zones exist, from tropical to temperate forests and from prairies to deserts.[3] Nonetheless, as Service notes, there is great similarity in the cultures of the native Australians.[4]

Of central importance, Australian Aborigines share the same basic economic strategy: *hunting-and-gathering*. Of course, local variations exist in the types of food eaten and the specific techniques used to obtain their meals, but all of Australia's hunter-gatherers live in bands and share food.[5] In parallel to Service, Robert Tonkinson explains that an overarching Australian constellation of cultural features is clearly recognizable. Widespread cultural traits include, with some variability, the recognition of band territories, the high value placed on ceremonial exchange among groups, elaborate male initiation ceremonies, belief in a period of creation called Dreamtime that is of critical significance in Aboriginal worldview, the exclusion of the women by the men from important aspects of religion, concern with the manner that body and spirit separate after death, and the totemic identification with particular plants, animals, and supernatural creative beings.[6]

"The amazing thing about the Australians," writes Hoebel, "is their luxuriant proliferation of the nuances of kinship."[7] Totems, clans, moieties, and marriage class groups crosscut not only local bands but also tribal lines.[8] Thus Aborigine societies have more social segmentation than is typical of nomadic foragers, yet, as we will see, they nonetheless tend to be nonwarring. One reason for this may be that the members of the same kinship segments, such as clans, can reside in different bands. L. Hiatt notes, for instance, how the members of a particular band belonged to *six* different clans.[9]

An additional feature of Australian Aborigine culture overall is the richness of its spirituality. As the Aboriginal belief system explains the origin and nature of the world, it emphasizes the bonds among people, to the earth itself, to all other living creatures, and to a pantheon of spiritual beings.[10] Tonkinson explains that an Aboriginal group typically attributes geographical features in its area to the activities of Dreamtime creatures: "Creative and world-ordering acts of the first beings [of Dreamtime] are narrated in myths, acted out in dance, condensed into song, and proven by a host of landforms of all kinds, as well as by portable stone objects intimately connected to the beings themselves." Dreamtime exists not only in the past, but also in the present and the future.

Australian Aborigines believe that they should follow a system of rules, "the Law," that originates from the part-human, part-animal spiritual beings active during the Dreamtime period of creation. In the various Aboriginal belief systems, the Law specifies proper behavior, including correct patterns of exchange, appropriate interaction patterns with kin and others, marriage rules, and rituals to be performed. A whole range of proper, customary activities stem from Dreamtime and are thus in accordance with the Law.[12]

Aboriginal Australia is an intriguing and important case to consider because over the millennia predating the arrival of colonizing Europeans, the entire population on the continent lived as hunter-gatherers. Thus Australia provides an example of how hunter-gatherer bands interact with each other in the absence of the plethora of changes brought about by the development of agriculture and ensuing new forms of social organization beginning, as we have seen, about 10,000 years ago elsewhere in the world. An entire continent exclusively comprised of hunting-and-gathering bands has relevance for understanding how prehistoric bands of humans—during the long hunter-gatherer stage of human existence—interacted with each other prior to the rise of tribes, chiefdoms, states, empires, colonialism, nationalism, and, most recently, globalism.

Australian Aborigines are important to our consideration of peace and war for several reasons. First, an examination of the Aboriginal cultures of Australia shows warfare to have been the rarest of anomalies. Whether we mean war as popularly conceived or use the more precise Prosterman definition, warring was a rare anomaly among Australian Aborigines.[13] On this point, as we shall see, the anthropological evidence is unequivocal. In Aboriginal times in Australia, lethal violence took the form of murder, vengeance killings, and feud (more accurately called individual self-redress in most cases). Some deaths also occurred in the administration of Aboriginal law: during juridical fights, duels, and the punishment or execution of wrongdoers. However, lethal intergroup violence that could be considered warfare was truly the exception to the well-established peace system of the Australian Aborigines.

The second point of importance is that the Aboriginal Australians traditionally employed a rich set of social and legal mechanisms to prevent conflict and to resolve disputes within and among social groups.[14] Much physical aggression was controlled and loss of life prevented. By no means was Aboriginal society free of aggression.[15] However, the natives developed multiple, creative ways to limit and minimize the seriousness of fighting and to keep revenge killings and feuding in check. This feature of the Australian Aborigine peace system was highlighted by Edward Westermarck almost 100 years ago: "Contrary to generally held ideas on the subject, war is not the normal condition . . . [among] the Australian Aborigines; . . . there are among them germs of what is styled 'international law'; . . . there has been something like an anticipation of the Geneva Convention even in the Australian bush."[16] Before examining some of the ingenious ways that Australian Aborigines handle disputes so as to prevent and limit violence, first it makes sense to document the near absence of warfare in Aboriginal Australia. Following a consideration of these two topics, I will review social factors that are important in maintaining the Australian Aborigine peace system.

THE PAUCITY OF WARFARE

Sir Baldwin Spencer and Francis Gillen studied the Arunta (also called Aranda) of Central Australia before very much culture contact with Europeans had taken place. Based on several years of observation, they wrote:

> As a general rule the natives are kindly disposed to one another—that is, of course, within the limits of their own tribe; and, where two tribes come into contact with one another on the borderland of their respective territories, there the same amicable feelings are maintained between the members of the two. There is no such thing as one tribe being in a constant state of enmity with another so far as these Central tribes are concerned. Now and again, of course, fights do occur between the *members* of different local groups who may or may not belong to the same or different tribes.[17]

Murdock and later Service conducted extensive reviews of the ethnographic information on the Arunta and independently concluded that warfare basically was absent. Murdock expresses that "relations between groups, even of different tribes, are almost equally amicable. No such thing as a chronic state of hostility exists. . . . Actual warfare is all but unknown."[18]

In reference to the Yolngu (also known as the Murngin) from Arnhem Land in northern Australia, Nancy Williams explains that the term "Yolngu war" actually refers *only* to blood revenge.[19] In fact, as we considered in the previous chapter, loosely applying martial vocabulary like "war" and "battle" to individual self-redress, feuds, punishment of wrongdoers, and even regulated fights, which serve as a form of conflict resolution, occurs with some regularity in the literature on Australia and elsewhere.[20] For example, W. Lloyd Warner tallied up violent deaths among the Murngin, lumping together those that resulted from individual fights, group fights, revenge homicides, and even capital punishment. Compounding the confusion, Warner titled his chapter "Warfare" and therein stated that "there are six distinct varieties of *warfare* among the Murngin."[21] Such labeling muddles the issue, for as Ronald and Catherine Berndt point out about Warner's six types, "Not all can be termed warfare."[22] In accordance with Williams' assessment that Murngin violence is actually blood revenge, Warner reports that the majority of the killings stemmed from revenge seeking.[23] One of Warner's six types of so-called warfare, the *makarata,* actually is, in his own words, "a ceremonial peacemaking fight."[24] According to Warner's observations over a 20-year period, no deaths resulted from *makarata* ceremonies.[25] It is very confusing to call a nonlethal peacemaking ceremony "warfare."

Only one type of Murngin fighting, called the *gaingar,* actually resembles warfare. Tactically, men from different clans face off and throw spears to kill. Seeking revenge for previous unavenged killings is a major motivation for this "spear fight to end spear fights." Over the 20-year period investigated by Warner, two *gaingar* fights took place, which resulted in a combined total of 29 deaths. The Murngin *gaingar,* whether labeled war or feud, represents perhaps the bloodiest exception to the typical Australian Aborigine pattern characterized by a dearth of lethal intergroup encounters.[26]

In reference to another northern Australian culture, the Tiwi, C. W. M. Hart and Arnold Pilling weigh the evidence and emphasize that "The bands were not firm political entities and therefore could not do battle, as bands, with each other. . . . Hence warfare, in the sense of pitched battles between groups aligned through territorial loyalties, did not occur and could not occur among the Tiwi."[27] Shortly, we will return to the interesting case of how the Tiwi expressed grievances in juridical fights that, although *superficially resembling* warfare, actually amounted to the expression of individual grudges in accordance with established juridical procedures.

Speaking of both the Walmadjeri and the Gugadja of the Western Desert, Ronald Berndt notes the absence of any group fighting. Related to the Mardudjara, or Mardu, of the Western Desert, Tonkinson states that feuding and war are absent and points out that "there is no word for either feud or warfare in the language of the desert people" (see Figure 12.1).[28]

For another desert culture, the Walbiri, Mervyn Meggitt documents how one group challenged another over a water hole—an event Meggitt refers to as a "war of conquest."[29] Birdsell points out that by the time the incident occurred, European colonists had already disrupted the Walbiri population, and he suggests that such fights were "unlikely to have been frequent in pre-contact times."[30] Meggitt himself makes clear that this event is at odds with the *overall pattern* of intergroup interaction among Australian Aborigines. Meggitt's description of Walbiri culture reflects the typicality of feuding and blood revenge as opposed to struggling over territory. Meggitt explains that numerous factors counteract warfare, and his observations on the Walbiri also are apropos to the preponderance of Australian Aborigine societies:

> Walbiri society did not emphasize militarism—there was no class of permanent or professional warriors; there was no hierarchy of military command; and groups rarely engaged in wars of conquest. Every man was (and is still) a potential warrior, always armed and ready to defend his rights; but he was also an individualist, who preferred to fight independently. In some disputes kinship ties aligned men into opposed groups, and such a group may occasionally have comprised all the men of a community. But there were no military leaders, elected or hereditary, to plan tactics and ensure that others adopted the plans.

Figure 12.1 A Mardu hunter from Australia's Western Desert in 1965 carries spears and a carving tool. The Mardu sometimes fight, verbally and physically, but they do not feud or wage war. Sometimes disputes are resolved at the beginning of "big meetings" as several bands come together to socialize and enact rituals. (Photo courtesy of Robert Tonkinson; see Tonkinson 1978, 2004.)

> . . . There was in any case little reason for all-out warfare between communities. Slavery was unknown; portable goods were few; and the territory seized in a battle was virtually an embarrassment to the victors, whose spiritual ties were with other localities.
>
> . . . The fact that wrongdoers could often find refuge in another community also indicates that the communities usually respected each other's boundaries; and indeed the punitive party was likely to confine itself to performing sorcery at a distance. Nevertheless, attempts to avenge deaths sometimes led to incursions into the territories of neighboring communities or tribes. In the former instance, the men of the revenge party in a sense represented their community against another community and went out with their countrymen's approval. But the raids and counter-raids usually concerned only specified groups of kinsmen and could thus be kept within manageable limits; rarely would the whole community arm. The members not directly involved often acted as informal referees; by inviting men of the other community to visit them for ceremonies, they created opportunities for the public settlement of grievances.[31]

Several authors express their conclusions as to the paucity of warfare in intergroup relations in Aboriginal Australia overall. David Horton notes the lack of supporting evidence for a 19th-century European view that Aborigines lived in a state of constant hostility. Horton points instead to the prevalence of symbolic, controlled displays of aggression in Aboriginal Australia and the absence of typical causes of warfare such as "territorial expansion, securing economic advantage, differences in political and religious ideologies, and the urge to devastate and annihilate."[32] Maurice Davie writes:

> The native Australians are far from being a warlike race in spite of their frequent affrays. These arise chiefly over women and are settled bloodlessly. . . . Real war does not exist among Australians because [quoting William Sumner 1911:4] "they have no property that is worth pillaging; no tribe has anything to tempt the cupidity of another. They have no political organization, so there can be no war for power."[33]

In 1910, Gerald Wheeler thoroughly considered all of the material then available on Aboriginal society. Wheeler concluded that in Aboriginal Australia, there were no wars for conquest, few attempts to take women by force, and what so-called war there was amounted to blood feuding. Fifty years later, now with additional ethnographic reports such as Meggitt's Walbiri material at his disposal, Service likewise equates Aboriginal "war" with revenge killing. He also notes that exacting revenge "seldom results in much bloodshed and never involves taking land or any other possessions."[34]

The Berndts reach a similar conclusion, writing that "warfare in the broader sense is infrequent in Aboriginal Australia, and most examples which have been classified as such are often no more than feud." Hoebel concurs: "Among the Australians it is clearly a matter of feud, because although it is nominally within the discretion of each local group to decide what course of action will be taken, all local groups accede at some times to utilization of an institutionalized intergroup procedure for settling quarrels between their members." Again speaking for Aboriginal culture generally, Catherine Berndt states that "it is important to remember that territorial defense and territorial conquest were not salient issues in Aboriginal Australia. The land was regarded as God-given, not subject to negotiation." Separately, Ronald Berndt expresses for Aboriginal societies overall that "fights of conquest, attempts to impose the government of one group or tribe upon another, were virtually unknown."[35]

From this body of data on Australian Aborigine societies, an overall conclusion is clear. With very occasional exceptions, disputes that might at first seem to be between communities in fact turn out to be *personal grievances between individuals* living in different communities. Sometimes such grievances lead to revenge against *particular individuals* or their close kin, thus constituting personal self-redress, which if reciprocated amounts to feuding, *not war between communities.* Events that could be considered warfare are extremely few and far between in the ethnographic record of Aboriginal Australia, and in some exceptional cases may have been prompted by territorial loss and other changes caused by the arrival of Europeans.[36] At contact, the Aboriginal hunting-and-gathering societies on this island continent were functioning within a peace system wherein each society generally respected the territorial rights of its neighbors. Whereas it would probably be an exaggeration to claim that warfare never happened before

European contact, the evidence clearly supports the conclusion that warfare was a very rare anomaly among native Australian societies.[37]

CONFLICT MANAGEMENT

Turning to a consideration of dispute prevention and resolution, some processes are similar within and across group boundaries. The first point to emphasize is that individuals are supposed to follow the rules of society, the Law, as decreed originally by the spiritual beings during Dreamtime and as passed down over the generations.[38] The rules specify appropriate and inappropriate marriages, sexual partners, obligations and patterns of interaction inherent in particular kinship relations, and thus, in general, correct ways to behave. Australian Aborigine society is egalitarian relative to class-differentiated societies; however, all members are not exact equals. Australian Aborigine societies tend to be less egalitarian than nomadic hunter-gatherers from other parts of the world. Women defer to men, and young men obey certain decisions of older men.[39] Elders play an important role in the maintenance of law and order in these societies where formal political authority is minimal.[40]

Concern with sorcery is pervasive. Typically, the most serious disputes between individuals stem from *corpse trouble* and *women trouble*.[41] Deaths other than those of infants and the very old are attributed to sorcery. In the Aboriginal belief system, deaths should be avenged. Thus theoretically, every death demands another. However, as we shall soon consider, the seeking of vengeance and counter-vengeance through feuding is generally kept in check. Similarly, disputes over women have multiple causes (for example, jealousy, elopements, adultery, and unfulfilled betrothals) and likewise multiple solutions besides violence.

A recurring theme reverberates through the literature on native Australia: The seeking of vengeance through violent self-redress is the *least favored* path to justice. As a general portrait, possibly overlapping alternatives to self-redress include the following:

1. Hearings, such as "big meetings," for accusers and defendants alike to make their cases before the juries of public opinion or to talk about a problem so that elders can arrive at a lawful solution.[42]
2. Compensation of aggrieved parties for damages.[43]
3. Duels, contests, juridical fights, and the like.[44]
4. The venting of emotions through public insults, harangues, and arguments.[45]
5. Punishment of wrongdoers, often by administering a nonlethal spear wound to the thigh.[46]
6. The reconciliation of antagonists via participation in joint rituals and ceremonies, such as the *makarata*.[47]

Of course, the specifics of such procedures vary from region to region and from culture to culture. Many pages could be devoted to providing examples of Australian Aborigine intergroup dispute resolution processes, but three examples will suffice to illustrate some of the six general processes just listed.

Example 1. The Kopara *Debt: A Creative Interpretation of "A Life for a Life"*

As is typical in Aboriginal Australia, among the Lakes Tribes of South Australia most adult deaths are attributed to sorcery.[48] In the Aboriginal system of thought, a death in one's own group must be avenged, or balanced, ideally by the death of the sorcerer. However, in most cases, conducting a revenge expedition is the choice of last resort. There are other preferred options to balance a death. A *kopara* is a debt and may refer to gifts, deaths, injuries, women, or initiation ceremonies. The Lakes Tribes evoke their *kopara* system to prevent the bloodshed of vendettas and to preserve friendly relations among people living in different groups.

A typical pattern runs like this. A dying person dreams of a particular man and tells his relatives of the dream. The person's kin then suspect that that individual, or in some cases a clan, has caused their relative's death by sorcery. They hold an inquest to validate their suspicions. The corpse is balanced on the heads of two squatting men. An elder taps two *inquest sticks* together and asks the deceased whether the person in the dream is responsible. The corpse answers in the affirmative by falling off the two squatting men's heads. Once the inquest has revealed the identity of the guilty party or parties, the relatives of the deceased perceive that they are owed a *kopara* debt related to this death. The relatives may attempt to balance the death, in other words, to collect the *kopara* debt, in various ways.

One option is for the accused murderer's clan to give a woman as a wife to a member of the dead person's clan—thus preventing a revenge expedition. A more intriguing option involves the exchange of *a life for a life,* but in a ceremonial way so that no one is actually killed. In order to become a man, a youth must be circumcised and initiated into manhood. When this rite of passage occurs, the youth is "killed," symbolically speaking, and replaced by his new adult identity that is more valued in society. The *kopara* debt incurred by the original sorcery killing can be balanced if one of the dead person's relatives circumcises a youth from the accused killer's group, thus symbolically "killing" the youth. Elkin writes: "This is a strange sort of punishment or revenge, but the discipline associated with the period of initiation, together with the increased importance and responsibility felt by the individual is no doubt, in most cases, a very wise course and of great social value. The Aborigines certainly prefer it to quarrelling and fighting."[49]

Example 2. Tiwi Juridical Fights: Letting Off Steam

Among the Tiwi of northern Australia, individual and group grievances are expressed at intergroup gatherings via the delivery of harangues, duels, and juridical fights. The public nature of these events and the established rules of conduct allow for the venting of emotions and the solving of some disputes (although also perhaps the creation of new ones) in a relatively harmless manner compared to the dangers associated with vengeance-seeking.[50]

Wheeler calls this type of event a *regulated or juridical fight* and explains that participants "avoid any bloodshed other than that due to wounds; the first blood that flows puts an end to the fight and settles the dispute."[51] Wheeler also emphasizes that juridical fights are a strictly regulated form of justice and occur in many Australian Aborigine cultures.[52] In this account, certain members of two Tiwi bands, the Tiklauila and the

Rangwila, express their grievances against particular members of the Mandiimbula band. Since the exact language of the original description is critical, I quote Hart and Pilling verbatim, adding italics for emphasis in some places.*

> Some of these [disputes] were seduction cases but some of them involved charges by elder against elder, of non-delivery of bestowed daughters, or other types of broken promises. Some of these cases had been going on for years, and settlement of them at the level of the individual duel had failed. The aggrieved individuals in the two Bathurst Island bands therefore pooled their grievances, persuaded many of their relatives and friends who were not aggrieved to join them, and a large party of men of all ages set off for the Mandiimbula territory.
>
> This party, comprising about thirty fighting men all heavily armed and all wearing the white paint indicative of anger and hostile intent, was a "war" party, and its coming to their territory was recognized as such by the Mandiimbula. On arrival at the place where the latter, duly warned of its approach, had gathered, the war party announced its presence. Both sides then exchanged a few insults and agreed to meet formally the next day in an open space where there was plenty of room. *After a night mostly spent by both sides in individual visiting and renewing old acquaintances,* the two armies met next morning in battle array, with the thirty Tiklauila-Rangwila warriors drawn up at one end of the clearing, and about sixty local warriors at the other end. Immediately the *familiar patterns* of the duel imposed themselves. A senior individual on one side began a harangue directed at an *individual* on the other. When he ran out of breath, *another individual* began his complaint. Since each accused Mandiimbula replied individually to the charges made against him, *the whole proceeding remained at the level of mutual charges and replies between pairs of individuals.* Angry old men on both sides often seemed to be trying to find a basis that would justify or provoke a general attack by one group upon the other, but always failed to find it because of the particularity of the charges. *The rules of Tiwi procedure compelled the accuser to specify the sources of his charges and his anger,* and those always turned out to be directed not at the Mandiimbula band, but at one, or at most two or three, individual members of the band. And when another old man took the center of attention, his anger would be directed at quite different individuals. *Hence when spears began to be thrown, they were thrown by individuals for reasons based on individual disputes.* Unlike the seduction duels [that generally involved an elder wounding a young man in the arm or thigh as punishment for seducing a wife], these duels occurred mostly between two senior men, and the danger of a direct hit was much reduced because of the poor marksmanship of both parties. On the other hand, the danger of somebody getting hurt was increased because a fight between two old men was likely to spread as other old men were drawn into it to support one or the other side—in which case, a wild melee occurred with badly thrown spears flying in all directions. This was probably a good thing, because soon somebody was bound to be hit, thus ending the fight. Not infrequently the person hit was some innocent noncombatant or one of the *screaming old women who weaved through the fighting men, yelling obscenities at everybody,* and whose reflexes for dodging spears were not as fast as those of the men.
>
> As soon as somebody was wounded, even a seemingly irrelevant crone, *fighting stopped immediately* until the implications of this new incident could be assessed by

* From "The Tiwi of North Australia" Fieldwork Edition by Hart & Pilling, copyright 1979. Reprinted with permission of Wadsworth, a division of Thomson Learning: www.thomsonrights.com. Fax 800-730-2215.

both sides. For the crone was never really irrelevant; she was somebody's mother and somebody else's wife and somebody else's sister and therefore the question of who threw the spear that wounded her gave rise to a new series of wrangles which had to be integrated into all the old ones. A man who had been quietly sitting, minding his own business and having no quarrels with anybody, would suddenly leap into the center of the stage and announce that the damaged old lady was his mother and therefore he wanted the hide of the rat that had damaged her, and a whole new argument was in progress.

If the person wounded in the first flurry of spear throwing was a senior male, that similarly led the arguments off in some new direction since his kinsmen in *both* war parties [italics in original] felt compelled to support him or revenge his wound or inflict a wound on his wounder. Frequently it appeared that the original matters of dispute, which had brought the two war parties together in the first place, were forgotten and lost in the new disputes and fights that originated on the field of battle. Such a view was supported by the frequency with which one found at the end of the day that the main causalities and the main headline performers had been people who had gone to the field of battle in the morning with no quarrel with anybody, and not even wearing white paint. Even the most peaceful spectator in the most remote corner of the gallery was likely to find himself in the center of the ring before the day was over at a Tiwi "battle."

Despite this apparent confusion and near anarchy of procedure, however, *the main outlines were quite clear. The bands were not firm political entities and therefore could not do battle, as bands, with each other. Everybody, on both sides, was interrelated in the same kinship system.* An angry old Tiklauila, abusing and throwing spears at an angry old Mandiimbula, might have as the basis of his complaint the fact that the Mandiimbula father had promised but not delivered one of his daughters. Since Tiwi bestowals were from mother's brother to sister's son, the spear throwing was patently a case of a sister's son abusing his mother's brother, and the fact that the two men belonged to different bands was not germane to their dispute. The angry Tiklauila elder could not demand support from other Tiklauila *as Tiklauila* [emphasis in original] in the case at issue for it involved a dispute between kinsmen whose band affiliations were irrelevant to the subject matter. Mainly for this reason *the so-called war party of one band against another band turned out to be only a loose collection of individuals,* each with his own case to argue, who found it convenient, and safer, to travel together into the territory of another band and argue all their individual cases on the same day at the same place. *Tiwi interpersonal relations were primarily kin relations between members of all bands, territorial loyalties* [that is, band loyalties] *were shifting ones, temporary and necessarily quite subordinate to kin loyalties. Hence warfare, in the sense of pitched battles between groups aligned through territorial loyalties, did not occur and could not occur among the Tiwi.*[53]

Example 3. Penis-Holding and Coitus: Reaffirming Bonds of Trust

In one usage, the penis-holding rite of the Aranda reaffirms peaceful relations among the male participants. In another context, the penis-holding rite is incorporated within a dispute resolution procedure. A variation of the dispute resolution procedure includes sexual intercourse in place of penis-holding if the accused individual is a woman. In either case, the standing of the social relationship is expressed by engaging in or abstaining from acts of physical intimacy (penis contact or intercourse). Reconciliation is symbolically reinforced by the reestablishment of intimate contact within ritual contexts.[54]

The primary purpose of the penis-holding rite is to resolve a grievance; however, a simplified version of the rite is associated with demonstrating good fellowship and a lack of enmity among men from divergent groups who unite to conduct a ritual. Each man belonging to one group in turn approaches each man belonging to a second group and pulls the hand of each partner so as to feel the underside of his penis. Only subincised men can take part in the penis-holding rite, since the incisure on the underside of the penis, not the penis itself, is the important feature in the rite. Subincision is a critical aspect of initiation into manhood in some Australian societies. In this operation, traditionally conducted with a sharp stone flake knife, the underside of a youth's penis is cut so as to split the urethra all the way to the scrotum. Once his wound heals, the male is considered an adult. During the rite, it is the urethral incision that is touched.

If a particular man is suspected of having caused the death by sorcery of another, a meeting may be called to determine his guilt or innocence. Two groups gather at a particular camp. The suspected man sits in the camp in the company of his friends and relatives, whereas the person or persons who are accusing him wait just outside the main camp. In turn, each man in the group in which the death has occurred carries out the penis-holding rite with all the men of the suspect's group, but not with the suspect himself. However, in all likelihood, one man of the suspect's group refuses to participate in the rite with the members of the accusing group until he has a chance to speak on behalf of his comrade. The advocate for the accused then delivers a speech in defense of his fellow. As his speech progresses, the defender first moves toward an elder man of his own group and penis-touches with him, and then he moves to an elder man of the accuser's group and penis-touches with him as well. As the defender reiterates his arguments, he moves from man to man in both groups engaging in the rite with all of them, except with the accused. "On completion of this procedure he would, so to speak, have offered his own life for that of his friend, as a result of his firm conviction of the latter's innocence."[55]

When the defender concludes his speech, the entire group sits in silence contemplating for some 15 minutes or so. When the leaders of each group reach a decision, the nature of the decision is relayed to the others by hand signal. The leaders then rise, walk over to where the defender of the accused is sitting, and engage in penis-holding with him. This means that the accused has been acquitted of the charges. All the other men then touch-penis with both the defender and the accused himself. With this outcome, the accused is considered to be cleared of the charges against him and no one can accuse him again of the same death. "Later that night, the man who had previously been accused would come to his defender and offer his penis to the latter 'for saving his life.' The defender would in turn get up and offer his penis, at the same time saying, 'I could not see them accusing you wrongly.' "[56]

If charges were brought against a woman, she might arrange for a male relative to stand for her. However, many women were not afraid to defend themselves. Berndt and Berndt describe the situation:

> She herself would be present at such a meeting where her accusers were gathered; rising and going among the latter group, she would touch the arms of those men who had accused her; then, returning to her own group, she would touch those men who would if necessary be called upon to defend her. Later she would tell her friend's husband to notify all those men whose arms she had touched that she would be ready for them at some

> particular place. At the appointed time she would go alone to this spot, situated outside the main camp, and offer herself for coitus to each of the men concerned [both her accusers and defenders]. At the time of coitus, and during the actual act when they were lying close together, the man must tell her that "he won't kill her," or in any way accuse her again in that particular affair (or should he be the defender, that he would stand by her). Should there be one man who did not appear at the arranged place for coitus, she would know that he still considered her to be in the wrong—i.e. "he won't give himself to her." . . . In this case another meeting might be called, a male relative of the woman standing for her. Should the matter not be settled in this way, the accuser might instigate a fight (i.e. should he consider himself to be in the right), or flee the camp, or be involved in a spearing (should he stubbornly refuse to accept the evidence of the woman or of her male defender). Should the accuser be in the wrong, and finally relent when matters have gone too far, he would arrange for his wife, a female relative, or a friend standing in relationship to him as a wife or sister, to stand for him. He would arrange matters with all the men concerned in the case so that at an appointed time they would go out, one by one, and copulate with the chosen representative of the man, at the same time telling her that the whole affair would be dropped; the matter would then be considered almost settled, the latter woman "squaring" the case, both parties having now put forth a woman. To finalize the affair completely, the original accuser must copulate with the first woman, telling her at the same time that he had wrongly accused her.[57]

SUMMING UP

In conclusion, a long list of features traditionally militated against warfare in Aboriginal Australia. First, although opinions and decisions of elder men carried more weight than those of younger men and the women, Australian societies were not greatly hierarchical. Consequently, no one held enough coercive power to command or direct military actions either of their own local band or any larger tribal unit.[58]

Second, as nomadic hunter-gatherers, the Aborigines were regularly on the move in search of food. Consequently, they had few material possessions or caches of stored food that others might be tempted to plunder.[59]

Third, groups were interconnected with one another through ties of kinship, religion, ceremonial exchanges, and trade. The importance of intergroup ties and interdependencies has been thoroughly documented.[60]

Fourth, band membership was not static, but open. Individuals and families could exercise the option of shifting band residence in the short term or long term. The fluidity of band composition is one feature that contributed to interconnections among bands (see point three). Virtually every person had relatives and personal contacts in other groups, and these overlapping social and kinship networks that spanned the flexible bands served to dampen intergroup hostility (see Figure 12.2).[61]

Fifth, in the typical Australian Aborigine belief system, tribal territories originated in Dreamtime and theoretically were not changeable. Such beliefs can be seen as one of many factors discouraging warfare for territorial gain.[62]

Sixth, resources often were reciprocally shared across band territories. Reciprocity came into play when a band with an abundance of some resource—a good harvest of a particular food plant, for example—invited neighboring bands to come and share the windfall. Such generosity was reciprocated in the future as another group experienced

Figure 12.2 A group of Mardu from western Australia in 1964. Among the Mardu, as among hunter-gatherer bands generally, group composition fluctuates over time. The people pictured here would, undoubtedly, have relatives spread over other bands. As illustrated in the Tiwi example discussed in this chapter, kinship ties do not stop at the band's edge, but instead interconnect people across bands. This characteristic of nomadic band society is one of many features that hinders violence between entire groups. (Photo courtesy of Robert Tonkinson.)

an abundance of some resource. In accordance with social custom, when use of a particular resource, whether abundant or not, was requested, permission was generally granted. To the contrary, poaching in the absence of permission could be considered a serious crime. The Aborigine belief system that promoted generosity and resource sharing and the typical compliance with the social rules (the Law) regarding, for example, asking and granting permissions helped to make trespassing, stealing, poaching, or fighting over resources all the less likely.[63]

Seventh, a well-developed legal system existed that served to settle many personal disputes within bands and also between persons living in different bands or tribes. Aboriginal cultures generally shared certain emphases: obey the Law (the rules and customs) originating during Dreamtime, punish wrongdoers who disregarded the Law, attempt to obtain justice via sorcery, or try to resolve disputes through a variety of mechanisms, for example, via duels, contests, and juridical fights; meetings and discussions; arrangements of *kopara* debts; enactment of reconciliation ceremonies; and so forth.[64]

Eighth, the most common grievances involved accusation of sorcery, rights to women, and, less often, trespass or poaching of a resource. Such grievances tended to be directed at particular *individuals,* not entire bands.[65]

Ninth, the preferred means of dealing with grievances was to handle them via the legal procedures available (see point seven), but the seeking of revenge through individual self-redress, sometimes resulting in the counter-vengeance of feuding, also occurred in some Aboriginal societies. As discussed in chapters 7 and 8, the revenge killings and feuding that stem from personal grievances tend not to pit political communities against one another in the kind of intergroup lethal combat that results in indiscriminant, multiple casualties that legitimately can be called warfare.[66]

Taking into consideration the forgoing points, I suggest that with exceedingly rare exceptions, the types of physical aggression that traversed Australian Aborigine group boundaries cannot be called war. Instead, such aggression consisted on the one hand of *vengeance-seeking through violent self-redress,* an activity that if reciprocated could become feuding, and on the other hand, a class of *legal procedures* consisting of physical punishment, duels, juridical fights, and the like, whose purpose was to deliver justice with *a minimal amount of violence.* These latter approaches were mechanisms for keeping the peace, *and certainly not warfare* (see Box 12.1).

BOX 12.1 ABORIGINAL ROCK ART: IS WARFARE MERELY IN THE EYES OF THE (WESTERN) BEHOLDER?

We have seen that the Murngin of Arnhem Land in northern Australia engaged in a ceremonial peacemaking fight called the *makarata.* Warner explains, "It is a kind of general duel and a partial ordeal which allows the aggrieved parties to vent their feelings by throwing spears at their enemies or by seeing the latter's blood run in expiation."[1] Whereas the ceremony does not always succeed in restoring the peace, over the 20-year period of Warner's study, no one was ever killed during a *makarata.* During the expiation ceremony, the elders continuously remind those throwing spears "to be careful not to kill or hurt anyone."[2] Clearly the *makarata* is not warfare; it is an example of conflict resolution, Australian Aborigine style.[3]

Exquisite rock art showing animals, humans, and mythological beings is spread across Arnhem Land. Dating to perhaps 10,000 years ago in the oldest cases, most of the human scenes portray tranquil daily activities, but some show figures amidst flying spears and boomerangs. Archaeologists Paul Tacon and Christopher Chippindale advance the seemingly obvious interpretation that such scenes portray warfare. The main title of their article, for instance, is "Australia's Ancient Warriors." They explain that "some of the paintings depict fighting, warriors, aspects or the results of warfare, and even elaborate, detailed battle scenes."[4]

However, to question the seemingly obvious, there are at least two reasons to doubt whether most of the rock art actually portrays warfare at all. The first is the overall rarity of war among Aboriginal Australians, the pattern that we have been considering in this chapter. The second stems from the scenes themselves and what is known about Australian Aborigine conflict resolution procedures. The majority of the rock art depictions of aggression are consistent with ethnographically described events that have nothing to do with *warfare:* revenge killings, the punishment of wrongdoers by delivering spear wounds to the thigh, and, especially, ceremonial expiatory duels, such as the *makarata,* as a typically Australian form of conflict resolution. For example, in one scene, a *single* figure has a spear penetrating its torso, an image more concordant with the aftermath of a killing than a battle—there is, after all, only one victim portrayed.[5] In another case, a single figure has been speared in the thigh, an image consistent with an inflicted punishment.[6]

Figure 12.3 As portrayed in Aboriginal rock art from northern Australia, two figures appear to be fighting with boomerangs. The arrow points to a boomerang that is "in flight" between the two figures. (Redrawn with permission from P. Tacon & C. Chippindale, 1994, "Australia's ancient warriors: Changing depictions of fighting in the rock art of Arnhem Land, N.T.," *Cambridge Archaeological Journal* 4:211–248.)

Significantly, most rock art scenes that portray aggression show only a few individuals, a pattern reminiscent of punishments and duels, *not intergroup warfare.*[7] In speaking of rock art called Dynamic Figures, Tacon and Chippindale write, "In most cases where actual combat is suggested only two or three figures are engaged in some sort of encounter. *There are many examples of two opposed figures* [see Figure 12.3]. . . . At a site above Jim Jim Falls, two opposed Dynamic Figures appear to be engaged in a boomerang fight."[8] By contrast to the abundant two-person dueling scenes, images of groups facing off against one another are relatively rare. Additionally, recalling the way that the Tiwi meet in groups to haggle, throw spears, and vent their emotions, it would seem unwise to jump to the conclusion, on the basis of rock art alone, that bloody battles rather than juridical fights and duels are being presented *even in group scenes.*

In short, the corpus of ethnographic data on Australian Aborigines contradicts the a priori assumption that most of these rock art fighting scenes are actually portraying *warfare.* Instead, even when multiple individuals are shown, the ethnographic data would suggest that, more probably, group-sanctioned punishments, expiatory duels, and similar grievance settlement procedures are being depicted.[9] When viewed from this ethnographic contextualizing perspective, certain speculations offered by Tacon and Chippindale about the supposed intensification of prehistoric *warfare* in this part of Australia become superfluous: There is not much point in speculating about an intensification of warfare if the events pictured are not actually warfare.[10] Given the individual nature of disputes in band society overall, the duels, contests, and other ritualized modes of conflict resolution regularly used by native Australians in particular, and the paucity of warfare in the Australian Aborigine context, shouldn't presumptions that rock art *shows war* elicit some healthy skepticism?

I suspect that the *concept of war* enters the picture, not so much from the minds of the original artists themselves as from the interpretations imposed on the artwork by cultural outsiders. Westerners tend to take war for granted. In their article, the Western archaeologists use the word "warfare" 37 times, "war" 12 times, "warring" twice, "military" or "militarily" 8 times, "battle" or "battles" 22 times, and "warrior" or "warriors" 6 times (which totals to 87 war words), whereas they refer to "resolution of disputes," "settle grievances," and "settling arguments" one time each and "conflict resolution" only twice (for a total of 5 dispute resolution terms). There also are many aggressive terms in the article that could be applied to individual or group aggression, such as violence, fight, combat, skirmish, clash, and enemy. The counting of particular words can provide only a rapid and rough reflection of which topics receive emphasis. By this count, Tacon and Chippindale employ unambiguous war terms about *17 times* more often than they use conflict resolution terminology (87 versus 5). This ratio is greatly out of step with what is ethnographically known about the widespread use of conflict resolution procedures in Australian Aborigine societies, on the one hand, and the paucity of war, on the other. Could Tacon and Chippindale's decision to use "warriors" in the title of their article and the fact that their article overflows with war terminology, while virtually neglecting a consideration of indigenous conflict resolution procedures, reflect, once again, the influences of a cultural tradition on scientific interpretation in which the naturalness and antiquity of war are simply taken for granted?

Sources: 1. Warner 1969:163. 2. Warner 1969:164. 3. See Berndt 1965. 4. Tacon & Chippindale 1994:214. 5. Tacon & Chippindale 1994: Figure 3, page 218. A few scenes do show more than one victim. 6. Tacon & Chippindale 1994:220; see also Knauft 1994; Warner 1969:165; Tonkinson 1978, 2004. 7. See Knauft 1994. 8. Tacon & Chippindale 1994:220, italics added. 9. See Berndt 1965; Berndt & Berndt 1996; Goodale 1974; Hart & Pilling 1979; Kaberry 1973; Spencer & Gillen 1927; Tonkinson 2004; Warner 1969; Wheeler 1910 10. Tacon & Chippindale 1994:225.

CHAPTER 13

WAR-LADEN SCENARIOS OF THE PAST

Uncovering a Heap of Faulty Assumptions

> For more than 99 percent of the approximately two million years since the emergence of a recognizable human animal, man has been a hunter and gatherer. . . . Questions concerning territorialism, the handling of aggression, social control, property, leadership, the use of space, and many other dimensions are particularly significant in these contexts. To evaluate any of these focal aspects of human behavior without taking into consideration the socioeconomic adaptation that has characterized most of the span of human life on this planet will eventually bias conclusions and generalizations.
>
> M. G. Bicchieri[1]

My sister Mollie once told me a joke about a chicken farmer who was eager to increase egg production. Hoping to benefit from the latest scientific knowledge, the farmer paid a visit to the university. He eventually ended up talking with a good-natured physicist. After hearing the problem, the physicist said, "Let me work on this for awhile. Can you come back in a week or two?" The farmer agreed and returned two weeks later. "Good news. I solved your problem," announced the physicist. Producing a thick pile of papers filled with equations and calculations, she continued, "First of all, we assume a two-dimensional chicken. . . ."

In science, whether designing an experiment or developing a theoretical model, we make certain initial assumptions because we can't investigate everything all at once. The physicist in my sister's joke begins by stating an *explicit* assumption, which has the advantage of holding it up for review. Obviously, making unrealistic assumptions can lead to unrealistic conclusions. We can assess at the onset that the physicist's recommendations for increasing egg production are based on a seemingly dubious assumption about the two-dimensionality of chickens.

Another class of assumptions—*implicit* assumptions—can be even more problematic in scientific endeavors because they are simply taken for granted. Implicit assumptions creep into theoretical modeling, research design, and scientific interpretations. We have already considered some cases involving implicit assumptions, such as when Blanc just seemed to have assumed that prehistoric hyenas had no relevance to understanding the condition of the Neanderthal skull in the Monte Circeo cave.

Overall, the more implicit assumptions we can identify, the better, because this allows us to assess whether they are in fact realistic. In this chapter and the next, I will attempt to bring out into the open some of the typical assumptions that lie behind recent writings on warfare and human evolution. The first step in this process is to summarize several recent discussions on this topic and to compile a list of recurring assumptions made in these works.

MAKING THE IMPLICIT EXPLICIT

Biologist Richard Alexander proposes a "balance of power" hypothesis.[2] Unlike most writers, Alexander is clear that he is proposing a hypothesis, as opposed to a conclusion: "At some early point in our history the actual function of human groups—their significance for their individual members—was protection from the predatory effects of other human groups. . . . Multi-male bands . . . stayed together largely or entirely because of the threat of other, similar, nearby groups of humans."[3] Assumptions underlying Alexander's thinking are that prehistoric groups were hostile and predatory toward their neighbors.[4] Pervasive intergroup hostility, in turn, accounted for groups staying together. His model also implies that group membership would have been largely fixed and stable due to the inherent hostility among different groups.

Economists Paul Shaw and Yuwa Wong assume that "warfare propensities are deeply entrenched in human nature."[5] Shaw and Wong apply a biological theorem—*the competitive exclusion principle* that explains why *two species* that rely on the same resources tend not to coexist—to different human groups, that is, *within the same* species.[6] Referring to the last one to two million years, Shaw and Wong describe the ancestors of present day humans as living in "small, tight-knit groups" of kin, numbering at most 100 persons, which they call *nucleus ethnic groups*.[7] According to their model, "relationships between nucleus ethnic groups were shaped *largely by conflict* in an environment of scarce resources."[8] Shaw and Wong supportively summarize Alexander's "balance of power" hypothesis, adding, "intergroup competition and warfare over scarce resources would have had to be *widely prevalent* throughout evolution."[9] In short, Shaw and Wong presume that tight-knit kin groups with propensities for war were engaged in ongoing fighting with one another. They also assume that resources were scarce and that humans regularly fought over them.

Biologist Bobbi Low continues in the same vein, asserting for example that "through evolutionary history, men [in contrast to women] have been able to gain reproductively by warring behavior."[10] Like Alexander and Shaw and Wong, Low assumes that war existed over long expanses of evolutionary time. Low explicitly asserts that in the evolutionary past, *lineages* of related men lived together and fought with other *lineages* of related, communally living men.[11] Reasons for past and present war include, according to Low, "women, revenge, agricultural lands, new territory, or any devised reason."[12] For Low, the key assumptions seem to be that engaging in war has lead to reproductive rewards for men during the evolution of the human species and that warring is facilitated when genetically related men live together.

Wrangham and Peterson echo the themes of the previous authors, using the term *male bonded* to refer to aggressive coalitions of patrilineal males—that is, individuals that are descended from a common ancestral male.[13] These authors compare humans and chimpanzees and focus on apparent similarities regarding male-initiated territorial aggression. They generalize the pattern to *all* human communities, assuming that, "In short, the system of communities defended by related men is a human universal that crosses space and time."[14]

As a final example, Ghiglieri assumes that warfare is ancient ("wars are older than humanity itself"), that warfare is natural ("*Wars erupt naturally everywhere humans are present*"), and that warfare has been critical in human evolution ("War vies with sex for the distinction of being the most significant process in human evolution").[15] By war, Ghiglieri means "*conflict between social groups that is resolved by individuals on one or both sides killing those on the opposite side.*"[16] According to Ghiglieri, war is a male reproductive strategy that was favored during human evolution.[17] He writes, "sexual selection and kin selection have designed human males—*compelled* human males—to wage war as a strategy to cooperatively seize the territory, resources, and women of other men and to use them reproductively. . . . According to the primeval conditions under which war evolved, a man could accrue more wives through war and thus raise his reproductive success by an order of magnitude."[18] In other words, Ghiglieri assumes that war is an *evolutionary adaptation* that has evolved expressly to fulfill specific functions.[19] Furthermore, he asserts that among other traits *male bonding*—in general and especially among groups of related males—and *leadership* "blend in natural selection's recipe for war."[20]

In these scenarios of prehistoric life, war is assumed to result from selection pressures operating over a long expanse of evolutionary time.[21] A careful analysis of these works, which I will refer to collectively as the Pervasive Intergroup Hostility Model, reveals interconnected assumptions about the human past.[22] War is extremely ancient. Intergroup relations tended to be hostile in the past. Group membership was largely fixed—the exception being that women were captured from neighboring groups as a goal of war. The males in a group were genetically related to one another, perhaps as members of a patrilineage. Related males readily *bonded* and cooperated with each other in warfare. Effective male bonding and cooperation in war paid off in terms of increased reproductive success for males engaging in these behaviors. Critical resources were scarce. War was waged to acquire scarce resources, territory, and women. Leadership and warrior behaviors correlated with reproductive success and thus were evolutionarily favored.

This evolutionary scenario might seem reasonable. First, the model seems internally coherent and logical. Second, when scientists evoke evolutionary concepts like sexual selection and the competitive exclusion principle, their status as experts and use of impressive jargon contribute a scientific air to the model. Third, the model may simply "feel right" in many ways. That is, it seems to be in agreement with our own everyday observations about the nature of warfare and human societies. We *know* from history and politics, for example, that intergroup hostilities often exist, social groups are bounded, relatives tend to support each other, wars are fought to conquer and defend territory or over scarce resources, leadership in war is important, and so on.

Despite the apparent plausibility of this scenario, I am going to propose that the assumptions underlying the Pervasive Intergroup Hostility Model are about as realistic as presuming the barnyard to be filled with two-dimensional chickens. Of course, that a model might "feel right" is not sufficient grounds for uncritically accepting the host of assumptions upon which it rests. For centuries, the model of a flat earth "felt right" to many Europeans. Instead, we must ask: Does the model match our best available observations of the facts? Are the implicit and explicit assumptions inherent in the explanation really reasonable when checked against observations of the real world? Additionally, in this case, we can question whether some of the evolutionary principles are really being applied in a sensible, logical manner.

Basically, insights about behavior and society during the evolutionary past come from three sources: (1) archaeology, (2) primate analogy, and (3) hunter-gatherer analogy. Each method has its strengths and weaknesses. Archaeology's contributions to understanding the past are significant and obvious. Archaeology provides material evidence, but unfortunately leaves out much detail. Related to warfare, we have already discussed in chapter 10 how war leaves an archaeological trail and how the worldwide archaeological record shows a steady spread and intensification of warfare only in the most recent millennia, the time period corresponding with a multitude of major changes in human social life following the agricultural revolution. We have also considered several cases that highlight the necessity of maintaining vigilance against accepting reconstructions of the past that deviate greatly from observable archaeological facts.

Primate analogy attempts to glean insights about the life of human precursors by studying living nonhuman primates, especially those species most closely related to humans. Features that are widely shared among primates, for example, living in social groups, are thought to be evolutionary ancient patterns. When two species such as humans and chimpanzees share certain features, it is often supposed that members of a common ancestral species also had these characteristics. However, this assumption may or may not be true depending on the feature in question. Similar features with similar functions also can evolve separately in different evolutionary lines—wings used for flight among certain insects and birds provide a classic illustration. Furthermore, features that appear similar may have evolved to fulfill different functions from one species to the next. Finally, some similarities between species may not constitute evolved adaptations at all, but mere fortuitous effects. For example, the observation that both chimpanzees and humans can offer skilled comic performances in front of large audiences at the circus does not suggest that *comic circus performing* is an ancient evolutionary adaptation stemming from an ancestral species common to chimpanzees and humans.

In the following discussion, rather than speculating about common ancestral features among humans and their closest living primate relatives—chimpanzees, bonobos, and gorillas—I am going to keep the focus directly on humans. My premise is that we will learn a great deal more about *human warfare and society* by studying *humans* than by studying other species. As Ferguson points out, "If chimps do make war, that tells us something about chimps, not humans."[23]

With hunter-gatherer analogy, the evolutionary time frame is shorter than with primate analogy, and insights relate directly to the human line. The rationale for drawing hunter-gatherer analogies is that the social and physical environments of current-day simple nomadic foragers are similar in many ways to those under which early humans evolved. The lifestyle *patterns* that recur across contemporary hunter-gatherer bands approximate past patterns better than those of any other type of society, a point emphasized in the chapter epigraph by Bicchieri. As Boehm expresses: "such people can serve as rough proxies for the foragers in whose groups our genes evolved."[24]

We must not assume that today's foragers live *exactly* as our ancestors lived. Various forces in world history have influenced current-day nomadic hunter-gatherers.[25] Over recent millennia, many simple hunter-gatherers have had varying degrees of contact with sedentary neighbors.[26] Nonetheless, compared to other choices for comparison, ranging from tribal peoples, such as the much-discussed Yanomamö, to the citizens of modern nation-states—or, for that matter, chimpanzees and bonobos if we engage in primate analogy—the *most basic, nomadic, hunter-gatherer societies clearly are the best choice for gaining insights about the societies of our ancestors*. First, as members of the same genus, *Homo,* existing simple nomadic hunter-gatherers are much more closely related to ancestral humans of the last one or two million years than are any living apes. Second, band social organization and reliance on foraging are critical features that most closely match those of ancestral humans. Our goal will be to compare the *assumptions* of the Pervasive Intergroup Hostility Model with our *best information* about the human past, as gleaned from archaeological findings and especially hunter-gatherer analogy.

In considering hunter-gatherers, our focus will be on the "simplest of the simple," the nomadic bands, as our best model. Thus we will favor information on *nomadic bands* over societies that have adopted a sedentary lifestyle, on *horseless hunter-gatherers* over those that have adopted the horse for hunting—an extremely recent practice, by the way—and *nonhierarchical* groups over socially ranked cases.[27] To best recreate the past, we will focus on the types of forager societies that most closely mirror the types of social organization and subsistence patterns of ancestral hunting-and-gathering humans, the way of life for *all humanity* over the numerous millennia prior to the recent development of agriculture.[28]

Additionally, the challenge is to assess *recurring patterns,* or *themes,* apparent in simple hunter-gatherer societies, rather than to grab idiosyncratic ethnographic tidbits from a few cultures. Boehm refers to this approach as an assessment of *central tendencies*. Robert Foley expresses a similar idea: "It is the *patterns, processes,* and *principles* derived from contemporary studies, not the events themselves, that should be extrapolated back in time. In this way the present can serve as a source of expectations about the past, without acting as a strait-jacket."[29]

How does the Pervasive Intergroup Hostility Model correspond with the facts derived from archaeology and an examination of simple hunter-gatherers? We have already seen that the oldest archaeological evidence of warfare dates to around 10,000 years ago, or only slightly older if we count the ambiguous Jabel Sahaba site near the Nile River. Earlier than this, there are only sporadic cases of homicide evident in the worldwide archaeological record, but no clear-cut evidence of *warfare*.[30]

Do data on the simple nomadic hunter-gatherer lifestyle support the cluster of assumptions that during human evolution, hostile, tightly knit, closed groups of related males regularly made war on neighboring groups over scarce resources, including territory and women? To separate the issues for analysis, are ethnographic data on forager bands supportive of the following assumptions about the past? (1) Groups consisted of male-bonded patrilineages in common residence. (2) Groups were tight-knit and bounded. (3) Intergroup hostility and warfare were *prevalent*. (4) Chronic resource scarcity caused wars. (5) More specifically, wars were waged over territory and to abduct women. (6) Military virtues and leadership were valued and prevalent.

THE PATRILINEAL–PATRILOCAL ASSUMPTION

Groups of related males, linked via a common ancestral male into a *patrilineage* and living together in what anthropologists refer to as *patrilocality,* are by no means universal features of nomadic hunter-gatherer bands. First Steward and later Service proposed such ideas, but other studies of hunter-gatherer societies have shown patrilineal, patrilocal assumptions to be at odds with reality.[31] Reviewing the issue in 1983, Alan Barnard concludes that "new generations of scholars gave the *coup de grace* to the patrilocal model. All over the world, societies of small community size were shown to be neither essentially virilocal nor patrilineal in any sense."[32] Virilocal reflects a mixed pattern of residence wherein patrilocality is prevalent.

Knauft provides quantitative data from a sample of 39 simple hunter-gatherer societies that show the assumption of predominant patrilineal-patrilocality to be untenable.[33] A majority of Knauft's societies recognize descent from both male and female ancestors—in anthropological terms, *ambilineal* or *bilateral* descent. Additionally, nearly three-quarters of these simple hunter-gatherer societies lack any form of patrilineal kin group. Finally, only about one-quarter exhibit patrilocal residence.

An examination of the same features for the 21 hunter-gatherer band societies in the SCCS (see chapter 8) yields somewhat similar results. The two samples define simple hunter-gatherers slightly differently and are *not* independent of each other since undoubtedly many societies appear within both lists. The SCCS sample has the advantage of representing world cultural provinces, but the disadvantage of being only about half the size of Knauft's group. The corresponding findings from both samples are summarized in Table 13.1.

The overall evaluation is this. Some simple hunter-gatherers are patrilineal or patrilocal, but most are not. Contradicting the assumption of the Pervasive Intergroup Hostility Model, bilateral descent is most typical, which means that kinship to mother's

TABLE 13.1 Descent and residence data for two samples of simple foraging societies that run counter to the Pervasive Intergroup Hostility Model's patrilineal–patrilocal assumption

Murdock Codes[a]	Knauft Sample[b] (n = 39)	SCCS Sample (n = 21)
Descent		
Bilateral or ambilineal descent (col. 24, codes B or K)	59%	71%
Lack patrilineal kin groups of any type (col. 20, code O)	72%	86%
Residence		
Patrilocal (col. 16, code P)	26%	10%
Virilocal (col. 16, code V)	–	40%

Note: Patrilocal residence is when residence is normally with or near a husband's male patrilineal relatives. *Virilocal* connotes a mixed pattern of residence in society that favors living near male kin, but in situations where paternal kin are neither aggregated into patrilineages nor patrilocal kin groups.[c] The sample of simple hunter-gatherers from the SCCS (see chapter 8) includes the !Kung (Ju/'hoansi), Hadza, Mbuti, Semang, Andamanese, Vedda, Tiwi, Aranda, Gilyak, Yukaghir, Ingalik, Copper Eskimo, Montagnais,[d] Micmac, Northern Saulteaux, Slave, Kaska, Paiute, Botocudo, Aweikoma, and Yahgan.

[a] From Murdock 1981.

[b] Knauft 1991; Knauft does not report a percentage for virilocality.

[c] Murdock 1981:94.

[d] The Montagnais codes are from Murdock 1967.

and father's relatives are on equal terms.[34] Furthermore, rather than male relatives clustering together in patrilocal residence, a great deal of flexibility exists among nomadic hunter-gatherers regarding residence patterns.

THE ASSUMPTION OF THE TIGHT-KNIT, BOUNDED GROUP

The mental image of a stable, tight-knit, bounded hunter-gatherer band is strictly that, a *mental* image. In the real world of nomadic bands, Shaw and Wong's "nucleus ethnic group" simply doesn't exist.[35] In actuality, hunter-gatherer bands have fluctuating memberships and tend to be interconnected with other bands through ties of kinship and friendship.[36] Giving several ethnographic examples, Turnbull draws anthropological attention to the "flux" of hunter-gatherer bands, noting "the constant changeover of personnel between local groups and the frequent shifts of campsites through the seasons."[37] Richard Lee and Irven DeVore agree: "Flexibility of living arrangements presents at first a confusing and disorderly picture. Brothers may be united or divided, marriage may take place within or outside the local group, and local groups may vary in numbers from one week to the next."[38]

In his review article, Barnard summarizes that by the 1960s and 1970s, "'Flux,' 'flexibility,' and 'fluidity' became the new buzz words to describe their [nomadic hunter-gatherer] social organization."[39] As more and more simple foragers have been studied, the interconnections among bands and the flexible, changing nature of band composition have become indisputably established, for example, for the Aché (Guayaki) and Cuiva of South America; the Chipewyan, Dogrib, Sanpoil, Washo, Western Shoshone and various Inuit groups of North America; the G/wi, Ju/'hoansi, Hadza, and Mbuti of Africa; and the Birhor, Batek Semang, Chenchu, Hill Pandaram and Paliyan of Asia (see Figure 13.1).[40]

Tim Ingold notes that ethnographic findings show that "flux in the composition of co-residential groups, far from being exceptional, is a widespread and striking feature of hunter-gatherer social arrangements. . . . We arrive at a view of the band as a *loose and unbounded association* of individuals or families, each related to one or more others through immediate kinship."[41] The fact that, among the Chipewyan of Sub-Arctic North America, bands were interlinked by bonds of affinity and kinship and band composition was fluid caught the attention of the second European to travel among the Chipewyan in the late 1700s, Samuel Hearne, who noted that his native guides invariably had friends in almost every band they encountered over a huge geographic distance.[42] James Downs reports that among the Washo of North America "with intermarriages relatively common, it was possible to extend the network of kinship relations beyond the tribe in finding 'relatives' among foreigners."[43] Among local groups of Andaman Islanders, whether of the same or different tribes, "friendly relations were kept alive by several of the customs of the Andamanese, by the intermarriage of members of different groups, by the adoption of children from one group to another, and by the fact that a man of one group might take up his residence more or less permanently with another."[44] Of Australian Aborigines overall, Birdsell reports a modal (or most common) rate of intermarriage among bands that speak *different* language dialects to have been 15 percent in pre-contact times.[45] This is a substantial amount of intermarriage interlinking bands from

Figure 13.1 The fluctuating nature of forager band composition applies to the Batek of Malaysia. The photo shows a family building a raft in 1981. The Batek use blow pipes and poison darts to hunt, but they do not use these weapons against people. They appear on both the nonwarring and internally peaceful society lists in chapters 5 and 7. (Photo courtesy of Kirk Endicott.)

different language groups. In conclusion, to assume that ancestral human groups were tight-knit kin groups closed off from other such groups is extremely unrealistic in light of the evidence from simple nomadic forager societies in various parts of the world. The *overall pattern* among nomadic foragers of flux and flexibility in group composition is extremely well documented and unambiguous.

THE ASSUMPTION OF PERVASIVELY HOSTILE INTERBAND RELATIONS

Undoubtedly, relations between certain foraging bands were hostile on occasion in the evolutionary past.[46] The important question, however, is whether or not assuming pervasive, or even typical, intergroup hostility and warfare is really justified. To gain insight on this issue, we can examine the evidence on typical patterns of interaction among bands.[47] The ethnographic evidence provides various reasons for questioning the assumption of pervasive intergroup hostility among ancestral bands.

Observations of nomadic hunter-gatherers suggest that *typical patterns* of interband interaction can aptly be characterized as benign coexistence or friendly contact, with pervasive intergroup hostility and warfare being relatively rare. Recall that nomadic foragers are well represented on the nonwarring societies list presented in chapter 7. Furthermore, in recent times, it seems that when bands do engage in acts of war, the violence often is directed against intruding agriculturalists, herders, or European colonists.[48] Tribal peoples generally, of course, not only nomadic hunter-gatherers, felt the impact of European colonial expansion. As Driver notes regarding North America, "The pressure of White settlement on the East Coast pushed the Eastern Indians toward the west and stirred up a host of conflicts between them and those tribes already located in the new land."[49]

Returning to band–band interaction, most of the Southern Paiute groups of western North America were on friendly terms: "They visited, hunted, and gathered in one another's territory, occasionally intermarried and, on a small scale, traded."[50] Birdsell notes how totemic and religious beliefs linked even widely separate Australian Aborigine groups of the Western Desert region, and he quotes Strehlow's observation that "in severe drought times it was possible for a stricken group to travel hundreds of miles, if necessary, and still be assured of the welcoming hospitality of a local group with which it was linked by religious ties."[51]

The fact that band membership and composition actually are flexible and fluctuating is also relevant to evaluating the assumption of pervasive intergroup hostility. At any given moment in time, individuals in one band have relatives and exchange partners living in other bands. That is, the members of any given flexible band are linked with persons living in other flexible bands through ties of kinship and friendship. Michael Jochim notes that among hunter-gatherers—ranging from the Australian Aborigines to the Ju/'hoansi (!Kung) of Africa—individuals establish trading partnerships with persons in other bands: "Partnerships link individuals across the landscape, with the social relations, rather than the gifts themselves, having the greatest importance in these transactions. One benefit of these exchanges is subsistence security: individuals can call upon their partners for support in times of need, such as drought."[52] Lee explains that the type of gift exchange, called *hxaro,* among the Ju/'hoansi contributes to friendly ties among members of different bands.[53]

Downs notes the linking effects of intermarriage among the Washo and the Paiute. "Along the edges of the Washo country, where there was a great deal of interaction between the Washo and their Paiute neighbors, bunches or bands existed in which intermarriage was so common as to cause them to be identified as 'half Paiute' by the Washo."[54] Again and again, the *pattern* observed among simple nomadic foragers is one in which intermarriage, ceremonial association, and exchange of gifts and favors create webs of interrelationships among bands.

When conflicts arise in band society, as we considered in chapters 11 and 12, they tend to be between individuals, not entire groups. Furthermore, among nomadic foragers, individuals tend to have relatives and friends living in other bands, whose flexible composition remains in flux. All these features inhibit band-to-band hostility. Individual conflicts that span (flexible) group membership may result in avoidance, dispute resolution procedures, or interpersonal violence, including, in some cases, lethal self-redress.[55] Simultaneously, however, ties of friendship, bonds of kinship, ceremonial interactions, and exchange relationships continue to link the groups overall as other persons besides the disputants interact in a variety of positive ways. In fact, third parties *from different bands* that are linked to one or both disputants may work actively to help them find a solution to their problem, as we have seen in chapter 12 related to Australian Aborigines.

It is worth noting that researchers who actually study hunter-gatherers tend *not* to portray intergroup enmity as the typical pattern among simple foragers. Lee and Daly write:

> Hunter-gatherers are generally peoples who have lived until recently without the overarching discipline imposed by the state. They have lived in relatively small groups, without centralized authority, standing armies, or bureaucratic systems. Yet the evidence indicates that they have lived together surprisingly well, solving their problems among themselves largely without recourse to authority figures and without a particular propensity for violence. It was *not* the situation that Thomas Hobbes, the great seventeenth-century philosopher, described in a famous phrase as "the war of all against all."[56]

Hunter-gatherer specialist Steward has this to say: "There have been many contentions that primitive bands own territories or resources and fight to protect them. Although I cannot assert that this is never the case, it is probably very uncommon." Knauft reaches the overall assessment related to simple hunter-gatherers: "With emphasis on egalitarian access to resources, cooperation, and diffuse affiliative networks, contrary emphasis on intergroup rivalry and collective violence is minimal." Finally, John Gowdy concludes, "Judging from historical accounts of hunter-gatherers, for most of the time humans have been on the planet we have lived in relative harmony with the natural world and with each other. Our minds and cultures evolved under these conditions."[57]

The assumption that pervasive intergroup hostility is the *typical* pattern of interaction among simple foraging bands is simply not supported by the bulk of ethnographic data on nomadic hunter-gatherers from around the world.[58] This does not mean that hostility never exists among simple foragers. Clearly, at times it does. However, *an assumption of pervasive, typical hostility among bands is untenable*. The *typical* pattern of contact among nomadic hunter-gatherers encompasses positive interaction and "live-and-let-live" policies.[59] Furthermore, as we have seen, most conflicts that occur tend to be between particular individuals, not entire groups. Interpersonal violence in many cases is averted as disputants simply maintain their distance, a practice that is not difficult to accomplish in *nomadic* forager societies with their *flexible* band form of social organization.

CHAPTER 14

MORE FAULTY ASSUMPTIONS

The danger has always been that the prehistoric world will simply be a reflection of the world in which we ourselves live.

ROBERT FOLEY[1]

To recap some essential points, the picture of intergroup relations among nomadic bands is taking shape. First, in chapter 8, an examination of the simple foragers in the SCCS showed the majority to be nonwarring. Second, the type of war practiced by the minority of simple hunter-gatherers in the sample seems relatively mild when compared with descriptions of fighting among equestrian and complex hunter-gatherers. Third, some so-called war reported for band societies in fact reflects nothing more than a misapplication of martial language to homicides, revenge killings, or juridical contests—remember, for instance, the so-called battle among the Tiwi.[2] Fourth, some "warfare" reported for simple foragers stems from an avalanche of social disruptions directly or indirectly caused by the spread of Europeans around the globe in recent centuries. Fifth, the data from Aboriginal Australia show warfare to be atypical of this continent of nomadic hunter-gatherers. Finally, as we began to consider in the previous chapter, a great deal of ethnographic data from around the world shows simple forager bands normally to interact without much hostility. Overall, the emerging picture is that warring at the nomadic band level of society is pretty rare and not very severe. All the forgoing observations cast doubt on the Pervasive Intergroup Hostility Model's presumption that warfare played a leading role in humanity's evolutionary past. However, before moving on to consider other assumptions, we must clear up an *apparent* contradiction between all the lines of evidence that support an unwarlike picture of band society and one particular cross-cultural study that, at first glance, appears to show the opposite.

In 1978, Carol Ember wrote, "I wish to address myself to one other view of hunter-gatherers that I have reason to believe is erroneous—namely, the view that hunter-gatherers are relatively peaceful." Ember reported that only ten percent of her "sample of hunter-gatherers . . . were rated as having no or rare warfare."[3]

Many writers continue to cite this study, and therefore it is important to address this apparent contradiction. Political scientist Joshua Goldstein, for instance, relies on Ember's findings to assert:

> The evidence from modern-day gathering-hunting societies, whose supposed peaceful nature was assumed to reflect peaceful human origins, in fact shows the opposite: modern gathering-hunting societies are *not* generally peaceful. Of 31 gathering-hunting societies surveyed in one study, 20 typically had warfare more than once every two years,

> and only three [10 percent] had "no or rare warfare." . . . If typical gathering-hunting societies found today represent the typical societies found before the rise of the state—as advocates of peaceful origins have claimed—then those original societies were warlike.[4]

Is Goldstein's conclusion really justified? In addition to keeping in mind all the ethnographic data on simple nomadic hunter-gatherers that contradict it, one must look carefully at the sample of societies and the methods used in the original cross-cultural study.

First, as Sponsel points out, Ember defines war so as to include feuding and even revenge killings directed against a *single individual*.[5] Under this definition, personal grudges that result in a killing can be counted as acts of "war." Furthermore, the fact that Ember is using such a sweeping definition of war, encompassing acts of feud and revenge homicide, is *not* apparent within the article itself.[6] The reader must seek out a different article to discover that acts of feud and revenge have been counted along with war in one catchall category: "An attack by a party from one community on *even a single person* from another community would be classified by us as warfare."[7] Obviously, counting instances of feud and revenge directed against a single individual as "war" increases the tally of so-called war, as we already have considered in chapter 7. *This point alone, which again is not at all apparent from the article itself, is sufficient to cast a totally different light on the findings.*

A second serious issue is that *almost half of the societies in Ember's sample are not simple nomadic hunter-gatherers at all!*[8] Seven equestrian cultures are included: the Ute, Kutenai, Coeur D'Alene, Gros Ventre, Comanche, Crow, and Tehuelche. These societies represent *23 percent* of the sample of 31. The use of horses to hunt game, such as bison on the North American plains, was a very recent cultural development, occurring only after the Spanish introduced the horse into the Americas.[9]

Prior to becoming *horse cultures,* some societies practiced horticulture and others hunted and gathered. The arrival of Europeans brought a multitude of changes to these societies, such as a shift in their economies to mounted hunting. *Increased militarism was another dramatic change.*[10]

Regarding, for instance, one of the equestrian cultures in Ember's sample, the Comanche, Hoebel explains that a great transformation occurred regarding warring and raiding. Prior to adopting the horse, the Comanche, as a subgroup of Shoshoneans, had nomadically foraged in small bands. "War was a thing to be avoided, for the Basin Shoshoneans had no military organization and were wholly lacking in fighting prowess," writes Hoebel. After adopting the horse, they became the "Spartans of the Prairies," and "gave trouble to all their enemies and to themselves."[11]

W. Newcomb lists various interactive factors that contributed to the overall pattern of warfare on the North American plains:

> There was a decrease in the available amount of game and in adequate hunting territories, which taken together with the shrinkage of the bison herds and the increasing white and native pressure from all sides further engendered conflict. Finally, there was the competition of tribes for European weapons, particularly guns, and the European policy of playing off one tribe against another.[12]

Clearly, there are important social, economic, and military differences between the equestrian hunters and simple nomadic hunter-gatherers. Equestrian hunters in the midst of a dramatic social upheaval initiated by the arrival of Europeans in the Americas by no means typify the prehistoric nomadic hunter-gatherer lifeways that existed prior to the origin of agriculture or the state. Such societies certainly do *not* constitute a very good model of humanity's past.

Furthermore, a substantial number of the societies in Ember's sample are neither egalitarian nor nomadic but instead are hierarchical and partially or totally sedentary.[13] The latter features characterize complex hunter-gatherers. As we have seen, the *overall pattern* is that complex hunter-gatherers tend to be *warlike* (and, archaeologically speaking, very recent), in contrast to simple hunter-gatherers, who tend to be *unwarlike* (and represent the oldest form of human social organization).[14] Three *sedentary* societies (Aleut, Yurok, and Bellacoola) and five *semi-sedentary* societies (Squamish, Maidu, Nootka, Eastern Pomo, and Pekangekum) are included in the sample, representing *another 26 percent* of the total. Furthermore, seven of the eight sedentary and semi-sedentary societies have some degree of hierarchical class stratification.[15]

Together, *48 percent* of the sample either are partly or totally sedentary or are equestrian hunters. *Therefore, the findings of Ember's study cannot legitimately be used to draw inferences about simple hunter-gatherer bands or the nomadic foraging past.*

The selection of this mixed sample may reflect the fact that when Ember published her study back in 1978, the important differences between simple and complex hunter-gatherers had not yet received much attention.[16] In any event, conclusions to be drawn from Ember's study must be carefully qualified, as follows:

> In a small sample that intermingles simple, complex, and equestrian hunter-gatherer societies, the majority of this *heterogeneous* collection of societies engage in revenge killings, feuds *or* warfare. However, it is not possible to determine how many of the societies engage in revenge killings *only,* feuding *only,* warfare *only,* or some combination of these activities. Furthermore, about half the sample are *not* simple nomadic band societies at all. Consequently, this study cannot be taken as evidence that *warfare* is common among simple nomadic hunter-gatherers, the type of society that we are focusing on to provide insights about the nomadic hunting-and-gathering past.

I emphasize these points because writers continue to make assertions, based on this study, as to the prevalence of war in the evolutionary past.[17] Authors who cite the article in this way simply may be unaware of how so-called warfare actually is being defined in the study and how almost half the sample are not simple forager bands. These factors greatly impact what can and what cannot logically be concluded from the findings.[18] It is important and timely to point out that all is not what it seems.

THE ASSUMPTION OF WARRING OVER SCARCE RESOURCES

This assumption actually entails a subset of other assumptions, all of which are open to debate. First, we can question assumptions about the nature and value of material goods. Second, related to natural resources, we can raise issues about presumed shortages in ancestral environments. Third, we can question the assumption that humans would be inclined to cope with resource scarcity via war. An examination of the *patterns* within ethnographic material on simple hunter-gatherers calls all these assumptions into question. Finally, we can ask whether assuming conditions of scarcity to have existed in the human evolutionary past makes sense given the earth's meager population for most of prehistory.

Few Bones for Contention

Simple hunter-gatherers are highly mobile. As a Ju/'hoansi man expressed to Lee, "We are here today, tomorrow over there, and the next day still elsewhere."[19] When camped for some days or weeks in a given location, simple foragers may build temporary shelters that they abandon when they move to a new location. They do not store food, and they do not accumulate much personal property.[20] When they shift campsites, they must carry their few possessions along with them. In other words, simple nomadic hunter-gatherers have virtually no material property or stored food supplies for other groups to plunder (see Figure 14.1).[21]

Nomadic hunter-gatherers are spread out over the landscape for most of the year. On occasion they may aggregate into temporary larger groups for ceremonial and social reasons, but as the resources are used up near the large camp, small groups re-form, perhaps with shifts in membership, and disperse once again. The population densities of simple hunter-gatherer societies tend to be very low relative to all other forms of social organization.[22]

A Shortage of Shortages

One surprising discovery made in recent decades is that foragers have a great deal of leisure time.[23] Simple foragers such as the Cuiva, !Kung, and Hadza can obtain all the

Figure 14.1 A Batek father entertains his children with a beetle dangling from a string. Note the construction and size of the shelter. (Photo courtesy of Kirk Endicott.)

food they need working about 20–28 hours per week, or less.[24] Even in environments that at first seem harsh to outsiders, hunter-gatherers with knowledge of what to eat and how to obtain it rather easily put food in their stomachs.[25] Of the Ju/'hoansi, Lee writes, "in assuming that their life must be a constant struggle for existence, we succumb to the ethnocentric notions that place our own Western adaptation at the pinnacle of success and make all others second or third best."[26] Similarly, Gowdy generalizes that "the notion of scarcity is largely a social construct, not a necessary characteristic of human existence or human nature. Hunter-gatherers may be considered affluent because they achieve a balance between means and ends by having everything they need and wanting little more."[27] Clearly, Shaw and Wong's assumption that tight-knit ancestral bands lived under conditions of resource scarcity should not just be accepted at face value.[28]

Moving and Sharing

We also can evaluate the assumption that *warring* over scarce resources would have been a pervasive strategy of forager groups. Whereas there are reasons to doubt that *pervasive or chronic* resources scarcities existed, however, *on occasion* certain resources such as water holes during a drought may have been in short supply.[29] Do such circumstances lead to warfare among simple foragers? A scrutiny of the ethnographic accounts leads to this answer: *perhaps rarely, but not usually.*

Rather than warring, *typical responses to resource scarcity among simple hunter-gatherers are to move to a new area or else to share resources.* Lee and DeVore summarize:

> Local groups as groups do not ordinarily maintain exclusive rights to resources. Variations in food supply from region to region and from year to year create a fluid situation that can best be met by flexible organizations that allow people to move from one area to another. The visiting patterns create intergroup obligations, so that the hosts in one season become the guests in another. We think that reciprocal access to food resources would rank as equal in importance with exchange of spouses as a means of communication between groups.[30]

The African Ju/'hoansi, North American Shoshone, and Australian Walbiri live in some of the *least* abundant environments occupied by hunter-gatherers. Contrary to what Shaw and Wong assume, in times of environmental stress these groups do not go to war.[31] Instead, they share. Eric Wolf describes the pattern for the three societies as follows:

> What we learn from these examples is that among some human groups organized conflict between groups is absent or rare, and we can perhaps specify the conditions that account for the absence of war among them. All three populations—[!Kung] San, Shoshoneans, Walbiri—live in environments where strategic resources are widely scattered and seasonably variable. To survive, a person periodically needs to gain access to resources in other locations, and he gains such access through ties of kinship, marriage, friendship, and exchange. The !Kung build these networks of friendship and neighborliness with people at different waterholes through marriage, visiting, and the good will that comes with being someone's namesake or giving them gifts of ostrich-eggshell, bead necklaces or arrows, spears, and knives. . . . There are no surpluses to maintain a permanent leisure class, and mechanisms other than those of kinship and friendship to gain access to other people's services. . . . What we can do is note the possible

> correspondence of resource scarcity and scatter and a tendency to expand interpersonal ties to reduce the risks and increase survival chances. Under such circumstances there may well exist a motivation to limit violence, since it is unwise to make enemies of potential friends and allies.[32]

Robert Kelly offers a thorough review of land use and resource sharing among both complex and simple hunter-gatherers.[33] Simple nomadic foragers regulate access to resources though kinship, trade-relationships, spiritual beliefs, and various other cultural mechanisms that have nothing to do with defending boundaries through physical force, even when resources are limited.[34]

Intergroup sharing also occurs in times of local abundance. Wheeler notes a pattern of sharing windfalls, such as abundant harvests of bunya nuts or raspberries, among Australian Aborigines.[35] When a coastal group of Australian Aborigines discovered a beached whale with meat enough for many, they lit signal fires and neighboring groups flocked to the site to share in the bounty. The reciprocal sharing of periodic bounties such as these among neighbors means that over the long haul everyone benefits more than had each group simply hoarded abundant food.

The *intergroup* sharing of resources such as water holes in times of drought or periodic food bounties mirrors the ubiquitous *within*-group sharing observed among simple hunter-gatherers. Uniformly, hunters share meat.[36] For example, the Guayaki of South America have a food taboo: A hunter should never eat the meat of the animals he has killed. This taboo reinforces the fact that people are interdependent and must share with each other; each hunter gives his game to others and in return receives meat from other hunters.[37]

Leacock notes how sharing among Montagnais hunter-gatherers increases food security: "Owing to the uncertainty of the hunt, several families were necessarily dependent upon each other, thus providing [in Steward's words], 'a kind of subsistence insurance or greater security than individual families could achieve.'" Lee explains the Ju/'hoansi system of social security: "If one has good relations with in-laws at different waterholes, one will never go hungry."[38]

We can conclude that sharing among *different* bands is facilitated by at least three factors. First, simple foragers are already accustomed to following an ethos of sharing within their own bands, so extending the ethos to people in other bands is congruent with prevailing practices and beliefs about what constitutes proper human conduct. Second, foragers understand the advantages of reciprocal sharing. "I may need 'your' water hole some day just as you now need to use 'mine' today. We need to share to survive." Third, sharing among groups is promoted by the fact that bands are interconnected via ties of kinship, friendship, marriage, and exchange.[39] Thus networks of relationships cut across band membership, including at times bands from different language groups.[40] Shifting band composition also tilts decisions toward reciprocal sharing and away from hostile competition for scarce resources.[41] Clearly, the assumption of hostile intergroup competition over scarce resources does not correspond very well with empirical observations of simple hunter-gatherer societies.

Sparse People, Not Sparse Resources

A brief mention of the human population is at least tangentially relevant to the assumption that prehistoric groups regularly fought over scarce resources. As Elizabeth Cashdan observes, "Competition results not simply from scarcity of resources in any absolute sense, but from scarcity relative to population density."[42] Today, humans flood the planet. This was far from the case during prehistory. Perhaps at times the converse—finding other people—even presented a problem! Lewis Binford has carefully estimated the human population of the entire world as recently as 11,000–12,000 years ago to have been about seven million persons, *and before that even less*.[43] "We must imagine a patchily inhabited world in which large, uninhabited areas separated localizations of very mobile, adaptively successful populations that exploited extensively areas in order to maintain their subsistence security."[44] The worldwide population figure of seven million averages out to about one person per every eight square miles. If even up to half of the Earth's landmass remained uninhabited 11,000–12,000 years ago, then the population density for seven million people worldwide would still have been very low, averaging about one person per every four square miles. It may be hard for 21st-century humans even to visualize such a sparsely populated planet. An additional frame of reference for contemplating the meaning of an average worldwide population density of only one person per every eight square miles is provided by Birdsell's calculations that in the *worst* desert conditions of Australia, the same amount of land, approximately eight square miles, is needed to support one nomadic forager.[45] Of course, many habitats on earth are substantially more plentifully endowed for foraging than Australia's harshest desert.

THE ASSUMPTION OF WARRING OVER LAND

Robert Netting, who studied human–environment interaction, summarizes regarding nomadic foragers: "Food resources appear adequate even during periods of climatic adversity, continuous subsistence effort is not required, and there is little evidence of intense competition for hunting and gathering areas."[46] Kelly writes in his book on foragers that "A strong tendency toward permission-granting rather than active perimeter defense gives human land tenure its own particular character."[47] Hunter-gatherer specialist James Woodburn reaches the conclusion for simple nomadic hunter-gatherers such as the Ju/'hoansi, Hadza, Mbuti, Paliyan, Hill Pandaram, and Batek Semang that "in every case individuals have full rights of access to camps in several of these areas and there is no question of tightly defined groups monopolizing the resources of their areas and excluding outsiders."[48] Correspondingly, after a career of studying foragers, Steward concludes that territorial warfare—in fact any kind of warfare—is almost nonexistent among simple hunter-gatherers:

> First, the primary groups [small bands] that comprise the larger maximum bands intermarry, amalgamate if they are too small or split off if too large. Second, . . . there is no more than a tendency for primary groups to utilize special areas. Third, most so-called "warfare" among such societies is no more than revenge for alleged witchcraft or continued interfamily feuds. Fourth, collecting is the main resource in most areas. Primary bands did not fight one another, and it is difficult to see how a maximum band could assemble its manpower to defend its territory against another band or why it should do so.[49]

Verne Ray reports for the Sanpoil of North America:

> The use of common territory was a matter of expediency made possible by the friendly relations existing between villages. The area, fairly definitely bounded, was considered

> by the Sanpoil as their proper range for food gathering but no effort was made to keep outsiders from making use of it also. Neighboring groups, however, were reasonably considerate and encroachment was slight.[50]

Woodburn states, "The boundaries of Hadza areas are . . . undefined: in effect there are no boundaries."[51] Of the Gilyak of Asia, C. H. Hawes observes that

> the division of creeks and tracks for snaring had been made in olden times; and the customary boundaries sanctioned by time are seldom transgressed. The abundance of game, coupled with the prowess of the pioneers, yielded little cause for quarrel, and spots were simply annexed according to the number of snares which the owner of the hut possessed.[52]

Overall, responses to trespass and resource use by persons from neighboring groups vary, probably for numerous reasons such as whether or not permission to use resources is requested in advance, the history and tenor of relations among the particular individuals or groups in question, belief systems related to nonviolence and violence, and the nature of the area or resources in question. Consequently, some nomadic hunter-gatherers such as the Semang, Kubu, Siriono, Hill Pandaram, and Hare simply avoid strangers by moving to a different location.[53] In other cases, such as among certain Australian Aborigines, the Ona of South America, or the Ju/'hoansi, resource use is granted to outsiders if permission is sought ahead of time.[54] In still other situations, trespassers and poachers are ambushed, as Hobhouse reports for the Vedda and Ray Kelly recounts for some Andaman Islanders of Asia, and also for the Slavey of Canada after they had been partially displaced from their homelands by the westward expansion of the Cree.[55] In sum, the use of force to attack a trespasser may or may not occur. The assumption that territorial warfare was *the chronic condition* among hunter-gatherers over past millennia ignores the variability and complexity of how hunter-gatherer bands interact regarding resources and land.

Again, it should also be kept in mind that competition over land and resources has gradually increased, largely since the agricultural revolution and most dramatically in recent centuries, as population densities worldwide have soared many times over what they were in aboriginal environments inhabited *only* by mobile hunter-gatherers. Currently there are over *six billion* people in the world. Unlike today, for most of humanity's existence on the planet, there has been a great deal of space for a relatively small number of people, even if not evenly distributed. Additionally, it is interesting to contemplate that territorial warfare among Australian Aborigines was virtually absent on this isolated continent inhabited for millennia solely by hunter-gatherers.[56] This observation offers a valuable insight into the *regular, typical pattern* of intergroup relations within a pure hunter-gatherer *world system*.

THE ASSUMPTION OF WARRING OVER WOMEN

What about the proposition that women were the scarce resources over which men of prehistoric bands warred? In some simple nomadic hunter-gatherer societies, men do fight over women from time to time. However, most ethnographic accounts of such disputes are not variations on a Helen of Troy theme: Disputes over women invariably involve *particular men and particular women, but rarely entire bands warring with other bands.* A husband may be upset about his wife's adultery. If the suspected lover is in another group, the husband may seek him out, but such personal disputes are not grounds for launching a war of group-against-group. A wife may run off with her lover, the couple seeking refuge in another band. A girl may elope rather than marry a man of a neighboring band to whom she has been promised. Again, these types of individual grudges may or may not lead to interpersonal *violence,* but they rarely lead to anything resembling *war* between entire nomadic bands. In future chapters, we will consider individual male competition and aggression over women in more detail. For now, the relevant point is that in some *nomadic forager societies,* individual men may fight over *a woman,* but groups of men tend not to march off to war over *women.*

Of relevance to this topic, the simplest foraging societies tend to have high levels of gender egalitarianism.[57] To simply assume that women are the spoils of men's battles—to "use them reproductively," as Ghiglieri puts it—hardly takes female autonomy and decision-making into account.[58] In an overview of gender relations, Karen Endicott concludes that "rather than assigning all authority in economic, political, or religious matters to one gender or the other, hunter-gatherers tend to leave decision-making about men's work and areas of expertise to men, and about women's work and expertise to women, either as groups or individuals."[59] For instance, among the Polar Eskimo, "men and women had more or less equal status."[60] Among the Yahgan "the woman was largely her own mistress, particularly in such provinces of her own as child rearing, food gathering, and canoe managing. Some men domineered over their wives, but not a few husbands were under the thumbs of their spouses."[61] Leacock observes, "those who came to know the Montagnais more intimately saw women as holding 'great power.' "[62] Gardner writes of the Paliyan, "Neither spouse can order the other and neither, by virtue of sex or age, is entitled to a greater voice in matters of mutual concern."[63] Finally, Lee states, "women are a force to be reckoned with in Ju/'hoan society."[64]

Generally speaking, women have great freedom to divorce and remarry in simple band societies.[65] Among the Paliyan, for example, Gardner reports that "Spouses separate at the first quarrel, which results in the serial marriages. . . . One girl of fifteen rotated between three men, moving after each quarrel; she had experienced eight unions, each of which was referred to as a marriage." In Montagnais bands, "divorce was easy and at the desire of either partner."[66]

Another reflection of the high level of gender egalitarianism and female autonomy that is *typical* of nomadic bands involves sexual relations. The assumption that women are the subordinate, passive victims of capture, rape, abduction, and forced marriage is at odds with most ethnographic accounts. These types of male domination over women's sexual and personal lives may occur within other types of social organization, but they are incongruent with the female autonomy that typifies simple hunter-gatherer bands.[67] In many nomadic forager societies, females exercise considerable choice and freedom in sexual behavior.[68] Allan Holmberg explains that Siriono "women enjoy about the same privileges as men. They get as much or more food to eat, and they enjoy the same sexual freedom."[69] Adultery is common yet tends to be ignored if engaged in discreetly.

> A woman is allowed to have intercourse not only with her husband but also with his brothers, real and classificatory, and with the husbands and potential husbands of her own and classificatory sisters. Thus, apart from one's real spouse, there may be as many as eight or ten potential spouses with whom one may have sex relations. There is,

moreover, no taboo on sex relations between unmarried potential spouses, provided the women have undergone the rites of maturity. Virginity is not a virtue. Consequently unmarried adults rarely, if ever, lack for sexual partners and frequently indulge in sex.[70]

A quotation on nomadic Ona hunter-gatherers of South America illustrates several points from the foregoing discussion—the *individual* nature of disputes over women, participation of a *woman herself* in decision-making, and the absence of *warfare* to capture women:

> Raids and wars to capture women for wives were not a feature of Ona culture. Forcible abductions of women from their husbands, by men of influence and power, occurred occasionally, *usually more or less by agreement and understanding with the woman herself,* sometimes with the help of her relatives.[71]

The ethnographically recurring pattern of hunter-gatherer gender equality calls into question the assumption that forager women are "war trophies," typically subjected to capture by groups of *warring* men. Of course it would be absurd to suggest that no nomadic hunter-gatherer woman has ever been violently abducted.[72] On the other hand, the ethnographic data do not support a generalization that waging war to abduct women is in any way typical or pervasive among egalitarian nomadic forager societies.[73]

THE ASSUMPTION OF LEADERSHIP

Nomadic hunter-gatherer societies are characterized by egalitarian values, high levels of personal autonomy, and the lack of formal leaders.[74] Woodburn writes "in these societies there are either no leaders at all or leaders who are very elaborately constrained to prevent them from exercising authority or using their influence to acquire wealth or prestige."[75] Leacock goes even further, explaining that "what is hard to grasp about the structure of the egalitarian band is that leadership as we conceive it is not merely 'weak' or 'incipient,' as is commonly stated, but irrelevant."[76]

Whereas military virtues and leadership capacities are sometimes valued among tribal and other kinds of peoples, by contrast, the cherished virtues among simple nomadic foragers include *generosity, humility,* and often *nonaggressiveness*.[77] The data contradict assertions that members of nomadic foraging bands have martial values, reward military leadership, or emphasize warrior skills. Assumptions that in the evolutionary past, military success correlated with reproductive success or that natural selection selected for leadership abilities are simply not substantiated by data on nomadic forager societies.[78] Cooper's statement about the Ona applies generally to simple nomadic hunter-gatherers: "No man recognized authoritative headship of or accepted orders from any other."[79] Boehm, who has read extensively in the cross-cultural literature, doesn't beat around the bush: "Egalitarian foragers uniformly eschew strong, authoritative leadership."[80] Clearly, the assumption that leadership, military or otherwise, is important in an egalitarian forager context is a very poor one.

SUMMING UP

Ethnographic data on simple nomadic hunter-gatherers provide the best basis for drawing inferences about the lifeways of ancestral humans. The archaeological record substantiates a nomadic hunting-and-gathering existence over humanity's evolutionary past. There were no villages or cities, no herding of animals, no horticulture, and no agriculture. These were the conditions under which the genus *Homo* appeared about two million years ago and more recently under which modern *Homo sapiens* emerged roughly 40,000–50,000 years ago. Therefore, if we want a window to the past, we should look for recurrent patterns among extant simple foragers. This decision is logical and defensible, even while acknowledging that simple current-day hunter-gatherers are not identical to ancestral groups. Combining archaeological findings and a careful study of nomadic foraging societies represents our best bet for gaining useful inferences about our past.

Turning to ethnographic information on simple nomadic foragers, the picture that emerges is that they live in small bands most of the time, but occasionally congregate into larger groupings for social and ceremonial purposes.[81] The membership of the small bands is flexible and changing. Individuals and families visit other bands, join other bands, and on occasion may forage as family units. At any given time, a person will have friends and relatives in various other bands. Decisions to join a new group for a short or long time may depend upon an individual having at least one close relative already residing within the band. The most common form of descent among simple hunter-gatherers is bilateral, a system that considers both mother's and father's lines rather than only one line, as in a patrilineal system. Bilateral systems tend to emphasize more kinship ties than do unilateral systems. This also means that each person has a unique kinship network. As was clearly evident in the Tiwi case explored in chapter 12, the fact that each person's network of relations in band society differs to some degree from those of everyone else strongly militates against concerted group-versus-group fighting. In nomadic foraging groups, individual autonomy is emphasized and group leadership is minimal. No one has the authority to order others to do anything, such as to go to war. Sharing, cooperation, and egalitarianism are prevalent aspects of the simple hunter-gatherer ethos. Reciprocal sharing crosscuts different groups; intergroup sharing is facilitated because people have trade partners, family members, and friends in other bands.

A fair number of nomadic hunter-gatherer societies have nonviolent values. Gardner provides examples of hunter-gatherers who are nonaggressive both *internally and externally:* the Paliyan, Kadar, Malapandaram, Semang, Yanadi, Siriono, and Ju/'hoansi [!Kung].[82] Drawing on the findings presented in chapters 5 and 7, we can expand this list of nonaggressive *and* nonwarring nomadic hunter-gatherers by adding, for instance, the Birhor and Nayaka (Naikens) of India, certain Canadian Inuit groups, the Greenland Inuit and Polar Eskimos, the Jahai of Malaysia, the Mbuti of Africa, the Vedda of Sri Lanka, and the Saulteaux of North America.

Bands usually move within somewhat loosely defined territories, with neighboring groups being linked in the aforementioned networks of friendship, kinship, and trade partnerships. Such ties interconnect not only bands that have a common language but also, to a lesser degree, more distant groups. Serious conflicts within bands may result in band fission. Disputes tend to be between particular individuals, often arising from jealousy or competition over a mate, but this type of dispute rarely pits an entire group against another entire group. Intergroup territorial fighting also is very rare among simple foragers.

The ethnographic patterns just summarized show virtually all the assumptions of the Pervasive Intergroup Hostility Model to be flawed. Contrary to the patrilocal/patrilineal assumption, most simple hunter-gatherer bands lack patrilineal descent groups and many are neither patrilocal nor virilocal. Contrary to the closed group assumption, the bands are *not* tightly knit, but instead, flexible and fluctuating in membership. Contrary to the assumptions of pervasive hostile intergroup relations and recurring warfare over scarce resources, the *typical* pattern is for groups to get along rather well, relying on resources within their own areas and respecting the resources of their neighbors. Intergroup marriages contribute to positive ties within and across language boundaries that are augmented through gift exchange, visiting, and the reciprocal sharing of resources, the last pattern being especially important in times of scarcity. Contrary to the warring over women and territory assumption, disputes over women, when occurring between members of different bands, tend to be individual affairs rather than the foundation for intergroup warfare. Instances of nomadic bands fighting over territory are atypical. Contrary to the leadership assumption, high levels of individual autonomy and egalitarianism are hallmarks of forager bands. Militaristic or warrior values are rarely if ever emphasized. *In sum, an examination of the actual ethnographic information on simple nomadic foragers suggests that the Pervasive Intergroup Hostility Model rests not on facts but on a heap of faulty assumptions and overzealous speculation.*

The rarity of warfare among simple hunter-gatherers also corresponds with the global archaeological record that shows no evidence of war until recent millennia. Both lines of evidence converge to suggest that warfare was extremely rare or nonexistent for most of the human past. This conclusion may run counter to conventional wisdom in Western societies. Whereas conventional wisdom does tend to be *conventional,* it cannot be considered *wisdom* when it drastically diverges from observable facts. We all make implicit assumptions within the context of our own cultural belief systems, and sometimes our assumptions are simply wrong. This also occurs in science. Nonetheless, one benefit of using a scientific approach to gaining knowledge about the world involves the ongoing process of questioning assumptions, gathering information to test hypotheses, reaching *tentative* conclusions, and then starting over again.

CHAPTER 15

MUCH ADO ABOUT THE YANOMAMÖ

> If an experimental model is chosen on the basis of apparent resemblances to only one or two aspects of a complex human phenomenon, without any systematic effort to determine if this resemblance is valid and functional, then the use of this model may provide only an illusion of information.
>
> CAROLINE AND ROBERT BLANCHARD[1]

Why do new variations of the Pervasive Intergroup Hostility Model repeatedly appear despite the paucity of evidence to support them? What is the strong appeal of this particular view of the human past? Perhaps John Durant's observation that reconstructions of the past in fact also tell us about the present applies.[2] Today, of course, we humans live in largely *closed,* socially *bounded, territorial* groups called countries. We all know that territorial integrity is paramount in *our* current world. We also know that relations between countries are sometimes *hostile*—and that wars are always raging somewhere. With hardly an exception, nations have armaments, a military, and "prudently" prepare for the "next war," even when not actually engaged in a current one. Within our territorial limits, we identify ourselves as Mexicans, Finns, Americans, and so on. We wave literal and figurative flags, we are proud, and we set ourselves apart from people of other nations. Furthermore, many of us come to suspect from what we see of current events that *competition for resources* such as oil lies at the root of at least some wars. We also take for granted that nations have *leaders* who manage affairs during peace and war. We honor our war heroes.

Thus the Pervasive Intergroup Hostility Model corresponds closely with *our* current social and political world. Even the name Alexander selected for his hypothesis, "balance of power," is, of course, currently used in talking about international relations.[3] Thus one explanation for the appeal of the Pervasive Intergroup Hostility Model is that it retells us a current-day tale that is comfortably familiar and easy to accept.

Are there other explanations for this blatant mismatch between beliefs and facts? In contrast to the specialists who have devoted their academic careers to actually studying foragers, Pervasive Intergroup Hostility theorists may simply lack knowledge of the relevant data. The model has advocates from disciplines like biology, primatology, economics, and evolutionary psychology, fields that traditionally do not study hunter-gatherers.

Another point worth mentioning is that Pervasive Intergroup Hostility theorists tend to ignore social organization and draw ethnographic examples from a cacophony of cultures including those with complex forms of organization—and sometimes from primate studies, too. One primatologist stirs together an Arab proverb, reference to World War II Kamikaze pilots, war stories from Vietnam, and a portrayal of "chimpanzeecide" into his evolutionary discussion of war.[4] Similarly, a biological discussion of war includes examples from equestrian hunters like the Blackfoot, the cattle-herding Meru, ancient Greeks, and present-day Basque terrorists, among other diverse illustrations.[5] A problem with serving a mixed platter of proverb, anecdote, history, and ethnography to bolster speculations about the evolution of war is that nearly all the tidbits come from social contexts and types of social organization that are dramatically different from the conditions under which humans evolved. As we have seen, when it comes to warfare, social organization matters.

THE FAMOUS YANOMAMÖ *UNOKAIS*

One particular society, the tribal Yanomamö (also spelled Yanomami to reflect linguistic variations), has become a favorite, yet questionable, example in discussions of the evolution of warfare. The Yanomamö are tribal horticulturalists, *not* nomadic hunter-gatherers. They live in *sedentary* villages, have a *patrilineal* system of descent, and sometimes raid other villages, occasionally, but not usually, abducting women in the process.[6] The Yanomamö fit the Pervasive Intergroup Hostility Model rather closely—clearly much better than do simple nomadic foragers—and this undoubtedly is one reason that proponents of the model like to discuss the Yanomamö.[7] In particular, one article by Chagnon has become a popular source for proponents of the Pervasive Intergroup Hostility Model, being approvingly cited for instance by Low, Wrangham and Peterson, Ghiglieri, and a host of other authors, sometimes with speculations as to what the findings might imply about human nature or the evolution of human aggression.[8]

In his article, Chagnon reports that Yanomamö men who have *participated* in a killing have more wives and children than men who have not.[9] When a Yanomamö man is involved in a killing, he must undergo a purification ceremony. After the ceremony, the man is referred to as *unokai*.[10] The majority of *unokais* (about 60 percent) have participated in only one killing and the overwhelming majority (79 percent) have participated in one or two killings, but a minority of the *unokais* have participated in multiple killings. Almost two-thirds (243/380) of the men studied by Chagnon, however, *never participated* in killing anybody. Chagnon explains that *unokais* average more than two-and-a-half times the number of wives and more than three times the number of children as non-*unokais of the same age*.[11]

The notoriety that this particular article has achieved is really astounding. Whereas the overwhelming majority of scientific articles are read and cited by only a few specialists in a given field, on rare occasions an article gains a much wider audience. Immediately upon publication, the reports that killers have more children caught the attention of the popular and scientific press well beyond anthropology.[12] The author of an article in *U.S. News and World Report* proposed that Chagnon's study "lends new credence" to the idea that "war arises from individuals struggling for reproductive success."[13] And about a decade-and-a-half after the article's publication, references to this one study, often mentioning *unokai* reproductive success, are too numerous to track.[14] The article has recently been republished, without data tables, in a book called

Understanding Violence edited by psychologist David Barash.[15] There are many other examples of the article's proliferating message. Buss discusses the *unokai* reproductive success findings in his textbook, *Evolutionary Psychology,* as do both Judith Harris in *The Nurture Assumption* and Steven Pinker in his best-selling *How the Mind Works.*[16]

Chagnon himself has referred to the Yanomamö as "our contemporary ancestors."[17] Buss sees Yanomamö warfare as highlighting "key themes in the evolution of human aggression."[18] And some proponents of the Pervasive Intergroup Hostility Model discuss Chagnon's study in support of their contention that war evolved as a male reproductive strategy, with warriors leaving more offspring over millennia than nonwarriors.[19] However, the problems with applying the Yanomamö findings in this way are manifold; they involve both questionable reasoning and, as we shall see, serious shortcomings of the original study. Starting with a broader view in the first part of this chapter, I will mention several reasons why one article comparing Yanomamö men who have participated in a killing with those who have not is of limited utility for understanding the evolution of human aggression. Then, narrowing the focus in the second section of the chapter, I will turn a critical eye toward the methodology and analysis of the article itself. It is also interesting to contemplate why a study that suggests that killers have more children has attracted such widespread attention.

BROADER ISSUES

In my opinion, the exuberance over these Yanomamö findings is misplaced. The first issue involves *spurious correlation,* a concept easily illustrated by example.[20] If we observe that years of cigarette smoking correspond, or *correlate,* with degree of baldness in men, before we attribute a causal link between smoking and going bald, it would be wise to ask if some other variable might also correlate with baldness. In other words, is the correlation between smoking and baldness merely spurious and of no meaningful consequence? In fact, years of smoking and degree of baldness obviously correlate with a third variable: age. If we control for the effect of age, then the apparent link between smoking and baldness disappears. Similarly, attaining *unokai* status and reproductive success also may correlate with some other causal variable or *variables*—having certain social skills, being an industrious cultivator, belonging to a large kin group, achieving headman status, or simply age, for example. Consequently, *participating* in killing per se may have about as much influence on the number of wives and offspring a man has as smoking has on baldness.

Chagnon is clearly aware of the possibility of spurious correlation.[21] He writes, for example: "Additional variables not fully investigated might help account for the correlations."[22] Nonetheless, Chagnon also expresses: "I believe that it is safe to say . . . that headmanship and being *unokai* are prestigious statuses among the Yanomamö and they are correlated with both striving and differences in reproductive success."[23] Notice that Chagnon mentions *both* headman and *unokais* statuses.[24] However, he does not systematically investigate the relative influences of these variables. It is also important to keep in mind that correlation by itself does *not* establish that one variable causes the other.

It is not uncommon for proponents of the Pervasive Intergroup Hostility Model, and sometimes other persons who discuss Chagnon's findings, to ignore the possibility of spurious correlation altogether and phrase their discussions *exclusively* in terms of "The Importance of Being *Unokai*" (apologies to Oscar Wilde).[25] We will return to the issue of spurious correlation later in this chapter and estimate the degree to which age and headman status affect Chagnon's *unokai* results.[26] It seems clear that some of the reproductive advantage that is often attributed *solely* to *unokai* status probably in large part reflects spurious correlations of *unokai* status with headman status and with age.

Second, the idea of using a sedentary, horticultural, tribal culture like the Yanomamö as a model for ancestral human society or for gaining evolutionary insights is problematic. Low does not discuss this issue but simply includes a wide range of ethnographic material, like the Yanomamö study, under the catchall label "preindustrial societies."[27] Wrangham and Peterson adopt a different approach, putting forth a dubious justification for stressing the Yanomamö findings: "As subsistence farmers, of course, Yanomamö are not typical of humans at the trailing edge of the Pleistocene, before agriculture was invented. But then human society varies too much for any single group to be perfectly representative of humans at any stage or state."[28] As we have discussed, simple nomadic hunter-gatherers clearly *are* the most appropriate type of society to use for drawing inferences about past ways of life. While they are not *perfect* representations of ancestral humans, nonetheless, simple nomadic foragers are much better proxies for human ancestors than are sedentary horticulturalists.[29]

Third, the emphasis on findings from *only one* study, from *only one* culture, to bolster speculations on the reproductive success of warriors versus nonwarriors related to "all social groups on Earth," as does Ghiglieri, for example, surely is not convincing.[30] Emphasizing what a single study might or might not suggest about broader issues of war, evolution, and human reproduction becomes even more problematic when contradictory findings exist. John Moore found that among two types of Cheyenne chiefs, war chiefs had *lower* reproductive success than did peace chiefs.[31] Ethnohistorical and census data consistently point to the same conclusion for the warlike Cheyenne: Warriors lived shorter lives and had fewer offspring than nonwarriors. Based on three different types of demographic analysis, Moore documents the lower fitness of warriors compared to nonwarriors.[32] The main point is this: Speculating on the basis of either Chagnon's Yanomamö study or Moore's Cheyenne study, *or any single study* for that matter, as to what the findings say about humanity overall is a very dubious proposition.[33] To be taken seriously, theories and models must be consistent with *bodies of knowledge,* not simply one or two particular studies.

METHODOLOGICAL AND ANALYTICAL ISSUES: QUESTIONING THE "OBVIOUS"

In addition to the foregoing issues, there are additional, specific reasons to suggest that much too much fuss is being made over the reported reproductive success of Yanomamö *unokais.* The key question is: *Does this highly publicized study actually show what it seems to show?* Do men who have participated in a killing really have three times the number of children and over twice as many wives as their same-aged peers?

Even raising such questions might seem absurd. After all, the findings were published in a leading science journal. Therefore, almost certainly reviewers and editors studied the article before publication and presumably would have caught any major flaws. Additionally, as we have seen, numerous authors have cited the findings. This implies that many readers have seen nothing wrong with the analysis. I can include myself among those who basically took the findings at face value upon the first reading. However, there is much more to interpreting these findings than at first meets the eye.

I am by no means the first person to raise questions about the article.[34] A set of critiques by Brian Ferguson are especially thorough. From the onset, Ferguson doubted whether the reported findings actually support Chagnon's conclusions about *unokais* having more wives and offspring than do non-*unokais*. I will now draw on the observations of Ferguson and others as well as offer some reanalyses of my own that draw on data from several of Chagnon's other publications. The following discussion will focus on three analytical issues: the *age effect,* the *headman effect,* and the *dead man effect.*[35]

In reanalyzing the data, I note that *unokais* and non-*unokais* are members of the *same Yanomamö population* for which demographic and reproductive data already have been published by Chagnon.[36] Data on age and reproduction available in other articles by Chagnon, which are not repeated in Chagnon's article, provide a way to address some critically important yet unanswered questions about *unokais* versus non-*unokais*.[37] A mathematical reanalysis demonstrates that neither the effects of age nor headman status were adequately controlled for in the original study. This returns us to the key question: *Does this highly publicized study actually show what it seems to show?*

Age Effects

Outside the modern art museum in Helsinki is a statue of former President C. G. E. Mannerheim (1867–1951) mounted on horseback. Also near the museum on most days between April and October are a flock of skateboarders, making good use of a low wall to perform various jumps and slides under the watchful eyes of President Mannerheim. I imagine that most readers can form a mental image of the age of these skateboarders, since skateboarders of similar appearance can be found elsewhere in the Western world. I also imagine that readers can rather easily form a visual image of persons at another Western setting: a golf course. Suppose that you read that male golfers average three times the number of children as male skateboarders. Based on your images of golfers and skateboarders, might you wonder if age has something to do with this reported finding? By contrast, the categories *unokais* and non-*unokais,* as novel concepts from an unfamiliar culture, are unlikely to evoke in most Western readers images as clear as those of *skateboarders* and *golfers*. In other words, I am suggesting that the likelihood that a group of *unokais* will be older than a group of non-*unokais* is *unlikely* to come to mind if a person lacks intimate knowledge of Yanomamö culture. And if someone familiar with the culture states that *unokais* and non-*unokais* are of comparable ages, then this further reduces the chance that readers will contemplate the possibility of age differences between the two groups.[38]

Ferguson nonetheless doubted whether *unokais* and non-*unokais* really are of comparable ages.[39] He pointed out that contrary to what Chagnon claims, some of the differences in the number of wives and children between *unokais* and non-*unokais* seems to be related to *age differences*. When Chagnon responded to Ferguson's commentary, he sidestepped the age question.[40] Are *unokais* and non-*unokais* of comparable ages or not?

TABLE 15.1 Numbers of offspring and wives among *unokais* and non-*unokais*

For each age interval as well as the total, "average number of offspring ratios" and "average number of wives ratios" have been calculated. Note that the only age interval in which *unokais* have more than three times the offspring and more than two-and-a-half times the wives of non-*unokais* is the 20–24 age group, which is based on only five *unokais*. The data in this table have not been corrected to take into account age or headman effects. See the chapter text for further discussion and Table 15.2 for a set of corrected overall ratios.

Age Intervals in Years	Average Number of Offspring: Unokais (# offspring/ # unokais)	Average Number of Offspring: Non-Unokais (# offspring/ # non-unokais)	Average Number of Offspring Ratio: Unokais/ Non-Unokais	Average Number of Wives: Unokais (# wives/ # unokais)	Average Number of Wives: Non-Unokais (# wives/ # non-unokais)	Average Number of Wives Ratio: Unokais/ Non-Unokais
20–24	5/5 = 1.00	14/78 = 0.18	**5.56**	4/5 = 0.80	10/78 = 0.13	**6.15**
25–30	22/14 = 1.57	50/58 = 0.86	**1.83**	13/14 = 0.93	31/58 = 0.53	**1.75**
31–40	122/43 = 2.83	123/61 = 2.02	**1.40**	49/43 = 1.14	59/61 = 0.97	**1.18**
≥ 41	524/75 = 6.99	193/46 = 4.19	**1.67**	157/75 = 2.09	54/46 = 1.17	**1.79**
Total	*n* = 137; 4.91	*n* = 243; 1.59	**3.09**	*n* = 137; 1.63	*n* = 243; 0.63	**2.59**

Source: The data used to create this table are from Chagnon 1988: Tables 2 and 3.

If not, why is this fact *not* readily apparent in Chagnon's original article? And, if some of the reported differences between *unokais* and non-*unokais* can be attributed to age differences between the two groups of men, then how much does this alter the meaning of the originally reported findings?

At first view, Chagnon's findings appear to speak for themselves.[41] The number of offspring and number of wives of *unokais* and non-*unokais* are compared, group-for-group, across four separate age intervals. The *unokais* outreproduce and outwed the non-*unokais* in all four pairs of age interval comparisons: 1 offspring versus 0.18; 1.57 versus 0.86; 2.83 versus 2.02; and a whopping 6.99 versus 4.19 (see Table 15.1). Based on this presentation of the data, it seems obvious that *unokais* average more children than non-*unokais*. The same pattern holds for wives. *Unokais* average more wives than non-*unokais* for each of the four age intervals: 0.80 versus 0.13; 0.93 versus 0.53; 1.14 versus 0.97; and 2.09 versus 1.17 (see Table 15.1).[42] These "facts" seem as clear as the sun's rising in the east. However, this mode of data presentation, *highlighting pairs of averages,* ushers the reader toward a fallacious conclusion—at least it did for me when I originally read the article. I suspect that this is one reason that many readers of the original article have accepted the validity of the findings. As we shall see, this way of presenting the data contributes to a false impression that age is being taken into consideration as differences in averages hold strongly across *all* the age groups.

Several observations about how the data are presented, which may at first appear to be of little or no consequence, are critical to interpreting the results. First, it is imperative to study the relative number of *unokais* and non-*unokais* within each of the age categories. Overall, there are fewer *unokais* than non-*unokais:* 137 versus 243. The following numbers of men (*unokais* versus non-*unokais,* respectively) are being compared within the four age intervals: 5 versus 78; 14 versus 58; 43 versus 61; and 75 versus 46. A data cell with only five individuals can be problematic in and of itself, but this is not the main point.[43] Some calculating based on these numbers reveals that 56 percent of the non-*unokais* are 20–30 years of age, but only 14 percent of the *unokais* are this young. These are pretty uneven percentages! This evokes images of *skateboarders* versus *golfers*. For Chagnon's oldest age category, men age 41 and older, the pattern is reversed. *Thus the age distributions are roughly mirror images of each other*. This criss-crossing pattern is shown in percentages in Figure 15.1 and in numerical values in Figure 15.2.

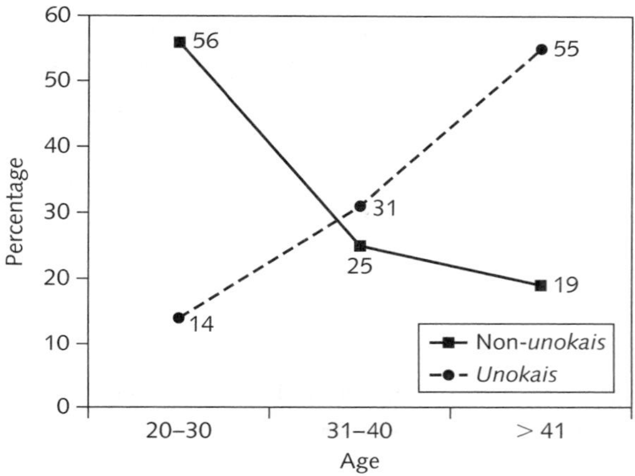

Figure 15.1 Age distributions for non-*unokais* and *unokais* expressed in terms of percent for each distribution separately. Notice that 56% of the non-*unokais* are 20–30 years of age; by contrast, 55% of *unokais* are at least 41 years of age. As a group, *unokais* are older than non-*unokais*. (Data from Chagnon 1988: Tables 2 and 3.)

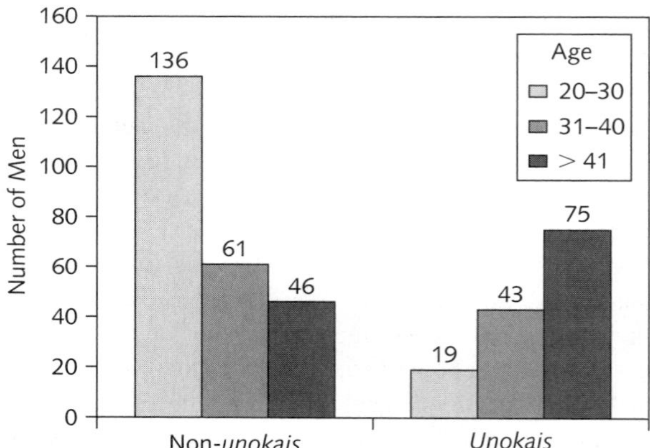

Figure 15.2 Age distributions for non-*unokais* ($n = 243$) and *unokais* ($n = 137$) plotted from the data in Chagnon 1988: Tables 2 and 3. The age distributions are very different. On the average, *unokais* are older than non-*unokais*. Note also that the third age category (> 41 years) is "open-ended."

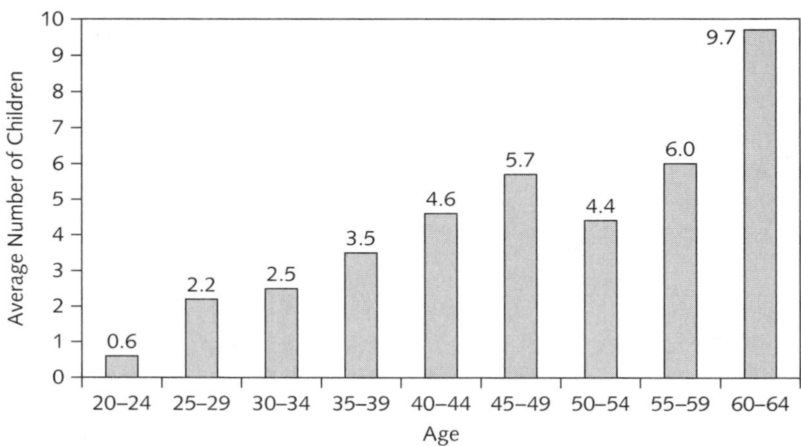

Figure 15.3 Male age and reproductive success. On the average, the older the man, the more children he has. For example, Yanomamö men in the 55- to 59-year age bracket average 6 children compared to an average 2.2 children for men in the 25- to 29-year age bracket. The age intervals shown here are of uniform width—namely, 5 years each. (These data are reported by Chagnon 1979a:384, Table 14.3, pertaining to 294 men 20 years and older, for the Yanomamö population most intensively studied by Chagnon.)

Should we be impressed that one group of men in which over half of the members are *41 years old or over* have more children (and wives in this polygynous society) than a second group of men from the same population in which over half the group members are *30 years old or younger?* The surprise would be if an older group of men did *not* average more offspring and wives than a younger group of men!

But we don't simply have to trust in common sense; in a different publication, Chagnon provides data on the average number of children men have at different ages.[44] I have graphed these data in Figure 15.3. Not surprisingly, older Yanomamö men have more children on the average than younger men. And young Yanomamö men are less likely to have attained *unokais* status than older men.[45] *Clearly, age of the fathers must be taken into account when comparing the number of children of unokais versus non-unokais.* As we shall see, the original manner in which the data are presented doesn't adequately do this.

A second noteworthy feature of the original data presentation involves the nature of the age categories. There are only four age intervals, and *each one differs from the rest*. The fourth one even lacks range information, but can be estimated from data in a different publication by Chagnon to be *around 33 years*.[46] Thus the first interval is 5 years, the second is 6 years, the third jumps to 10 years, and the last interval, which again is probably about 33 years, is simply given as >41.[47] Working on this mathematical puzzle, I gradually realized that the greatly uneven age intervals also play a part in obscuring the true divergent nature of the *unokai* and non-*unokai* age distributions. To visually emphasize this point, Figure 15.4 compares the percentage of *unokais* and percentage of non-*unokais* in bars that correspond to the *relative widths* of each of Chagnon's four intervals.[48] If this bar chart appears unconventional, that's exactly the

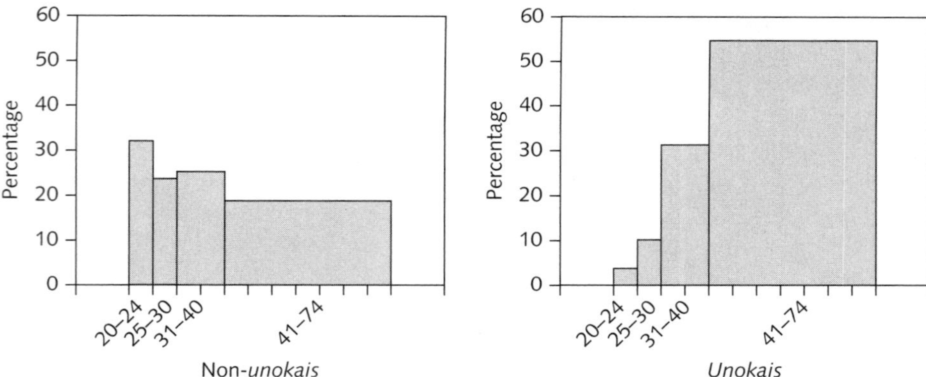

Figure 15.4 Paired bar charts showing the relative percentages of non-*unokais* (left chart) and *unokais* (right chart) in each age group; these charts also graphically reflect the unequal widths of the four age intervals. As reflected in Figure 15.1, the two charts show the marked differences between the age patterns of the two groups. Additionally, this figure visually portrays how the widths of the age intervals used in Chagnon 1988 (Tables 2 and 3) are markedly different from one another, a point that may not be as apparent if looking at the tables in the original article (also see Table 15.1). Note: The range of the fourth age interval, 41–74, is an estimate based on Yanomamö population data in Chagnon et al. 1979 (p. 311).

point. Conventionally, age intervals used in tables and presented in bar charts are of equal widths, as Chagnon has done in other publications.[49] Figure 15.4 highlights the fact that the original age intervals are markedly uneven, a point that may not be as apparent in the tabular presentations of the same numbers in Chagnon's original article.[50]

As in the Holmes and Watson "new neighbor" story in chapter 1, it now also may be revealing to consider "what is *not* there." After several days of focusing on this puzzle, as I sat down to dinner one evening it suddenly occurred to me what was *missing* from Chagnon's article.[51] When two groups are compared in social science publications, it is very standard practice for statistical tests to be employed. However, in this case, no statistical test results comparing *unokais* and non-*unokais* are presented. And there are no basic age-related statistics—that is, no means, standard deviations, and range information for the *age* of the *unokais* and the *age* of the non-*unokais*. As a consequence, the reader must make "eyeball" comparisons of pairs of averages: *unokais* versus non-*unokais* for the four different age subgroups. Merely comparing *averages* that are derived from *unequal* numbers of men, in age categories of grossly *unequal* size, that reflect *fundamentally different* age distributions with *very different* average ages will very likely lead to erroneous interpretations. In this case, our own eyes—and minds—can readily deceive us; age may seem to be controlled for, but in fact it is not.

Repeatedly, Chagnon has reported that *unokais* have *over three times* the number of offspring as non-*unokais*.[52] We have seen that the majority of the *unokais* in his sample are over 41 years old, whereas the majority of non-*unokais* in his study are 30 years old or younger. How much does the *real* age difference between *unokais* and non-*unokais* affect the findings? How many children among the *unokais* exist *simply because the fathers are older* than are the non-*unokai* fathers?

Let's consider a mathematical approach to these questions.[53] Further details and calculations are provided in the Notes. Chagnon presents data on the number of *unokais* and number of non-*unokais* in each of the four age brackets; therefore, estimates of the average age for *unokais* and non-*unokais* can be calculated using this published information.[54]

We will consider three sets of calculations that correct for the influence of age. The first, a very conservative approach for estimating average ages, is to use the same age bracket midpoint values for both groups of men.[55] This approach almost certainly *underestimates* the actual differences in average ages between *unokais* and non-*unokais* because it completely ignores age differences *within age categories*. In reality, differences in average age between *unokais* and non-*unokais* occurring *within* age intervals also should be taken into account. Although classified within the *same* age grouping, "a 40-year-old man, for example, is more likely to be *unokai* and to have more children than a 31-year-old man."[56] The second and third approaches estimate the age differences *within* age intervals to be two years and four years, respectively, since the exact extent of this difference is not known.

The first approach that simply ignores age differences *within* age intervals—the very conservative method—finds the average age of the *unokais* to be 42.5 years compared to 32.1 years for the non-*unokais*—*a difference of 10.4 years*. The second approach assumes that within age-category age differences amount to two additional years of actual age difference between the two groups; therefore, 12.4 years of age difference is used in the second set of calculations. A third set of calculations is conducted using 14.4 years of average age difference between *unokais* and non-*unokais*. It is not possible to know whether the 12.4 calculations or the 14.4 calculations are closest to reality without having access to the actual data. Based on scrutinizing this mathematical puzzle, I think the 12.4-year estimate is very plausible, and the 14.4-year estimate less likely, but still possible. *In any case, there is a high level of certainty that the conservative 10.4 estimate is too small because it totally ignores within age interval differences.* Exactly how much "too small" remains an open question in the absence of the actual data, and that is why I also present calculations for the two other possibilities, 12.4 and 14.4 years of difference. By the way, I am focusing more on children than on wives because more data on offspring than on wives are available in Chagnon's publications.[57]

How many "extra" children—that is, age-effect offspring—would the *unokai* group have simply because they have *at least* 10.4 years of additional child-producing experience over the men in the non-*unokai* group? To address the issue, it is necessary to assess how many children Yanomamö men average per year. Three different estimation methods, using two different census years, yield virtually identical results: The average Yanomamö man gains 0.182 offspring per year, or about one child every five-and-a-half years.[58]

The next step is to standardize the sizes of the two groups of Yanomamö men to facilitate the subtraction of age effect–related offspring. In my calculating, I've standardized the number of *unokais* and non-*unokais* to 137 men each, the original sample size for the *unokais*.[59] Based on Chagnon's data and before any age effect corrections, 137 non-*unokais* would have 214 offspring to the 673 offspring reported for the 137 *unokais*.[60] In other words, the *unokais* hold a 459 offspring lead over the non-*unokais*—that is, 673 minus 214 equals 459—before any age effect corrections are made.

The conservative 10.4-year calculations reduce the *unokais'* advantage by 56 percent. In numbers of children, the *unokais'* lead over the non-*unokais* drops to 200, again, when both groups are standardized to 137 men each.[61] Under the 12.4-year calculations, the *unokais'* advantage is cut by 67 percent; in raw numbers, the *unokais* now lead by 150 children.[62] And under the 14.4-year calculations, the *unokais'* advantage drops by 78 percent of its starting value, and thus the *unokais'* offspring lead shrinks to only 100 children.[63]

Clearly, correcting for age differences between the *unokais* and non-*unokais* dramatically alters the findings. Even if we adopt the very conservative 10.4-year age effect correction, the much-reported *over three-to-one unokai*–to–non-*unokai* offspring ratio drops to *less than two-to-one*. But age corrections, while very important, are only the first part of the story.

The Headman Effect

Headmen in tribal societies tend to have more wives than other men *whether or not warfare is present*.[64] Let's further examine the problem of spurious correlation by comparing the reproductive success of Yanomamö headmen and nonheadmen. In 1979, Chagnon and his colleagues reported that the 20 Yanomamö headmen in this study population had over twice as many children as did nonheadmen (8.6 versus 4.16), on the average.[65] The men in both groups were 35 years of age or over. The 20 headmen also averaged one-third more wives, 3.6 for headmen versus 2.4 for the nonheadmen.[66] Nine years later, Chagnon reported the differences in *unokai* and non-*unokai* reproductive success and number of wives without controlling for the fact that headmen were already known to average more wives and children than other men.[67] Ever-watchful Ferguson was quick to point out:

> It is common place in Amazonian ethnography . . . that headmen have more wives and more children, regardless of the presence or absence of war. The Yanomamö certainly follow this pattern, with one headman reportedly (Chagnon 1988:988) having 43 children by 11 wives. The greater number of offspring associated with headman status thus distorts the advantage attributable to *unokais* status by an unknown amount.[68]

Chagnon responded to Ferguson, not by using his data to calculate the "unknown amount" of headman influence, but rather by arguing that *unokais* still have more wives and children if 13 headmen (12 *unokais* and 1 non-*unokai*) are dropped out of the analysis.[69] Chagnon offers no explanation as to why he removes *only* 13 headmen, instead of the 20 reported for the same population a few years earlier.[70] Whereas clearly particular headmen would be expected to be *replaced* over a decade, the number of *headman positions* might not be expected to decrease so rapidly in the same population.[71] By the way, after Ferguson raised the *age issue,* Chagnon did *not* present any age-related recalculations either, but retained his original four age groups, now with headmen data for 13 men removed from the tables.[72]

By referring to data from several of Chagnon's articles, it is possible to estimate the approximate amount that the inclusion of headmen in the original analysis distorted the comparison of *unokais* and non-*unokais*.[73] Calculations that compensate for 13 headmen suggest that about 21 percent of the reported *unokai* offspring advantage over non-*unokais* can be attributed to the higher than average reproductive success of headmen. Calculations that compensate for the 20 headmen reported earlier by Chagnon and his colleagues lead to an estimate that about 33 percent of the initially reported *unokai* reproductive advantage in fact results from a headman effect.[74] However, headmen status is also correlated with age. Therefore, since the age effect and the headman effect are

TABLE 15.2 Estimations of the reproductive advantage of *unokais* over non-*unokais* under several *age effect* and *combined age and headman effect* conditions, with both groups standardized to the same size (137 men)

Number of Offspring: Unokais/Non-Unokais	Equivalent Ratio	Unokai-Advantage: Unokais' Offspring Minus Non-Unokais' Offspring	% Reduction in the Initial Unokai Advantage
Initial Condition			
673/214	3.14-1	459	0%
10.4-Year Age Correction			
414/214	1.93-1	200	56%
10.4-Year Age Correction Plus a Correction for 13 Headmen			
325/209	1.56-1	116	75%
10.4-Year Age Correction Plus a Correction for 20 Headmen			
276/205	1.35-1	71	84%
12.4-Year Age Correction			
364/214	1.70-1	150	67%
12.4-Year Age Correction Plus a Correction for 13 Headmen			
278/209	1.33-1	69	85%
12.4-Year Age Correction Plus a Correction for 20 Headmen			
230/205	1.12-1	25	95%
14.4-Year Age Correction			
314/214	1.47-1	100	78%
14.4-Year Age Correction Plus a Correction for 13 Headmen			
231/209	1.11-1	22	95%
14.4-Year Age Correction Plus a Correction for 20 Headmen			
185/205	0.90-1	–20	104%

not totally independent of one another, it makes sense to integrate headman effect calculations with the age effect calculations.[75] This approach *reduces* the magnitude of the headman effect as calculated independently of age, and hence is more realistic. Results of these integrated age effect and headman effect calculations as well as age effect calculations alone are summarized in Table 15.2.

As discussed, an age difference estimate between *unokais* and non-*unokais* of 10.4 years, based on an assumption of equal age interval midpoints, is certainly too small. If I were a gambler, I'd place my bet on the estimate of 12.4 years of age difference between *unokais* and non-*unokais* integrated with a headman effect that corrects for 20 headmen—see the seventh row in Table 15.2. The calculations expressed in this seventh row of the table correct simultaneously for a realistic number of headmen and for a reasonable age effect that adds two years of additional age difference to the 10.4-year figure to compensate for a modest amount of *within age-interval* age difference between *unokais* and non-*unokais*. Under these conditions, *95 percent of the originally reported unokai advantage disappears*. That is, 95 percent of the initial *unokai* advantage actually can be attributed to the fact that the group of *unokais* are older *and* have more headmen than do the non-*unokais*. Even when the *unrealistically conservative* age calculation and the *smaller* headman calculation are used (see row three of Table 15.2), 75 percent of the originally reported *unokai* advantage disappears. *This is a huge change in the picture.*

If my "bet" on row seven is close to correct, then of course some 5 percent of the *unokai* advantage is *not* attributable to a combination of these two effects. However, before we conclude that *unokais* in fact have some slight reproductive advantage over non-*unokais due to their unokai status,* it would be prudent to keep in mind at least three cautions. First, the age effect may be even larger than the 12.4 years reflected in row seven. Second, any slight remaining correlation between reproductive success and being *unokai* still does not demonstrate that a *causal* relationship actually exists. Third, there is still at least one other problem to be considered.

The Dead Man Effect

Chagnon presents findings based only on *unokais* that were *still alive* at the time of the study.[76] Ferguson emphasizes that this methodological decision could lead to extremely erroneous findings, since in a revenge-seeking culture such as the Yanomamö, *unokais* may get bumped off in vengeance attacks more often than non-*unokais*.[77] Obviously this could take a bite out of a person's lifelong reproductive success and, in terms of population dynamics, could lower the overall reproductive success for *unokais,* dead *and* alive, as a group. However, focusing only on living *unokais* and ignoring the dead ones obscures any lowering of reproductive success for *unokais* overall.

That *unokais* are at a greater risk of being killed than are non-*unokais* is plausible in light of ethnographic observations. Jacques Lizot, who has worked with the Yanomamö, expresses: "We should remember the tragic end of most of the famous warriors in the very region where Chagnon worked. . . . Very few of these men died a 'natural' death."[78] As Chagnon himself explains, vengeance motivates much Yanomamö raiding, and furthermore, raiders target particular individuals for revenge, although they are not always successful in disposing of the person they had hoped to kill.[79] In a culture where revenge plays a role in raiding, the Yanomamö men who "live by the sword"—the *unokais*—may more often "die by the sword," cutting short their reproductive careers as they become victims of vengeance-seekers. These dead *unokais* are not represented in Chagnon's study at all.[80] They fall through a crack in the methodology.

A sounder approach would be to compare the lifetime reproductive success and number of wives of deceased *unokais* with deceased non-*unokais*. Simply knowing mortality rates for the two types of men also would be enlightening. Ferguson writes that "adding in deceased men and their offspring could lower the *unokai's* measured reproductive advantage; it is certainly within the realm of possibility that *unokai* men would be found to have fewer offspring than non-*unokais*."[81] And of course this methodological issue is in *addition to* the problems of age effects and headman effects.

As we shall consider in coming chapters, an evolutionary model of human aggressive behavior can lead to a more general suggestion, namely, that in evolutionary terms, the fitness costs of killing have probably been greater than the benefits. Of scientific interest, and perhaps also human interest, Box 15.1 recounts some of the debate over killing and lifetime reproductive success in the words of Chagnon, Ferguson, and others.

BOX 15.1 IN THEIR OWN WORDS: DO *UNOKAIS* RISK AN EARLY GRAVE?

In his original article, Chagnon writes,

> It is possible that many men strive to be *unokais* but die trying and that the apparent higher fertility of those who survive may be achieved at an extraordinarily high mortality rate. . . . The data do not appear to lend support to this possibility. Of 15 recent killings, four of the victims were females: there are no female *unokais*. Nine of the males were under 30 years of age, of whom four were under an estimated 25 years of age. Although I do not have the *unokai* histories of these individuals, their ages at death and the political histories of their respective villages at the time they were killed suggest that few, if any of them, were *unokais*.[1]

Bruce Albert comments on the question of *unokai* mortality risks as follows:

> Chagnon raises this question only to reject it on the basis of anecdotal information (1988:990) or of "impressions" (1989b:566). No conclusive evidence has yet been provided. This is a crucial question in view of the fact that many Yanomami ethnographers (including Chagnon) have stressed that men taken to be responsible for deaths in warfare (especially the multi-"*unokaid*" warriors) are preferred targets for revenge raids.[2]

Ferguson points out that Chagnon's data on reproductive success pertains only to living men: "What is the effect of becoming *unokai* on life chances? Does the average *unokai* live and breed longer than the average non-*unokai*?"[3]

Chagnon agrees about the significance of the issue: "When I submitted my paper to *Science* in 1987, I did not have enough appropriate data to resolve the question. The data I had suggested that *unokais* were *not* at greater risk of violent death. I subsequently collected more data relevant to that question on a recent field trip and, as my schedule permits, I will publish them."[4]

Another specialist on the Yanomamö, Lizot weighs in with his assessment: "Successful warriors do not enjoy a higher status than others, but they do enjoy a certain notoriety. . . . The men who have a reputation of being *waitheri* [fierce] . . . are also the favorite targets for enemy arrows, for many reasons."[5]

Ferguson revisits the issue in his book *Yanomami Warfare,* published in 1995:

> Does the average *unokai* live and breed longer than the average non-*unokai?* After compiling the case material presented in this book, I emphasize this question even more. . . . Most of the men identified as war leaders were killed in war, including Ruwahiwe of the Konabuma-teri, Fusiwe of the Wanitima-teri, Rashawe of the Bisaasi-teri, Riokowe of the Iwahikoroba-teri, Kohawe of the Shitari, and Damowa of the Monou-teri. . . . Chagnon states that he now has data to address this question. . . . At the time of this writing, over four years have passed and the new data have not yet appeared in any publication with which I am familiar.[6]

Sources: 1. Chagnon 1988:990. 2. Albert 1990:560. 3. Ferguson 1989b:564. 4. Chagnon 1989:566. 5. Lizot 1994:854. 6. Ferguson 1995:361–362.

THE HEART OF THE MATTER

To return to the key question: Does this highly publicized study actually show what it seems to show? *Clearly it does not. Unokais* do not average over three times the offspring and two-and-a-half times the wives as do non-*unokais*. In actuality, there are multiple reasons for doubting that *unokais* have any real advantage over non-*unokais* at all. And if any such advantage does actually exist, it clearly is only a small fraction of the amount reported by Chagnon.[82]

We have seen that the *unokais* as a group are substantially older than are the non-*unokais*. This fact is self-evident from viewing the two distributions in terms of either relative percentages (Figure 15.1) or numerical values (Figure 15.2). In Chagnon's original article, specifications about the two age distributions, such as the means and standard deviations, were not provided.[83] Furthermore, the findings were displayed within four *unequal* age-brackets—of 5 years, 6 years, 10 years, and probably about 33 years. I have followed up on some of Ferguson's concerns and attempted to estimate the extent of age and headman effects.[84] I have opted for conservative decisions in calculating estimates, so my corrections may be too small. *Even so, calculations show that the combined effects of age and headmanship are substantial.* Even the most conservative calculation (age alone) cuts the originally reported *unokai* advantage by 56 percent, whereas the most liberal (yet plausible) calculation combining corrections for age and headman effects totally eliminates any *unokai* advantage (see Table 15.2). But the results of these mathematical estimates, while impressive, are not the final story. Correcting for a dead-man effect of *unknown magnitude* might reverse the direction of the original findings, since comparing only living *unokais* with living non-*unokais* problematically obscures a likely higher mortality rate among *unokais*. These three methodological and analytical issues are complementary and additive. In light of the combined weight of these concerns, any assertion that *unokais* have more offspring and wives than non-*unokais* rests on extremely shaky ground.

At the beginning of this chapter, I proposed three general reasons why Chagnon's Yanomamö article has much less relevance to the evolution of human aggression than some Pervasive Intergroup Hostility theorists assert.[85] First, the issue of spurious correlation is not satisfactorily addressed in Chagnon's original article.[86] Obviously, age and headmanship are two additional variables that also must be taken into consideration. Moreover, any remaining *unokai* advantage may have nothing whatsoever to do with *unokai*-ness per se, but may reflect instead the influences of other variables, for instance, ambitiousness, industriousness, social skills, and so forth.[87] Second, using a sedentary, horticultural, tribal society structured in terms of patrilineages as a model for ancestral human society is problematic. Third, findings from *one* study on *one* society have only limited generalizability. Thus even before probing whether the study actually demonstrates a reproductive advantage for Yanomamö *unokais,* a combination of factors caution against making a big deal about the findings.

WHY SO MUCH ADO?

As part of the scientific process, erroneous conclusions should be corrected, if possible. The extremely problematic findings from this one study have proliferated in an absolutely astounding way as they are mentioned or recounted in publication after publication.[88] The widespread distribution of highly dubious findings makes a corrective discussion all the more important.

Ferguson's cautions about age differences, headmen effects, and the like seem not to have become widely known, or appreciated, at least judging from the number of writers who continue to report the *unokai* reproductive advantage without any caveats or acknowledgments that problems may exist.[89] However, the age issue is so serious that it should be neither forgotten nor ignored. This point is all the more poignant when compounded by the other methodological and analytical problems discussed in this chapter.

An interesting question to consider is why the study has gained such notoriety in the first place. Could one reason be that the original uncorrected findings reflect a theme that we have explored in previous chapters? Can at least some of the enthusiastic reception and bountiful reiteration of these findings result from a perception that this study offers a "scientific confirmation" of widely shared cultural beliefs about violent, warlike human nature? Do assumptions that warfare is ancient, natural, or perhaps even an evolutionary adaptation explain at least some of the enthusiasm generated over Chagnon's findings?[90] Like the tenets of the Pervasive Intergroup Hostility Model generally, the Yanomamö findings go hand-in-hand with the cultural belief, as expressed by the senior citizen in Florida, that "there always has been war and always will be war."

Perhaps another reason that these findings have been so eagerly embraced is because of a resurgent interest in evolutionary explanations for violence and war. Unfortunately, the *unokai* model leads us astray. Not only does it lack solid supporting evidence, but it also comes up short in terms of evolutionary logic. Soon we will consider why the proposal that *warfare* has been designed by natural selection is extremely dubious. The idea that war has evolved to enhance male reproductive success confuses *adaptation* with *fortuitous effect* and also muddles the social institution of *warfare* with *interpersonal aggression*. We will consider an alternative evolutionary perspective on human aggression that is more solidly grounded theoretically and in much closer agreement with observable facts than are proposals derived either from *unokai* findings or, more generally, from the Pervasive Intergroup Hostility Model. In preparation, we need first to look at additional relevant facts—at patterns of conflict, violence, and conflict management that typically occur within simple hunter-gatherer societies.

CHAPTER 16

WINDOWS TO THE PAST

Conflict Management Case Studies

> Other [Ju/'hoansi] people will intervene before a person can act in a hot rage with possible serious injury to his enemy. Also, any other adult in camp is related to any would-be aggressor by dozens of overlapping ties of kinship and marriage. Once a person attacks his victim he is like a fly that attacks an insect already caught in a spider's web. Immediately both are caught. If the combatants forget the sticky web in the heat of their anger, the onlookers do not.
>
> PATRICIA DRAPER[1]

In previous chapters, salient aspects of nomadic hunter-gatherer societies were considered using relevant data from around the world. This chapter continues the exploration of simple forager lifestyle by focusing directly on *conflict and conflict management* among five such societies. These societies are selected from different regions of the world and especially from cases where ample information is available on conflict and its management. The societies are the Siriono, Montagnais-Naskapi, Paliyan, Netsilik, and Ju/'hoansi.

SIRIONO

The semi-nomadic Siriono inhabit a tropical area in Bolivia, speak a Tupian language, and have few material possessions. At the time they were studied in the mid-20th century by Allan Holmberg, they numbered approximately 2,000.[2] Whereas good hunters have slightly higher status than do poor hunters, Siriono society is basically egalitarian. Holmberg reports that "a form of chieftainship does exist, but the prerogatives of this office are few."[3] *Best hunter* might be a better term than chief, for "little attention is paid to what is said by a chief" and the chief lacks the power to demand compliance with his wishes.[4] One mark of the chief's position is the tendency, in contrast to other men, to have more than one wife. This puts further burden on a chief's hunting skills.

Women have about the same privileges as men, and both sexes engage in about the same amount of work.[5] Women take part in drinking feasts and ceremonies. Both women and men enjoy active sex lives. "While lying naked in their hammocks, husband and wife are frequently observed fondling each other, and if desire mounts to a sufficient pitch (if, for instance, a man begins to feel an erection), the couple may retire to the bush for immediate sexual intercourse."[6]

In terms of conflict, verbal quarreling is common, especially between spouses, but physical aggression is not. Of 75 disputes among various persons, 44 involved food, 19 were related to sex, and 12 resulted from other causes.[7] Congruent with the weak authority of the chief, he tends not to get involved in the disputes of others. Holmberg states that "the handling of one's affairs is thus largely an individual matter; everyone is expected to stand up for his own rights and to fulfill his own obligations."[8] Consequently, the participants usually settle quarrels themselves.[9] Avoidance is also employed when people get angry. A typical male response is to go hunting: "If they shoot any game their anger disappears; even if they do not kill anything they return home too tired to be angry."[10]

The Siriono do not engage in war. "We find neither the organization, the numbers, nor the weapons with which to wage war, aggressive or defense. Moreover, war does not seem to be glorified in any way by the culture."[11] When foreigners such as rubber tappers began to encroach on areas occupied by Siriono and to kill them early in the 20th century, the Siriono reciprocated on several occasions by killing intruders.[12] Overall, the Siriono strategy has been to avoid warlike peoples such as the Yanaigua and the Baure: "Both tribes are equated by the Siriono under one term, *kurúkwa,* a kind of monster, and are carefully avoided by them whenever possible."[13]

Siriono bands interact peacefully. They do not claim exclusive territories. If hunters from one band come across signs that another band is occupying a given area, the hunters abstain from hunting in the vicinity, thus respecting the rights of the first band to any game in the area.[14] Within Siriono society, murder is almost unknown, as is sorcery, rape, and theft of non-food items.[15] As is typical among nomadic hunter-gatherers, if conflict becomes intense between individuals or families within a band, one party simply joins another group.[16] Most conflicts are resolved short of band fission, however.

Adultery is common. If the adulterers are discreet and their partners are appropriate, such as one's spouse's siblings, the affairs may be ignored.[17] However, too frequent extramarital flings that arouse public attention can lead to jealousy.

> The Siriono say of a person in whom sexual desire is aroused that he is *ecimbasi*. To be *ecimbasi* [aroused or lustful] is all right when sexual activity is confined to intercourse with one's real spouse, and occasionally with one's potential spouses, but one who takes flagrant advantage of his sex rights over potential spouses to the neglect of his real spouses is accused of being *ecimbasi* in the sense of being promiscuous. Such accusations not infrequently lead to fights and quarrels.[18]

Another interesting aspect of Siriono sexuality involves how women and men at times engage in reciprocal exchanges. Acíba-eóko had several times tried to seduce one of his potential wives—that is, a socially legitimate extramarital sex partner. This woman had refused because she did not want to provoke a quarrel with her husband. One day the woman saw Acíba-eóko returning from the hunt with a fat peccary and other game. Acíba-eóko's potential wife was eager to get some of the meat.

> She waited until Acíba-eóko was alone—his wives had gone for palm cabbage and water—and approached him with the following request: "*ma nde sóri tai etíma; sediákwa*" ("Give me a peccary leg; I am hungry"). He replied, "*éno, cúki cúki airáne*" ("O.K., but first sexual intercourse"). She replied, "*ti, manédi gadí*" ("No, afterward, no

> less"). He said, "*ti, námo gadí*" ("No, now, no less"). She replied, "*eno, maNgíti?*" ("O.K., where?"). He answered, "*aiíti*" ("There"), pointing in the direction of the river. Both of them set out, by different routes, for the river, and returned, also by different routes, the woman carrying firewood, about half an hour later. He secured his prize; she, hers.[19]

Asymmetry exists in how jealous Siriono men and women deal with adultery. A husband tends to express anger toward his wife; a wife tends to express her anger at her female rival. On occasion, women attack rivals with their digging sticks. As mentioned, angry men may "go hunting" to cool off. Male-male disputes may be settled through wrestling matches at periodic drinking feasts.[20] The wrestling matches have rules that limit aggression, and, generally, participants use self-restraint and adhere to the rules. If not, others intervene. Holmberg explains that "aggression at drinking feasts is limited to wrestling matches; any other type of fighting is frowned upon and is usually stopped by non-participant men and women. On one occasion Eantándu when drunk, struck an opponent with his fists. Everyone began to clamor that he was fighting unfairly, 'like a white man.' He stopped immediately."[21]

Holmberg reports that murder is "almost unknown."[22] He heard of only two killings, one in which a man killed his wife at a drinking feast and the other in which a man, perhaps accidentally, killed his sister when he threw a club at her while perched in a tree.

MONTAGNAIS-NASKAPI

Broadly speaking, Montagnais-Naskapi refers to all the semi-nomadic hunter-gatherer peoples of the 625,000-square-mile Labrador Peninsula in Canada that speak Algonkian languages.[23] This includes East Main Cree, Montagnais, and Naskapi bands.[24] In the mid-1800s, there were about 24 bands on the Labrador Peninsula, with a total Algonkian population close to 4,000.[25] Traditionally, three or four families camped together in a lodge group for the long winter season, but joined numerous other groups during large festive summer gatherings.[26] Frank Speck vividly portrays native life: "Sheltered only in draughty caribou-skin or bark tents, clad in caribou-skin raiment, using mostly bone and wooden implements, and processing neither political institutions nor government, they follow no occupation or industry other than hunting wild animals and fishing amid the most physically exacting and rigorous climatic environments of the continent."[27]

By the mid-1700s, the Montagnais-Naskapi were engaged in the fur trade with Europeans, which affected traditional life in a number of ways. Leacock argues convincingly that participation in the fur trade led to the development of "hunting territories."[28] In aboriginal and early historical times, notions of ownership and restrictive use of resources among Montagnais-Naskapi were unknown. Thus the trapping and trading economy brought alterations to a free-use system. As in traditional times, fishing, berrying, bark-collecting, and hunting of game animals still could be conducted anywhere, as could the killing of fur animals such as beaver *for food*. However, in the new system, hunting or trapping animals in someone else's hunting ground in order to sell the pelts constituted an infringement.

Jesuit missionary Paul Le Jeune recorded many aspects of the traditional life when he spent the winter of 1633–1634 with a Montagnais band. He observed that cooperation, sharing, and generosity were highly valued and that good will, helpfulness, and a lack of jealousy characterized everyday life.[29] Le Jeune also noted the high level of equality in social relations generally, as well as between men and women, and that leadership, as among the Siriono, was all but lacking: "All the authority of their chief is in his tongue's end; for he is powerful in so far as he is eloquent; and, even if he kills himself talking and haranguing, he will not be obeyed unless he pleases the Savages."[30]

Observing that the native women participated in group decisions, went about their tasks unmolested by male supervision, and enjoyed sexual and other freedoms, Le Jeune became concerned.[31] He lectured men to constrain the independence of the women and implored the women to obey the men, apparently to slight avail. Le Jeune was vexed by the manner in which members of both sexes "imagine that they ought by right of birth, to enjoy the liberty of wild ass colts, rendering no homage to any one whomsoever," a poetic statement of what anthropologist nowadays call *individual autonomy*.[32] In the end, Le Jeune received lectures in turn from the Montagnais about being more tolerant, as he himself recorded: "They said that when I prayed [to] God, they greatly approved of it, as well as of what I told them; and hence, that I must also approve of their customs, and I must believe in their ways of doing things; that one of their number was going to pray in their way, soon, and that I should listen patiently."[33]

Julius Lips reports that murder and manslaughter are considered crimes, whereas killing in self-defense is exempt from punishment.[34] In native legal thinking, the appropriate punishment for homicide is death. The death sentence ought to be carried out by the *victim's close male relatives*.[35] Furthermore, the murderer himself, not one of his relatives, is the *only person* subject to revenge.

Lips reports that "the kin feeling among the Naskapi is not strong enough to develop into a regular blood feud."[36] In general, natives report that murderers are killed in revenge and that is the end of the affair, but in the following case reported by Lips, the murderer escaped with his life. In about 1850, a man named Chachiow killed Naytowcaneyoo "to get hold of the latter's wife."[37] After sharing a meal, Chachiow simply stood up and shot Naytowcaneyoo as his wife looked on. Chachiow didn't even bother to bury Naytowcaneyoo properly, but simply piled some snow on the body. The woman remained with Chachiow through the winter, and he went about hunting and trapping as usual. The next summer, several of his own band happened to pass by just as Chachiow was about to dine on a rabbit. They shot him in the leg, but did not pursue him as he fled. They brought Naytowcaneyoo's wife back to the summer gathering point and she married another man. A year later, the killer rejoined his band, and no one punished him further.

Each individual was more or less on his or her own in dealing with conflicts.[38] Gerald Reid notes that band leadership was ephemeral and that no governing structures existed.[39] The strongest force was that of public opinion. Ideally, a person should be generous and cooperative, exercise self-restraint, and avoid disturbing the peace.[40] Quarreling between spouses was exceedingly rare.[41] Individuals avoided showing enmity, it seems, in part due to the pressure of public opinion and in part out of fear that by expressing anger toward another person they might subject themselves to retribution via supernatural means. Finally, as Lips explains, mutual dependency seemed to inhibit the open expression of anger: "The toilsome and lonely life of the Indian in the woods made him inclined to accept a compromise in any legal dispute. His dependence upon his neighbor's aid and good will strengthened this tendency to work out an amicable solution, *even with members of other bands*."[42]

Thus social control was maintained largely by rewarding and encouraging positive behavior and also by applying ridicule as a reflection of public opinion.[43] In response to the most serious transgressions, such as committing incest, constant trouble-making, or murder (if not punished by the victim's kin), the guilty party could be ostracized from the band. This was a severe punishment reserved for the most serious crimes, for "in Naskapi society, expulsion is equal to a death sentence," writes Lips.[44] He recounts how a man named Ámechíchi was banished from his band in about 1870 due to his repeated violations of hunting rules and then starved to death.[45]

Regarding interband relations, Lips explains that territories are clear and that borders "are respected by the neighboring bands. However, it is considered permissible to trespass the borderline and to pass through the territory of a foreign band, without any legal or bodily harmful consequences."[46] As is typical among nomadic hunter-gatherers, subgroup composition is in a constant state of flux as families shift from one group to another.

Recall that the label "Montagnais-Naskapi" actually refers to East Main Cree, Naskapi, and Montagnais bands. "The different Montagnais-Naskapi bands maintain the friendliest relations with each other; they have never fought each other in any wars."[47] I did not rate the Montagnais-Naskapi as nonwarring—see chapters 7 and 8—however, because Lips also reports that they defended themselves from Iroquois encroachment from the south and considered trespassing Eskimos their enemies as well.[48] However, Leacock clarifies that Montagnais-Naskapi warring amounted in actuality to "sporadic raiding," and her overall assessment was that "warfare was minimal or nonexistent."[49]

Moreover, Leacock points out that the hostilities between the Montagnais-Naskapi and the Iroquois originated from the introduction of the fur trade by Europeans, prompting the Iroquois to intrude into Montagnais-Naskapi territories in search of pelts.[50] Reid adds: "Confrontations with European settlers and missionaries, the spread of epidemic diseases, the easy availability of alcohol through French traders, and the concentration of people at trading posts and mission stations all contributed to an increase in social friction and conflict."[51] In sum, the hunter-gatherer bands of the Labrador Peninsula continued their tradition of interacting peacefully with each other, without war, following the arrival of Europeans; however, the encroachment of outsiders searching for furs prompted some fighting by the Montagnais-Naskapi against intruders.

PALIYAN

The Paliyan of southern India have a population of over 3,000.[52] Some Paliyan now live in settled communities, but others remain in mobile foraging bands, usually between 15 and 30 persons in size.[53] To focus on the nomadic bands that move camp every few days, by now it will come as no surprise that "the membership of a Paliyan band is always in flux."[54] Peter Gardner reports that nomadic Paliyan subsist totally on the foods they forage, which consist of over 100 species of plants and animals, with wild yams being the staple.[55] About three times a year, hunters cooperatively kill a wild pig, less often an elk-sized sambar deer, and more often a variety of smaller prey.[56] Members of both sexes gather yams, hunt, fish, collect honey, and prepare food. Food is not a scarce resource. Gardner explains that people spend only three to four hours a day in the pursuit of food and show "no anxiety whatsoever about its supply."[57]

Paliyan prefer to live in a band with their primary relatives. Gardner discovered that virtually equal numbers of persons were living with maternal kin as with paternal kin—hence they are not patrilocal.[58] Additionally, "if a husband and wife come from different groups they may move back and forth irregularly."[59] Most marriages are monogamous, and interestingly, the age differences between husband and wife average 14.3 years; husbands were older than their wives in 69 percent of the marriages.[60]

The Paliyan place great value on individual autonomy, equality, and respect. The emphasis on respect is not simply a cultural ideal.[61] In daily behavior, Paliyan avoid competition, shy away from interpersonal comparisons, and shun the seeking of prestige. Moreover, there are no real leaders, and the Paliyan usually deal with conflicts through avoidance rather than confrontation. To Paliyan thinking, anyone who interferes with the individual autonomy of another person is acting disrespectfully. The value of equality comes into play because "everyone merits equal respect by virtue of being a human being."[62] Gardner specifically illustrates gender equality by noting that, "If a woman decides to bring her lover into the household as a second husband, and if her original partner elects to go along with the change (instead of moving out), her polyandry is her own concern."[63] As this instance reflects, the broader principle is that neither a wife nor a husband has the right to give orders to the other.

Another reflection of Paliyan individual autonomy and equality involves hunting groups. As in social relations generally, no one dominates the decision-making; the members of the hunting group operate via discussion and consensus.[64] At the end of the hunt, the game is meticulously apportioned into equivalent piles. Not only are the shares of meat equal, but also each contains identical *types* of meat. "When all have agreed that the piles are of equal size, each hunter takes one, whatever his role in the hunt" (see Figure 16.1).[65]

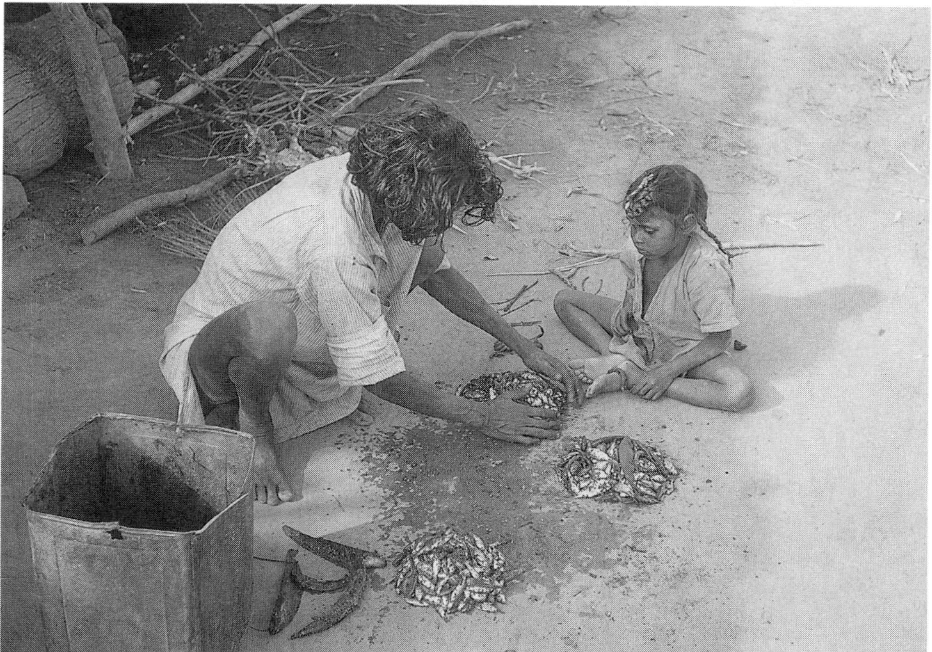

Figure 16.1 After three Paliyan families from southern India went fishing together, a man and his young son make an initial division of the catch into three equal-sized piles. (Photo courtesy of Peter Gardner.)

The Paliyan live in accordance with a nonviolent ethos.[66] Aggression is incompatible with the values of respect, equality, and individual autonomy. For the most part, the Paliyan use effective nonviolent techniques to deal with interpersonal conflict.[67] First, individuals employ self-restraint, as reflected in the ideal, "If one strikes [a man], the struck man keeps still. It is our main motto."[68] Second, Paliyan avoid drinking alcohol, which would be available as palm toddy in some circumstances. Third, people remove themselves from conflict situations. Temporary and longer-term avoidance is relatively easy in this individually autonomous, nomadic society. Fourth, a third-party conciliator may assist in relieving tension. In line with the values of this culture, "a self-appointed conciliator distracts with wit or sooths with diplomacy, this is done in a respectful way, never at the expense of the principals."[69]

Gardner recorded only 20 episodes of conflict—or, more accurately, of *disrespect*—including those in which children were involved, over a four-and-a-half month period in a largely foraging band. Most instances of disrespect were rather mild, as when adults lightly slapped children or when someone whose feelings had been hurt simply left the band in total silence.[70]

Even the most serious cases, such as those involving marital jealousy, are very mild from a culturally comparative perspective. The vast majority of the disrespect cases involved no physical contact whatsoever, and sometimes no verbal exchange either, such as when one party responded by leaving.[71] Overall, the rate of disrespect cases comes out to be *just under one case per person per year*. Gardner reports that the Paliyan have strong beliefs against murder and reports no actual cases of homicide. They do not engage in feuds or war and respond to threats of violence from outsiders by moving away.[72]

NETSILIK INUIT

Arctic Eskimos, or Inuit, are remarkably uniform in language and culture from Siberia to Greenland.[73] Inuit camps in traditional times rarely had more than 100 persons and often considerably less.[74] Across the Arctic, population densities were low, ranging between 0.5 and 1.5 persons per 100 square miles. Government was lacking and band leadership was weak. The best hunters were respected, but even these men lacked the power to exert their will on others.[75] Shamans, who were thought to possess supernatural powers, were respected and perhaps feared. Among the Netsilik, for example, the shaman has been described as half-priest and half-sorcerer, someone "who could fall into trance and evoke helpful spirits to cure the sick, aid the community, or satisfy *personal grievances*."[76]

The Netsilik Inuit are one of many groups in the Central Canadian Arctic.[77] Traditionally, the Netsilik population resided in small nomadic bands with variable membership.[78] In the winter, the Netsilik harpooned seals on the frozen sea; in the summer, they engaged in fishing and communal caribou hunts.[79]

Traditionally, male infants were valued over female infants because they eventually would become hunters.[80] Probably for this reason, more female infants than male infants were killed. The sick and the old were sometimes left to die, not out of cruelty, but out of necessity in the harsh Arctic environment. In 1923, out of 259 persons, 150 were males and only 109 females.[81]

The Netsilik strongly believed that every man should hunt and had clear rules for sharing meat. Asen Balikci explains how lazy men were disliked, criticized, and sometimes even ostracized. By contrast, if a productive hunter who regularly shared with others became ill, he and his family were aided with gifts of food.[82]

Along with cooperation and sharing, a great deal of competition existed among Netsilik men. "In the chase for caribou and musk oxen, during the watch for seals, and in wrestling matches, every man tried to outdo his neighbor, to obtain more food and appear stronger."[83] The competition clearly extended to having and keeping a wife. Balikci reports that many incidences of wife stealing occurred: "Having a wife could not be taken for granted at any time."[84] Only the most skilled hunters could support two wives.[85] As a rule, co-wives got along quite well.[86] Polyandry also existed, probably as a response to a shortage of women, but it created tensions. In contrast to the amiable relations between co-wives, sexual jealousy among co-husbands often was difficult to conceal and in recent history had contributed to two murders.[87]

In accordance with a nomadic way of life, the Netsilik had few material possessions.[88] Furthermore, the Netsilik did not claim exclusive rights to natural resources. Balikci emphasizes that among the Netsilik, as among most Inuit, people had the right to hunt anywhere they pleased; no person or family was entitled to attempt the exclusion of others from hunting or fishing in a particular location.[89] Hoebel explains, "Anyone, whatever his local group, may hunt where he pleases, for the idea of restricting the pursuit of food is repugnant to all Eskimos, except to some extent in Western Alaska, where the individualistic or familistic notions of the Northwest Coast Indians are said to have influenced Eskimo practices."[90]

Physical aggression periodically occurred in Netsilik society: "Men fight among themselves for a wife, for a simple consequence of the shortage of women is that young men must take women by force if their parents have not been so prudent as to betroth them to an infant girl."[91] As indicated in the quotation, wife stealing among the Netsilik was an individual affair involving a claim to a particular woman.[92] In other words, groups of Netsilik men did not raid other groups for women.[93] Pertaining not only to the Netsilik but also to other Central Canadian Inuit, C. Irwin emphasizes that obtaining a wife by husband-killing "was never done on a mass scale, involving war."[94]

Turning to murder, Balikci reports that the most frequent cause of homicide and attempted homicide among the Netsilik was "the desire to steal a *certain* woman."[95] This motive is typical among Inuit generally.[96] In six out of seven Netsilik murder cases, the killers were male. The one female killer shot her sleeping husband apparently to get out of the marriage, although generally speaking Netsilik women were free to divorce.[97] Hoebel searched the Inuit literature for homicide cases and found that in 26 out of 27 cases, the killer was a male.[98] Balikci tells how Netsilik killers use the element of surprise, murdering their victims while they sleep or attacking them from behind.

> Ikpagittoq was married to Oksoangutaq's sister. They were Netsilik. . . . Not far from their camp lived Saojori, a particularly strong man from the Aivilik [a different Inuit group] country, with his two wives. . . . Ikpagittoq encouraged Oksoangutaq, who was single, to kill Saojori and take his wives. . . . The two men went out and found Saojori on the ice at the very moment when he was about to catch a seal. Saojori guessed the evil intentions of his visitors, and so he held the seal with one hand and kept the other free to grab his knife if he needed to defend himself. The visitors apparently were very

> friendly and helped to drag the seal to the shore, where Saojori extracted the liver for a quick meal. Then he went down to the beach to wash his hands, still holding his knife between his teeth, ready for defense. As he knelt down at the water, Ikpagittoq attacked him from behind, trying to throw him to the ground. A struggle developed, while Oksoangutaq stood by watching until the embattled Ikpagittoq shouted at him, "You said you wanted to kill this man, what are you waiting for?" Oksoangutaq stepped up and pushed his knife into Saojori's neck, killing him on the spot. After the murder the two men went inland to hunt caribou; on returning home, they sent Oksoangutaq's sister to Saojori's tent to inform his two wives about the murder. One of the wives was very frightened and ran away with her child. Oksoangutaq had no trouble catching her, and made her his wife.[99]

Irwin notes that about half of the 36 Netsilik myths he collected focus on the *wrongness* of homicide and the *certainty* that a victim's relatives will seek revenge on the perpetrator.[100] In such myths, the clear "moral to the story," that homicide doesn't pay, may discourage some potential murderers. In actuality, avenging a close relative's murder was a possibility, not an absolute obligation among the Netsilik. A frequently used alternative to physically killing a murderer was to extract revenge through supernatural means.[101] Fear of supernatural retribution also may have prevented some contemplated homicides. Fearing revenge, murderers often fled to some distant area and did not return for several years, hoping that with time the passions of their victim's family would subside.

The Netsilik language contains no word for war.[102] Speaking of the Central Canadian Inuit, including the Netsilik, Irwin concludes that warfare was nonexistent: "Intertribal conflict amongst the Inuit of the Central Arctic was limited to murder, and revenge killing, or execution, as is suggested by their semantics."[103] For the Netsilik, Balikci describes several murders and kin-based revenge expeditions.[104] After thoroughly reviewing the literature, Hoebel reached a conclusion similar to Irwin's regarding the lack of real warfare among the Inuit of the Central Canadian Arctic.[105] Based on fieldwork among Central Eskimos, Franz Boas concluded, "Real wars or fights between settlements, I believe, have never happened, but contests have always been confined to single families."[106] Furthermore, Irwin notes that although certain locations could have abundant food resources, "the ethnographic record suggests that the Inuit did not fight wars over these 'oases of protein' that are scattered across their habitat."[107]

Interpersonal conflicts were handled in many ways. Avoidance was practiced. Gossip and mockery were used to check deviancy.[108] Quarreling and fighting were prevented or limited, because people feared aggressive retaliation, loss of beneficial relationships, or sorcery by an opponent. Moreover, the Netsilik utilized ritualized contests to settle disputes without bloodshed. If all else failed, the community could issue a death sentence against a person considered to be dangerously antisocial.

Contests had definite rules. In a stylized physical fight, a man who challenged another had to receive the first blow.[109] The two opponents struck each other on the forehead or shoulder until one man gave up. A Netsilik man explained, "After the fight, it is all over; it was as if they had never fought before."[110]

The song duel was another ritualized contest for settling disputes. The community-wide audience eagerly laughed and joked as they listened to the lyrics composed by each opponent. Each man's wife sang the song her husband had composed as he accompanied her by beating a drum and dancing for the audience. Scathing lyrics included "accusations of incest, bestiality, murder, avarice, adultery, failure at hunting, being henpecked, lack of manly strength, etc."[111] Under the rules of song dueling, opponents could blast their antagonists in verse but not make direct reference to the details of their dispute.

Virtues in Netsilik society included sharing, strength, and industriousness; deviance included laziness, failure to share, and gratuitous aggressiveness. Killing on one occasion demonstrated a man's strength and courage; killing on multiple occasions showed that he was a danger to others.[112] Decisions to kill dangerous deviants were made by the person's own family.[113] The fact that a deviant's own kin undertook the task of removing the violent or otherwise antisocial person from society had the advantage of preventing revenge.[114] Knud Rasmussen describes an execution of a man who had become mentally disturbed and violent:

> [Arnaktark] . . . stabbed his wife Kakortingnerk in her stomach. She fled on foot with her child on her shoulders, and after arriving at the main camp she told what had happened.
>
> They started to fear that he might stab again at someone they loved, and they discussed what should be done. The discussion was held among family, and it was felt that Arnaktark, because he had become a danger to them, should be killed. Kokonwatsiark [one of Arnaktark's brothers] said that he would carry out the verdict himself and the others agreed. . . . Kokonwatsiark said to him: "Because you do not know very well any more (have lost control of your mind), I am going to 'have' you." Then he aimed at his heart and shot him through the chest.[115]

The Netsilik engaged in homicide, revenge killings, executions, and occasionally feuds, but not war. Disputes generally were of a personal nature, and many were between two men over a particular woman. Occasionally, disputes led to homicide, but more often, conflict was handled through ritualized fights, song duels, sorcery, toleration, and avoidance. Netsilik social norms included obligations related to hunting, sharing, and open access to natural resources. "When camp stability was endangered by individuals who disregarded these community interests, or upset the social balance by disruptive aggressive activity or by evil sorcery or insanity, the community did take action—even to the extreme of execution, if it was needed."[116]

JU/'HOANSI

For many years, anthropologists have referred to the Ju/'hoansi of the Kalahari Desert in Africa as the Kung, !Kung, !Kung San, or !Kung Bushmen. Richard Lee suggests that it is more suitable and respectful to call the people by the name they use for themselves, Ju/'hoansi, which is pronounced *zhu-twasi* and means real people.[117] The Ju/'hoansi language includes click sounds created by pulling the tongue sharply away from the roof of the mouth. The name *Ju/'hoansi* and some other words used in quotations include linguistic symbols (for instance: /, =/, !, and //) to designate different types of clicks. Traditionally, the Ju/'hoansi were nomadic. In recent decades, many Ju/'hoansi have adopted a settled way of life.[118]

Our focus here is on the traditional nomadic hunter-gathering lifestyle of the Ju/'hoansi, especially on the populations in the vicinity of Dobe and Nyae Nyae, because they have been well studied. The Ju/'hoansi have a low population density—about 10 persons per 100 square miles.[119] Archaeological findings show that nomadic hunter-gatherers have lived in this part of the Kalahari Desert for thousands of years.[120]

"Among the !Kung [Ju/'hoansi] *and other hunter-gatherers, good fences do not make good neighbors,"* emphasizes Lee.[121] The Ju/'hoansi word *n!ore* refers to the area surrounding a water hole, which generally ranges in size from 300 to 600 square kilometers.[122] Each *n!ore* has a core group of owners. Realizing that individuals sometimes disagreed about which *n!ore* they were in while travelling, Lee concludes that *n!ores* lack clear boundaries.[123] Ownership of a *n!ore* is collective, not individual. Any person within a core group of owners and their visiting guests can use resources within the *n!ore*.[124] Neighboring groups also can use the resources, but custom requires them to advise the *n!ore* owners as to their movements. Finally, even more distant groups are allowed to use the *n!ore* resources, but they should follow certain rules of etiquette.[125] They must first ask permission of the owners. They must not stay too long. And they must arrive in modest numbers. Lee explains: "The Ju/'hoansi regard the *n!ore* as their storehouse or larder, and if food runs out in one *n!ore* all people have a claim on the resources of several other *n!ores*."[126]

Disputes over food or land are rare and seldom entail aggression. They are much less common than quarrels over betrothals and adultery.[127] Instead, the Ju/'hoansi have a nonexclusive, collective pattern of land ownership and reciprocally share resources. As discussed in chapter 14, reciprocal sharing among fluctuating and interconnected groups benefits everyone.

Researchers agree that leadership and authority structures are very weak in Ju/'hoansi society. Cashdan notes the existence of social pressures against authority among Kalahari hunter-gatherers, including the Ju/'hoansi.[128] Thomas also comments on the lack of authority.[129] Lee states that "leaders have no formal authority," and relates the answer he received to a question about leadership: " 'Of course we have headmen!' he replied, to my surprise. 'In fact, we are all headmen,' he continued slyly, 'each one of us is headman over himself!' "[130]

The nomadic Ju/'hoansi do not engage in warfare.[131] Lee points out: "It is extremely interesting and significant that the traditional Ju/'hoansi did not attempt to fortify or stockade their village sites in any way. They slept in the open, protected only by their sleeping fires, which keep the carnivores at bay, and by their mutual trust of the peaceful relations with their human neighbors."[132]

Making war would be antithetical to the mutually beneficial pattern of reciprocal sharing across indistinct, interreliant group lines wherein each person is linked to individuals in other *n!ores* as relatives, in-laws, trading partners, and friends.[133] There is no reason to risk death by going to war over resources when one can exchange favors instead! Furthermore, each person has only a few personal possessions, so basically there is nothing to plunder.[134]

What about raiding other groups for women? As among the Netsilik, this simply does not occur. In parallel to the Alacaluf and Tiwi examples presented in chapter 11, fighting over *a* woman is a personal matter among the Ju/'hoansi. Mislabeling this type

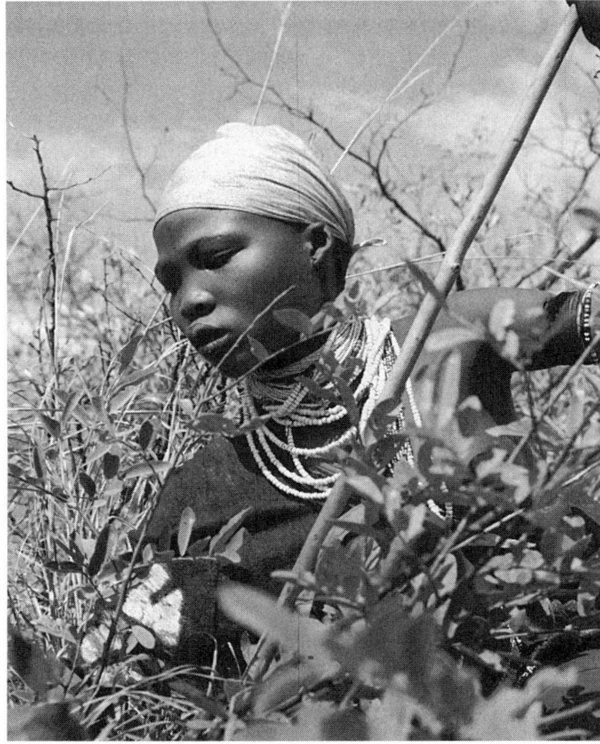

Figure 16.2 Among the Ju/'hoansi of the African Kalahari, women gather a variety of vegetable foods. The woman pictured is on a gathering expedition and carries her digging stick. The plentiful mongongo, which provides both fruit and nuts, is the most important vegetable food gathered. When away from camp on gathering trips, married women may rendezvous with their lovers. Richard Lee concludes that, on balance, neither sex exploits the other in Ju/'hoansi society, but to the contrary, there is relative equality between the sexes. (Photo courtesy of Harvard University's Peabody Museum of Archaeology and Ethnology; see Lee 1993:48, 92; Shostak 1983).

of dispute as a *battle* or as *warfare* only confuses the situation and obscures the individual nature of such contests. Moreover, disputes over women are seldom lethal.

A lack of war does not mean that all other forms of lethal aggression are absent from Ju/'hoansi society. The Ju/'hoansi commit homicides. They sometimes avenge previous killings and may execute extreme deviants. These forms of violence, however, *are not war*. Failure to clearly distinguish between warfare on the one hand and various other types of lethal aggression arising from personal grievances on the other has contributed to confusion about the Ju/'hoansi.[135]

We have seen that nomadic hunter-gatherers typically promote cooperation, sharing, and egalitarianism, including female–male equality.[136] The Ju/'hoansi are no exception (see Figure 16.2).[137] Lee writes, "On balance, the evidence shows a relatively equal role in society for the two sexes."[138] Men and women work equally hard. Men discuss political matters more than do women, but women initiate divorce more often than do men.[139] Marjorie Shostak relates the life story of a woman she calls Nisa.[140] Certainly, Ju/'hoansi women are not merely at the beck-and-call of the men:

> Sex with a lover [who] a woman really likes is very pleasurable. So is sex with her husband, the man of her house. The pleasure they both give is equal. Except if a woman has pulled her heart away from her lover, then there is little pleasure with him.
>
> When a woman has a lover, her heart goes out to him and also to her husband. Her heart feels strong toward both men. But if her heart is small for the important man and big for the other one, if her heart feels passion only for her lover and is cold toward her husband, that is very bad. Her husband will know and will want to kill her and the lover. A woman has to want her husband and her lover equally; that is when it is good.
>
> Women are strong; women are important. . . . [Ju/'hoansi] men say that women are the chiefs, the rich ones, the wise ones. . . . A woman can bring a man life, even if he is almost dead. She can give him sex and make him alive again. If she were to refuse, he would die! If there were no women around, their semen would kill men. Did you know that? If there were only men, they would all die. Women make it possible for them to live. Women have something so good that if a man takes it and moves about inside it, he climaxes and is sustained.[141]

Although Nisa mentions that a neglected husband might feel like committing homicide, several researchers conclude that the Ju/'hoansi strongly devalue aggression and for the most part are very peaceful.[142] Based largely on his work among a different Kalahari society, the !Ko San, ethologist Irenäus Eibl-Eibesfeldt argues, however, that verbal aggression such as mockery and insults, sorcery, sibling rivalry among children, and children's aggression refute Ju/'hoansi peacefulness. He points out that !Ko San, and by extension the Ju/'hoansi, are not *aggression-free*.[143]

The first observation is that Ju/'hoansi and !Ko are different societies![144] Melvin Konner makes another important point: From a culturally comparative view, the Ju/'hoansi are *relatively* peaceful, not *absolutely* nonviolent.[145] Using terms like *aggression-free* implies a dichotomy—that is, either having *aggression* or being *aggression-free*. By contrast, notice that Lee uses the word relative in his assessment: "The Ju/'hoansi managed to live in *relative* harmony with a few overt disruptions."[146] Likewise, Thomas, who titled her book about the Ju/'hoansi *The Harmless People,* describes aggressive incidents.[147] Although Thomas is impressed with the relative tranquility of Ju/'hoansi daily life, she clearly is not proposing that the Ju/'hoansi are aggression-free. Neither is Lee, who reports 22 homicide cases between 1920 and 1955.[148] Similarly, Draper concludes that physical aggression among the Ju/'hoansi is extremely rare, but nonetheless obviously does occur—as reflected, for instance, in Draper's epigraph for this chapter.[149]

The Ju/'hoansi themselves specify three types of conflict.[150] The least serious is talking. Next comes physical fighting without deadly weapons. Finally, there is fighting with lethal weapons. Fighting with words ranges from innocuous to serious. Lorna Marshall calls the Ju/'hoansi the most loquacious people she knows and concludes that all the talking helps to maintain the peace "by keeping everyone in touch with what others are thinking and feeling, releasing tensions, and keeping pressures from building up until they burst out in aggressive acts."[151] In the most serious verbal altercations, a plethora of sexual insults are exchanged.

Lee observed 34 physical altercations that lasted from less than a minute to five minutes (see Table 16.1).[152] Friendly peacemakers typically attempted to separate the

TABLE 16.1 Initiators and recipients of physical aggression among the Ju/'hoansi

	Victim		
Attacker	**Male**	**Female**	**Total**
Male	11	14	25
Female	1	8	9
Total	12	22	34

Note: In 10 of the 14 cases involving a male attacking a female, the principals were husband and wife. In the one case of a female attacking a male, the principals were husband and wife.

Source: This table is created from data in Lee 1979:377, Table 13.1.

antagonists. Adultery was the most common reason for the fights, but sometimes the causes of physical encounters remained obscure.

Some features of verbal and physical fighting appear in Nisa's life story as told to Shostak. Nisa had separated from her husband, Besa, and was living with Bo.

> I cursed him as he held me, "Besa-Big-Testicles! Long-Penis! First you left me and drank of women's genitals elsewhere. Now you come back, see me, and say I am your wife?" He pushed me toward the fire, but I twisted my body so I didn't land in it. Then he went after Bo. Bo is weaker and older than Besa, so Besa was able to grab him, pull him outside the hut, and throw him down. . . . My younger brother woke and ran to us, yelling, "Curses to your genitals!" He grabbed them and separated them. Bo cursed Besa. Besa cursed Bo, "Curses on your penis!" He yelled, "I'm going to kill you Bo, then Nisa will suffer! If I don't kill you, then maybe I'll kill her so that you will feel pain! Because what you have that is so full of pleasure, I also have. So why does her heart want you and refuse me?"
>
> . . . The next time, Besa came with his quiver full of arrows, saying, "I'm going to get Nisa and bring her back with me." . . . People heard us fighting and soon everyone was there, my younger and older brothers as well. Besa and I kept arguing and fighting until, in a rage, I screamed, "All right! Today I'm no longer afraid!" and I pulled off all the skins that were covering me—first one, then another, and finally the leather apron that covered my genitals. I pulled them all off and laid them down on the ground. I cried, "There! There's my vagina! Look, Besa, look at me! This is what you want!"
>
> The man he had come with said, "This woman, her heart is truly far from you. Besa, look. Nisa refuses you totally, with all her heart. She refuses to have sex with you. Your relationship with her is finished. See. She took off her clothes, put them down, and with her genitals is showing everyone how she feels about you. She doesn't want you, Besa. If I were you, I'd finish with her today." Besa finally said, "Eh, you're right. Now I am finished with her."
>
> . . . Bo and I married soon after that. We lived together, sat together, and did many things together. Our hearts loved each other very much and our marriage was very very strong.[153]

In the account, several aspects of Ju/'hoansi verbal and physical fighting are portrayed. The sexual insults flow freely. Nisa's brother plays the role of friendly peacemaker by separating Bo and Besa, and later other people come to the scene of Besa and Nisa's verbal fight and thus are on hand to intervene if necessary.[154] Besa arrives with deadly arrows, but does not use them. Besa's own companion takes part in persuading him to give up and leave. Nisa exercises her rights to divorce and is not intimidated by Besa. She finally resorts to a dramatic genital display to get her message across. Finally, a husband and wife obviously can have very warm feelings for each other, judging from the way Nisa speaks about Bo.

The third type of Ju/'hoansi fighting involves weapons and can result in injuries and death. Lee documents 22 homicides committed by 25 persons in the Ju/'hoansi areas called Dobe, Nyae Nyae, and /Du/da over a 35-year period.[155] All killers were men, and all but three victims were men. Only five of the 22 killings were premeditated; most were crimes of passion.[156] Typically, victims were killed by spears or arrows. The Ju/'hoansi cover the tips of their hunting arrows with poison from *Diamphidia* beetles.[157] Quite probably this practice increased the fatality rate. Furthermore, homicide victims were not always the adversaries themselves, but supporters, peacemakers, or unfortunate bystanders. Some homicides were conducted in revenge for a prior killing. Finally, both attempted and successful executions of killers resulted in deaths.[158]

Close biological relatives tended not to kill each other. The closest biological relationship between killer and victim was when a nephew dispatched his uncle.[159] Lee's data suggest that successful revenge-killings and successful executions of recidivist murderers tended to bring an end to lethal violence.[160] In other words, killing a killer restores a balance, preventing further violence. For instance, the following revenge killing of a murderer provoked no counter-revenge:

> One evening D2 walked right into G's camp and without saying a word shot three arrows into G, one in the left shoulder, one in the forehead, and the third in the chest. G's people made no move to protect him. After the three arrows were shot, G still sat facing his attacker. Then D2 raised his spear as if to stab him. But G said, "You have hit me three times. Isn't that enough to kill me, that you want to stab me too?"[161]

Draper explains that the Ju/'hoansi are uncomfortable around unpredictable persons or those with violent tempers.[162] Aggressiveness is *not* appreciated. Lee makes a similar point in a different context—the personality features that parents look for in a potential son-in-law: "He should be a good hunter, he should *not* have a reputation as a fighter, and he should come from a congenial family of people who like to do *hxaro,* the Ju/'hoan form of traditional exchange."[163]

As Boehm emphasizes about foragers overall, group members may execute "a bullying recidivist killer, possibly a psychotic, who in effect intimidates his group."[164] For instance, a Ju/'hoansi man named =/Gau was described as a lion—who "ate people." After he had killed three people, a young in-law of =/Gau stabbed him in the heart as he slept. =/Gau jumped up to attack his assailant but dropped dead in his tracks. A second recidivist killer was named /Twi and, like =/Gau, was a notorious man and possibly psychotic. He was finally put to death by group action. "He had killed two people already, and on the day he died he stabbed a woman and killed a man. . . . No one came to his aid because all those people had decided he had to die. . . . Then they all fired on him with poison arrows till he looked like a porcupine."[166] In all, at least 11 homicides (50 percent of the total) stemmed directly or indirectly from the actions of only two overly aggressive men, =/Gau and /Twi. It is very understandable that the Ju/'hoansi do not like violent-tempered persons.

All this discussion of homicidal violence must be balanced by again noting that social relationships seldom involve physical aggression. Ju/'hoansi manage the overwhelming majority of their conflicts through talk, humor, short and long-term avoidance, friendly peacemaking, and recently by appealing to non- Ju/'hoansi mediators.[167] Both Richard Lee and Susan Kent point out that traditionally the nomadic Ju/'hoansi could easily "vote with their feet."[168] The Ju/'hoansi not only prevent many conflicts from escalating to violence, but also know how to reconcile following a dispute.[169]

In the following events, friendly peacemaking, temporary avoidance, and reconciliation are apparent. A young wife, whom Lee refers to as N=/isa, was jealous and, spewing nasty sexual insults, accused several other women of having had sex with her husband.[170] Finally, one woman slapped N=/isa, and they began to grapple. Other women pulled them apart. A consensus developed that N=/isa's suspicions were ungrounded. The next day, N=/isa and her husband left for another waterhole. When they came back, N=/isa made overtures of friendship to the women she had insulted. They readily forgave her.

LESSONS FROM THE CASE STUDIES

The Siriono, Montagnais-Naskapi, Paliyan, Netsilik, and Ju/'hoansi were selected for examination because ample data exist on conflict and its management for these societies. The first essential point is that group violence is minimal in all five of these nomadic hunter-gatherer cultures. *Clearly none of these societies could be characterized as warlike*. In none of the cases do groups of men from one band attempt to capture women from other bands. Group-level fighting over natural resources is not reported and appears to be most unusual. Revenge killings and executions occur in some cases. One factor that militates against warfare is that positions of authority are lacking.

Second, the fact that conflicts are personal deserves special attention. The case studies reinforce that disputes tend to be between individuals, *not* between entire bands, a pattern previously pointed out in chapters 11 and 12. In simple foraging societies, characterized by high levels of individual autonomy, each individual is held personally responsible for his or her own behavior, including acts of violence, theft, adultery, incest, disrespect toward others, failure to share, and so forth. Three typical conflict scenarios, apparent in the case studies, are when two men compete for the same woman, when two women compete for the same man, and when jealousy sparks quarreling between spouses. Many, probably most, interpersonal disputes involve little or no actual violence. Homicides are sometimes left unavenged. When undertaken, revenge killings again show the *personal quality* of disputes in simple forager society. If revenge is sought, the predominant pattern is for the *killer alone* to be targeted by *family members* of the victim.

A third point to highlight is the variability among simple nomadic foragers regarding aggressiveness. The Paliyan exhibit extremely low levels of physical aggression, the Montagnais-Naskapi and the Siriono are slightly more aggressive but still rather peaceful, and the Ju/'hoansi and the Netsilik, while not overly violent on a daily basis, nonetheless are markedly more prone to periodic lethal violence than are the first three societies. In many situations, male sexual competition is behind fighting contests, song duels and murders among the Netsilik and arguments, physical fights, and homicides among the Ju/'hoansi. The Montagnais-Naskapi, Siriono, and especially the Paliyan express rivalry and jealousy with far less aggression.

Fourth, when viewed in a broader cross-cultural framework, the kinds of aggression discussed in all five simple forager case studies *is relatively harmless*.[171] Sensibly, none of the anthropologists who have studied these band societies have called them *aggression-free*. However, the most lethal yet relatively rare form of violence involves the homicide-then-revenge sequence that originates from personal grievances. Some hunter-gatherers, such as the Siriono, are reported to attack foreign trespassers, whereas others, such as the Paliyan, simply avoid intruders. Warfare is absent among the Siriono, Paliyan, Netsilik, and Ju/'hoansi and of not much consequence among the Montagnais-Naskapi. The Montagnais-Naskapi bands did not war amongst themselves, but, following the changes set in motion by the arrival of Europeans in the New World, sometimes attacked intruders.

We are now ready to integrate data on the nature of band societies with evolutionary principles in order to offer a reconstruction of likely conflict processes in the human past. In contrast to the Pervasive Intergroup Hostility Model, with its numerous faulty assumptions, this alternative evolutionary perspective draws on *empirical observations* of simple band societies.

CHAPTER 17

UNTANGLING WAR FROM INTERPERSONAL AGGRESSION

> If conflict induces anxieties in both parties, this means that conflict is not just about fight or flight, and winning or losing, but also about the future of the relationship. Conflict is thus, also emotionally, at the interface of competition and cooperation, which is the interface at which morality develops. Thus moral systems, from an evolutionary viewpoint, can be looked at as an elaborate form of conflict resolution seeking fairness and social integration in a competitive world.
>
> MELANIE KILLEN AND FRANS DE WAAL[1]

This chapter and the next explore *concepts* and *fallacies*. I will introduce a number of evolutionary propositions that enlighten much of the aggressive behavior observed in animals, including humans.[2] Useful theoretical concepts include natural selection, sexual selection, inclusive fitness, evolutionary adaptation, the environment of evolutionary adaptation, evolutionary stable strategy, and evolutionary cost-benefit analyses. In terms of fallacies, we have a central fallacy around which a handful of others orbit. The central fallacy is that *warfare* is an evolutionary adaptation. Satellite fallacies involve the types of evidence and reasoning used to support this dubious proposition. I will be proposing an *alternative* evolutionary perspective, *not* arguing that evolution is irrelevant to the study of human aggression. My critique of arguments and assumptions that war serves evolutionary functions does not constitute a blanket denial of evolutionary theory or disciplines such as evolutionary psychology. Rather, I am arguing that widely publicized assertions that warring behavior has evolved through natural selection are probably wrong for a number of reasons.

We have seen how aggressive conflicts at the hunter-gatherer band level of social organization tend to be between particular individuals, not between entire groups. We will now consider an evolutionary analysis of the patterns of *interpersonal aggression* in nomadic hunter-gatherer societies and suggest that the forces of natural selection and sexual selection have shaped such behaviors in humans as they have in a great number of other species. Evolutionary theory, models of aggression based on game theory, studies of animal aggression, and data on nomadic band societies converge toward a similar assessment: During human evolution, *restraint* and *limited* interpersonal aggression have been favored by selective forces over more extreme aggression. This assessment pertains to *interpersonal aggression*. If we shift the focus to warfare, *neither the observable facts nor the application of evolutionary principles supports the notion that war is an evolutionary adaptation.*

NATURAL SELECTION

The process of *natural selection* encompasses three basic tenets.[3] First, variation exists among the members of a population. Second, reproductive fitness varies among individuals. In other words, some variants survive and produce more offspring than do others. Third, fitness is inheritable to some degree and thus is transmissible from parents to offspring. Charles Darwin explains the working of natural selection, using protective coloration as an illustration:

> It may metaphorically be said that natural selection is daily and hourly scrutinizing throughout the world, the slightest variations; rejecting those that are bad, preserving and adding up all that are good; silently and insensibly working, *whenever and wherever opportunity offers,* at the improvement of each organic being in relation to its organic and inorganic conditions of life. . . . When we see leaf-eating insects green, and bark-feeders mottled-gray; the alpine ptarmigan white in winter, the red-grouse the colour of heather, we must believe that these tints are of service to these birds and insects in preserving them from danger.[4]

Natural selection operates on the *variation* among *individuals* within a population favoring some forms over others *under particular environmental conditions*. If the cases of protective coloration referred to by Darwin have evolved in these species due to selection favoring the survival and reproduction of the bearers of these particular traits over other individuals lacking such traits, then these instances of protective coloration can be referred to as *adaptations*. They have been *designed* by natural selection to fulfill *specific functions*.[5] The concept of adaptation applies to behavioral as well as physical traits. In other words, behavioral traits, such as those involving aggression, also are the products of natural selection operating on the variation in behaviors among individuals across generations in the ancestral environment of the species.[6]

How does evolutionary reasoning apply to aggression? What are the evolutionary "costs" and "benefits" of aggressive behavior? Some hypothesized costs include being injured, getting killed, harming relatives if fighting with them, losing friends, taking time and energy away from other necessary pursuits such as finding food or mating, and, among humans, getting yourself expelled from the group.[7] A central point is that engaging in aggression can be *dangerous* and has the potential for reducing an individual's fitness in various ways.[8] Individuals sometimes die as a result of injuries sustained in fights, as observed, for instance, among hyenas, lions, and various primates, but as ethologist Robert Hinde assesses, "death and injury are less common than might be expected."[9] Aggression researchers Caroline and Robert Blanchard add: "In evolutionary terms . . . successful individuals will be those with techniques which enable them to avoid agonistic situations involving serious possibilities of defeat or injury, while leaving them to continue in more promising situations."[10]

Evolutionary benefits of aggression include, depending on species and circumstances, obtaining food, territory, or mates; protecting oneself and one's offspring and other relatives from injury or death; and gaining dominance and hence better access to resources or mates.[11] Thus aggression seems to have various evolutionary functions.

Furthermore, the severity, frequency, and specific functions of aggressive behavior vary from species to species.[12] For instance, some species engage in territorial defense whereas others do not, and some species fight primarily during mating season whereas others are aggressive in other contexts.

The essential point is that although aggression can be risky, clearly it can be beneficial to individual fitness in certain circumstances. Theoretically speaking, we would expect that *natural selection, operating over many generations, has shaped the aggressive behavior engaged in by the members of a given species, including humans, so as to maximize fitness benefits and minimize fitness costs under conditions of the ancestral evolutionary environment.* We will return to this topic shortly, but first we must consider some other important evolutionary principles.

NATURAL ENVIRONMENTS AND THE EEA CONCEPT

"The hunting and gathering way of life is the only stable, persistent adaptation humans have ever achieved."[13] Donald Symons points out that over the evolutionary history of any species, natural selection has operated to produce adaptations within a certain range of environmental conditions.[14] Symons calls these "natural environments," a concept roughly equivalent to the Environment of Evolutionary Adaptation (or EEA).[15] The EEA concept does *not* simply refer to a particular environmental habitat, but is "a statistical composite of the adaptation-related properties of the ancestral environments encountered by members of ancestral populations, weighted by their frequency and fitness-consequences."[16] To express this idea less abstractly, archaeology and analogies drawn from nomadic foraging bands suggest that some noteworthy features of the human EEA, as weighted by *typicality and fitness consequences,* might include the presence of animal predators, group-living, regular presence of relatives, nomadism, very low population densities, variable diet, concealed ovulation, bipedal locomotion, long periods of infant dependency, sexual division of labor, a socially complex environment, and so forth. Again, the EEA concept implies much more than a particular environmental habitat, or geographical place; it implies a *composite of regularly occurring features,* including those related to group life, relevant to the development of adaptations in a species' past.[17]

Typically, the behaviors observed among individuals living within a *natural environment*—that is, an environment with conditions similar to those of the EEA—are expected to reflect adaptations, while at the same time, it cannot be assumed that behaviors observed in *unnatural environments*—those markedly different from the EEA—reflect adaptations, although they also might.[18] *For this reason, as we evaluate whether particular behaviors are adaptations, we should keep in mind the kind of environments under which the species has evolved.* Natural selection shaped *Homo sapiens* within natural environments characterized by small nomadic hunter-gatherer bands living at low population densities spanning a variety of different eco-zones. Group living in band-level social organization is a feature of the ancestral social environment. Adaptations typically stem from conditions encountered over the long-term ancestral past rather than from the diversity of social circumstances that have confronted some humans only over the most recent millennia, centuries, and decades.

This is one reason why constructing evolutionary explanations for warfare-as-an-adaptation based on a Yanomamö model of the past with its sedentary, village-living, horticultural, patrilocal features gets us off to a false start. Clearly, the social institutions and behaviors of people living in societies with various forms of social organization—complex hunter-gatherers, tribal peoples, archaic states, modern nations, and so on—differ dramatically from those of simple nomadic hunter-gatherers. From an evolutionary point of view, these constitute very recent and remarkable shifts away from the typical living conditions in the evolutionary past. These forms of social organization, arising almost exclusively within the last 12,000 years and in many cases much more recently, are unnatural human environments in the sense that they differ in certain ways from conditions under which the species evolved. Consider just a few of the myriad unnatural features of some 21st-century environments: town and city living; dependency on farming; daily contact with hundreds or thousands of strangers; birth control; HIV; an abundance of fatty foods, sugar, and salt; professional armies; microwave ovens; nuclear weapons; hand guns; hospitals; synthetic chemicals; mass-media; alcohol; nation-states; and so on. So, the most relevant data on human adaptations come from simple nomadic hunter-gatherers, not from complex hunter-gatherers such as sedentary, hierarchical fisherfolk of the Northwest Coast of North America, *not* from equestrian hunters of the plains of North and South America, *not* from tribal peoples such as the Yanomamö, and *not* from any other recently developed complex forms of human society based on horticulture, animal husbandry, or agriculture. While some useful insights about adaptation, as we will see in the next section, sometimes *can* be gained by observations in such unnatural environments, it also is important to keep in mind that simple nomadic hunter-gatherer bands most closely reflect *ancestral conditions*.[19]

"FLEXIBLE" ADAPTATIONS, SEXUAL SELECTION, AND SEX DIFFERENCES IN AGGRESSION

Biologist George Williams points out that some adaptations are relatively fixed or invariable (obligate) while others are more flexible (facultative) in their expression depending upon environmental situations.[20] Humans are adapted to walk upright and nearly always do so, as opposed to creeping, crawling, rolling along, or walking on their hands, regardless of cultural and ecological circumstances. Thus walking bipedally constitutes a relatively fixed adaptation in *Homo sapiens*. On the other hand, human language use is a more flexible adaptation. Whereas humans in every culture use language to communicate, which language or languages a young child begins to speak depend on the particular linguistic environment. Whereas obligate adaptations would be expected to occur across a wide range of natural and unnatural environments, facultative (more flexible) adaptations would be expected to show more variability of expression across a range of different environmental conditions. Many adaptations in humans tend toward the flexible end of a flexible-to-firm continuum. Before applying this concept to the variability that exists regarding the expression of human aggression, we need to consider the concept of sexual selection.

Sexual selection results from the variation among individuals in their abilities to acquire mates.[21] Sexual selection can occur in two manners. First, the members of one sex can choose some members of the opposite sex over others; second, the members of one sex can compete with other members of their own sex for mating access to members of the other sex. The first type of sexual selection can be used to explain the evolution of ornamentation—the huge and colorful tail feathers of male peacocks being a classic example.[22] The second kind of sexual selection accounts for the fighting structures and behaviors observed in many animal species, typically within the male sex. Larger male than female body size, muscle mass, and structures such as antlers are explained as adaptations for male–male competition evolved via sexual selection. Darwin writes, "It is the males that fight together and sedulously display their charms before the females; and the victors transmit their superiority to their male offspring."[23] Why do males tend to compete over females rather than vice-versa?

Biologist Robert Trivers suggests that the answer lies in the unequal amounts of *parental investment* typically made by females and males in offspring.[24] Darwin realized that "the female often differs from the male in having organs for the nourishment or protection of her young, such as the mammary glands of mammals, and the abdominal sacks of the marsupials."[25] Among mammals, a male at the minimum can mate and be gone, whereas the female continues to "invest" in offspring at the minimum through periods of pregnancy and nursing. Parental investment entails time, energy, and risk and can be defined as any contribution "by the parent in an individual offspring that increases the offspring's chance of surviving (and hence reproductive success) at the cost of the parent's ability to invest in other offspring."[26]

Darwin suggested that the observable sex differences in humans, as in a variety of animals, resulted from sexual selection to a great extent: "There can be little doubt that the greater size and strength of man, in comparison with woman, together with his broader shoulders, more developed muscles, rugged outline of the body, his greater courage and pugnacity, are all due in chief part to inheritance from his half-human male ancestors."[27] Symons observes that in humans female body weight is 80–89 percent of male body weight on the average.[28] Drawing on the work of one of his teachers, Sherry Washburn, Symons concludes that "If one focuses on the anatomy that is primarily responsible for sex differences, it becomes clear . . . that human males have evolved roughly *twice* the aggressive apparatus of females."[29] In accordance with the evolutionary concepts of sexual selection and parental investment, Symons proposes that men fight more than women because men are evolutionarily adapted to compete over women more than vice versa.[30]

I must emphasize one point to avoid any misunderstandings. The suggestion that certain sex differences in humans, including body size, muscular strength, and fighting ability, are in substantial part attributable to the second type of sexual selection, same-sex competition, *cannot* be taken as evidence that *warfare* has evolved via sexual selection. After all, larger male body size, strength, and other fighting attributes have evolved in numerous animal species that lack any type of aggression remotely resembling warfare. Furthermore, these types of sex differences in humans, as in a host of other animals, are the evolutionarily result of competition among *individuals*. It is not necessary, and in fact theoretically problematic, to propose that sex differences evolved in humans as a result of competition among groups. Such a view, which is referred to as group selection, lacks empirical support.[31]

The cross-cultural evidence, including data from simple nomadic foraging societies, shows an *overall pattern*. Men tend to engage in more severe physical aggression than do women. With cross-cultural regularity—from the type of nomadic band settings that are most similar to those of the evolutionary past to a range of relatively unnatural social environments—men tend to commit more homicides than do women.[32] In comparing male–male homicides to female–female homicides, Daly and Wilson conclude that "intrasexual competition is far more violent among men than among women in every human society for which information exists."[33] Moreover, behavioral findings and crime statistics repeatedly show that physical aggression is both *more frequent* and *more severe* in men than in women.[34] Generally, even beyond simple nomadic hunter-gatherer society, it is virtually always men who extract violent revenge or engage in feuds, with great variation across cultures, as we have seen, and in social circumstances where war is present, it is men who meet on the battlefields.[35] The sex differences among humans, including larger male body size, greater strength, and *overall pattern* of disproportionate male participation in aggressive behavior of various types, suggest that Darwin was right: Sexual selection in the form of male–male competition has operated on ancestral humans.[36]

From the simple nomadic hunter-gatherer case studies, we saw that two Siriono killers were both male, although one killing (and perhaps the other one as well) may have been accidental. In any case, males were the perpetrators in both incidents. In the Montagnais-Naskapi case, where homicides are not common, we considered an example involving a male killer. Homicides by women apparently are rare. Homicide is not reported among the Paliyan. Among the Netsilik, the killers of adults tended to be men. All 22 killers among the Ju/'hoansi were male. Again, the Ju/'hoansi rate may be atypically high for nomadic hunter-gatherers due to the ready availability of poisoned arrows (see Figure 17.1).

Several conclusions about lethal aggression in simple hunter-gatherer societies are noteworthy. First, the case study material shows that men commit most homicides. Thus the cross-cultural *pattern* of sex differences in lethal aggression holds widely across natural and unnatural environments, from conditions resembling the EEA to those markedly different from ancestral conditions. Second, rates of homicide vary, being low in some cases (for example, the Siriono, Paliyan, and Montagnais-Naskapi) and more common in other cases (for example, the Netsilik and Ju/'hoansi). Third, the case studies suggest that most disputes stem from individual grievances. Recurring reasons for homicide include competition between two men over a particular woman and close relatives of a victim avenging the death of a family member. *These types of dispute are not war*. Fourth, it is important that only a small fraction of disputes actually end in homicide, even among the Netsilik and the Ju/'hoansi. Most disputes among simple nomadic hunter-gatherers are *not* lethal, being handled instead in a variety of other ways, as the case studies illustrate. As a generalization derivable from the ethnographic literature on simple forager band societies, the majority of men in such societies never kill anybody.[37]

As pointed out at the beginning of chapter 9, the fact that men have a tendency to engage in more aggression than women does not prove "the ubiquity of warfare and violence across time and space."[38] In a substantial number of societies—the Saami, Sanpoil, Saulteaux, Semai, Semang, Sherpa, and Siriono, to take a sibilant sample—neither men nor women engage in very much aggression. Thus, one major difficulty with this claim of ubiquitous violence is the existence of a substantial number of nonwarring cultures and societies with very low levels of internal aggression. The claim of ubiquitous violence simply collides with too much data to the contrary. At the same

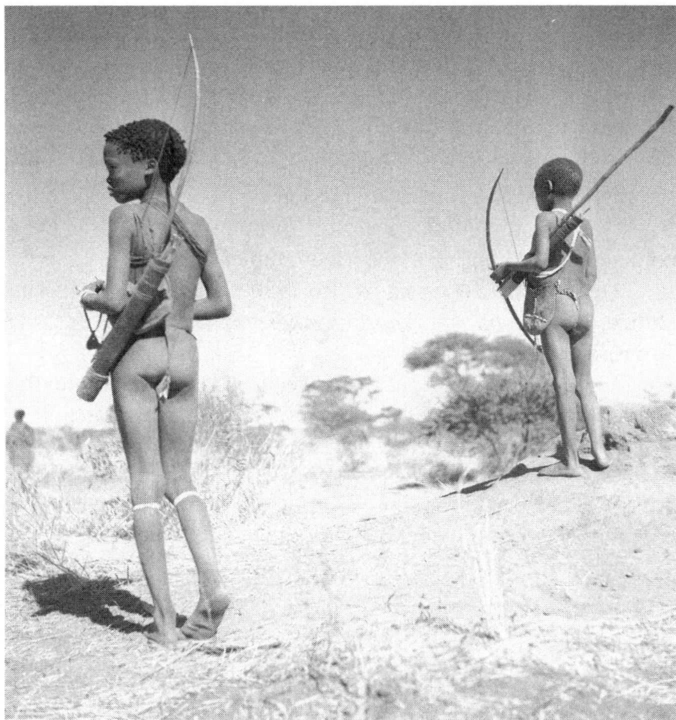

Figure 17.1 Two Ju/'hoansi boys practice hunting. Like nomadic foragers everywhere, the Ju/'hoansi share meat. The "owner of the meat" has the right, and obligation, to distribute the meat to others, and ownership is determined by who made the arrow used in the kill. Since men avidly exchange hunting arrows, the owner of a kill is generally *not* the person who actually shot the lethal arrow. Thus a good hunter does not necessary distribute more meat than does an average or poor hunter. This practice, interestingly, equalizes the glory of meat ownership and distribution among hunters and reflects in a practical sense the Ju/'hoansi's strong ethos of egalitarianism. (Photo courtesy of Harvard University's Peabody Museum of Archaeology and Ethnology; see Lee 1993.)

time, the data clearly show that the male capacity for serious violence *is* greater than the female capacity for such violence, and as we have seen, this pattern makes theoretical sense and corresponds with a great deal of data on animal aggression.

There is a rather easy way to deal with both these observations that does not require a claim that warfare and violence are ubiquitous in the face of indisputable evidence to the contrary. The continuum between fixed, or obligate, adaptations on one end and flexible, or facultative, adaptations on the other can help us out of this conceptual cul-de-sac. Human aggression is a facultative adaptation, somewhat like the capacity to learn language, not a rigid, obligate adaptation like bipedal locomotion. Everywhere, human males tend to be larger in size, have greater strength, perhaps have a greater tendency as children to practice aggression, and as adults possess a greater *potential* to act aggressively than do females.[39] However, the adaptation for male–male aggressivity in humans is *flexible—facultative*—and therefore significantly open to environmental influence.[40]

This perspective parallels that of a discipline called human behavioral ecology, which also acknowledges variability and focuses on evolutionary adaptation in ecological contexts.[41] Among the hunter-gatherer case studies, we have seen a range of variation from the nonviolent Paliyan to the sometimes-violent Netsilik. In other words, the *implicit assumption* that sexual selection has produced the rigid obligate type of adaptation for human male–male aggressive competition is not defensible in light of the high degree of variability in levels of male aggression that occurs across cultural environmental conditions. Such an assumption runs into difficulty even among the five nomadic hunter-gatherer societies comprising the case studies, before even referring to the dozens of highly peaceful societies known to exist or before considering the cross-cultural variability in *peacefulness–aggressiveness* apparent in Ross' sample of the 90 societies discussed in chapter 5.[42]

Alternatively, if male–male competition is seen as a facultative, flexible adaptation that varies with ecological and social contexts, then theory and facts fit very well together.[43] The observation that some hunter-gatherer societies have very low levels of aggression and others have higher levels of aggression does not create any major obstacle for sexual selection theory. It is no longer necessary to turn a blind eye to the fact that many simple nomadic hunter-gatherer societies, as well as some other types of societies, have minimal amounts of physical aggression.

THE COSTS AND BENEFITS OF AGGRESSION TO INDIVIDUAL FITNESS

Additional insights about human aggression can be gained from evolutionary studies of animal aggression. Animal studies suggest that much of the aggression occurring within a species does not entail all-out fighting, but rather is *restrained*.[44] Rattlesnakes inject prey with deadly venom and may use their lethal fangs in self-defense against predators, including unlucky humans from time to time. However, when two male rattlers compete for a female they do not use their venomous fangs. Instead they wrestle with intertwined necks until one is pinned by the other. The winner then releases the loser unharmed.[45] Male mule deer "fight furiously but harmlessly by crashing or pushing antlers against antlers, while they refrain from attacking when an opponent turns away, exposing the unprotected side of its body."[46] Overall, studies show that for the most part animals use *nonlethal, restrained patterns* of competition.[47] By evolutionary reasoning, the use of *threat displays* in place of actual fighting, the employment of *ritualized competitions* (as is common among ungulates), and the display of *submission and appeasement signals* (as observed among many primates) exist because they have benefited *individuals* who have engaged in these kinds of *restrained aggression* over those who have not.[48] As we shall consider, the same evolutionary logic can be applied to explain patterns of restraint observed among humans as well.

Game theory provides three conceptual models, dubbed *hawk–dove, sequential assessment,* and *war of attrition* games, that have been usefully applied to different aspects of animal conflict.[49] When it comes to nomadic hunter-gatherers, a lack of detailed data makes sequential assessment models—such as those that focus on escalation during fights—difficult to evaluate. The war of attrition model is most applicable to noninjurious contests, such as displays, as opposed to physical aggression. This leaves us with variations of the hawk–dove model, which although simple, provides some tantalizing insights.

John Maynard Smith and G. R. Price used computer simulations to gain insights into the evolution of aggression by comparing the relative success of different fighting strategies. They used the term *evolutionary stable strategy,* or ESS for short, to refer to a particular behavioral strategy that, "if most of the members of a population adopt it, there is no 'mutant' strategy that would give higher reproductive fitness." An ESS is roughly comparable to a behavioral adaptation. The ESS concept rests on the idea that a particular behavioral response will evolve, *not* because it is good for the group or species as a whole, but rather because the given behavior is best for any *individual* to engage in as a way to maximize *individual* fitness. We also should keep in mind that the results of simulations depend on the initial parameters, such as the types of strategies, which are programmed into the computer.[50]

The individual fitness costs and benefits were compared using computer simulations for actors that pursued several different behavioral strategies. The researchers found that neither belligerent (hawk) nor timid (dove) strategies are as evolutionarily successful as an approach dubbed the *retaliator* strategy. The retaliator strategy involves being nonaggressive unless attacked, in which case the retaliator fights back. In the evolutionary simulations, individuals that retreated too readily from a fight did not fare very well in comparison to more aggressive individuals; however, fighting entails risks and thus bellicose individuals also accrued evolutionary penalties. The conclusion is that limited, or judiciously applied, aggression is more advantageous than either pacifistic or overly belligerent strategies.[51]

Game theorist Robert Axelrod used computer simulations to compare 62 different strategies for cooperation and defection between pairs of players matched in a cyberspace tournament.[52] With a change of terminology, *cooperation* can be viewed as somewhat analogous to engaging in restrained, relatively safe fighting, whereas *defection* can be seen as employing injurious fighting techniques. Interestingly, one strategy, called TIT FOR TAT, outperformed all the other strategies. The TIT FOR TAT strategy always cooperates as a first "move" and thereafter does exactly what the other player did on the previous move. If the other player defects rather than cooperates, TIT FOR TAT also defects next time. If the other player then cooperates, the TIT FOR TAT strategy then also cooperates. Thus the TIT FOR TAT approach parallels in some ways the *retaliator* strategy from the hawk–dove simulations, which never attacks (defects) first, but responds to an attack (defection) by fighting back. Axelrod explains TIT FOR TAT's robust success in outperforming a multitude of alternative strategies: "[It is] nice, retaliatory, forgiving, and clear. Its niceness prevents it from getting into unnecessary trouble. Its retaliation discourages the other side from persisting whenever defection is tried. Its forgiveness helps restore mutual cooperation. And its clarity makes it intelligible to the other player, thereby eliciting long-term cooperation."[53]

As we examine human aggression, especially within the comparatively natural environment of hunter-gatherer bands, it may be useful to keep these insights from animal studies and game theory in mind. We can ask, for instance, what is the *typical pattern* of aggression in nomadic forager bands? Does aggression tend to be restrained or of a "no-holds-bared" variety? In other words, in this natural context, is aggression *typically* hawkish, dovish, or retaliatory?

INCLUSIVE FITNESS

One more evolutionary concept will prove useful to our theorizing. In 1964, biologist William Hamilton suggested that the degree of biological relatedness between individuals affects the manner in which they interact with each other.[54] The more closely individuals are related, the more examples of helping, sharing, and caring should be expected, whereas harmful behaviors such as aggression should be minimized in accordance with the closeness of the genetic relationship. Alleles are alternative forms of a particular gene, and because of common inheritance, relatives are likely to have many identical alleles. Hamilton proposed that since relatives share many identical alleles, helping relatives is an indirect way of enhancing one's own fitness. Hamilton called this idea *inclusive fitness,* reasoning that "the social behaviour of a species evolves in such a way that in each behaviour-evoking situation the individual will seem to value his neighbours' fitness against his own according to the coefficients of relationship appropriate to that situation."[55] Hamilton was *not* suggesting that individuals *consciously* calculate the degree to which they are related to others before behaving altruistically or selfishly, but rather that natural selection performs this fitness cost–benefit analysis over many generations. Behavioral adaptations that serve particular evolutionary functions are thus designed through these selective processes.

Hamilton's concept of inclusive fitness extends the evaluation of an individual's fitness beyond the self to include also the individual's relatives, those who carry many of the same alleles. When an individual protects and cares for close relatives, thereby increasing their chances to survive and reproduce, the actor enhances simultaneously his or her own *inclusive fitness* because kin have multiple alleles in common. It is now time to integrate these evolutionary concepts with data on simple foragers.

CHAPTER 18

AN ALTERNATIVE EVOLUTIONARY PERSPECTIVE

The Nomadic Forager Model

> I want to hunt eland, kudu, and gemsbok, but hunting men is what gets you killed.
>
> JU/'HOANSI MAN, QUOTED BY RICHARD LEE[1]

As we consider the five simple hunter-gatherer case studies in light of evolutionary concepts and models, we first can ask, are the data on conflict in simple forager societies congruent with the findings from game theory? Second, does an evolutionary cost–benefit model offer insights about conflict in nomadic band society? Third, do humans at this band level of social organization show patterns of restraint during conflict that are similar to those apparent in numerous other species? Fourth, does the concept of inclusive fitness have any applicability to conflict situations within nomadic hunter-gatherer societies?

HUMAN HAWKS, DOVES, AND RETALIATORS

Computer simulations comparing different fighting strategies found that *retaliators* outcompete *hawks* and *doves*. In none of the five band societies does a hawk approach to conflict predominate. Acts of gratuitous aggression violate the emphasis that nomadic foragers place on egalitarianism, sharing, and generosity.[2] In correspondence with the computer simulation, the occasional hawk does not fare very well. Among the Ju/'hoansi, the two notorious killers, =/Gau and /Twi, both met violent ends. Among the Netsilik, a man executed his own brother who had become unpredictably violent and mentally unbalanced. Balikci summarizes: "When camp stability was endangered by individuals who disregarded these community interests, or upset the social balance by disruptive aggressive activity or by evil sorcery or insanity, the community did take action—even to the extreme of execution."[3] The Montagnais-Naskapi sometimes indirectly imposed a death sentence by ostracizing a serious malcontent, an act that could result in the starvation of the troublemaker.

In fact, the execution of violent persons and bullies is pervasively reported for band societies.[4] David Damas' assessment for the Copper Inuit also applies to many other nomadic forager societies: "Certain men were feared for their aggressiveness or violent tendencies, but they almost invariably met with violent ends themselves."[5] Hoebel explains the usual fate of the recidivist killer:

> As a general menace, he becomes a public enemy. As a public enemy, he becomes the object of public action. The action is legal execution: a privilege-right of the executioner. The single murder is a private wrong redressed by the kinsmen of the victim. Repeated murder becomes a public crime punishable by death at the hands of an agent of the community.[6]

Based on an extensive consideration of the literature, Boehm writes that "reports of execution of individuals who behave too aggressively are available for Eskimos, North American Indians, Australian Aborigines, and African foragers. . . . My suspicion is that the *pattern* may be generalized to nomadic foragers in general."[7] To return for a moment to the tribal Yanomamö and the Pervasive Intergroup Hostility Model, the recurring pattern wherein recidivist killers are executed in nomadic hunter-gatherer society coupled with the fate of the hawks in evolutionary computer simulations provide additional empirical and theoretical reasons, respectively, for seriously doubting the plausibility of the scenario, as often derived from Chagnon's *unokai* findings, that killers have been favored over nonkillers (or warriors over nonwarriors) during human evolution.[8] Has the elimination of overly aggressive persons in band society over millennia actually constituted an additional selection pressure against hawks during human evolution? And if so, does the execution of hawkish individuals in band societies constitute an additional, uniquely human selection pressure against overly aggressive persons?

What about the retaliator (or TIT FOR TAT) approach to life? Recall that retaliators act peacefully unless attacked but then fight back. The case studies suggest that nomadic hunter-gatherers overall behave in rough accordance with the retaliator strategy. The first part of the retaliator strategy, to act peacefully, is clearly evident in everyday social behavior. Most foragers interact nonaggressively most of the time. Typically, they *are* harmless. None of these five societies place a high value on aggression, and this generalization holds for most nomadic forager societies.[9] To the contrary, generosity, calmness, and industriousness are appreciated, reinforced, and emphasized during the socialization of children and in social life overall. At the same time, these societies are characterized by high levels of individual autonomy, wherein individuals defend their own rights. Recall how justice seeking among the Montagnais-Naskapi, Netsilik, and Ju/'hoansi is largely an individual affair. This constitutes a *pattern* in band society.[10]

While a certain amount of conflict among simple hunter-gatherers fits the retaliator strategy rather closely, at the same time real band-dwellers are more flexible than computer simulated retaliators. In real life, for example, instead of automatically retaliating as in a computer model, nomadic foragers are renowned for voting with their feet in response to conflict or attack. Furthermore, many grievances are resolved verbally, often with the involvement of third parties, rather than through physical retaliation. The dealing with conflict via avoidance, toleration, and other nonphysical means like discussion and mediation suggests that among nomadic foragers, a great deal of conflict behavior is either dovelike or retaliatorlike.[11]

Interestingly, the Paliyan, with their nonviolent belief system and corresponding peaceful behavior, at first glance seem worthy of being characterized as a population of doves. But are they true doves or are they really retaliators who rarely encounter any acts of aggression to retaliate against? The ESS simulations suggest that peaceful behavior among the Paliyan and similar nonviolent bands probably stems from retaliators engaging in the first part of their strategy, since a population of true doves theoretically would not fare well if invaded by hawks (but, of course, neither would the hawks in comparison to retaliators). Again we see that viewing aggressive behavior as a facultative, flexible adaptation is more consistent with the data than is viewing it in an obligate way.

COSTS AND BENEFITS OF AGGRESSION

In considering costs and benefits of aggression, it may be useful to assess what the case study material shows about reasons for conflicts. Among the nonviolent Paliyan, the most serious *disrespect* cases involved sexual jealousy between husbands and wives. In Siriono society, the majority of disputes involved food or sex. Among the Montagnais-Naskapi, we considered a case wherein a man murdered a husband to get his wife. A common cause of disputes in Ju/'hoansi society was adultery leading to physical fights between men over a woman, between women over a man, and between wives and husbands.[12] Lee points out how adultery and sexual rivalry play a part in some Ju/'hoansi homicides: "A man attacked and killed a non-San [non- Ju/'hoansi] who had been sleeping with his wife . . . a man killed another and ran away with his wife . . . a man who had slept with another's wife was attacked by the husband but killed the husband . . . and a man killed his wife in an argument over her adultery."[13] Competition among Netsilik men over a particular woman also was a typical reason for conflict and sometimes resulted in aggression. Thus the case studies suggest that much fighting at the band level of social organization stems from sexual jealousy or competition between men over a woman, and also competition between women over men, although the latter is less injurious. This overall pattern is in accordance with predictions derived from sexual selection and parental investment theory.[14]

Additionally, among the Ju/'hoansi, Netsilik, and Montagnais-Naskapi, homicides at times led to revenge killings by close family members of the victim. The overall conclusion from the case studies is that serious aggression tends to result most typically from *women and corpses,* as some specialists on Australian Aborigine culture express it, although of course a miscellany of other reasons also can underlie aggression.[15] Anthropologists have reached similar conclusions about the typical reasons for homicide in simple hunter-gatherer band societies elsewhere in the world as well.[16]

The fighting of two men over a woman has obvious parallels in other species. We can speculate that the evolutionary benefits to be gained by defending or usurping a woman depend on a number of variables such as the age and health of the woman and an availability of other mates in the population.[17] Interestingly, Netsilik society has a sex ratio imbalance, largely because of the practice of female infanticide, and among the Netsilik we see more lethal fighting over women than in the other four case study societies. In humans, belief systems regarding the acceptability or nonacceptability of aggression also figure into the equation, as indicated by the rarity of physical aggression and the paucity of homicides among the Paliyan. Some Paliyan obviously feel jealousy, but the nonviolent values and patterns of respectful interaction that individuals internalize during socialization are highly successful at preventing homicide.

The fact that close family members of a victim sometimes avenge homicide in certain nomadic forager societies represents, as far as I know, a uniquely human motive for *killing*. Revenge killings are reported in three of the five case studies, the Montagnais-Naskapi, Netsilik, and Ju/'hoansi. However, not all homicides are avenged.[18] It is important to emphasize a recurring pattern among nomadic foragers. When revenge is undertaken, *the tendency is for family members of the victim to target the killer personally*.[19] This pattern is apparent in Ju/'hoansi homicide data.[20] Recall that 11 out of a total of 22 killings were initial homicides.[21] Subsequently, revenge was sought against four original killers, whereas seven killings went unavenged. During retaliation attempts, the attacks sometimes went awry, resulting in the death of an attacker or a bystander rather than (or in addition to) the original malefactor. A cross-cultural study of vengeance by Ericksen and Horton also reflects the pattern among nomadic foragers wherein individuals, as opposed to kin groups, engage in self-redress against killers.[22] In a majority of the nomadic band societies (11 of 17) for which information was available, Ericksen and Horton found that a malefactor was either the only target or the preferred target of vengeance, or else that the society exhibited the "highly individual," that is, *not* kin-group-based, pattern of individual self-redress. "The actions taken in case of a killing, an injury, or other transgressions are highly individual and depend on the specific circumstances of the individuals involved."[23]

Killing is risky business and nomadic hunter-gatherers certainly understand this, judging from the use of certain risk-reduction tactics. Balikci concludes that Netsilik "murderers were evidently careful to avoid a struggle."[24] A prevalent homicidal tactic is to surprise the intended victim, as illustrated by Montagnais-Naskapi, Netsilik, and premeditated Ju/'hoansi homicides as well as numerous others in the ethnographic record.[25] Killers attack their victims from behind or while they are asleep. For example, "/Toshe sneaked up on =/Gau in the dead of night while he was sleeping and stabbed him in the heart with a spear."[26] A second homicidal tactic involves outnumbering the victim, as illustrated by the murder of the man who was living with another fellow's wife by *two* Alacaluf brothers, the killing of a husband by *two* Netsilik brothers-in-law, and several planned Ju/'hoansi revenge killings that involved multiple perpetrators.

Due to the possibility of becoming the victim of revenge, a common tactic used by killers in nomadic forager society is to flee or hide upon committing a homicide, as was typical among the Netsilik.[27] The Montagnais-Naskapi killer, to mention a specific example, remained hiding in the woods with the wife of the man he killed rather than making his whereabouts known to others.

RESTRAINT

An examination of conflict and aggression in nomadic hunter-gatherer society, as among animal species, shows that individuals practice a great deal of *restraint*. Of the Yahgan, Martin Gusinde expresses: "A person will literally foam with rage. . . . Nevertheless, he can muster astonishing self-control when he realizes that he is too weak to stand against his opponent."[28]

The widely practiced "voting with one's feet" approach to conflict by nomadic foragers obviously reflects restraint. Pertaining to the Netsilik, Balikci calls this technique a "*very important* strategy for conflict resolution."[29]

Figure 18.1 This particular group of Australian Mardu women and children were visited by Bob Tonkinson in 1963. As an overall observation, self-restraint and ritualization are apparent in the way that the Mardu handle grievances. Tonkinson explains that "when men fight each other, the unstated aim of the many conventions surrounding their conflicts is to allow maximum opportunity for the dispute to be aired verbally. This takes place in an atmosphere of great public drama and menace, so that honor is seen to be satisfied, but with a minimum of physical violence." (Photo courtesy of Robert Tonkinson; quote from Tonkinson 1978:124.)

A second indication of the typicality of restraint is that a great number of disputes simply never escalate to the level of physical aggression. In evolutionary terms, if a conflict can be handled without incurring the risks associated with physical fighting, so much the better. Recall that animals sometimes employ low-risk *threat displays* in place of actually fighting. Humans, with language at their disposal, can employ verbal threats in a parallel manner (see Figure 18.1). More generally, we have seen that the Ju/'hoansi, for example, deal verbally with a great number of disputes.[30]

Third, the ritualized aggression of various animal species has analogs among nomadic foragers, as illustrated by the song dueling among the Netsilik, the formal pattern of spear-throwing and dodging among the Tiwi, or the *makarata* peacemaking ceremony of the Murngin. Another example of ritualized restraint comes from the Siriono and their rules for fighting that permit wrestling, but not punching "like a white man." We saw that Siriono bystanders enforce the cultural rules of fair fighting. Such aggression-limiting rules and ritualized contests are regularly mentioned in the ethnographic literature on simple foragers.[31]

A fourth indication of restraint is that even within societies where revenge killing is socially allowed or advocated, as among the Netsilik, nonetheless, *many killings simply go unavenged.* The fact that killers tend to flee in part accounts for this, but another reason may be due to restraint on the part of would-be avengers, a strategy that would seem to keep them out of risky situations. Alternatively, revenge is sometimes exacted through supernatural means, a very low risk method, since it can be done from a safe distance and the target may never know that sorcery has been directed against him. Considerable patience may be required. The Netsilik, for instance, are aware that "the evil spell may take a long time, sometimes years, before reaching the culprit and accomplishing the original intention of revenge."[32] Finally, the circumstances of the killing and the character of the victim come into play. Among the Yahgan—and I suspect also more generally—the danger of a revenge killing may be "even greater in the case of a murder for an *insignificant reason*."[33] At the same time, there seem to be circumstances wherein family members of a homicide victim acknowledge that "he had it coming," or assess that a lethal duel "was a fair fight," and thus seek no revenge.[34]

As an important aside, I must comment that a focus on restraint also puts a new spin on tribal Yanomamö aggression. As among nomadic foragers, Yanomamö men minimize risks. They often take revenge through sorcery rather than by physically attacking an enemy, many disputes are handled through contests that curtail serious injury and the loss of life, raiding is undertaken in groups instead of individually, men find excuses to drop out of raiding expeditions, ambushing a single unsuspecting victim is a favored tactic, women usually are *not* captured during a raid because they slow down the rate of retreat thus endangering the raiders, villages sometimes simply move away from aggressive neighbors, and so forth.[35] As in many animal species, the use of restraint by humans is apparent across a variety of evolutionarily natural and unnatural environments. *Exercising restraint during aggressive encounters may well be the outcome of strong selective forces operating over evolutionary time.*

In summary, the anthropological material on patterns of aggression in nomadic hunter-gatherer settings is *not* consistent with an image of Hobbesian hawks. To the contrary and in parallel with studies of aggression in various animal species, *a great deal of restraint on aggression is evident in nomadic forager societies.* Conflicts are handled by toleration, avoidance, and a plethora of safer, nonphysical approaches such as verbal harangues, arguments, discussions, reprimands, song duels, and mediations assisted by others. Some groups have developed social rules that help to limit the severity of physical fighting or ritualized contests that allow for the venting of emotions without serious injury. In band-level societies, onlookers, as *interested* third parties, stand ready to intervene to enforce the rules or pull contestants apart should fighting escalate. Such interventions are often unnecessary because both contestants of their own accord simply follow the rules of restraint. It is in their interests to do so because following the rules minimizes risks to both of them.[36] As is observable elsewhere in the animal kingdom, the restrained or limited use of aggression among nomadic foragers is readily apparent.

INCLUSIVE FITNESS

The concept of inclusive fitness also has the potential for elucidating some aspects of aggression among nomadic hunter-gatherers. Various authors have noted that inclusive fitness theory predicts that close relatives will come to each other's aid during aggressive conflicts.[37] We have seen an example of such aid as an Alacaluf brother assisted his sibling in a murderous maneuver to recoup his wife.[38]

While I do not doubt the validity of this proposition, I think the application of inclusive fitness theory to conflict situations in humans has been too narrowly conceived, focusing almost exclusively on *fighting support*. Coming to the aid of a threatened relative does *not* automatically imply that fighting shoulder-to-shoulder is the only tactic or the best tactic as weighed by inclusive fitness enhancement. Perhaps a more effective aid-giving approach, in some circumstances, involves talking some sense into an infuriated relative and dragging him away from a risky situation. I am reminded of the idea behind a slogan used in the United States intended to reduce drunk-driving tragedies: "Friends don't let friends drive drunk." In this case: "Kin don't let kin fight foolishly." My speculating is based in part on a recurring theme in ethnographic accounts: In nomadic bands, and also in other types of societies, third parties routinely distract and separate disputants (see Box 3.3). How does inclusive fitness theory apply here? In nomadic band society, third parties are generally *relatives* to some degree of *one or both* antagonists. For the Ju/'hoansi, Lee provides an example of relatives intervening to stop a fight. "At this point, Kashe's *father* and Bo's *uncle,* who had been restraining the boys, exchanged looks and broke into laughter as if to say, 'What a mess! The boys were trying to kill each other!' This released the tension, and the danger of more outbreaks subsided."[39]

Inclusive fitness theory also leads to the prediction that biological relatives should not kill or harm one another.[40] Seemingly counter to this prediction, we have seen that a Netsilik man killed his violent, insane brother and that one of the two Siriono killers threw a wooden club from a tree, killing his sister. In the Netsilik case, the entire family and other members of the band saw the act as necessary for the safety of everybody. In short, this is an unusual situation wherein the victim, while a relative, represents a deadly threat to everybody else. As mentioned, the Siriono killing may have been an accident. These two incidents reinforce a broader epistemological point. In attempting to assess *overall patterns,* we should not lose sight of the forest when confronted by an occasional exceptional tree. Unfortunately, ethnographic reports are often sketchy as to the degree of relatedness between killer and victim, but regarding the Ju/'hoansi, Lee specifies that the closest biological relationship between killer and victim was nephew and uncle: "Close kin do not kill one another. No case concerns killing a parent, a child, or a sibling, and only one describes a husband killing a wife."[41] Given the fact that biologically related family members are regularly in proximity to each other in band society, Ju/'hoansi killings would seem to disproportionately represent nonkin and distant kin over close family members.

ASSESSING THE OVERALL PATTERNS AND RECURRING THEMES

The *overall patterns* of aggression observable in these case study societies, and reinforced by many less detailed accounts of conflict in other band societies, show numerous similarities with aggressive behavior observed in other species. Furthermore, the typical patterns of aggression in nomadic forager social settings are largely consistent with predictions from evolutionary theory. In accordance with ESS modeling, for example, hawks do not fare well in these real-life settings. The majority of conflicts are dealt with *without* the use of physical aggression. Sex differences in aggression match predictions from sexual selection and parental investment theory. The reasons for disputing, whether through nonphysical or physical means, tend to be highly personal at this level of social organization. Most disputes result from *individual* interests, often of a sexual nature. This corresponds with much aggression among animals. It seems likely that the patterns of interaction among simple foragers are in accordance with predictions of inclusive fitness theory, although data on this point are fragmentary. Close relatives sometimes support each other in aggressive actions, but perhaps of equal importance, close relatives, in third-party roles, help each other avoid and retreat from aggressive altercations, thus minimizing the risks. The intervention by friendly peacemakers, whether relatives or friends, is widespread. This pattern, by the way, also has been observed among other primate species.[42]

Aggression among nomadic hunter-gatherers also has some features unique to humans. First, language facilitates a vast array of options for dealing with conflict verbally, from threatening to apologizing. Second, the killing of someone is felt to be an affront to the victim's family, and they sometimes kill the perpetrator in revenge.[43] Revenge killing, while not universal across simple band societies, is nonetheless a common social feature associated with this type of social organization. And avenging the death of a close relative seems to be uniquely human. The exaction of revenge against killers would seem to represent *an additional* powerful selection force against killers, especially gratuitous killers, which can be hypothesized to have operated in the social world of ancestral humans.[44]

Contrary to the assumptions of the Pervasive Intergroup Hostility Model, nomadic forager societies tend *not* to be subdivided into groups like patrilineages. Nomadic foragers do tend to track descent bilaterally—from both mother's and father's side of the family—and this provides each individual with a unique set of interpersonal kinship links that are not exactly shared by anyone else. Moreover, band composition is ephemeral and fluctuating, not closed and enduring. Consequently, nomadic foragers, living in a weakly partitioned or unpartitioned social world, perceive homicides and lesser disputes in terms of individual grievances, not as occasions for making war, group against group.

WARRING AS AN ADAPTATION? THE TWIN PROBLEMS OF CONFUSING *FUNCTION* WITH *EFFECT* AND *AGGRESSION* WITH *WARFARE*

In 1966, Williams attempted a theoretical house cleaning. His quest has much relevance today for evaluating the proposition that war is an evolutionary adaptation. Williams begins his discussion by proposing a ground rule: "Adaptation is a special and onerous concept that should be used only where it is really necessary."[45] Adaptations result from the evolutionary forces of natural selection operating over time; hence adaptations have evolutionary *functions*. Williams cautions that functions should not be confused with *fortuitous effects*.[46] Take apples for example. Observation and experimentation reveal that the reproduction and dispersal of apple trees are the evolved functions of apples. By contrast, as Williams explains, "the apple's contribution to Newtonian inspiration and the economy of Kalamazoo County are merely fortuitous effects and of no biological interest."[47]

Picking up on Williams' idea, Symons discusses how functional explanations (or adaptations) can be assessed by investigating whether structures or behavior patterns are *designed* to produce predicted consequences:

> Evidence that a structure or behavior pattern evolved through the process of natural selection to serve a particular purpose or function is to be found in the design of the structure or behavior pattern. For example, the detailed structure of the vertebrate eye provides overwhelming evidence of functional design for effective vision, and indicates continued selection for this purpose throughout the evolutionary history of vertebrates.[48]

A popular view of warfare, reflected in various recent writings, is that war has served evolutionary functions in the human past. This proposition, sometimes implied and sometimes stated, holds that either war itself or else psychological mechanisms assumed to be useful for making war have resulted in higher fitness for individuals bearing such traits and *for this reason* have been favored by selection over past millennia.[49] For instance, Wrangham sees "warfare as adaptive and rooted in genetic predispositions" and refers to such predispositions as "lethal raiding psychology."[50] Wrangham writes that "our history of raiding has given us the tendency to attack *whenever* the costs appear sufficiently low."[51] In a similar vein, Buss asserts that selection favored psychological traits "*designed* to lead men to war."[52] Buss further proposes that "women would have been the key reproductive resource that selected for men to evolve a psychology of warfare" and tentatively concludes that "men have evolved specific psychological mechanisms for engaging in warfare."[53] What is the nature of the evidence that warfare itself or psychological mechanisms for warfare have evolved *directly* due to natural or sexual selection favoring such traits?

First, a frequently used argument in proposing specific evolved functions of war is to refer to its widespread occurrence across cultures and throughout history.[54] However, the mere fact that history and ethnography show a plenitude of wars does not prove war-making to be an evolutionary adaptation. We must consider what can and cannot legitimately be concluded from the widespread occurrence of a trait. Paralleling adaptations, fortuitous effects *also* can be widespread. Consider, for example, that apples have economic value across many cultural circumstances; this is simply a fortuitous effect and not evidence that natural selection designed an *economic* function of apples. Similarly, the widespread use of computer keyboards, literally in every country of the world today, cannot be taken as evidence of a specifically evolved adaptation for keyboard use in humans. Obviously the ability to use computer keyboards is a fortuitous effect of various adaptations and *not* an evolved function in and of itself. The prevalence of a particular trait—selling apples, computer keyboard use, reading, or waging war—across various cultural landscapes (markedly different from those of ancestral conditions, by the way) does not in and of itself show that such traits are adaptations. The proposal that the widespread occurrence of war demonstrates its evolutionary function is fallacious.

A second, more specific argument for the evolutionary function of warfare alleges that raiding in humans and chimpanzees has a shared, ancient origin, dating to a common ancestor of both species.[55] Wrangham argues that chimpanzees' and humans' warring behavior (coalitionary aggression) must be at least five million years old and therefore must have evolutionary functions.[56]

Several problems confront using chimpanzees to reconstruct ancestral human behavior.[57] A series of lethal attacks on lone chimpanzee victims, well documented at two locations, Gombe and Kibale, have prompted, nonetheless, a plethora of speculation about what such behavior might show about the origin of *human* warfare. Obviously, chimpanzees and humans are different species. At best, chimpanzees provide only tangential insights about human behavior in the evolutionary past. Additionally, one problem with interpreting the acts of violence among chimpanzees, particularly at Gombe, is that killings may have been exacerbated by the destruction of chimpanzee habitats.[58] In locations other than Gombe and Kibale, the evidence for lethal raiding among chimpanzees is not clear-cut.[59] Wilson and Wrangham note, for instance, that "in contrast to Gombe, observers at Mahale neither directly observed intergroup killing nor found bodies of victims."[60]

Second, bonobos (an ape species that is about as closely related to humans as are chimpanzees) are *nonraiding*.[61] This raises the question: Why emphasize the common ancestry of humans and chimpanzees while neglecting a comparably close relationship with the peaceful bonobos? Linking humans to chimpanzees instead of to bonobos is an arbitrary decision that is begging for a *convincing* rationale. In any case, the data *most* relevant to understanding humans are on humans, whereas data on other species, while also useful at times, nonetheless, provide less direct insights.

Third, as we have seen, the worldwide archaeological evidence, including clear temporal sequences for particular locations, contradicts the proposed scenario of over five million years of warfare among human ancestors. Fourth, the fact that simple nomadic hunter-gatherers typically are nonwarring also poses a major problem for this assertion of a psychological predisposition for rampant raiding over millions of years.

Fifth, the proposed psychological mechanisms underlying war—what Wrangham calls "an evolutionarily selected 'propensity for lethal raiding'"—are derived merely from speculation, not psychological research.[62] Some proposed psychological mechanisms include, for example, "the experience of a victory thrill, an enjoyment of the chase, a tendency for easy dehumanization . . . ready coalition formation, and sophisticated assessment of power differentials."[63] It seems likely to me, partly based upon reading numerous ethnographies, that some or all of these proposed psychological mechanisms, rather than being universal human traits, more likely represent attitudes and ideas circulating within the culture of the theorist. Proposing, for instance, that the Paliyan experience a "victory thrill" is at odds with the value they place on nonviolence and respect. To take another example, this time regarding the presumption of coalition formation as an aspect of the psychology of lethal raiding, we have seen that Australian Tiwi in particular and nomadic band societies in general do not readily form coalitions at all. To the contrary, the nature of band-level social organization makes coalition formation difficult.[64]

Wrangham speculates that

> selection has favored various complex traits, such as a tendency to classify others as in-group or out-group, to regard members of out-groups as potential prey, to be alert to (or search for) power asymmetries between in-group and out-group parties, and to be ruthless in attacking out-group parties when the perceived power asymmetry is sufficiently great.[65]

Do such traits even exist with any regularity in humans? Maybe some do and maybe others do not. Either way, Wrangham presents *no evidence* that such traits regularly exist. Of equal importance, the assertion that "selection has favored various complex traits" such as the ones listed also lacks convincing *evidence*. Rather than assuming traits to have evolutionary functions, it is best to view such traits as fortuitous effects until a clear and logical argument for their adaptive design can be presented. Listing psychological traits that *might or might not* be widespread in humans and that *might or might not* have evolutionary functions does not move scientific understanding forward. Such speculation should not be mistaken for evidence that a "lethal raiding propensity" really exists. Overall, for the various reasons mentioned, the suggestion that propensities for warfare among chimpanzees and humans share an ancient origin and have been directly favored by selection *lacks credibility on numerous grounds*.

Another war-as-adaptation argument falters due to an erroneous assumption about what logically can be concluded from observations of current-day reproductive success. This argument returns us briefly to the famous Yanomamö *unokais*.[66] We have seen how the *unokai* findings continue to be cited to bolster the idea that, over evolutionary time, the risks of warfare must have been outweighed by fitness benefits that warriors are presumed to have accrued.[67]

One problem with evoking the *unokai* findings in support of a functional interpretation of war is that these observations about reproductive success are derived from a type of social organization that did not exist in ancestral times. As we have seen, social organization affects patterns of lethal aggression.[68] Ignoring for the moment the dubious nature of the proposition that *unokais* have any reproductive advantage over non-*unokais* to begin with, the point at hand is that data on reproductive success in one sedentary tribal population provide a pretty weak foundation from which to propose an evolutionary function for killing or war-making in humanity generally.[69]

By analogy, suppose we find out that males who contribute to sperm banks in Finland average three times the offspring by two-and-a-half times the number of women (including artificially inseminated women, in this case) as men who are nondonors to sperm banks. As Symons points out, the enhanced reproductive success achieved by contributing to a sperm bank is *not* evidence that such behavior constitutes an evolutionary adaptation.[70] Clearly, sperm banks and artificial insemination did not exist in the evolutionary past. These recent practices occur only within an environment that is markedly different from conditions under which adaptations arose. By the same reasoning, it is also problematic to assert that an elevation in *unokai* reproductive success among living Yanomamö men reflects pan-human *adaptations* for killing, warfare, fierceness, bravery, and so forth. Thus assertions that Chagnon's *unokai* findings provide valid grounds for arguing that war evolved as an adaptation to enhance male reproductive success are theoretically ill founded.[71] This critique totally leaves aside the important issue as to whether the findings actually show what they have been claimed to show in the first place.

A final problem arises when discussions of sex differences and adaptation shift back and forth from the aggressive behavior of *individuals* to the coalitionary aggression of *groups* during warfare.[72] In the previous chapter, we considered that sex differences in aggression are widespread among animals, including humans, and evoked

Trivers' concept of parental investment and Darwin's insights about sexual selection to explain this general pattern.[73] Similar sex differences in aggression occur in many species *that do not make war*. Therefore, it is illogical to argue that if men on the average tend to be more severely aggressive than are women, then *warfare* is an adaptation. In my view, a reasonable case *can* be made that some forms of aggressive behavior have evolved in humans as facultative adaptations, but the existence of sex differences alone does not lend any support to an assertion that *warfare* is an evolutionary adaptation. Furthermore, switching back and forth between aggression and war, as if these types of behavior constitute a unified concept, further muddies the already murky waters swirling around evolutionary discussions of warfare.[74]

In sum, all four of the commonly used arguments that warfare is an adaptation have major problems. First, the widespread occurrence of warfare does not provide support for the war-as-adaptation argument because fortuitous effects also can be widespread. Moreover, the widespread occurrence of warfare is almost certainly very recent in an evolutionary time frame. Second, the ancient common ancestor argument linking the presumed warring propensities of humans and chimpanzees is suspect for multiple reasons, five of which were just mentioned. Third, the *unokai* reproductive success findings, whether valid or not, relate to one population of sedentary tribal horticulturalists, a form of social organization that is *not* the best choice for deriving a model of evolutionary function under ancestral conditions. Finally, sex differences in aggressiveness cannot logically be used to argue that war or warring is an adaptation. Sex differences in aggressiveness are in accordance with sexual selection and parental investment theories, but the fact that similar sex differences exist among countless nonwarring animal species highlights that the mere existence of sex differences in humans provides neither a convincing nor a logical argument that *warfare* is an adaptation.

Writers who *suppose* that either warfare or psychological propensities for engaging in warfare are adaptations—that warring has been designed by natural selection to fulfill specific evolutionary functions—are confusing function with fortuitous effects. Clearly humans have a variety of attributes and capacities—from designing weapons to smoothly cooperating with each other—that make war possible. But this does not mean that such traits specifically evolved for warring. This would be analogous to suggesting that the design of human hands reflect an evolutionary adaptation expressly for using computer keyboards or that the vertebrate eye is an adaptation for reading. Observations that humans are *capable* of reading, keyboard use, chasing prey, being ruthless, and waging war are indisputable; however, such observations are *not* valid grounds for concluding that these actions have been designed through natural selection expressly to fulfill the specific functions of reading, computer use, or waging war. If we apply Williams' ground rule and reserve the concept of evolutionary *adaptation* for situations where it is really necessary, then we lack any reasonable grounds for concluding that war is an adaptation.[75]

CONCLUSIONS

Some of the ideas presented here may turn out to be correct or nearly so. Of course, I hope this is the case for the majority. Other ideas certainly will need to be refined, and perhaps still others tossed out. This is normally the way scientific understanding progresses. In previous chapters, I have expressed dissatisfaction when writers have selectively included material that corresponds with their speculations while ignoring (or even misrepresenting) findings that contradict their views. Darwin wisely realized his own tendency to more readily forget information that went against his theorizing than confirmatory facts:

> I had, also, during many years, followed a golden rule, namely, that whenever a published fact, a new observation or thought came across me, which was opposed to my general results, to make a memorandum of it without fail and at once; for I have found by experience that such facts and thoughts were far more apt to escape from the memory than favorable ones.[76]

I have tried my best to learn from Darwin.

As I step back and review this book as a whole, I consider the ideas presented in this chapter to be more tentative than the material in other chapters, basically for two reasons. First, although it is clear that ancestral humans and proto-humans were nomadic and foraged for a living, no one has *direct* data on the social life of the ancestral nomadic hunter-gatherers extending back one or two million years. Therefore, as discussed in previous chapters, we must rely primarily on archaeology and insights derived *indirectly* from observations of existing nomadic hunter-gatherers to reconstruct by analogy the most likely ancestral ways of life.

If the social life of current-day nomadic foragers had turned out to be extremely variable from one group to the next, then it probably would have been best to have given up the entire endeavor of using hunter-gatherer analogy to gain insights about the past. However, as we have seen, nomadic hunter-gatherers turn out to show a number of recurring social and behavioral characteristics. This is good news, since the existence of numerous recurring patterns in the social life of present-day simple foragers strongly suggests that ancestral patterns also may have been similar to the social patterns that currently are universal or nearly so among nomadic hunter-gatherers.

Nearly universal features of nomadic foragers include relatively low population densities, small band size (typically between 25 and 50 members), mobility, flexibility and fluctuations in group composition, concentration–dispersion patterns, interconnections among bands (especially among those that speak the same or similar languages), social emphasis on sharing and cooperation, high values placed on individual autonomy, bilateral systems of descent that emphasize connections to both maternal and paternal relatives, minimal leadership within groups, no overarching authority among groups, high levels of egalitarianism in both an ethos and as manifested in social relations, high levels of gender egalitarianism, decision-making by consensus, sexual division of labor, hunting as primarily (but not exclusively) a male activity (with hunting large game being a male activity) and gathering as primarily (but not exclusively) a female activity, minimal material property, minimal private ownership of resources, loosely defined territorial ranges, patterns of reciprocal exchange among individuals within and between groups, a tendency to find spouses in other groups, the personal nature of disputes (e.g., involving sexual jealousy), group fission or interpersonal avoidance as a response to conflict (especially serious conflict), a devaluation of physical aggression, lack of warrior values, and exertion of social control via gossip, ridicule, withdrawal of support, and, in extreme cases, ostracism and execution (see Figure 18.2).[77]

Figure 18.2 A Paliyan woman from southern India uses a digging stick to unearth yams. The high level of personal autonomy and sexual egalitarianism apparent in Paliyan society is typical of simple nomadic hunter-gatherer society generally. (Photo courtesy of Peter Gardner.)

The second reason that I consider the ideas in this chapter to be more tentative than those in other parts of the book is because the ethnographic data on aggression, conflict, conflict management, and reconciliation in simple hunter-gatherer societies tend to be sporadic and vary greatly in level of detail. In essence, I faced the same problem encountered by Boehm when he attempted to find information on egalitarianism in the ethnographic record. Boehm explains, "Because data on egalitarian behavior are relatively scarce, I did not undertake a typical cross-cultural survey with careful reliance on sampling techniques. Rather, I looked for any source that provided useful information on the above topics."[78] Adopting a similar approach, I have attempted to locate as much information as possible on aggression, conflict management, and related topics among nomadic hunter-gatherers. Some *overall patterns* can be extracted from the sources. Nonetheless, the lack of relevant data for some simple forager societies and variability in amount of data for other such groups must be borne in mind. Consequently, conclusions must be viewed somewhat tentatively.

In attempting to learn from Charles Darwin, I have been alert to any bits of information that contradict my suppositions. Any researcher is a filterer of information. As I studied information on nomadic hunter-gatherers presented by other observers, I interpreted the observations that already have undergone distillation by the original writers. This situation is less than ideal, but unavoidable.

What I promise the reader is that I have tried to be true to the facts. My approach has been not to sweep contradictory information under the rug. Although acknowledging that I am a filterer, organizer, and interpreter of information, nonetheless, I have attempted to weigh the information fairly to reach conclusions that are in accordance with the available information. Weighing the information also involves an assessment of *context* and *patterns*.[79] An occasional exception to a general pattern should not cause us to lose sight of the regularities and throw out a model or an explanation that fits most of the facts. On the other hand, numerous exceptions suggest that one's model is not very close to reality. In science, when observations do not support a hypothesis, the hypothesis should be rejected or modified in light of the findings. Science does not advance by clinging to pet speculations that are contradicted by numerous facts. Therefore, in this chapter, as in science generally, interpretations should be in accordance with empirical observation.

The validity of the major thesis of this book—that humans have a tremendous yet underappreciated potential for getting along and dealing with conflict without violence—can be looked at as being independent of my hypothesizing in this chapter. If time does show my evolutionary reasoning to be more or less on target, the overall thesis of the book gains additional support. However, if time demonstrates my reasoning to be faulty, the overall thesis of the book is by no means demolished on this basis alone. Data in other chapters on peaceful societies, nonwarring cultures, the archaeologically recent development of war, and the vast array of conflict management and prevention processes developed by human beings clearly document that *whatever the evolutionary basis,* humans have a substantial capacity for living in peace and resolving their differences without bloodshed.

CHAPTER 19

WEIGHING THE EVIDENCE

> Up until the time of Kepler, all major ideas concerning the motions of the planets used circles. The possibility that other curves might be necessary was never seriously considered. It was Kepler who first proposed that an ellipse and not a circle must be used in describing the orbit of a planet.
>
> WILLIAM KAUFMANN III[1]

Some guys were hunting when one spied a moose.[2] They shot through the brush until all sounds ceased. Upon investigation, they discovered only the body of a man. Then they remembered hearing, during their salvo, someone shouting, "Don't shoot. I'm not a moose." They also now realized that the "moose" had been waving a red cap, and the light finally dawned on them what they had done. This tragic story illustrates dramatically that sometimes people can become so fixed in their ideas that they become oblivious to even blaring contradictory information.

A couple of years ago, my brother-in-law, Dale, and I were driving on a small country road and came across a Chevy van with its right wheels lodged in the gully on the side of the road. Fortunately no one in the vehicle had been hurt in this little mishap that had taken place at low speed. Dale and I inspected the situation and determined that this was a job for a tow truck, since the underbelly of the van was lodged solidly on the pavement as the vehicle listed to the right.

While inspecting for damages, I realized that brake fluid was leaking from the *left* front wheel area onto the ground. This seemed just a little peculiar to me because it was the *right* side of the car that was in the gully, but I didn't let this contradictory fact disturb my diagnosis. From my mechanical experience, limited though it is, I *knew* that the only fluid to be found in the wheel-tire areas would be brake fluid. However, just to be sure that something like windshield washing fluid wasn't dripping from a leak higher up, I checked. There was no dripping from above. Now I noticed something else that was a little bit odd. The brake fluid was on the hubcap side—that is, the outside—of the wheel with no obvious source from inside the wheel. Strange.

Provoked by creeping doubts about my brake fluid diagnosis, I now saw *for the first time* that the liquid was yellow. I'd never seen yellow brake fluid before, but then I'm not a connoisseur. Come to think of it, I thought, I *have* seen yellow liquid that looks like this. To gather more data, I got down on my hands and knees and smelled. Ah-ha!

If it looks like dog pee and it smells like dog pee. . . . Standing up, I looked around and noted a fact that previously had seemed irrelevant to the mechanical puzzle. One of the passengers of the stranded van was a male Labrador retriever, now joyfully running to and fro. Bingo! Life makes sense.

I imagine that every reader could tell a story or two of how they were absolutely convinced that something was one way when in fact is was not, but that their *preconceptions* blinded them to a more plausible interpretation of events. Such experiences can give us more empathy for the moose hunters and also may provide us with some humbling insights related to scientific interpretation.

Notice that at first, I simply dismissed *odd* or *contradictory* bits of information, such as liquid dripping from the undamaged *left* side of the car, and clung firmly instead to my erroneous interpretation that brake fluid was leaking. Good thing I wasn't moose-hunting! However, the alternative explanation, the one I now accept as genuine—dare I pun "gen-urine"—explains each and every odd, contradictory observation. With all observations accounted for, I'm satisfied with the new interpretation, but at the same time recognize that a *slim possibility* exists that the yellow fluid dripping off the hubcap was not Labrador retriever urine. In science also, there always remains at least a little doubt that "we got it exactly right."

This doubt returns us to the sleuthing analogy presented in the first chapter of the book. An initial "reading" of the evidence led to the conclusion that Holmes and Watson's new neighbor was a man. However, after gathering more data and weighing the totality of the evidence, Holmes and Watson reversed their conclusion. But recall that they never actually met the neighbor, and so their revised interpretation, which was based on an overall assessment of the available evidence, is best thought of as *likely* rather than *certain.* Shortly, we will apply a similar approach as we review the evidence presented in this book. First, however, the sleuthing story can be used to reinforce another point about the insidious effects of preexisting beliefs.

Take a couple seconds and think about the mental image that you formed of Holmes and Watson when reading chapter 1. What were they wearing? Did they have accents? If you are picturing Holmes and Watson as British men, you probably are familiar with books and films featuring Sir Arthur Conan Doyle's Sherlock Holmes and Dr. Watson. Were your images of Holmes and Watson male? Were your images some sort of rendering of Doyle's famous sleuths?

The point of this thought experiment is to reinforce, in a subjective way, one of this book's themes: Preexisting cultural knowledge and beliefs provide each of us with a host of *initial, implicit assumptions* that in turn affect our interpretations of the world. If you go back to chapter 1 and look for any *factual* information about whether Watson and Holmes are male or female and what they look like, you won't find any. If you *assumed* that they were men without really giving the matter any thought, it is probably because we all *know* that Holmes and Watson are male, British, fictional detectives. This information is in our shared cultural fund of knowledge. It does not even come to mind to question these points because, based on our past *cultural experiences* with books, films, jokes, conversations, and perhaps even a visit to number 221b Baker Street in London, we already know, *or just assume,* based on their names and the context of the story, that the Holmes and Watson in the first chapter fit the image of the familiar characters.

Many people in Western societies also already know, *or just assume* based on their cultural experiences, that warfare is extremely ancient, natural, and part-and-parcel of human nature—that humans are the descendants of killer apes. But it's time to smell the brake fluid. It's time to look afresh at the available evidence and try to untangle the facts from implicit assumptions and preconceptions, for many of the so-called facts are actually culturally derived presumptions and lead to interpretations that are *not* necessarily very accurate.

Western culture is replete with Hobbesian beliefs that war is natural.[3] Prehistoric life is often assumed to have been as Hobbes envisioned in *Leviathan:* "nasty, brutish, and short."[4] Such beliefs are manifested in many ways: in everyday conversations, in entertainment, and in politics.[5] Recall that a substantial number of university students in the United States agree that humans have "an instinct for war" and that "war is an intrinsic part of human nature."[6] From television shows to motion pictures like *2001: A Space Odyssey,* or from writings by scientists such as Raymond Dart to those of playwrights like Robert Ardrey, such messages are reiterated in Western culture.[7] Sometimes people who question this prevailing view of human nature are even labeled as naïve, foolish, unrealistic, or utopian.[8]

The Hobbesian beliefs extend into science. After all, scientists are people too, and like everybody else they tend to adopt the belief system of the culture within which they are born and raised. We have seen many examples in this book of how Hobbesian beliefs manifest themselves in science. In the case of Dart, his own explicitly stated views about human nature corresponded with his initial violence-laden interpretations of the australopithecine fossil material. According to Dart, humans bear the blood be-splattered mark of Cain and so did the australopithecines. In a similar vein, Richards expressed openness to "the possibility of some built-in tendency towards war in man's genes or in some universal characteristic of human life" and in the same passage argued for the antiquity of warfare.[9]

We also have considered how scratch marks on a fossil skull were interpreted as evidence of prehistoric scalping. In reality, the marks on the skull had been caused by careless laboratory practices. The excavator of Monte Cicero cave saw foul play where there was none, misperceiving a natural rockfall and the gnawing of hyenas as evidence of murder and cannibalism.[10]

Wright's cross-cultural classificatory scheme, which applied the label *war* to all societies, even nonwarring ones, would once again seem to reflect assumptions stemming from a Hobbesian cultural belief system. Under this labeling scheme, *all cultures war*![11] And the examples continue. Ember sought to disprove "that hunter-gatherers are relatively peaceful."[12] She cited four scholarly sources as reflecting this so-called myth.[13] In all four publications, however, the anthropologists in question were explicitly writing about the relative peacefulness of a particular type of hunter-gatherer society—*simple nomadic hunter-gatherer bands*—not equestrian or complex hunter-gatherers. These anthropologists used the term "band" and the phrase "band level of society" and referred by name to the !Kung (Ju/'hoansi), Mbuti, and Hadza, all nomadic *band* societies.[14] However, Ember first lumped together complex hunter-gatherers and equestrian hunters with nomadic band societies to create a heterogeneous sample.[15] This decision may have seemed more reasonable some 27 years ago than it does today. Recall that Ember also defined "war" so broadly as to encompass revenge killings and feuds. Not surprisingly, she discovered a lot of so-called war. And as we have seen, these problematic findings continue to be cited in support of Hobbesian views of the past.[16]

In a somewhat similar manner, Keeley mixed archaeological evidence of homicide and some ambiguous cases of death with the evidence of prehistoric war to create an impression of more warfare and older warfare than actually exist.[17] We have considered, moreover, how some ethnographic descriptions liberally employ the language of war while describing individual fights or even conflict resolution procedures. We saw, for example, that Goodale spoke of juridical procedures used by the Tiwi as "battles," and Bird told of an angry Alacaluf husband who made a "declaration of war" before committing a *homicide.*[18] Tacon and Chippindale filled their article on Australian Aborigine rock art with war words and labeled the human figures "warriors," while virtually ignoring a huge body of contextualizing information about the nature of conflict management in Aboriginal Australian societies.[19]

We explored the Pervasive Intergroup Hostility Model in detail. We saw that Pervasive Intergroup Hostility scenarios rest on a heap of faulty assumptions and, regarding warfare, basically project present-day beliefs and circumstances onto the past. We also considered the tremendous interest in Yanomamö *unokais* and the ready acceptance of the purported link between reproductive success and killing.

The main point of reviewing this litany of examples, from Dart's assumptions about blood be-splattered killer-apes to the eager retelling that *unokai* "warriors" outreproduce their peers, is that they simultaneously *represent and reinforce* deep-seated and largely taken-for-granted cultural beliefs about the antiquity and naturalness of warfare and violence. Cultural beliefs creep into scientific and other writings, affecting perceptions, descriptions, and interpretations. In the real world of global politics, they may also affect decisions whether or not to wage war.

Are dark-sided, demonic interpretations of humanity really grounded in science? Are such neo-Hobbesian interpretations congruent with the available evidence? Are they really based on sound reasoning? My intention in this book has been to raise questions that have been largely ignored—to open this pile of implicit assumptions about war, peace, and human nature to more careful scrutiny.

We have a situation roughly analogous to the problem Holmes and Watson faced. An initial reading of the facts pointed to their new neighbor being male. However, after further investigation, the preponderance of the evidence suggested that their neighbor actually was female. One implication of the analogy is the importance of considering *all* of the available data—the magazines, clothing, key ring, multivitamins, paucity of masculine items, and so forth—not simply a few selective facts such as those involving a pickup truck. Another implication is that some observations carry more theoretical weight than do others. In the sleuthing analogy, for instance, observations about items inside the house deserve more weight than observations about a vehicle parked on the street. In regards to understanding warfare and human nature, analogously, I suggest that the findings from one problematic article on *unokai* reproductive success, for instance, carry much less weight than do the entire body of research studies on nomadic forager societies. Or, similarly, the behavior of chimpanzees carries less weight for understanding humans than does the actual behavior of humans.

As in the Holmes and Watson story, we must evaluate the available evidence anew and reach an overall assessment as to what the preponderance of the data suggests. Obviously we must consider all of the available facts, not simply a few that happen to fit preconceived ideas, like the regular occurrence of warfare in Western history. We also must be aware that, as in the Holmes and Watson story, first impressions can be misleading. We have seen, for instance, how ethnographic descriptions sometimes put a warlike slant on disputes, that, upon more careful examination, turn out to be interpersonal conflicts. Ultimately, we must base our conclusions on the facts, not on preconceived notions, as difficult as this may be at times. This is where it may be helpful to remember the lessons learned from Dr. Virchow and his microscope, the moose-hunting tragedy, and the leaking "brake fluid," in order to remain on our guard against jumping too quickly to preconceived conclusions.

If we step back and assess the big picture, the data suggest that humans, while very capable of engaging in warfare, also have a strong capacity for getting along peacefully. Thus warfare is not inevitable, and the view that warfare is ancient, natural, and an intrinsic part of human nature wilts under the light of fresh scrutiny. When many different observations, experimental results, and data point to the same conclusion, support for the conclusion becomes overwhelming. Scenarios portraying the naturalness of war are contradicted across the board by the information we have considered in this book from archaeology, hunter-gatherer studies, comparative ethnography, the study of social organization, cross-cultural research findings on war and justice seeking, research on animal aggression, evolutionary theory, and, last but not least, a consideration of the powerful biasing effects that cultural belief systems continue to have on Western thinking about war and peace. *Findings and insights from these multiple areas complement and reinforce one another when viewed as a comprehensive body of relevant information.* If we weigh the totality of the evidence, we arrive at a new conclusion: Humans are not really so nasty after all. War is *not* part-and-parcel of human nature or human societies. In the next chapter, we will explore some of the implications that this conclusion holds for creating and guaranteeing peace.

CHAPTER 20

ENHANCING PEACE

> We share a planet and we need common rules to guide our actions. . . . We are becoming more and more dependent on each other and I hope this will lead to our understanding and respecting each other better than we have done in the past. I wish you boldness of spirit and fresh ideas.
>
> TARJA HALONEN, PRESIDENT OF FINLAND[1]

Anthropology provides many insights on war and peace, but by far the most important, for it pertains directly to the future of the species, is that war, like slavery before it, *can* be abolished. With wars continuing to erupt in different quarters of the planet, this idea might seem implausible. The elimination of war, however, is starkly *realistic* in two senses of the word. First, an anthropological perspective suggests that the human species, realistically, has the *capacity* to accomplish this goal. Second, the serious challenges facing humanity, including the spread of weapons of mass destruction, suggest that, realistically, we must abolish war before it abolishes us. Replacing war with alternative ways to ensure security and resolve conflicts is the only rational way to proceed into the 21st century and beyond.

As an institution, war is already obsolete, and this fact is becoming ever more apparent. As a means of ensuring a nation's *safety and security,* war is outmoded, for it does little or nothing to protect people from the very real threats of global environmental degradation, human rights abuses, nuclear proliferation, and terrorism. It can be argued that the acceptance and the waging of war even contribute to these problems. The presence of nuclear weapons on the planet makes war increasingly risky, not merely for soldiers and civilians in combat zones but for every person on Earth. For these reasons, war is obsolete. Alternative ways of handling conflict must be implemented and cooperation enhanced in order to deal effectively in the 21st century with problems such as global warming and the proliferation of ever more deadly weapons that threaten not only the citizens of any particular country but human survival overall.

Anthropology offers a broad perspective on humanity that spans evolutionary time and crosses cultural space. In this sense, anthropology is *macroscopic.* What does the anthropological material considered in this book tell us about the possibility of eliminating war? For starters, clearly war is not immutably fixed in "human nature." Nor is war an unchangeable social institution. The flexibility of both human behavior and social forms makes a transition from war to other forms of conflict resolution conceivable.

In this chapter, we will focus on some anthropological lessons for promoting and maintaining peace. In my view, specific peace-promoting possibilities include enhancing crosscutting relations; recognizing interdependence; promoting new values, attitudes, and beliefs; implementing overarching levels of governance; and expanding the use of conflict management mechanisms. From this list, creating structures for effective global governance and expanding institutions for preventing and resolving conflicts without going to war are critically important. We cannot rely on fostering goodwill alone.

In the 21st century, the price tag for continuing to deal with intergroup conflict through war, as a form of self-redress, is simply too high. Instead, humanity must replace the dangerous, costly, and often ineffective institution of warfare with new international conflict resolution institutions—regional and global courts, for example. Within nations, this transition from seeking justice through self-redress to reliance on legal institutions has been made repeatedly in human history, offering hope that a similar transition is possible internationally. We are faced with the challenge of bringing the sheriff and the judge to the global Wild West.

A MACROSCOPIC PERSPECTIVE: THE HUMAN CAPACITY TO MOVE BEYOND WAR

As we have seen, a long-standing belief in the Western tradition blames a bellicose human nature for war. Obviously, the anthropological data do not support the validity of such a view. Numerous internally peaceful and nonwarring societies exist, sometimes within nonwarring peace systems such as among Aboriginal Australians, the Upper Xingu River basin tribes, and the Todas and their neighbors in India's Nilgiri Hills. Correspondingly, in a substantial number of societies for which warfare has been reported, the fighting really does not amount to much. Recall that in Wright's landmark study of war, the *majority* of 590 societies, 64 percent, were classified as either nonwarring or unwarlike, that is, as having *defensive war* or *social war* in Wright's terminology.[2] However, this important finding seems to have "fallen through a crack," as many people continue to presume that war is natural, ubiquitous, and unavoidable.

The worldwide archaeological record, data on simple forager societies, and cross-cultural studies combine to suggest that warfare is only a few thousand years old, arising along with social complexity and greatly intensifying with the birth of states, as economic and political motives for war moved to the forefront.[3] In recent centuries, as Europeans colonized the world, warfare was exacerbated cross-culturally by a barrage of dramatic changes—the crowding and rearranging of native peoples; the usurpation of native land; the introduction of firearms, trade goods, and slavery; and the waging of wars of extermination against native peoples.[4] The idea is not to blame the arrival of European colonial powers for *all* indigenous warfare, but rather to point out how time and again the flames of war have been fanned by social, political, and economic forces set into motion only within the last several centuries.

Now, at the dawn of the 21st century, the social institution called war has become too dangerous and too costly to continue. The historical hour has arrived for shifting from a state of imperfect security, as elusively sought through military means in a self-redress system, writ large, to a more effective system for providing justice through international legal structures and viable mechanisms of conflict management (see Figure 20.1).

Can such a transition be accomplished? A macroscopic anthropological view reveals *Homo sapiens* to be an extremely flexible species. The fact that human beings

Figure 20.1 East of Oaxaca City in southern Mexico, a large mosaic tribute to Benito Juárez alludes to his role in implementing social reforms in the mid-1800s. Juárez's credo, "respect for the rights of others is peace," appears in Spanish in the middle of the scene. On the right side of the mosaic, Lady Justice, blindfolded, holds balanced scales in this familiar symbolic depiction of impartiality under the law. Courts of law and legal protection of individual rights typify today's democracies. Could the same principles also be implemented to protect human rights and provide impartial justice within the global neighborhood? (D. P. Fry photo collection.)

are capable of living in a variety of markedly different types of social organization offers testimony to this behavioral and social plasticity. Consider the immense differences between life in a nomadic hunter-gatherer band and a modern industrial nation-state. Today's urban dweller could easily see over a thousand persons in a *single day,* more than a band member might see in her entire *lifetime.* And the modern urbanite encounters numerous strangers, whereas the band member moves with a small number of relatives and friends, only rarely encountering an unknown person. As we have seen, the members of nomadic band society are linked to one another through webs of reciprocity and kinship, place a high premium on sharing, and are egalitarian in their social relations. The socioeconomic hierarchy, generally taken for granted by citizens of modern states living in a world of ranked social roles—for instance, CEOs, middle management, and workers; school principals, teachers, and teachers' aids; generals, lieutenants, and privates; and doctors, nurses, and orderlies—is an alien concept in the social world of egalitarian nomadic foragers. Particular persons may be admired for certain abilities, but nomadic hunter-gatherer society lacks hierarchical positions of authority.[5]

The essential point is that members of the same species, *Homo sapiens,* are capable of living in the dramatically different social worlds of bands, tribes, chiefdoms, and states. The transition from the millennia-old lifeways of the nomadic forager band

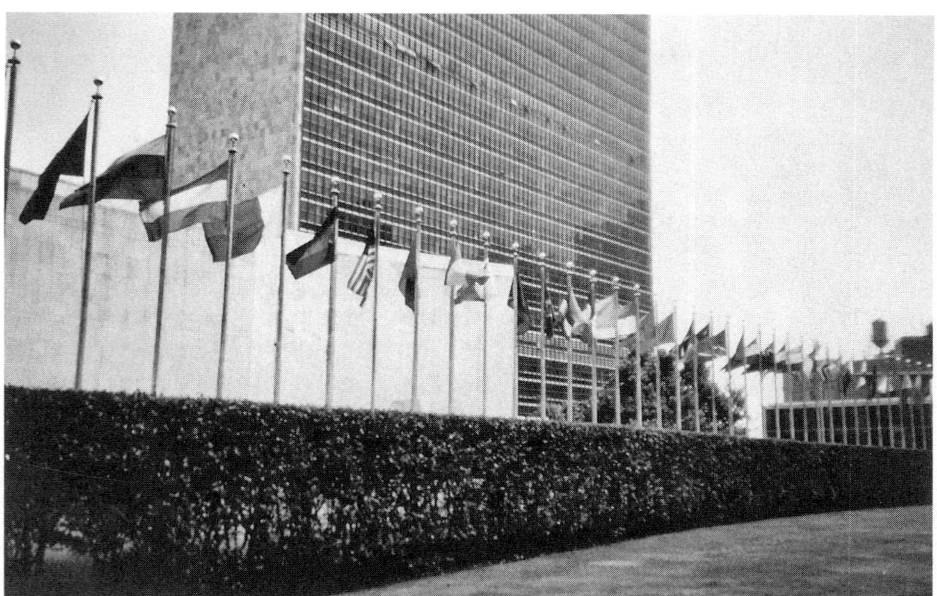

Figure 20.2 The United Nations provides a forum for discussion and conflict resolution among nations. This conflict-resolving potential, while currently important, could be greatly expanded. There is a pressing need for expanded international governance in the 21st century to effectively address global issues: Global problems require global solutions. (D. P. Fry photo collection.)

to the conditions of the urban, industrial nation is truly staggering! Yet we high-tech folks of the 21st century rarely pause to consider the immense plasticity in the nature of our species that allows a hunter-gatherer primate to live in this Internet world of strangers, stock exchanges, and cruise missiles. A macroscopic anthropological perspective highlights the human capacity for creating and adjusting to immense social changes.

An appreciation of the immensity of social changes that humans have undergone in recent millennia leads to the observation that there is nothing sacred about the institution of war. War is, after all, a rather recent development. Nation-states and an international system that accept the waging of war are younger still. A species as flexible as *Homo sapiens* certainly can create alternative ways to deal with international conflicts (see Figure 20.2). As illustrated in this book, humans have a solid repertory of conflict management skills to draw upon. Not only are we humans capable of fighting the bloodiest of wars, but we also have a substantial potential for peace. Across societies, people are apt preventers and avoiders of violence. Over a vast array of societal circumstances, humans deal with most conflicts without any physical aggression at all. Regularly, the language-using primate "talks it out," airs grievances verbally in the court of public opinion, negotiates compensation, focuses on restoring relationships bruised by a dispute, convenes conflict resolution assembles, and listens to the wisdom of the elders or other third parties, who, acting as peacemakers, strive to end the tension within the group and among disputants. As we have considered, humans also routinely show a great deal of self-restraint against acting aggressively. Such restraint makes evolutionary sense and has numerous parallels in other animal species.

Some societies have developed ways to reduce violence to extremely low levels. While not denying the obvious human capacity to wreak great carnage, nonetheless, there is bountiful anthropological evidence that the label *peacemaking primate,* on balance, is far more fitting an appellation than is *killer-ape.* After all, peaceful social life and the handling of conflict without violence predominate across societies. As Robert Hinde expresses in the foreword to this book:

> We do indeed have propensities to behave assertively and aggressively, but we also have propensities to behave prosocially and cooperatively, with kindness and consideration for others. Social life would not be possible if these prosocial tendencies did not predominate over selfish assertiveness and aggressiveness.

Another observation about human nature derivable from anthropological material is that cultures can become more peaceful, sometimes quite rapidly.[6] Shifts away from violence can be externally imposed (as when colonial rulers or national governments put an end to tribal warfare) or internally enacted. As considered in chapter 5, the Waorani of Ecuador ended a pattern of chronic feuding and Chatino villagers in Mexico took constructive action to restore the peace in their community.[7]

A macroscopic view can lead to new insights. In this book, we have examined the proposition that individuals tend to accept the belief system of their culture without much question. I have argued that Western cultural beliefs about the naturalness and acceptability of war are commonly just taken for granted.[8] Widespread beliefs that war is natural can hinder the search for alternatives—and thus the inevitably of war becomes a self-fulfilling prophecy. Such beliefs may be detrimental both to avoiding particular wars and to abolishing the institution of war. However, history and anthropology demonstrate that immense social and institutional changes are possible.

A careful reassessment of the anthropological data is extremely important for challenging the self-fulfilling prophecy that war is ancient, natural, and inevitable.[9] As William Ury expresses:

> Perhaps the principal obstacle to preventing destructive conflict lies in our own minds—in the fatalistic beliefs that discourage people from even trying. The story that humans have always warred, and always will, is spread unchallenged from person to person and from parent to child. It is time, in our everyday conversations, to question and refute this story and its embedded assumptions about human nature. It is time to give our children—and ourselves—a more accurate and more positive picture of our past and our future prospects. From realistic hope springs action.[10]

SPECIFIC INSIGHTS FOR KEEPING THE PEACE

Anthropology offers a variety of specific insights for building and preserving peace. These include the development of crosscutting ties among social units; the recognition and promotion of interdependence among social groups; the reinforcement of peace-focused values, attitudes, and beliefs (as opposed to values, attitudes, and beliefs that support and encourage war); implementation of superordinate authority structures that promote justice; and the greater utilization of conflict management mechanisms at the international level. There certainly are other anthropological insights relevant to creating a more peaceful world, but let's begin by considering these.

Crosscutting Ties

Humans often perceive themselves in terms of "us" and "them"—a feature that can be exploited to make killing "them" easier. However, the perception of differences among groups does not automatically lead to violence. Ethnocentrism is *not* equivalent to war. Who exactly constitutes "us" and "them" is flexible and subject to ongoing reevaluation and redefinition. Consider how in today's political world, countries that fought each other as bitter enemies during World War II—France and Germany or Japan and the United States, for instance—are now friends, allies, and trade partners. Furthermore, the ethnocentrism of "us" and "them" does not in and of itself *cause* warfare. Playing up differences can ferment conflict and violence; however, building bridges and recognizing common interests can contribute to peace and cooperation.

Intermarriage between groups, which promotes crosscutting kin, social, and economic relations, may contribute to maintaining the peace.[11] Recall that the tribes of the Upper Xingu River basin in Brazil, which speak different languages, have developed a pattern of exchange and interaction based on peace, not warfare. Gregor describes how "intertribal marriage is a major source of peaceful contact with each of the Xingu villages."[12] More generally, Robin Fox explains that "you would not try to exterminate a band whose wives were your daughters and whose daughters were your potential wives; you would become, in one sense at least, one people."[13] The crosscutting ties need not be based on intermarriage.[14] Ilsa Glazer describes how *special purpose friendships* can link members of agonistic ethnic groups, contributing to a common group identity, and thus prevent violence.[15] Using examples as diverse as New Guinea tribes and the ancient Scottish Celtic clans, Kenneth Smail reports that leaders sometimes formed crosscutting ties by sending their own sons to live in other groups to reduce tensions, deter aggression, and build friendly alliances.[16]

This anthropological insight is straightforward. Relationships that link groups tend to reduce intergroup violence. The more crosscutting ties, the less the chance of war. As Mead once expressed:

> Our organizational task may then be defined as reducing the strength of all mutually exclusive loyalties, whether of nations, race, class, religion or ideology, and constructing some quite different form of organization in which the memories of these loyalties and the organization residues of these former exclusive loyalties cannot threaten the total structure.[17]

As implied by Mead, crosscutting ties are relevant to reducing the threat of war and terrorism at different social levels within and among nations. Applications also range from *preventing* the development of tensions between groups to *reducing* existing tensions. Ways to encourage and promote crosscutting ties are as bountiful as human ingenuity itself, so a couple of illustrative examples will suffice. First, international student exchange programs could be increased manyfold (perhaps drawing on a fraction of the funds currently allocated to military budgets), especially involving the exchange of students between countries with a history of hostility. Daughters, sons, and other close relatives of leaders of such countries should be encouraged to take part in such programs.[18]

Smail proposes the utility of ongoing citizen exchange programs that include transferring substantial numbers of businesspeople, academics, political leaders, military personnel, artists, and so on among nations in order to reduce tensions and promote mutual friendship.[19] He explains:

> The exchange of "peace hostages" thus represents an approach to deterrence that is quite different from any currently in use, an approach that increases in inhibitory power the greater its public visibility, the longer it is in place, the larger its participatory scope, and the more pressing the need. In addition to its ability to inhibit warlike or destabilizing acts in the short term, particularly on the part of the leadership, it is important to note that such a program would also incorporate the simultaneous capacity to enhance transnational understanding (mutual respect) over the longer term, at all levels of the body politic.[20]

Additionally, *within* countries when racial, ethnic, or political hostility threaten the peace, positive interaction could be promoted within existing organizations (schools, community organizations, local government) through such mechanisms as heterogeneous cooperative learning groups and workshops or community-bridging activities and projects.[21]

Interdependence and Cooperation

Related to the idea of crosscutting ties is the peace-maintaining potential of interdependence among individuals and social units. O'Nell reached the conclusion that among Zapotec villagers of La Paz the "needs for reciprocity and cooperation fundamentally serve to inhibit interpersonal violence between people who are ostensibly interdependent."[22]

Tonkinson explains that nomadic hunter-gatherer Mardu bands *need each other.* The Mardu are interdependent for ecological reasons, and are well aware of this fact. They strive to maintain positive relations among bands.

> In the Western Desert, . . . there *is* an important underlying ecological factor, the irregularity of spread and unreliability of rainfall in a region having no permanent waters. . . . It necessitates a strong cultural stress on the permeability of boundaries and the maintenance of open and peaceful movement and inter-group communication within a huge area of desert. In these circumstances, to permit inter-group conflict or feuding to harden social and territorial boundaries would be literally suicidal, since no group can expect the existing water and food resources of its territory to tide it over until the next rains; peaceful inter-group relations are imperative for long-term survival. . . . It is not surprising, then, that the Mardu have no word for either "feud" or "warfare" and there is no evidence for the kinds of longstanding inter-group animosity one associates with feuding. The situation is one of small and scattered highly mobile groups moving freely within large territories rather than highly localized, solitary corporate groups contesting resources and maintaining boundaries.
>
> Thanks to their open boundaries and the multiple linkages (shared values, religion, worldview, Law, kinship, friendship and marriage alliances) [that is, crosscutting ties] joining every Mardu band to all others in their society, the arena of shared understandings is huge when groups need to resolve their differences. Everyone is mindful also of how much their survival rests on mutual hospitality and unfettered access to their neighbors' natural resources in both lean and bountiful times.[23]

The Mardu recognize their state of mutual dependence. They understand that fighting would be extremely detrimental, potentially even suicidal, and therefore suppress it. In this case, ecological factors contribute to interdependence, and *interdependence contributes to peace.*

In other contexts, factors such as common external threats or economic specialization contribute to interdependence and the maintenance of peaceful relations. For instance, solidarity for the common defense within Comanche society was enhanced by the presence of hostile neighbors so that "general fighting within the tribe was not to be countenanced when there were always outside enemies to be confronted."[24] Similarly, Boehm explains that among feuding Montenegrins, truces were expeditiously enacted and feuds subjugated to the necessity of maintaining military alliances if common enemies appeared on the horizon.[25] However, individuals and groups can become interdependent for a variety of reasons having nothing to do with the presence of a common enemy. The Xingu societies' pattern of intertribal trade provides a good example of economic interdependence. Recall that each Xingu tribe produces and exchanges goods not manufactured by the other tribes, for instance, ceramics, hardwood bows, belts, necklaces, and potassium chloride salt.[26] Each group has a monopoly on items that the members of the other groups desire, contributing to the creation of an economically interdependent system. It is interesting that the Xingu themselves have created and continue to nurture the interdependent exchange relationships. The ties and mutual dependencies are viewed in a positive light, and one beneficial effect involves the maintenance of peaceful relations among the villages.

Interdependence per se does not automatically lead to peaceful interaction. The parties whose fates are intertwined must recognize the nature of the situation. Interdependence has a huge potential for contributing to peace in the 21st century and beyond. Considerable interdependence already exists among the peoples of the earth and continues to grow in the realms of economics, security, and the environment. Awareness also is on the rise that interdependence brings common challenges necessitating cooperation.

The reality of global *economic interdependence* is reflected in the growth and proliferation of transnational corporations and the effects that economic growth and decline in one region have on the economies of other world regions. A commentator for the BBC expressed the interdependence of the global economy: "The American economy sneezes and the world catches a cold."[27]

The reality of global *security interdependence* is also multidimensional. Nuclear weapons link the fate of all peoples of the world. Even a "small" nuclear exchange, if setting off a nuclear winter, would prove disastrous for all humanity. Radiation from a large, medium, or small-scale nuclear war would encircle the globe. Use of biological and chemical weapons also could have geographically broad-reaching disastrous effects. Thus the very presence of weapons of mass destruction links the peoples and nations of the world in an interdependent fate.

Bulging military expenditures and the waging of more conventional wars also relate to interdependence. Spending $2 billion a day worldwide on military expenditures diverts huge amounts of financial and other resources from promoting sustainable development, protecting the environment, and fulfilling a host of human and humanitarian needs—again issues that span borders.[28] The waging of wars pollutes both local and common environments simultaneously, for war-caused environmental devastation can have ecological impacts regionally and even on the global ecosystem.[29]

Figure 20.3 A Greek fishing boat returns to harbor in Heraklion, Crete. The overexploitation of the world's fisheries and pollution of the earth's oceans are but two critical issues that simultaneously reflect global environmental interdependence and the necessity of implementing cooperative solutions to shared problems. No nation, for instance, can unilaterally protect the seas. It is in the long-range self-interest of each interdependent nation to cooperate in solving common problems. (D. P. Fry photo collection.)

A third reality of interdependence, just alluded to, involves the environment. All persons and nations on the planet are *environmentally interdependent,* being affected by pollution of the oceans, greenhouse warming, ozone depletion, species loss, radioactivity, and so on (see Figure 20.3).

Thus interdependence in the areas of economy, security, and environment *already exists.* Realization of the *implications* of interdependence also exists in some quarters. For example, in recent years the idea of *common security* has gained increasing attention. Sociologists Lester Kurtz and Jennifer Turpin explain that common security assumes that "no one is secure until everyone is, because we all live in the same 'global village.'"[30] Another important concept that is gaining a foothold in security deliberations is *comprehensive security*—the idea that military factors are only part of the story and that a host of nonmilitary influences, such as social inequities, ecological deterioration, poverty, and migration pressures, have major peace and security ramifications.[31] Such inequities would seem to provide a ripe breeding ground for terrorism.

A potential peace-promoting insight involves enhancing awareness of the new realities of global interdependence among leaders and citizens. Anthropology suggests that when individuals clearly perceive their interdependence, replacing violent competition with cooperation is a possible outcome.[32] However, as Michael Renner points out, interdependence in and of itself may not necessarily promote cooperation.[33] The *realization* of mutual interdependence is a critical variable. Thus one step toward doing away with war is to promote awareness, among leaders and citizens alike, that as an institution war is outdated, counterproductive, and extremely dangerous to *all* persons living on an interdependent planet. Raising awareness that *all* humans share the threats posed by terrorists with weapons of mass destruction, global environmental degradation, global warming, oceanic pollution, and the worldwide loss of biodiversity—coupled with the realization that *all* persons on the planet are ever-increasingly linked within an interdependent global economic system—leads to a *rational* approach of resolving conflicts without war and of cooperatively addressing common problems. In short, it is in every person's and every nation's self-interest to move humanity beyond war. It is "neither realistic, nor rational, nor reasonable to be prepared to destroy ourselves to defend ourselves."[34] In today's world, military approaches no longer actually provide the *safety and security* that people desire. The most pressing challenges to human survival in the 21st century simply are not amenable to military solutions.

Values, Attitudes, and Beliefs

Anthropological research clearly demonstrates the importance of cultural values, attitudes, and beliefs in influencing how conflicts are handled.[35] Values, attitudes, and beliefs are internalized during socialization and reinforced in daily life. Examples of peace-promoting belief systems can be seen in the values and attitudes held, for example, by the Semai, Mehinaku, and La Paz Zapotec. The Semai simultaneously devalue physical violence and value harmony.[36] Of the Mehinaku, Gregor writes, "The concept of good is tied to peacefulness. A villager's reputation and moral worth depend on being circumspect in behavior, avoiding confrontations, and rarely showing anger."[37] The La Paz Zapotec uphold the values of social tranquility, respect, responsibility, and cooperation—all of which are incompatible with expressing violence.[38]

The anthropological observation that attitudes, values, and beliefs can either promote peaceful, nonviolent behavior or, to the contrary, facilitate aggression and warfare has implications for abolishing war. The prevalent belief among national leaders and citizens is that the institution of warfare is permissible and at times necessary.[39] Such beliefs facilitate the waging of war. As Adams and Bosch demonstrate, holding such beliefs discourages people from taking action for peace.[40] This pattern contributes to a self-fulfilling prophecy wherein the war institution continues, in part because large numbers of people, believing that war is natural, even inevitable, do not insist that intergroup conflicts be handled in new ways.

Albert Einstein expressed that in the nuclear age "everything has changed, save our modes of thinking."[41] One implication is that new attitudes, values, and beliefs—new modes of thinking—are relevant to replacing war with other approaches to seeking security. The tremendous variation in cultural belief systems apparent in the ethnographic record, including those in peaceful societies, suggests that shifting to beliefs that favor nonviolent forms of conflict management instead of war are certainly within the range of human possibilities.

An alternative belief system could embrace concepts of common security and comprehensive security and therefore advocate cooperation over competition in dealing with the shared threats to human safety and well-being. An alternative belief system could emphasize that all nations, all humans, share a common fate, and that warfare is no longer acceptable, and, furthermore, that it no longer provides an effective route to any nation's security. David Krieger suggests one critically important attitude change: "Warfare must be de-legitimized as a means of settling disputes."[42] Thus a new belief system based on an appreciation of global interdependence would recognize that warfare is an obsolete social institution.

It is possible to imagine a global system wherein conflicts are managed by institutions other than war and common environmental, developmental, and security concerns are cooperatively addressed.[43] If implementing changes of this magnitude seems impossible, then an anthropological time perspective may help to put the truly immense human potential for social change in focus. The same species that began as a politically acephalous band-living hunter-gatherer has managed to create a system of nation-states, some operating as democratic polities with millions of citizens. The immensity of this shift in social and political complexity from band to nation is truly staggering. It shows without a doubt that humans are an amazingly flexible species capable of creating diverse social institutions.

In the 1990s, a group of world leaders convened in Stockholm and produced a report called the *Stockholm Initiative*. The document makes a number of recommendations to the people and leaders of the world regarding peace and security, environment and development, human rights and democracy, and global cooperation and governance. The *Stockholm Initiative* calls for a new worldview and attitudes that recognize the interdependence of humanity and the absolute necessity of cooperation.

> Cooperation on issues that require countries to act in accordance not only with national interest but also according to global norms will demand a system that more clearly defines rights and obligations of nations. When agreed upon, such rights and obligations must be respected. Norms must gradually acquire the status of law. . . . The reality of the human neighborhood requires us urgently to seek a compact on establishing a strengthened system of global governance.[44]

The essential point of this discussion is *not* that peace can be achieved *simply* through modifying beliefs, attitudes, and values, but rather as *one* ingredient in a complex recipe for abolishing war, beliefs, attitudes, and values that promote peace can be fostered as alternatives to traditional views that war is acceptable, even inevitable. Elie Wiesel raises questions that challenge status quo thinking: "Why not glorify something else? Why not give a medal to those who oppose and prevent war? Give *them* a Medal of Honor! Why don't we write poetry, drama, and plays about the triumph of peace instead of victory in war?"[45]

Overarching Authority: The Benefits of Governance over Anarchy

Robarchek and Robarchek suggest that the absence of an overarching authority among the Waorani was one factor that contributed to feuding in the past and made the marked reduction in fighting a "fragile peace."[46] Ferguson concludes: "The point that a strong overarching authority will prevent or diminish internal warfare is valid, but obvious."[47] In chapter 8, I related an anecdote about a Yanomamö man who enthusiastically realized the potential of police, courts, and a code of law for achieving justice without raiding and revenge killings.[48] The point, which obviously excited the Yanomamö man, is that a superordinate authority with viable judicial institutions can replace the violent self-redress patterns of individual revenge killings, feuding, or warring.

At this moment in history, the international war system is roughly analogous to the individual self-redress system typical of band society or the feuding system typical of tribal social organization. The scale is different, but the self-redress patterns are similar. In self-redress systems, third parties may intervene as friendly peacemakers or mediators and attempt to prevent bloodshed, but ultimately no one has the authority to prevent disputants from using force. Any nation in the current acephalous world system can seek justice via military means—in the same way that a wronged Alacaluf hunter pursues self-redress or a group of Yanomamö set out on a revenge raid in an attempt to even the score. As pointed out in chapter 8, seeking justice via self-redress has the major disadvantage of potentially leading to the escalation or prolongation of violence, as occurs during feuding among socially segmented groups. *Anthropology shows that an effective way to stop violence within an acephalous self-redress system is to create or impose a higher level of judicial authority.* New mechanisms, such as courts, take over the administration of justice, and in the process reduce the violence inherent in self-redress justice seeking. Thus the Yanomamö man eagerly realized the benefits of courts and police.

One variety of superordinate authority that halts warfare is what van der Dennen labels *peace by incorporation or subjugation* and Black calls *repressive peacemaking.*[49] Peace is imposed by an authority that treats killing, feuding, or warring as offenses punishable in and of themselves. For instance, at the state level of social organization individuals rarely are permitted to use violent self-redress to extract justice personally. The punishment of offenders becomes the duty of the state, not individual citizens.

The pacification of warring indigenous groups by a colonial power or national government exemplifies this type of superordinate approach to feuding or warfare. Keeley points out that some of the most warlike tribal cultures eagerly accepted pacification, or in other cases pacified themselves, once European contact had been made. Correspondingly, Meggitt notes how the Mae Enga were willing to give the government courts a try as an alternative to warfare until it became clear, in this particular case, that the colonial courts were not effectively handling their grievances.[50]

This type of peace by incorporation or subjugation—repressive peacemaking—has the danger of replacing the devil with the witch. The benefits of a repressive peace may come with a hefty price tag: losses to rights, freedoms, and independence.

Superordinate authority, however, need not be repressive.[51] Democratic superordinate authorities present positive alternatives to repressive regimes. A superordinate authority structure can be formed through the action of the subunits themselves, as with the creation of confederations or federations. Such structures may increase the internal peace among the composite units, but not necessarily increase the peace beyond the confederacy or federation. For instance, the Iroquois confederacy (consisting of the Cayuga, Mohawk, Oneida, Onondaga, Seneca, and Tuscarora) was founded with one of its main objectives "to break up the spirit of warfare, and to live in harmony with the neighboring peoples."[52] The confederacy brought internal peace, but subsequently contributed, it seems, to external warfare. We have noted a similar limitation of the Xingu peace system: It did not protect the member tribes from attacks by "wild Indians" living outside the Upper Xingu River basin. The moral is that an effective system for conflict resolution among nations would need to encompass all the nations of the world, not merely some of them—although regional federations may constitute an intermediate step in the right direction.

Anthropology lends support to the *Stockholm Initiative*'s call for additional global structures of governance. In a confederate system, the locus of authority remains primarily in the constituent units. In the case of the Iroquois League, this seems to have been sufficient to prevent warring among the member tribes. In a federal system, greater authority is transferred from the constituent units to an overarching institution.

Various authors have suggested that the United Nations could be reformed to make it more democratic and to shift it from a confederate status toward a federal model with greater authority. The United States, it will be remembered, went through just such a transformation in giving up the ineffective Articles of Confederation in favor of the federal system of governance created by the U.S. Constitution. Is there a lesson here? As modest initial changes, the authors of the *Stockholm Initiative* propose that "the United Nations takes on a broadened mandate at the Security Council level, following the wider understanding of security which has developed, and that its composition and the use of the veto be reviewed" and furthermore that "the Secretary-General be given a stronger position and the means to exercise authority, and that the method of appointment of the Secretary-General and of higher-level staff be reviewed."[53]

The implementation of overarching authority structures also can occur at the regional level. The European Union (EU) is an example par excellence. The European Commission, European Parliament, and European Court of Justice provide an overarching level of governance to the 25 member countries that includes new political, legislative, and judicial mechanisms for handling disputes and for facilitating cooperation on shared concerns (see Figure 20.4). A common currency, the euro, has already replaced national currencies within about half of the EU countries. The possibility of war within the Union has become about as unlikely as war breaking out between Indiana and Illinois. "Peace is therefore the primary achievement of the process of European integration."[54] Although presenting additional difficulties in scale, a global union through the United Nations or other global institutions could be implemented. Another lesson of European integration is that it does not occur overnight; in fact, the "two steps forward and one step back" saying has been applied to the process. A similar view seems appropriate when considering the potential of creating greater global governance.

Conflict Management Mechanisms

The human potential for peace is omnipresent. Conflict abounds in human societies, but even in the most violent societies, people handle most disputes without bloodshed. The anthropological material presented in this book illustrates the ingenuity through which people deal with conflict without violence and restore the peace following disputes. Some cultures have developed regulated contests that prevent serious injury, as illustrated by Netsilik song duels, Xingu wrestling matches, and the shoving fights of the Siriono. As an alternative to violence, the Oraibi Hopi settled a serious dispute with a contest:

> The leaders of these factions met and agreed to hold a pushing contest in the plaza, the losing faction then being obliged to leave the village. The leaders drew a line in the sand, with the members of one faction on one side and their enemies on the other. Then the two groups of men confronted each other until one was able to push the other back and surge over the line.

Figure 20.4 The European Union Parliament building in Brussels, Belgium, and the national flags of the member states. In 2004, ten new countries joined the European Union, which now consists of 25 member nations. In the wake of the devastating destruction suffered by Europe in World War II, postwar leaders envisioned how a more integrated Europe could prevent future wars. The European Union has not destroyed national traditions, but it has reduced the chance of war *within the Union.* The European Union also has added a level of governance to benefit member countries in terms of enhancing commerce and trade, providing added food and product safety, limiting regional air and water pollution, preventing crime and terrorism, and so forth. (D. P. Fry photo collection.)

> The losers, with their wives and children, packed up their belongings and left Oraibi as agreed. For a short time, they camped outside the village. After suffering much hardship, they eventually built their own village a little to the north. At no time, as far as reported, did any brawling break out or were guns or other weapons used defensively or offensively. This is self-control on a massive scale.[55]

In mediation, recall that a more or less neutral third party attempts to assist disputants in reaching a mutually acceptable agreement. Neil Whitehead tells of how one tribal group, the Yao, engaged in mediation between Aricoure and Carib warriors in 1624. The Yao intervened because they were friends of both groups; following the attainment of peace, they hosted both groups of warriors in their village for eight days.[56]

An anthropological perspective demonstrates that humans are capable of devising and employing a great diversity of conflict prevention and management techniques.[57] Warfare, a form of group level self-redress, can be seen as just one option among others in a general conflict management typology that also includes avoidance, toleration, negotiation, and third-party settlement procedures of various types. Clearly there are alternative approaches for dealing with intergroup conflict besides war.

Moreover, as applied work by William Ury, Jeanne Brett, and Stephen Goldberg demonstrates, nonviolent systems for dealing with conflict can be designed and implemented. These practitioners demonstrate that it is possible to shift from power contests (and war is the ultimate power contest) to a system that focuses on reconciling the interests and rights of disputants through any number of creative procedures. Ury and his colleagues suggest that an effective conflict management system should have a set of successive layers so that "if one procedure fails, another is waiting."[58]

Third-party conflict management options such as mediation, arbitration, and adjudication can be used in place of war. In an international system that has abolished war, trained mediators and arbitrators, operating under the auspices of the United Nations or other international and regional organizations, could assist with the handling of disputes among nations. International courts could be reserved for more serious cases, especially those dealing with violations of international law or human rights issues.

Although currently referred to as the International Court of Justice, or the World Court, this United Nations–affiliated tribunal actually engages in arbitration, not adjudication, because it lacks enforcement power, relying instead on voluntary appearances and voluntary compliance with rulings. Shifting the procedure of this important international tribunal from arbitration to adjudication, a change that would also require shifts in attitudes and perceptions, would advance global governance.

Anthropological studies show that such shifts in thinking are indeed possible. Recall that the Waorani chose to give up their system of violence and counterviolence when presented with a new view of reality by outside influences. The transition may serve as a parable for the overall abandonment of warfare by the peoples of the earth, who, we must remember, are still living under the ominous shadow of existing nuclear arsenals and weapons of ever greater mass destruction:

> Once contact was established, they [more distant hostile Waorani bands] too were presented an alternative reality premised on peacefulness and a glimpse of a world without constant fear of violent death. . . . The result was that new cultural knowledge—new information and new perceptions of reality—allowed people to visualize new options and new goals. . . . The killing stopped because the Waorani themselves made a conscious decision to end it.[59]

Renner provides some specific redesign proposals for improving the conflict prevention and resolution system of the United Nations.[60] With an eye to prevention, an early warning office could monitor potential conflicts. Early warning reports spanning the globe could allow United Nations mediation and arbitration teams to respond quickly to prevent brewing disputes from escalating. Eventually, such teams should be prepared to defuse internal as well as external disputes.

Humans use a variety of conflict management techniques that do not entail violence.[61] Humans also are capable of implementing and trying new conflict management procedures.[62] As illustrated by the planned creation of the European Union, humans can exercise foresight and ingenuity to eliminate the threat of war through the design of higher levels of democratic government, complete with built-in conflict management procedures. Although more complicated, the same process conceivably could be accomplished at the global level. To argue otherwise is to belittle human ingenuity.

CONCLUSIONS

One important, general contribution that anthropology holds for ending "the scourge of war" lies in demonstrating that warfare is not a natural, inevitable part of human nature. Ferguson has stated clearly why this message is of great importance:

> The image of humanity, warped by bloodlust, inevitably marching off to kill, is a powerful myth and an important prop of militarism in our society. Despite its lack of scientific credibility, there will remain those "hard-headed realists" who continue to believe in it, congratulating themselves for their "courage to face the truth," resolutely oblivious to the myth behind their "reality."[63]

In suggesting that war is an obsolete social institution that *can* and *must* be abolished, I have not dwelled on the doom and gloom of the current conflagrations raging in the world, the threat of terrorism, or the peril of nuclear holocaust that has slipped into the background of daily consciousness but nonetheless remains a grave obstacle to long-term human survival. An interview project with environmental activists led to the conclusion that at least a glimmer of hope is critical to motivate an individual to try to bring about social change.[64] In this chapter, by adopting a macroscopic anthropological view, I have concentrated on many glimmers of hope that I think shine toward the same conclusion: *Potentially, war can be eliminated and replaced by effective and just conflict management procedures and institutions.*

In *The Descent of Man,* Charles Darwin observed: "No tribe could hold together if murder, robbery, treachery, etc., were common; consequently such crimes within the limits of the same tribe 'are branded with everlasting infamy;' but excite no such sentiment beyond these limits."[65] Anthropology has borne out Darwin's observation; murder, violence, and rape within a social group are condemned by the members of the group.[66] Darwin also observed that with the advent of nation-states, the constitution of the "tribe" had broadened dramatically. This development suggested a new possibility to Darwin:

> As man advances in civilization, and small tribes are united into larger communities, the simplest reason would tell each individual that he ought to extend his social instincts and sympathies to all the other members of the same nation, though personally unknown to him. This point being once reached, there is only an artificial barrier to prevent his sympathies extending to the men of all nations and races.[67]

Anthropology shows clearly that through millennia and across continents humans experience tremendous variation in ways of life and social organization. In foraging bands, individuals identify with their relatives and friends in their own and neighboring bands; in nation-states, as Darwin noted, the level of identification generally rises to the country as a whole. This shows that both the social organization and the unit of identification—in other words, the "us" compared to the "them"—are extremely malleable. A global identification, "all of us," *in addition to* lower-level "us" identifications, seems well within the realm of human capacities, especially when our common survival depends on at least enough common identification to put a halt to war and cooperate to solve global problems that threaten *all of us.*

Immense social change on numerous dimensions is indisputably possible, as illustrated by the transformation from a nomadic hunting-and-gathering existence to a global system comprised of nation-state polities, the institution of slavery being totally given up in Western thinking and practice, and the creation of the European Union as a regional level of government complete with its own courts, legislators, and laws. And the existence of peace systems and numerous societies that do not engage in war illustrates the flexibility of humans and their social systems as well as demonstrates the human capacity to live without war. At a more specific level, anthropology suggests a full palette of often-complementary approaches that could be implemented to move humanity beyond war—enhance crosscutting ties; recognize the new reality of mutual interdependence and the necessity of using international cooperation to address common challenges; adopt new attitudes, values, and beliefs appropriate to an interdependent world that promote nonviolent conflict resolution; create overarching authority structures for effective governance; and utilize conflict management processes in place of war. Abolishing war in the 21st century is not only realistic in the sense that it is possible, but also realistically necessary for human survival and well-being. The peacemaking primate has the capacity to do so.

APPENDIX

ORGANIZATIONS TO CONTACT

Around the planet, many of the world's indigenous peoples, including some societies mentioned in this book, are struggling for survival. Readers who would like to find out more about the current challenges faced by indigenous peoples and what can be done to offer assistance may want to contact Cultural Survival, 215 Prospect Street, Cambridge, MA 02139, USA (www.cs.org). The goal of Cultural Survival is to promote "the rights, voices, and visions of indigenous peoples."

Similarly, readers who would like to find out more about ongoing efforts to replace war with viable security alternatives can obtain useful information from Citizens for Global Solutions, 418 Seventh Street, Washington, DC 20003, USA (www.globalsolutions.org). The group's mission statement reads: "Citizens for Global Solutions envisions a future in which nations work together to abolish war, protect our rights and freedoms, and solve the problems facing humanity that no nation can solve alone. This vision requires effective democratic global institutions that will apply the rule of law while respecting the diversity and autonomy of national and local communities."

Notes

To reduce the number of notes, a single note at the end of a paragraph will supply all the references relevant to the paragraph in situations where this does not result in citation ambiguities.

CHAPTER 1: QUESTIONING THE WAR ASSUMPTION

1. Ehrlich 2001:10, 3.
2. de Waal 1989. Except for anthropologists, whose works constitute the vast majority of sources cited, the academic discipline of a researcher, if known, is provided the first time that the person's name is mentioned.
3. Ghiglieri 1999:246; Keeley 1996; Buss 1999:298; Wrangham & Peterson 1996:63.
4. Keeley 1996:30–31; Wrangham & Peterson 1996:75.
5. Ehrlich 2001:3.
6. Douglass 1986; on racial beliefs: Gould 1978.
7. See Ferguson 1984a; Fry 1985; Hobbes 1946.
8. Wright 1942, 1964:40.
9. Chagnon 1988.
10. de Waal & Lanting 1997:2.
11. Ehrlich 2001:11
12. Chagnon 1988, 1990a, 1990b, 1992a, 1992b.
13. See Buss 1999; Ghiglieri 1999; Pinker 1997.
14. Chagnon 1979a:384.
15. Mead 1967:224–225.

CHAPTER 2: THE PEACE SYSTEM OF THE UPPER XINGU

1. Ireland 1988:159.
2. Fry 1999a:719, following Rubin, Pruitt, & Kim 1994.
3. Fry 2000.
4. Gardner & Resnik 1996:169.
5. Haghighi & Sorensen 1996:20–21.
6. Robarchek & Robarchek 1998a:19, 20, 57, 58; Robarchek & Robarchek 1996a:66.
7. Knauft 1987.
8. Murphy & Quain 1955:2.
9. Murphy & Quain 1955:10.
10. Basso 1973:2; Gregor 1990:105.
11. Gregor 1990:105–106; see also Basso 1973:1, 5; Dole 1966.
12. Gregor 1990:109; Gregor 1994a:235.

13. Carneiro 1994a:206; see also Basso 1973:3 and frontispiece map. Sometimes different names or spellings are used for the same society. For example, Yawalapití and Yaulapití are variations referring to the same culture. At times, however, the variations reflect more than differences in spelling or pronunciation. Ireland 1991 advocates dropping the Waurá variation of Wauja, because the people themselves find it incorrect and derogatory. I will use Wauja unless the alternative appears in a direct quotation.

14. Basso 1973:vii.

15. See Carneiro 1983.

16. See Dole 1966.

17. Gregor 1990:114.

18. Gregor 1985:37.

19. Gregor 1985:201; Murphy & Quain 1955:93.

20. Basso 1973:104 note 10.

21. Murphy & Quain 1955:48; see also Dole 1966; Gregor 1985:30; Zelený 1994:379.

22. Gregor 1985:30.

23. Basso 1973:73.

24. Murphy & Quain 1955:94.

25. Basso 1973:163; Gregor 1985:35–36; Murphy & Quain 1955:94.

26. Gregor 1990:110.

27. Gregor 1994a:237; Gregor 1985:29.

28. Murphy & Quain 1955:48.

29. Zelený 1994:379.

30. Murphy & Quain 1955:48; Zelený 1994:379; Gregor 1985:31.

31. Dole 1966:73.

32. Gregor 1985:31.

33. Murphy & Quain 1955:57–58, 48.

34. Gregor 1985, 1994b:255.

35. Basso 1973:55–56; Carneiro 1994a:207; Gregor 1990:111–112, 1994a:237, 1994b:244; Murphy & Quain 1955:18–19; Zelený 1994:378.

36. Murphy & Quain 1955:19.

37. Gregor 1990:111–112.

38. For example, Basso 1973.

39. Zelený 1994:379.

40. Kuikuru: Carneiro 1994a:208; Mehinaku: Gregor 1990:112.

41. Gregor & Robarchek 1996:173.

42. Gregor 1994b.

43. Gregor 1994a:239.

44. Gregor 1990:113.

45. See Basso 1973:3.

46. See Gregor 1990:110, 1994a:238; Basso 1973:5–7, 12–14.

47. Gregor 1994b:246.

48. Carneiro 1994a:208.

49. For example, see Basso 1973:129–130; Gregor & Robarchek 1996:178.

50. Gregor & Robarchek 1996:162.

51. Carneiro 1977; Basso 1973:124–131; Dole 1966.

52. See photographs in Chapter 8 of Basso 1973 and in Gregor 1985:97.

53. Gregor & Robarchek 1996:180.

54. Murphy & Quain 1955:15; Gregor 1990:117, see also Gregor & Robarchek 1996:162; Ireland 1991:58.

55. Gregor 1990:116; see also Gregor 1994b:247–248.

56. Gregor 1990:116.
57. Gregor 1994b:248.
58. Wilbert 1994:187.
59. Ireland 1991:58.
60. Gregor 1994b:249.
61. Service 1971a; see also Reyna 1994; Boehm 1999.
62. Service 1971a.
63. Boehm 1999; for example, Kelly 1995 uses complex hunter-gatherers.
64. Kelly 1995:302.
65. Price & Brown 1985.
66. Boehm 1999:146; Service 1971a:166–169.
67. Boehm 1999:146.

CHAPTER 3: TAKEN FOR GRANTED: THE HUMAN POTENTIAL FOR PEACE

1. Fernea 2004:114.
2. Avruch 1991.
3. Koch 1974, 1979; Black 1993; Nader & Todd 1978.
4. On avoidance: see Koch 1974 and Black 1993; Ferguson 1989a:195, 196; Dentan 2004.
5. Turnbull 1961:120–121.
6. Arcand 1994:144.
7. Quote is from Nader & Todd 1978:9; Black 1993:88.
8. Matteson 1994:280.
9. Norberg-Hodge 1991:46.
10. On negotiation: see Gulliver 1979; G/wi: Silberbauer 1972:318; Japanese: Ohbuchi et al. 1989; Fijians: Hickson 1979; Koch et al. 1977.
11. All Kpelle quotes are from Gibbs 1963:4, 5.
12. Bennett & Zingg 1976:212–213.
13. Redfield 1967:9–10.
14. Comanche: Hoebel 1967a; the quote is from page 190.
15. For example, see Brögger 1968 on Italian peasants; Caplan 1995 on the Limbus of Nepal; Colson 1995 for a general observation; Gibbs 1963 on the Kpelle of Liberia; Gibson 1989:66 on the Buid of the Philippines; Gluckman 1967 on the Lozi of Zambia; Hickson 1979, 1986 on Fijians; Hollan 1988 on the Toraja of Indonesia; Just 1991:117 on the Dou Donggo of Indonesia; Koch 1974, 1979 and Koch et al. 1977 on the Jalé of New Guinea; Lederach 1991 on Costa Ricans; Nader 1969, 1990 on Talean Zapotecs of Mexico; Noland 1981 on Iranians; Robarchek 1997 on the Semai of Malaysia; Shook 1985 on Hawaiians; and Turnbull 1961 on the Mbuti of central Africa.
16. Black 1993.
17. On friendly peacemaking: see Black 1993; Fox 1989:161.
18. Meggitt 1977:119; see also Black 1993; Coon 1971.
19. Berndt 1965:181–182; quote is from W. Lloyd Warner in Berndt 1965:182.
20. Gulliver 1979; on lacking authority: Koch 1974; Black 1993; on coercion: Barton 1967; Merry 1982; Podolefsky 1990.
21. Fry 2000, 2001a, 2001b; Gibbs 1963; Greenhouse 1985:97; Merry 1982; Takala 1998.
22. Fiji: Brenneis 1990; Paliyan: Gardner 2004; Dou Donggo: Just 1991; Limbus: Caplan 1995; Abkhazians: Garb 1996; Nubians: Fernea 2004.
23. Boggs & Chun 1990; quote is from Shook & Kwan 1991:220.

24. Shook 1985; Shook & Kwan 1991.
25. Shook 1985:14.
26. Dentan 1968, 1978, 1992, 2001a, 2004; Robarchek 1986, 1990, 1994, 1997.
27. Dentan 2004; Robarchek 1979, 1997.
28. Robarchek 1979, 1997; quote is from Robarchek 1997:55.
29. Bedouin: Stewart 1990; quote is from page 394.
30. Boehm 1987.
31. Vuk Vrcevic 1890 quoted in Boehm 1987:127–128.
32. Boehm 1987:157.
33. Black 1993:115.
34. Gluckman 1967:77–78.
35. Tarahumara: Bennett & Zingg 1976; Pastron 1974; Huichol: Schaefer 1995; Zapotec: Fry 2004b; Nader 1969, 1990.
36. Bennett & Zingg 1976:332.
37. Black 1993; Fry & Fry 1997.
38. Koch 1974:223; see also Force 1960:80 on Palau Islanders.
39. Jochelson 1926:132; see also page 383.
40. See Hollan 1988; O'Nell 1981, 1989.
41. Bonta 1996; Semai: Dentan 1968; Robarchek 1997; Chewong: Howell 1989:53–54.
42. Amish and Hutterites: Bonta 1993, 1997; Dentan 1994; Hostetler 1974, 1983a, 1983b; Kidder & Hostetler 1990; Longhofer 1991; Montagu 1976; lack of homicide: Hostetler 1983b:3, 14; Panare: Henley 1982:113, 228; Wáiwai: Howard 1994:348.
43. Robarchek 1997:54; Andamanese: Coon 1971; Zapotec: Fry 1994; Semang: Endicott 1988, 1993; Bukidon: Edgerton 1993:55; Doukhobors: Mealing 1991; Ladakh: Norberg-Hodge 1991; Montagnais-Naskapi: Leacock 1981; Seri: Bowen & Moser 1995:234; Sherpa: Paul 1992; Fürer-Haimendorf 1984; Tanna: Lindstrom 1991.
44. Finnish Gypsies: Grönfors 1977:119, 122; Hill Pandaram: Morris 1992:100; Thai: Martin & Levinson 1993:69.
45. Hallowell 1974; Gregor 1994b.
46. West Greenlanders: Kleivan 1991:377–378; Canadian Inuit: Briggs 1994:165; Ju/wasi: Thomas 1994:75; Toraja: Hollan 1988:59; see also Hollan 1997; Thai: Phillips 1974:170; Tarahumara: Pastron 1974:387–388; Zapotec: O'Nell 1981:360.
47. de Waal 1989, 1996; Aureli & de Waal 2000.
48. Cords & Aureli 2000.
49. de Waal 1996:173, italics in original.

CHAPTER 4: MAKING THE INVISIBLE VISIBLE: BELIEF SYSTEMS IN SAN ANDRÉS AND LA PAZ

1. Benito Juárez in Dublan & Lozano 1876:27.
2. Quirk 1971.
3. Fry 1992a:192.
4. See Fry 1987, 1988, 1990, 1992a, 1992b, 1993a, 1994, 2004b, and 2005.
5. Fry 1994.
6. O'Nell 1979:302; judicial records: Paddock 1982 and personal communication 1986.
7. Paddock 1982 and personal communication 1986.
8. Archer & Gartner 1984; Daly & Wilson 1988:275; *Statistical Abstract of the United States* 1996:204; *Uniform Crime Reports* 1993:284.
9. Fry 1993a.

10. O'Nell's 1969 interview schedule was adopted for this study. Sixteen questions pertain to child discipline. With the help of field assistants, 18 fathers in La Paz and 31 fathers in San Andrés were interviewed. All interviews were tape-recorded, transcribed, and verb usage related to child discipline analyzed. See Fry 1993a for details.

11. Fry 1993a.

12. O'Nell 1969:263, italics added.

13. Fry 1994.

14. Guerra et al. 1997:203.

15. See Fry 1988, 1992b, 1994, 2005.

16. A full description of the ethological methodology appears in Fry 1988, 1990. Systematic behavior observations began after rapport had been established and parents had granted me permission to observe their children in and around their homes. Forty-eight three- to eight-year-old children, 24 from each community, were observed using a procedure called *focal individual sampling*. The majority of the focal observations (84 percent) were conducted within family compounds, with the remainder occurring in streets, schoolyards, fields, and elsewhere. Total observation time per child averaged about three hours. I switched back and forth between the two communities to collect data on a weekly to biweekly basis. The behavioral data were narrated into a tape recorder, or, in a minority of observation sessions, jotted on paper. I recorded a running commentary of the behaviors engaged in by each focal child, including aggression, play aggression, and discipline received. If the child switched locations, I shifted my vantage point so as to maintain continuous visual contact. I did not remain close enough to the child to interfere with his or her actions or to attract attention. One of several Zapotec field assistants accompanied me on nearly all observation sessions. The relevant data were transcribed, coded, and analyzed statistically.

17. See Fry 1988, 1992b, 1994.

18. Steinmetz 1977.

19. See Bandura 1973; Eron & Huesmann 1984; Huesmann 1988; Straus 2001.

20. Fry 1994, 2004b.

21. Huesmann 1988:19.

22. For example, Friedrich 1972; Greenberg 1981, 1989.

23. Fry 1992b.

24. Fry 1989.

25. Fry 1992a, 1992b.

26. Fry 1988, 1992b, 1994.

27. See Fry 1998.

CHAPTER 5: THE CROSS-CULTURAL PEACEFULNESS–AGGRESSIVENESS CONTINUUM

1. Daly & Wilson 1988:275, italics added.

2. Dennen 1995.

3. Sponsel 1996a; see also Bonta 1996.

4. See Ghiglieri 1999; Wrangham & Peterson 1996.

5. Ross 1993a. Ross' sample of societies is a subsample taken from the Standard Cross-Cultural Sample (SCCS) of 186 mostly preindustrial societies from around the globe. The entire SCCS contains ethnographic information on representative, well-described societies from the world's major cultural provinces. At about half the size, Ross' sample of 90 represents many but not all of these cultural provinces.

6. External and internal conflict correlation: $r = .39$; $p < .001$; $N = 90$, Ross 1993a:84.

7. Ross 1993a: Appendix A.

8. Ross 1993a:90–91, italics added.
9. Ross 1993a:86–87.
10. Dentan 1994, 2001b; Fry 1998, 1999a.
11. Robarchek & Robarchek 1996a, 1998a.
12. Robarchek & Robarchek 1996a:72.
13. Greenberg 1989:231.
14. Willis 1989:137.
15. See also Haas 1999 for an archaeological example.
16. Fry 2004a.
17. Bonta 1993, 1996, 1997; Dennen 1995: Chapter 7; Fabbro 1978; Fry 1999a, 2004a; Gregor 1996a; Howell & Willis 1989; Kemp & Fry 2004; Levinson 1994; Montagu 1978a; Sponsel 1996a, 1996b; Sponsel & Gregor 1994; Ross 1993a, 1993b.
18. Gregor & Sponsel 1994:xv.
19. Sponsel 1994:18.
20. Thoden van Velzen & van Wetering 1960; Fabbro 1978.
21. Montagu 1978a.
22. Montagu 1982:293.
23. For example, Montagu 1951, 1963, 1964, 1972, 1973, 1976, 1989, 1999; see also Sperling 2000.
24. Howell & Willis 1989; O'Nell 1989; see also O'Nell 1969, 1979, 1981, 1986.
25. Levinson 1989:98, 103; Ross 1993a.
26. Bonta 1993; Sponsel & Gregor 1994; Dennen 1995.
27. Gregor 1996a; Sponsel 1996a, 1996b; Bonta 1996, 1997; Dentan 2001a, 2001b; Gardner 2000a, 2000b; Robarchek 1997; Fry 1998, 1999a, 2001b; Kemp & Fry 2004; Gregor forthcoming.
28. Fry 2004a.
29. Levinson 1994:122.
30. Fry 1998.
31. Overing 1989:79, 92.
32. Thoden van Velzen & van Wetering 1960; Masumura 1977; Ross 1993a; Minturn et al. 1969; Levinson 1989; Palmer 1965; Ember & Ember 1992a.
33. Thoden van Velzen & van Wetering 1960:191.
34. Masumura 1977:393.
35. Ross 1993a.
36. Minturn et al. 1969:315–318.
37. Levinson 1989:103.
38. Palmer 1965.
39. Palmer 1965:320, 322.
40. Ember & Ember 1992a.
41. Burrows 1952; Lutz 1982, 1983, 1988; Spiro 1952; Thoden van Velzen and van Wetering 1960; Minturn et al. 1969; Palmer 1965.
42. Fry 2004a; for examples, see Kemp & Fry 2004.

CHAPTER 6: PEACE STORIES

1. Koskela 1997:307.
2. Koskela 1997:302.
3. Fry & Takala 2001.
4. See *Yearbook of Nordic Statistics* 1994:338; *Statistical Abstract of the United States* 1996, calculated from data on page 205; Honkatukia 2001:26; King et al. 1991:361.

5. Bonta 1996.

6. Robarchek 1997:51; Dentan 1968:6.

7. Dentan 1968, 1978:97, 1995, 2000, 2004.

8. Dentan 2000:212.

9. For example, Clayton Robarchek 1979, 1980, 1989, 1990, 1994, 1997; Clayton & Carole Robarchek 1992, 1996a, 1998a, 1998b, quote is from 1996a:64.

10. Robarchek & Robarchek 1998b:124, note 2.

11. Dentan 1988:626; for comparative homicide rates: Table 6.1, this volume; see also Knauft 1987.

12. Robarchek & Robarchek 1998b:124.

13. Dentan 1988:626; also see Dentan 1995:230, note 2; Dentan 2004.

14. Kelly 2000:20; Keeley 1996:31.

15. See Dentan 1968:58, 1999; Robarchek & Dentan 1987; Gregor & Robarchek 1996:161. In the communist insurgency following World War II, some Semai were removed from their social world, given weapons, and ordered to kill. They obeyed, sometimes with wild abandon. Clearly this event does not demonstrate that *Semai culture* is warlike. In an interesting consideration of this topic, Robarchek & Dentan 1987 effectively lay to rest what they refer to as the myth of the bloodthirsty Semai.

16. Robarchek 1980:113.

17. Robarchek 1990:72–73.

18. Dentan 1978; Robarchek 1980, the quote is from page 114.

19. Robarchek 1980.

20. Robarchek 1997:54.

21. Dentan 1968:55.

22. Robarchek 1979:106.

23. Burrows 1952:25; see also Burrows 1963:424–428.

24. Spiro 1952:497, 498; Minturn et al. 1969:317.

25. Lutz 1982:114.

26. Lutz 1988:199.

27. For example, see Ghiglieri 1999; Wrangham & Peterson 1996.

28. Betzig & Wichimai 1991 argue that Ifaluk is not such a peaceful place, despite the fact that they also acknowledge that "Betzig, Turke, Rodseth and Harrigan, in six months of combined observation, never saw any physical violence among adults, and saw adults punish children physically only twice." In evaluating the type of information that Betzig & Wichimai use in attempting to debunk Ifaluk peacefulness, Bonta 1997:318 concludes that their argument is "singularly unconvincing." I might add that Betzig & Wichimai are not simply considering physical aggression, but also more generally discuss social inequality and conflicts of interest (for example, the paying of tribute to chiefs) to argue that Ifaluk is not bereft of conflict. As discussed in chapter 2, *conflict and physical aggression are not identical concepts*. Conflict would be expected on Ifaluk, as in any society. Betzig & Wichimai point out that Ifaluk chiefs take tribute from the commoners, Ifaluk traditionally paid tribute to Yap, legends of ancient wars exist on Ifaluk, people on Ifaluk sometimes have land disputes, and people fear sorcery; in short, they propose, on page 245, that "there is no question that conflicts of interest exist on Ifaluk." True enough. But this does *not* imply that conflicts regularly take a violent form—that "individual differences were not infrequently resolved by violence" as they put it (page 249). This assertion about violence widely oversteps the facts and is contradicted not only by the observations by Burrows 1952, Spiro 1952, and Lutz 1982, 1983, 1988, but interestingly also by Betzig's own firsthand observations—see Betzig & Wichimai 1991:240. Ifaluk does not lack all forms of conflict; people do get angry and hostile and have disputes. However, an overall assessment of the various reports from Ifaluk suggests that *physical aggression* very rarely occurs and that *violence,* manifested in acts such as murder, is practically nonexistent.

29. Lutz 1988:199 for both quotes.

30. Burrows 1952:17; Lutz 1982:114, 1983:248.

31. Lutz 1982:114.

32. Lutz 1983:248, 253, 1988:137–140.

33. Lutz 1983:253.

34. Lutz 1988:17.

35. Lutz 1983:249, 1988.

36. Gullestad 1991:46; Ross 1993a:161; see also Dobinson 2004: Of course, even a homogeneous society such as Norway reflects some intra-societal variation in aggressiveness–-peacefulness. The homicide rate for Oslo, the capital, exceeds the national average, for example.

37. Smith 1999.

38. Seager 1997.

39. Ross 1993a:160.

40. *Yearbook of Nordic Statistics* 1994:338; Archer & Gartner 1984; Dobinson 2004.

41. Dobinson 2004:160.

42. Hollos 1970:156; Ross 1993b:57; Ross 1993a:164.

43. Dobinson 2004; Gullestad 1991; Hollos 1974; Larson 1992:182.

44. Hollos 1974.

45. Barth 1952.

46. Hollos 1974:74; Gullestad 1991:46; see also Fry 1994.

47. Hollos 1974:73, 41.

48. See Dobinson 2004.

49. Barth 1952:35.

50. Gullestad 1991:46.

51. Hollos 1974:67.

52. Barth 1952; Hollos 1974.

53. Gregor 1990:109.

54. Ghiglieri 1999:133, italics in original, page 147, page 149, italics added, page 103, page 30; Pilbeam is quoted in Lewin 1987:43.

55. Ghiglieri 1999.

56. Aubert 1969; Larson 1992.

CHAPTER 7: A HOBBESIAN BELIEF SYSTEM? ON THE SUPPOSED NATURALNESS OF WAR

1. Hobbes 1946:82.

2. Grunkemeyer 1996:126; see also Geertz 1973.

3. Grunkemeyer 1996:125.

4. Adams & Bosch 1987; Fry & Welch 1992.

5. See Barash 1991; Carneiro 1994b.

6. See Robarchek 1989.

7. Fry 2004b.

8. Thomas Huxley quoted in Holsti 1913:14.

9. Henry Maine quoted in Wheeler 1910:129.

10. William James 1910:272 quoted in Carneiro 1994b:7.

11. Dart 1953:207–208.

12. Wilson 2001:14.

13. Wrangham & Peterson 1996:84.

14. Low 1993:13.

15. Ghiglieri 1999:164, 165, italics in original.
16. Hobbes 1946.
17. Lesser 1967:94, 95.
18. Montagu 1976:59, 60.
19. Malinowski 1941:540.
20. Carneiro 1994b:6, italics in original.
21. Ferguson 1984a:12, italics in original.
22. Sponsel 1996b:114–115, italics in original.
23. Kelly 2000:2.
24. Keeley 1996:31, 32.
25. Barash 1991: Chapter 6.
26. Ehrlich 2001:11.
27. Textor 1967: variable 417; two societies are not coded.
28. Textor 1967: variable 418.
29. See Otterbein 1994, 1999.
30. Otterbein 1968, 1970.
31. Otterbein & Otterbein 1965:1470; see also Otterbein 1968:279.
32. Otterbein 1970:3.
33. Otterbein 1968.
34. Ferguson 1989a:196, 1995:47–48.
35. Gibson 1989, 1990.
36. Forbes 1885.
37. Endicott 1983.
38. Otterbein 1968:277, 280.
39. The coding of internal war among the Tiwi of Australia should be reconsidered, for, as will be discussed in chapter 12, the material upon which the coding is based (in Hart & Pilling 1960) does not pertain to "armed combat between political communities." The Tiwi sometimes engage in a type of juridical fight as a way to express individual grievances that upon the first glance might seem like a battle, but as ethnographers Hart and Pilling 1960, 1979 make clear, this process is *not* combat between political communities as political communities. Among the Tiwi, the so-called battle actually involves individuals expressing personal grudges and grievances—see chapter 12 as well as Wheeler 1910; Wolf 2001:196–197; and Reyna 1994:57. A clarification of this issue and recoding this society means that 10 percent of Otterbein's sample lack any type of war.
40. Otterbein 1970:11; Otterbein did not drop a society if the ethnographer stated clearly and directly that war is absent, but he did drop a substantial number of societies for which information on war was lacking.
41. Otterbein 1999:802.
42. Driver 1969:310, 312–320; quote is from page 312.
43. Jorgensen 1980:241.
44. Ember & Ember 1992a, 1992b, 1994a, 1997; see White 1989 related to the SCCS.
45. Ember & Ember 1997.
46. Otterbein 1968, 1970, 1973.
47. Ember & Ember 1992a:172, 1992b:248, 1994a:627, 1997:3.
48. Ember & Ember 1992a:172, italics added; note the word "combatants."
49. Boehm 1987:221.
50. Radcliffe-Brown 1922:84; Gusinde 1937:885, 893.
51. Radcliffe-Brown 1922:84.
52. Radcliffe-Brown 1922:86; Lesser 1967; Hobhouse 1956:105; Service 1966:110.
53. Cooper 1946a:95; Gusinde 1937:893; Service 1971b:35. The following additional citations correspond with those already noted as to the absence of warfare among the

Andamanese and the Yahgan: Dennen 1995:623, 672; Hobhouse 1956:111; Nag 1972:7; Pandya 1992:10; Service 1966:97, 1971b:49. However, Kelly 2000: Chapter 3 follows Ember & Ember's 1992b, 1994b, 1997 approach of including feuding within a definition of war and consequently refers to Andaman Islander feuding or revenge killings as "war." See also note 55 in this chapter.

54. Ember & Ember 1997; Ferguson 1997:331. The sources quoted by Ferguson also are in the bibliography.

55. Dennen 1995:93. War and feud are differentiated, for example, by Boehm 1987: Chapter 11; Carneiro 1994b:6; Driver 1969: Chapter 18; Evans-Pritchard 1940:151, 161; Irwin 1990; Jorgensen 1980:210; Lesser 1967:95; Malinowski 1941; Otterbein 1968; Pospisil 1971:1–10; Schneider 1950 quoted in Dennen 1995:88; Tefft & Reinhardt 1974:154; also see Turney-High 1971: Chapter 2.

56. Otterbein & Otterbein 1965: Table 3; Ericksen & Horton 1992.

57. Boehm 1987:243.

58. Ericksen & Horton 1992:62, 74.

59. Low 1993:13.

60. Dennen 1995:92.

61. Prosterman 1972:140.

62. Prosterman 1972:140–141; Otterbein 1970.

63. Du Bois 1960.

64. Steward quoted in Wolf 2001:195.

65. Gregor & Robarchek 1996:161.

66. See Bonta 1993, 1996, 1997; Dentan 1994; Fabbro 1978; Hostetler 1974, 1983a:25, 38, 1983b.

67. Sweden: Keeley 1996:32; Switzerland: Fry 1985:160; Keeley 1996:32; Iceland: Levinson 1994;137; Durrenberger & Beierle 1992.

68. Levinson 1994:137.

69. Arias 1997:148.

70. For example, Brown 1991 does *not* include war in his lengthy compilation of human universals. Brown 1991:138 does include, as a universal human trait, having ways to handle conflict (for instance, consultation or mediation). Earlier in the chapter, quotations to the effect that war is not a human universal were presented by Lesser 1967:94, 95 and Montagu 1976:59, 60 (see also Montagu 1978b; Malinowski 1941:540; Carneiro 1994b:6; Ferguson 1984a:12; Sponsel 1996b:114–115; Kelly 2000:2; Keeley 1996:32). The conclusions of various other anthropologists could be added. Gregor 1996b:xiv notes that "the existence of at least a few peaceful cultures, and the human desire for peace are powerful arguments against an inherently aggressive human nature." Wolf 2001:194, 195 writes: "Interpersonal violence may be triggered by the wish to interfere with the activities of another person or to avenge some real or imagined wrong. It may result in killing, but it is not war. War proper involves entire social groups organized as political communities, and—intentionally or unintentionally—its outcomes affect the balance of power between such social groups and communities. . . . There are people who do not carry on war in the sense I have defined it." Dennen 1995:506, 595–610 (also see pages 620–673) provides a list of approximately 200 cultures that are "Highly Unwarlike," that is, "War [is] reported as absent or mainly defensive," and concludes, "The evidence of a substantial number of peoples without warfare, or with mainly defensive and/or low-level warfare (that is, seldom exceeding the level of petty feuding) does not support the view of universal human belligerence." Ury 1999:xviii–xiv (an anthropologist and coauthor of *Getting to Yes* by Fisher & Ury 1981), writes: "Destructive conflict, which disrupts our homes, work organizations, communities, and world, is thus widely accepted as an inevitable and prominent part of human existence. . . . Even in this most deadly of centuries, most people around the planet have lived most of their lives in a condition of peace, not

war. Peace is the norm." We can top off this list by noting Margaret Mead's 1967:216 basic proposition that war is "a cultural invention."

71. Otterbein 1968, 1970; Ember & Ember 1992a, 1992b, 1994a, 1994b, 1997.

72. Burrows 1963:421.

CHAPTER 8: SOCIAL ORGANIZATION MATTERS!

1. Endicott 1988:122.

2. Wright 1942; Hobhouse, Wheeler, & Ginsberg 1915.

3. Wright 1942: Appendix IX.

4. Wright 1942:546, Appendix IX.

5. See Wright 1942: Appendix IX, Tables 5 & 11.

6. Wright 1942:546.

7. Endicott 1983; Dentan 2004; Forbes 1885; Gregor & Robarchek 1996; Schebesta 1929:280, 1978:187. The term *Sakai* is a pejorative term that nowadays is avoided by anthropologists; see Endicott 1983:218.

8. Nansen 1893:162.

9. Aweikoma: Henry 1941:55; Buid: Gibson 1989:71; Chewong: Howell 1989:50; Dorobo: Huntingford 1954:134; Guayaki: Clastres 1972:143, 165; Jahai: Sluys 1999:307, 310, 2000; Dene: Helm 1956:131–132; Panare: Henley 1982:10–11; Shoshone: Wolf 2001:195; Siriono: Holmberg 1969:157–158; Wáiwai: Fock 1963:6–7, 9; Others: Birdsell 1971:340–341; Ferguson 1989a:196.

10. Dentan 2004.

11. Wright 1942.

12. Wright 1942; Gardner 1966; Dick 1992; Hockings 1992:15, 17; Raghaviah 1962.

13. Gardner 1966, 2000a, 2000b, 2004; Sinha 1972.

14. Gorer 1967.

15. Hockings 1980, 1992:15, 17; Murdock 1934:110; Rivers 1986; Walker 1992:297; Wolf 1992:137.

16. Montagu 1976:268–269.

17. See Tonkinson 1978:2004.

18. Wright 1942.

19. Reyna 1994.

20. Boehm 1999, 2000.

21. See Haas 2001; Hobhouse et al. 1915; Johnson & Earle 1987; Leavitt 1977; Malinowski 1941; Simmons 1937; Reyna 1994; Dennen 1995: Chapter 2; Wright 1942:66. Regarding the cross-cultural relationship between war and subsistence patterns (for instance, foraging or practicing agriculture), Ember & Ember 1997:5 reach the mixed conclusion that "foragers in the ethnographic record had warfare fairly often on average, but they do seem to have had less than nonforagers." The first part of this interpretation must be evaluated in light of the Embers' use of a broad definition of war that counts feuding and certain kinds of revenge killings as acts of war (see chapters 7 and 14 for further discussion).

22. Dennen 1995:142.

23. Haas 2001:343. Haas 2001 does not view complexity in and of itself as a cause of war, nor do I. Haas 2001:343 writes, "Warfare is an integral part of the power structure, organization, and operation of all early chiefdom and state societies recognizable in the archaeological record. Chiefs and state rulers used warfare and the associated military apparatus to exercise power at home and to expand/defend their boundaries against outside enemies—real or perceived. The

higher frequency of warfare in states and chiefdoms is not necessarily a product of organizational complexity; rather, the economic and demographic conditions that are conducive to warfare also are conducive to the development of complex, centralized polities."

24. Reyna 1994.

25. Thomas 1959.

26. Malinowski 1941:538.

27. Reyna 1994.

28. Reyna 1994:40.

29. Chagnon 1988.

30. Buck 1957:417; Hickson 1986:284; Reyna 1994:44; Service 1978:268–272.

31. Mead 1961b, 1969.

32. Carneiro 1990:199, 200, 205; the quote is from page 199.

33. Binford 2001:219; Ferguson 1984b; Kelly 1995:302; Service 1971a:143–145, 1971b: 207, 1978.

34. Knauft 1991.

35. Service 1971b, the quote is from pages 207–208; Ferguson 1984b.

36. Ferguson 1984b:272.

37. Kelly 1995:293, italics added.

38. Kelly 1995:293, italics added; see also Binford 2001:432.

39. For example, Gat 2000a, 2000b; Goldstein 2001:24.

40. Kelly 1995.

41. Murdock & White 1969; White 1989.

42. Murdock 1967, 1981.

43. Murdock 1967, 1981.

44. Prosterman 1972. Classifying the societies in the sample as either *warring* or *nonwarring* was straightforward for the overwhelming majority, but there were a few exceptions. The Yurok of California, basically complex hunter-gatherers, deserve mention as a comparatively *simple, complex* hunter-gatherer society. On the basis of ethnographic descriptions, I classified the Yurok as *warring,* noting for instance that on occasion one *village* fought with another *village*. This type of fighting seemed closer to the definition of war than feud. At the same time, several ethnographers—including Spier 1930:24; Elmendorf 1974:466, note 4; and Kroeber 1953:49—state that the Yurok did *not* have true war but, for the most part, only engaged in feuding between kin groups or in "private quarrels." However, this fighting cost lives and on occasion resulted in the burning of entire villages, as reported by Kroeber 1953:51. This case represents a judgment call, obviously, but the scale of the fighting and mention of some village-versus-village fighting tilted my decision toward a *warring* classification rather than considering the aggression to be simply feuding (*nonwarring*).

Several cases involving simple nomadic hunter-gatherers (specifically, the Aweikoma, Botocudo, and Gilyak) that were coded as *warring* also merit special mention, *because the type of fighting may actually have constituted only self-redress or feuding*. If this is true, *nonwarring* actually would be the appropriate classification. Unfortunately, the descriptions are not clear-cut enough to determine with certainty the presence of war, feuding, self-redress, or some combination of these, so, *conservatively*—that is, against my predictions—these simple nomadic societies were rated as *warring* even though the actual evidence for war is sketchy or ambiguous.

45. If the five equestrian hunter-gatherer societies are dropped from the analysis, the results of a Fisher's exact test for warring/nonwarring by simple foragers/complex foragers is also statistically significant ($p = .0017$, one-tailed).

46. Leacock 1978:249.

47. Henry 1941:55.

48. Shternberg 1933:247.

49. Haida: Murdock 1934:241; see also Swanton 1975; Klamath: M. Martin 1991:192; see also Spier 1930; Comanche and Chiricahua Apache: Hoebel 1967a, 1967b; Basso 1971: for example, page 20; Wallace & Hoebel 1952.

50. Reyna 1994.

51. Renner 1993:50; see also Sivard 1993.

52. Chagnon 1988:987.

53. Reyna 1994:49.

54. Fry 2006.

55. Tikopia: Firth 1957:396–397; Nootka: Ferguson 1984b:289.

56. See Black 1993; Brown 1991:138; Greenhouse 1985.

57. Semai: Robarchek 1997; Hawaiians: Shook 1985; Indians on Fiji: Brenneis 1990; Buid: Gibson 1989:66; Finland: Takala 1998; Norway: Dobinson 2004; United States: McCormick 1988.

58. Fry 2000, 2001a, 2001b, 2004a.

59. Brögger 1968:231.

60. Boehm 1987:159.

61. Hobhouse et al. 1915:71; the quote is from page 254.

62. Hoebel 1967b:327, italics added.

63. Hobhouse et al. 1915; Hoebel 1967b; Ericksen & Horton 1992:73–74.

64. Chagnon 1988:990.

65. See Knauft 1991:405.

66. See Kelly 2000.

67. Kelly 2000:47.

68. Kelly 2000.

69. Kelly 2000; for example, see Du Bois 1960.

70. Gusinde 1937:898–905; Janetski 1991:362; Kelly 2000; Peterson 1991:375.

71. Lee 1979:382–396.

72. Lee 1979:389.

73. Lee 1979.

74. Fry 2006.

75. For example, Black 1993; Boehm 1987; Ericksen & Horton 1992; Hobhouse et al. 1915; Hoebel 1967b; Malinowski 1941; Reyna 1994; Dennen 1995.

76. Brögger 1968.

77. Rubin et al. 1994.

78. Fry 2000, 2001a, 2001b.

79. Hoebel 1967a:193.

80. Chagnon 1988.

81. Reyna 1994.

CHAPTER 9: PARADISE DENIED: A BIZARRE CASE OF SKULLDUGGERY

1. Dennen 1995:497.
2. Wrangham & Peterson 1996:63.
3. Wrangham & Peterson 1996:108–109.
4. Fry 1998.
5. Wrangham & Peterson 1996:108.
6. Wrangham & Peterson 1996:84.
7. See Sussman 1999:124–127.
8. Freeman 1983.

9. Montagu 1978a; Howell & Willis 1989; Bonta 1993; Sponsel & Gregor 1994; Wrangham & Peterson 1996:75.

10. Sussman 1999:126–127.

11. Wrangham & Peterson 1996:81.

12. Ferguson 1997:338.

13. See Rivers 1986:5–6, 628; also see Bird 1987:177; Hockings 1992:15.

14. Hockings 1992:17; Murdock 1934:110; Walker 1992:297; Wolf 1992:137.

15. Rivers 1986:628.

16. Wrangham & Peterson 1996:81.

17. Otterbein 1970:20.

18. For instance, see Lutz 1988:19.

19. Huntingford 1951:1, 2–7, 48, 1954:124.

20. Damas 1991:76.

21. Irwin 1990.

22. Wrangham & Peterson 1996:104.

23. Lesser 1967; Montagu 1978a, 1978b, 1994; Sponsel 1996a, 1996b.

24. Freeman 1983; Wrangham & Peterson 1996.

25. Mead 1973:202.

26. Freeman 1983:89, 165, and 173.

27. Freeman 1983:157.

28. Freeman's 1983 footnote, on page 335, for the quoted paragraph reads as follows: "M. Mead, *Sex and Temperament in Three Primitive Societies,* in *From the South Seas,* (New York, 1939), 285; idem, review of Samoa under the Sailing Gods by N. A. Rowe, *The Nation* 133 (1931): 138; idem, *Male and Female* (Harmondsworth, 1962, orig. 1950), 220, 360."

29. Mead 1963.

30. Mead 1963:285, italics added.

31. Freeman 1983:157, italics added.

32. Mead 1961b:309–310.

33. Mead 1961b:310.

34. Mead 1961b:299.

35. Mead 1973:44.

36. Mead 1973:53.

37. Mead 1973:71; see also pages 33, 77.

38. Freeman 1983:157; Mead 1931.

39. Mead 1931:138.

40. Mead 1931:138; Freeman 1983:157, 165; Wrangham & Peterson 1996:102, 105.

41. Mead 1931:138.

42. See Côté 1994; Shankman 1996, 2000.

43. For example, Caton 1990; Côté 2000a, 2000b; Ember 1985; Feinberg 1988; Grant 1995; Holmes 1987; Marshall 1993; Scheper-Hughes 1984; Schwartz 1983; Weiner 1983; but see as exceptions: Côté 1994, for instance pages 14–15; Feinberg 1988.

44. See Mead 1961b:302, note 2; 1969:168; Freeman 1983.

45. Freeman 1983; Mead 1969:168.

46. Mead 1969:168.

47. Mead 1961b:302, note 2.

48. For example, Mead 1961b, 1969.

49. For example, Mead 1973:12, 199, 1961b:282, 1950:405, 406; see Ember 1985; Holmes 1987:148–151.

50. Mead 1973:199.

51. Wrangham & Peterson 1996:104, italics added.

52. For example, Mead 1973:146, 1950:405.

53. Daly & Wilson 1988:282.
54. Wrangham & Peterson 1996; Freeman 1983; Wrangham & Peterson 1996:104.
55. Shankman 1996:555.

CHAPTER 10: RE-CREATING THE PAST IN OUR OWN IMAGE

1. Carl Sagan quoted in Clark 2002:50.
2. For example, Pottenger 1938, 1948.
3. Pottenger 1952:67, 68, 69–70, italics added.
4. Low 1993:13.
5. Lewin 1987:47–84; Weiss & Mann 1990:317–322.
6. Joseph Birdsell quoted in Dennen 1995:199; Dart 1949, 1953, 1958; see also Roper 1969:430–433, 449.
7. Dart 1953:207.
8. Dart 1949:5.
9. Dart 1949:13–14; see Brain 1970.
10. Ury 1999:33.
11. Dart 1949:12.
12 Dart 1949:38.
13. Dart 1949:38.
14. Dart 1953:209.
15. For example, Ardrey 1961, 1966.
16. Roper 1969:432–433.
17. Brain 1970.
18. John Durant quoted in Lewin 1987:312.
19. Ury 1999:33.
20. See Dennen 1995:199; Ury 1999:31–33; Walker 2001.
21. Smith 1997.
22. Maschner 1997.
23. Keeley 1996:ix.
24. See also Marcus 1992:391–394; Sabloff 1990:52–53.
25. Binford & Ho 1985.
26. Bahn 1992:330.
27. Stiner 1991; White & Toth 1991.
28. Stiner 1991:116.
29. White & Toth 1991:123.
30. White & Toth 1991; Stiner 1991; Dennen 1995:207.
31. Ury 1999:34.
32. White & Toth 1989:367.
33. Sponsel 1996b:105.
34. Roper 1975:304–309.
35. Roper 1975.
36. Richards 1975:342, 343, emphasis in original; Roper 1975.
37. Richards 1975:343.
38. Bar-Yosef 1986.
39. Bar-Yosef 1986:161.
40. Bar-Yosef 1986:161.
41. Keeley 1996:39, italics added; Roper 1969; see also Haas 2001.
42. Otterbein 1997.
43. Keeley 1996:36–39.

44. Otterbein 1997:271.
45. Kelly 2000:157, italics added.
46. Binford 2001; Kelly 1995:302.
47. Knauft 1991:392.
48. Service 1971a:143, 1971b.
49. Kelly 1995:294; see also Knauft 1991.
50. Knauft 1991:392; see also Alvard & Kuznar 2001:295; Cohen 1985; Henry 1985.
51. Alvard & Kuznar 2001:295; Cohen 1985:100; Henry 1985:366; Kelly 1995:304; Knauft 1991:392.
52. Henry 1985:365.
53. Henry 1985:365.
54. Brown & Price 1985:437; see Soffer 1985.
55. Henry 1985.
56. Henry 1985:376.
57. Maschner 1997.
58. Maschner 1997:293–294.
59. Maschner 1997:270.
60. Roper 1975:300.
61. Roper 1975.
62. Roper 1975:323.
63. Roper 1975:324.
64. John Garstang quoted in Roper 1975:326.
65. Roper 1975:329.
66. Haas 1999:16.
67. Haas 1999.
68. Haas 1999:19.
69. Haas 1999:21.
70. Flannery & Marcus 2003.
71. Flannery & Marcus 2003:11,805.
72. Haas 2001.
73. Keeley 1996.
74. Haas 1996:1360.
75. Roper 1969:448; see also Roper 1975.
76. Kelly 2000; Keeley 1996:39; Haas 1996:1360; Roper 1969:448; as well as Boehm 1999:94–95; Ferguson 1997, 2000; Otterbein 1997; Sponsel 1996b; Ury 1999.
77. Kelly 2000:1, 2.
78. See Haas 2001.
79. Ferguson 2000:6.
80. Haas 1999:13, 2001; Hobhouse et al. 1915; Johnson & Earle 1987; Leavitt 1977; Malinowski 1941; Simmons 1937; Reyna 1994; Wright 1942:66.
81. Ferguson 1997:322, 326.
82. Sponsel 1996b:104, emphasis in original.
83. Keeley 1996:39.

CHAPTER 11: CULTURAL PROJECTIONS

1. Jung 1983:242.
2. Bird 1946:71, italics added.
3. Goodale 1974:133–134, italics added.

4. Karok society blended simple and complex hunter-gatherer characteristics—see Bright 1978 and Murdock 1967. Traditionally, the Karok subsisted on a combination of gathering, fishing, and hunting and lived in relatively permanent villages along the Klamath River in Northern California. Food was abundant. In terms of complex features, salmon fishing was more important than hunting, and the Karok spent most of the year in villages located near the river. The Karok also ranked people in terms of wealth, assessed by possession of items like shells, woodpecker scalps, and obsidian knife blades. In terms of simple hunter-gatherer features, leadership was undeveloped and there were no chiefs, egalitarian values coexisted alongside the prestige attained through having wealth, and some seasonal movement of small camps of people corresponded with the collecting of the annual acorn harvest. In sum, the Karok had some features that are *atypical* of simple nomadic hunter-gatherers generally.

5. Bright 1978:185, italics added.

6. Hart & Pilling 1979:81–82; Burbank 1992:266, 1994:35.

7. Burbank 1992:266.

8. Bright 1978:185; see also Bright 1991:177.

9. For example, see Cooper 1946b:117–118; Lebzelter 1934:30; Spencer & Gillen 1927; Warner 1969.

10. Service 1966:60.

CHAPTER 12: ABORIGINAL AUSTRALIA: A CONTINENT OF UNWARLIKE HUNTER-GATHERERS

1. Tonkinson 1978:11–12.

2. Service 1966:103; Tonkinson 1978:1–6; Walsh 1993:1; White & Mulvaney 1987:115–117.

3. Birdsell 1971:337–339, 345; Tonkinson 1978:3.

4. Service 1966:104.

5. Tonkinson 1978:6.

6. Tonkinson 1978:6.

7. Hoebel 1967b:301.

8. Hoebel 1967b:301–302; see Hiatt 1968.

9. Hiatt 1968:101.

10. Tonkinson 1978:14.

11. Tonkinson 1978:18.

12. Berndt 1965:174; Tonkinson 1978:140.

13. Prosterman 1972:140–141.

14. Berndt & Berndt 1996: Chapter 10; see also Williams 1988.

15. Burbank 1994; Warner 1969.

16. Westermarck 1910:vi.

17. Spencer & Gillen 1927:27–28, italics added.

18. Murdock 1934:45; Service 1971b:18.

19. Williams 1987:31, 39; see also 99, 152–153.

20. See Gat 2000a:27 for a recent reiteration of Warner's 1969 interchangeable use of *war* and *feud* for the Murngin; see also Goodale 1974:133–134 and Hart & Pilling 1979 on the Tiwi; Spencer & Gillen 1927: 447 on the Arunta.

21. Warner 1969:144–179, quote is from page 155, italics added.

22. Berndt & Berndt 1996:358.

23. Williams 1987; Warner 1969:148.

24. Warner 1969:155.

25. Warner 1969:155–156.

26. Warner 1969: quote is from page 162, see pages 161–163; see also Berndt & Berndt 1996:358.

27. Hart & Pilling 1979:85.

28. Berndt 1972:203; Tonkinson 1978:118, 127; see also Tonkinson 2004.

29. Meggitt 1965:245–246.

30. Birdsell 1971:341.

31. Meggitt 1965:245–246.

32. Horton 1994:1153.

33. Davie 1929:52.

34. Wheeler 1910:149; Service 1966:103.

35. Berndt & Berndt 1996:362; Hoebel 1967b:306; Berndt 1978:159; Berndt 1965:202.

36. Birdsell 1971:341.

37. See Birdsell 1971:340–341; Berndt & Berndt 1996. In my opinion, when Gat 2000a emphasizes Australian Aborigine *warfare,* he does not weigh the totality of the evidence. Instead, he cites *exceptions* as if they represent a typical pattern for Australia. Additionally, he does not clearly distinguish between war and other forms of violence such as homicide and revenge killings. This is why Gat's perspective on Australian Aborigine *warfare* is at odds with what others who have examined this issue in depth have concluded, for example, Catherine Berndt 1978; Ronald Berndt 1965; Birdsell 1971; Davie 1929; Hoebel 1967b; Service 1966; Westermarck 1910; Wheeler 1910. Gat 2000a:23–24 refers to the atypical Walbiri waterhole "war of conquest" from Meggitt's 1965 book (which occurred after the disruption of the native population by Europeans) in such a way that implies that such events were *common* in Aboriginal Australia. Additionally, Gat 2000a:27 overlooks the personal, homicidal nature of most of the so-called Murngin warfare, granted, something that might be easy to do given Warner's 1969 inconsistent and contradictory use of terminology, as pointed out in the chapter.

38. Berndt 1965:174.

39. Tonkinson 1978.

40. Berndt 1965:167; Berndt & Berndt 1996; Hoebel 1967b:302–303.

41. Berndt 1965:176; Kaberry 1973:179.

42. For example, Berndt 1965:176, 185; Berndt & Berndt 1996: Chapter 10; Tonkinson 2004:102–104.

43. Elkin 1931; Berndt 1965:185; Berndt & Berndt 1996:346.

44. Berndt 1965:181, 194–197; Berndt & Berndt 1996:350–353; Goodale 1974:133–134; Hart & Pilling 1979:80–87; Kaberry 1973:143–153; Wheeler 1910:134–135, 140–147.

45. For example, Berndt 1965:177; Kaberry 1973:150–151; see also Williams 1987:97, 1988:200.

46. Berndt & Berndt 1996:347; Burbank 1994:32, 69; Hart & Pilling 1979:79–83; Spencer & Gillen 1927:446; Tonkinson 1978:118, 124, 2004:98; Wheeler 1910:135–138.

47. For example, Berndt 1965:187–190; Berndt & Berndt 1945:262–266, 1996:349–350; Warner 1969:163–165.

48. Example 1 is from Elkin 1931.

49. Elkin 1931:197.

50. Example 2 is from Hart & Pilling 1979:83–87.

51. Wheeler 1910:140–147, 148.

52. Wheeler 1910; see also Berndt & Berndt 1996: Chapter 10.

53. Warner 1969:179 (italics added) reaches a similar conclusion about the Murngin: "The history of the feud shows clearly that although clan solidarity is of considerable importance, and at times it is even possible that two or more clans may ally themselves for a short period, *the kinship system tends to break down these solidarities and make a feud almost the activity of one individual.*"

Turning to a different issue, is Hart & Pilling's 1979 use of language poetic or just plain confusing? Otterbein 1968 coded the Tiwi as having infrequent *external war* and frequent *internal war* (see chapter 7 and also Otterbein 1970). A careful reading of the Tiwi material, as just quoted in length, suggests that Otterbein (or his student coders) actually misinterpreted juridical fighting—that is, conflict resolution—as internal war. Otterbein defines internal war as armed conflict between political communities within the same culture. Hart & Pilling, however, conclude that the Tiwi did not and could not wage war, band versus band as political communities. It is understandable that such a misunderstanding could happen in light of Hart & Pilling's 1979:83–87 poetic and apparent contradictory use of language. For example, as we have just seen, they sometimes put the words *war* and *battle* in quotes and at other times do not, they sometimes refer to *so-called battles* and other times simply *battles,* and finally, under the chapter subheading "Warfare," they arrive at the paradoxical conclusion that warfare did not occur. However, when read carefully in its entirety, Hart & Pilling's portrayal corresponds with Wheeler's conclusion that such events are juridical in nature. Reyna 1994:57, note 10, independently suggests a similar conclusion. Hart & Pilling 1979 themselves, by the way, use legal terminology in their description (for example, "the rules of Tiwi procedure," on page 84) and categorized the whole topic (including the subsection "Warfare") under the label "Legal Affairs" (page 79). Otterbein's 1999:799 recent comments on the Tiwi, however, side-step this central point. The fact that the Tiwi used sneak attacks during *blood feuds,* for example, seems fairly clear—see Pilling 1968:158; Hart, Pilling, & Goodale 1988:93–95—and is *not* the issue here. As noted earlier in this chapter, Warner's 1969 (see also Spencer & Gillen 1927:447) description of Murngin revenge seeking and juridical processes also uses the same type of confusing terminology in a chapter dubiously titled "Warfare"—see his Chapter VI.

54. Example 3 is from Berndt & Berndt 1945:262–266; see also Tonkinson 1978:119.

55. Berndt & Berndt 1945:263.

56. Berndt & Berndt 1945:262.

57. Berndt & Berndt 1945:265.

58. Berndt 1965:174; Hart & Pilling 1979; Meggitt 1965:245; Warner 1969:163; Wheeler 1910:116.

59. Berndt & Berndt 1996:340–341; Meggitt 1965:246; Service 1966:105.

60. Berndt 1965:170, 172, 203; Berndt 1978:159; Birdsell 1971:349, 353, 357; Elkin 1931: for instance, see pages 197–198; Hart & Pilling 1979:85–86; McKnight 1986:146; Myers 1982:181; Service 1966:104; Tonkinson 1978:6, 2004; Warner 1969: for example, see pages 145–146; Wheeler 1910:160 and Chapter V.

61. Berndt & Berndt 1996; for example, see pages 145–146; Birdsell 1971:351–352, 357; Hart & Pilling 1979:84–85; Meggitt 1965:242, 246; Tonkinson 1978:118, 2004.

62. Berndt 1978:159; Berndt & Berndt 1996:140; Birdsell 1971; Doolan 1979; Kaberry 1973:179; Meggitt 1965:42, 241; Wheeler 1910:65, 86.

63. Birdsell 1971:339–350; Myers 1982: for example, see page 184; Williams 1982: for example, see pages 148–151; Wheeler 1910:66–69.

64. Berndt 1965:174, 185–190, 202, 204–205, 1972:203; Berndt & Berndt 1945:260–266, 1996: Chapter 10; Elkin 1931; Kaberry 1973: for example, see pages 143–153; Meggitt 1965:251–263; Spencer & Gillen 1927: Chapter 18; Tonkinson 1978: Chapter 6, 2004; Warner 1969: for example, see pages 156–157, 163–165; Wheeler 1910:130–147; Williams 1987.

65. Berndt 1965:176, 1972:199, 203; Elkin 1931:194; Goodale 1974:132–133; Kaberry 1973:179; McKnight 1986:146–147; Meggitt 1965:242, 245–246; Spencer & Gillen 1927: Chapter 18; Warner 1969:148.

66. See Berndt 1978:158; Berndt 1965:173, 178, 190–191; Berndt & Berndt 1996: Chapter 10; Birdsell 1971:347, 351; Elkin 1931:197; Spencer & Gillen 1927: Chapter 18; Warner 1969: 166–179; Wheeler 1910:130, 148–165.

CHAPTER 13: WAR-LADEN SCENARIOS OF THE PAST: UNCOVERING A HEAP OF FAULTY ASSUMPTIONS

1. Bicchieri 1972:iii, iv–v.
2. Alexander 1979:222–230; 1987:78–79, 107–110.
3. Alexander 1979:222, 223; see also Alexander 1987:107.
4. For example, Alexander 1987:78–79, 104, 107–108, 110.
5. Shaw & Wong 1989:17, see also pages 3–9, 14–15.
6. Shaw & Wong 1989:50.
7. Shaw & Wong 1989:14.
8. Shaw & Wong 1989:50, italics added.
9. Shaw & Wong 1989:54, italics added.
10. Low 1993:19.
11. Low 1993:43, see also page 20.
12. Low 1993:36.
13. Wrangham & Peterson 1996.
14. Wrangham & Peterson 1996:25.
15. Ghiglieri 1999, quotes are from pages 161, 163 (italics in original), and 162.
16. Ghiglieri 1999:160–161, italics in original.
17. Ghiglieri 1999:165, 197.
18. Ghiglieri 1999:197, italics in original.
19. Ghiglieri 1999:196.
20. Ghiglieri 1999:196.
21. See Tooby & Cosmides 1990; Williams 1966.
22. See also Borgia 1980:183–185; Gat 2000a, especially pages 24–25.
23. Ferguson 2000:11.
24. Boehm 1999:13; see also Boehm 2005; Marlowe 2002:271.
25. Wolf 2001:197; Woodburn 1988.
26. Kent 2002:1; Woodburn 1988.
27. See Boehm 1999, 2000, 2005; Kelly 2000; Knauft 1991; Murdock 1968. The Spanish introduced the horse into the Americas some 500 years ago—see Métraux 1946b:202–203. Some of the North American cultures that adopted the horse for hunting some 300 years ago were sedentary agriculturalists prior to contact—see Hoebel 1967b:289; Kehoe 1999. Following Murdock 1968 and Knauft 1991, among others, I think it is critically important *not* to lump complex horse-riding hunters or sedentary, socially hierarchical fisherfolk together with simple nomadic hunter-gatherers, as does Ember 1978, for example (see Chapter 14, this volume, for details). Especially for the purposes of reconstructing past lifeways, we should draw analogies from simple foragers, rather than from more complex and relatively recent cultural forms.
28. Boehm 1999:13, 95, 221, 2005; Knauft 1991:392; Marlowe 2002:248, 271; Sponsel 1996b:104.
29. Boehm, 2005; quote is from Foley 1992:338, italics added.
30. Haas 2001; Roper 1969; Boehm 1999; Ury 1999.
31. For example, see Service 1971a; for other studies see Barnard 1983:195–197; Hiatt 1968; Ingold 1999.
32. Barnard 1983:196.
33. Knauft 1991:405.
34. Hoebel 1967b:293.
35. Shaw & Wong 1989:14–15.
36. For example: Binford 2001; Birdsell 1971:348–357; Downs 1966:51, 54; Guenther 2002; Hart & Piling 1979; Netting 1986:13–17; Silberbauer 1972; Tonkinson 1978:49; Woodburn 1982.

37. Turnbull 1968a:132.

38. Lee & DeVore 1968a:9.

39. Barnard 1983:196.

40. See Arcand 1999:98–99 on the Aché; Damas 1968 on Inuit societies; Downs 1966:45, 49 on the Washo; Endicott 1988 on the Batek Semang; Gardner 1972:404–405, 422, 2000b, on the Paliyan; Helm 1968, 1972 on the Dogrib; Hill 1994:4 on the Aché; Kaare & Woodburn 1999:202 and Woodburn 1968b, 1982 on the Hadza; Lee 1979, 1993 on the !Kung; Morris 1977, 1982 on the Hill Pandaram; Ray 1980:109–110 on the Sanpoil; Silberbauer 1972 on the G/wi; Smith 1981:276 on the Chipewyan; Thomas, Pendleton, & Cappannari 1986:276 on the Western Shoshone; Turnbull 1968a on the Mbuti; Fürer-Haimendorf 1985:10 on the Chenchu; Williams 1968 on the Birhor; and on various societies, see Birdsell 1971:351 and Woodburn 1982.

41. Ingold 1999:403, italics added; see also Boehm 1999:36–37; Gardner 1991; Helm 1961, 1972:56; Jochim 1996:625; Knauft 1991:397, 402; Lee & DeVore 1968a:7–9; Woodburn 1982.

42. Smith 1981:273, 276.

43. Downs 1966:54.

44. Radcliffe-Brown 1922:82; see also Hoebel 1967b:301–302 on the Aborigines of Central Australia; Warner 1969:179 on the Murngin; Hart & Pilling 1979, for instance page 89, on the Tiwi.

45. Birdsell 1971:357.

46. For example, see Gardner 1966:403–404, Jochim 1996:626, and, for specific examples, Kelly 2000:141 on the Cree raiding the Slavey; Krech 1991:139 on the Hare's fear of the Inuit; Lips 1947:399 on the hostility between Montagnais-Naskapi and the Eskimo and Iroquois; Downs 1966:52–54 on the Washo's reaction to trespassers; and Warner 1969:161–162 on the Murngin *gaingar,* a group fight among clans.

47. Boehm 2005, Foley 1992.

48. See Birdsell 1971:341; Driver 1969:309; Ferguson 1990a, 1995; Ferguson & Whitehead 1992a; Guenther 2002; Helm 1956:131–132; Kelly 2000:141; Kent 2002:8; Marlowe 2002; Reid 1991:245; Smith 1991:80; Woodburn 1988.

49. Driver 1969:309.

50. Kelly & Fowler 1986:368–369.

51. Birdsell 1971:349; see also Murdock 1934:45, italics added; Tonkinson 1978:116.

52. Jochim 1996:625.

53. Lee 1993; see also Wiessner 1982.

54. Downs 1966:51; see also Kelly & Fowler 1986:368–369; Radcliffe-Brown 1922:82.

55. For example, Gusinde 1937; Hoebel 1967b: Chapter 12.

56. Lee & Daly 1999:1.

57. Steward 1968:333–334; see also Turnbull 1968b:341; Knauft 1991:402; Gowdy 1999:397.

58. See also Service 1966:55, 60; Reyna 1994.

59. For example, Clastres 1972:165; Gusinde 1937:633–634, 885; Holmberg 1969:132; Ray 1980:110; Hawes 1903.

CHAPTER 14: MORE FAULTY ASSUMPTIONS

1. Foley 1992:335.

2. See note 44 in chapter 8, this volume.

3. Ember 1978; both quotes are from page 443.

4. Goldstein 2001:24, italics in original.

5. Sponsel 1996b:110.

6. Ember 1978.

7. Ember & Ember 1971:578, italics added.

8. Ember 1978:443, also Table 5.

9. Llewellyn & Hoebel 1941; Secoy 1992; see also Ewers 1967.

10. Fried 1973:360; Hoebel 1967b; Leacock 1982; Newcomb 1950; Secoy 1992; see also Métraux 1946b:202–203.

11. Ember 1978; Hoebel 1967b:129; see also Fried 1973:360.

12. Newcomb 1950:328.

13. Ember 1978.

14. See Binford 2001:219; Kelly 1995: Table 8-1 on page 294.

15. The sedentary, semi-sedentary, and class stratification ratings are from Murdock's 1967 cross-cultural codes. Specifically, code "V" in column 30 of Murdock's codes applies to the three sedentary societies, code "T" for column 30 applies to the five semi-sedentary societies, and either a "D" or a "W" code in column 69 indicates class stratification for seven societies out of the eight.

16. For example, see Binford 2001; Kelly 1995:294 (Table 8-1); Knauft 1991; but also see Murdock 1968. To forestall any confusion, Kelly's 1995:23 (and see also his corresponding endnote 17 in his Chapter 1) discussion of "hunter-gatherer" fighting and raiding is directed toward *complex hunter-gatherers,* such as the Nootka, Haida, Tlingit, Tsimshian, and other North American Northwest coastal groups, and thus his comment about violence on page 23 must be contextualized in light of his assessment of warfare in Chapter 8 of the same book.

17. For example, see Alexander 1979:222–230; Goldstein 2001:24; Ghiglieri 1999:164; Keeley 1996:31; Wrangham & Peterson 1996:75.

18. For example, of the aforementioned five sources, only Goldstein 2001 also cites the earlier article, that is, Ember & Ember 1971, the source that contains the definition of war not provided in Ember's 1978 study itself.

19. Lee 1979:347.

20. Hoebel 1967b:290.

21. Holmberg 1969:17; Meggitt 1965:246; Fürer-Haimendorf 1985:12.

22. Jochim 1996:625; see also Binford 2001; Kelly 1995.

23. Gowdy 1999:392; Netting 1986:9–13.

24. Arcand 1999:98; Gowdy 1999:393; Lee 1993:41, 56–60; see also Kelly 1995:21, Table 1.1.

25. Kent 2002; Netting 1986:10.

26. Lee 1993:60.

27. Gowdy 1999:392.

28. Shaw & Wong 1989.

29. See Lee 1979.

30. Lee & DeVore 1968a:12.

31. Shaw & Wong 1989.

32. Wolf 2001:196.

33. Kelly 1995: Chapters 5 & 8.

34. Kelly 1995:189; see also Birdsell 1971; Cashdan 1983.

35. Wheeler 1910:67; see also Birdsell 1971:346.

36. Birdsell 1971:355; Boehm 1999:183, 2005; Knauft 1991:393–394; Hobhouse 1956:114; Ingold 1999; Lee & Daly 1999:4; Lee & DeVore 1968a:12; for examples, see Balikci 1968; Clastres 1972; Damas 1968; Downs 1966:51; Gurven, Allen-Arave, Hill, & Hurtado 2000; Gusinde 1937:910, 913; Helm 1961; Honigmann 1954:89; Leacock 1954:7, 33; Lee 1993; Marshall 1961; Service 1971b:75; Sluys 2000; Woodburn 1982.

37. Clastres 1972:169.

38. Leacock 1954:7; Lee 1993:88; see also Cashdan 1983; Wiessner 1982; on the Australian Gidjingali: Hiatt 1968:101–102; on the G/wi: Silberbauer 1972:296–304; on the Mardu: Tonkinson 2004.

39. For example, see Birdsell 1971.

40. Birdsell 1971:349, 357; Hoebel 1967b:301–302.

41. See Rubin, Pruitt, & Kim 1994:134–141 for a discussion and citations of empirical studies on the conflict-inhibiting effects of crosscutting ties.

42. Cashdan 1983:48.

43. Binford 2001: Chapter 5.

44. Binford 2001:453.

45. Birdsell 1971:338.

46. Netting 1986:19.

47. Kelly 1995:192–193.

48. Woodburn 1982:435.

49. Steward 1968:334.

50. Ray 1980:110.

51. Woodburn 1982:437; see also Holmberg 1969:132; Honigmann 1954:88.

52. Hawes 1903:300–301; see also Lee 1979:350, 370.

53. Forbes 1885:122; Hobhouse 1956; Morris 1977:230, 237; Sandbukt 1988:111; Holmberg 1969:132; Krech 1991:139, 141.

54. Birdsell 1971:340–341, 348–349; Myers 1982; Williams 1982; Wheeler 1910:66–69; Cooper 1946b:118–119; Lee 1979:337.

55. Hobhouse 1956:105, 106–107; Kelly 2000:141; see also Birdsell 1971:348.

56. C. Berndt 1978:159; R. Berndt 1965:202; Birdsell 1971:340–341; Wheeler 1910: Chapter 4.

57. Endicott 1999.

58. Ghiglieri 1999:197.

59. Endicott 1999:415.

60. Gilberg 1984:585.

61. Cooper 1946a:93; see also Gusinde 1937:462–463, 475, 626–627.

62. Leacock 1981:191.

63. Gardner 1972:422.

64. Lee 1993:85.

65. Endicott 1999:415; for example, see Arcand 1999:99 on the Cuiva; Cooper 1946a:93 on the Yahgan; Fürer-Haimendorf 1985:11 on the Chenchu; Gilberg 1984:585 on the Polar Eskimo; Lee 1993:83–84 on the Ju/'hoansi; Marlowe 2002:266 on the Hadza.

66. Leacock 1981:192.

67. See Martin & Voorhies 1975.

68. For example, Hill 1994:5 on the Aché; Fürer-Haimendorf 1985:11 on the Chenchu; Gardner 1972 on the Paliyan.

69. Holmberg 1969:147.

70. Holmberg 1969:164, 165.

71. Cooper 1946b:115, italics added.

72. For example, see Honigmann 1954:95 on the Kaska; Osgood 1958:63–65 on the Ingalik.

73. Manson & Wrangham 1991 interchangeably use the terms *intergroup aggression, lethal raiding,* and *warfare* as they argue that intergroup aggression occurs over women in some foraging societies. These authors also lump various kinds of disputes over women together, which makes it impossible to determine if anything more organized or more serious than personal grudge resolution over cases of adultery, elopement, and breaking of betrothal promises is being included under their catchall conceptual category *intergroup aggression over women as scarce resources*. For example, Manson & Wrangham 1991:375 report that in four Australian Aborigine foraging societies—the Aranda, Gidjingali, Murngin, and Tiwi—women are the "cause of intergroup aggression." However, readers are not told any of the relevant cultural particulars. My reading of Australian ethnography leads me to suspect that the overwhelming majority of instances of

"adultery, the abduction of women, or failure to deliver a promised bride" (Manson & Wrangham 1991:374) do *not* amount to warfare at all, but actually are *interpersonal* disputes between parties who sometimes happen to be living in different bands (see chapters 11, 12, and 16, this volume). The flexible and "in flux" nature of nomadic band composition discussed in the previous chapter also argues against *warring* over women. Furthermore, especially in light of the well-documented egalitarian status of women and men in nomadic hunter-gatherer societies, I must wonder if what Manson & Wrangham call *abduction,* more often than not, amounts to what might better be called *seduction, elopement,* or *divorce*—in other words, events in which the women are *coparticipants* in liaisons rather than the mere *victims* of abduction during "intergroup aggression" or "lethal raiding," as implied by these authors. A variety of ethnographic accounts on simple foragers show women's choice in such matters—see chapter 16, this volume; Berndt 1965; Cooper 1946b:118; Marlowe 2002:266.

To mention a specific society in Manson & Wrangham's sample, as we saw in chapters 11 and 12, Tiwi men become embroiled in *personal* disputes over betrothals, the affairs of their wives, and so on. But clearly these are disputes between *individual* men over *particular* women. To imply that the Tiwi engage in *intergroup aggression* (or *war* or *lethal raiding*) over women as scarce resources is to misrepresent the nature of these disputes and to ignore how such complaints are dealt with under Tiwi legal procedure. In sum, various implicit assumptions congruent with the Pervasive Intergroup Hostility Model yet incongruent with ethnographic descriptions of nomadic bands appear in Manson & Wrangham's 1991 article.

74. Boehm 1999:67, 2000, 2005; Helm 1956; Kelly 1995; Service 1966:51; Woodburn 1982.

75. Woodburn 1982:444.

76. Leacock 1978:249.

77. See Boehm 1999:71, 112; Service 1966:51; Woodburn 1982:445.

78. On the proposed evolutionary selection for leadership, see, for example, Ghiglieri 1999:196; Low 1993:35, 40.

79. Cooper 1946b:116.

80. Boehm 1999:208.

81. Nomadic hunter-gatherers come together periodically to conduct joint ceremonies, exchange items they have made, arrange marriages, socialize, and so forth. Subsequently, small groups disperse once again—for instance, see Birdsell 1971:347. Lee 1979:360–361 notes that such a concentration–dispersion pattern has been observed among Australian Aborigines, North American sub-Arctic groups, foragers of the Great Basin, African Mbuti and Ju/'hoansi foragers, and other simple hunter-gatherers. The central point, according to Lee 1979, is that this coming together and separating pattern facilitates reciprocal access to important resources. Lee 1979:361 concludes, "The concentration–dispersion pattern with its flexibility of group structure and rules of reciprocal access reveals the underlying spatial dynamic of the foraging mode of production. Such a dynamic makes much more sense of the foragers' adaptation than does the patrilocal band model."

82. Gardner 1966:402–403.

CHAPTER 15: MUCH ADO ABOUT THE YANOMAMÖ

1. Blanchard & Blanchard 1989:94.

2. John Durant is quoted in chapter 10, this volume; see Lewin 1987:312; see also Fried 1973.

3. Alexander 1979, 1987.

4. Ghiglieri 1999:170, 168.

5. Low 1993.

6. Chagnon 1988, 1990a:51; 1992a.

7. Alexander 1979:53, 178, 215, 242, 252–253; Shaw & Wong 1989:22, 25, 33–34, 52; see also Manson & Wrangham 1991:369.

8. Chagnon 1988; approvingly cited: Low 1993:21, 26, 31; Wrangham & Peterson 1996:64–74; Ghiglieri 1999:144, 192–194; regarding human aggression: see, for example, Buss 1999:300.

9. Chagnon 1988.

10. Chagnon 1988:987.

11. Chagnon 1990b:95, 1992a:205, 1992b:239–240. In one source, Chagnon 1990b:95 (italics added) claims only "over twice" as many wives for the *unokais:* "A recent analysis of marital and reproductive correlates of Yanomamö men who are *unokais* (those who have killed) indicates that they, compared to *same age* non-*unokai,* have over twice as many wives and over three times as many children." In a second publication, Chagnon 1992a:205 (italics added) explains that "*Unokais* (men who have killed) are more successful at obtaining wives and, as a consequence, have more offspring than *men their own age* who are not *unokais*." He specifies that "*Unokais* had, on the average, more than two-and-a-half times as many wives as non-*unokais* and over three times as many children." The wording is essentially the same in Chagnon 1992b:239–240. The calculations presented in Table 15.1 show that these statements apply only to comparisons between the entire two groups, *not same-aged men* (see Ferguson 1995), but more importantly, as we will consider shortly, presenting the findings in this way is extremely misleading because it obscures the fact that the *unokais* are substantially older than the non-*unokais.*

12. For example, see Moore 1990:323.

13. Chagnon 1988; the quotes are from Allman 1988:57.

14. As examples, see Barash 2001:165–174; Booth 1989; Burnham & Phelan 2000:88; Buss 1999:304–305; Campbell 1999:212; Cronk 1999:80; Daly & Wilson 1994:274; Gat 2000a:21, 2000b:75, 76, 87 note 4; Geary 1998:317–318; Ghiglieri 1999:144, 193–194; Harris 1999:185; Low 1993:21, 26, 31; Manson & Wrangham 1991:369, 374; McCarthy 1994:107; Pinker 1997:510; Symons 1990:436–437; Wrangham & Peterson 1996:64–74.

15. Barash 2001.

16. Buss 1999:304–305; Harris 1999:185; Pinker 1997:510.

17. Chagnon 1983:214.

18. Buss 1999:300.

19. Chagnon 1988; for example, Ghiglieri 1999:193–194.

20. Ferguson 1989b, 1995.

21. Chagnon 1988:989, 990; 1990b:95.

22. Chagnon 1988:990.

23. Chagnon 1990b:95.

24. Chagnon 1990b.

25. Chagnon 1988; for example, see Low 1993:26, 31; Buss 1999:305; Harris 1997:185; Pinker 1997:510.

26. Chagnon 1988.

27. Low 1993.

28. Wrangham & Peterson 1996:68.

29. Boehm 1999; see also Marlowe 2002.

30. One study: Chagnon 1988; quote is from Ghiglieri 1999:194. Chagnon himself makes no such claims about the wide applicability of the findings. See Moore 1990.

31. Moore 1990.

32. Moore 1990.

33. Chagnon 1988; Moore 1990.

34. For example, Albert 1989, 1990; Ferguson 1989b, 1995, 2000; Lizot 1994; Robarchek & Robarchek 1998a.

35. Ferguson 1989b, 1995:358–362, 2000.

36. For example, Chagnon 1974, 1979a, 1979b, 1988, 1989, 1992a; Chagnon et al. 1979.

37. Chagnon 1988.

38. Chagnon 1990a:53, 1990b:95, 1992a:205, 1992b:239–240.

39. Ferguson 1989b:564, 1995:359–360.

40. Chagnon 1989; Ferguson 1989b.

41. Chagnon 1988: Tables 2 & 3.

42. Chagnon 1988: Table 3.

43. Suppose you read in the newspaper that 50 percent of dentists reject fluoride treatments. You might be surprised given the widely known benefits of fluoride. However, if the same information were expressed that *one of the two* dentists interviewed by the newspaper reporter rejects fluoride, chances are that you have a different reaction to the information, now knowing that *only two* dentists were consulted. Extremely small samples are more open to the vagaries of chance—sampling error—than are larger groups. We should keep this point in mind regarding *average* numbers of offspring and wives that Chagnon 1988 calculates on the basis of *only five persons*. Furthermore, the manner in which Chagnon 1988 reports his findings suggests an equivalent "weight" to *averages* based on only *five* killers and those calculated for 78 nonkillers. This type of data presentation is misleading. As a minor point of curiosity, it would be interesting to know how the five offspring of these five *unokais* are distributed among these young men. The *average* of 1.00 child each could result, at an extreme, from four childless men and one man with five children (by two wives?). We have no way of knowing about the *distribution* of children based only on an average.

44. Chagnon 1979a:384, Table 14.3.

45. See Chagnon 1988:990.

46. Chagnon 1979a.

47. Presumably >41 actually means ≥41, because there would be no logical reason to drop all the 41-year-old men out of the analysis. Therefore, I add the "±" sign (that is, to read: ">41±") to reflect this ambiguity, and when calculating, I include the 41-year-olds, changing ">41" to "≥41" when appropriate.

48. Chagnon 1988.

49. For example, Chagnon et al. 1979:311; Chagnon 1992a:229.

50. Chagnon 1988: Tables 2 & 3.

51. Chagnon 1988.

52. Chagnon 1990a, 1990b, 1992a, 1992b.

53. This mathematical analysis makes use of the fact that Chagnon has published elsewhere demographic and reproductive data on the same Yanomamö population used in his *unokai* versus non-*unokai* study. This mathematical approach is geared toward providing *estimates* because access to Chagnon's database would be needed to calculate the actual values. Some of the demographic and reproductive data used in the calculations are from a census conducted by Chagnon in 1975, whereas data in his 1988 article reflect a census he conducted *of the same population* in 1987. In using data from both censuses in my calculations, I am making an *explicit assumption* that certain demographic and reproductive values have not markedly changed in the relatively short 12-year period between the two censuses. I do *not* assume all values are identical, but simply that the 1975 data are a reasonable approximation of unavailable 1987 data. The calculations presented later in note 58 suggest that this is a reasonable assumption regarding reproductive success.

54. Chagnon 1988: Table 2.

55. The average age for each age bracket can be estimated by multiplying the midpoint value of the age bracket by the number of men within the age bracket. (This is a conservative approach given the pattern of *within* age-bracket variation suggested by Figures 15.1 and 15.2.) Separate estimates of the average age of the *unokais* and non-*unokais* can then be obtained by adding up

the respective four age bracket products and dividing each sum by the number of men in the relevant group—the usual way to calculate averages, in other words.

Since one age bracket is open-ended (age >41±), the midpoint must be estimated. Demographic data provided in Chagnon et al. 1979:311 (Figure 12.3) on the Yanomamö age and sex pyramid for 1,336 persons show that about 60 percent of the male ≥41 age group would be in their forties, another 25 percent or so in their fifties, and the remaining 15 percent in their sixties and seventies. An estimated average age for the ≥41 age bracket from the Yanomamö demographic data is *50.7* years. This is calculated as follows: For the 40- to 44-year age interval, there are 25 men. To subtract the 40-year-olds (since the interval in question begins with 41-year-olds), assume the 25 men are evenly distributed over this 5-year interval. Therefore, 25 − 5 = 20. This is the only 5-year interval that requires an adjustment in order to estimate the midpoint of the 33-year interval of 41–74 years. There are a total of 71 men between the ages of 41 and 74. Therefore:

Age interval	Number of men		Interval midpoint		Product
41–44	20	×	42.5	=	850
45–49	21	×	47	=	987
50–54	10	×	52	=	520
55–59	9	×	57	=	513
60–64	6	×	62	=	372
65–69	0	×	67	=	0
70–74	5	×	72	=	360

850 + 987 + 520 + 513 + 372 + 360 = 3,602
3,602/71 = 50.7

Therefore, I use 50.7 in my calculations as a plausible midpoint estimate.

The age calculations are as follows:

20- to 24-year age interval midpoint value = 22 years
25- to 30-year age interval midpoint value = 27.5 years
31- to 40-year age interval midpoint value = 35.5 years
estimated ≥41-year age interval midpoint = 50.7 years

Unokais

22 × 5 men = 110
27.5 × 14 men = 385
35.5 × 43 men = 1,526.5
50.7 × 75 men = 3,802.5
110 + 385 + 1,526.5 + 3,802.5 = 5,824
5,824/137 *unokais* = 42.5 years as the estimated average age for *unokais*

Non-*unokais*

22 × 78 men = 1,716
27.5 × 58 men = 1,595
35.5 × 61 men = 2,165.5
50.7 × 46 men = 2,332.2
1,716 + 1,595 + 2,165.5 + 2,332.2 = 7,808.7
7,808.7/243 non-*unokais* = 32.1 years as the estimated average age for non-*unokais*

The difference in estimated average ages therefore is 42.5 – 32.1 = 10.4 years.

For curiosity, I ran a Mann-Whitney U-Test using midpoint age values as the scores for each age interval to see whether a 10.4-year difference in the mean ages of these two groups would be statistically significant. Not surprisingly, the results were extremely significant ($p < .0001$, two-tailed). In other words, due to chance alone, finding an average age difference of 10.4 years between two groups under these estimated circumstances is extremely unlikely—the odds are less than 1 in 10,000. An age difference of this magnitude thus is deemed to be very meaningful, statistically.

56. Ferguson 1995:360.

57. A comparison of census data *for the same population only 12 years apart in time* (1975 and 1987) presents a challenge of interpretation regarding "average numbers of wives." In 1975, the total population was 1,336, as calculated from Chagnon et al. 1979: Figure 12.3. By 1987, the total population was 1,394, as calculated from Chagnon 1988: Table 1, thus showing an increase of 58 persons in 12 years.

Chagnon's 1988: Table 3 data show a pattern wherein the average number of wives increases with age for both *unokais* and non-*unokais* (see also Table 15.1). The data provided by Chagnon 1988: Table 3 allows the average number of wives for the entire population of men (*unokais* and non-*unokais*) together to be calculated, for different minimum ages of men. Note the pattern of increased number of wives as the ages of the subgroups progressively constitute older and older men (see the "Average no. of wives" column) in the following chart:

Age of men	No. of wives	No. of men	Average no. of wives
≥20 years	377	380	0.99
≥25 years	363	297	1.22
≥31 years	319	225	1.42
">41±" years	211	121	1.74

The challenge of interpretation arises if data based on the 1975 census from Chagnon et al. 1979: Table 12.9 are used to calculate a value for "Average no. of wives" for men 35 years of age and older and this value is then compared to the calculations in my table in this note. Logically, based on the averages in my table, a value for average number of wives for men 35 years and older would be expected to fall between the values of 1.42 and 1.74, because age ≥35 years falls between ≥31 years and ≥41± years. However, the value for ≥35 years is not even close to the logical expectation. It is way beyond this range, at 2.57 average number of wives. The calculations are as follows, based on data in Chagnon et al. 1979: Table 12.9 (see also Chagnon et al. 1979: Figure 12.3):

Age of men	No. of wives	No. of men	Average no. of wives
≥35 years	329	128	2.57

Can there be this much change in average number of wives in just 12 years? And if so, why?

58. The average number of children per man per year was estimated by using the information from Chagnon's 1988 article, based on a 1987 census, and also in two other ways—as a check on the estimate—using data from a 1975 census reported in an earlier publication, Chagnon's 1979a. Both censuses pertain to the same population of Yanomamö most intensively studied by Chagnon—see Chagnon 1979a:380, note 5, page 383, Chagnon 1979b:95, and Chagnon 1988:986. Significantly, the two methods based on the earlier census yield virtually identical results as the estimate from the later census.

Method 1: Based on the findings reported in Chagnon 1988 for the 1987 census. This method has the *disadvantage* that there are only four data points—that is, see Chagnon's 1988 Tables 2 & 3—to estimate from, and the *advantage* that the reproduction rate estimate is for the same census year as the rest of the study's data.

Age subgroups for the entire male population 20 years old and over:

20- to 24-year-olds: 5 *unokais* + 78 non-*unokais* = 83 men
25- to 30-year-olds: 14 *unokais* + 58 non-*unokais* = 72 men
31- to 40-year-olds: 43 *unokais* + 61 non-*unokais* = 104 men
>41-year-olds: 75 *unokais* + 46 non-*unokais* = 121 men

Number of offspring per age subgroup for the entire male population 20 years old and over:

20- to 24-year-olds: 5 *unokai* offspring + 14 non-*unokai* offspring = 19 offspring
25- to 30-year-olds: 22 *unokai* offspring + 50 non-*unokai* offspring = 72 offspring
31- to 40-year-olds: 122 *unokai* offspring + 123 non-*unokai* offspring = 245 offspring
>41-year-olds: 524 unokai offspring + 193 non-unokai offspring = 717 offspring
19 offspring/83 men = 0.23
72 offspring/72 men = 1.00
245 offspring/104 men = 2.36
717 offspring/121 men = 5.93

By the way, Chagnon 1990a (Figure 2, page 52) reports the average reproductive success of men in 1988, age *40 years or older,* to be 5.82. This figure is very close to the 5.93 estimate just calculated for men age *41 years or older,* thus corroborating the estimate calculated here. Since the age groups differ by 1 year (40-plus years versus 41-plus years), we would *not* expect *exactly identical* figures.

We can assign each offspring value to the relevant age interval midpoint:

22-year-olds = 0.23 offspring average
27.5-year-olds = 1.00 offspring average
35.5-year-olds = 2.36 offspring average
50.7-year-olds = 5.93 offspring average (the 50.7 midpoint was calculated in note 55)

The midpoints are irregular numbers of years apart from each other, calculated as follows:

27.5 – 22 = 5.5 years difference
35.5 – 27.5 = 8 years difference
50.7 – 35.5 = 15.2 years difference

The differences in average offspring between midpoints are as follows:

1.00 (at age 27.5) – 0.23 (at age 22) = 0.77 in 5.5 years
0.77/5.5 = 0.14 offspring/year
2.36 (at age 35.5) – 1.00 (at age 27.5) = 1.36 in 8 years
1.36/8 = 0.17 offspring/year
5.93 (at age 50.7) – 2.36 (at age 35.5) = 3.57 in 15.2 years
3.57/15.2 = 0.235 offspring/year

A rough estimate of the average number of offspring per man per year results from averaging the three rates:

$$0.14 + 0.17 + 0.235 = 0.545/3 = 0.182 \text{ offspring per year on the average.}$$

Method 2: Based on 1975 census data for the same population discussed in Chagnon 1988. From Figure 15.3, this method takes the average of all possible 10-year differences. That is:

$9.7 - 4.4 = 5.3$
$6.0 - 5.7 = .3$
$4.4 - 4.6 = -.2$
$5.7 - 3.5 = 2.2$
$4.6 - 2.5 = 2.1$
$3.5 - 2.2 = 1.3$
$2.5 - .6 = 1.9$
Then: $5.3 + .3 + (-.2) + 2.2 + 2.1 + 1.3 + 1.9 = 12.9/7 = 1.84$

This yields 1.84 offspring per average 10-year period, or 0.184 offspring per year.

Method 3. Again based on 1975 census data from the same population as discussed in Chagnon 1988. This method simply subtracts the average number of children of the youngest age interval (the 20–24 value of 0.6) from that of the oldest age interval (the 70–74 value of 9.7): 9.7 – 0.6 = 9.1. Taking the difference in age between the midpoints of the two intervals (22 years and 72 years) results in a period of 50 years. That is: 72 – 22 = 50 years. The yearly average over the 50 year period is: 9.1/50 = 0.182.

(As an aside, a comparison of the information in two publications—Chagnon 1979a and Chagnon et al. 1979—reveals that the last three 5-year age groups—spanning 60–74 years—have been combined into one category in the chapter with the reproductive data. If this fact is *not* taken into consideration a slightly higher yearly rate of 0.22 offspring per year is obtained when 9.1 is divided by only 40 instead of 50. In other words, a higher rate of 0.22 offspring per year results from the fact that Chagnon 1979a combined several age intervals. This artificially inflated rate is *not* used in the calculations because it is simply an artifact of combining data from three age groups).

In conclusion, three different methods based on data from the Yanomamö population most intensively studied by Chagnon yield very similar estimates for the average number of offspring per man per year: 0.182, 0.184, and again, 0.182.

59. To make comparable comparisons, we can mathematically reduce the number of non-*unokais* or increase the number of *unokais*. The final corrected ratio of *unokai* offspring to non-*unokai* offspring comes out the same either way. The following calculations reduce the number of non-*unokais* to 137 to be equivalent to the 137 *unokais:* 137/243 = .56379

So:

	Unokais	**Non-*unokais***		
20–24	5	78	×	.56379 = 43.98
25–30	14	58	×	.56379 = 32.70
31–40	43	61	×	.56379 = 34.39
>41±	75	46	×	.56379 = 25.93
Total:	137	243		137.00

60. Chagnon 1988 reports that 243 non-*unokais* have 380 offspring, whereas 137 *unokais* have 673 offspring. To calculate the equivalent number of offspring for 137 non-*unokais:*

137/243 = .56379
.56379 × 380 = 214.24 non-*unokai* offspring for 137 non-*unokais*

Thus 137 non-*unokais* have 214 offspring, whereas the same number of *unokais* have 673 offspring, based on the numbers presented in Table 2 of Chagnon's 1988 original article.

Note that 673/214 yields 3.14, or the "over three times" relationship noted by Chagnon. In numbers of offspring, the "*unokai* advantage" over the non-*unokais* is 459 offspring. That is, 673 *unokai* offspring minus 214 non-*unokai* offspring equals 459 additional *unokai* offspring over non-*unokai* offspring. We can refer to this as the "*unokai* advantage" when both groups are standardized to 137 members each.

61. In order to correct for a difference between the average age of the *unokais* and the average age of the non-*unokais,* we first can calculate how many offspring are attributable to the age difference between the two groups. Second, we can subtract these age-effect offspring from the number of *unokai* offspring. Third, we can calculate the drop in "*unokai* advantage." The following calculations are for the conservative estimate of 10.4 years average age difference between *unokais* and non-*unokais*. A certain number of *unokai* offspring result simply from the older average age of this subgroup. How many *unokai* offspring can be attributed to a 10.4-year average age advantage over the non-*unokais?*

First: In note 58, we calculated that Yanomamö males average between 0.182 and 0.184 children each year. It is conservative to use the slightly smaller figure. Therefore:

.182 (offspring per year) × 10.4 (years) = 1.893 offspring per *unokai* in 10.4 years

Second:

1.893 × 137 (*unokais*) = 259.3, or 259 "extra" offspring due to an average of 10.4 years of "extra" reproductive time for *unokais* over non-*unokais*

To complete the comparison, we next subtract the "extra" offspring from the *unokai* total offspring to compensate for age effects (see note 60).

673 *unokai* offspring for 137 *unokais* − 259 "extra" age effect offspring = 414 *unokai* offspring, versus 214 non-*unokai* offspring

The *unokai* advantage changes as follows:

414 −214 = 200

The ratio of *unokai* offspring to non-*unokai* offspring decreases from the *initial over 3-to-1* to *slightly less than 2-to-1.*

414/214 = 1.93

And the *unokai* advantage decreases as follows:

259/459 = .564

In other words, under the 10.4 years of age correction calculations, 56 percent of the initial "*unokai* advantage" (459 offspring) actually stems from an age effect equivalent to 259 offspring.

62. How many age effect offspring do 137 *unokais* have in 12.4 years?

First:

0.182 (offspring per year) × 12.4 (years) = 2.257 offspring per *unokai* in 12.4 years

Second:

> 2.257 × 137 (*unokais*) = 309.2, or 309 "extra" offspring due to an average of 12.4 years of "extra" reproductive time for *unokais* over non-*unokais*

To complete the comparison, we next subtract the "extra" offspring from the initial number of *unokai* offspring to compensate for age effects (see note 60).

> 673 *unokai* offspring for 137 *unokais* − 309 "extra" age effect offspring = 364 *unokai* offspring, versus 214 non-*unokai* offspring

The *unokai* advantage changes as follows:

> 364 − 214 = 150

The ratio of *unokai* offspring to non-*unokai* offspring decreases from the *initial over 3-to-1* to noticeably *less than 2-to-1*.

> 364/214 = 1.70

And the *unokai* advantage decreases as follows:

> 309/459 = .673

In other words, under the 12.4 years of age correction calculations, 67 percent of the initial "*unokai* advantage" (459 offspring) actually stems from an age effect equivalent to 309 offspring.

63. How many age effect offspring do 137 *unokais* have in 14.4 years?

First:

> 0.182 (offspring per year) × 14.4 (years) = 2.621 offspring per *unokai* in 14.4 years

Second:

> 2.621 × 137 (*unokais*) = 359.1, or 359 "extra" offspring due to an average of 14.4 years of "extra" reproductive time for *unokais* over non-*unokais*

We next subtract the "extra" offspring from the number of initial *unokai* offspring to compensate for age effects (see note 60).

> 673 *unokai* offspring for 137 *unokais* − 359 "extra" age effect offspring = 314 *unokai* offspring, versus 214 non-*unokai* offspring

The *unokai* advantage changes as follows:

> 314 − 214 = 100

The ratio of *unokai* offspring to non-*unokai* offspring decreases from the *initial over 3-to-1* to only *about 1.5-to-1*.

> 314/214 = 1.47

And the initial *unokai* advantage decreases markedly:

> 359/459 = .782

In other words, under the 14.4 years of age correction calculations, 78 percent of the initial "*unokai* advantage" (459 offspring) actually stems from an age effect equivalent to 359 offspring.

64. Ferguson 1989b:564.

65. Chagnon et al. 1979:317–318.

66. Chagnon et al. 1979:318.

67. Chagnon 1988.

68. Ferguson 1989b:564.

69. Chagnon 1989; Ferguson 1989b.

70. No explanation: Chagnon et al. 1979; earlier: see Chagnon 1979a, 1979b.

71. Chagnon et al. 1979 list 20 Yanomamö headmen in 13 villages. They explain on page 318 (italics added) that "in some villages there are several 'headmen' as described above, a situation that *often* emerges when a village's composition includes several large descent groups." Separately, Chagnon 1979a:385 (italics added) states, "If there are two comparatively large lineages in the village, it is *common* to find two headmen, one from each descent group, and *quite common* for most of the village social activities to reflect the interests and desires of the *two leaders*." Similarly, nine years later and related to the same Yanomamö population that he has most intensively studied, Chagnon 1988:988 (italics added) states that if a "village has two descent groups of approximate equal size *it will have two (or more) leaders*."

Chagnon 1988:988 also states that "all headmen in this study are *unokai*." In writing a rebuttal one year later to Ferguson's 1989b commentary on his 1988 *Science* article, Chagnon 1989, in note 2, reports that his statement about all headmen being *unokai* was wrong, and so he removes one non-*unokai* headman along with 12 headmen from the *unokai* group (as part of his argument that the headman effect does not compromise his reported findings). This, of course, amounts to removing a total of 13 men from the analysis to adjust for a headman effect, not the 20 headmen from the earlier reports. Chagnon 1989 does not explain why *only* 13 headmen, instead of 20, are removed (nor does he offer any information about the implied loss of seven *headman positions* as descent group leaders).

72. Ferguson 1989b; Chagnon 1989.

73. Chagnon 1988, 1989; Chagnon et al. 1979. Due to the fact that different Chagnon publications list different numbers of lineage headmen for the same study population (see note 71), headman effect corrections (independent of any age correction) will be calculated twice, first using the 13 headmen figure reported in Chagnon 1989 and second using the 20 headmen figure reported by Chagnon et al. 1979. Obviously individual headmen may die or be replaced, but it is difficult to imagine why seven headman *positions* would disappear so quickly. Calculations based on 20 headmen involve an assumption that the same ratio of one non-*unokai* headman to 12 *unokai* headmen applies also to the group of 20 headmen.

Chagnon et al. 1979:318 (Table 12.8) report that the average headman reproductive success is 8.6 offspring. The first step is to remember that 12 *unokai* headmen occur within the original number of 137 *unokais* and one non-*unokai* headman occurs within 243 non-*unokais*. Therefore, to base calculations on equal numbers of *unokais* and non-*unokais* (137 men in each group), we need to proportionately decrease the one non-*unokai* headman (or actually the estimate of his offspring) as follows: The average number of offspring for headmen is 8.6. So we can estimate 8.6 offspring for one non-*unokais* headman among 243 non-*unokais*. To convert this to 137 men:

$137/243 = .56379$

8.6 offspring $\times$ .56379 = 4.8 or 5 headman offspring to be discounted from the non-*unokai* group.

There are 12 *unokai* headmen among the 137 *unokais*. Therefore:

8.6 offspring $\times$ 12 *unokai* headmen = 103.2, or, 103 headmen offspring to be discounted from the *unokai* group

Recall that 137 *unokais* have 673 offspring and 137 non-*unokais* have 214 offspring, once both groups are standardized to the same number of men (137) and *before* any corrections whatsoever have been made (see note 60).

Therefore, for *unokais:*

673 initial offspring − 103 discounted headman offspring = 570

And for non-*unokais:*

214 initial offspring − 5 discounted headman offspring = 209

The initial "*unokai* advantage" before any corrections, as we have seen in note 60, is 459 offspring (673 – 214 = 459). After the headman correction, we have an adjusted "*unokai* advantage" of 361 offspring (570 – 209 = 361).

Finally, therefore, 361/459 = .786. Thus 78.6 percent of "*unokai* advantage" remains, or, saying this the other way around, 21.4 percent of the "*unokai* advantage" is removed by calculating a headman correction by removing only 13 headmen.

These procedures will be repeated, this time removing 20 headmen from the analysis instead of 13. As in the previous calculations, the average headman reproductive success is 8.6 offspring, as reported by Chagnon et al. 1979 (Table 12.8).

Based on Yanomamö ethnography, it seems reasonable to assume (explicitly) that nearly all the headman are *unokais,* but we don't know exactly how many headmen, if any, are not. Recall that Chagnon 1988 stated that all headmen are *unokais,* but then in 1989 reported that 12 out of 13 headmen are *unokais*. As the best estimate, therefore, we can use the same ratio of 12/13 (92.3 percent) in our calculations:

20 headmen × .923 = 18.46 *unokai* headmen out of 20, total

And:

20 − 18.46 = 1.54 non-*unokai* headmen out of 20

The next step is to convert 1.54 non-*unokai* headmen for a population of 243 non-*unokais* into the equivalent number for a population of 137 non-*unokais*. The 18.46 *unokai* headmen need no conversion because the *unokai* group already consists of 137 members. Therefore, to base calculations on equal numbers of *unokais* and non-*unokais* (137 men in each group), we need to proportionately decrease the number of non-*unokai* headmen as follows:

137/243 = .56379,

1.54 non-*unokai* headmen × .56379 = .868 headmen among 137 non-*unokais,* or, rounding-off, 1 headman,

1 non-*unokai* headman × 8.6 offspring = 8.6 offspring, or 9 headmen offspring to be discounted from the non-*unokai* group

There are 18.46 *unokai* headmen among 137 *unokais*. Therefore:

18.46 *unokai* headmen × 8.6 offspring = 158.76, or 159 headmen offspring to be discounted from the *unokai* group

Recall that 137 *unokais* have 673 offspring and 137 non-*unokais* 214 offspring, once both groups are standardized to the same number of men and *before* any type of corrections have been made (see note 60).

Therefore, for *unokais:*

673 initial offspring − 159 discounted headman offspring = 514

And for non-*unokais:*

214 initial offspring − 9 discounted headman offspring = 205

The initial "*unokai* advantage" before any corrections, as we have seen, is 459 offspring (673 – 214 = 459). After the headman correction, we have an adjusted "*unokai* advantage" of 309 offspring (514 – 205 = 309).

Finally, therefore, 309/459 = .673. Thus 67 percent of "*unokai* advantage" remains, or, saying this the other way around, 33 percent of the "*unokai* advantage" is removed by calculating a headman correction based on 20 headmen.

In summary, in calculating the extent of a headman effect, we have two estimates. If we use the 13 headman figure from Chagnon 1989, then *21 percent* of the offspring difference between *unokais* and non-*unokais* can be attributed to a headman effect by itself. If we use the 20 headmen figure from Chagnon et al. 1979, then *33 percent* of the offspring difference between *unokais* and non-*unokais* can be attributed to a headman effect by itself. As stated in the text of the chapter, it is probably better to evaluate age effects and headman effects simultaneously, as will be done shortly, since headmanship is associated with age.

74. Chagnon et al. 1979.

75. Estimating age effects and headman effects together involves several steps. The overall idea is to figure out how many offspring to subtract from the initial uncorrected number of *unokai* offspring to compensate *simultaneously* for the effects of age and headmanship. As for age effect estimations alone (see notes 61–63), three sets of estimations will be provided that simultaneously correct for age and headmanship effects. The 10.4-year estimate is almost certainly too low, as discussed in the chapter text. Since we do not know the actual extent of age differences within age intervals between *unokais* and non-*unokais,* the two additional age estimates are provided to show how the calculations come out under these conditions also.

Following Chagnon 1989, the first series of calculations pertains to removing only 13 headmen. Following Chagnon et al. 1979, the second series of calculations pertains to removing 20 headmen. The final results of these and previous age effect calculations are summarized in Table 15.2.

First Simultaneous Correction Series: Age Effect with 13 Headmen Removed. The first step is to recalculate an estimate of the average number of offspring expected per man per year in the overall population under the new condition of removing 13 headmen and their offspring. This estimation method draws on the findings reported in Chagnon 1988 and 1989 (Table 1) and is referred to as Method 1 in note 58.

If 1 non-*unokai* headman is removed, and if 12 *unokai* headmen are removed—see Chagnon 1989: Table 1—we have, first, the following numbers of men:

20- to 24-year-olds: 5 *unokais* + 78 non-*unokais* = 83 men
25- to 30-year-olds: 13 *unokais* + 58 non-*unokais* = 71 men
31- to 40-year-olds: 42 *unokais* + 60 non-*unokais* = 102 men
>41±-year-olds: 65 *unokais* + 46 non-*unokais* = 111 men

Next we can remove offspring attributable to the removed headmen.
20- to 24-year-olds (with no headmen to remove):

5 – 0 = 5 *unokai* offspring + 14 – 0 = 14 non-*unokai* offspring = 19 offspring

25- to 30-year-olds (with 1 headman removed):

22 – 8.6 = 13.4 *unokai* offspring + 50 – 0 = 50 non-*unokai* offspring
= 63.4 offspring

31- to 40-year-olds (with 2 headmen removed):

122 – 8.6 = 113.4 *unokai* offspring + 123 – 4.8 = 118.2 non-*unokai* offspring
= 231.6 offspring

>41±-year-olds (with 10 headmen removed):

524 – 86 = 438 *unokai* offspring + 193 – 0 = 193 non-*unokai* offspring
= 631 offspring

Summing the offspring for each group, there are altogether 570 *unokai* offspring + 375 non-*unokai* offspring = 945 offspring total.

19 offspring/83 men = .23
63.4 offspring/71 men = .89
231.6 offspring/102 men = 2.27
631 offspring/111 men = 5.68

If we assign each offspring value to the relevant age interval midpoint:

22-year-olds = 0.23 offspring average
27.5-year-olds = 0.89 offspring average
35.5-year-olds = 2.27 offspring average
50.7-year-olds = 5.68 offspring average (the 50.7 midpoint was calculated in note 55)

The midpoints are irregular numbers of years apart from each other, calculated as follows:

27.5 − 22 = 5.5 years difference
35.5 − 27.5 = 8 years difference
50.7 − 35.5 = 15.2 years difference

The differences in average offspring between midpoints are as follows:

.89 (at age 27.5) − .23 (at age 22) = .66 in 5.5 years; .66/5.5 = 0.12 offspring/year
2.27 (at age 35.5) − .89 (at age 27.5) = 1.38 in 8 years; 1.38/8 = 0.173 offspring/year
5.68 (at age 50.7) − 2.27 (at age 35.5) = 3.41 in 15.2 years;
3.41/15.2 = 0.224 offspring/year

A rough estimate of the average number of offspring per man per year results from simply averaging the three rates:

0.12 + 0.173 + 0.224 = 0.517/3 = 0.172 offspring per year on the average.

In the second step, for each of the three age difference estimates (10.4, 12.4, and 14.4 years) between *unokais* and non-*unokais,* we calculate the age effects.
For 10.4 years:

0.172 (offspring per year) × 10.4 (years) = 1.789 offspring per *unokai* in 10.4 years

Second:

1.789 × 137 (*unokais*) = 245 *"extra" offspring* due to an average of 10.4 years of "extra" reproductive time for *unokais* over non-*unokais*

For 12.4 years:

0.172 (offspring per year) × 12.4 (years) = 2.133 offspring per *unokai* in 12.4 years

Second:

2.133 × 137 (*unokais*) = 292 *"extra" offspring* due to an average of 12.4 years of "extra" reproductive time for *unokais* over non-*unokais*

For 14.4 years:

0.172 (offspring per year) × 14.4 (years) = 2.477 offspring per *unokai* in 14.4 years

Second:

2.477 × 137 (*unokais*) = 339 *"extra" offspring* due to an average of 14.4 years of "extra" reproductive time for *unokais* over non-*unokais*

In the third step, we calculate the estimate of the headman effect. Related to removing only 13 headmen, these calculations have already been provided in note 73. The results were that 103 *unokais'* offspring should be subtracted to correct for the headman effect and 5 non-*unokais'* offspring should be subtracted for the same reason.

In the fourth step, we subtract offspring to compensate for the age effect and the headman effect simultaneously (for the three different age effect estimates and the removal of 13 headmen condition).

For the 10.4-year estimation:
Unokais:

673 *unokai* offspring for 137 *unokais* − 245 (age effect offspring, step 2)
= 428 − 103 (headman effect offspring, step 3) = 325

Non-*unokais:*

214 non-*unokai* offspring for 137 *unokais* − 0 (age effect)
= 214 − 5 headman effect offspring, step 3) = 209

The "*unokai* advantage" drops to *25 percent* of its initial value, calculated as follows:

325 – 209 = 116

Recall that the initial, uncorrected *unokai* advantage was 459 offspring. Therefore:

116/459 = .253

and

.253 × 100 = 25.3 percent

For the 12.4-year estimation:
Unokais:

673 *unokai* offspring for 137 *unokais* − 292 (age effect offspring, step 2)
= 381 − 103 (headman effect offspring, step 3) = 278

Non-*unokais:*

214 non-*unokai* offspring for 137 *unokais* − 0 (age effect) = 214 −5 (headman effect offspring, step 3) = 209

The "*unokai* advantage" drops to *15 percent* of its initial value, calculated as follows:

$$278 - 209 = 69$$

Recall that the initial, uncorrected *unokai* advantage was 459 offspring. Therefore:

$$69/459 = .15$$

and

$$.15 \times 100 = 15 \text{ percent}$$

For the 14.4-year estimation:
Unokais:

673 *unokai* offspring for 137 *unokais* − 339 (age effect offspring, step 2) = 334 − 103 (headman effect offspring, step 3) = 231

Non-*unokais:*

214 non-*unokai* offspring for 137 *unokais* − 0 (age effect) = 214 − 5 (headman effect offspring, step 3) = 209

The "*unokai* advantage" drops to *5 percent* of its initial value, calculated as follows:

$$231 - 209 = 22$$

Recall that the initial, uncorrected *unokai* advantage was 459 offspring. Therefore:

$$22/459 = .048$$

and

$$.048 \times 100 = 4.8 \text{ percent}$$

Second Simultaneous Correction Series: Age Effect with 20 Headmen Removed. The estimation for the correction of 20 headmen must be done differently from the correction for 13 headmen because the nature of the available data is different. The first step estimates the number of offspring per year with 20 headmen removed by making use of previously calculated rates of average yearly reproduction.

The average number of offspring per year with all headmen included in the population was calculated to be 0.182 (see notes 58 and 61). Previously in this note, the average number of offspring per year with 13 headmen removed was calculated to be 0.172.

How much further would the average yearly number of offspring in the population be reduced by removing 20 headmen instead of 13? One way to estimate this is simply to make use of the ratio of 20:13 and then apply it to the average number of offspring per year figures.

$$20/13 = 1.538$$

From the number of offspring per year rates calculated earlier: $0.172/0.182 = 0.945$.

$$1.00 - 0.945 = 0.055$$

Remembering the ratio $20/13 = 1.538$,

$$1.538 \times 0.055 = 0.085$$
$$0.085 \times 0.182 = 0.015$$
$$0.182 - .015 = .167$$

Hence with 20 headmen removed from the population, the average number of offspring per man per year for the entire adult male population is estimated to be 0.167.

In the second step, for each of the three age difference estimates (10.4, 12.4, and 14.4 years) between *unokais* and non-*unokais,* we calculate the age effects with the 20 headmen removed.

For 10.4 years:

0.167 (offspring per year) × 10.4 (years) = 1.737 offspring per *unokai* in 10.4 years

Second:

1.737 × 137 (*unokais*) = 238 *"extra" offspring* due to an average of 10.4 years of "extra" reproductive time for *unokais* over non-*unokais*

For 12.4 years:

0.167 (offspring per year) × 12.4 (years) = 2.071 offspring per *unokai* in 12.4 years

Second:

2.071 × 137 (*unokais*) = 284 *"extra" offspring* due to an average of 12.4 years of "extra" reproductive time for *unokais* over non-*unokais*

For 14.4 years:

0.167 (offspring per year) × 14.4 (years) = 2.405 offspring per *unokai* in 14.4 years

Second:

2.405 × 137 (*unokais*) = 329 *"extra" offspring* due to an average of 14.4 years of "extra" reproductive time for *unokais* over non-*unokais*

In the third step, we calculate the estimate of the headman effect. These calculations have already been provided in the second part of note 73, related to removing 20 headmen.

The results were that 159 *unokais'* offspring should be subtracted to correct for the headman effect and 9 non-*unokais'* offspring should be subtracted for the same reason.

In the fourth step, we subtract offspring to compensate for the age effect and the headman effect simultaneously (for the three different age effect estimates and the removal of 20 headmen condition).

For the 10.4-year estimation:

Unokais:

673 *unokai* offspring for 137 *unokais* − 238 (age effect offspring, step 2)
= 435 − 159 (headman effect offspring, step 3) = 276

Non-*unokais:*

214 non-*unokai* offspring for 137 *unokais* − 0 (age effect)
= 214 − 9 (headman effect offspring, step 3) = 205

The "*unokai* advantage" drops to *16 percent* of its initial value:

$276 - 205 = 71$
$71/459 = .155$
$.155 \times 100 = 15.5$ percent

For the 12.4-year estimation:
Unokais:

673 *unokai* offspring for 137 *unokais* − 284 (age effect offspring, step 2) = 389 − 159 (headman effect offspring, step 3) = 230

Non-*unokais:*

214 non-*unokai* offspring for 137 *unokais* − 0 (age effect) = 214 −9 (headman effect offspring, step 3) = 205

The "*unokai* advantage" drops to *5 percent* of its initial value:

$230 - 205 = 25$
$25/459 = .054$
$.054 \times 100 = 5.4$ percent

For the 14.4 year estimation:
Unokais:

673 *unokai* offspring for 137 *unokais* − 329 (age effect offspring, step 2) = 344 − 159 (headman effect offspring, step 3) = 185

Non-*unokais:*

214 non-*unokai* offspring for 137 *unokais* − 0 (age effect) = 214 − 9 (headman effect offspring, step 3) = 205

The "*unokai* advantage" drops to −4 *percent, or, in other words, the non-unokais now hold a slight advantage over the unokais:*

$185 - 205 = -20$
$-20/459 = -.435$
$-.435 \times 100 = -4.4$ percent

76. Chagnon 1988.
77. Ferguson 1989b, 1995.
78. Lizot 1994:855.
79. Chagnon 1988:986, 987.
80. Chagnon 1988.
81. Ferguson 1995:361.
82. Chagnon 1988, 1990a, 1990b, 1992a, 1992b.
83. Chagnon 1988.
84. Ferguson 1989b, 1995.

85. Chagnon 1988.

86. Chagnon 1988.

87. See Cronk 1999:80.

88. See, for example, Barash 2001:165–174; Burnham & Phelan 2000:88; Buss 1999:304–305; Campbell 1999:212; Cronk 1999:80; Daly & Wilson 1994:274; Gat 2000b:75, 76, 87 note 4; Geary 1998:317–318; Ghiglieri 1999:144, 193–194; Low 1993:21, 26, 31; Manson & Wrangham 1991:369, 374; McCarthy 1994:107; Pinker 1997:510; Symons 1990:436–437; Wrangham & Peterson 1996:64–74.

89. Ferguson 1989b, 1995. Given the proliferation of citation and discussion of the article in question, it would seem that a substantial number of writers either are unaware of the existing critiques or else do not take them seriously. In *Understanding Violence,* Barash 2001 republishes a shortened version of Chagnon's 1988 piece. He also republishes an edited version of a chapter from Ferguson's 1995 book, but removes Ferguson's critique of Chagnon's article before republishing the rest of the chapter in his own book. Low 1993 (see pages 22 & 36) cites Moore's 1990 article on the Cheyenne in such a way as not to inform her readers that the main point of Moore's article is to question the Yanomamö findings.

90. Chagnon 1988.

CHAPTER 16: WINDOWS TO THE PAST: CONFLICT MANAGEMENT CASE STUDIES

1. Draper 1978:43.
2. Holmberg 1969:1, 10, 13, 17.
3. Holmberg 1969:144.
4. Holmberg 1969:148.
5. Holmberg 1969:138, 140, 147, 161, 165.
6. Holmberg 1969:141.
7. Holmberg 1969:154.
8. Holmberg 1969:151.
9. Holmberg 1969:151, 153.
10. Holmberg 1969:157.
11. Holmberg 1969:158.
12. Holmberg 1969:159.
13. Holmberg 1969:160.
14. Holmberg 1969:132.
15. Holmberg 1969:151–153.
16. Holmberg 1969:157.
17. Holmberg 1969:152.
18. Holmberg 1969:161.
19. Holmberg 1969:166.
20. Holmberg 1969:156.
21. Holmberg 1969:156.
22. Holmberg 1969:152.
23. Lips 1947:397.
24. Reid 1991:243–244; see also Speck 1935:13–16.
25. Lips 1947:397; Reid 1991:244; Speck 1935:14.
26. Reid 1991:244, 245.
27. Speck 1935:15–16.
28. Leacock 1954.

29. Leacock 1981:193; see also Leacock 1954:33, 1978; Lips 1947:472–475; Reid 1991:245; Speck 1935:44.
30. Leacock 1981:191.
31. For example, Leacock 1978:249.
32. Leacock 1978:249.
33. Leacock 1981:195.
34. Lips 1947:470.
35. Lips 1947:470.
36. Lips 1947:470.
37. Lips 1947:470.
38. Lips 1947:469, 470.
39. Reid 1991:245.
40. Leacock 1981:193; Lips 1947:469, 471–472.
41. Leacock 1978:249.
42. Lips 1947:402; italics added.
43. See Reid 1991:245; Speck 1935:44.
44. Lips 1947:469.
45. Lips 1947:469; see also Fry 2006.
46. Lips 1947:398.
47. Lips 1947:399; see also Speck 1935:31.
48. Lips 1947:399.
49. Leacock 1978:249–250.
50. Leacock 1954:43, 1978:250, 253.
51. Reid 1991:245.
52. Gardner 1972:407.
53. Gardner 2000b:23.
54. Gardner 1972:422, 1985:413.
55. Gardner 2000b:23, 33.
56. Gardner 2000b:39.
57. Gardner 1972:414.
58. Gardner 2000b:103.
59. Gardner 2000b:103.
60. Gardner 1999:263, 2000b:104–111.
61. Gardner 2000b:83.
62. Gardner 2000b:85, see also 1999:263.
63. Gardner 2000b:3.
64. Gardner 1972:415.
65. Gardner 1972:415–416.
66. Gardner 1972:425, 1995, 1999:263, 2000a, 2000b:93.
67. Gardner 2000a, 2000b.
68. Gardner 1999:263.
69. Gardner 2000a:224.
70. Gardner 1995, 2000a:225.
71. Gardner 1972:439.
72. Gardner 1966:402, 1985:413–416, 421, 1999:263, 2004.
73. Hoebel 1967b:67, 68; see also Irwin 1990.
74. Hoebel 1967b:67.
75. Hoebel 1967b:82.
76. Balikci 1970:xvi, italics added.
77. Balikci 1970:xvii.

78. Balikci 1970:xx; O'Leary & Levinson 1991:254.
79. O'Leary & Levinson 1991:254.
80. Balikci 1970:151–152.
81. Balikci 1970:148.
82. Balikci 1970:176–177.
83. Balikci 1970:170.
84. Balikci 1970:169.
85. Balikci 1970:156; see also Irwin 1990:200–202.
86. Balikci 1970:156.
87. Balikci 1970:157.
88. Balikci 1970:178.
89. Balikci 1970:176.
90. Hoebel 1967b:79; see also Irwin 1990:202.
91. Knud Rasmussen quoted in Eckert & Newmark 1980:209–210.
92. See also Balikci 1970:179.
93. Irwin 1990:201.
94. Irwin 1990:201.
95. Balikci 1970:179, italics added.
96. Hoebel 1967b.
97. Balikci 1970:180.
98. Hoebel 1967b:87.
99. Balikci 1970:180–181.
100. Irwin 1990:196–197.
101. Balikci 1970:179, 181.
102. Irwin 1990:194–199.
103. Irwin 1990:199.
104. Balikci 1970:182–184.
105. Hoebel 1967b:82–83; Irwin 1990.
106. Boas 1964:57.
107. Irwin 1990:202.
108. Balikci 1970:185.
109. Balikci 1970:185–186.
110. Balikci 1970:186.
111. Balikci 1970:186.
112. See Hoebel 1967b:88–90.
113. Balikci 1970:192.
114. See Hoebel 1967b:89.
115. Knud Rasmussen quoted in Balikci 1970:190–191.
116. Balikci 1970:193.
117. Lee 1993:ix.
118. Draper 1978:35; Lee 1993:10. Lee 1993:9 provides an historical context: "As White settlement expanded north in the eighteenth century, bitter conflicts arose with the native peoples, conflicts that escalated into genocidal warfare against the San [of which the Ju/'hoansi are but one group]. By the late nineteenth century the San had been virtually exterminated within the boundaries of the present-day Republic of South Africa, and most writers of the day spoke of them as a dying race. As exploration pushed father north, however, the grim obituary of the San proved, happily, to be premature. In the security of the Kalahari Desert, thousands of San continue to live as hunter-gatherers in relatively peaceful proximity to a variety of neighboring Black herders and farmers."
119. Draper 1978:39.

120. Lee 1993:18–19.
121. Lee 1979:335, italics in original.
122. Lee 1979:335.
123. Lee 1979:335.
124. Lee 1979:337.
125. Lee 1979:337–338.
126. Lee 1993:93.
127. Lee 1979:338, 370, 1993:93.
128. Cashdan 1980:116.
129. Thomas 1994:71.
130. Lee 1979:343, 348.
131. Draper 1975:86; Konner 1982:204; Lee 1979:398; Marshall 1976:53; see also Thomas 1959:21–24.
132. Lee 1993:35–36.
133. Wiessner 1982; see also Smith 1988.
134. See Lee 1979:456; Cashdan 1980:116.
135. See Konner 1982:204; Fry 2004a.
136. See Boehm 1999: Leacock 1978; Woodburn 1982.
137. Draper 1978:44–47; Lee 1979:460; Marshall 1961; Shostak 1983; Thomas 1994:71, 74, 75.
138. Lee 1979:454.
139. Lee 1979:454.
140. Shostak 1983.
141. Shostak 1983:287–288.
142. Draper 1975, 1978:33; Kent 1989:704; Konner 1982:204; Lee 1993:93; Marshall 1961, 1976; Thomas 1994:71, 75.
143. Eibl-Eibesfeldt 1974, 1979.
144. See Kent 2002; Fry 2004a.
145. Konner 1982:204.
146. Lee 1993:93, italics added.
147. Thomas 1959:24, 186.
148. Lee 1979, 1993.
149. Draper 1978:33.
150. Lee 1979: Chapter 13, 1993:97–102.
151. Marshall 1961: 235.
152. Lee 1979:377.
153. Shostak 1983:258, 259, 261.
154. See Draper 1978:33, 43–44; Lee 1979:376, 380, 1993:98–99; Thomas 1959:186; 1994:76.
155. Lee 1979, 1993.
156. Lee 1979:382, 397.
157. Lee 1979:388.
158. Lee 1979; see also Draper 1978:40; Thomas 1994:78.
159. Lee 1979:383.
160. For example, see Lee 1979: Tables 13.2 & 13.3, codes K2, K6, K17, & K19.
161. Lee 1979:393, Case number 6.
162. Draper 1978:40; see also Thomas 1994:75.
163. Lee 1993:81, italics in original.
164. Boehm 1999:80; see also Boehm 2000:94; Draper 1978:40.
165. Lee 1979:390.

166. Lee 1979:394.
167. Draper 1978; Lee 1979: Chapter 13, 1993: Chapter 7; Marshall 1961; Thomas 1994.
168. Lee 1979:367; Kent 1989.
169. Fry 2000:339, 348.
170. Lee 1993:96.
171. Reyna 1994:38, 40.

CHAPTER 17: UNTANGLING WAR FROM INTERPERSONAL AGGRESSION

1. Killen & de Waal 2000:364.

2. An anthropological rendition of the nature–nurture fallacy entails dichotomizing between evolutionary and more proximate cultural analysis as mutually exclusive perspectives. However, such polarization of explanations is unfortunate because aggression, altruism, and other multifaceted behaviors are too complex to be accounted for exclusively through any single perspective. Biological and cultural perspectives can contribute to an understanding of aggression, and to acknowledge a contribution from biology does not automatically imply determinism or reductionism, nor does it diminish the obviously important influences of culture and learning. Furthermore, evolutionary and proximate interpretations are at times quite complementary.

3. Lewontin 1970:1.

4. Darwin 1958a:90, 91, italics in original.

5. Symons 1990.

6. Symons 1990:427–428.

7. Archer & Huntingford 1994: see, for example, page 10; Boehm 1999, 2005; Hamilton 1971; Riechert 1998:82; Service 1966; van Schaik & Aureli 2000.

8. Archer 1988; de Waal 2000; Blanchard & Blanchard 1989:104–105; Huntingford & Turner 1987; Preuschoft & van Schaik 2000; Riechert 1998:82.

9. Schaller 1972; Wilson 1973, 1975:246; Hinde 1974:268.

10. Blanchard & Blanchard 1989:104.

11. Archer 1988; Wilson 1975:242–243.

12. For example, de Waal 1989.

13. Symons 1979:35.

14. Symons 1979:31–38.

15. See Tooby & Cosmides 1990, 1992.

16. Tooby & Cosmides 1990:386–387.

17. See Tooby & Cosmides 1990:387–388.

18. Symons 1979:35.

19. Symons 1979, 1990. Whereas behaviors observed in unnatural environments may not reflect adaptations as clearly as behavior occurring in natural settings that correspond with the EEA, they still might in some cases. As Symons 1990—also see Irons 1998—points out, unnatural environments can be viewed as natural experiments that may contribute to a further understanding of adaptations. Additionally, as Irons 1998:198 notes, particular adaptations interact with different environmental features. Therefore, unnatural environmental conditions might be expected to interact with some adaptations more than others.

20. Williams 1966:82–83.

21. Darwin 1998.

22. See Darwin 1998.

23. Darwin 1998:229.

24. Trivers 1972.

25. Darwin 1998.

26. Trivers 1972:139.

27. Darwin 1998:583.

28. Symons 1979:142.

29. Symons 1979:142, emphasis in original.

30. Symons 1979:153, 163; see also Buss, 1992; Daly & Wilson, 1988, 1994; Jolly, 1985:247–248.

31. See Fry 1980; Maynard Smith 1997; Riechert 1998:65; Williams 1966.

32. See Balikci 1970; Brown 1991:137; Burbank 1992, 1994:202; Daly & Wilson 1988; Lee 1979.

33. Daly & Wilson 1988:161.

34. For example, Burbank 1987, 1994; Daly & Wilson 1988; Fry 1992a, 1998; Hines & Fry 1994; Kuschel 1992; Lee 1979; Maccoby & Jacklin 1974:368; Romanucci-Ross 1973; Taylor 1979.

35. Adams 1983; Burbank 1987:71, 1994:202.

36. Darwin 1998.

37. To return for a moment to the tribal Yanomamö (who, of course, are not nomadic foragers), despite the huge amount of ink that has been devoted to discussing killing and other violence within this society as a predominant feature, if we consider all the men age 20 years and over in Chagnon's 1988 study population, *only* 14 percent (54/380) of the men have participated in more than one killing and 22 percent (83/380) have participated in *only* one killing, whereas the majority, 64 percent (243/380), have not participated in any killings at all (see Chagnon's Figure 1 & Table 2). These percentages suggest first that only a minority of men are involved in the bulk of the killings and second that *the vast majority of men are not raiders or murderers* at all. It is also relevant to keep in mind that the phrase "participated in a killing" often reflects a shared event with several or numerous other men (see chapter 15, this volume). This can produce multiple "participants in a killing" per single victim. Ethnographic descriptions of nomadic forager societies, such as those considered in chapter 16, suggest that even *lower* levels of killing typifies band society.

38. Wrangham & Peterson 1996:84.

39. For example, see Fry 1990, 2005.

40. In fact, pertaining to animal aggression generally, Huntingford & Turner 1987:79 note *facultative* elements: "Animals do not respond to the agonistic stimuli provided by an opponent in an absolute mechanical way; whether two animals fight and if so what form this takes is influenced by various aspects of the environment in which the encounter occurs. The influential factors tend to be those which indicate the costs of fighting, the probability of victory and the rewards gained by the winner." For examples of variable behavioral responses from the discipline of human behavioral ecology, see Dyson-Hudson & Smith 1978; Winterhalder & Smith 2000.

41. See Winterhalder & Smith 2000.

42. Ross 1993a.

43. See Dyson-Hudson & Smith 1978; Winterhalder & Smith 2000; Williams 1966.

44. See Archer & Huntingford 1994; Eibl-Eibesfeldt 1961, 1979:37–40; Le Boeuf 1971; Maynard Smith & Price 1973; Riechert 1998:65; Schaller 1972:55. Ethologist Konrad Lorenz 1966 emphasized the restraint in animal fighting. He interpreted such restraint as good for the species, a group selection type of explanation. This is not the theoretical model adopted here. For an overview and critique of group selection, see Fry 1980.

45. Eibl-Eibesfeldt 1961; Wilson 1975:243.

46. Maynard Smith & Price 1973:15.

47. Archer & Huntingford 1994; Borgia 1980:169; Hinde 1974:269; Riechert 1998:65.

48. Ritualized competition: Archer & Huntingford 1994:3–4; Maynard Smith & Price 1973; see also Fry 2005; submission and appeasement signals: see Aureli & de Waal 2000; Hinde 1974:270; restrained aggression: see Fry 1980; Hinde 1974:272; Maynard Smith & Price 1973.

49. Riechert 1998; see also Archer and Huntingford 1994; Riechert 1986.

50. Maynard Smith & Price 1973; Maynard Smith 1974; quote is from Maynard Smith & Price 1973:15.

51. Archer 1988; Archer & Huntingford 1994; Fry 1980:73; Riechert 1998.

52. Alexrod 1984.

53. Alexrod 1984:54.

54. Hamilton 1964, 1971.

55. Hamilton 1964:19.

CHAPTER 18: AN ALTERNATIVE EVOLUTIONARY PERSPECTIVE: THE NOMADIC FORAGER MODEL

1. Lee 1979:391.

2. For example, see Balikci 1968, 1970; Boehm 1999, 2000, 2005; Briggs 1994; Damas 1972:24–25; Downs 1966:51; Fowler 1991:331; Hill 1994:5; Service 1966; Sluys 2000.

3. Balikci 1970:193.

4. For example, see Boas 1964:57; Damas 1972:33, 1991:78; Hallowell 1974:279; Hill 1994:6; Hobhouse 1956:102; Hoebel 1967b:88–89; Nansen 1893:163; Service 1966:50; Spencer & Gillen 1927:444.

5. Damas 1991:78.

6. Hoebel 1967b:88.

7. Boehm 1999:82, italics added.

8. Chagnon 1988.

9. For example, see Endicott 1979, 1983, 1988; Fowler 1991; Gusinde 1937:633–634, 635, 908, 911, 1031; Hallowell 1974; Helm 1961, 1972; Hill 1994; Krech 1991; Morris 1977, 1982, 1992; Sinha 1972; Tonkinson 1978, 2004; Sluys 1999, 2000.

10. For example, see Gusinde 1937:635, 886.

11. Voting with their feet: see, for example, Arcand 1999:99; Damas 1991:78; Gilberg 1984:583, 585; Gusinde 1937:888, 984; Kleivan 1991:378; Lee 1979:367; David Martin 1991:378–379; Rushforth 1991:320; verbal resolutions: see, for example, Berndt 1965; Fowler 1991:332; Gratton 1991:266; Rushforth 1991:320; Silberbauer 1972, 1982:30; Sinha 1972; Tonkinson 1978, 2004; Williams 1991:226.

12. Lee 1979:377.

13. Lee 1979:392.

14. Given the typicality of sexual affairs in many band societies (as reflected in the Siriono, Paliyan, and Ju/'hoansi case studies, for example), obviously, the overwhelming majority of sexual affairs do *not* lead to homicides.

15. For example, see Berndt 1965; Gratton 1991:266; Peterson 1991:375. Based on Lee's 1979 data, a fair number of Ju/'hoansi homicides seem to be crimes of passion. It seems likely that some attacks would not otherwise have resulted in lethal injuries if the readily available poisoned arrows had not been used to inflict wounds.

16. See Boehm 1999:7, 80–81; Hosley 1991:158; Knauft 1991; Rushforth 1991:320; Turnbull 1965a:202–210.

17. See Winterhalder & Smith 2000 for a review of the influences of ecological and demographic factors on various types of human behavior.

18. Balikci 1970:181; Lee 1979.

19. Fry 2006; for example, see Gusinde 1937:887, 398–905; Kelly 2000; Peterson 1991:375; Janetski 1991:362.

20. Lee 1979:383.

21. See Lee 1979:389.

22. Ericksen & Horton 1992.

23. Ericksen & Horton 1992:63; see also their Table 2, for the codings for 17 nomadic band societies for which information was available, SCCS numbers 2, 13, 77, 79, 90, 91, 119, 122, 124, 125, 126, 127, 128, 129, 137, 180, 186.

24. Balikci 1970:180.

25. See also Downs 1966:51; Hobhouse 1956:102; Hoebel 1967b:307; Murdock 1934:46; Spencer & Gillen 1927:445, 450.

26. Lee 1979:390.

27. Balikci 1970:182; see also Gusinde 1937:899–900.

28. Gusinde 1937:887.

29. Balikci 1970:192, italics added.

30. Marshall 1961; Lee 1979, 1993.

31. For example, Asch 1981:343 on the Slavey; Damas 1972:33 on the Copper Eskimo; Gould 1991:241 on the Ngatatjara; Gratton 1991:266 on the Pintupi; Gusinde 1931 on the Ona; Hobhouse 1956:101 generalizing about Australian Aborigines; Hoebel 1967b:92 generalizing about Inuit societies; Murdock 1934:210–211 on the Polar Eskimo; Peterson 1991:375 on the Walpiri; Tonkinson 1978, 2004 on the Mardu; Turnbull 1965a:188–189 on the Mbuti; Warner 1969:163 on the Murngin.

32. Balikci 1970:181.

33. Gusinde 1937:890.

34. See Fry 2006.

35. Chagnon 1988, 1990a, 1992a, 1996. The film *The Ax Fight* by Asch & Chagnon 1975 also illustrates Yanomamö restraint. As the film begins, self-control is clearly apparent during a long standoff that follows a brief pole fight between two men. Later, self-restraint is also shown by a number of Yanomamö engaged in a melee. For example, attackers hit their victims with the flat side of machetes rather than with the cutting edges and with the dull sides of axes rather than using the chopping side. Various third-party peacemakers are also apparent in the footage, including the headman. When a young man is knocked unconscious by an ax blow, with the dull side, to his back, all fighting stops until the extent of his injuries can be determined.

36. Archer & Huntingford 1994.

37. For example, Asch & Chagnon 1975; Chagnon & Bugos 1979; Ghiglieri 1999.

38. See also Gusinde 1937:886, 987.

39. Lee 1979:380, italics added.

40. Hamilton 1971; see Daly & Wilson 1988; Dunbar et al. 1995; Maynard Smith 1974.

41. Lee 1979:391. A wife and husband are unlikely to be more closely related to each other than as first cousins. First cousin marriage occurs fairly frequently in many societies. Sometimes ethnographic descriptions do not clearly distinguish between biological and social relatives. Inclusive fitness theory pertains to biological relatives. A report, for example, that a man killed his brother-in-law does not necessarily contradict inclusive fitness theory, since brothers-in-law may not be closely related biologically.

42. See de Waal 1996, 2000.

43. See Westermarck 1924:479.

44. Fry 2006.

45. Williams 1966:4.

46. Williams 1966:8.

47. Williams 1966:9.

48. Symons 1978:4.

49. For example, Alexander 1987:107–110, 232; Buss 1999:300, 301, 306; Buss & Shackelford 1997:609; Ghiglieri 1999:165, 197; Low 1993:19, 40; Pinker 1997:509–517; Wrangham 1999a:5–6, 14, 1999b:19.

50. Wrangham 1999b:19, 22.

51. Wrangham 1999a:14, italics added.

52. Buss 1999:300, 301, italics added.

53. Buss 1999:306.

54. Alexander 1987: for example, see page 79; Buss 1999:298, 302; Buss & Shackelford 1997:609; Ghiglieri 1999: for example, see pages 163, 164, 170, 196; Low 1993:43; Pinker 1997: 509–510; Wrangham 1999b:18, 19; Wrangham & Peterson 1996: for example, see pages 24, 81.

55. Ghiglieri 1999:165–177; Wilson & Wrangham 2003; Wrangham 1999a, 1999b: for example, see page 20; Wrangham & Peterson 1996:22, 71.

56. Wrangham 1999a, 1999b.

57. Carneiro 1994b; Ferguson 2000; Sussman 1999.

58. See Sussman 1999:126.

59. Sussman 1999:126–127; Wilson & Wrangham 2003:372–375, see Table 1.

60. Wilson & Wrangham 2003:374.

61. Wilson & Wrangham 2003:265.

62. Wrangham 1999b:23.

63. Wrangham 1999b:22.

64. See, for example, Hart & Pilling 1979:85–86; Holmberg 1969:158; Knauft 1991:402; Meggitt 1965:24; Steward 1968:334.

65. Wrangham 1999b:23.

66. Chagnon 1988.

67. Buss 1999:305, 306; Daly & Wilson 1994:268, 274; Ghiglieri 1999:197–198; Low 1993:21, 26, 31, 36, 40; Pinker 1997:509–517; Wrangham & Peterson 1996:68.

68. See also Fry 2006.

69. Symons 1979, 1990, 1992; Tooby & Cosmides 1990.

70. Symons 1979.

71. Chagnon 1988, 1990a, 1990b, 1992a, 1992b, 1996. "To claim that a trait is an adaptation," points out Symons 1990:428, "is to make a claim about the *past*" (italics in original). The basic claim in question is that warfare was a regular, pervasive feature in the human past. As we have seen, a variety of observations cast doubt on this assertion. First, the archaeological data worldwide show a paucity of evidence for war beyond the 10,000 B.P. year mark. Second, local archaeological time sequences show as a *general pattern* the rise of social complexity (almost always within the last 13,000 years), especially state-level social organization (less than 5,000–6,000 years ago), to have been accompanied by the development of war. Thus war leaves archaeological tracks and appears along with new forms of social organization that have originated only very recently in a prehistoric time scale. Third and corresponding with the second point, cross-cultural studies show a correlation between nonwarring and band-level social organization, the form of social organization that characterized the EEA. Fourth, the paucity of warfare on the entire continent of Aboriginal Australia is also indicative of a relatively nonwarring past. Fifth, nomadic band society has social structural features (for example, nomadism, flux, flexibility, lack of social segmentation, and high degrees of individual autonomy) that are inconsistent with making war. Sixth, according to Binford 2001, the entire world population was extremely low in the past, only reaching seven million people for the entire planet by about 11,000– 12,000 years ago. This suggests an overall human-to-resource balance over prior millennia that is not in accord with presumptions that pervasive scarcity resulted in chronic warfare. Obviously, people were not equally distributed everywhere. Nonetheless, there was plenty of space and ample resources for a global population of only a few million persons. Together, all of these observations *constitute mutually reinforcing reasons* for seriously doubting the presumption that warfare was *typical* in the human evolutionary past. In this way, sperm banks and warfare probably have something in common.

72. See Symons 1990:436–438; Tooby & Cosmides 1990:420.

73. Trivers 1972; Darwin 1998.

74. For example, Buss 1999; Buss & Shackelford 1997:608; Daly & Wilson 1994:264–268; Shaw & Wong 1989:14.

75. Williams 1966.

76. Darwin 1958b:123.

77. Bicchieri 1972; Binford 2001; Boehm 1999, 2000, 2005; Karen Endicott 1999; Gardner 1966, 1991; Guenther 2002; Ingold 1999; Ingold et al. 1988a, 1988b; Kelly 1995; Kent 2002; Knauft 1991; Leacock 1978, 1982; Leacock & Lee 1982; Lee & Daly 1999; Lee & DeVore 1968a, 1968b; Murdock 1968; Service 1966; Steward 1968; Woodburn 1982.

78. Boehm 1999:66.

79. Kent 2002.

CHAPTER 19: WEIGHING THE EVIDENCE

1. Kaufmann 1977:3.

2. Orma 1986:14–15.

3. Barash 1991:16–17, 422.

4. Hobbes 1946:82.

5. See Kemp 2004.

6. Adams & Bosch 1987; Fry & Welch 1992.

7. Dart 1949, 1953, 1958; Ardrey 1961.

8. For example, see Ghiglieri 1999:178–179.

9. Richards 1975:343.

10. White & Toth 1989, 1991; Stiner 1991.

11. Wright 1942.

12. Ember 1978:443.

13. Lee & DeVore 1968a:9; Service 1966:60; Steward 1968:334; Turnbull 1968b:341.

14. Band: Lee & DeVore 1968a:9; Steward 1968:334; band level of society: Service 1966:60; specific bands: Lee & DeVore 1968a:9; Turnbull 1968b:341.

15. Ember 1978.

16. Alexander 1979:222–230; Goldstein 2001:24; Ghiglieri 1999:164; Keeley 1996:31; Wrangham & Peterson 1996:75.

17. Keeley 1996:36–39.

18. Goodale 1974:133–134; Bird 1946:71.

19. Tacon & Chippindale 1994.

CHAPTER 20: ENHANCING PEACE

1. Halonen 2000.

2. Wright 1942.

3. See Hobhouse et al. 1915; Johnson & Earle 1987; Leavitt 1977; Malinowski 1941; Simmons 1937; Reyna 1994; Wright 1942:66.

4. See Ferguson & Whitehead 1992a, 1992b; Leacock 1982; Mead 1961b; Newcomb 1950; Ross 1984.

5. Boehm 1999.

6. Fry 1999b; Keeley 1996:158; Robarchek & Robarchek 1996a, 1996b, 1998a, 1998b; Sponsel 1996b:113.

7. Greenberg 1989; Robarchek & Robarchek 1996a, 1998a.
8. See Hinde 2001.
9. Hinde 2001.
10. Ury 1999:199.
11. Koch 1974; Koch et al. 1977.
12. Gregor 1990:113; see also Gregor 1994b.
13. Robin Fox quoted in Dennen 1995:522; see also Boehm 1987:172; Ury 1999.
14. Koch 1974:168; Dennen 1995.
15.Glazer 1997.
16. Smail 1997:82.
17. Mead 1967:224.
18. Smail 1985.
19. Smail 1985, 1997.
20. Smail 1997:78–79.
21. See Johnson et al. 1983; Slavin 1983; Glazer 1997.
22. O'Nell 1989:125.
23. Tonkinson 2004:101.
24. Hoebel 1967b:139.
25. Boehm 1987:119.
26. Gregor 1994b.
27. BBC World Business Report, March 18, 2003.
28. Kurtz & Turpin 1997:222.
29. Renner 1991.
30. Kurtz & Turpin 1997:216.
31. Renner 1999:164.
32. Boehm 1987; Dennen 1995; Gregor 1994b; Meggitt 1977; O'Nell 1989; Tonkinson 2004.
33. Renner 1999:167.
34. Mellon et al. 1994:269.
35. For example, Briggs 1994; Fry 1992b, 1994; Gregor 1990, 1994b; Robarchek & Robarchek 1996a, 1996b, 1998a, 1998b.
36. Dentan 1968; Robarchek 1997; Robarchek & Robarchek 1996a, 1996b.
37. Gregor 1994b:246.
38. Fry 1992b, 1994, 1999a; O'Nell 1981, 1989.
39. Fry & Fry 1997; Hinde 2001; Hinde & Groebel 1989.
40. Adams & Bosch 1987.
41. Albert Einstein quoted in Krieger 1994:319.
42. Krieger 1994:319.
43. See French 1992, 1995, 2000; Fry 1985; Fry & Fry 1997; Johansen 1984; Ury et al. 1988.
44. *Stockholm Initiative* 1991:36–37.
45. Wiesel & Fry 1997:239–240, emphasis in original.
46. Robarchek & Robarchek 1996a.
47. Ferguson 1984a:20.
48. Chagnon 1988.
49. Dennen 1995:519; Black 1993.
50. Keeley 1996:145; Meggitt 1977.
51. See Boehm 1999, 2003.
52. A. Hale quoted in Dennen 1995:503.
53. *Stockholm Initiative* 1991:38.
54. Bertens 1994:2.

55. Schlegel 2004:25.

56. Whitehead 1990:155.

57. See Fry 2000; Ury 1999.

58. Ury et al. 1988; see also Ury 1999; quote is from Ury et al. 1988:172.

59. Robarchek & Robarchek 1996b:72–73.

60. Renner 1993.

61. Fry 2001a, 2001b, 2001c.

62. Greenberg 1989; Robarchek & Robarchek 1996a, 1996b, 1998a, 1998b; Ury et al. 1988, Ury 1999.

63. Ferguson 1984a:12.

64. Fry 1993b.

65. Darwin 1998:120.

66. See Brown 1991:138; Hoebel 1967b.

67. Darwin 1998:126–127.

References

Adams, David B. (1983) "Why there are so few women warriors." *Behavior Science Research,* 18:196–212.

Adams, David and Bosch, Sarah (1987) "The myth that war is intrinsic to human nature discourages action for peace by young people," in J. M. Ramírez, R. A. Hinde, and J. Groeble (eds.), *Essays on Violence,* pp. 121–137. Seville: University of Seville Press.

Albert, Bruce (1989) "Yanomami 'violence': Inclusive fitness or ethnographer's representation?" *Current Anthropology,* 30:637–640.

——— (1990) "On Yanomami warfare: Rejoinder." *Current Anthropology,* 31:558–563.

Alexander, Richard (1979) *Darwinism and Human Affairs.* Seattle: University of Washington Press.

——— (1987) *The Biology of Moral Systems.* New York: Aldine de Gruyter.

Allman, William F. (1988) "A laboratory of human conflict." *U.S. News and World Report* (April 11):57–58.

Altschuler, Milton (1964) *The Cayapa: A Study in Legal Behavior.* Unpublished doctoral dissertation, Department of Anthropology, University of Minnesota.

——— (1967) "The sacred and profane realms of Cayapa law." *International Journal of Comparative Sociology,* 8:44–54.

——— (1970) "Cayapa personality and sexual motivation," in D. S. Marshall and R. C. Suggs (eds.), *Human Sexual Behavior: Variations in the Ethnographic Spectrum,* pp. 38–58. New York: Basic Books.

Alvard, Michael S. and Kuznar, L. (2001) "Deferred harvests: The transition from hunting to animal husbandry." *American Anthropologist,* 103:295–311.

Anderson, Myrdene and Beach, Hugh (1992) "Saami," in D. Levinson (ed. in chief), *Encyclopedia of World Cultures,* L. A. Bennett (volume ed.), *Volume IV, Europe (Central, Western, and Southeastern Europe),* pp. 220–223. Boston: G. K. Hall.

Anderson, Robert and Anderson, Stanley (1992) "Danes," in D. Levinson (ed. in chief), *Encyclopedia of World Cultures,* L. A. Bennett (volume ed.), *Volume IV, Europe (Central, Western, and Southeastern Europe),* pp. 88–91. Boston: G. K. Hall.

Annan, Kofi H. E. (1997) "Secretary-General Kofi Annan's Closing Plenary Address." *World Federalist: The Quarterly Newsletter of the World Federalist Association,* July (special insert, following page 6).

Arcand, Bernard (1994) "Cuiva," in D. Levinson (ed. in chief), *Encyclopedia of World Cultures,* J. Wilbert (volume ed.), *Volume VII, South America,* pp. 142–145. Boston: G. K. Hall.

——— (1999) "Cuiva," in R. B. Lee and R. Daly (eds.), *The Cambridge Encyclopedia of Hunters and Gatherers,* pp. 97–100. Cambridge: Cambridge University Press.

Archer, Dane and Gartner, Rosemary (1984) *Violence and Crime in Cross-National Perspective.* New Haven, CT: Yale University Press.

Archer, John (1988) *The Behavioural Biology of Aggression.* Cambridge: Cambridge University Press.

Archer, John and Huntingford, Felicity (1994) "Game theory models and escalation of animal fighting," in M. Potegal and J. F. Knutson (eds.), *The Dynamics of Aggression: Biological and Social Processes in Dyads and Groups,* pp. 3–31. Hillsdale, NJ: Lawrence Erlbaum.

Ardrey, Robert (1961) *African Genesis.* New York: Dell.

——— (1966) *The Territorial Imperative.* New York: Atheneum.

Arias, Oscar (1997) "Esquipulas II: The management of a regional crisis," in D. P. Fry and K. Björkqvist (eds.), *Cultural Variation in Conflict Resolution: Alternatives to Violence,* pp. 147–158. Mahwah, NJ: Lawrence Erlbaum.

Asch, Michael I. (1981) "Slavey," in W. C. Sturtevant (general ed.), *Handbook of North American Indians,* J. Helm (volume ed.), *Volume 6, Subarctic,* pp. 338–349. Washington, DC: Smithsonian Institution.

Asch, Michael and Smith, Shirleen (1999) "Slavey Dene," in R. B. Lee and R. Daly (eds.), *The Cambridge Encyclopedia of Hunters and Gatherers,* pp. 46–50. Cambridge: Cambridge University Press.

Asch, Tim and Chagnon, Napoleon A. (1975) *The Ax Fight.* 16 mm film. Somerville, MA: Documentary Educational Resources.

Aubert, Vilhelm (1969) "Law as a way of resolving conflicts: The case of a small industrial society," in L. Nader (ed.), *Law in Culture and Society,* pp. 282–303. Chicago: Aldine.

Aureli, Filippo and de Waal, Frans B. M. (eds.) (2000) *Natural Conflict Resolution.* Berkeley: University of California Press.

Avruch, Kevin (1991) "Introduction: Culture and conflict resolution," in K. Avruch, P. W. Black, and J. A. Scimecca (eds.), *Conflict Resolution: Cross-Cultural Perspectives,* pp. 1–17. New York: Greenwood Press.

Axelrod, Robert (1984) *The Evolution of Cooperation.* New York: Basic Books.

Bahn, Paul G. (1992) "Cannibalism of ritual dismemberment?" in S. Jones, R. Martin, and D. Pilbeam (eds.), *The Cambridge Encyclopedia of Human Evolution,* p. 330. Cambridge: Cambridge University Press.

Balikci, Asen (1968) "The Netsilik Eskimos: Adaptive processes," in R. B. Lee and I. DeVore (eds.), *Man the Hunter,* pp. 78–82. Chicago: Aldine.

——— (1970) *The Netsilik Eskimo.* Garden City, NY: The Natural History Press.

Bandura, Albert (1973) *Aggression: A Social Learning Analysis.* Englewood Cliffs, NJ: Prentice-Hall.

Bar-Yosef, O. (1986) "The walls of Jericho: An alternative interpretation." *Current Anthropology,* 27:157–162.

Barash, David P. (1991) *Introduction to Peace Studies.* Belmont, CA: Wadsworth.

——— (ed.) (2001) *Understanding Violence.* Boston: Allyn and Bacon.

Barnard, Alan (1983) "Contemporary hunter-gatherers: Current theoretical issues in ecology and social organization." *Annual Review of Anthropology,* 12:193–214.

Barrett, S. A. (1925) *The Cayapa Indians of Ecuador.* Indian Notes and Monographs, Volume 40. New York: Museum of the American Indian, Heyes Foundation.

Barth, Fredrik (1952) "Subsistence and institutional system in a Norwegian mountain village." *Rural Sociology,* 17:26–38.

Barton, R. F. (1967) "Procedure among the Ifugao," in P. Bohannan (ed.), *Law and Warfare: Studies in the Anthropology of Conflict,* pp. 161–181. Austin: University of Texas Press.

Basso, Ellen B. (1973) *The Kalapalo Indians of Central Brazil.* New York: Holt, Rinehart, and Wilson.

Basso, Keith H. (ed.) (1971) *Western Apache Raiding and Warfare: From the Notes of Grenville Goodwin.* Tucson: University of Arizona Press.

Benjamin, Geoffrey (1993) "Temiar," in D. Levinson (ed. in chief), *Encyclopedia of World Cultures,* P. Hockings (volume ed.), *Volume V, East and Southeast Asia,* pp. 265–273. Boston: G. K. Hall.

Bennett, Wendell C. and Zingg, Robert M. (1976) *The Tarahumara: An Indian Tribe of Northern Mexico.* Glorieta, NM: The Rio Grande Press. Originally published in 1935.

Berndt, Catherine H. (1978) "In Aboriginal Australia," in A. Montagu (ed.), *Learning Non-Aggression: The Experience of Non-Literate Societies,* pp. 144–160. Oxford: Oxford University Press.

Berndt, Ronald M. (1965) "Law and order in Aboriginal Australia," in R. M. Berndt and C. H. Berndt (eds.), *Aboriginal Man in Australia: Essays in Honour of Emeritus Professor A. P. Elkin,* pp. 167–206. London: Angus and Robertson.

——— (1972) "The Walmadjeri and Gugadja," in M. G. Bicchieri (ed.), *Hunters and Gatherers Today,* pp. 177–216. Prospect Heights, IL: Waveland.

Berndt, Ronald and Berndt, Catherine (1945) "A preliminary report on field work in the Ooldea region, Western South Australia." *Oceania,* 15:239–266.

——— (1996) *The World of the First Australians,* 5th ed. Canberra: Aboriginal Studies Press.

Bertens, Jan-Willem (1994) "The European movement: Dreams and realities." Paper presented at the seminar "The EC after 1992: The United States of Europe?" Maastricht, The Netherlands, January.

Betzig, Laura and Wichimai, Santus (1991) "A not so perfect peace: A history of conflict on Ifaluk." *Oceania,* 61:240–256.

Bicchieri, M. G. (ed.) (1972) *Hunters and Gatherers Today.* Prospect Heights, IL: Waveland.

Billings, Dorothy K. (1991) "Cultural style and solutions to conflict." *Journal of Peace Research,* 28:249–262.

Binford, Lewis R. (2001) *Constructing Frames of Reference: An Analytical Method for Archaeological Theory Building Using Hunter-Gatherer and Environmental Data Sets.* Berkeley: University of California Press.

Binford, Lewis R. and Ho, Chuan K. (1985) "Taphonomy at a distance: Zhoukoudian, 'The cave home of Beijing man' "? *Current Anthropology,* 26:413–442.

Bird, Junius (1946) "The Alacaluf," in J. H. Steward (ed.), *Handbook of South American Indians, Volume 1, The Marginal Tribes,* pp. 55–80 plus plates. Washington, DC: U.S. Government Printing Office.

Bird, Nurit (1987) "The Kurumbas of the Nilgiris: An ethnographic myth?" *Modern Asian Studies,* 21:173–189.

Bird-David, Nurit (1992) "Nayaka," in D. Levinson (ed. in chief), *Encyclopedia of World Cultures,* P. Hockings (volume ed.), *Volume III, South Asia,* pp. 194–196. Boston: G. K. Hall.

Birdsell, Joseph B. (1971) "Australia: Ecology, spacing mechanisms and adaptive behaviour in aboriginal land tenure," in R. Crocombe (ed.), *Land Tenure in the Pacific,* pp. 334–361. New York: Oxford University Press.

Birket-Smith, Kaj and de Laguna, Frederica (1938) *The Eyak Indians of the Copper River Delta, Alaska.* Copenhagen: Levin and Munksgaard.

Black, Donald (1993) *The Social Structure of Right and Wrong.* San Diego: Academic Press.

Blackburn, Roderic H. (1982) "In the land of milk and honey: Okiek adaptations to their forests and neighbors," in E. Leacock and R. Lee (eds.), *Politics and History in Band Society,* pp. 283–305. Cambridge: Cambridge University Press.

Blanchard, D. Caroline and Blanchard, Robert J. (1989) "Experimental animal models of aggression: What do they say about human behaviour?" in J. Archer and K. Browne (eds.), *Human Aggression: Naturalistic Approaches,* pp. 94–121. London: Routledge.

Boas, Franz (1964) *The Central Eskimo.* Lincoln: University of Nebraska Press. Originally published in 1888.

Boehm, Christopher (1987) *Blood Revenge: The Enactment and Management of Conflict in Montenegro and Other Tribal Societies,* 2nd paperback ed. Philadelphia: University of Pennsylvania Press.

——— (1999) *Hierarchy in the Forest: The Evolution of Egalitarian Behavior.* Cambridge: Harvard University Press.

——— (2000) "Conflict and the evolution of social control," in L. D. Katz (ed.), *Evolutionary Origins of Morality: Cross-Disciplinary Perspectives,* pp. 79–101. Bowling Green, OH: Imprint Academic.

——— (2003) "Global conflict resolution: An anthropological diagnosis of problems with world governance," in R. W. Bloom and N. Dess (eds.), *Evolutionary Psychology and Violence: A Primer for Policymakers and Public Policy Advocates,* pp. 203–237. Westport, CT: Praeger.

——— (2005) "Variance reduction and the evolution of social control." Available: http://www.santafe.edu/files/gems/behavioralsciences/variance.pdf (Accessed: January 2005).

Boggs, Stephen T. and Chun, Malcolm N. (1990) "*Ho'oponopono:* A Hawaiian method of solving interpersonal problems," in K. A. Watson-Gegeo and G. M. White (eds.), *Disentangling: Conflict Discourse in Pacific Societies,* pp. 122–160. Stanford: Stanford University Press.

Bonta, Bruce D. (1993) *Peaceful Peoples: An Annotated Bibliography.* Metuchen, NJ: Scarecrow Press.

——— (1996) "Conflict resolution among peaceful societies: The culture of peacefulness." *Journal of Peace Research,* 33:403–420.

——— (1997) "Cooperation and competition in peaceful societies." *Psychological Bulletin,* 121:299–320.

Booth, William (1989) "Warfare over Yanomamö Indians." *Science,* 243:1138–1140.

Borgia, Gerald (1980) "Human aggression as a biological adaptation," in J. S. Lockard (ed.), *The Evolution of Human Social Behavior,* pp. 165–191. New York: Elsevier.

Bowen, Thomas and Moser, Mary Beck (1995) "Seri," in D. Levinson (ed. in chief), *Encyclopedia of World Cultures,* J. W. Dow and R. van Kemper (volume eds.), *Volume VIII, Middle America and the Caribbean,* pp. 232–235. Boston: G. K. Hall.

Brain, C. K. (1970) "New finds at the Swartkrans australopithecine site." *Nature,* 225:1112–1119.

Brenneis, Donald (1990) "Dramatic gestures: The Fiji Indian *Pancayat* as therapeutic event," in K. A. Watson-Gegeo and G. M. White (eds.), *Disentangling: Conflict Discourse in Pacific Societies,* pp. 214–238. Stanford: Stanford University Press.

Briggs, Jean L. (1970) *Never in Anger: Portrait of an Eskimo Family.* Cambridge: Harvard University Press.

——— (1978) "The origins of nonviolence: Inuit management of aggression (Canadian Arctic)," in A. Montagu (ed.), *Learning Non-Aggression: The Experience of Non-Literate Societies,* pp. 54–93. Oxford: Oxford University Press.

——— (1994) " 'Why don't you kill your baby brother?' The dynamics of peace in Canadian Inuit camps," in L. E. Sponsel and T. Gregor (eds.), *The Anthropology of Peace and Nonviolence,* pp. 155–181. Boulder, CO: Lynne Rienner.

Bright, William (1978) "Karok," in W. C. Sturtevant (general ed.), *Handbook of North American Indians,* R. F. Heizer (volume ed.), *Volume 8, California,* pp. 180–189. Washington, DC: Smithsonian Institution.

——— (1991) "Karok," in D. Levinson (ed. in chief), *Encyclopedia of World Cultures,* T. O'Leary and D. Levinson (volume eds.), *Volume I, North America,* pp. 175–178. Boston: G. K. Hall.

British Broadcasting Corporation, *BBC World Business Report,*" broadcast on March 18, 2003.

Brögger, Jan (1968) "Conflict resolution and the role of the bandit in peasant society." *Anthropological Quarterly,* 41:228–240.

Brown, Donald E. (1991) *Human Universals.* New York: McGraw-Hill.

Brown, James A. and Price, T. Douglas (1985) "Complex hunter-gatherers: Retrospect and prospect," in T. D. Price and J. A. Brown (eds.), *Prehistoric Hunter-Gatherers: The Emergence of Cultural Complexity,* pp. 436–442. New York: Academic Press.

Buck, Peter H. (1957) *Arts and Crafts of Hawaii.* In the electronic Human Relations Area Files, Hawaii, Doc. 2. New Haven, CT: HRAF, 2003, computer file.

Burbank, Victoria K. (1987) "Female aggression in cross-cultural perspective." *Behavior Science Research,* 21:70–100.

——— (1992) "Sex, gender, and difference: Dimensions of aggression in an Australian Aboriginal community." *Human Nature,* 3:251–278.

——— (1994) *Fighting Women: Anger and Aggression in Aboriginal Australia.* Berkeley: University of California Press.

Burnham, Terry and Phelan, Jay (2000) *Mean Genes: From Sex to Money to Food—Taming Our Primal Instincts.* New York: Penguin.

Burrows, Edwin G. (1952) "From value to ethos on Ifaluk Atoll." *Southwestern Journal of Anthropology,* 8:13–35.

——— (1963) *Flower in My Ear: Arts and Ethos on Ifaluk Atoll.* Seattle: University of Washington Press.

Buss, David (1992) "Mate preference mechanisms: Consequences for partner choice and intrasexual competition," in J. H. Barkow, L. Cosmides, and J. Tooby (eds.), *The Adapted Mind: Evolutionary Psychology and the Generation of Culture,* pp. 249–266. New York: Oxford University Press.

——— (1999) *Evolutionary Psychology: The New Science of the Mind.* Boston: Allyn and Bacon.

Buss, David M. and Shackelford, T. (1997) "Human aggression in evolutionary psychological perspective." *Clinical Psychology Review,* 17:605–619.

Campbell, Alan T. (1995) *Getting to Know Waiwai: An Amazonian Ethnography.* London: Routledge.

Campbell, Anne (1999) "Staying alive: Evolution, culture and women's intra-sexual aggression," with commentaries. *Behavioral and Brain Sciences,* 22:203–252.

Caplan, Lionel (1995) "The milieu of disputation: Managing quarrels in East Nepal," in P. Caplan (ed.), *Understanding Disputes: The Politics of Argument,* pp. 137–159. Oxford: Berg.

Carneiro, Robert L. (1977) "Recent observations on shamanism and witchcraft among the Kiukuru Indians of Central Brazil." *Annals of the New York Academy of Sciences,* 293:215–228.

——— (1983) "The cultivation of manioc among the Kuikuru of the Upper Xingú," in R. B. Hames and W. T. Vickers (eds.), *Adaptive Responses of Native Amazonians,* pp. 65–111. New York: Academic Press.

——— (1990) "Chiefdom-level warfare as exemplified in Fiji and the Cauca Valley," in J. Haas (ed.), *The Anthropology of War,* pp. 190–211. Cambridge: Cambridge University Press.

——— (1994a) "Kuikuru," in D. Levinson (ed. in chief), *Encyclopedia of World Cultures,* J. Wilbert (volume ed.), *Volume VII, South America,* pp. 206–209. Boston: G. K. Hall.

——— (1994b) "War and peace: Alternating realities in human history," in S. P. Reyna and R. E. Downs (eds.), *Studying War: Anthropological Perspectives,* pp. 3–27. Amsterdam: Gordon and Breach.

Cashdan, Elizabeth A. (1980) "Egalitarianism among hunters and gatherers." *American Anthropologist,* 82:116–120.

——— (1983) "Territoriality among human foragers: Ecological models and an application to four Bushman groups." *Current Anthropology,* 24:47–66.

Caton, Hiram (ed.) (1990) *The Samoa Reader: Anthropologists Take Stock.* New York: Lanham.

Chagnon, Napoleon A. (1974) *Studying the Yanomamö.* New York: Holt, Rinehart and Winston.

——— (1979a) "Is reproductive success equal in egalitarian societies?" in N. A. Chagnon and W. Irons (eds.), *Evolutionary Biology and Human Social Behavior: An Anthropological Perspective,* pp. 374–401. North Scituate, MA: Duxbury Press.

——— (1979b) "Mate competition, favoring close kin, and village fissioning among the Yanomamö Indians," in N. A. Chagnon and W. Irons (eds.), *Evolutionary Biology and Human Social Behavior: An Anthropological Perspective,* pp. 86–132. North Scituate, MA: Duxbury Press.

——— (1983) *Yanomamö: The Fierce People,* 3d ed. New York: Holt, Rinehart and Winston.

——— (1988) "Life histories, blood revenge, and warfare in a tribal population." *Science,* 239:985–992.

——— (1989) "Response to Ferguson." *American Ethnologist,* 16:565–570.

——— (1990a) "On Yanomamö violence: Reply to Albert." *Current Anthropology,* 31:49–53.

——— (1990b) "Reproductive and somatic conflicts of interest in the genesis of violence and warfare among tribesmen," in J. Haas (ed.), *The Anthropology of War,* pp. 77–104. Cambridge: Cambridge University Press.

——— (1992a) *Yanomamö,* 4th ed. Fort Worth: Harcourt Brace Jovanovich College Publishers.

——— (1992b) *Yanomamö: The Last Days of Eden.* San Diego: Harcourt Brace & Co.

——— (1996) "Chronic problems in understanding tribal violence and warfare," in G. R. Bock and J. A. Goode (eds.), *Genetics of Criminal and Antisocial Behaviour,* plus discussion, pp. 202–236. Chichester: John Wiley and Sons.

Chagnon, Napoleon A. and Bugos, Paul E., Jr. (1979) "Kin selection and conflict: An analysis of a Yanomamö ax fight," in N. A. Chagnon and W. Irons (eds.), *Evolutionary Biology and Human Social Behavior: An Anthropological Perspective,* pp. 213–238. North Scituate, MA: Duxbury Press.

Chagnon, Napoleon A., Flinn, Mark V., and Melancon, Thomas F. (1979) "Sex-ratio variation among the Yanomamö Indians," in N. A. Chagnon and W. Irons (eds.), *Evolutionary Biology and Human Social Behavior: An Anthropological Perspective,* pp. 290–320. North Scituate, MA: Duxbury Press.

Clark, G. A. (2002) "Neandertal archaeology—implications for our origins." *American Anthropologist,* 104:50–67.

Clastres, Pierre (1972) "The Guayaki," in M. G. Bicchieri (ed.), *Hunters and Gatherers Today,* pp. 138–174. Prospect Heights, IL: Waveland.

Cohen, Mark N. (1985) "Prehistoric hunter-gatherers: The meaning of social complexity," in T. D. Price and J. A. Brown (eds.), *Prehistoric Hunter-Gatherers: The Emergence of Cultural Complexity,* pp. 99–119. New York: Academic Press.

Colson, Elizabeth (1995) "The contentiousness of disputing," in P. Caplan (ed.), *Understanding Disputes: The Politics of Argument,* pp. 65–81. Oxford: Berg.

Conklin, Harold C. (1954) *The Relation of Hanunóo Culture to the Plant World.* Unpublished doctoral dissertation, Anthropology Department, Yale University.

Coon, Carleton S. (1971) *The Hunting Peoples.* Boston: Little, Brown and Co.

Cooper, John M. (1946a) "The Yahgan," in J. H. Steward (ed.), *Handbook of South American Indians, Volume 1, The Marginal Tribes,* pp. 81–106. Washington, DC: U.S. Government Printing Office.

——— (1946b) "The Ona," in J. H. Steward (ed.) *Handbook of South American Indians, Volume 1, The Marginal Tribes,* pp. 107–125. Washington, DC: U.S. Government Printing Office.

Cords, Marina and Aureli, Filippo (2000) "Reconciliation and relationship qualities," in F. Aureli and F. B. M. de Waal (eds.), *Natural Conflict Resolution,* pp. 177–198. Berkeley: University of California Press.

Côté, James E. (1994) *Adolescent Storm and Stress: An Evaluation of the Mead-Freeman Controversy.* Hillsdale, NJ: Lawrence Erlbaum Associates.

——— (2000a) "The Mead-Freeman controversy in review." *Journal of Youth and Adolescence,* 29:525–538.

——— (2000b) "The implausibility of Freeman's hoaxing theory: An update." *Journal of Youth and Adolescence,* 29:525–538.

Cox, Bruce A. (1968) *Law and Conflict Management among the Hopi.* Doctoral dissertation, Department of Anthropology, University of California at Berkeley.

Cronk, Lee (1999) *That Complex Whole: Culture and the Evolution of Human Behavior.* Boulder, CO: Westview.

Daly, Martin and Wilson, Margo (1988) *Homicide.* New York: Aldine de Gruyter.

——— (1994) "Evolutionary psychology of male violence," in J. Archer (ed.), *Male Violence,* pp. 253–288. London: Routledge.

Damas, David (1968) "The diversity of Eskimo societies," in R. B. Lee and I. DeVore (eds.), *Man the Hunter,* pp. 111–117. Chicago: Aldine.

——— (1972) "The Copper Eskimo," in M. G. Bicchieri (ed.), *Hunters and Gatherers Today,* pp. 3–49. Prospect Heights, IL: Waveland.

——— (1991) "Copper Eskimo," in D. Levinson (ed. in chief), *Encyclopedia of World Cultures,* T. O'Leary and D. Levinson (volume eds.), *Volume I, North America,* pp. 76–79. Boston: G. K. Hall.

Dart, Raymond A. (1949) "The predatory implemental technique of australopithecines." *American Journal of Physical Anthropology,* 7:1–38.

——— (1953) "The predatory transition from ape to man." *International Anthropological and Linguistic Review,* 1:201–218.

——— (1958) "The minimal bone-breccia content of Makapansgat and the australopithecine predatory habit." *American Anthropologist,* 60:923–931.

Darwin, Charles (1958a) *The Origin of Species: By Means of Natural Selection of the Preservation of Favoured Races in the Struggle for Life,* Mentor paperback ed. New York: New American Library, Times Mirror. Originally published in 1859.

——— (1958b) *The Autobiography of Charles Darwin, 1809–1882.* New York: W. W. Norton. Originally published in 1887.

——— (1998) *The Descent of Man.* New York: Prometheus Books. Originally published in 1871.

Davie, Maurice R. (1929) *The Evolution of War: A Study of Its Role in Early Societies.* New Haven, CT: Yale University Press.

de Waal, Frans B. M. (1989) *Peacemaking among Primates.* Cambridge: Harvard University Press.

——— (1996) *Good Natured: The Origin of Right and Wrong in Humans and Other Animals.* Cambridge: Harvard University Press.

——— (2000) "The first kiss: Foundations of conflict resolution research in animals," in F. Aureli and F. B. M. de Waal (eds.), *Natural Conflict Resolution,* pp. 15–33. Berkeley: University of California Press.

de Waal, Frans B. M. and Lanting, F. (1997) *Bonobo: The Forgotten Ape.* Berkeley: University of California Press.

Dennen, J. M. G. van der (1995) *The Origin of War,* 2 volumes. Groningen, The Netherlands: Origin Press.

Dentan, Robert Knox (1968) *The Semai: A Nonviolent People of Malaya.* New York: Holt, Rinehart, and Winston.

——— (1978) "Notes on childhood in a nonviolent context: The Semai case (Malaysia)," in A. Montagu (ed.), *Learning Non-Aggression: The Experience of Non-Literate Societies,* pp. 94–143. Oxford: Oxford University Press.

——— (1988) "Discussion and criticism: On reconsidering human violence in simple societies." *Current Anthropology,* 29:625–629.

——— (1992) "The rise, maintenance, and destruction of peaceable polity: A preliminary essay on political ecology," in J. Silverberg and J. P. Gray (eds.), *Aggression and Peacefulness in Humans and Other Primates,* pp. 214–270. New York: Oxford University Press.

——— (1993) "Senoi," in D. Levinson (ed. in chief), *Encyclopedia of World Cultures,* P. Hockings (volume ed.), *Volume V, East and Southeast Asia,* pp. 236–339. Boston: G. K. Hall.

——— (1994) "Surrendered men: Peaceable enclaves in the Post-Enlightenment West," in L. E. Sponsel and T. Gregor (eds.), *The Anthropology of Peace and Nonviolence,* pp. 69–108. Boulder, CO: Lynne Rienner.

——— (1995) "Bad day at Bukit Pekan." *American Anthropologist,* 97:225–231.

——— (1999) "Spotted doves at war." *Asian Folklore Studies,* 58:397–434.

——— (2000) "Ceremonies of innocence and the lineaments of ungratified desire: An analysis of a syncretic Southeast Asian taboo complex." *Bijdragen tot de Taal-, Land- en Volkenkunde (Journal of the Humanities and Social Sciences of Southeast Asia and Oceania),* 156:193–232.

——— (2001a) "Ambivalence in child training by the Semai of Peninsular Malaysia and other peoples." *Crossroads: An Interdisciplinary Journal of Southeast Asian Studies,* 15:89–129.

——— (2001b) "Peace and nonviolence: Anthropological aspects," in U. Hannerz (ed.), *Encyclopedia of the Social and Behavioral Sciences, vol. 3, Anthropology,* pp. 11140–11144. London: Elsevier Science.

——— (2004) "Cautious, alert, polite, and elusive: Semai of Central Peninsular Malaysia," in G. Kemp and D. P. Fry (eds.), *Keeping the Peace: Conflict Resolution and Peaceful Societies around the World,* pp. 167–184. New York: Routledge.

Dentan, Robert Knox and Williams-Hunt, Bah Tony (Anthony) (1999) "Untransfiguring death: A case study of rape, drunkenness, development and homicide in an apprehensive void." *Review of Indonesian and Malaysian Affairs,* 33:17–65.

Dick, Sara J. (1992) "Kurumbas," in D. Levinson (ed. in chief), *Encyclopedia of World Cultures,* P. Hockings (volume ed.), *Volume III, South Asia,* pp. 142–143. Boston: G. K. Hall.

DiMaggio, Jay (1992) "Lepcha," in D. Levinson (ed. in chief), *Encyclopedia of World Cultures,* P. Hockings (volume ed.), *Volume III, South Asia,* pp. 148–149. Boston: G. K. Hall.

Dobinson, Kristin (2004) "Rethinking peace and conflict: The Norwegians of Europe," in G. Kemp and D. P. Fry (eds.), *Keeping the Peace: Conflict Resolution and Peaceful Societies around the World,* pp. 149–166. New York: Routledge.

Dole, Gertrude E. (1966) "Anarchy without chaos: Alternatives to political authority among the Kuikuru," in M. J. Swartz, V. W. Turner, and A. Tuden (eds.), *Political Anthropology,* pp. 73–87. Chicago: Aldine.

Dolhinow, Phyllis (1999) "Review of *Demonic Males: Apes and the Origins of Human Violence* by R. Wrangham and D. Peterson." *American Anthropologist,* 101:445–446.

Donald, Leland (2000) "Patterns of war and peace among complex hunter-gatherers: The case of the Northwest Coast of North America," in P. P. Schweitzer, M. Biesele, and R. K. Hitchcock (eds.), *Hunters and Gatherers in the Modern World: Conflict, Resistance, and Self-Determination,* pp. 164–179. New York: Berghahn.

Doolan, J. K. (1979) "Aboriginal concept of boundary: How do Aboriginals conceive 'easements'—How do they grant them?" *Oceania,* 49:161–168.

Douglass, Frederick (1986) *Narrative of the Life of Frederick Douglass, an American Slave.* New York: Penguin. Originally published in 1845.

Downs, James F. (1966) *The Two Worlds of the Washo: An Indian Tribe of California and Nevada.* New York: Holt, Rinehart and Winston.

Dozier, Edward P. (1983) *The Pueblo Indians of North America,* Waveland ed. Prospect Heights, IL: Waveland Press.

Draper, Patricia (1975) "!Kung women: Contrasts in sexual egalitarianism in foraging and sedentary contexts," in R. R. Reiter (ed.), *Toward an Anthropology of Women,* pp. 77–109. New York: Monthly Review Press.

——— (1978) "The learning environment for aggression and anti-social behavior among the !Kung (Kalahari Desert, Botswana, Africa)," in A. Montagu (ed.), *Learning Non-Aggression: The Experience of Non-Literate Societies,* pp. 31–53. Oxford: Oxford University Press.

Driver, Harold. E. (1969) *Indians of North America,* 2d ed. Chicago: University of Chicago Press.

Drower, E. S. (1962) *The Mandaeans of Iraq and Iran: Their Cults, Customs, Magic Legends, and Folklore.* Leiden: E. J. Brill.

Du Bois, Cora (1960) *The People of Alor: A Social-Psychological Study of an East Indian Island.* New York: Harper and Brothers.

Dublan, Manuel and Lozano, José María (eds.) (1876) *Legislacíon Mexicana O, Colecćon Complete de las Disposiciones Legistativas Expedidas Desde la Independencía de la Republica,* in 34 volumes published between 1876 and 1904. Mexico City: Imprenta del Comercío de Dublan y Chávez.

Dunbar, R. I. M., Clark, Amanda, and Hurst, Nicola (1995) "Conflict and cooperation among the Vikings: Contingent behavioral decisions." *Ethology and Sociobiology,* 16:233–246.

Durrenberger, E. Paul and Beierle, John (1992) *Cultural Summary: Icelanders.* In the electronic Human Relations Area Files, Icelanders. New Haven, CT: HRAF, 2004, computer file.

Dyson-Hudson, R. and Smith, Eric Alden (1978) "Human territoriality: An ecological reassessment." *American Anthropologist,* 80:21–41.

Eckert, Penelope and Newmark, Russell (1980) "Central Eskimo song duels: A contextual analysis of ritual ambiguity." *Ethnology,* 19:191–211.

Edgerton, Ronald K. (1993) "Bukidnon," in D. Levinson (ed. in chief), *Encyclopedia of World Cultures,* P. Hockings (volume ed.), *Volume V, East and Southeast Asia,* pp. 52–55. Boston: G. K. Hall.

Ehrlich, Robert (2001) *Nine Crazy Ideas in Science: A Few Might Even Be True.* Princeton, NJ: Princeton University Press.

Eibl-Eibesfeldt, Irenäus (1961) "The fighting behavior of animals." *Scientific American,* 205:112–122.

——— (1974) "The myth of the aggression-free hunter and gatherer society," in R. L. Holloway (ed.), *Primate Aggression, Territoriality, and Xenophobia: A Comparative Perspective,* pp. 425–457. New York: Academic Press.

——— (1979) *The Biology of Peace and War: Men, Animals, and Aggression,* trans. E. Mosbacher. New York: Viking.

Elkin, A. P. (1931) "The kopara: The settlement of grievances." *Oceania,* 2:191–198.

Elmendorf, William W. (1974) *Structure of Twana Culture.* New York: Garland.

——— (1993) *Twana Narratives: Native Historical Accounts of a Coast Salish Culture.* Seattle: University of Washington Press.

Ember, Carol (1978) "Myths about hunter-gatherers." *Ethnology,* 17:439–448.

Ember, Carol R. and Ember, Melvin (1992a) "Warfare, aggression, and resource problems: Cross-cultural codes." *Behavior Science Research,* 26:169–226.

——— (1992b) "Resource unpredictability, mistrust, and war." *Journal of Conflict Resolution,* 36:242–262.

——— (1994a) "War, socialization, and interpersonal violence: A cross-cultural study." *Journal of Conflict Resolution,* 38:620–646.

——— (1997) "Violence in the ethnographic record: Results of cross-cultural research on war and aggression," in D. L. Martin and D. W. Frayer (eds.), *Troubled Times: Violence and Warfare in the Past,* pp. 1–20. Amsterdam: Gordon and Breach.

Ember, Melvin (1985) "Evidence and science in ethnography: Reflections on the Freeman-Mead controversy." *American Anthropologist,* 87:906–910.

Ember, Melvin and Ember, Carol (1971) "The conditions favoring matrilocal versus patrilocal residence." *American Anthropologist,* 73:571–594.

——— (1994b) "Cross-cultural studies of war and peace: Recent achievements and future possibilities," in S. P. Reyna and R. E. Downs (eds.), *Studying War: Anthropological Perspectives,* pp. 185–208. Amsterdam: Gordon and Breach.

Endicott, Karen L. (1984) "The Batek De' of Malaysia." *Cultural Survival Quarterly,* 8:6–8.

——— (1999) "Gender relations in hunter-gatherer societies," in R. B. Lee and R. Daly (eds.), *The Cambridge Encyclopedia of Hunters and Gatherers,* pp. 411–418. Cambridge: Cambridge University Press.

Endicott, Kirk (1979) *Batek Negrito Religion: The World-View and Rituals of a Hunting and Gathering People of Peninsular Malaysia.* Oxford: Clarendon Press.

——— (1983) "The effects of slave raiding on the Aborigines of the Malay Peninsula," in A. Reid (ed.), *Slavery, Bondage and Dependency in Southeast Asia,* pp. 216–245. New York: St. Martin's Press.

——— (1988) "Property, power and conflict among the Batek of Malaysia," in T. Ingold, D. Riches, and J. Woodburn (eds.), *Hunters and Gatherers 2: Property, Power, and Ideology,* pp. 110–127. Oxford: Berg.

——— (1993) "Semang," in D. Levinson (ed. in chief), *Encyclopedia of World Cultures,* P. Hockings (volume ed.), *Volume V, East and Southeast Asia,* pp. 233–236. Boston: G. K. Hall.

Ericksen, Karen P. and Horton, Heather (1992) "'Blood feuds': Cross-cultural variations in kin group vengeance." *Behavior Science Research,* 26:57–85.

Eron, Leonard and Huesmann, L. Rowell (1984) "The control of aggressive behavior by changes in attitudes, values, and the conditions of learning," in R. Blanchard and D. C. Blanchard (eds.), *Advances in the Study of Aggression, Volume 1,* pp. 139–171. Orlando, FL: Academic Press.

Estevez, Fernando (1992) "Canarians," in D. Levinson (ed. in chief), *Encyclopedia of World Cultures,* L. A. Bennett (volume ed.), *Volume IV, Europe (Central, Western, and Southeastern Europe),* pp. 50–53. Boston: G. K. Hall.

Evans-Pritchard, E. E. (1940) *The Nuer: A Description of the Modes of Livelihood and Political Institutions of a Nilotic People.* Oxford: Oxford University Press.

Ewers, John (1967) "Blackfoot raiding for horses and scalps," in P. Bohannan (ed.), *Law and Warfare,* pp. 327–344. Austin: University of Texas Press.

Fabbro, David (1978) "Peaceful societies: An introduction." *Journal of Peace Research,* 15:67–83.

Feinberg, Richard (1988) "Margaret Mead and Samoa: *Coming of Age* in fact and fiction." *American Anthropologist,* 90:656–663.

Ferguson, R. Brian (1984a) "Introduction: Studying war," in R. B. Ferguson (ed.), *Warfare, Culture, and Environment,* pp. 1–81. Orlando, FL: Academic Press.

——— (1984b) "A reexamination of the causes of Northwest Coast Warfare," in R. B. Ferguson (ed.), *Warfare, Culture, and Environment,* pp. 267–328. Orlando, FL: Academic Press.

——— (1989a) "Game wars? Ecology and conflict in Amazonia." *Journal of Anthropological Research,* 45:179–206.

——— (1989b) "Do Yanomamö killers have more kids?" *American Ethnologist,* 16:564–565.

——— (1990a) "Blood of the Leviathan: Western contact and warfare in Amazonia." *American Ethnologist,* 17:237–257.

——— (1990b) "Explaining war," in J. Haas (ed.), *The Anthropology of War,* pp. 26–55. Cambridge: Cambridge University Press.

——— (1995) *Yanomami Warfare: A Political History.* Santa Fe, NM: School of American Research Press.

——— (1997) "Violence and war in prehistory," in D. L. Martin and D. W. Frayer (eds.), *Troubled Times: Violence and Warfare in the Past,* pp. 321–355. Amsterdam: Gordon and Breach.

——— (2000) "Is war in our genes? Evidence vs. speculation on the antiquity and biology of war." Phi Beta Kappa lecture, Rutgers University, Newark, New Jersey, February 16.

Ferguson, R. Brian and Farragher, L. (1988) *The Anthropology of War: A Bibliography.* New York: Harry Frank Guggenheim Foundation.

Ferguson, R. Brian and Whitehead, Neil (eds.) (1992a) *War in the Tribal Zone: Expanding States and Indigenous Warfare.* Santa Fe, NM: School of American Research Press.

——— (1992b) "The violent edge of empire," in R. B. Ferguson and N. Whitehead (eds.), *War in the Tribal Zone: Expanding States and Indigenous Warfare,* pp. 1–30. Santa Fe, NM: School of American Research Press.

Fernea, Elizabeth W. and Fernea Robert A. (1991) *Nubian Ethnographies.* Prospect Heights, IL: Waveland Press.

Fernea, Robert (1973) *Nubians in Egypt: Peaceful People.* Austin: University of Texas Press.

——— (2004) "Putting a stone in the middle: The Nubians of Northern Africa," in G. Kemp and D. P. Fry (eds.), *Keeping the Peace: Conflict Resolution and Peaceful Societies around the World,* pp. 105–121. New York: Routledge.

Firth, Raymond (1957) *We, the Tikopia: A Sociological Study of Kinship in Primitive Polynesia,* 2d ed. London: George Allen and Unwin.

——— (1967) *Tikopia Ritual and Belief.* London: George Allen and Unwin.

Fisher, Roger and Ury, William L. (1981) *Getting to Yes: Negotiating Agreement without Giving In.* Boston: Houghton Mifflin.

Flannery, Kent V. and Marcus, Joyce (2003) "The origin of war: New ^{14}C dates from ancient Mexico." *Proceedings of the National Academy of Sciences,* 100:11,801–11,805.

Fock, Niels (1963) *Waiwai: Religion and Society of an Amazonian Tribe.* Copenhagen: The National Museum.

Foley, Robert (1992) "Studying human evolution by analogy," in S. Jones, R. Martin, and D. Pilbeam (eds.), *The Cambridge Encyclopedia of Human Evolution,* pp. 335–340. Cambridge: Cambridge University Press.

Forbes, H. O. (1885) "On the Kubus of Sumatra." *Journal of the Anthropological Institute of Great Britain and Ireland,* 14:121–127.

Force, Roland (1960) "Leadership and Culture Change in Palau." *Fieldiana Anthropology,* 50:1–211.

Fowler, Catherine S. (1991) "Southern Paiute (and Chemehuevi)," in D. Levinson (ed. in chief), *Encyclopedia of World Cultures,* T. O'Leary and D. Levinson (volume eds.), *Volume I, North America,* pp. 329–333. Boston: G. K. Hall.

Fox, Robin (1989) *The Search for Society: Quest for a Biosocial Science and Morality.* New Brunswick, NJ: Rutgers University Press.

Frake, Charles O. (1960) "The Eastern Subanun of Mindanao," in G. P. Murdock (ed.), *Social Structure in Southeast Asia,* pp. 51–64. New York: Wenner-Gren Viking Fund Publications in Anthropology.

——— (1980a) "Litigation in Lipay: A study of Subanun law," in A. S. Dil (ed.), *Language and Cultural Description: Essays by Charles O. Frake,* pp. 132–143. Stanford: Stanford University Press.

——— (1980b) "The diagnosis of disease among the Subanun of Mindanao," in A. S. Dil (ed.), *Language and Cultural Description: Essays by Charles O. Frake,* pp. 104–117. Stanford: Stanford University Press.

——— (1993) "Subanun," in D. Levinson (ed. in chief), *Encyclopedia of World Cultures,* P. Hockings (volume ed.), *Volume V, East and Southeast Asia,* pp. 243–246. Boston: G. K. Hall.

Freeman, Derek (1983) *Margaret Mead and Samoa: The Making and Unmaking of an Anthropological Myth.* Cambridge: Harvard University Press.

French, Hilary (1992) "Strengthening global environmental governance," in L. Brown, H. Brough, A. Durning, C. Flavin, H. French, J. Jacobson, N. Lenssen, M. Lowe, S. Postel, M. Renner, J. Ryan, L. Starke, and J. Young (eds.), *The State of the World 1992,* pp. 155–173. New York: W. W. Norton.

——— (1995) "Forging a new global partnership," in L. Brown, D. Denniston, C. Flavin, H. French, H. Kane, N. Lenssen, M. Renner, D. Roodman, M. Ryan, A. Sachs, L. Starke, P. Weber, and J. Young (eds.), *The State of the World 1995,* pp. 170–189. New York: W. W. Norton.

——— (2000) *Vanishing Borders: Protecting the Planet in the Age of Globalization.* New York: W. W. Norton.

Fried, Morton (1973) "On human aggression," in C. Otten (ed.), *Aggression and Evolution,* pp. 355–362. Lexington, MA: Xerox College Publishing.

Friedrich, Paul (1972) "Political homicide in rural Mexico," in I. K. Feierabend, R. L. Feierabend, and T. R. Gurr (eds.), *Anger, Violence and Politics,* pp. 269–282. Englewood Cliffs, NJ: Prentice-Hall.

Fry, Douglas P. (1980) "The evolution of aggression and the level of selection controversy." *Aggressive Behavior,* 6:69–89.

——— (1985) "Utilizing human capacities for survival in the nuclear age." *Bulletin of Peace Proposals,* 16:159–166.

——— (1987) "Differences between playfighting and serious fighting among Zapotec children." *Ethology and Sociobiology,* 8:285–306.

——— (1988) "Intercommunity differences in aggression among Zapotec children." *Child Development,* 59:1008–1019.

——— (1990) "Play aggression among Zapotec children: Implications for the practice hypothesis." *Aggressive Behavior,* 16:321–340.

——— (1992a) "Female aggression among the Zapotec of Oaxaca, Mexico," in K. Björkqvist and P. Niemalä (eds.), *Of Mice and Women: Aspects of Female Aggression,* pp. 187–199. Orlando, FL: Academic Press.

——— (1992b) "'Respect for the rights of others is peace': Learning aggression versus non-aggression among the Zapotec." *American Anthropologist,* 94:621–639.

——— (1993a) "Intergenerational transmission of disciplinary practices and approaches to conflict." *Human Organization,* 52:176–185.

——— (1993b) "The relationship of environmental attitudes and knowledge to environmental behavior." Paper presented at the meeting of the American Anthropological Association, Washington, DC, November 17–21.

——— (1994) "Maintaining social tranquility: Internal and external loci of aggression control," in L. E. Sponsel and T. Gregor (eds.), *The Anthropology of Peace and Nonviolence,* pp. 133–154. Boulder, CO: Lynne Reinner.

——— (1998) "Anthropological perspectives on aggression: Sex differences and cultural variation." *Aggressive Behavior,* 24:81–95.

——— (1999a) "Peaceful societies," in L. R. Kurtz (ed.), *Encyclopedia of Violence, Peace and Conflict, Volume 3,* pp. 719–733. San Diego: Academic Press.

——— (1999b) "Aggression and altruism," in L. R. Kurtz (ed.), *Encyclopedia of Violence, Peace and Conflict, Volume 1,* pp. 17–33. San Diego: Academic Press.

——— (2000) "Conflict management in cross-cultural perspective," in F. Aureli and F. B. M. de Waal (eds.), *Natural Conflict Resolution,* pp. 334–351. Berkeley: University of California Press.

——— (2001a) "Aggression prevention in cross-cultural perspective: From Finns to Zapotecs," in M. Martinez (ed.), *Prevention and Control of Aggression and the Impact on Its Victims,* pp. 313–321. New York: Kluwer Academic/Plenum.

——— (2001b) "Is violence getting too much attention? Cross-cultural findings on the ways people deal with conflict," in J. M. Ramirez and D. S. Richardson (eds.), *Cross-Cultural Approaches to Research on Aggression and Reconciliation,* pp. 123–148. Huntington, NY: Nova Science Publishers.

——— (2001c) "Developing alternatives to war," in M. Martinez (ed.), *Prevention and Control of Aggression and the Impact on Its Victims,* pp. 339–346. New York: Kluwer Academic/ Plenum.

——— (2004a) "Conclusion: Learning from peaceful societies," in G. Kemp and D. P. Fry (eds.), *Keeping the Peace: Conflict Resolution and Peaceful Societies around the World,* pp. 185–204. New York: Routledge.

——— (2004b) "Multiple paths to peace: The "La Paz" Zapotec of Mexico," in G. Kemp and D. P. Fry (eds.), *Keeping the Peace: Conflict Resolution and Peaceful Societies around the World,* pp. 73–87. New York: Routledge.

——— (2005) "Rough-and-tumble social play in humans," in A. D. Pellegrini and P. K. Smith (eds.), *The Nature of Play: Great Apes and Humans,* 54–85. New York: Guilford.

——— (2006) "Reciprocity: The foundation stone of morality," in M. Killen and J. Smetana (eds.), *Handbook of Moral Development.* Mahwah, NJ: Lawrence Erlbaum.

Fry, Douglas P. and Fry, C. Brooks (1997) "Culture and conflict resolution models: Exploring alternatives to violence," in D. P. Fry and K. Björkqvist (eds.), *Cultural Variation in Conflict Resolution: Alternatives to Violence,* pp. 9–23. Mahwah, NJ: Lawrence Erlbaum.

Fry, Douglas P. and Takala, Jukka-Pekka (2001) "Who's afraid of Helsinki at night?" Paper presented at the meetings of the European Sociological Association, Helsinki, Finland, August 28–September 1.

Fry, Douglas P. and Welch, James N. (1992) "Beliefs about human nature and conflict: Implications for peace education." Paper presented at the meetings of the American Anthropological Association, San Francisco, December.

Fry, Kathy M. (1989) *Women's Status and Their Contribution to the Household Economy: A Study of Two Zapotec Communities.* Unpublished master's thesis, Department of Anthropology, Indiana University.

Fürer-Haimendorf, von Christoph (1984) *The Sherpas Transformed: Social Change in a Buddhist Society of Nepal.* New Delhi: Sterling.

——— (1985) *Tribal Populations and Cultures of the Indian Subcontinent.* Leiden-Köln: E. J. Brill.

Garb, Paula (1996) "Mediation in the Caucasus," in A. W. Wolfe and H. Yang (eds.), *Anthropological Contributions to Conflict Resolution,* pp. 31–46. Athens: University of Georgia Press.

Gardner, Peter (1966) "Symmetric respect and memorate knowledge: The structure and ecology of individualistic culture." *Southwestern Journal of Anthropology,* 22:389–415.

——— (1972) "The Paliyans," in M. G. Bicchieri (ed.), *Hunters and Gatherers Today,* pp. 404–447. Prospect Heights, IL: Waveland.

——— (1985) "Bicultural oscillation as a long-term adaptation to cultural frontiers: Cases and questions." *Human Ecology,* 13:411–432.

——— (1991) "Foragers' pursuit of individual autonomy." *Current Anthropology,* 32:543–572.

——— (1995) "Escalation avoidance and persistent Paliyan nonviolence." Paper presented at the meeting of the American Anthropological Association, Washington, DC, November 15–19.

——— (1999) "The Paliyan," in R. B. Lee and R. Daly (eds.), *The Cambridge Encyclopedia of Hunters and Gatherers,* pp. 261–264. Cambridge: Cambridge University Press.

——— (2000a) "Respect and nonviolence among recently sedentary Paliyan foragers." *Journal of the Royal Anthropological Institute* (N. S.), 6:215–236.

——— (2000b) *Bicultural Versatility as a Frontier Adaptation among Paliyan Foragers of South India.* Lewiston, NY: Edwin Mellen Press.

——— (2004) "Respect for all: The Paliyans of South India," in G. Kemp and D. P. Fry (eds.), *Keeping the Peace: Conflict Resolution and Peaceful Societies around the World,* pp. 53–71. New York: Routledge.

Gardner, S. E. and Resnik, H. (1996) "Violence among youth: Origins and a framework for prevention," in R. L. Hampton, P. Jenkins, and T. P. Gullotta (eds.), *Preventing Violence in America,* pp. 157–177. Thousand Oaks, CA: Sage.

Gat, Azar (2000a) "The human motivational complex: Evolutionary theory and the causes of hunter-gatherer fighting. Part I. Primary somatic and reproductive causes." *Anthropological Quarterly,* 73:20–34.

——— (2000b) "The human motivational complex: Evolutionary theory and the causes of hunter-gatherer fighting. Part II. Proximate, subordinate, and derivative causes." *Anthropological Quarterly,* 73:74–88.

Gayton, Anna H. (1948) *Yokuts and Western Mono Ethnography.* In the electronic Human Relations Area Files, Klamath, Doc. 1. New Haven, CT: HRAF, 2002, computer file.

Geary, David C. (1998) *Male, Female: The Evolution of Human Sex Differences.* Washington, DC: American Psychological Association.

Geertz, Clifford (1973) *The Interpretation of Cultures.* New York: Basic Books.

Ghiglieri, Michael P. (1999) *The Dark Side of Man: Tracing the Origins of Male Violence.* Reading, MA: Perseus.

Gibbs, James L. (1963) "The Kpelle moot: A therapeutic model for the informal settlement of disputes." *Africa,* 33:1–11.

——— (1965) "The Kpelle of Liberia," in J. L. Gibbs (ed.), *Peoples of Africa,* pp. 199–240. New York: Holt, Rinehart, and Winston.

Gibson, Thomas (1989) "Symbolic representations of tranquility and aggression among the Buid," in S. Howell and R. Willis (eds.), *Societies at Peace: Anthropological Perspectives,* pp. 60–78. London: Routledge.

——— (1990) "Raiding, trading, and tribal autonomy in insular Southeast Asia," in J. Haas (ed.), *The Anthropology of War,* pp. 125–145. Cambridge: Cambridge University Press.

Gifford, Edward W. (1926) *Clear Lake Pomo Society.* In the electronic Human Relations Area Files, Pomo, Doc. 7. New Haven, CT: HRAF, 2000, computer file.

Gilberg, Rolf (1984) "Polar Eskimo," in D. Damas (volume ed.) and W. C. Sturtevant (ed.), *Handbook of North American Indians, Volume 5, Arctic,* pp. 577–594. Washington, DC: Smithsonian Press.

——— (1991) "Inughuit," in D. Levinson (ed. in chief), *Encyclopedia of World Cultures,* T. O'Leary and D. Levinson (volume eds.), *Volume I, North America,* pp. 159–161. Boston: G. K. Hall.

Glazer, Ilsa (1997) "Beyond the competition of tears: Black-Jewish conflict containment in a New York neighborhood," in D. P. Fry and K. Björkqvist (eds.), *Cultural Variation in Conflict Resolution: Alternatives to Violence,* pp. 137–144. Mahwah, NJ: Lawrence Erlbaum.

Gluckman, Max (1967) "The judicial process among the Barotse," in P. Bohannan (ed.), *Law and Warfare: Studies in the Anthropology of Conflict,* pp. 59–91. Austin: University of Texas Press.

Goldman, Irving (1961) "The Zuni of New Mexico," in M. Mead (ed.), *Cooperation and Competition among Primitive Peoples,* revised paperback ed., pp. 313–353. Boston: Beacon Press. Originally published in 1937.

Goldstein, Joshua (2001) *War and Gender: How Gender Shapes the War System and Vice Versa.* Cambridge: Cambridge University Press.

Goodale, Jane C. (1974) *Tiwi Wives: A Study of the Women of Melville Island, North Australia,* first paperback ed. Seattle: University of Washington Press.

——— (1991) "Tiwi," in D. Levinson (ed. in chief), *Encyclopedia of World Cultures,* T. E. Hays (volume ed.), *Volume II, Oceania,* pp. 327–330. Boston: G. K. Hall.

Gorer, Geoffrey (1967) *Himalayan Village: An Account of the Lepchas of Sikkim,* 2d ed. New York: Basic Books. Originally published in 1938.

Gould, Richard A. (1991) "Ngatatjara," in D. Levinson (ed. in chief), *Encyclopedia of World Cultures,* T. E. Hays (volume ed.), *Volume II, Oceania,* pp. 238–241. Boston: G. K. Hall.

Gould, Stephen Jay (1978) "Morton's ranking of races by cranial capacity." *Science,* 200:503–509.

Gowdy, John (1999) "Hunter-gatherers and the mythology of the market," in R. B. Lee and R. Daly (eds.), *The Cambridge Encyclopedia of Hunters and Gatherers,* pp. 391–398. Cambridge: Cambridge University Press.

Grant, Nicole (1995) "From Margaret Mead's field notes: What counted as 'sex' in Samoa?" *American Anthropologist,* 97:678–682.

Gratton, Nancy E. (1991) "Pintupi," in D. Levinson (ed. in chief), *Encyclopedia of World Cultures,* T. E. Hays (volume ed.), *Volume II, Oceania,* pp. 264–267. Boston: G. K. Hall.

Greenberg, James B. (1981) *Santiago's Sword: Chatino Peasant Religion and Economics.* Berkeley: University of California Press.

——— (1989) *Blood Ties: Life and Violence in Rural Mexico.* Tucson: University of Arizona Press.

Greenhouse, Carol (1985) "Mediation: A comparative approach." *Man,* 20:90–114.

Gregor, Thomas (1985) *Anxious Pleasures: The Sexual Lives of an Amazonian People.* Chicago: University of Chicago Press.

——— (1990) "Uneasy peace: Intertribal relations in Brazil's Upper Xingu," in J. Haas (ed.), *The Anthropology of War,* pp. 105–124. Cambridge: Cambridge University Press.

——— (1994a) "Mehinaku," in D. Levinson (ed. in chief), *Encyclopedia of World Cultures,* J. Wilbert (volume ed.), *Volume VII, South America,* pp. 235–239. Boston: G. K. Hall.

——— (1994b) "Symbols and rituals of peace in Brazil's Upper Xingu," in L. E. Sponsel and T. Gregor (eds.), *The Anthropology of Peace and Nonviolence,* pp. 241–257. Boulder, CO: Lynne Rienner.

——— (1996a) *A Natural History of Peace.* Nashville, TN: Vanderbilt University Press.

——— (1996b) "Introduction," in T. Gregor (ed.), *A Natural History of Peace,* pp. ix–xxiii. Nashville, TN: Vanderbilt University Press.

——— (forthcoming) Untitled book on the Upper Xingu peace system.

Gregor, Thomas and Robarchek, Clayton A. (1996) "Two paths to peace: Semai and Mehinaku nonviolence," in T. Gregor (ed.), *A Natural History of Peace,* pp. 159–188. Nashville, TN: Vanderbilt University Press.

Gregor, Thomas and Sponsel, Leslie E. (1994) "Preface," in L. E. Sponsel and T. Gregor (eds.), *The Anthropology of Peace and Nonviolence,* pp. xv–xviii. Boulder, CO: Lynne Rienner.

Grönfors, Martti. (1977) *Blood Feuding among Finnish Gypsies: Sociology Research Report No. 213.* Helsinki: University of Helsinki.

Grunkemeyer, Marilyn T. (1996) "Belief systems," in D. Levinson and M. Ember (eds.), *Encyclopedia of Cultural Anthropology, Volume 1,* pp. 125–130. New York: Henry Holt and Company.

Gudjónsson, G. H. and Pétursson, H. (1990) "Homicide in the Nordic countries." *Acta Psychiatrica Scandinavia,* 82:49–54.

Guenther, Mathias (2002) "Independence, resistance, accommodation, persistence: Hunter-gatherers and agropastoralists in the Ghanzi Veld, early 1800s to mid-1900s," in S. Kent (ed.), *Ethnicity, Hunter-Gatherers, and the "Other,"* pp. 127–149. Washington, DC: Smithsonian Institution Press.

Guerra, Nancy G., Eron, Leonard D., Huesmann, L. Rowell, Tolan, Patrick H., and van Acker, Richard (1997) "A cognitive/ecological approach to the prevention and mitigation of violence and aggression in inner-city youth," in D. P. Fry and K. Björkqvist (eds.), *Cultural Variation in Conflict Resolution: Alternatives to Violence,* pp. 199–213. Mahwah, NJ: Lawrence Erlbaum.

Gullestad, Marianne (1991) "Doing interpretive analysis in a modern large scale society: The meaning of peace and quiet in Norway." *Social Analysis: Journal of Cultural and Social Practice,* 29:38–61.

Gulliver, P. H. (1979) *Disputes and Negotiations: A Cross-Cultural Perspective.* New York: Academic Press.

Gurven, Michael, Allen-Arave, Wesley, Hill, Kim, and Hurtado, Magdalena (2000) "It's a Wonderful Life": Signaling generosity among the Ache of Paraguay. *Evolution and Human Behavior,* 21:263–282.

Gusinde, Martin (1931) *The Fireland Indians, Volume 1: The Selk'nam, on the Life and Thought of a Hunting People of the Great Island of Tierra del Fuego.* In the electronic Human Relations Area Files, Ona, Doc. 1. New Haven, CT: HRAF, 1996, computer file.

——— (1937) *The Yahgan: The Life and Thought of the Water Nomads of Cape Horn,* trans. Frieda Schütze. In the electronic Human Relations Area Files, Yahgan, Doc. 1. New Haven, CT: HRAF, 2003, computer file.

Haas, Jonathan (1996) "War," in D. Levinson and M. Ember (eds.), *Encyclopedia of Cultural Anthropology, Volume 4,* pp. 1357–1361. New York: Henry Holt and Company.

——— (1999) "The origins of war and ethnic violence," in J. Carman and A. Harding (eds.), *Ancient Warfare: Archaeological Perspectives,* pp. 11–24. Gloucestershire, UK: Sutton Publishing.

——— (2001) "Warfare and the evolution of culture," in G. Feinman and T. D. Price (eds.), *Archaeology at the Millennium: A Sourcebook,* pp. 329–350. Kluwer Academic/Plenum: New York.

Haghighi, Bahram and Sorensen, Jon (1996) "America's fear of crime," in T. J. Flanagan and D. R. Longmire (eds.), *Americans View Crime and Justice: A National Public Opinion Survey,* pp. 16–30. Thousand Oaks, CA: Sage.

Hallowell, A. Irving (1974) "Aggression in Saulteaux society," in A. I. Hallowell (ed.), *Culture and Experience,* pp. 277–290. Philadelphia: University of Pennsylvania Press.

Halonen, Tarja (2000) "Speech by President of the Republic Tarja Halonen at the 18th general International Peace Research Association conference," Tampere, Finland, August 5. Online at www.copri.dk/copri/ipra/halonen.htm, August 16, 2004.

Hamilton, William D. (1964) "The genetical evolution of social behaviour, II." *Journal of Theoretical Biology,* 7:17–52.

——— (1971) "Selection of selfish and altruistic behavior in some extreme models," in J. F. Eisenberg and W. S. Dillon (eds.), *Man and Beast: Comparative Social Behavior.* Washington, DC: Smithsonian Press.

Harner, Michael J. (1972) *The Jívaro: People of the Sacred Waterfall.* Garden City, NY: Anchor Books/Doubleday.

Harris, Judith R. (1999) *The Nurture Assumption: Why Children Turn Out the Way They Do,* first Touchstone ed. New York: Simon and Schuster.

Hart, C. W. M. and Pilling, Arnold (1960) *The Tiwi of North Australia.* New York: Holt, Rinehart, and Winston.

——— (1979) *The Tiwi of North Australia,* fieldwork ed. New York: Holt, Rinehart, and Winston.

Hart, C. W. M., Pilling, Arnold R., and Goodale, Jane C. (1988) *The Tiwi of North Australia,* 3d ed. New York: Holt, Rinehart, and Winston.

Hawes, C. H. (1903) "Gilyak," in the Human Relations Area Files, code 721. New Haven, CT: HRAF Press.

Heider, Karl G. (1979) *Grand Valley Dani: Peaceful Warriors.* New York: Holt, Rinehart, and Winston.

Heinen, H. Dieter (1994) "Warao," in D. Levinson (ed. in chief), *Encyclopedia of World Cultures,* J. Wilbert (volume ed.), *Volume VII, South America,* pp. 356–359. Boston: G. K. Hall.

Helm, June (1956) "Leadership among the Northeastern Athabascans." *Anthropologica,* 2:131–163.

——— (1961) *The Lynx Point People: The Dynamics of a Northern Athapaskan Band.* Ottawa: National Museum of Canada, Bulletin Number 176, Anthropology Series Number 53.

——— (1968) "The nature of Dogrib socioterritorial groups," in R. B. Lee and I. DeVore (eds.), *Man the Hunter,* pp. 118–125. Chicago: Aldine.

——— (1972) "The Dogrib Indians," in M. G. Bicchieri (ed.), *Hunters and Gatherers Today,* pp. 51–89. Prospect Heights, IL: Waveland.

——— (1991) "Dogrib," in D. Levinson (ed. in chief), *Encyclopedia of World Cultures,* T. O'Leary and D. Levinson (volume eds.), *Volume I, North America,* pp. 87–90. Boston: G. K. Hall.

Henley, Paul (1982) *The Panare: Tradition and Change on the Amazonian Frontier.* New Haven, CT: Yale University Press.

——— (1994) "Panare," in D. Levinson (ed. in chief), *Encyclopedia of World Cultures,* J. Wilbert (volume ed.), *Volume VII, South America,* pp. 264–267. Boston: G. K. Hall.

Henry, Donald O. (1985) "Preagricultural sedentism: The Natufian example," in T. D. Price and J. A. Brown (eds.), *Prehistoric Hunter-Gatherers: The Emergence of Cultural Complexity,* pp. 365–384. New York: Academic Press.

Henry, Jules (1941) *Jungle People: Kaingáng Tribe of the Highlands of Brazil.* New York: J. J. Augustin.

Hester, Thomas R. (1991) "Yurok," in D. Levinson (ed. in chief), *Encyclopedia of World Cultures,* T. O'Leary and D. Levinson (volume eds.), *Volume I, North America,* pp. 393–396. Boston: G. K. Hall.

Hiatt, L. R. (1968) "Ownership and use of land among Australian Aborigines," in R. B. Lee and I. DeVore (eds.), *Man the Hunter,* pp. 99–102. Chicago: Aldine.

Hickson, Letitia (1979) "Hierarchy, conflict, and apology in Fiji," in K.-F. Koch (ed.), *Access to Justice, Volume 4, The Anthropological Perspective, Patterns of Conflict Management: Essays in the Ethnography of Law,* pp. 17–39. Alphen aan den Rijn: Sijthoff and Noordhoff.

——— (1986) "The social context of apology in dispute settlement: A cross-cultural study." *Ethnology,* 25:283–294.

Hill, Kim (1994) "Ache," in D. Levinson (ed. in chief), *Encyclopedia of World Cultures,* J. Wilbert (volume ed.), *Volume VII, South America,* pp. 3–7. Boston: G. K. Hall.

Hinde, Robert A. (1974) *Biological Bases of Human Social Behaviour.* New York: McGraw-Hill.

——— (2001) "Why is war acceptable?" in M. Martinez (ed.), *Prevention and Control of Aggression and the Impact on Its Victims,* pp. 323–330. New York: Kluwer Academic/Plenum.

Hinde, Robert A. and Groebel, J. (1989) "The problem of aggression," in J. Groebel and R. A. Hinde (eds.), *Aggression and War: Their Biological and Social Bases,* pp. 3–9. Cambridge: Cambridge University Press.

Hines, Nicole J. and Fry, Douglas P. (1994) "Indirect modes of aggression among women of Buenos Aires, Argentina." *Sex Roles,* 30:213–236.

Hobbes, Thomas (1946) *Leviathan: Or the Matter, Forme and Power of a Commonwealth Ecclesiasticall and Civil.* Oxford: Basil Blackwell. Originally published in 1651.

Hobhouse, L. T. (1956) "Part II. Peace and order among the simplest peoples." *British Journal of Sociology,* 7:96–119.

Hobhouse, L. T., Wheeler, G. C., and M. Ginsberg (1915) *The Material Culture and Social Institutions of the Simpler Peoples: An Essay in Correlation.* London: Chapman and Hall.

Hockings, Paul (1980) *Ancient Hindu Refugees: Badaga Social History 1550–1975.* The Hague: Mouton.

——— (1992) "Badaga," in D. Levinson (ed. in chief), *Encyclopedia of World Cultures,* P. Hockings (volume ed.), *Volume III, South Asia,* pp. 14–18. Boston: G. K. Hall.

——— (1993) "Hanunóo," in D. Levinson (ed. in chief), *Encyclopedia of World Cultures,* P. Hockings (volume ed.), *Volume V, East and Southeast Asia,* pp. 90–91. Boston: G. K. Hall.

Hoebel, E. Adamson (1967a) "Law-ways of the Comanche Indians," in P. Bohannan (ed.), *Law and Warfare: Studies in the Anthropology of Conflict,* pp. 183–203. Austin: University of Texas Press.

——— (1967b) *The Law of Primitive Man: A Study in Comparative Legal Dynamics.* Cambridge: Harvard University Press.

Hollan, Douglas (1988) "Staying 'cool' in Toraja: Informal strategies for the management of anger and hostility in a nonviolent society." *Ethos,* 16:52–72.

——— (1997) "Conflict avoidance and resolution among the Toraja of South Sulawesi, Indonesia," in D. P. Fry and K. Björkqvist (eds.), *Cultural Variation in Conflict Resolution: Alternatives to Violence,* pp. 59–68. Mahwah, NJ: Lawrence Erlbaum.

Hollos, Marida C. (1970) *Community, Family, and Cognitive Development in Rural Norway.* Unpublished doctoral dissertation, Department of Anthropology, University of California at Berkeley.

——— (1974) *Growing up in Flathead: Social Environment and Cognitive Development.* Oslo: Universitetsforlaget.

Holmberg, Allan (1969) *Nomads of the Long Bow: The Siriono of Eastern Bolivia.* New York: American Museum of Natural History. Originally published in 1950.

Holmes, Lowell D. (1987) *Quest for the Real Samoa: The Mead/Freeman Controversy and Beyond.* South Hadley, MA: Bergin and Garvey.

Holsti, Rudolf (1913) "The Relation of War to the Origin of the State." *Annales Academiæ Scientiarum Fennicæ, Series B, Volume XII.* Helsinki: Finnish Academy of Science.

Honigmann, John J. (1954) *The Kaska Indians: An Ethnographic Reconstruction.* New Haven, CT: Yale University Publications in Anthropology, no. 51.

Honkatukia, Päivi (2001) *"Ilmoitti tulleensa raiskatuksi": Tutkimus Poliisin Tietoon Vuonna 1998 Tulleista Raiskausrikoksista,* Oikeuspoliittisen tutkimuslaitoksen tutkimuksia 180. Helsinki: Statistics Finland.

Horton, David (1994) "Warfare," in D. Horton (ed.), *The Encyclopedia of Aboriginal Australia: Aboriginal and Torres Strait Islanders History, Society, and Culture, Volume 2,* pp. 1152–1154. Canberra: Aboriginal Studies Press.

Hose, C. (1894) "The natives of Borneo." *Journal of the Anthropological Institute of Great Britain and Ireland,* 23:156–172.

Hosley, E. H. (1991) "Ingalik," in D. Levinson (ed. in chief), *Encyclopedia of World Cultures,* T. O'Leary and D. Levinson (volume eds.), *Volume I, North America,* pp. 156–159. Boston: G. K. Hall.

Hostetler, John A. (1974) *Hutterite Society.* Baltimore: Johns Hopkins University Press.

——— (1983a) *Amish Life.* Scottdale, PA: Herald Press.

——— (1983b) *Hutterite Life.* Scottdale, PA: Herald Press.

——— (1991) "Hutterites," in D. Levinson (ed. in chief), *Encyclopedia of World Cultures,* T. O'Leary and D. Levinson (volume eds.), *Volume I, North America,* pp. 153–155. Boston: G. K. Hall.

Hostetler, John A. and Huntington, Gertrude E. (1968) "Communal socialization patterns in Hutterite society." *Ethnology,* 7:331–355.

Howard, Alan (1990) "Dispute management in Rotuma." *Journal of Anthropological Research,* 46:263–292.

——— (2004) "Restraint and ritual apology: The Rotumans of the South Pacific," in G. Kemp and D. P. Fry (eds.) *Keeping the Peace: Conflict Resolution and Peaceful Societies around the World,* pp. 35–51. New York: Routledge.

Howard, Catherine (1994) "Wáiwai," in D. Levinson (ed. in chief), *Encyclopedia of World Cultures,* J. Wilbert (volume ed.), *Volume VII, South America,* pp. 345–348. Boston: G. K. Hall.

Howe, L. E. A. (1989) "Peace and violence in Bali: Culture and social organization," in S. Howell and R. Willis (eds.), *Societies at Peace: Anthropological Perspectives,* pp. 100–116. London: Routledge.

Howell, Nancy (1979) *Demography of the Dobe !Kung.* New York: Academic Press.

Howell, Signe (1988) "From child to human: Chewong concepts of self," in G. Jahoda and I. M. Lewis (eds.), *Acquiring Culture: Cross Cultural Studies in Child Development,* pp. 147–168. London: Croom Helm.

——— (1989) "'To be angry is not to be human, but to be fearful is': Chewong concepts of human nature," in S. Howell and R. Willis (eds.), *Societies at Peace: Anthropological Perspectives,* pp. 45–59. London: Routledge.

Howell, Signe and Willis, Roy (1989) *Societies at Peace: Anthropological Perspectives.* London: Routledge.

Huesmann, L. Rowell (1988) "An information processing model for the development of aggression." *Aggressive Behavior,* 14:13–24.

Huntingford, Felicity and Turner, Angela (1987) *Animal Conflict.* London: Chapman and Hall.

Huntingford, G. W. B. (1951) "The social institutions of the Dorobo." *Anthropos,* 46:1–48.

——— (1954) "The political organization of the Dorobo." *Anthropos,* 49:123–148.

Ingold, Tim (1976) *The Skolt Lapps Today.* Cambridge: Cambridge University Press.

——— (1999) "On the social relations of the hunter-gatherer band," in R. B. Lee and R. Daly (eds.), *The Cambridge Encyclopedia of Hunters and Gatherers,* pp. 399–410. Cambridge: Cambridge University Press.

Ingold, Tim, Riches, David, and Woodburn, James (eds.) (1988a) *Hunters and Gatherers, 1, History, Evolution, and Social Change.* Oxford: Berg.

——— (1988b) *Hunters and Gatherers, 2, Property, Power, and Ideology.* Oxford: Berg.

Ireland, Emilienne (1988) "Cerebral savage: The whiteman as symbol of cleverness and savagery in Waurá myth," in J. Hill (ed.), *Rethinking History and Myth: Indigenous South American Perspectives on the Past,* pp. 158–173. Urbana: University of Illinois Press.

——— (1991) "Neither warriors nor victims: The Wauja peacefully organize to defend their land." *Cultural Survival Quarterly,* 15:54–60.

Irons, William (1998) "Adaptively relevant environments versus the environment of evolutionary adaptedness." *Evolutionary Anthropology,* 6:194–204.

Irwin, C. (1990) "The Inuit and the evolution of limited group conflict," in J. van der Dennen and V. Falger (eds.), *Sociobiology and Conflict: Evolutionary Perspectives on Competition, Cooperation, Violence and Warfare,* pp. 189–240. London: Chapman and Hall.

Itkonen, Toivo I. (1984) *The Lapps in Finland up to 1945, volume 1,* trans. Eeva K. Minn. In the electronic Human Relations Area Files, Lapps, Doc. 2. New Haven, CT: HRAF, 1996, computer file. Originally published in Finnish in 1948.

Jacobs, Sue-Ellen (1991) "Tewa Pueblos," in D. Levinson (ed. in chief), *Encyclopedia of World Cultures,* T. O'Leary and D. Levinson (volume eds.), *Volume I, North America,* pp. 347–350. Boston: G. K. Hall.

Jamison, Paul L. (1978) "Anthropometric variation," in P. L. Jamison, S. L. Zegura, and F. A. Milan (eds.), *Eskimos of Northwestern Alaska: A Biological Perspective,* pp. 40–78. Stroudsburg, PA: Dowden, Hutchinson, and Ross.

Janetski, Joel C. (1991) "Ute," in D. Levinson (ed. in chief), *Encyclopedia of World Cultures,* T. O'Leary and D. Levinson (volume eds.), *Volume I, North America,* pp. 360–363. Boston: G. K. Hall.

Jochelson, Waldemar (1926) *The Yukaghir and the Yukaghirized Tungus.* The Jesup North Pacific Expedition Memoir of the American Museum of Natural History, Volume IX. New York: G. E. Stechert.

Jochim, Michael (1996) "Hunting and gathering societies," in D. Levinson and M. Ember (eds.), *Encyclopedia of Cultural Anthropology,* Volume 2, pp. 624–629. New York: Henry Holt.

Johansen, Robert C. (1984) "Toward an alternative security system," in B. H. Weston (ed.), *Toward Nuclear Disarmament and Global Security,* pp. 569–603. Boulder, CO: Westview.

Johnson, Allen (1983) "Machiguenga gardens," in R. B. Hames and W. T. Vickers (eds.), *Adaptive Responses of Native Amazonians,* pp. 29–63. New York: Academic Press.

Johnson, Allen W. and Earle, Timothy (1987) *The Evolution of Human Societies: From Foraging Group to Agrarian State.* Stanford: Stanford University Press.

Johnson, David W., Johnson, Roger T., and Maruyama, Geoffrey (1983) "Interdependence and interpersonal attraction among heterogeneous and homogeneous individuals: A theoretical formulation and a meta-analysis of the research." *Review of Educational Research,* 53:5–54.

Jolly, Alison (1985) *The Evolution of Primate Behavior,* 2d ed. New York: Macmillan.

Jorgensen, Joseph G. (1980) *Western Indians: Comparative Environments, Languages, and Cultures of 172 Western American Indian Tribes.* San Francisco: W. H. Freeman.

Jung, Carl G. (1983) *The Essential Jung: Selected Writings,* selected and introduced by Anthony Storr. London: Fontana Press.

Just, Peter (1991) "Conflict resolution and moral community among the Dou Donggo," in K. Avruch, P. W. Black, and J. A. Scimecca (eds.), *Conflict Resolution: Cross-Cultural Perspectives,* pp. 107–143. New York: Greenwood Press.

Kaare, Bwire and Woodburn, James (1999) "Hadza," in R. B. Lee and R. Daly (eds.), *The Cambridge Encyclopedia of Hunters and Gatherers,* pp. 200–204. Cambridge: Cambridge University Press.

Kaberry, Phyllis M. (1973) *Aboriginal Woman: Sacred and Profane.* New York: Gordon Press.

Kaufmann, William J., III (1977) *Relativity and Cosmology,* 2d ed. New York: Harper and Row.

Keeley, Lawrence H. (1996) *War before Civilization: The Myth of the Peaceful Savage.* Oxford: Oxford University Press.

Kehoe, Alice B. (1999) "Blackfoot/Plains," in R. B. Lee and R. Daly (eds.), *The Cambridge Encyclopedia of Hunters and Gatherers,* pp. 36–40. Cambridge: Cambridge University Press.

Kelly, Isabel T. and Fowler, Catherine S. (1986) "Southern Paiute," in W. D'Azevedo (volume ed.) and W. Sturtevant (ed.), *Handbook of North American Indians, Volume 11, Great Basin,* pp. 368–397. Washington, DC: Smithsonian Press.

Kelly, Raymond C. (2000) *Warless Societies and the Origin of War.* Ann Arbor: University of Michigan Press.

Kelly, Robert L. (1995) *The Foraging Spectrum: Diversity in Hunter-Gatherer Lifeways.* Washington, DC: Smithsonian Institution Press.

Kemp, Graham (2004) "The concept of peaceful societies," in G. Kemp and D. P. Fry (eds.), *Keeping the Peace: Conflict Resolution and Peaceful Societies around the World,* pp. 1–10. New York: Routledge.

Kemp, Graham and Fry, Douglas P. (eds.) (2004) *Keeping the Peace: Conflict Resolution and Peaceful Societies around the World.* New York: Routledge.

Kent, Susan (1989) "And justice for all: The development of political centralization among newly sedentary foragers." *American Anthropologist,* 91:703–712.

——— (2002) "Interethnic encounters of the first kind: An introduction," in S. Kent (ed.), *Ethnicity, Hunter-Gatherers, and the "Other,"* pp. 1–27. Washington, DC: Smithsonian Institution Press.

Kidder, Robert and Hostetler, John A. (1990) "Managing ideologies: Harmony as ideology in Amish and Japanese societies," *Law and Society Review,* 24:895–922.

Killen, Melanie and Frans B. M. de Waal (2000) "The evolution and development of morality," in F. Aureli and F. B. M. de Waal (eds.), *Natural Conflict Resolution,* pp. 352–372. Berkeley: University of California Press.

King, Bruce M., Camp, Cameron J., and Downey, Ann M. (1991) *Human Sexuality Today.* Englewood Cliffs, NJ: Prentice Hall.

Kirch, Patrick V. (1997) "Microcosmic histories: Island perspectives on 'global' change." *American Anthropologist,* 99:30–42.

Kleivan, Inge (1991) "West Greenland Inuit," in D. Levinson (ed. in chief), *Encyclopedia of World Cultures,* T. O'Leary and D. Levinson (volume eds.), *Volume I, North America,* pp. 376–379. Boston: G. K. Hall.

Knauft, Bruce (1987) "Reconsidering violence in simple human societies." *Current Anthropology,* 28:457–500.

——— (1991) "Violence and sociality in human evolution." *Current Anthropology,* 32:391–428.

——— (1994) "Comment" [on "Australia's ancient warriors" by Paul Tacon and Christopher Chippindale]. *Cambridge Archaeological Journal,* 4:229–231.

Koch, Klaus-Friedrich (1974) *War and Peace in Jalémó: The Management of Conflict in Highland New Guinea.* Cambridge: Harvard University Press.

——— (1979) "Introduction: Access to justice: An anthropological perspective," in K.-F. Koch (ed.), *Access to Justice, Volume 4, The Anthropological Perspective, Patterns of Conflict Management: Essays in the Ethnography of Law,* pp. 1–16. Alphen aan den Rijn: Sijthoff and Noordhoff.

Koch, Klaus-Friedrich, Altorki, S., Arno, A., and Hickson, Letitia (1977) "Ritual reconciliation and the obviation of grievances: A comparative study in the ethnography of law." *Ethnology,* 16:270–283.

Konner, Melvin (1982) *The Tangled Wing: Biological Constraints on the Human Spirit.* New York: Henry Holt.

Koskela, Hille (1997) "'Bold walk and breakings': Women's spatial confidence versus fear of violence." *Gender, Place and Culture,* 4:301–319.

Krammerer, Cornelia A. (1993) "Akha," in D. Levinson (ed. in chief), *Encyclopedia of World Cultures,* P. Hockings (volume ed.), *Volume V, East and Southeast Asia,* pp. 11–13. Boston: G. K. Hall.

Krauss, Ellis S., Rohlen, Thomas P., and Steinhoff, Patricia G. (eds.) *Conflict in Japan.* Honolulu: University of Hawaii Press.

Krech, S. (1991) "Hare," in D. Levinson (ed. in chief), *Encyclopedia of World Cultures,* T. O'Leary and D. Levinson (volume eds.), *Volume I, North America,* pp. 139–142. Boston: G. K. Hall.

Krieger, David (1994) "Ending the scourge of war," in R. Elias and J. Turpin (eds.), *Rethinking Peace,* pp. 318–325. Boulder, CO: Lynne Rienner.

Kroeber, A. L. (1953) "The Yurok: Law and custom," in A. L. Kroeber (ed.), *Handbook of the Indians of California,* pp. 20–52. Berkeley: California Book Company.

Kurtz, Lester R. and Turpin, Jennifer (1997) "Conclusion: Untangling the web of violence," in J. Turpin and L. R. Kurtz (eds.), *The Web of Violence: From Interpersonal to Global,* pp. 207–232. Urbana: University of Illinois Press.

Kuschel, Rolf (1992) "'Women are women and men are men': How Bellonese women get even," in K. Björkqvist and P. Niemalä (eds.), *Of Mice and Women: Aspects of Female Aggression,* pp. 173–185. Orlando, FL: Academic Press.

Larson, Karen A. (1992) "Norwegians," in D. Levinson (ed. in chief), *Encyclopedia of World Cultures,* L. A. Bennett (volume ed.), *Volume IV, Europe (Central, Western, and Southeastern Europe),* pp. 180–182. Boston: G. K. Hall.

Le Boeuf, B. J. (1971) "The aggression of the breeding bulls." *Natural History,* 80:83–94.

Le Clercq, Chrétien (1910) "New Relation of Gaspesia," in W. F. Ganong (trans. and ed.), *Publications of the Champlain Society, Volume 5,* pp. 1–452. Toronto: The Champlain Society.

Leacock, Eleanor (1954) *The Montagnais "Hunting Territory" and the Fur Trade.* Memoirs of the American Anthropological Association, *American Anthropologist,* 56(2), part 2, memoir number 78.

——— (1978) "Women's status in egalitarian society: Implications for social evolution." *Current Anthropology,* 19:247–275.

——— (1981) "Seventeenth-century Montagnais social relations and values," in W. C. Sturtevant (general ed.), *Handbook of North American Indians,* J. Helm (volume ed.), *Volume 6, Subarctic,* pp. 190–195. Washington, DC: Smithsonian Institution.

——— (1982) "Relations of production in band society," in E. Leacock and R. Lee (eds.), *Politics and History in Band Society,* pp. 159–170. Cambridge: Cambridge University Press.

Leacock, Eleanor and Lee, Richard (eds.) (1982) *Politics and History in Band Society.* Cambridge: Cambridge University Press.

Leavitt, Gregory C. (1977) "The frequency of warfare: An evolutionary perspective." *Sociological Inquiry,* 47:49–58.

Lebar, Frank M. (1975a) "Hanunóo," in F. M. Lebar (ed. and compiler), *Ethnic Groups of Insular Southeast Asia, Volume 2, Philippines and Formosa,* pp. 74–76. New Haven, CT: Human Relations Area Files Press.

——— (1975b) "Subanun," in F. M. Lebar (ed. and compiler), *Ethnic Groups of Insular Southeast Asia, Volume 2, Philippines and Formosa,* pp. 32–34. New Haven, CT: Human Relations Area Files Press.

——— (1975c) "Yami," in F. M. Lebar (ed. and compiler), *Ethnic Groups of Insular Southeast Asia, Volume 2, Philippines and Formosa,* pp. 108–114. New Haven, CT: Human Relations Area Files Press.

Lebar, Frank M., Hickey, Gerald C., and Musgrave, John K. (1964) "Semang," in F. M. Lebar, G. C. Hickey, and J. K. Musgrave (eds.), *Ethnic Groups of Mainland Southeast Asia,* pp. 181–186. New Haven, CT: Human Relations Area Files Press.

Lebra, Takie S. (1984) "Nonconfrontational strategies for management of interpersonal conflicts," in E. S. Krauss, T. P. Rohlen, and P. G. Steinhoff (eds.), *Conflict in Japan,* pp. 41–60. Honolulu: University of Hawaii Press.

Lebzelter, Viktor (1934) *Eingeborenenkulturen in Südwest-und Südafrika* [*Native Cultures in Southwest and South Africa*], trans. Richard Neuse. In the Human Relations Area Files, Id Number FX10, Document Number 3. New Haven, CT: Human Relations Area Files.

Lederach, John Paul (1991) "Of nets, nails, and problems: The folk language of conflict resolution in a Central American setting," in K. Avruch, P. W. Black, and J. A. Scimecca (eds.), *Conflict Resolution: Cross-Cultural Perspectives,* pp. 165–186. New York: Greenwood Press.

Lee, Richard B. (1972) "The !Kung Bushmen of Botswana," in M. G. Bicchieri (ed.), *Hunters and Gatherers Today,* pp. 327–368. Prospect Heights, IL: Waveland.

——— (1979) *The !Kung San: Men, Women, and Work in a Foraging Community.* Cambridge: Cambridge University Press.

——— (1993) *The Dobe Ju/'hoansi,* 2d ed. Fort Worth: Harcourt Brace College Publishers.

——— (2002) "Solitude or servitude? Ju/'hoansi images of the colonial encounter," in S. Kent (ed.), *Ethnicity, Hunter-Gatherers, and the "Other,"* pp. 184–205. Washington, DC: Smithsonian Institution Press.

Lee, Richard B. and Daly, Richard (1999) "Introduction: Foragers and Others," in R. B. Lee and R. Daly (eds.), *The Cambridge Encyclopedia of Hunters and Gatherers,* pp. 1–19. Cambridge: Cambridge University Press.

Lee, Richard B. and DeVore, Irven (1968a) "Problems in the study of hunters and gatherers," in R. B. Lee and I. DeVore (eds.), *Man the Hunter,* pp. 3–12. Chicago: Aldine.

——— (eds.) (1968b) *Man the Hunter.* Chicago: Aldine.

Lesser, Alexander (1967) "War and the state," in M. Fried, M. Harris, and R. Murphy (eds.), *War: The Anthropology of Armed Conflict and Aggression,* pp. 92–96. Garden City, NY: The Natural History Press.

Levinson, David (1989) *Family Violence in Cross-Cultural Perspective.* Newbury Park, CA: Sage.

——— (1994) *Aggression and Conflict: A Cross-Cultural Encyclopedia.* Santa Barbara: ABC-CLIO.

Levy, Robert I. (1975) *Tahitians: Mind and Experience in the Society Islands.* Chicago: University of Chicago Press.

——— (1978) "Tahitian gentleness and redundant controls," in A. Montagu (ed.), *Learning Non-Aggression: The Experience of Non-Literate Societies,* pp. 222–235. Oxford: Oxford University Press.

Lewin, Roger (1987) *Bones of Contention: Controversies in the Search for Human Origins.* New York: Simon and Schuster.

Lewontin, R. C. (1970) "The units of selection." *Annual Review of Ecology and Systematics,* 1:1–18.

Lindstrom, Lamont (1991) "Tanna," in D. Levinson (ed. in chief), *Encyclopedia of World Cultures,* T. E. Hays (volume ed.), *Volume II, Oceania,* pp. 313–315. Boston: G. K. Hall.

Lips, Julian (1947) *Naskapi Law.* Philadelphia: American Philosophical Society.

Lizot, Jacques (1994) "On warfare: An answer to N. A. Chagnon," trans. by Sarah Dart. *American Ethnologist,* 21:845–862.

Llewellyn, Karl N. and Hoebel, E. Adamson (1941) *The Cheyenne Way.* Norman: University of Oklahoma Press.

Lock, Margaret (1993) "Japanese," in D. Levinson (ed. in chief), *Encyclopedia of World Cultures,* P. Hockings (volume ed.), *Volume V, East and Southeast Asia,* pp. 104–111. Boston: G. K. Hall.

Longhofer, Jeffrey L. (1991) "Mennonites," in D. Levinson (ed. in chief), *Encyclopedia of World Cultures,* T. O'Leary and D. Levinson (volume eds.), *Volume I, North America,* pp. 216–220. Boston: G. K. Hall.

Lorenz, Konrad (1966) *On Aggression.* New York: Bantam.

Loudon, J. B. (1970) "Teasing and socialization on Tristan da Cunha," in P. Mayer (ed.), *Socialization: The Approach from Social Anthropology,* pp. 293–332. London: Tavistock.

Low, Bobbi S. (1993) "An evolutionary perspective on war," in W. Zimmerman and H. Jacobson (eds.), *Behavior, Culture, and Conflict in World Politics,* pp. 13–55. Ann Arbor: University of Michigan Press.

Lutz, Catherine (1982) "The domain of emotion words on Ifaluk." *American Ethnologist,* 9:113–128.

——— (1983) "Parental goals, ethnopsychology, and the development of emotional meaning." *Ethos,* 11:246–262.

——— (1988) *Unnatural Emotions: Everyday Sentiments on a Micronesian Atoll and Their Challenge to Western Theory.* Chicago: University of Chicago Press.

Maccoby, Eleanor and Jacklin, C. (1974) *The Psychology of Sex Differences.* Stanford: Stanford University Press.

Maceda, Marcelino N. (1975) "Mamanua," in F. M. Lebar (ed. and compiler), *Ethnic Groups of Insular Southeast Asia, Volume 2, Philippines and Formosa,* pp. 29–31. New Haven, CT: Human Relations Area Files Press.

MacGaffey, Wyatt (1995) "Kongo," in D. Levinson (ed. in chief), *Encyclopedia of World Cultures,* J. Middleton and A. Rassam (volume eds.), *Volume IX, Africa and the Middle East,* pp. 166–168. Boston: G. K. Hall.

Malinowski, Bronislaw (1941) "An anthropological analysis of war." *American Journal of Sociology,* 46:521–550.

Man, Edward H. (1932) *On the Aboriginal Inhabitants of the Andaman Islands.* London: The Royal Anthropological Institute of Great Britain and Ireland.

Mann, R. S. (1986) *The Ladakhi: A Study in Ethnography and Change.* Calcutta: Anthropological Survey of India, Indian Government.

Manson, Joseph H. and Wrangham, Richard W. (1991) "Intergroup aggression in chimpanzees and humans." *Current Anthropology,* 32:369–390.

Marcus, Joyce (1992) *MesoAmerican Writing Systems: Propaganda, Myth, and History in Four Ancient Civilizations.* Princeton, NJ: Princeton University Press.

Marlowe, Frank (2002) "Why the Hadza are still hunter-gatherers," in S. Kent (ed.), *Ethnicity, Hunter-Gatherers, and the "Other,"* pp. 247–275. Washington, DC: Smithsonian Institution Press.

Marshall, Lorna (1961) "Sharing, talking, and giving: Relief of social tensions among !Kung Bushmen." *Africa,* 31:231–249.

——— (1976) *The !Kung of Nyae Nyae.* Cambridge: Harvard University Press.

Marshall, Mac (1993) "The wizard from Oz meets the wicked witch of the East: Freeman, Mead, and ethnographic authority." *American Ethnologist,* 20:604–617.

Martin, David F. (1991) "Wik Mungkan," in D. Levinson (ed. in chief), *Encyclopedia of World Cultures,* T. E. Hays (volume ed.), *Volume II, Oceania,* pp. 376–379. Boston: G. K. Hall.

Martin, M. Kay and Voorhies, Barbara (1975) *Female of the Species.* New York: Columbia University Press.

Martin, M. Marlene (1991) "Klamath," in D. Levinson (ed. in chief), *Encyclopedia of World Cultures,* T. O'Leary and D. Levinson (volume eds.), *Volume I, North America,* pp. 190–192. Boston: G. K. Hall.

——— (1993) "Javanese," in D. Levinson (ed. in chief), *Encyclopedia of World Cultures,* P. Hockings (volume ed.), *Volume V, East and Southeast Asia,* pp. 111–114. Boston: G. K. Hall.

Martin, M. Marlene and Levinson, David (1993) "Central Thai," in D. Levinson (ed. in chief), *Encyclopedia of World Cultures,* P. Hockings (volume ed.), *Volume V, East and Southeast Asia,* pp. 69–72. Boston: G. K. Hall.

Maschner, Herbert D. G. (1997) "The evolution of Northwest Coast warfare," in D. L. Martin and D. W. Frayer (eds.), *Troubled Times: Violence and Warfare in the Past,* pp. 267–302. Amsterdam: Gordon and Breach.

Masumura, Wilfred (1977) "Law and violence: A cross-cultural study." *Journal of Anthropological Research,* 33:388–399.

Matteson, Esther (1994) "Piro," in D. Levinson (ed. in chief), *Encyclopedia of World Cultures,* J. Wilbert (volume ed.), *Volume VII, South America,* pp. 278–281. Boston: G. K. Hall.

Maybury-Lewis, David (1974) *Akwe-Shavante Society.* New York: Oxford University Press.

Maynard Smith, J. (1974) "The theory of games and the evolution of animal conflicts." *Journal of Theoretical Biology,* 47:209–221.

——— (1997) "The objects of selection." *Proceedings of the National Academy of Science,* 94:2091–2094.

Maynard Smith, J. and Price, G. R. (1973) "The logic of animal conflict." *Nature,* 246:15–18.

McCarthy, Barry (1994) "Warrior values: A socio-historical survey," in J. Archer (ed.), *Male Violence,* pp. 105–120. London: Routledge.

McCauley, Ann P. (1993) "Bali," in D. Levinson (ed. in chief), *Encyclopedia of World Cultures,* P. Hockings (volume ed.), *Volume V, East and Southeast Asia,* pp. 35–38. Boston: G. K. Hall.

McCorkle, Thomas (1978) "Intergroup conflict," in W. C. Sturtevant (general ed.), *Handbook of North American Indians,* R. F. Heizer (volume ed.), *Volume 8, California,* pp. 694–700. Washington, DC: Smithsonian Institution.

McCormick, M. Melissa (1988) *Mediation in the Schools: An Evaluation of the Wakefield Pilot Peer-Mediation Program in Tucson, Arizona.* Chicago: American Bar Association.

McKnight, David (1986) "Fighting in an Australian Aboriginal supercamp," in D. Riches (ed.), *The Anthropology of Violence,* pp. 136–163. Oxford: Basil Blackwell.

Mead, Margaret (1931) "'Progress' hits Samoa." *The Nation,* 133 (3488):138.

——— (1950) *Male and Female: A Study of the Sexes in a Changing World.* London: Victor Gollancz.

——— (1961a) "The Arapesh of New Guinea," in M. Mead (ed.), *Cooperation and Competition among Primitive Peoples,* revised paperback ed., pp. 20–50. Boston: Beacon Press. Originally published in 1937.

——— (1961b) "The Samoans," in M. Mead (ed.), *Cooperation and Competition among Primitive Peoples,* revised paperback ed., pp. 282–312. Boston: Beacon Press. Originally published in 1937.

——— (1963) *Sex and Temperament in Three Primitive Societies,* 1963 ed. New York: William Morrow. Originally published in 1935.

——— (1967) "Alternatives to war," in M. Fried, M. Harris, and R. Murphy (eds.), *War: The Anthropology of Armed Conflict and Aggression,* pp. 215–228. Garden City, NY: The Natural History Press.

——— (1969) *Social Organization of Manu'a,* 2d ed. Honolulu: Bernice P. Bishop Museum.

——— (1973) *Coming of Age in Samoa,* Laurel ed. New York: Dell. Originally published in 1928.

Mealing, T. Mark (1991) "Doukhobors," in D. Levinson (ed. in chief), *Encyclopedia of World Cultures,* T. O'Leary and D. Levinson (volume eds.), *Volume I, North America,* pp. 90–93. Boston: G. K. Hall.

Meggitt, Mervyn (1965) *Desert People: A Study of the Walbiri Aborigines of Central Australia.* Chicago: University of Chicago Press.

——— (1977) *Blood Is Their Argument: Warfare among the Mae Enga Tribesmen of the New Guinea Highlands.* Mountain View, CA: Mayfield.

Mellon, Christian, Muller, Jean-Maria, and Semelin, Jacques (1994) "Civil Deterrence," in R. Elias and J. Turpin (eds.), *Rethinking Peace,* pp. 269–275. Boulder, CO: Lynne Rienner.

Merry, Sally E. (1982) "The social organization of mediation in nonindustrial societies: Implications for informal community justice in America," in R. L. Abel (ed.), *The Politics of Informal Justice, Volume 2: Comparative Studies,* pp. 17–45. New York: Academic Press.

Métraux, Alfred (1946a) "The Caingang," in J. Steward (ed.), *Handbook of South American Indians, Volume 1, The Marginal Tribes,* pp. 445–475. Washington, DC: U.S. Government Printing Office.

——— (1946b) "Ethnography of the Gran Chaco," in J. Steward (ed.), *Handbook of South American Indians, Volume 1, The Marginal Tribes,* pp. 197–370. Washington, DC: U.S. Government Printing Office.

——— (1946c) "The Bodocudo," in J. Steward (ed.), *Handbook of South American Indians, Volume 1, The Marginal Tribes,* pp. 531–540. Washington, DC: U.S. Government Printing Office.

Minturn, Leigh, Grosse, Martin, and Haider, Santoah (1969) "Cultural patterning of sexual beliefs and behavior." *Ethnology,* 8:301–318.

Mitchell, William E. (1978) "On keeping equal: Polity and reciprocity among the New Guinea Wape." *Anthropological Quarterly,* 51:5–15.

——— (1991) "Wape," in D. Levinson (ed. in chief), *Encyclopedia of World Cultures,* T. E. Hays (volume ed.), *Volume II, Oceania,* pp. 370–373. Boston: G. K. Hall.

——— (1999) "Why Wape men don't beat their wives: Constraints toward domestic tranquility in a New Guinea society," in D. A. Counts, J. K. Brown, and J. C. Campbell (eds.), *To Have and to Hit: Cultural Perspectives on Wife Beating,* pp. 100–109. Urbana: University of Illinois Press.

Montagu, Ashley (1951) *Statement on Race.* New York: Abelard-Schuman.

——— (1963) *Race, Science and Humanity.* Princeton, NJ: van Nostrand.

——— (1964) *The Concept of Race.* New York: Free Press.
——— (1972) *Touching: The Human Significance of the Skin.* New York: Harper and Row.
——— (ed.) (1973) *Man and Aggression,* 2d ed. New York: Oxford University Press.
——— (1976) *The Nature of Human Aggression.* Oxford: Oxford University Press.
——— (ed.) (1978a) *Learning Non-Aggression: The Experience of Non-Literate Societies.* Oxford: Oxford University Press.
——— (1978b) "Introduction," in A. Montagu (ed.), *Learning Non-Aggression: The Experience of Non-Literate Societies,* pp. 3–11. Oxford: Oxford University Press.
——— (1982) "Edward Westermarck: Recollections of an old student in young age," in T. Stroup (ed.), *Edward Westermarck: Essays on His Life and Works, Acta Philosophica Fennica, Volume 34,* pp. 63–70. Helsinki: The Philosophical Society of Finland.
——— (1989) *Growing Young.* Grandby, MA: Bergen and Garvey.
——— (1994) "Foreword," in L. E. Sponsel and T. Gregor (eds.), *The Anthropology of Peace and Nonviolence,* pp. ix–xiv. Boulder, CO: Lynne Rienner.
——— (1999) *The Natural Superiority of Women,* 5th ed. Walnut Creek, CA: Alta Mira/Sage.
Moore, John H. (1990) "The reproductive success of Cheyenne war chiefs: A contrary case to Chagnon's Yanomamö." *Current Anthropology,* 31:322–330.
Morey, Robert V., Jr. and Marwitt, John P. (1975) "Ecology, economy, and warfare in lowland South America," in M. A. Nettleship, R. Dale Givens, and A. Nettleship (eds.), *War, Its Causes and Correlates,* pp. 439–450. The Hague: Mouton.
Morris, Brian (1977) "Tappers, trappers and the Hill Pandaram (South India)." *Anthropos,* 72:225–241.
——— (1982) "Economy, affinity and the inter-cultural pressure: Notes around Hill Pandaram group structure." *Man,* 17:542–461.
——— (1992) "Hill Pandaram," in D. Levinson (ed. in chief), *Encyclopedia of World Cultures,* P. Hockings (volume ed.), *Volume III, South Asia,* pp. 99–101. Boston: G. K. Hall.
Munch, Peter A. (1974) "Anarchy and *anomie* in an atomistic community." *Man* (N.S.), 9:243–261.
Munch, Peter A. and Charles E. Marske (1981) "Atomism and social integration." *Journal of Anthropological Research,* 37:158–171.
Murdock, George P. (1934) *Our Primitive Contemporaries.* New York: Macmillan.
——— (1967) "Ethnographic Atlas: A Summary." *Ethnology,* 6:109–236.
——— (1968) "The current status of the world's hunting and gathering peoples," in R. B. Lee and I. DeVore (eds.), *Man the Hunter,* pp. 13–20. Chicago: Aldine.
——— (1981) *Atlas of World Cultures.* Pittsburgh: University of Pittsburgh Press.
Murdock, George P. and White, Douglas R. (1969) "Standard Cross-Cultural Sample." *Ethnology,* 8:329–369.
Murphy, Robert F. (1957) "Intergroup hostility and social cohesion." *American Anthropologist,* 59:1018–1035.
Murphy, Robert F. and Quain, Buell (1955) *The Trumai Indians of Central Brazil.* Seattle: University of Washington Press.
Murra, John (1948) "The Cayapa and Colorado," in J. H. Steward (ed.), *Handbook of South American Indians, Volume 4, The Circum-Caribbean Tribes,* pp. 277–291. Washington, DC: U.S. Government Printing Office.
Musters, G. C. (1873) *At Home with the Patagonians,* 2d ed. In the Human Relations Area Files, Id Number, SH5. New Haven, CT: Human Relations Area Files.
Myers, Fred R. (1982) "Always ask: Resource use and land ownership among Pintupi Aborigines of the Australian Western Desert," in N. M. Williams and E. S. Hunn (eds.), *Resource Managers: North American and Australian Hunter-Gatherers,* pp. 173–195. Boulder, CO: Westview.

Nader, Laura (1969) "Styles of court procedure: To make the balance," in L. Nader (ed.), *Law and Culture in Society,* pp. 69–91. Chicago: Aldine.

——— (1990) *Harmony Ideology: Justice and Control in a Zapotec Mountain Village.* Stanford: Stanford University Press.

Nader, Laura and Todd, Harry F., Jr. (1978) "Introduction: The disputing process," in L. Nader and H. F. Todd, Jr. (eds.), *The Disputing Process: Law in Ten Societies,* pp. 1–40. New York: Columbia University Press.

Nag, Moni (1972) "Andamanese," in F. M. Lebar (ed. and compiler), *Ethnic Groups of Insular Southeast Asia, Volume 1, Indonesia, Andaman Islands, and Madagascar,* pp. 4–7. New Haven, CT: Human Relations Area Files Press.

Nansen, Fredtjof (1893) *Eskimo Life,* trans. William Archer. London: Longmans, Green, and Company.

Needham, Rodney (1972) "Penan," in F. M. Lebar (ed. and compiler), *Ethnic Groups of Insular Southeast Asia, Volume 1, Indonesia, Andaman Islands, and Madagascar,* pp. 176–180. New Haven, CT: Human Relations Area Files Press.

Netting, Robert McC. (1986) *Cultural Ecology,* 2d ed. Prospect Heights, IL: Waveland Press.

Newcomb, W. W., Jr. (1950) "A re-examination of the causes of Plains warfare." *American Anthropologist,* 52:317–330.

Noble, William A. and Jebadhas, A. William (1992) "Irula," in D. Levinson (ed. in chief), *Encyclopedia of World Cultures,* P. Hockings (volume ed.), *Volume III, South Asia,* pp. 104–109. Boston: G. K. Hall.

Noland, S. (1981) "Dispute settlement and social organization in two Iranian rural communities." *Anthropology Quarterly* 54:190–202.

Nooy-Palm, C. H. M. (1972) "Mentaweians," in F. M. Lebar (ed. and compiler), *Ethnic Groups of Insular Southeast Asia, Volume 1, Indonesia, Andaman Islands, and Madagascar,* pp. 41–44. New Haven, CT: Human Relations Area Files Press.

Norberg-Hodge, Helena (1991) *Ancient Futures: Learning from Ladakh.* San Francisco: Sierra Club Books.

Ohbuchi, Ken-ichi, Kameda, Masuyo, and Agarie, Nariyuki (1989) "Apology as aggression control: Its role in mediating appraisal of and response to harm." *Journal of Personality and Social Psychology,* 56:219–227.

O'Leary, Timothy J. and Levinson, David (1991) "Netsilik Inuit," in D. Levinson (ed. in chief), *Encyclopedia of World Cultures,* T. O'Leary and D. Levinson (volume eds.), *Volume I, North America,* p. 254. Boston: G. K. Hall.

O'Nell, Carl W. (1969) *Human Development in a Zapotec Community with an Emphasis on Aggression Control and Its Study in Dreams.* Unpublished doctoral dissertation, Department of Anthropology, University of Chicago.

——— (1979) "Nonviolence and personality dispositions among the Zapotec." *Journal of Psychological Anthropology,* 2:301–322.

——— (1981) "Hostility management and the control of aggression in a Zapotec community." *Aggressive Behavior,* 7:351–366.

——— (1986) "Some primary and secondary effects of violence control among the nonviolent Zapotec." *Anthropological Quarterly,* 59:184–190.

——— (1989) "The non-violent Zapotec," in S. Howell and R. Willis (eds.), *Societies at Peace: Anthropological Perspectives,* pp. 117–132. London: Routledge.

Orma, Esko (1986) *Huoli Ihmisestä: Uudistuvaa Psykiatriaa.* Helsinki: Therapeia-säätiö.

Ortner, Sherry B. (1978) *Sherpas through Their Rituals.* Cambridge: Cambridge University Press.

——— (1989) *High Religion: A Cultural and Political History of Sherpa Buddhism.* Princeton, NJ: Princeton University Press.

Osgood, Cornelius (1958) *Ingalik Social Culture.* New Haven, CT: Yale University Publications in Anthropology, no. 53.

Oswalt, Robert L. (1991) "Pomo," in D. Levinson (ed. in chief), *Encyclopedia of World Cultures,* T. O'Leary and D. Levinson (volume eds.), *Volume I, North America,* pp. 292–296. Boston: G. K. Hall.

Otterbein, Keith F. (1968) "Internal war: A cross-cultural study." *American Anthropologist,* 70:277–289.

——— (1970) *The Evolution of War: A Cross-Cultural Study.* New Haven, CT: Human Relations Area Files Press.

——— (1973) "The anthropology of war," in J. Honigmann (ed.), *Handbook of Social and Cultural Anthropology,* pp. 923–927. Boston: Houghton Mifflin.

——— (ed.) (1994) *Feuding and Warfare: Selected Works of Keith F. Otterbein.* Langhorne, PA: Gordon and Breach.

——— (1997) "The origins of war." *Critical Review,* 2:251–277.

——— (1999) "A history of research on warfare in anthropology." *American Anthropologist,* 101:794–805.

Otterbein, Keith F. and Otterbein, Charlotte S. (1965) "An eye for an eye, a tooth for a tooth: A cross-cultural study of feuding." *American Anthropologist,* 67:1470–1482.

Overing, Joanna (1986) "Images of cannibalism, death and domination in a 'non-violent' society," in D. Riches (ed.), *The Anthropology of Violence,* pp. 86–102. Oxford: Basil Blackwell.

——— (1989) "Styles of manhood: An Amazonian contrast in tranquility and violence," in S. Howell and R. Willis (eds.), *Societies at Peace: Anthropological Perspectives,* pp. 79–99. London: Routledge.

Paddock, John (1982) "Anti-violence in Oaxaca, Mexico: Archive research." Paper presented at the meetings of the American Society for Ethnohistory, Nashville, TN, October.

Palmer, Stuart (1965) "Murder and suicide in forty non-literate societies." *Journal of Criminal Law, Criminology, and Police Science,* 56:320–324.

Pandya, V. (1992) "Andamanese," in D. Levinson (ed. in chief), *Encyclopedia of World Cultures,* P. Hockings (volume ed.), *Volume III, South Asia,* pp. 8–12. Boston: G. K. Hall.

Pastron, A. G. (1974) "Collective defenses of repression and denial: Their relationship to violence among the Tarahumara Indians of northern Mexico." *Ethos,* 2:387–404.

Paul, Robert A. (1977) "The place of the truth in Sherpa law and religion." *Journal of Anthropological Research* 33:167–184.

——— (1992) "Sherpa," in D. Levinson (ed. in chief), *Encyclopedia of World Cultures,* P. Hockings (volume ed.), *Volume III, South Asia,* pp. 257–260. Boston: G. K. Hall.

Pelto, Pertti (1962) *Individualism in Skolt Lapp Society.* In the electronic Human Relations Area Files, Lapps, Doc. 20. New Haven, CT: HRAF, 1996, computer file.

Peterson, Nicolas (1991) "Warlpiri," in D. Levinson (ed. in chief), *Encyclopedia of World Cultures,* T. E. Hays (volume ed.), *Volume II, Oceania,* pp. 373–376. Boston: G. K. Hall.

Phillips, Herbert P. (1974) *Thai Peasant Personality: The Patterning of Interpersonal Behavior in the Village of Band Chan.* Berkeley: University of California Press.

Pilling, Arnold (1968) "Discussions, part III, 17.g: Predation and warfare," in R. B. Lee and I. DeVore (eds.), *Man the Hunter,* pp. 157–158. Chicago: Aldine.

Pinker, Steven (1997) *How the Mind Works.* New York: W.W. Norton.

Podolefsky, A. (1990) "Mediator roles in Simbu conflict management." *Ethnology,* 29:67–81.

Pospisil, Leopold (1971) *Anthropology of Law: A Comparative Theory.* New York: Harper and Row.

Pottenger, Francis M. (1938) *Symptoms of Visceral Disease: A Study of the Vegetative Nervous System in Its Relationship to Clinical Medicine,* 5th ed. St. Louis: C. V. Mosby.

——— (1948) *Tuberculosis: A Discussion of Phthisiogenesis, Immunology, Pathogic Physiology, Diagnosis, and Treatment.* St. Louis: C. V. Mosby.

——— (1952) *The Fight against Tuberculosis: An Autobiography.* New York: Henry Schuman.

Preuschoft, Signe and van Schaik, Carel P. (2000) "Dominance and communication: Conflict management in various social settings," in F. Aureli and F. B. M. de Waal (eds.), *Natural Conflict Resolution,* pp. 77–105. Berkeley: University of California Press.

Price, T. Douglas and Brown, James A. (eds.) (1985) *Prehistoric Hunter-Gatherers: The Emergence of Cultural Complexity.* New York: Academic Press.

Prosterman, Roy L. (1972) *Surviving to 3000: An Introduction to the Study of Lethal Conflict.* Belmont, CA: Duxbury-Wadsworth.

Quirk, R. (1971) *Mexico.* Englewood Cliffs, NJ: Prentice-Hall.

Radcliffe-Brown, Alfred R. (1922) *The Andaman Islanders.* Cambridge: Cambridge University Press.

Raghaviah, V. (1962) *The Yanadis.* New Delhi: Bharatiya Adimjati Sevak Sangh.

Ray, Verne (1980) *The Sanpoil and Nespelem: Salishan Peoples of Northeastern Washington.* New York: AMS Press.

Redfield, Robert (1967) "Primitive law," in P. Bohannan (ed.), *Law and Warfare: Studies in the Anthropology of Conflict,* pp. 3–24. Austin: University of Texas Press.

Reid, Gerald (1991) "Montagnais-Naskapi," in D. Levinson (ed. in chief), *Encyclopedia of World Cultures,* T. O'Leary and D. Levinson (volume eds.), *Volume I, North America,* pp. 243–246. Boston: G. K. Hall.

Renner, Michael (1991) "Assessing the military's war on the environment," in L. Brown, A. Durning, C. Flavin, H. French, J. Jacobson, N. Lenssen, M. Lowe, S. Postel, M. Renner, J. Ryan, L. Starke, and J. Young (eds.), *The State of the World 1991,* pp. 132–152. New York: W. W. Norton.

——— (1993) *Critical Juncture: The Future of Peacekeeping,* Worldwatch Paper no. 114. Washington, DC: The Worldwatch Institute.

——— (1999) "Ending violent conflict," in L. Brown, C. Flavin, H. French, J. Abramovitz, S. Dunn, G. Gardner, A. Mattoon, A. Platt McGinn, M. O'Meara, M. Renner, D. Roodman, P. Sampat, L. Starke, and J. Tuxill (eds.), *The State of the World 1999,* pp. 151–168. New York: W. W. Norton.

Reyna, S. P. (1994) "A mode of domination approach to organized violence," in S. P. Reyna and R. E. Downs (eds.), *Studying War: Anthropological Perspectives,* pp. 29–65. Amsterdam: Gordon and Breach.

Richards, C. (1975) "Comment," in M. A. Nettleship, R. Dalegivens, and A. Nettleship (eds.), *War, Its Causes and Correlates,* pp. 342–343. The Hague: Mouton.

Riechert, Susan E. (1986) "Spider fights as a test of evolutionary game theory." *American Scientist* 74:604–609.

——— (1998) "Game theory and animal contests," in L. A. Dugatkin and H. K. Reeve (eds.), *Game Theory and Animal Behavior,* pp. 64–93. New York: Oxford University Press.

Rivers, W. H. R. (1986) *The Todas,* first Indian ed. Jaipur, India: Rawat. Originally published in 1906.

Rivière, Peter (1994) "Trio," in D. Levinson (ed. in chief), *Encyclopedia of World Cultures,* J. Wilbert (volume ed.), *Volume VII, South America,* pp. 334–337. Boston: G. K. Hall.

Robarchek, Clayton A. (1979) "Conflict, emotion, and abreaction: Resolution of conflict among the Semai Senoi." *Ethos,* 7:104–123.

——— (1980) "The image of nonviolence: World view of the Semai Senoi." *Federated Museums Journal (Malaysia),* 25:103–117.

——— (1986) "Helplessness, fearfulness, and peacefulness: The emotional and motivational context of Semai social relations." *Anthropology Quarterly,* 59:177–183.

——— (1989) "Hobbesian and Rousseauan images of man: Autonomy and individuality in a peaceful society," in S. Howell and R. Willis (eds.), *Societies at Peace: Anthropological Perspectives,* pp. 31–44. London: Routledge.

——— (1990) "Motivations and material causes: On the explanation of conflict and war," in J. Haas (ed.), *The Anthropology of War,* pp. 56–76. Cambridge: Cambridge University Press.

——— (1994) "The psychocultural dynamics of Semai peacefulness," in L. E. Sponsel and T. Gregor (eds.), *The Anthropology of Peace and Nonviolence,* pp. 183–196. Boulder, CO: Lynne Rienner.

——— (1997) "A community of interests: Semai conflict resolution," in D. P. Fry and K. Björkqvist (eds.), *Cultural Variation in Conflict Resolution: Alternatives to Violence,* pp. 51–58. Mahwah, NJ: Lawrence Erlbaum.

Robarchek, Clayton A. and Dentan, Robert Knox (1987) "Blood drunkenness and the bloodthirsty Semai: Unmaking another anthropological myth." *American Anthropologist,* 89:356–365.

Robarchek, Clayton A. and Robarchek, Carole (1992) "Cultures of war and peace: A comparative study of Waorani and Semai," in J. Silverberg and J. P. Gray (eds.), *Aggression and Peacefulness in Humans and Other Primates,* pp. 189–213. New York: Oxford University Press.

——— (1996a) "Waging peace: The psychological and sociocultural dynamics of positive peace," in A. W. Wolfe and H. Yang (eds.), *Anthropological Contributions to Conflict Resolution,* pp. 64–80. Athens: University of Georgia Press.

——— (1996b) "The Acuas, the cannibals, and the missionaries: From warfare to peacefulness among the Waorani," in T. Gregor (ed.), *A Natural History of Peace,* pp. 189–212. Nashville, TN: Vanderbilt University Press.

——— (1998a) *Waorani: The Contexts of Violence and War.* Fort Worth, TX: Harcourt Brace College Publishers.

——— (1998b) "Reciprocities and realities: World views, peacefulness, and violence among the Semai and Waorani." *Aggressive Behavior,* 24:123–133.

Romanucci-Ross, Lola (1973) *Conflict, Violence and Morality in a Mexican Village.* Palo Alto, CA: National Press.

Roper, Marilyn K. (1969) "A survey of the evidence for intrahuman killing in the Pleistocene." *Current Anthropology,* 10:427–459.

——— (1975) "Evidence of warfare in the Near East from 10,000–4,300 B.C.," in M. A. Nettleship, R. Dalegivens, and A. Nettleship (eds.), *War, Its Causes and Correlates,* pp. 299–340. The Hague: Mouton.

Roseman, Marina (1990) "Head, heart, odor, and shadow: The structure of the self, the emotional world, and the ritual performance among Senoi Temiar." *Ethos,* 18:227–250.

Ross, Jane B. (1984) "Effects of contact on revenge hostilities among the Achuarä Jívaro," in R. B. Ferguson (ed.) *Warfare, Culture, and Environment,* pp. 83–109. Orlando, FL: Academic Press.

Ross, Marc Howard (1993a) *The Culture of Conflict: Interpretations and Interests in Comparative Perspective.* New Haven, CT: Yale University Press.

——— (1993b) *The Management of Conflict: Interpretations and Interests in Comparative Perspective.* New Haven, CT: Yale University Press.

Rubin, Jeffrey Z., Pruitt, Dean G., and Kim, Sung Hee (1994) *Social Conflict: Escalation, Stalemate, and Settlement,* 2d ed. New York: McGraw-Hill.

Ruby, Robert H. and Brown, John A. (1989) *Dream-Prophets of the Columbia Plateau: Smohalla and Skolaskin.* Norman: University of Oklahoma Press.

Rushforth, Scott (1991) "Slavey," in D. Levinson (ed. in chief), *Encyclopedia of World Cultures,* T. O'Leary and D. Levinson (volume eds.), *Volume I, North America,* pp. 318–320. Boston: G. K. Hall.

Sabloff, Jeremy A. (1990) *The Cities of Ancient Mexico: Reconstructing a Lost World,* first paperback ed. New York: Thames and Hudson.

Sandbukt, Øyvind (1988) "Tributary tradition and relations of affinity and gender among the Sumatran Kubu," in T. Ingold, D. Riches, and J. Woodburn (eds.), *Hunters and Gatherers, 1, History, Evolution, and Social Change,* pp. 107–116. Oxford: Berg.

Sather, Clifford (1975) "Bajau Laut," in F. M. Lebar (ed. and compiler), *Ethnic Groups of Insular Southeast Asia, Volume 2, Philippines and Formosa,* pp. 9–12. New Haven, CT: Human Relations Area Files Press.

——— (1993) "Bajau," in D. Levinson (ed. in chief), *Encyclopedia of World Cultures,* P. Hockings (volume ed.), *Volume V, East and Southeast Asia,* pp. 30–35. Boston: G. K. Hall.

——— (2004) "Keeping the peace in an island world: The Sama Dilaut of Southeast Asia," in G. Kemp and D. P. Fry (eds.), *Keeping the Peace: Conflict Resolution and Peaceful Societies around the World,* pp. 123–147. New York: Routledge.

Savishinsky, Joel S. (1974) *The Trail of the Hare: Life and Stress in an Arctic Community.* Human Relations Area Files, Id Number ND9, document number 10. New Haven, CT: Human Relations Area Files.

Schaefer, Stacy B. (1995) "Huichol," in D. Levinson (ed. in chief), *Encyclopedia of World Cultures,* J. W. Dow and R. van Kemper (volume eds.), *Volume VIII, Middle America and the Caribbean,* pp. 124–128. Boston: G. K. Hall.

Schaller, George B. (1972) *The Serengeti Lion.* Chicago: University of Chicago Press.

Schebesta, Paul (1929) *Among the Forrest Dwarfs of Malaya.* London: Hutchinson and Company.

——— (1978) *My Pygmy and Negro Hosts,* first AMS edition reprinted from the 1936 edition. New York: AMS Press.

Scheper-Hughes, Nancy (1984) "The Margaret Mead controversy: Culture, biology and anthropological inquiry." *Human Organization,* 43:85–93.

Schlegel, Alice (2004) "Contentious but not violent: The Hopi of Northern Arizona," in G. Kemp and D. P. Fry (eds.), *Keeping the Peace: Conflict Resolution and Peaceful Societies around the World,* pp. 19–33. New York: Routledge.

Schneider, Mary Jane (1991) "Mandan," in D. Levinson (ed. in chief), *Encyclopedia of World Cultures,* T. O'Leary and D. Levinson (volume eds.), *Volume I, North America,* pp. 213–215. Boston: G. K. Hall.

Schwartz, Theodore (1983) "Anthropology: A quaint science." *American Anthropologist,* 85:919–929.

Seager, Joni (1997) *The State of Women in the World Atlas.* New York: Penguin Books.

Secoy, Frank (1992) *Changing Military Patterns of the Great Plains Indians.* Lincoln: University of Nebraska Press.

Seligmann, C. G. and Seligmann, Brenda Z. (1969) *The Veddas.* Oosterhout, N. B., The Netherlands: Anthropological Publications. Originally published in 1911.

Service, Elman R. (1966) *The Hunters.* Englewood Cliffs, NJ: Prentice-Hall.

——— (1971a) *Primitive Social Organization: An Evolutionary Perspective,* 2d ed. New York: Random House.

——— (1971b) *Profiles in Ethnology,* rev. ed. New York: Harper and Row.

——— (1978) *Profiles in Ethnology,* 3d ed. New York: Harper and Row.

Shankman, Paul (1996) "The history of Samoan sexual conduct and the Mead-Freeman controversy." *American Anthropologist,* 98:555–567.

——— (2000) "Culture, biology, and evolution: The Mead-Freeman controversy revisited." *Journal of Youth and Adolescence,* 29:539–556.

Shaw, R. Paul and Wong, Yuwa (1989) *Genetic Seeds of Warfare: Evolution, Nationalism, and Patriotism.* Boston: Unwin Hyman.

Shook, Victoria E. (1985) *Ho'oponopono: Contemporary Uses of a Hawaiian Problem-Solving Process.* Honolulu: University of Hawaii Press.

Shook, Victoria E. and Kwan, L. K. (1991) "*Ho'oponopono:* Straightening family relationships in Hawaii," in K. Avruch, P. W. Black, and J. A. Scimecca (eds.), *Conflict Resolution: Cross-Cultural Perspectives,* pp. 213–229. New York: Greenwood Press.

Shostak, Marjorie (1983) *Nisa: The Life and Words of a !Kung Woman.* New York: Vintage/Random House.

Shternberg, Lev I. (1933) *Semya I Rod U Narodov Severo-Vostochnoi Azii.* English translation in the Human Relations Area Files, Id Number RX2. New Haven, CT: Human Relations Area Files.

——— (1999) *The Social Organization of the Gilyak,* ed. Bruce Grant. Anthropological Papers of the American Museum of Natural History, no. 82. Seattle: University of Washington Press.

Silberbauer, George B. (1972) "The G/wi Bushmen," in M. G. Bicchieri (ed.), *Hunters and Gatherers Today,* pp. 271–326. Prospect Heights, IL: Waveland.

——— (1981) *Hunter & Habitat in the Central Kalahari Desert.* Cambridge: Cambridge University Press.

——— (1982) "Political processes in G/wi bands," in E. Leacock and R. Lee (eds.), *Politics and History in Band Society,* pp. 23–35. Cambridge: Cambridge University Press.

Simmons, Leo W. (1937) "Statistical correlations in the science of society," in G. P. Murdock (ed.), *Studies in the Science of Society,* pp. 495–517. New Haven, CT: Yale University Press.

——— (1942) *Sun Chief: The Autobiography of a Hopi Indian.* New Haven, CT: Yale University Press.

Sinha, D. P. (1972) "The Birhors," in M. G. Bicchieri (ed.), *Hunters and Gatherers Today,* pp. 371–403. Prospect Heights, IL: Waveland.

Sivard, Ruth L. (1993) *World Military and Social Expenditures, 1993.* Leesburg, VA: World Priorities Press.

Slavin, Robert E. (1983) *Cooperative Learning.* New York: Longman.

Sluys, Cornelia M. I. van der (1999) "Jahai," in R. B. Lee and R. Daly (eds.), *The Cambridge Encyclopedia of Hunters and Gatherers,* pp. 307–311. Cambridge: Cambridge University Press.

——— (2000) "Gifts from the immortal ancestors," in P. P. Schweitzer, M. Biesele, and R. K. Hitchcock (eds.), *Hunters and Gatherers in the Modern World: Conflict, Resistance, and Self-Determination,* pp. 427–454. New York: Berghahn.

Smail, J. Kenneth (1985) "Building bridges via reciprocal 'hostage exchange': A confidence-enhancing alternative to nuclear deterrence. *Bulletin of Peace Proposals,* 16:167–177.

——— (1997) "The giving of hostages." *Politics and the Life Sciences,* 16:77–85.

Smith, Dan (1999) *The State of the World Atlas.* London: Penguin.

Smith, Eric Alden (1988) "Risk and uncertainty in the 'original affluent society': Evolutionary ecology of resource-sharing and land tenure," in T. Ingold, D. Riches, and J. Woodburn (eds.), *Hunters and Gatherers, 1, History, Evolution, and Social Change,* pp. 222–231. Oxford: Berg.

Smith, James G. E. (1981) "Chipewyan," in J. Helm (volume ed.) and W. C. Sturtevant (general ed.), *Handbook of North American Indians, Volume 6, Subarctic,* pp. 271–284. Washington, DC: Smithsonian Institution Press.

——— (1991) "Cree, Western Woods," in D. Levinson (ed. in chief), *Encyclopedia of World Cultures,* T. O'Leary and D. Levinson (volume eds.), *Volume I, North America,* pp. 79–82. Boston: G. K. Hall.

Smith, Maria O. (1997) "Osteological indications of warfare in the Archaic Period of the western Tennessee Valley," in D. L. Martin and D. W. Frayer (eds.), *Troubled Times: Violence and Warfare in the Past,* pp. 241–265. Amsterdam: Gordon and Breach.

Soffer, Olga (1985) "Patterns of intensification as seen from the Upper Paleolithic of the Central Russian Plain," in T. D. Price and J. A. Brown (eds.), *Prehistoric Hunter-Gatherers: The Emergence of Cultural Complexity,* pp. 235–270. New York: Academic Press.

Speck, Frank G. (1935) *Naskapi: The Savage Hunters of the Labrador Peninsula.* Norman: University of Oklahoma Press.

Spencer, Baldwin and Gillen, Francis J. (1927) *The Arunta: A Study of a Stone Age People.* London: Macmillan.

Sperling, Susan (2000) "Obituaries: Ashley Montagu (1905–1999)." *American Anthropologist,* 102:583–588.

Spier, Leslie (1930) *Klamath Ethnography.* In the electronic Human Relations Area Files, Klamath, Doc. 1. New Haven, CT: HRAF, 1998, computer file.

Spiro, Melford E. (1952) "Ghosts, Ifaluk, and teleological functionalism." *American Anthropologist,* 54:497–503.

Sponsel, Leslie E. (1994) "The mutual relevance of anthropology and peace studies," in L. E. Sponsel and T. Gregor (eds.), *The Anthropology of Peace and Nonviolence,* pp. 1–36. Boulder, CO: Lynne Rienner.

——— (1996a) "Peace and nonviolence," in D. Levinson and M. Ember (eds.), *Encyclopedia of Cultural Anthropology, Volume 3,* pp. 908–912. New York: Henry Holt and Company.

——— (1996b) "The natural history of peace: A positive view of human nature and its potential," in T. Gregor (ed.), *A Natural History of Peace,* pp. 95–125. Nashville, TN: Vanderbilt University Press.

Sponsel, Leslie E. and Gregor, Thomas (eds.) (1994) *The Anthropology of Peace and Nonviolence.* Boulder, CO: Lynne Rienner.

Statistical Abstract of the United States 1996 (1996). Washington, DC: U.S. Department of Commerce.

Stegeborn, Wiveca (1999) "Wanniyala-aetto," in R. B. Lee and R. Daly (eds.), *The Cambridge Encyclopedia of Hunters and Gatherers,* pp. 269–273. Cambridge: Cambridge University Press.

Steinmetz, Suzanne (1977) "The use of force for resolving family conflict: The training ground for abuse." *Family Coordinator,* 26:19–26.

Steward, Julian (1968) "Causal factors and processes in the evolution of pre-farming societies," in R. B. Lee and I. DeVore (eds.), *Man the Hunter,* pp. 321–334. Chicago: Aldine.

Stewart, Frank H. (1990) "Schuld and Haftung in Bedouin law," in T. Mayer-Maly, D. Nörr, W. Waldstein, A. Laufs, W. Ogris, M. Heckel, P. Mikat, and K. W. Nörr (eds.), *Zeitschrift der Savigny-Stiftung für Rechtsgeschichte, Hundertsiebenter Band, CXX,* pp. 393–407. Vienna: Hermann Böhlaus Nachf.

Stiner, Mary C. (1991) "The cultural significance of Grotta Guattari reconsidered. I. The faunal remains from Grotta Guattari: A taphonomic perspective," plus commentary. *Current Anthropology,* 32:103–117, 124–138.

Stinson, Sara (2000) "Growth variation: Biological and cultural factors," in S. Stinson, B. Bogin, R. Huss-Ashmore, and D. O'Rourke (eds.), *Human Biology: An Evolutionary and Biocultural Perspective,* pp. 425–464. New York: Wiley-Liss.

Stockholm Initiative on Global Security and Governance—Common Responsibilities in the 1990s (1991). Stockholm: Prime Minister's Office.

Straus, Murray A. (2001) "Physical aggression in the family: Prevalence rates, links to non-family violence, and implications for primary prevention of societal violence," in M. Martinez (ed.), *Prevention and Control of Aggression and the Impact on Its Victims,* pp. 181–200. New York: Kluwer Academic/Plenum.

Sumner, W. G. (1911) *War and Other Essays.* New Haven, CT: Yale University Press.

Sussman, Robert W. (1999) "The myth of man the hunter/man the killer and the evolution of human morality," in R. W. Sussman (ed.), *The Biological Basis of Human Behavior: A Critical Review,* 2d ed. pp. 121–129. Upper Saddle River, NJ: Prentice Hall.

Swanton, John R. (1975) "Contributions to the ethnography of the Haida." The Jesup North Pacific Expedition Memior of the American Museum of Natural History, Volume V (reprint of 1905 edition). New York: G. E. Stechert.

Symons, Donald (1978) *Play and Aggression: A Study of Rhesus Monkeys.* New York: Columbia University Press.

——— (1979) *The Evolution of Human Sexuality.* New York: Oxford University Press.

——— (1990) "Adaptiveness and adaptation." *Ethology and Sociobiology,* 11:427–444.

——— (1992) "On the use and misuse of Darwinism in the study of human behavior," in J. H. Barkow, L. Cosmides, and J. Tooby (eds.), *The Adapted Mind: Evolutionary Psychology and the Generation of Culture,* pp. 137–159. New York: Oxford University Press.

Tacon, P. and Chippindale, C. (1994) "Australia's ancient warriors: Changing depictions of fighting in the rock art of Arnhem Land, N.T." *Cambridge Archaeological Journal* 4:211–248.

Takala, Jukka-Pekka (1998) *Moraalitunteet Rikosten Sovittelussa,* Oikeuspoliittisen Tutkimuslaitoksen Julkaisuja 151 [*Moral Emotions in Victim-Offender Mediation*—with a summary in English]. Helsinki: Oikeuspoliittinen Tutkimuslaitos [Department of the Finnish Ministry of Justice].

Taylor, William B. (1979) *Drinking, Homicide, and Rebellion in Colonial Mexican Villages.* Stanford: Stanford University Press.

Tefft, Stanton K. and Reinhardt, Douglas (1974) "Warfare regulation: A cross-cultural test of hypotheses among tribal peoples." *Behavior Science Research,* 9:151–172.

Textor, Robert B. (1967) *A Cross-Cultural Summary.* New Haven, CT: Human Relations Area Files Press.

Thoden van Velzen, H. U. E. and van Wetering, W. (1960) "Residence, power groups and intra-societal aggression." *International Archives of Ethnography,* 49:169–200.

Thomas, David H., Pendleton, Lorann S. A., and Cappannari, Stephen C. (1986) "Western Shoshone," in W. D'Azevedo (volume ed.) and W. Sturtevant (ed.), *Handbook of North American Indians, Volume 11, Great Basin,* pp. 262–283. Washington, DC: Smithsonian Press.

Thomas, David John (1982) *Order without Government: The Society of the Pemon Indians of Venezuela.* Urbana: University of Illinois Press.

——— (1994) "Pemon," in D. Levinson (ed. in chief), *Encyclopedia of World Cultures,* J. Wilbert (volume ed.), *Volume VII, South America,* pp. 271–273. Boston: G. K. Hall.

Thomas, Elizabeth M. (1959) *The Harmless People.* New York: Vintage, Random House.

——— (1994) "Management of violence among the Ju/wasi of Nyae Nyae: The old way and a new way," in S. P. Reyna and R. E. Downs (eds.), *Studying War: Anthropological Perspectives,* pp. 69–84. Amsterdam: Gordon and Breach.

Tiger, Lionel (2000) "The Internal Triangle," in L. D. Katz (ed.), *Evolutionary Origins of Morality: Cross-Disciplinary Perspectives,* pp. 146–148. Bowling Green, OH: Imprint Academic.

Tonkinson, Robert (1978) *The Mardudjara Aborigines: Living the Dream in Australia's Desert.* New York: Holt, Rinehart, and Winston.

——— (1991) "Mardudjara," in D. Levinson (ed. in chief), *Encyclopedia of World Cultures,* T. E. Hays (volume ed.), *Volume II, Oceania,* pp. 179–182. Boston: G. K. Hall.

——— (2004) "Resolving conflict within the law: The Mardu Aborigines of Australia," in G. Kemp and D. P. Fry (eds.), *Keeping the Peace: Conflict Resolution and Peaceful Societies around the World,* pp. 89–104. New York: Routledge.

Tooby, John and Cosmides, Leda (1990) "The past explains the present: Emotional adaptations and the structure of ancestral environments." *Ethology and Sociobiology,* 11:375–424.

——— (1992) "The psychological foundation of culture," in J. H. Barkow, L. Cosmides, and J. Tooby (eds.), *The Adapted Mind: Evolutionary Psychology and the Generation of Culture,* pp. 19–136. New York: Oxford University Press.

Trivers, Robert L. (1972) "Parental investment and sexual selection," in B. G. Campbell (ed.), *Sexual Selection and the Descent of Man, 1871–1971,* pp. 136–179. Chicago: Aldine.

Turnbull, Colin M. (1961) *The Forest People: A Study of the Pygmies of the Congo.* New York: Simon and Schuster.

——— (1965a) *Wayward Servants: The Two Worlds of the African Pygmies.* Garden City, NY: The Natural History Press.

——— (1965b) "The Mbuti Pygmies of the Congo," in J. L. Gibbs, Jr. (ed.), *Peoples of Africa,* pp. 281–317. New York: Holt, Rinehart, and Winston.

——— (1968a) "The importance of flux in two hunting societies," in R. B. Lee and I. DeVore (eds.), *Man the Hunter,* pp. 132–137. Chicago: Aldine.

——— (1968b) "Discussions, part VII, 35.b: Primate behavior and the evolution of aggression," in R. B. Lee and I. DeVore (eds.), *Man the Hunter,* pp. 339–344. Chicago: Aldine.

——— (1978) "The politics of non-aggression (Zaire)," in A. Montagu (ed.), *Learning Non-Aggression: The Experience of Non-Literate Societies,* pp. 161–221. Oxford: Oxford University Press.

Turney-High, Harry H. (1941) "Ethnography of the Kutenai." *Memoirs of the American Anthropological Association, Number 56.* Menasha, WI: American Anthropological Association.

——— (1971) *Primitive War: Its Practice and Concepts.* Columbia: University of South Carolina Press.

Turrado Moreno, Angel (1945) *Ethnography of the Guarauno Indians.* In the electronic Human Relations Area Files, Warao, Doc. 6. New Haven, CT: HRAF, 2000, computer file.

Underhill, Ruth M. (1939) *Social Organization of the Papago Indians.* New York: AMS Press.

——— (1946) *Papago Indian Religion.* New York: Columbia University Press.

Uniform Crime Reports for the United States 1993 (1993) Washington, DC: Federal Bureau of Investigation, Department of Justice.

Ury, William (1999) *Getting to Peace: Transforming Conflict at Home, at Work, and in the World.* New York: Viking.

Ury, William L., Brett, Jeanne M., and Goldberg, Stephen B. (1988) *Getting Disputes Resolved: Designing Systems to Cut the Costs of Conflict.* San Francisco: Jossey-Bass.

van Schaik, Carel P. and Aureli, Filippo (2000) "The natural history of valuable relationships in primates," in F. Aureli and F. B. M. de Waal (eds.), *Natural Conflict Resolution,* pp. 307–333. Berkeley: University of California Press.

Veltre, Douglas W. (1991) "Aleut," in D. Levinson (ed. in chief), *Encyclopedia of World Cultures,* T. O'Leary and D. Levinson (volume eds.), *Volume I, North America,* pp. 14–16. Boston: G. K. Hall.

Walker, Anthony R. (1986) *The Toda of South India: A New Look.* Delhi: Hundustan Publishing Corporation.

——— (1992) "Toda," in D. Levinson (ed. in chief), *Encyclopedia of World Cultures,* P. Hockings (volume ed.), *Volume III, South Asia,* pp. 294–298. Boston: G. K. Hall.

Walker, Phillip L. (2001) "A bioarchaeological perspective on the history of violence." *Annual Review of Anthropology,* 30:573–596.

Wallace, Ernest and Hoebel, E. Adamson (1952) *The Comanches: Lords of the Southern Plains.* Norman: University of Oklahoma Press.

Wallis, Wilson D. and Wallis, Ruth S. (1955) *The Micmac Indians of Eastern Canada.* Minneapolis: University of Minnesota Press.

Walsh, Michael (1993) "Languages and Their Status in Aboriginal Australia," in M. Walsh and C. Yallop (eds.), *Language and Culture in Aboriginal Australia,* pp. 1–13. Canberra: Aboriginal Studies Press.

Ward, Barbara E. (1970) "Temper tantrums in Kau Sai: Some speculations upon their effects," in P. Mayer (ed.), *Socialization: The Approach from Social Anthropology,* pp. 109–125. London: Tavistock.

Warner, W. Lloyd (1969) *A Black Civilization: A Social Study of an Australian Tribe.* Gloucester, MA: Peter Smith. Originally published in 1937.

Warren, Charles P. (1975a) "Batak," in F. M. Lebar (ed. and compiler), *Ethnic Groups of Insular Southeast Asia, Volume 2, Philippines and Formosa,* pp. 68–70. New Haven, CT: Human Relations Area Files Press.

——— (1975b) "Palawan," in F. M. Lebar (ed. and compiler), *Ethnic Groups of Insular Southeast Asia, Volume 2, Philippines and Formosa,* p. 64. New Haven, CT: Human Relations Area Files Press.

——— (1975c) "Tagbanuwa," in F. M. Lebar (ed. and compiler), *Ethnic Groups of Insular Southeast Asia, Volume 2, Philippines and Formosa,* pp. 64–67. New Haven, CT: Human Relations Area Files Press.

Weiner, Annette B. (1983) "Ethnographic determinism: Samoa and the Margaret Mead controversy." *American Anthropologist,* 85:909–919.

Weiss, Mark L. and Mann, Alan E. (1990) *Human Biology and Behavior,* 5th ed. Glenview, IL: Scott Foresman.

Westermarck, Edward (1910) "Prefatory note," in G. C. Wheeler, *The Tribe, and Intertribal Relations in Australia.* London: John Murray.

——— (1924) *The Origin and Development of the Moral Ideas,* in two volumes, 2d ed. London: Macmillan.

Wheeler, Gerald C. (1910) *The Tribe, and Intertribal Relations in Australia.* London: John Murray.

White, Douglas R. (1989) "Focused ethnographic bibliography: Standard cross-cultural sample." *Behavior Science Research,* 23:1–145.

White, John P. and Mulvaney, Derek J. (1987) "How many people?" in D. J. Mulvaney and J. P. White (eds.), *Australians to 1788,* pp. 115–117. Sydney: Fairfax, Syme, and Weldon Associates.

White, Tim D. and Toth, Nicholas (1989) "Engis: Preparation damage, not ancient cutmarks. *American Journal of Physical Anthropology,* 78:361–367.

——— (1991) "The cultural significance of Grotta Guattari reconsidered. II. The question of ritual cannibalism at Grotta Guattari," plus commentary. *Current Anthropology,* 32:118–138.

Whitehead, Neil (1990) "The snake warriors—sons of the tiger's teeth: A descriptive analysis of Carib warfare ca. 1500–1820," in J. Haas (ed.), *The Anthropology of War,* pp. 146–170. Cambridge: Cambridge University Press.

Wiesel, Elie and Fry, Douglas P. (1997) "On respecting others and preventing hate: A conversation with Elie Wiesel," in D. P. Fry and K. Björkqvist (eds.), *Cultural Variation in Conflict Resolution: Alternatives to Violence,* pp. 235–241. Mahwah, NJ: Lawrence Erlbaum.

Wiessner, Polly (1982) "Risk, reciprocity and social influences on !Kung San economics," in E. Leacock and R. Lee (eds.), *Politics and History in Band Society,* pp. 61–84. Cambridge: Cambridge University Press.

Wilbert, Johannes (1993) *Mystic Endowment: Religious Ethnography of the Warao Indians.* Cambridge: Harvard University Press.

——— (1994) "Kalapalo," in D. Levinson (ed. in chief), *Encyclopedia of World Cultures,* J. Wilbert (volume ed.), *Volume VII, South America,* p. 187. Boston: G. K. Hall.

Williams, B. J. (1968) "The Birhor of India and some comments on band organization," in R. B. Lee and I. DeVore (eds.), *Man the Hunter,* pp. 126–131. Chicago: Aldine.

Williams, George C. (1966) *Adaptation and Natural Selection: A Critique of Some Current Evolutionary Thought.* Princeton, NJ: Princeton University Press.

Williams, Nancy M. (1982) "A boundary is to cross: Observations on Yolngu boundaries and permission," in N. M. Williams and E. S. Hunn (eds.), *Resource Managers: North American and Australian Hunter-Gatherers,* pp. 131–153. Boulder, CO: Westview.

——— (1987) *Two Laws: Managing Disputes in a Contemporary Aboriginal Community.* Canberra: Australian Institute of Aboriginal Studies.

——— (1988) "Studies in Australian Aboriginal Law 1961–1986," in R. M. Berndt and R. Tonkinson (eds.), *Social Anthropology and Australian Aboriginal Studies: A Contemporary Overview,* pp. 191–237. Canberra: Aboriginal Studies Press.

——— (1991) "Murngin," in D. Levinson (ed. in chief), *Encyclopedia of World Cultures,* T. E. Hays (volume ed.), *Volume II, Oceania,* pp. 223–227. Boston: G. K. Hall.

Willis, Roy (1989) "The 'peace puzzle' in Ufipa," in S. Howell and R. Willis (eds.), *Societies at Peace: Anthropological Perspectives,* pp. 133–145. London: Routledge.

——— (1995) "Fipa," in D. Levinson (ed. in chief), *Encyclopedia of World Cultures,* J. Middleton and A. Rassam (volume eds.). *Volume IX, Africa and the Middle East,* pp. 98–100. Boston: G. K. Hall.

Wilson, Edward O. (1973) "Book review." *Science,* 179:466–467.

——— (1975) *Sociobiology: The New Synthesis.* Cambridge: Harvard University Press.

——— (2001) "On human nature," in D. P. Barash (ed.), *Understanding Violence,* pp. 13–20. Boston: Allyn and Bacon.

Wilson, Michael L. and Wrangham, Richard W. (2003) "Intergroup relations in chimpanzees." *Annual Review of Anthropology* 32:363–392.

Winterhalder, Bruce and Smith, Eric Alden (2000) "Analyzing adaptive strategies: Human behavioral ecology at twenty-five." *Evolutionary Anthropology* 9:51–72.

Wolf, Eric (2001) "Cycles of violence: The anthropology of war and peace," in D. P. Barash (ed.), *Understanding Violence,* pp. 192–199. Boston: Allyn and Bacon.

Wolf, Richart K. (1992) "Kota," in D. Levinson (ed. in chief), *Encyclopedia of World Cultures,* P. Hockings (volume ed.), *Volume III, South Asia,* pp. 134–138. Boston: G. K. Hall.

Woodburn, James (1968a) "Discussions, part III, 17.g: Predation and warfare," in R. B. Lee and I. DeVore (eds.), *Man the Hunter,* pp. 157–158. Chicago: Aldine.

——— (1968b) "Stability and flexibility in Hadza residential groupings," in R. B. Lee and I. DeVore (eds.), *Man the Hunter,* pp. 103–110. Chicago: Aldine.

——— (1982) "Egalitarian societies." *Man,* 17:431–451.

——— (1988) "African hunter-gatherer social organization: Is it best understood as a product of encapsulation?" in T. Ingold, D. Riches, and J. Woodburn (eds.), *Hunters and Gatherers 1: History, Evolution and Social Change,* pp. 31–64. Oxford: Berg.

Wrangham, Richard W. (1999a) "Is military incompetence adaptive?" *Evolution and Human Behavior,* 20:3–17.

——— (1999b) "Evolution of coalitionary killing." *Yearbook of Physical Anthropology,* 42:1–30.

Wrangham, Richard and Peterson, Dale (1996) *Demonic Males: Apes and the Origin of Human Violence.* Boston: Houghton Mifflin.

Wright, Quincy (1942) *A Study of War.* Chicago: University of Chicago Press.

——— (1964) *A Study of War,* 2d ed., abridged by L. L. Wright. Chicago: University of Chicago Press.

Yearbook of Nordic Statistics 1994 (1994) Copenhagen: Nordic Statistical Secretariat.

Zelený, Mnislav (1994) "Yawalapití," in D. Levinson (ed. in chief), *Encyclopedia of World Cultures,* J. Wilbert (volume ed.). *Volume VII, South America,* pp. 377–380. Boston: G. K. Hall.

Zent, Stanford (1994) "Piaroa," in D. Levinson (ed. in chief), *Encyclopedia of World Cultures,* J. Wilbert (volume ed.), *Volume VII, South America,* pp. 275–278. Boston: G. K. Hall.

Zigmond, Maurice L. (1986) "Kawaiisu," in W. D'Azevedo (volume ed.) and W. Sturtevant (general ed.), *Handbook of North American Indians, Volume 11, Great Basin,* pp. 398–411. Washington, DC: Smithsonian Press.

Zvelebil, Kamil V. (1988) *The Irulas of the Blue Mountains.* Syracuse, NY: Syracuse University, Maxwell School of Citizenship and Public Affairs.

Name Index

Subject Index